Contemporary Supervision
MANAGING PEOPLE AND TECHNOLOGY

McGraw-Hill SERIES IN MANAGEMENT

CONSULTING EDITORS
Fred Luthans and Keith Davis

Dr. Betty Roper Ricks

Associate Professor of Management Emeritus
Old Dominion University
Norfolk, Virginia

Dr. Mary Lea Ginn

Consulting Editor and Writer
Cincinnati, Ohio

Dr. Anne Scott Daughtrey

Eminent Professor of Management Emeritus
Old Dominion University
Norfolk, Virginia

SECOND EDITION

Contemporary Supervision
MANAGING PEOPLE AND TECHNOLOGY

McGraw-Hill, Inc

New York   St. Louis   San Francisco   Aukland   Bogotá   Caracas   Lisbon   London   Madrid
Mexico City   Milan   Montreal   New Delhi   San Juan   Singapore   Sidney   Tokyo   Toronto

CONTEMPORARY SUPERVISION
Managing People and Technology

This book is printed on acid-free paper.

2 3 4 5 6 7 8 9 0   DOC   DOC   9 0 9 8 7 6 5

ISBN 0-07-052648-6

This book was set in Berkeley Oldstyle by The Clarinda Company.
The editors were Lynn Richardson, Dan Alpert, and Peggy Rehberger;
the designer was Leon Bolognese;
the production supervisor was Louise Karam.
R. R. Donnelley & Sons Company was printer and binder.

Cover painting: Westfal Landesmuseum, Munster/A. K. G., Berlin / Superstock

Library of Congress Cataloging-in-Publication Data

Ricks, Betty R.
    Contemporary supervision: managing people and technology / Betty
Roper Ricks, Mary Lea Ginn, Anne Scott Daughtrey. —2nd. ed.
        p.   cm. —(McGraw-Hill series in management)
    Rev. ed. of: Contemporary supervision / Anne Scott Daughtrey. 1st
ed. c1989.
    Includes bibliographical references and index.
    ISBN 0-07-052648-6
    1. Supervision of employees.   I. Ginn, Mary L. (Mary Lea), (date).
II. Daughtrey, Anne Scott.   III. Daughtrey, Anne Scott.
Contemporary supervision.   IV. Title.   V. Series.
HF5549. 12.D38   1995
658.3'02—dc20   94-14945

About the Authors

Dr. Betty Roper Ricks, Associate Professor of Management Emeritus, served 12 years in a supervisory capacity in public education prior to her appointment to the faculty of Old Dominion University, where she was a member of the faculty of the College of Business and Public Administration for 15 years. Dr. Ricks earned her masters and doctoral degrees from Virginia Polytechnic Institute and State University. She has been a speaker at national and international conferences and is the author of several business textbooks as well as numerous articles in professional journals. Dr. Ricks has received several awards of recognition for outstanding teaching at the college level. She has been active in professional organizations in the field of business.

Dr. Mary Lea Ginn, consulting editor and writer in the field of business, is an experienced business education textbook editor and author of several textbooks. She has been active in professional and volunteer organizations for many years and has taught at the community college and university level. Dr. Ginn earned a masters degree from the University of Arkansas at Fayetteville and a doctorate from Kansas State University.

Dr. Anne Scott Daughtrey, Eminent Professor of Management Emeritus, is a widely recognized author, speaker, and teacher. Among her many publications is a business textbook that has won a gold-book award for sales of over 1 million copies. She is also the recipient of a national award for outstanding teaching in business and economic principles. In addition to many years of teaching, she has conducted seminars in business and economics and teaching strategies in colleges and universities throughout the country. She also served in a supervisory capacity in a variety of settings totaling over 10 years. She holds masters and doctoral degrees from the University of South Dakota and was a member of the faculty of the College of Business and Public Administration at Old Dominion University in Norfolk, Virginia, for 29 years before her recent retirement, when she was awarded faculty emerita status.

Contents

Preface

In this time of increasing pressures for higher productivity on the one hand and greater attention to the desire of workers for more autonomy over their work lives on the other hand, managers are having a difficult time balancing these diverse interests and keeping the company moving forward. The supervisor, as a part of the management team, plays a critical role in this balancing act. *Contemporary Supervision: Managing People and Technology,* 2d edition, is designed not only to help supervisors maintain equilibrium in these changing times but also to prepare them to help as their companies make the transition from a more traditional to a more contemporary management focus

This text is appropriate for courses such as supervision, introduction to management, and educational supervision taught to freshmen, sophomores, and juniors in departments of business management, educational administration, and continuing education. It is an effective source for the practicing supervisor and for in-house training. This text presents complete and current coverage of topics involving the transition from the traditional to the participatory approach.

Special features of the second edition of *Contemporary Supervision: Managing People and Technology* include the following:

❏ Focuses on competencies throughout the book. All competencies are presented at the chapter opening; they are presented individually at the appropriate learning point within the chapter; and they form the basis for the competency review at the end of the chapter.

❏ Includes topics of interest to students preparing for transitional management (e.g., participative management) as well as students preparing to deal with current issues such as stress management, ethics, AIDS, diversity management, safety and health, sexual harassment, total quality management, decision making, and delegation.

❏ Provides activities and suggestions to aid the supervisor in translating theory into practice. In addition to realistic examples, these suggestions are featured throughout the text in sections entitled "What Can the Supervisor Do?"

❏ Integrates throughout the chapters both realistic case studies and those based on actual companies to illustrate chapter content. These cases are short enough to be easily covered in one class period.

❏ Addresses in detail topics often glossed over. There are entire chapters on decision making, delegation, health and safety, and total quality management. Special attention is paid to managing diversity and change, nondiscriminatory staffing, and participative management.

❏ Provides a wealth of learning aids, including numerous self-quizzes or questionnaires, forms, exercises, case studies, applications, illustrations, and more.

❏ Is written in an informal, easy-to-read style that makes learning enjoyable.

The supplements include an *Instructor's Manual* and a *Student Study and Activity Guide.*

1. The Instructor's Manual includes general and chapter-specific teaching suggestions, lecture outlines, additional cases and activities, solutions to end-of-chapter activities, solutions to additional cases and activities, a test bank, and solutions to additional cases and enrichment activities in the *Student Study and Activity Guide.*
2. The *Student Study and Activity Guide* provides material to help students review the content of the text as well a to direct their study of each chapter. For example, for each chapter there is a chapter outline and study questions in a variety of formats. In addition, there are applications, cases, and other activities which serve to enrich the students' learning process. Solutions to the Test Your Knowledge are also provided.

The authors are indebted to many people for their ideas and assistance with this publication. Among those who have made direct contributions are the following reviewers:

Lawrence Barry, *Cuyamaca College*
Charles Beavin, *Miami-Dade Community College*
Steve Byrd, *Southeast Missouri State University*
Tommy Gilbrath, *University of Texas at Tyler*
Linda Hite, *Indiana University-Purdue University at Fort Wayne*
Kimberly McDonald, *Indiana University-Purdue University at Fort Wayne*
Lee Munson, *Santa Rosa Junior College*
Joseph Platts, *Miami-Dade Community College*
James Rassi, *Paradise Valley Community College*
John Sinton, *Community College of the Finger Lakes*
Robert Vaughn, *Lakeland Community College*
Gary Wagenheim, *Purdue University*
Edward White, *Danville Community College*

And to Tom Ricks, for his unwavering patience and support.

Finally, no book could find its way to the marketplace without the able assistance of the editorial and production staff of the publisher. The authors gratefully acknowledge the guidance and support of Lynn Richardson, Dan Alpert, Josh Pincus, Peggy Rehberger, Louise Karam, and the many other professionals at the McGraw-Hill family who were always willing to assist in any way.

Betty Roper Ricks
Mary Lea Ginn
Anne Scott Daughtrey

Contemporary Supervision
MANAGING PEOPLE AND TECHNOLOGY

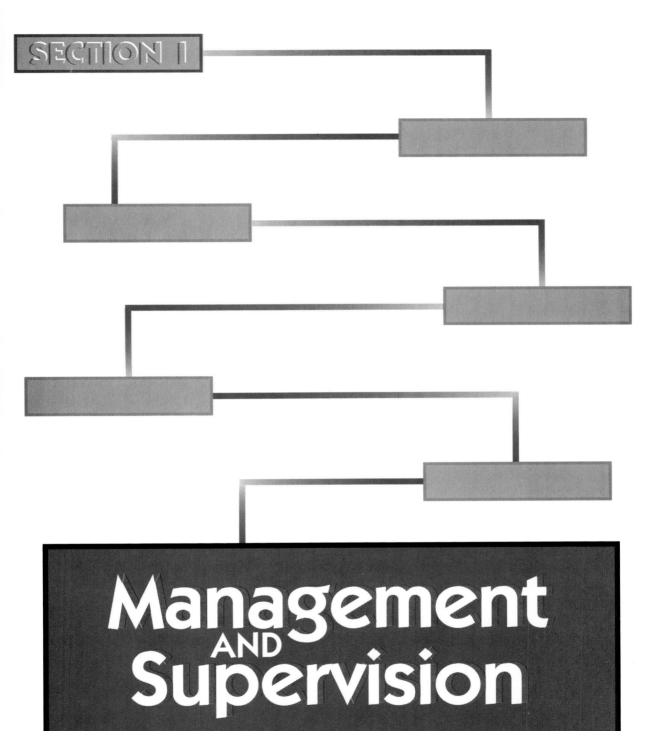

SECTION 1

Management AND Supervision

STUDYING THIS CHAPTER WILL ENABLE YOU TO:

1. Name the basic approaches in the evolution of management and give a feature of each.

2. Explain the integrative approaches to management.

3. Define *contemporary management.*

4. Describe participative management and give the premise on which it is based.

5. Describe team problem solving as a component of contemporary management.

6. Describe total quality management.

7. Explain how the supervisor is affected by the global nature of organizations.

8. Identify the levels of management and give an example of each.

9. Explain the functions of management.

10. Give an example of the supervisor's duties in each of the managerial functions.

11. Describe the skills needed by managers and show the importance of each to the levels of management.

CHAPTER OUTLINE

MANAGEMENT IS AN EVOLVING PROFESSION
- The Classical Approach
- The Behavioral Approach
- The Management Science Approach
- Integrative Approaches

CONTEMPORARY MANAGEMENT
- Participative Management
- Total Quality Management
- Global Management

THE LEVELS OF MANAGEMENT
- First-Line Management
- Middle-Level Management
- Upper-Level Management

THE FUNCTIONS OF MANAGEMENT
- Planning
- Organizing
- Staffing

- Leading and Motivating
- Controlling
- The Overlapping Nature of Managerial Functions

THE SUPERVISOR AS THE FIRST LINE OF MANAGEMENT
- The Role of the Supervisor
- Performing the Management Functions
- The Duties of the Supervisor
- The Skills Required
- The Skills of a Manager

Competency Review
Applications
Cases
References
Suggested Readings
Glossary

C   H   A   P

THE Supervisor's Role IN Management

T E R 1

Management is the process of working with and through other people, and using other available resources, to meet the goals of the organization and its people. Supervisors are the first line of management, and they make up the largest group in the management team. This group of workers is often called front-line managers, lower-level managers, first-line managers, forepersons, section heads, team leaders, or supervisors. In some small organizations where there are fewer layers of management, they may be referred to as managers, with titles such as office manager, shift manager, or sales manager. This chapter will build a framework through which you can examine an important part of the management team—the supervisor.

Management Is an Evolving Profession

Modern management is a product of the twentieth century, and it is still evolving. Today, approximately 8 million professional managers make up about 8 percent of employment in the United States.[1] Before the turn of the century, businesses in Europe and America were operated by their owners and their families. Decisions were made on the basis of experience and intuition. No principles had yet been developed to guide the decision makers. Owners relied mostly on hunches and true grit to run their companies. As the industrial revolution spread, it spawned the factory system, mass production, and unprecedented growth in the size of business enterprises. Owners began to hire managers for the day-to-day operations. After the turn of the century, research applications, especially in engineering, began to improve the efficiency of both workers and equipment in the workplace. This was the beginning of the concept of management as a profession. Principles of management that could serve as guidelines in decision making began to evolve.

To review the evolution of management, one might use the early to mid-1900s and the 1950s to the latter part of the twentieth century as broad time lines of development. Cumulative knowledge and overlapping of concepts and periods obviously occurred, especially after midcentury, but looking back, we can identify several distinct approaches that were focal points at various times as management evolved.

The Classical Approach

The **classical approach** to management is a combination of scientific management and classical organization theory. Each made a major contribution to modern management.

Scientific Management. Beginning in the late nineteenth century and finding its focus in the first quarter of the twentieth century, **scientific management** placed its emphasis on improving efficiency in the workplace. Researchers such as Frederick W. Taylor[2] and Frank and Lillian Gilbreth[3] studied jobs and the tools used by workers to perform those jobs. They sought "the one best way" to perform each job.

Taylor, an engineer, focused on time-and-motion studies, observing workers on the job and analyzing the tasks and the tools used. He then redesigned the tools for maximum efficiency. For example, after a study at Bethlehem Steel in which he observed workers shoveling raw materials, such as iron ore and coke, into an open furnace, Taylor tested shovels of various sizes and designed one for maximum efficiency. When his system was installed, it produced impressive results: The number of shovelers needed was reduced from between 400 and 600 to 140; productivity increased from 16 to 59 long tons per worker per day; costs were decreased from 7.1 cents to 3.2 cents per long ton; and worker wages, based on Taylor's piece rate and incentive system, increased from $1.15 to $1.88 per day. Taylor's concepts, with some modification, are still used in management.

Two other early scientific management pioneers, Frank and Lillian Gilbreth, also studied efficiency in the workplace. In their pursuit of "the one best way" to perform a task, they analyzed the motions of workers on the job. Frank Gilbreth first studied the motions of bricklayers in construction when he was a bricklayer himself. By analyzing the task, he was able to cut the number of motions required to lay a brick from 18 to 6 and managed to move, within a year, from being the slowest apprentice to being the fastest worker on the job. He opened his own construction company and installed his system. His success spread quickly internationally. With his wife, Lillian, one of the earliest industrial psychologists, assisting in the analysis, Gilbreth classified 17 basic motions, which he called "therbligs," his name spelled backwards with a slight change. Lillian Gilbreth was so involved in the research that historians have been unable to determine much of the authorship of his work. She also continued the work after his death. Today their time-and-motion analysis remains a core concept of management.

The scientific approach to designing tools and work flow and to measuring output gave the period the label "scientific management" and gave Taylor the title "father of scientific management." Scientific management focused on how to make lower-level jobs more productive.

Classical Organization Theory.   At the same time, in France, Henri Fayol,[4] an engineer who became a manager, was examining not the work on the shop floor but business activities. In his writing, he concentrated on the managerial functions. Fayol's management functions closely follow the current functions that are developed throughout this text: planning, organizing, staffing, leading and motivating, and controlling. Fayol's original five functions were planning, organizing, commanding, coordinating, and controlling. The coordinating function, although originally identified as a separate function, is now accepted as necessary in all of the functions; therefore, rather than being a separate entity, it is integrated into all of the other functions.

Fayol also developed a body of knowledge that can be taught, called the 14 principles of management. These principles can be used as guidelines for managing universally. Many of these principles, shown in Figure 1.1, are still relevant today. Fayol's work in management functions and principles became known as **classical organization theory,** sometimes referred to as administrative theory.

Other pioneers and their research, such as Henry L. Gantt and his scheduling of work, also contributed to the classical approach to management. You will learn more about Henry Gantt and his Gantt charts in Chapters 2 and 14. Together, the work of these researchers made major contributions to the evolving profession of management by focusing on these two elements of work:

The management of work—by studying the task, the tools, the skills of the worker, and the arrangement of the workstation into an efficient work flow (scientific management)

The work of management—by identifying the activities performed by managers and establishing principles of management that could be adapted to different situations (classical organization theory)

The emphasis on efficiency and productivity made the classical approach to management mechanistic and authoritarian. Recall Fayol's function called "commanding"? The worker was considered a tool of production, to be manipulated in whatever manner would best increase profits. This lack of humanistic concern eventually led to the behavioral approach.

The Behavioral Approach

Concerned by the overemphasis on the technical aspects of the workplace, social scientists began to give attention to the human side of management in an attempt to balance the two. The result became known as the **behavioral approach.**

Figure 1.1
FAYOL'S PRINCIPLES OF MANAGEMENT

1. *Division of work.*   This provides for specialization for the efficient use of labor. Fayol applies this to managerial as well as technical work.
2. *Authority.*   Authority and responsibility are related and should be equal.
3. *Discipline.*   Needed for developing obedience, application, energy, and respect. Fayol recommends that discipline be applied judiciously.
4. *Unity of command.*   Workers should receive orders from one superior only.
5. *Unity of direction.*   The entire organization should be moving in one direction toward a common objective.
6. *Subordination of individual interest to general interests.*   The interests of one individual or group should not have priority over the interests of the organization as a whole.
7. *Remuneration.*   Rewards and remuneration should be fair.
8. *Centralization.*   The degree of centralization or decentralization should depend on the organization; the rule should be the one that gives the best overall yield.
9. *Scalar chain.*   Fayol presents this as a chain of command from the highest to the lowest manager and says that this line of authority should be clearly communicated.
10. *Order.*   To promote efficiency and coordination, all materials and people related to a specific kind of work should be located in the same general area. Meaning "a place for everything and everything in its place," this principle is essentially the principle of organization.
11. *Equity.*   Workers should be treated with kindness and justice.
12. *Stability of tenure of personnel.*   Unnecessary turnover, both a cause and an effect of bad management, should be minimized because it is costly.
13. *Initiative.*   Workers should be encouraged to exercise initiative in improving their work, thereby improving their job satisfaction.
14. *Esprit de corps.*   Managers should encourage harmony and teamwork among workers.

Source: Henri Fayol, *General and Industrial Management,* copyright © 1987 by David S. Lake Publishers, Inc., Belmont, Calif. 94002. Reprinted by permission.

The Hawthorne studies, conducted between 1924 and 1932 by Elton Mayo[5] and others at the Western Electric Company, became an important milestone in the evolution of management thought. One phase of the research was to determine the relationship of the lighting in a relay assembly room to the productivity of the workers. Lighting was varied for one group and held constant for the other. The researchers were surprised to find that productivity increased in both groups during the period of the study whether the lighting was increased or decreased and that no consistent relationship existed between lighting and productivity. This led the researchers to interview the workers in an attempt to find the reason. They formulated these reasons for the higher productivity:

1. The workers enjoyed the experiment, which they considered to be an important and interesting study.
2. A new and more relaxed supervisor-worker relationship developed during the experiments.
3. The workers developed a friendlier group relationship.
4. The workers felt special because they had been singled out to participate in the study.

In other words, the positive response of the workers resulted not from their changed physical conditions but from their feeling that management was paying attention to them as human beings. This became known as "the Hawthorne effect."

The contribution of the behavioral approach is that it adds to scientific management's concern for the work itself a concern for the individual performing the work. This latter concern, as you will read later in this chapter, has intensified in contemporary management.

The Management Science Approach

Concepts formulated in the first half of the twentieth century continued to be applied in the second half, but now new research and technology began to influence management.

The introduction of the computer to the business scene in the 1950s had a profound impact on management theory. This new tool enabled managers to use the science of mathematics to manipulate great volumes of information to solve business problems at previously unheard of speeds. But the technology became a hard taskmaster and created some problems of its own, such as information overload, inflexibility, and worker stress. Computer technology and its rapid improvements and growth updated and expanded techniques from earlier scientific management, giving the period the label **management science**.

Growing out of the missile technology of World War II and military operations in which teams of experts were used to develop strategy, management science contributed both the use of statistics and technology and the team approach to problem solving. In England during World War II, for example, when confronted with the problem of dealing with antisubmarine warfare, the government put together teams of scientists, mathematicians, and physicists to develop the strategy. Management science is also known as **operations research** (OR).

COMPETENCY CHECK
Can you name three approaches in the early evolution of management and give an example of each?

Integrative Approaches

The proliferation of theories prompted Harold D. Koontz to note that a "management theory jungle" had been created, with each movement going its own way without regard for the others.[6] Modern management tries to cut through this jungle by integrating the findings of earlier movements. Two integrative approaches—the systems approach and the contingency approach—have emerged.

The Systems Approach.   The **systems approach** involves viewing the organization as a set of interrelated parts interacting with one another to accomplish a common goal. That is the meaning of *system*. The basic system consists of input (all resources used), process (transformation of inputs), and output (product, service, or information).

An enterprise, viewed as a system, will be more productive when its managers treat each part of the organization as important and interrelated. The interactions of the parts are more critical than are the separate actions of the parts. For example, a top sales force may be setting records in taking orders (input), but if the production department (process) is turning out only 60 percent of its production goals (output), the system is headed for trouble when deliveries are due.

The systems approach emphasizes management interrelationships in both the internal and external environments. The organization interacts with its external environment daily through its suppliers, customers, competitors, governmental agencies, and so on. This is more thoroughly discussed in Chapter 2.

The Contingency Approach.   The contingency approach refutes the "one best way" theme of scientific management, yet it was included in the writings of Mary Follett[7] in the 1920s. The **contingency**, or situational, **approach** takes into consideration various elements of the situation being managed and chooses the approach most appropriate for that situation.

The contingency approach to management suggests that there is no "cookbook" approach to solving business problems—a manager cannot identify the problem, turn to page 61 in a "how-to" book, and find the solution. Instead, managers must examine the forces in the situation, the forces within the subordinates, and the forces within the manager when attempting to solve any business problem.

The contingency approach enables managers to use knowledge from the classical, the behavioral, and the management science approaches as appropriate to the situation. Using all three of the approaches is sometimes referred to as **triangular management.** Today's management thinking continues to broaden the integrative process.

**COMPETENCY
CHECK**

Can you explain
the integrative
approaches to
management?

Contemporary Management

Management has been defined as the process of working with and through other people, using available resources, to accomplish the goals of the organization. Contemporary management may be defined in more comprehensive terms. *Contemporary management* is management that:

accomplishes the goals of the organization through the efforts of its people, recognizing that people perform best when meeting their own needs.

provides equal opportunity for employment, training, and promotion.

creates and maintains an environment that is physiologically and psychologically healthful.

promotes worker participation in decision making and problem solving and encourages innovation.

tries to balance the demands of technology with the needs of the workers.

rewards workers on the basis of their performance and shares productivity gains with those responsible for achieving the gains.

For contemporary management to be successful, it must be embraced by all levels of management.

Today's management is marked by its complexity. Managers must guide the internal mechanism of the organization, produce a competitive product, service, or information, and market that product, service, or information at a profit. They must also cope with a variety of external forces unknown to their counterparts in earlier periods. These new external forces may be economic, social, political, environmental, national, or global. They have also had an impact on workers, creating a new relationship between employer and employee. Some of these new forces are:

1. demand for greater productivity, resulting from national and international competition.
2. wide publicity given to other styles of management, especially those existing in Japan, whose success in international trade has had such an impact on the United States.
3. emergence of information as a major resource; it has been called a fourth sector of the economy, taking its place along with business, government, and the consumer.
4. expanding knowledge of behavioral and management science.
5. changing attitudes and values of today's workers.
6. changing legal environment, which has increased employer responsibility for the protection of employees' rights.
7. increasing recognition that the most important resource an organization has is its people.
8. changing workforce demographics.
9. emphasis on quality.

Today there is a greater emphasis on research into human behavior, especially as it affects and is affected by the workplace. How can managers motivate workers to be more productive? Many believe the answer lies in the degree to which workers are involved in the decisions that affect them. Contemporary management embraces participative management, team problem solving, total quality management, and global management.

started 1960's

COMPETENCY CHECK

Can you define contemporary management?

Participative Management

Participative management is management in which employees are involved, often in teams, in making decisions on such matters as goal setting, production process- es, scheduling, assignment distribution, and problem solving. Many organizations that have changed to participative management in recent years have done so in response to fierce competition and the resultant falling market share, lower quality of output, decreased customer satisfaction, and the recession of the early 1990s. Some companies have found that participative management works to cure these ills. LTV, Inc., a manufacturer of steel, aircraft products, missiles and electronics, and energy products, has experienced many benefits. One team working on a quality- related problem effected an 85 percent improvement in product quality and signif- icant cost reductions. Another team devised a microfiche records system that not only improved paper-flow efficiency but also resulted in a saving of $72,000.[8]

Participative management as a growing trend is a basic premise of this book. There is substantial evidence that participative management does improve the work environment and result in higher productivity. Participative management will be presented throughout the text as a more effective approach to managing. An overwhelming number of upper-level managers from large and small compa- nies (83 percent) responding to a New York Stock Exchange study agreed that par- ticipative management is effective in today's environment.[9] In the United States, emphasis on participative management has evolved largely from the Japanese style of management. Ouchi's Theory Z[10] attributes much of the success of Japanese businesses in world markets to their participative management style. Peters and Waterman,[11] in citing more than 40 highly successful U.S. companies, point out that employee involvement in management is a typical characteristic. In other evi- dence that it works, a study of 101 industrial companies found that the participa- tively managed among them outscored the others on 13 of 14 financial mea- sures.[12]

Team problem solving is not new, but it has been tried by more organizations since the wide publicity given to the Japanese use of teams they call "quality circles" (see Chapter 15). **Problem-solving teams** and **quality circles** are terms used for groups of employees who have responsibility for solving problems or addressing specific issues in their work units.

The innovative organization plan for General Motors' Saturn plant, located in Tennessee, incorporates a team approach throughout. This is a leading-edge organi- zational and operational plan whose implementation was anticipated with great interest by management and union leaders.[13]

In spite of its growing use, the team approach may be resisted. Some workers may resist because they don't want the extra responsibility; some supervisors resist because they believe their authority is being usurped. When it is attempted, it is sometimes abandoned because it was improperly initiated or administered.[14] Effec- tive team building requires that management align personal and corporate goals, find and build on employee strengths, reduce conflicts and politicking, and help all workers recognize their importance to the team. In using a team problem-solving approach, the supervisor's role sometimes changes from director to facilitator and coordinator. The success or failure of the team approach often hinges on the supervisor.

Increasingly documented as elements of job satisfaction are participation in decision making, whether individually or in teams, control of work lives, and gains the employer makes through worker efforts. One author refers to worker participation in management as "an ethical imperative."[15] Worker participation is looked upon as an essential element of contemporary management.

Total Quality Management

Total quality management (TQM) is the topic of Chapter 15, so at this point we will provide only a brief overview. **Total quality management** has been called "a prescription for quality" because it spreads the responsibility for quality across the entire organization—from the president to the file clerk. The fundamental engines for driving TQM are empowering, energizing, and enabling individuals to work with one another.[16] TQM emphasizes continuous improvement and has a customer-driven focus. The "customer" is whomever you normally deal with—the student who comes to the registrar to make an inquiry is the registrar's "customer"; the supervisor who asks her manager about the profits for the quarter is the manager's "customer"; the young man who asks the receptionist for an employment application is the receptionist's "customer."

The total quality management philosophy not only takes into account and accepts diversity and multiculturalism, it seeks the integration and contributions of all people.

Global Management

Global competition is forcing U.S. companies to come to grips with managing in a different environment—one that reaches far beyond the boundaries of the United States. **Global management** involves the management of organizations that operate in more than one country. Global management affects all levels of management, from the chief executive officer to the supervisor.

While top-level managers are involved in the overall strategies for competing in a global market, supervisors are involved in implementing those strategies while working with or for people of other nationalities and cultures. As shown in Figure 1.2, many companies are instituting programs for a global orientation for all levels of managers. Supervisors must be trained in supervising a diverse workforce (see Chapter 8) that includes workers of other nationalities. Honoring other cultures, while maintaining and increasing production and quality, is new to the supervisory role. In many cases, supervisors will be working under the direction of managers whose backgrounds and values are quite different, and they must learn to work as well with these managers as they have with those whose backgrounds and values are similar to their own.

COMPETENCY CHECK
Can you explain participative management, team problem solving, total quality management, and global management as a part of contemporary management?

Figure 1.2 HOW COMPANIES ARE TRAINING FOR GLOBAL MANAGEMENT	
Company	Program
American Express Co.'s travel related services	American business school students may work outside the United States for up to 10 weeks during summers. Junior managers with at least two years' experience may transfer to other countries.
Colgate-Palmolive Co.	15 recent college graduates are trained each year for 15 to 24 months prior to multiple overseas job assignments.
General Electric Co.'s aircraft-engine unit	Midlevel engineers and managers may be selected to participate in foreign language and cross-cultural training regardless of foreign assignments.
Honda of America Manufacturing, Inc.	U.S. supervisors and managers may be sent to Tokyo to work in parent company for up to three years. Six months of Japanese language lessons, cultural training and lifestyle orientation are provided before going to Tokyo.
PepsiCo Inc.'s international beverage division	Young foreign managers may be brought to the United States for one-year assignments in bottling plants.
Raychem Corp.	Inexperienced Asian clerks through middle managers may be assigned to the United States for six months to two years.

Source: Information reported in *The Wall Street Journal,* Mar. 31, 1992.

The Levels of Management

While all managers perform the same functions, there are differences among their jobs. The vertical relationship among these managers is called management levels.

The hierarchy of most organizations is composed of three levels: first-line, middle-level, and upper-level management. Figure 1.3 shows position titles of managers in each level. It also shows the relationship of management to workers; this nonmanagerial group is called operations.

The levels of management are also commonly called by other terms. Upper-level management is used synonymously with top-level or just top management and consists of chief executive officers, chief operating officers, presidents, and vice presidents. Middle-level management is sometimes abbreviated to mid-management, and includes department heads, division managers, and coordinators. The terms *first-* or *front-line manager* and *supervisor* are also used synonymously, as they will be in this text.

First-Line Management

First-line management—supervisors—works with the operating personnel who actually produce the product, service, or information the organization provides. As the term implies, first-line managers form the first line of contact with workers in

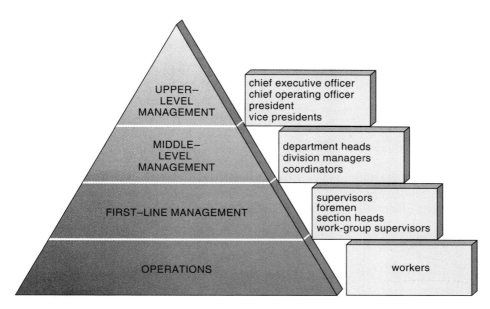

Figure 1.3
LEVELS OF MANAGEMENT AND OPERATIONS

operations. They direct the workers in carrying out the objectives of the organization and serve as the conduit through which workers communicate with management. They must also work with their peers and with superiors. Unlike middle- and upper-level managers, they do not supervise other managers. Their managerial tasks are marked by variety. The supervisor's job is expected to undergo changes in the future; it stands to become more important as the people-productivity link in the organization.[17]

Middle-Level Management   *most amount of stress - being cut*

Middle-level management forms a link between upper-level management, where policies are set, and first-line management, where operations are performed. Middle-level managers are the administrators who interpret and carry out plans and directives from upper-level management. They integrate and coordinate the work of the various departments so that the activities of all groups can be directed toward accomplishing company goals. In coordinating the activities of first-line management, they also serve as supervisors of these managers.

Middle-level management has been the focus of much upheaval in recent years. Japanese firms have few middle managers; American firms have traditionally had many managers at this level. Middle-level managers have served as information specialists in the past, but in many organizations computers are taking over this function. Managers who have been simply a link in the communication chain are finding that this is no longer enough. Organizational redesign and cost-cutting measures in the 1980s and 1990s have pared the middle level down significantly.

computers have replaced

Traditional middle managers, whose jobs have consisted mainly of passing on other people's work, will need to accept change or find their jobs in jeopardy.[18]

Upper-Level Management

COMPETENCY CHECK

Can you identify the levels of management and give an example of the titles and responsibilities of each?

The view from the top may be exhilarating, but in that rarified atmosphere responsibility sets heavily on the manager's shoulders. The "buck" stops here. First-line and middle-level managers have many peers, but there are only a few at the top. **Upper-level managers** establish the character, the mission, and the goals of the organization. They also plan broad strategies to implement the goals and secure the future of the organization. They use a broad brush to create the "big picture" and communicate the results downward to middle-level managers, who fill in the details of implementation by establishing objectives to meet each goal. In this way, upper-level managers also direct managers in the middle-management group.

As you have seen, all levels of management perform the same functions, but the emphasis differs. The following section will give you an overview of these functions.

The Functions of Management

The management process involves a set of activities called functions. As you have read, Fayol cited five functions of management early in this century. Only slightly modified, modern management theory identifies those functions as planning, organizing, staffing, leading and motivating, and controlling. These are shown in Figure 1.4. The time and effort devoted to each function will vary with the manager's position in the hierarchy. The supervisor's role in each of these functions will be dealt with in separate sections of this book. A brief discussion here will introduce you to these functions.

Planning

Planning includes identifying the mission, direction, and goals and objectives of the organization and determining the strategies for achieving them. Planning includes analyzing economic events and trends and forecasting their implications for the

Figure 1.4
FUNCTIONS OF MANAGEMENT BY LEVELS

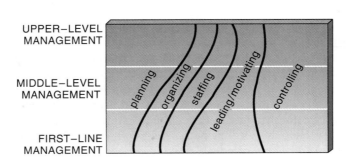

UPPER–LEVEL MANAGEMENT

MIDDLE–LEVEL MANAGEMENT

FIRST–LINE MANAGEMENT

planning   organizing   staffing   leading/motivating   controlling

organization. It also includes examining alternative uses of resources and choosing among them. Planning involves thinking, gathering and analyzing data, discussing concepts and ideas, creating innovative and entrepreneurial opportunities, and evaluating decisions. Note from Figure 1.4 that upper-level management devotes the largest portion of time to the planning function.

Organizing

Organizing means creating a structure for the organization. It involves identifying the tasks to be done and grouping those tasks into jobs. It includes establishing relationships among jobs and people and assigning managerial authority. Organizing also includes allocating the resources available to the organization. The organizing function usually results in a graphic organization hierarchy (illustrated in an organization chart) that shows how the efforts of the organization are interrelated and integrated. As shown in Figure 1.4, the participation of managers in the organizing function does not vary greatly from one level to another. Organizing puts the plans and strategies defined in the planning function into action.

Staffing

The process of selecting, training and developing, appraising, and rewarding employees is called **staffing.** Staffing is an integral part of the supervisor's responsibility. It was once considered a part of the organizing function, but with the increasing importance being assigned to human resources management, staffing itself is now commonly considered a major function. In companies with a human resources department, the supervisor will work in conjunction with that department in carrying out the staffing function. Section IV will address the supervisor's role in staffing.

Leading and Motivating

Influencing workers to act in a way that will lead to accomplishing the goals and objectives set in the planning function is a difficult task. By **leading** and **motivating**, managers try to create a climate in which workers will willingly perform their jobs and accept their share of responsibility for accomplishing the organizational goals. Leading and motivating means directing the work of people so that their tasks will be performed correctly, efficiently, and on time. This function requires the manager to understand human behavior and motivation and to be an excellent communicator. The supervisor spends a large proportion of time leading and motivating. Section V will address this function in depth.

Controlling

Controlling is the process through which management determines whether and how well it is accomplishing what it set out to accomplish. In controlling, managers compare actual performance with planned performance. The results determine what action should be taken. Regular monitoring is part of controlling. Monitoring reduces the potential for discovering deviations from plans only at the end of a fiscal period. If a company has planned a 5 percent sales increase for a quarter, for example, managers will compare sales each week or month to the sales projected in the plan. If sales are lower than expected, management may have a special sale to generate more revenue. If sales are higher than expected, sales personnel might be encouraged to push slow-moving or higher-profit products. Note that comparing and taking corrective action go hand in hand in controlling.

The controlling function, like the leading and motivating function, takes a large share of the supervisor's time. You will study the supervisor's role in controlling in Section VI.

The Overlapping Nature of Managerial Functions

coordinating ✓

Overlapping of functions is inherent in the managerial process. Although it is necessary to study each function as a separate entity before you can understand how they are integrated, managerial functions should not be considered as discrete, independent activities. In the real world, managers do not plan on Monday, organize on Tuesday, staff on Wednesday, lead and motivate on Thursday, and control on Friday. Planning, for example, goes on most of the time. During the planning stage, managers set standards, which are then used in controlling. For example, the 5 percent increase in sales discussed above was set during planning as a standard for growth. After comparing current sales with projected sales, the manager plans what corrective action, if any, needs to be taken, using the controlling function.

In orienting a new worker to a computer terminal workstation, the supervisor will observe whether the worker's skills are adequate to the task. These observations will guide the supervisor in planning for additional training, if needed, to upgrade the skills. If the skills are better than expected, the manager will plan an adjustment to the orientation period.

COMPETENCY CHECK

Can you explain the five functions of management?

In motivating a worker who rarely seems to complete assigned tasks, a manager might observe that the worker seems consistently to have more tasks to perform than other workers. This will call into play the organizing function of examining the job description and possibly redesigning the job.

X→ The Supervisor as the First Line of Management

Are supervisors part of management? In 1947, the Taft-Hartley Act placed supervisors unequivocally in the hierarchy of management. The act specifically prohibited X supervisors from joining unions of production or clerical workers. Hierarchical status does not always accrue from legal definition, however. "They remain today the bottom-most figure on what is essentially a totem pole," according to two researchers.[19]

A study of 225 plants employing over 9000 supervisors disclosed that 97 percent of top management surveyed considered supervisors an integral part of management.[20] They are not always successful in conveying this feeling to supervisors, however. Another study asked 250 supervisors if they truly felt a part of management. In response, 74 percent said yes, 24 percent said "sometimes," and 2 percent said no.[21] Clearly there is room for improvement on both sides to achieve a psychological as well as a hierarchical integration of the supervisor into management.

The Role of the Supervisor

The supervisor plays many roles. Some are well defined; some are not. One study found that supervisors spend more than two-thirds of their time relating with other people. What they do in these relationships covers a broad range of tasks and numerous roles.

One of the supervisor's roles is to serve as a connecting bridge between management and operations. Likert described supervisors as linking pins between the upper and lower planes of the organizational structure. This characteristic has been described as "a series of flexible couplings, transmitting orders and instructions from above while absorbing shocks and disturbances from below."[22] As you can see, a linking pin serves a critical function.

More recently, Keith Davis referred to supervision as "the keystone in the organizational arch,"[23] the supporting structural member that ties together management and workers. Davis's view and the bridging characterization connote less friction between the elements being joined. That is in keeping with what effective supervision should be. A bridge connecting two productive groups can be a facilitating element. While the bridge is subject to some stress, it can support a lot of traffic when properly planned.

Among the bridging tasks the supervisor performs are those of communicating and interpreting company objectives and policies to workers, appraising employee performance and making recommendations to upper management, identifying and communicating the needs of workers to management, and serving as a role model in interpreting and carrying out management's philosophy. As shown in Figure 1.5, supervisors spend much less of their time (15 percent) working with people in the same or higher levels than they do working with subordinates (55 percent); but this bidirectional interface will involve all the management functions.

COMPETENCY CHECK

Can you give examples of the various roles a supervisor plays?

Performing the Management Functions

The bridging characterization should not be interpreted as limiting the supervisor's role to that of facilitator, as important as that role is. The supervisor performs all five managerial functions: planning, organizing, staffing, leading and motivating, and controlling.

Look at Figure 1.5 again and note that 15 percent of supervisors' time is spent "thinking ahead." That is part of planning. So is part of the 15 percent of their time that is spent "doing work that cannot be delegated." The supervisor must plan for the long term (How will my department contribute to the company's 5-year plan?); for the intermediate term (Conduct a personnel-needs analysis for the biennium); and for the short term (Plan a meeting with work-team leaders for next week).

18   SECTION I   MANAGEMENT AND SUPERVISION

Figure 1.5
HOW MANAGERS
SPEND THEIR
TIME

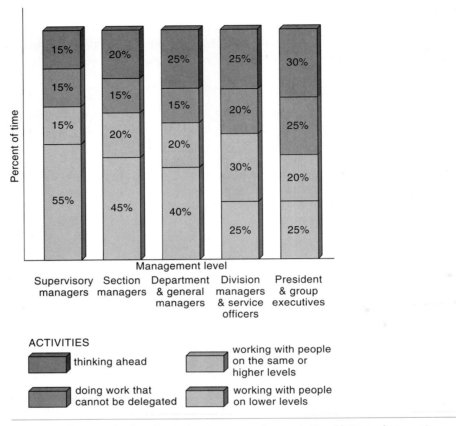

Source: Based on a study of an electrical appliance manufacturer in Donald C. Mosely, Leon C. Megginson, and Paul Pietri, *Supervisory Management,* South-Western Publishing Company, Cincinnati, 1993, p. 12. Copyright © 1993 by South-Western Publishing Co. All rights reserved.

The supervisor also organizes. Work must be analyzed and scheduled, and production goals must be met. Vacation requests must be coordinated with workers and with job demands. Conferences must be scheduled for a variety of purposes. Equipment maintenance schedules must be designed and maintained. Job design and job descriptions must be analyzed and kept up to date. Some of this organizing falls into the 15 percent of time spent "doing work that can't be delegated."

The staffing responsibility may be shared with the human resources department, but some tasks must be handled at the source—the unit supervisor. These tasks include determining labor needs, appraising performance, and making compensation and rewards recommendations.

The leading function is a subtle and difficult one. It involves the supervisor's personality and style as well as his or her background in management principles and human behavior. Creating conditions in which workers will be motivated to perform well and willingly is a critical component of leading. Conferring and counseling are also included in this function.

A study by the authors revealed that of the 52 percent of the time devoted to management functions by supervisors, over one-third is spent in leading and motivating.

Controlling involves continual follow-up on activities initiated in the course of performing the other four functions. Evaluation of a meeting held with work teams; checking to see that equipment is being maintained; determining whether production goals have been met; finding out whether the new self-appraisal system is really motivating workers; determining if quality standards are being met—all of these are controlling functions that the supervisor must perform.

The Duties of the Supervisor

Another way to look at what the supervisor does is to examine the activities performed on a daily basis without classifying them by function. From the numerous research studies being conducted today on supervision, many sets of supervisory tasks have been compiled. Organizations that have supervisory job descriptions have custom-made lists of duties for every supervisor classification.

Figure 1.6 shows a comprehensive list of duties of supervisors developed by a large corporation. The list resulted from a study of supervisory job content conducted by the organization over several years to aid in the selection of supervisors and to help prepare them for their new jobs. The result is a generic list of duties that could be applied to almost any supervisory position.

Figure 1.6 PRINCIPAL DUTIES OF SUPERVISORS (Ranked by proportion of time devoted to activity)	
Duties	**Frequency**
Controlling work	Every day
Problem solving and decision making	Every day
Planning work	Every day
Informal oral communications	Every day
General communications	Every day
Providing performance feedback	Every day
Training, coaching, developing employees	Every day
Providing written communications and documentation	Every day
Creating and maintaining a motivating atmosphere	Every day
Personal time management	Every day
Meetings and conferences	Twice monthly
Self-development activities	Weekly
Employee career counseling	Bimonthly
Representing the company to the community	Monthly

Source: Adapted from a major AT&T study reported in *Performance-Based Supervisory Development,* Human Resources Development Press, Amherst, Mass., 1982, p. 20.

**COMPETENCY
CHECK**
Can you give an
example of a
supervisory duty
in each of the five
management
functions?

The duties of the supervisor are varied and demanding. Carrying out these duties requires a variety of skills, as we shall see in the next section.

The Skills Required

How about the wisdom of Solomon and the patience of Job? Even such a formidable combination may not be enough if one is supervising in a technological environment. Certainly today's managers must be more skillful than their counterparts in the past.

The Skills of a Manager

Regardless of level in the hierarchy, today's manager must possess certain skills and be able to use them effectively. These can be classified as technical, conceptual, and human skills. Though all managers need all three skills, the importance of each skill varies with the level on which the manager operates, as shown in Figure 1.7.

Technical Skill.   **Technical skill** is the ability to use specific knowledge, methods, procedures, or techniques in performing a job. This ability is crucial to first-level managers. They must work in direct contact with operations workers and must be able to provide technical assistance when needed. Though there are exceptions, supervisors typically should be able to perform the jobs in their work units and to train others to do them. Much respect from workers is derived from supervisors' technical competence. Without this respect, a supervisor's ability to lead and motivate workers is seriously impaired.

As managers move up in the hierarchy, technical skill becomes less critical. The CEO need not know how to operate a jackhammer in order to manage a road construction company, but he or she should know what kind of equipment is needed for various construction jobs.

Conceptual Skill.   **Conceptual skill** is the ability to see the big picture, to understand or create abstract concepts, and to apply these concepts to specific situations.

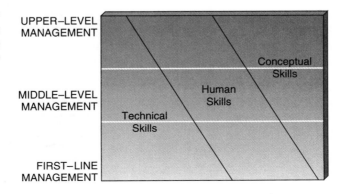

**Figure 1.7
SKILLS NEEDED
BY LEVELS OF
MANAGEMENT**

Conceptual skill is future-oriented and more important to upper-level managers than it is to lower-level managers. Top executives must be able to relate events and trends in the environment to their companies. They must be able to visualize the organization as a whole composed of interdependent parts, with the actions of any part having an impact on the whole.

Supervisors also need conceptual skills in order to visualize how their departments fit into the whole organization. While they are usually given specific guidelines for their units, their plans must mesh with all other units to work toward organizational goals.

Human Skill.   **Human skill** is the ability to understand, communicate with, work with, and interact harmoniously with people. It is the most important skill a manager can possess, and it is almost equally important at all levels of management. Human skills enable managers to understand themselves as well as others. Managers also need to understand and be tolerant of different views and values. Most important, they must understand the communications process and be skillful in using it in all their work relationships.

COMPETENCY CHECK
Can you cite three skills needed by managers and show their importance at the different levels?

COMPETENCY REVIEW

1. Name the three early approaches in the evolution of management and give a feature of each.
2. Explain the integrative approaches to management.
3. Define *contemporary management*.
4. Describe participative management and give the premise on which it is based.
5. Describe team problem solving as a component of contemporary management.
6. Describe total quality management.
7. Explain how the supervisor is affected by the global nature of organizations.
8. Identify the levels of management and give an example of a position in each.
9. Explain the functions of management.
10. Give an example of the supervisor's duties in each of the managerial functions.
11. Describe the skills needed by managers and show the importance of each to the levels of management.

APPLICATIONS

1. If you have not yet had the opportunity to demonstrate your leadership, you may have much more potential than you think. The following scale is designed to help you evaluate just how much potential you possess. Circle the number that indicates where you fall, from 1 to 10, on the scale. After you have finished, record your score in the space provided. Your instructor will help you interpret your score.

a. I can develop the talent and confidence to be an excellent speaker in front of groups.

10 9 8 7 6 5 4 3 2 1

I could never develop the confidence to speak in front of groups.

b. I have the capacity to build and maintain productive relationships with workers under my supervision.

10 9 8 7 6 5 4 3 2 1

I'm a loner. I do not want the responsibility of building relationships with others.

c. I intend to take full advantage of all opportunities to develop my leadership qualities.

10 9 8 7 6 5 4 3 2 1

I do not intend to seek a leadership role or to develop my leadership skills.

d. I can develop the skill of motivating others. I would provide an outstanding example.

10 9 8 7 6 5 4 3 2 1

I could never develop the skill of motivating others. I would be a poor example to follow.

e. I can be patient and understanding with others.

10 9 8 7 6 5 4 3 2 1

I have no patience with others and could not develop it.

f. I could learn to be good at disciplining those under me—even to the point of terminating a worker after repeated violations.

10 9 8 7 6 5 4 3 2 1

It would tear me up to discipline a worker under my supervision; I'm much too kind and sensitive.

g. I can make tough decisions.

10 9 8 7 6 5 4 3 2 1

I do not want decision-making responsibilities.

h. It would not bother me to isolate myself and maintain a strong line of discipline between workers and myself.

10 9 8 7 6 5 4 3 2 1

I have a great need to be liked; I want to be one of the gang.

i. I would make an outstanding member of a "management team."

10 9 8 7 6 5 4 3 2 1

I hate staff meetings and would be a weak or hostile team member.

j. In time, I would be a superior leader—better than anyone I have known.

10 9 8 7 6 5 4 3 2 1

My leadership potential is so low it is not worth developing.

TOTAL SCORE_____

Source: Adapted from "A Self-Paced Exercise Guide," *Supervisor's Survival Kit,* 2d ed., Science Research Associates, Inc., 1980.

2. Following are some of the activities that supervisors perform. By checking the appropriate column, classify each according to the predominant function. If you think that an activity falls within more than one function, check two or more columns as appropriate.

Activities	Plan	Organize	Staff	Lead/Motivate	Control
Met with team leaders					
Conferred with tardy worker					
Reviewed vacation requests; made tentative schedule					
Made T&D proposal					
Prepared budget					
Prepared speech					
Conducted two performance appraisal interviews					
Set up task force to review work standards					
Visited workstations; observed two with problems					
Reviewed draft of new policy statement					

CASES   Case I

"YOU CAN HAVE ANY COLOR CAR AS LONG AS IT IS BLACK"

In 1903, the first Ford motorcar went into production. An advertisement in Frank Leslie's *Popular Monthly* magazine of July 1903 called the Fordmobile the "latest and best." The advertisement described the car as being the "boss of the road" and declared:

"This new light touring car fills the demand for an automobile between a run-about and a heavy touring car. It is positively the most perfect machine on the market, having overcome all drawbacks such as smell, noise, jolt, etc. common to all other makes of Auto Carriages. It is so simple that a boy of fifteen can run it.

For beauty of finish it is unequaled—and we promise IMMEDIATE DELIVERY. We haven't space enough to enter into its mechanical detail, but if you are interested in the NEWEST and MOST ADVANCED AUTO manufactured today write us for particulars.

FORD MOTOR CO., 697 Mack Ave., Detroit, Mich."

Henry Ford is reported to have said, regarding the color of the car, that "you can have any color, as long as it is black." This, of course, made things easy for the paint department, for it had only one color of paint to use, which made the process move much more quickly.

However, when competition became greater as more companies began to produce cars, Ford was forced to offer a variety of exterior paint colors to meet the market demand. This, of course, affected the paint department in a major way.

1. Considering the manufacture of an automobile as a system, what are the inputs, the process, and the output of the system?
2. When Ford began to offer a variety of exterior paint colors, did this affect only the paint department? If not, what other parts of the Ford Motor Company were affected?
3. How does this change and its effect on other parts illustrate the systems approach to management?

Case II

BUT THE OPERATIONS RESEARCH TEAM DESIGNED THIS!

Marshall Insurance Company, located in a large metropolitan area, is expanding so rapidly that it is necessary to move their headquarters to a larger space. MIC has located a large warehouse and renovated the exterior. The interior space has been divided, and the offices for the upper- and middle-level managers have been defined. The floor that will house the file clerks and the clerks who post the policyholders' payments has been designed by the operations research (OR) team.

There are five file clerks and five accounts receivable clerks. The accounts receivable clerks are all separated by 4-foot-high modular dividers. The accounts receivable clerks post each payment, and the premium notice marked "Paid" is then given to the file clerks for storing in the 25 file cabinets provided. When the file cabinets are bulging at the seams, the file clerks purge the files. No one is

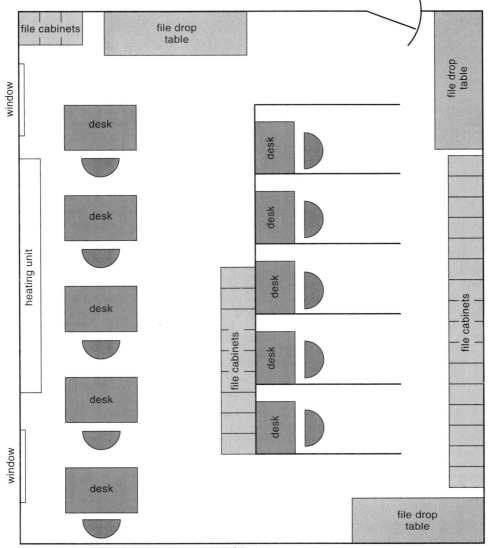

Scale ¼″ = 1′

assigned that responsibility; whoever can't stand the mess any longer begins the clean-out process.

The design that the operations research team has submitted to you is shown on page 25. Examine the design and then, using your knowledge of the classical and behavioral approach to management,

1. identify the problems caused by ignoring the classical approach to management.
2. identify the problems caused by ignoring the behavioral approach to management.
3. redraw the layout in such a way as to eliminate or minimize the problems identified in questions 1 and 2. You must work within the following parameters: room size remains the same as shown, and you may change job assignments, but you may not hire or fire anyone.
4. describe how your layout eliminates or minimizes the problems identified in questions 1 and 2.
5. explain the benefits managers receive from using information available to them through the various approaches to management.

REFERENCES

1. U.S. Bureau of Labor Statistics, *Occupational Outlook Handbook,* April 1986, p. 25.
2. Frederick W. Taylor, *The Principles of Scientific Management,* Harper & Row Publishers, Inc., New York, 1911.
3. Frank B. Gilbreth, *Motion Study,* D. Van Nostrand Company, Inc., New York, 1911. Also, Frank B. Gilbreth and Lillian M. Gilbreth, "Motion Study and Time Study Instruments of Precision," *Transactions of the International Engineering Congress,* vol. II, 1916; and Lillian M. Gilbreth, *The Quest of the One Best Way,* Society of Industrial Engineers, New York, 1924.
4. Henri Fayol, *General and Industrial Management,* Constance Storrs (trans.), Sir Isaac Pitman & Sons, Ltd., London, 1949.
5. Elton Mayo, *The Social Problem of Industrial Civilization,* Harvard Graduate School of Business Administration, Boston, 1945. See also Fritz Roethlisberger and William J. Dickson, *Management of the Worker: An Account of a Research Program Conducted by the Western Electric Company, Hawthorne Works, Chicago,* Harvard University Press, Cambridge, Mass., 1939.
6. Harold D. Koontz, "The Theory Jungle Revisited," *Academy of Management Review,* April 1980, pp. 175–187.
7. Henry C. Metcalf and Lyndall F. Urwich (eds.), *Dynamic Administration: The Collected Papers of Mary Parker Follett,* Harper & Row Publishers, Inc., New York, 1942.
8. William H. Wagel, "Opening the Door to Employee Participation," *Personnel,* April 1986, p. 6.
9. *People and Productivity—A Challenge to Corporate America,* a study by the New York Stock Exchange, Office of Economic Research, 1982, p. 27.
10. William Ouchi, *Theory Z: How American Business Can Meet the Japanese Challenge,* Addison-Wesley Publishing Company, Inc., Reading, Mass., 1981.

11. Thomas J. Peters and Robert H. Waterman, Jr., *In Search of Excellence: Lessons from America's Best-Run Companies,* Harper & Row Publishers, Inc., New York, 1982.
12. William Saporita, "The Revolt Against Working Smarter," *Fortune,* Jul. 21, 1986, pp. 58–65.
13. For one account, see "GM's $4 Billion Bet on a Car to Conquer Imports," *U.S. News and World Report,* Aug. 5, 1985, pp. 23–24.
14. Janice A. Klein, "Why Supervisors Resist Employee Involvement," *The Harvard Business Review,* September–October 1984, p. 88.
15. Jackson Ramsey and Lester R. Bittel, "Men and Women Who Turn the Key of American Productivity," *Journal of Organizational Behavior Management,* Spring–Summer 1985, p. 43.
16. Thomas H. Patten, Jr., "Beyond Systems—The Politics of Managing in a TQM Environment," *National Productivity Review,* Winter 1991/92.
17. For three observers' views, see Peter Drucker, "Twilight of the First-Line Supervisor?" *The Wall Street Journal,* June 7, 1983, p. 34; and Leonard A. Schlesinger and Janice A. Klein, "The First-Line Supervisor: Past, Present, and Future," *Handbook of Organizational Behavior,* Jay W. Lorsch (ed.), Prentice-Hall, Inc., Englewood Cliffs, N.J., 1986.
18. Rosabeth Moss Kanter, "The Reshaping of Middle Management," *Management Review,* January 1986, pp. 19–20.
19. Ramsey and Bittel, loc. cit.
20. Bradford Boyd, *Management-Minded Supervision,* 2d ed., McGraw-Hill Book Company, New York, 1976, p. 13.
21. Ibid., p. 14.
22. Rensis Likert, *New Patterns of Management,* McGraw-Hill Book Company, New York, 1961.
23. Keith Davis, "The Supervisory Role," *Supervisory Management: Tools and Techniques,* M. Gene Newport (ed.), West Publishing Company, St. Paul, Minn., 1976, p. 5.

SUGGESTED READINGS

Baker, Jack T.: "We're Lost, But We're Making Great Time," *IM,* November–December 1991, p. 6.
Crandall, Richard E.: "First-Line Supervisors: Tomorrow's Professionals," *Personnel,* November 1988, p. 24.
Hansen, Theodore L., Jr.: "Management's Impact on First-Line Supervisor Effectiveness," *SAM Advanced Management Journal,* Winter 1987, p. 41.
Magnet, Myron: "The Truth about the American Worker," *Fortune,* May 4, 1992, p. 48.
Piskora, Beth: "The Middle Management Trap," *Graphic Arts Monthly,* July 1989, p. 42.
Ruben, Douglas: "Managing Without Managers: The Participative Way," *Supervision,* November 1988, p. 17.
Sheridan, John: "Where Are the New Rules?" *Industry Week,* Feb. 3, 1992, p. 27.
"Who Needs Bosses Anyway?" *The Virginian-Pilot* and *The Ledger Star,* Norfolk, Va., Mar. 29, 1992.

GLOSSARY

behavioral approach   A management approach that is concerned with the human side of management and a balance between technical aspects of the workplace and the human side.

classical approach   A management approach that uses a combination of scientific management and classical organization theory.

classical organization theory   A body of work that includes a study of the management functions and the principles of management.

conceptual skill   The ability to see the big picture, to understand or to create abstract concepts, and to apply these concepts to specific situations.

contingency approach   An approach that takes into consideration various elements of the situation being managed and chooses the approach most appropriate for that situation.

controlling   The process through which management determines whether and how well it is accomplishing what it set out to accomplish.

first-line management   Managers who work with the operating personnel who actually produce the product, service, or information the firm provides.

global management   The management of organizations that operate in more than one country.

human skill   The ability to understand, communicate with, work with, and interact harmoniously with people.

leading and motivating   Creating a climate in which workers will willingly perform their jobs and accept their share of the responsibility for accomplishing the firm's goals.

management   The process of working with and through other people, and using other available resources, to meet the goals of the organization.

management science   An approach using computer technology and expanded techniques from earlier scientific management to solve business problems.

middle-level management   Forms a link between upper-level management, where policies are set, and first-line management, where operations are performed.

operations research   Another name for management science.

organizing   Creating a structure for the organization by identifying the tasks to be done and grouping the tasks into jobs, establishing relationships among jobs and people, assigning managerial authority, and allocating resources.

participative management   Employee involvement, often in teams, in making decisions on such matters as goal setting, production processes, scheduling, assignment distribution, and problem solving.

problem-solving teams (quality circles)   Terms used for groups of employees who have responsibility for solving problems or addressing specific issues in their work units.

planning   Identifies the mission, direction, and goals and objectives of the firm and determines the strategies for achieving them.

scientific management   A management approach that places its emphasis on improving efficiency in the workplace.

staffing   The process of selecting, training and developing, appraising, and rewarding employees.

systems approach   Viewing the organization as a set of interrelated parts interacting with one another to accomplish a common goal.

technical skill   The ability to use specific knowledge, methods, procedures, or techniques in performing a job.

total quality management   A management approach emphasizing continuous improvement with a customer-driven focus that spreads the responsibility for quality across the entire organization.

triangular management   Using combined knowledge from the classical, the behavioral, and the management science approaches.

upper-level management   The level of management that establishes the character, mission, and goals of the organization.

SECTION II

THE Planning Function

**STUDYING THIS CHAPTER
WILL ENABLE YOU TO:**

1. Describe the benefits and problems associated with planning.

2. Define the types of plans.

3. Show the relationship between organizational goals and the environment.

4. Distinguish between the external environments of upper-level and lower-level management.

5. Give an example of goal or objective setting by different levels of management.

6. Explain the planning focus of the supervisor.

7. Write objectives appropriate for the supervisory level.

8. Describe forecasting as it applies to supervisors.

9. Write an action plan for defined objectives.

10. Describe activities for which supervisors should plan.

11. Describe the tools and aids supervisors can use to help them plan.

WHY PLAN?
  Benefits
  Problems
  Supervisory Focus

TYPES OF PLANS
  Strategic Plans
  Short-Term Plans

HOW TO PLAN
  Understanding the Organizational
    Environment
  Forecasting
  Establishing Goals and Objectives
  Developing an Action Plan

WHAT TO PLAN
  Human Resources

  Physical and Material Resources
  Financial Resources
  Time Resources

PLANNING TOOLS AND AIDS
  Calendars
  Activity Lists
  Charts and Boards
  Computers
  Tickler Files

Competency Review
Applications
Cases
References
Suggested Readings
Glossary

THE Supervisor's Role IN Planning

Planning is the process of determining what you wish to accomplish (*goals and objectives*) and how you are going to accomplish them (*strategy*). Planning is deciding in advance what to do, how to do it, when to do it, and who is to do it. Planning bridges the gap from where we are to where we want to go.

Why Plan?

Planning provides direction. It helps you to know where you are going and requires that you develop a way to get there. As noted in *The Peter Principle*, "If you don't know where you are going, you will end up somewhere else."[1] Even if you do know where you are going, if you don't have a plan to get there, you will probably also end up somewhere else.

Benefits

The benefits of planning are many, and the following list is not all-inclusive. However, the list provides some insight into the benefits to be gained from the planning process. Planning

provides direction.
encourages managers to think ahead.
formally allocates resources.
requires a formal statement of what is to be accomplished.
provides, in writing, information for successors.
seeks to prevent problems.
allows managers at all levels to see how their departments or divisions fit into the total organizational plan.
lets each supervisor know what is expected of his or her group.
motivates by providing challenging and realistic goals for employees.
allows employees to provide input, thus making them a part of the organization.
leads to better coordination of organizational efforts.
leads to development of performance standards.
leads to more profitable organizational performance.

Problems

Although the benefits far outweigh the problems, supervisors must be aware that the planning process cannot be successful if any of the following problems exist:

- untrained planners
- lack of follow-through
- lack of upper-level management support
- lack of communication of expectations to employees
- lack of time; too busy putting out fires

People at the supervisory level are often asked to plan when they don't know how to plan, what to plan, or even why planning is important. Planning should answer these questions:

COMPETENCY CHECK
Can you identify the benefits and problems of planning?

1. What do we want to achieve? (goals and objectives)
2. What must we do to achieve our goals and objectives? (action plan)
3. When should each of the activities identified in the action plan be completed? (checkpoints and deadlines)
4. Who will work on each activity? (task and responsibility assignment)
5. Where should each activity take place? (location)
6. When should all activities be completed? (time frame)

No one should assume that planning always leads to success. It does not. However, a company with a good plan will beat out a company with no plan any time.

Supervisory Focus

Managers plan at all levels of an organization. However, the focus of their planning efforts, as well as the time frames and activities for which they plan, differ. Figure 2.1 shows the planning focus by hierarchical level for one activity.

As noted in Chapter 1, a study showed that 20.2 percent of the time supervisors spend on management functions is devoted to planning. The survey respondents, employed by both national and international organizations, indicated that their five top planning priorities were as follows:[2]

Making decisions	26.5%
Setting departmental activities	17.6%
Planning own work	14.7%
Planning work schedules	11.8%
Planning training and development	11.8%

Figure 2.1
THE HIERARCHICAL PLANNING PROCESS

Decision Level	Decision Process	Forecast Needed
Corporate (upper level)	Establish sales goals	Annual demand by product and region
Division sales manager (middle level)	Determine sales plan by product	Monthly demand for 2 years by product and region
Sales supervisor (first level)	Determine monthly sales objective by product	Monthly demand for 6 months by product

As you can see, the planning activities these supervisors are primarily involved in are the operational and daily types of plans.

Types of Plans

There are two basic types of plans—strategic, or long-term, plans and operational, or short-term, plans. Although first-level managers are concerned primarily with operational plans, they should be knowledgeable about how strategic plans fit into the planning process.

Strategic Plans

 Strategic plans are long-term plans that are formulated by upper-level management and reflect the vision of the organization for its future. The strategic plan flows from the mission statement of the company—that is, why is the company in business? What is its reason for being?

 Strategic plans are typically made for a period of 5 to 10 years. Several decades ago, when the business environment was not so volatile, strategic plans were often made for 15 to 20 years. Even today, companies that experience relatively little change in their products or services from year to year (such as manufacturers of matches or boxes) may still make strategic plans for longer periods. However, to companies such as those in the computer industry, which operate in a constantly changing, highly competitive market, "long term" may mean two years.

Strategic plans include standing plans and single-use plans. **Standing plans** are plans that seldom change and are used year after year. They include policies, procedures, rules, and other repetitive-use plans. **Single-use plans** are made for one activity or project and are "used up" once that project or activity is completed. An example of a single-use plan is one that is used to introduce a new product to the market or to add a wing to a building.

Short-Term Plans

 Short-term plans are typically made for 1 to 5 years, depending on the industry. These plans must "fit" the strategic plans and become one of the vehicles for accomplishing the long-term plan of the organization. Short-term plans include operational plans and daily plans.

Operational plans are plans that facilitate the accomplishment of the everyday activities of first-level managers. These and daily plans are the focus of this chapter. Work scheduling, preventive maintenance scheduling, and the design of new work methods are examples of operational plans.

Daily plans are plans that show a supervisor's actions for a particular day. Daily plans, of course, flow from operational plans, allowing the supervisor to work toward the accomplishment of the "bigger picture."

COMPETENCY CHECK
Can you describe the two major types of plans?

COMPETENCY
CHECK
Can you explain
the planning
focus of the
supervisor?

WHAT CAN THE SUPERVISOR DO?

The supervisor's focus is on the operational and daily levels of planning. Upper-level managers are concerned with strategic and long-term planning; middle-level managers are concerned with short-term and operational planning. As noted in Chapter 1, as one rises in a hierarchy, the time devoted to planning increases. Conversely, as one goes down in the hierarchy, the time devoted to the leading/motivating function increases and the time available for planning decreases.

It has been said that strategic planning is "doing the right things" and that operational planning is "doing things right." In this way, strategic and operational planning are interrelated and interdependent; the supervisor's role in "doing things right" is particularly important to the success of the strategic plan—"doing the right things."

How to Plan

The "how" of planning includes understanding the organizational environment, forecasting needs, establishing goals and objectives, and writing an action plan.

Understanding the Organizational Environment

The environment in which a business operates has both internal and external components. Internally, the **organizational environment** encompasses all the human and nonhuman resources in the organization and the interaction among these resources. The **human resources** are the people in the organization—their behaviors, attitudes, skills, motivations, and performance in getting the job done. The **nonhuman resources** are the organization's technology—its equipment, facilities, materials, information, money, and the processes involved in getting the work done. Integrating these resources into an effective operational system is what management is all about. As a supervisor, you will interact with your company's human and nonhuman resources as you manage its people and the technology within your assigned unit or department.

The major external environmental forces that affect company goals are shown in the outer frames of Figure 2.2, the environment of upper-level management, and Figure 2.3, the environment of lower-level management. Note the differences between the forces that influence upper-level management and the forces that influence lower-level management.

The forces that influence upper-level management are largely *outside* the firm: customers, creditors, suppliers, stockholders, competitors, the economy, government, unions and the labor market, and society. These all have an impact on what

Figure 2.2
ORGANIZATIONAL
GOALS AND THE
ENVIRONMENT:
UPPER-LEVEL
MANAGEMENT

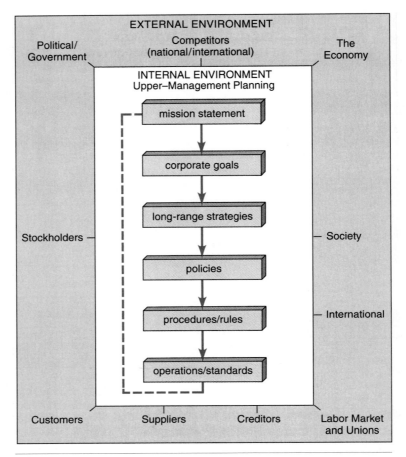

Source: Adapted from R. Wayne Mondy, Robert E. Holmes, and Edwin B. Flippo, *Management: Concepts and Practices,* Allyn and Bacon, Inc., Boston, 1980, p. 61.

COMPETENCY CHECK
Can you distinguish between the internal and external environments of upper- and lower-level management?

goals a company chooses to pursue. Upper-level management must be aware of changing conditions in any of these external forces.

The forces in the external environment that affect lower-level management are largely *inside* the organization; that is, they are outside the manager's specific unit or department but within the organization. These include the company's culture, structure, policies and procedures, standards, financial status, and technology as well as management philosophy, other departments, and peers.

Forces external to the organization affect all management to some degree. For example, as a supervisor, you may interface with suppliers and equipment vendors. But upper-level management will typically serve as a buffer between you and most external forces, such as creditors and stockholders.

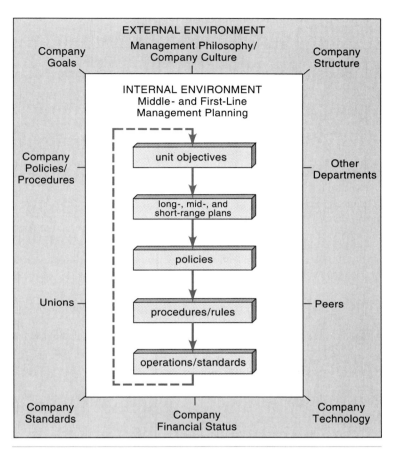

Source: Adapted from R. Wayne Mondy, Robert E. Holmes, and Edwin B. Flippo, *Management: Concepts and Practices,* Allyn and Bacon, Inc., Boston, 1980, p. 60.

**Figure 2.3
ORGANIZATIONAL
OBJECTIVES AND
THE
ENVIRONMENT:
LOWER-LEVEL
MANAGEMENT**

To aid managers in determining their needs and the probability of success for their plan, knowledge about future environmental forces is needed.

Forecasting

Forecasting is attempting to look into the future and predict future needs. The supervisor's role in forecasting involves projecting the future needs of her or his department. A supervisor who lacks experience in forecasting, if asked to "forecast the needs of your department for the short term (this year) and for the long term (the next 5 years)," might have, as a typical reaction, "What do I look like, a crystal ball? I'm no swami, and I don't own a Ouija board, so what do you expect from me?" However, if the supervisor were asked specific questions such as the ones in

**COMPETENCY
CHECK**
Can you describe forecasting as it applies to supervisors?

Figure 2.4
PLANNING QUESTIONS FOR FISCAL YEAR 1994–95

EQUIPMENT
1. What types of equipment, other than that in current use, will you need to perform the work in your department?
2. What pieces of equipment should be replaced?
3. What additional equipment will be required?
4. Will maintenance contracts expire? Should they be renewed?

PERSONNEL
1. Will additional employees be needed? If so, how many and in what capacity?
2. Will different skills be required by employees? If so, what skills? Do current employees have these skills?
3. Will it be necessary to reduce the workforce? If so, by how many and in what area?
4. Are any of the workers' skills obsolete? Identify.
5. Do workers need additional training? If so, in what areas? Identify the employees.
6. Which employees are ready for development and growth within their areas of expertise? What training and development should be provided?

FACILITIES
1. Are current space allocations adequate for current needs?
2. Will more or less space be required for future needs?
3. Is the current work-space layout efficient?
4. Is the current work-space layout safe?
5. Are the heating/cooling/lighting systems adequate?
6. Is the furniture ergonomically designed to reduce fatigue?

WORK METHODS AND PROCESSES
1. Are current work methods efficient?
2. Are materials required to complete the work available when needed?
3. Are materials of the quality required to produce a quality product?
4. Is the flow of work efficient?
5. Should new or different work methods be analyzed in order to increase efficiency?

Figure 2.4, the responses would be her forecast. She would probably feel more secure in her answers than if she were just asked to "forecast."

The supervisor's responses to these questions will be based on her knowledge in her area of expertise and her experience within the field. In addition, she might want to consult with staff specialists and with experienced employees to gain the benefit of their knowledge.

Forecasting is predicting the future. It is not an exact science, and of course there is no absolute way to predict what will happen. Too many outside influences over which supervisors have no control affect the accuracy of predictions. For example, if there is an unpredicted downturn in the economy and the demand for a product decreases, projected increases in personnel and equipment will be negatively affected. Forecasting, at best, is an educated guess, but an educated guess is better than no guess at all!

Establishing Goals and Objectives

Goals are the "end" to which a company aspires. A business sets the goals it wants to reach and then does everything it must to reach the goals.

The terms goal and objective are often used interchangeably. But goals are broader and less definitive than objectives: Goals may be stated in words such as *understand* and *know* and in other words that are not definite or quantitative. **Objectives** are more specific and focus on a particular ability, knowledge, or accomplishment. Objectives should be stated in words or phrases that allow the end result to be easily ascertained.

Goals and the Environment.   Goals are the rationale for an organization's existence. The environment plays a large role in shaping the organization.

The relationship of goals and the environment is evident in several ways. One way is through constraints in the environment. Forces in the environment determine, to a great extent, what an organization may and may not do. A company may sell almost anything that has not been cited by law as harmful to individuals or to society. Laws also govern the way a chemical plant may dispose of its waste materials. A company must dispose of chemical waste in such a way as to protect humans and the environment, and it must add the cost of doing this to the costs of doing business. Thus, the legal environment imposes many constraints on an organization.

Governments also impose constraints. Our federal government, for example, may not allow an organization to trade with certain countries whose actions it considers unacceptable. This is a constraint from the political environment.

Social disapproval may also affect company goals. Besides outright constraints, the environment sometimes dictates that certain objectives, while not illegal, may not be desirable. Companies that sell alcoholic products, for example, have certainly been affected by the recent actions of groups whose goal is to decrease highway fatalities.

Another factor in the environment that can affect organizational goals is the state of the economy. For example, foreign competition has greatly depressed the domestic electronics industry and caused its market share to plummet. In addition to competition, changing prices, the increased cost of capital, and a dwindling supply of resources are among many forces in the economic environment that can influence organizational goals. As you can see, there are many factors in the environment over which the organization has little control but must plan for anyway.

Internal forces can also affect management goals. A company that wishes to expand, for example, may find that it does not have the economic or human resources to do so. Goals sometimes must be modified or discarded because of internal environmental forces.

There are environmental/goal relationships other than the five cited above. Even

COMPETENCY CHECK

Can you show the relationship between organizational goals and the environment?

the weather can influence the goals a company chooses. For example, a retail store in northern Alaska would be foolhardy to specialize in swimwear and beach clothes. You will detect other relationships as we view the setting of goals by the management team.

Goals and the Hierarchy.   Differences in the levels of management affect how broad or how definitive the goal or objective statements must be. In setting goals, managers do not work in isolation but function as a team. When a goal is established, each manager must set objectives for his or her department that will feed into and help achieve the goal. Whether the manager focuses on goals or objectives depends largely on his or her level of management, as we shall see in the discussion that follows. However, no matter where the manager is in the hierarchy, the goals and objectives must tie back to the mission statement.

Upper-level managers, such as the board of directors, the chief executive officer (CEO), the president, and other executive officers look at the "big picture." They formulate goals that answer such questions as:

What is our company all about?
What product(s) or service(s) will we provide?
What level of profit shall we strive for?
What image do we wish to portray?
Where do we wish to be 5 or 10 years from today?
How will we get there?

When Chrysler said, "We want to be your car company," it meant that its goal was to develop customer loyalty that would keep its customers coming back for more cars and service. Upper-level management sets the broad goals that will enable the company to operate in a highly competitive national and international environment.

Before divestiture, AT&T operated in a protected political environment as a limited monopoly. As such, it reminded the public that "all we have to sell is service." Today, without this protected status, it has changed its goals. It now aims to be a competitive manufacturer and retailer of communications products, telecommunications systems, and computer technology. Environmental forces caused AT&T's top management to reshape the company and its goals.

 Upper-level managers are ultimately responsible for every goal and objective throughout the organization. They direct most of their efforts toward setting broad, long-term goals. Top managers also formulate strategies for achieving those goals. The setting and implementation of secondary and supporting objectives is delegated to the lower levels of management.

Middle-level managers, such as regional officers, division directors, and plant managers, set supportive objectives based on the broad goals that support those established by upper-level managers. At the middle level, objectives are greater in number and more focused than the broad company goals. Middle-level managers coordinate objectives with their peers and delegate to first-line managers the setting of additional supportive goals.

You have noted that a hierarchy of objectives is created as each level sets objec-

WHAT CAN THE SUPERVISOR DO?

A supervisor who is about to become a part of the planning process would first have to know and understand the goals of the organization and then determine how his department can contribute to accomplishing these goals. The supervisor would then begin to develop his own departmental objectives and an action plan. He may decide that his department's turn-around time for computer-generated reports could be reduced and that computer downtime could be reduced as well. Once the general direction of the department has been established, the specific objectives must be stated in writing.

tives to carry out the goals set at the top. The number increases from the few broad company goals at the top to more objectives with greater focus at the middle to more detailed and more narrowly aimed objectives at the supervisor's level.

First-line managers direct operations. This is the level at which products are made or services performed. Here the dreams and plans are given physical form. Objectives get more specific, such as:

Increase sales by 10 percent within a year.
Reduce employee turnover by 10 percent this year.
Reduce rejects to 1 percent by the end of the second quarter.
Cross-train four junior line workers by year's end.
Implement an incentive program to reduce absenteeism by 10 percent by midyear.
Reduce customer complaints by 10 percent within 6 months.

In general, objectives should

be related to the needs of the organization.
be measurable and quantifiable, whenever possible.
be designed to prevent rather than solve problems.
be challenging, but achievable.
consider internal and external constraints.
be innovative.
be written.
be consistent with one another and with organizational goals.

Writing Objectives. Techniques for writing meaningful objectives include (1) using specific terms, including what is to be achieved and within what time frame; (2) stating objectives in measurable terms; (3) using language that workers understand; and (4) stating objectives in terms of end results. Let's look at three objectives that have been identified and write these objectives in terms that meet the specific requirements for a "good" objective.

COMPETENCY CHECK
Can you give an example of goal or objective setting by each of the levels of management?

Thought	Objective
Increase productivity	Increase average output for computer operators by 5% over 1/1/94 measurement by 1/1/95
Reduce downtime	Reduce computer downtime by 10% over current levels by 1/1/95
Reduce turnaround time	Reduce average turnaround time for documents from current 4 hours to 3½ hours by 1/1/95

Other objectives may be added that are not so easily quantifiable.

COMPETENCY CHECK
Given general information, can you write an appropriate objective?

Writing qualitative objectives is much more difficult than writing quantitative ones. For example, an objective, to "increase the quality of work life of the computer operators" may be important. What is "quality of work life"? How do you know if you have it at all, and how do you know if it has increased? To write an objective relating to quality of work life, you must first decide what you want to accomplish (for example, to reduce operator fatigue), and then you must write the objective. The "how" will be included in the action plan.

Thought	Objective
Increase quality of work life	Reduce operator fatigue as measured by decreased absenteeism

Stating the objective in this way clearly shows what you expect to accomplish as well as how it can be measured. If you want to be even more precise, the objective might read "reduce absenteeism by 10 percent within a 6-month period."

4 ✳ Developing an Action Plan

COMPETENCY CHECK
Can you write an action plan to reach objectives previously written?

An **action plan** describes how objectives are to be accomplished. What specific actions must be taken, and by whom? What specific activities and tasks must be performed, and by whom? The action plan converts objectives into activities and tasks and assigns responsibility for achieving the objectives.

Let's look once more at the objectives on pages 41 and above and see how these objectives can be translated into an action plan.

1. *Objective:* Increase average output for computer operators by 5 percent over 1/1/94 measurement by 1/1/95.
   Action plan: Provide additional training in computer operation for four operators.
   Enroll supervisor in course for improving interpersonal skills.

2. *Objective:* Reduce computer downtime by 10 percent over current measurement by 1/1/95.
   Action plan: Institute preventive maintenance program.
   Develop in-house repair program for minor repairs.

3. *Objective:* Reduce average turnaround time for documents from current 4 hours to 3½ hours by 1/1/95.
   Action plan: Reschedule work assignments so that all operators become proficient in each type of document processing.
   Improve computer operator skills through training, as described above.

4. *Objective:* Reduce operator fatigue as measured by decreased absenteeism.
   Action plan: Provide increased lighting levels in checking area.
   Provide cushioned floor pads in high-traffic areas.
   Replace existing chairs with ergonomically designed chairs.

When the objectives have been determined and an action plan developed, all this information should be combined on a form such as the one shown in Figure 2.5.

Figure 2.5
DEPARTMENTAL PLANS

Supervisor Juan Perry   **Department** Information Processing

Objective	Action	Persons Involved	Date Begun	Target Date	Outcome
Increase average output for computer operators by 5% over 1/1/94 measurement by 1/1/95	Provide additional training in computer operation for four operators	Cox, McMills, Kennedy, Thu	1/15/94	1/1/95	
	Enroll supervisor in course for improving interpersonal skills	Knight			
Reduce computer downtime by 10% over current measurement by 1/1/95	Institute preventive maintenance program	All	1/15/94	1/1/95	
	Develop in-house repair program for minor repairs	Johnson, Szuka, Mathis, Bell			
Reduce average turnaround time for documents from current 4 hours to 3½ hours by 1/1/95	Reschedule work assignments so that all operators become proficient in each type of document processing	All computer operators (see above)	1/15/94	1/1/95	
	Improve computer operator skills through training, as described above				
Reduce operator fatigue as measured by decreased absenteeism	Provide increased lighting levels in checking area	All computer operators (see above)	1/15/94	1/1/95	
	Provide cushioned floor pads in high-traffic area				
	Replace existing chairs with ergonomically designed chairs				

WHAT CAN THE SUPERVISOR DO?

"Why should I plan? I spend all of my time 'putting out fires' and trying very hard to 'keep my head above water.' How can you expect me to find time to plan, too?"

Lack of planning often causes supervisors to spend all their time "putting out fires" and trying to "keep their heads above water." It's a vicious cycle, allowing no time to do the planning that would minimize the daily crisis management engaged in by so many supervisors. If supervisors understood that time invested in planning would ultimately pay dividends in daily efficiency, they might be convinced that it was worthwhile to learn how to plan and how to follow through on the planning process.

Note that there is space on the form to indicate the date action is to begin and the target date for completion, as well as space to identify the persons involved and the actual outcomes.

What to Plan

Supervisors are charged with the responsibility for using the resources available to them in the most efficient way. They must plan for the efficient use of their human, physical, material, financial, and time resources.

Human Resources

To allocate human resources most efficiently, supervisors should plan for staffing needs, improvement in productivity and quality of work life, and total quality management.

Staffing Needs.　Supervisors must plan for staffing needs in terms of the number of people needed to accomplish the objectives of their departments as well as the skills required of the workers both now and in the future. For example, the supervisor of the computer department may determine that there are enough workers to run an efficient department at the present time, but, if managers continue to increase their use of the information processing department, two additional computer operators and one additional clerk will be required next year. While the current skill level is adequate for current needs, new graphics equipment may require hiring more skilled operators or providing additional training for those already on the job.

Productivity Improvement.　Planning for productivity improvement may involve plans for improving the quality of work life of employees and planning for the implementation of a total quality management program.

Part of a supervisor's planning responsibility for human resources is to plan for improving the quality of their work life. Quality of work life is covered in Chapter 15.

One of the major purposes of total quality management is improving productivity, both in quantity and in quality. Chapter 15 is devoted to the total quality management concept.

Physical and Material Resources

Planning for physical and material resources includes plans for facilities and equipment and materials and supplies.

Facilities and Equipment.   Efficient use of facilities and equipment requires planning. Space must be properly allocated for most efficient work flow. To evaluate space use, the supervisor should examine the current floor layout. A scale drawing of the floor plan, with each piece of furniture and equipment placed in its current position, provides a basis for tracing work flow and evaluating efficiency. The supervisor can then analyze the allocation and use of space in relation to the tasks performed.

The allocation and use of equipment should also be evaluated. Equipment use should be maximized, with as little idle time as possible. (See the section on Gantt charts for information on scheduling.)

In addition to proper allocation and use, the supervisor must plan for the most efficient equipment to do the job. This will require staying up to date regarding new equipment. Reviewing trade journals and vendor literature, attending professional meetings, and having discussions with colleagues help supervisors stay current. While the resources to replace equipment will not always be available, supervisors should be prepared to make equipment recommendations when the opportunity arises. Records of equipment downtime and maintenance costs provide backup when requesting new or replacement equipment.

The supervisor also needs to plan for a safe place to work and for safe use of equipment. Providing a safe work environment is the topic of Chapter 16, "Maintaining a Safe and Healthy Workplace."

Materials and Supplies.   Supervisors also plan for the proper allocation, availability, use, and conservation of materials and supplies. For many companies, materials and supplies represent a major expenditure.

When materials and supplies are improperly allocated, not available when needed, or improperly used, or when waste is prevalent, costs increase. Additional costs are incurred when workers must wait for materials or supplies required for their work activities and when storage costs are incurred for excessive inventory. Implementing a just-in-time inventory system has proved invaluable in reducing costs associated with excessive inventory or inadequate inventory. The **just-in-time (JIT) inventory** system is a control technique that arranges for inventory to be delivered directly to the production facility as it is needed—"just in time" to be used. JIT was initiated in Japan and has been successful in other countries, including the United

States. Ford Motor Company, General Motors, American Motors, General Electric, and RCA are just a few of the companies that have adopted JIT.

Many companies experience increased costs due to careless use of materials and supplies. Use of materials and supplies must be planned to minimize costs and increase worker efficiency.

Financial Resources

Supervisors may have to plan and submit budgets for their departments. These budgets typically include projected salaries of workers, costs of proposed equipment purchases, allocations for materials and supplies, and training and development costs.

Time Resources

Peter Drucker wrote: "The output limits on any process are set by the scarcest resource . . . time is the scarcest resource, and unless it can be managed, nothing else can be managed."[3]

Most people complain that there is "just not enough time in a day," but time is a valuable resource over which supervisors have some control. To make maximum use of both workers' and supervisors' time, planning is a must. No good supervisor would dream of starting a new work method or ordering materials without careful planning, yet many supervisors (and others) think proper time use does not have to be planned—it will just happen. Nor do they consider that time is money and that they should be as accountable for its use as they are for the use of all other resources.

Supervisors may use either of two methods of scheduling. **Forward scheduling,** where the schedule results in a projected completion date, is preferred. This type of scheduling allows the supervisor to analyze the job to be completed, schedule tasks leading to project completion, and estimate when the project can be completed. More difficult to implement is **backward scheduling.** Here, the supervisor is given a completion date and must figure out how to get the work completed by that time.

Worker Time.   Planning worker time is a large part of many supervisors' duties. A plan must be developed for scheduling regular working time; overtime, when necessary and appropriate; worker absences; and holidays and vacations. In cases where temporary layoffs are an annual occurrence, this time must be anticipated and plans made to minimize work interruption.

In the 1985 survey of supervisors conducted by the authors,[4] 44.2 percent of the respondents reported that "planning work schedules" was one of their top five planning priorities; 11.8 percent indicated that "planning work schedules" was their *most* important planning activity.

Scheduling is deciding when activities will take place as well as their order, or when specific processes or procedures will begin and end, or when workers will begin and end their working day. Different jobs require different levels of scheduling. If the work of one individual or group of individuals affects the ability of others to complete their jobs, the supervisor must plan for coordination of activities. For example, on an assembly line, the task of the worker who installs the windshield wipers on a truck is dependent upon the person who installs the windshields. Until that portion of the truck is assembled, the windshield-wiper installer is idle.

Other jobs require a different type of scheduling. Each of the jobs that comes into a word processing center is assigned to an operator who is responsible for completing the job. If an extremely long or complicated job comes in to be processed, several operators may be assigned to complete selected portions and work together to complete the entire project.

Many companies provide breaks or rest periods during the day to help relieve worker fatigue. Breaks are taken by workers according to a predetermined schedule so that they will not all be away from their workstations at the same time.

During the past decade, flextime has become a popular type of work scheduling. **Flextime** allows employees some flexibility in the way they schedule their workday. There is usually a **core time,** a time during which all employees must be on the job, but beginning and ending work hours are flexible. For example, a company may set 10 A.M. to 2 P.M. as the core time—the busy time when it is important that all employees be available to work. The other 4 hours of an 8-hour day may then be set according to the personal needs of the workers, as long as the work can be accomplished and the job covered within the working hours of the company. Suzanne is a "day person," someone who is wide awake and full of energy early in the day. She may choose to come to work as soon as the doors open at 6:30 A.M. and work until 3:30 P.M. Julian is a single parent whose child must catch the school bus at 8:30 A.M. He may choose to report to work at 9:30 A.M. and work until 6:30 P.M.

Flextime requires very careful scheduling. Not everyone can work from 6:30 A.M. to 3:30 P.M., leaving the business unattended from 3:30 P.M. until closing. Nor can everyone work from 9:30 A.M. until 6:30 P.M. The supervisor must work with each individual to make a schedule that will maximize worker productivity and worker satisfaction.

Other companies have accommodated their requirements and worker needs through job sharing, permanent part-time, and telecommuting. *Job sharing* allows two people to share a particular job, with one person working part of a day and the other person assuming the job responsibilities during the remaining work time. Working parents are the most likely candidates for job sharing. In one large city, for example, the assistant commonwealth attorney's job is shared by two attorneys, one who performs the duties during the morning, the other during the afternoon. Permanent part-time differs from job sharing. Most regular part-time jobs are entry-level positions or temporary jobs. **Telecommuting** is working from a location other than the workplace. Most telecommuters work from their home using a computer for linkage to the workplace. All these alternative work modes require careful scheduling by the supervisor.

Planning for work beyond the regular workday is sometimes necessary. Planning for overtime should not be left to chance nor to the last minute. While supervisors may be unable to anticipate overtime weeks or even days in advance, they can have a plan ready when the need occurs. Knowing who is willing to work overtime hours, on what days, and for how many hours will simplify the task of scheduling overtime work. However, if overtime becomes a normal activity, an investigation of work methods and employee workloads should be made. Perhaps alternative work methods may be instituted, workloads adjusted, or more workers hired.

Just as overtime should be planned for, so should time when employees will not be at work due to absenteeism, tardiness, holidays, vacations, and temporary lay-offs. Workers who are able to do more than one job can often cover for absent workers by performing essential tasks. This, of course, will require an adjustment in the normal workload, but it will allow the department to continue to function without interruption. Unanticipated absences and tardiness cannot be scheduled, but they can be planned for. If the supervisor knows who is capable of doing other tasks, planning for absences is easier.

Planning for vacations is especially important. Employees get angry if they believe their vacation time has been unfairly scheduled. If the company has a vacation policy, the supervisor should adhere to both the letter and the intent of the policy. As with any other absence, the supervisor must be sure that there are enough people available to handle the work so that productivity will not suffer.

Supervisor Time. In the survey of supervisors cited previously,[5] 70.5 percent responded that "planning own work" ranked as one of the five top planning priorities; in fact, 14.7 percent indicated that "planning own work" was their *first* planning priority. Because of the importance of planning one's own work time efficiently, this section will be devoted to identifying time wasters and time leaks. Suggestions for improved use of time will also be provided. Planning tools and techniques for better use of both supervisors' and workers' time will be discussed in the next section.

Numerous studies identifying time wasters have been conducted. Most of the study results show common time wasters among people in different positions and different careers. For example, the same time wasters were identified by different groups of workers (including office managers, administrative assistants, engineers, school administrators, city managers, executive secretaries, university administrators, data processing managers, and funeral directors).[6] Figure 2.6 shows a cross-sectional profile of the common time wasters identified by this heterogeneous work group.

Figure 2.6 COMMON TIME WASTERS FOR GENERAL WORK GROUP	
Time Waster	**Ranked Importance**
Telephone	1
Drop-in-visitors	2
Meetings	3
Socializing	4
Failure to delegate	5
Lack of daily plan	6
Inability to say "no"	7
Incomplete information	8
Crisis management	9
Personal disorganization	10

Source: Dennis L. Mott, "Time Management," *NBEA Yearbook,* chap. 14, no. 18, National Business Education Association, Reston, Va., p. 145. Reprinted with permission.

Figure 2.7
TIME-AUDIT ANALYSIS

EVALUATE YOUR TIME

How am I presently spending my time? Note every major category on this time audit (meetings,telephone calls, planning daily work, work, etc.).

	How Much Time Do I Spend?		
	Too little	*Just right*	*Too much*
Activity			
_____			
_____			
_____			

Are you having a problem managing your time? Do you recognize any of the problems shown in Figure 2.6? If so, perhaps you should conduct a time audit. A time audit will help you identify the work time you have available and how you spend it. You may conduct a continuous time audit by dividing each workday over a 2-week period into 15- or 20-minute segments and recording how you spend each segment. Or you may conduct a periodic audit by appointing someone to randomly select (10 to 20 times weekly) a period of time in which to record your activity. Either way, the time audit will provide information about how you use your time and allow you to analyze the results for time wasters and time leaks—inefficient use of time. A simple form for *analyzing* the time audit is shown in Figure 2.7.

Here are some general guidelines for improving the use of your time:

Rank tasks in order of importance. Then work through the tasks, beginning with the most important ones.
Divide tasks into two groups—those for which you can control the timing and those over which you have no control.
Determine which tasks can be delegated. *Do it!*
Determine where time can be saved by taking the right steps.
Make a list or a chart to help you keep track of your progress on each item.
Follow up. At the end of each week, take a look at your time log and see how you actually spent your time. Was your time used effectively? Why, or why not?

COMPETENCY CHECK
Can you identify four major categories for which a supervisor must plan?

Planning Tools and Aids

Many planning tools and aids are available to supervisors to help them plan better and increase their efficiency. Among these tools and aids are calendars, activity lists, charts and boards, computers, and tickler files.

WHAT CAN THE SUPERVISOR DO?

Do you regularly practice timesaving techniques? Are the following techniques a part of your normal routine? Do you

1. arrive at your workplace half an hour early in order to take advantage of the quiet time before other employees arrive?
2. write a daily "to-do list" of your top priorities?
3. plan your week's activities on Monday?
4. sort out all important mail items and telephone messages?
5. delegate routine duties?
6. set deadlines for your subordinates when you delegate work?
7. set deadlines for yourself?
8. use waiting time to plan activities?
9. carry blank 3 × 5 cards to jot down spontaneous ideas and notes?
10. know why you procrastinate? (what you are avoiding?)
11. break down unpleasant tasks into smaller ones?
12. cut down on nonproductive activities—phone calls, rambling conversations, water-cooler breaks?
13. handle every piece of paper once by dealing with it, answering it, or throwing it away?
14. answer letters by writing on the bottom of the letter, when appropriate?
15. keep your work area cleared and ready for action? (Items waiting for attention should be placed in the center of the work area.)
16. schedule a meeting only when you can explain its purpose?
17. listen carefully? (Ask direct questions to obtain needed information quickly or for clarification.)
18. say no to additional tasks if you know you do not have the time to do a good job on them?
19. set aside your most productive time period every day to do creative work? know when your most productive time period is?
20. save all trivial matters for a 3-hour session once a month?
21. make an appointment with yourself for 15 minutes late in the afternoon? (Spend 5 minutes of that time assessing the day and how well you've used your time. Then identify the projects that are critical to tomorrow's success, and decide what time should be spent on which projects.)
22. on Friday, make a 30-minute appointment with yourself? (Plan for the coming week. Schedule the most important tasks for Monday, Tuesday, or Wednesday, when you should be refreshed from the weekend. Thursday and Friday are usually spent playing "catch up.")

Source: Adapted from Mary C. Lock, "25 Ways to Save Time," *Modern Secretary,* February 1983, p. 14.

Calendars

Calendars may range from one monthly sheet with 31 square blocks to separate pages for each day, with time segments marked and space provided for various other types of information. A simple pocket calendar can help you stay organized. By entering two dates for each task, a deadline and a warning date, you can remind yourself to start working on the task in time. Unless you put important dates and activities in writing, you may forget them in the rush of your day-to-day activities. However, even the best-kept calendar won't do you any good if you forget to refer to it. Figures 2.8 and 2.9 show two types of planning calendars.

Figure 2.8
PLANNING CALENDAR

DAILY PLANNING CALENDAR   *Date* _____

Priority   *Activity*
                  Letters to Write
_____   _____
_____   _____
_____   _____
_____   _____

                  People to See
_____   _____
_____   _____
_____   _____
_____   _____

                  Things to Be Done
_____   _____
_____   _____
_____   _____
_____   _____

                  Things to Be Planned
_____   _____
_____   _____
_____   _____

(Continued)

**Figure 2.8
(CONTINUED)**

Items to Be Obtained

_____   _____
_____   _____
_____   _____
_____   _____

Priority

Phone Calls to Make

_____   PERSON _____ TEL. NO.

_____   _____
_____   _____
_____   _____
_____   _____

Priority:

1. important and urgent (must be done now)
2. important but not urgent (separates effective managers from ineffective ones)
3. urgent but not important (clamor for attention, but on objective examination, have low priority)
4. busy work (marginally worth doing but not urgent or important)
5. wasted time (subjective—use as criterion for judging how you feel when task is completed)

Appointments

8:00 _____	1:00 _____
8:30 _____	1:30 _____
9:00 _____	2:00 _____
9:30 _____	2:30 _____
10:00 _____	3:00 _____
10:30 _____	3:30 _____
11:00 _____	4:00 _____
11:30 _____	4:30 _____
12:00 _____	5:00 _____
12:30 _____	5:30 _____

Figure 2.9
PLANNING CALENDAR

Date *Jan. 22, 199–*   Day *Tuesday*

	ACTIVITY	PRIORITY	EVALUATION
		1–Urgent 2–Important 3–Routine 4–Discretionary 5–Wasted	Could you have used your time more efficiently? (Example: delegate to ———; organize, plan, train someone else to handle it; combine, eliminate, etc.)
8:00	*Work on report for J.O.*	*1*	
8:30			
9:00			
9:30			
10:00	*Meeting with dept. heads*	*2*	
10:30			
3:30	*Performance appraisal-Sam*	*3*	
4:00	*Conference with vendors*	*4*	
4:30	*Return phone calls*	*3*	
5:00	*Order materials*	*3*	*Delegate to Max*
5:30	*Jim stopped by*	*5*	

Figure 2.10 ACTIVITY LIST				
Date assigned	Person responsible	Action	Due date	Completed

Figure 2.11 ACTIVITY LIST	

Things to Do Today

Activity	Notes about activity

Activity Lists

Activity lists, like calendars, come in many forms. The purpose of an activity list is to provide a form for recording tasks to be completed, either by you or by those who report to you. The form you choose to record the tasks on should suit your specific needs. Figures 2.10 and 2.11 show portions of two types of activity lists.

Charts and Boards

Charts provide a graphic representation—a visual interpretation—of activities. Charts allow supervisors to see, at a glance, the status of a project or the output of a worker, to track personnel, or to define activities.

Among the most frequently used charts is the Gantt chart, named for its founder, Henry Gantt. Gantt charts track activities in relation to time. Supervisors may use Gantt charts to track how each worker is progressing on assignments or to examine the status of a particular activity. Gantt chart computer software is now available for automating worker schedules and tracking progress.

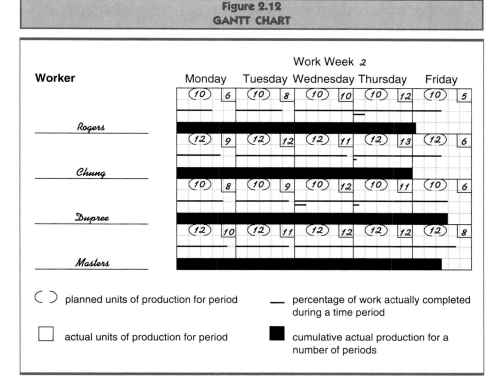

Figure 2.12
GANTT CHART

Worker	Work Week 2
	Monday · Tuesday · Wednesday · Thursday · Friday

Rogers: (10) 6 | (10) 8 | (10) 10 | (10) 12 | (10) 5

Chung: (12) 9 | (12) 12 | (12) 11 | (12) 13 | (12) 6

Dupree: (10) 8 | (10) 9 | (10) 12 | (10) 11 | (10) 6

Masters: (12) 10 | (12) 11 | (12) 12 | (12) 12 | (12) 8

( ) planned units of production for period

☐ actual units of production for period

— percentage of work actually completed during a time period

■ cumulative actual production for a number of periods

Figure 2.12 shows a Gantt chart for a 1-week period. In this case, the chart is used to schedule human resources. For week 10, Rogers and Dupree were scheduled to produce 10 units per day each for 5 days; Chung and Masters were scheduled to produce 12 units. The supervisor, by looking at the Gantt chart, can see immediately that there were days when some of the workers were on target and days when more or less work than scheduled was produced.

Visual control boards simplify many routine and time-consuming planning tasks. They also provide a quick overview of project status, can be used to schedule projects or workers, highlight problem areas, and perform a control function.

Computers

Computers can be used as planning tools in many different areas. They may be used to schedule space, maintenance, and personnel; to plan for inventory and ordering; to provide information on current levels of production; to provide information on personnel; and to do many other tasks. Periodic printouts (daily, weekly, or monthly) can provide the information needed to make planning decisions. If a computer database is available to you, use the information as you plan your departmental activities.

Tickler Files

A tickler file "tickles" your memory by reminding you of something you are supposed to do. Set up a tickler file by having divider tabs for each month of the year and tabs for 31 days behind the current month. As you think of things to do later in the month or year, put a note behind the tab for that day or month. At the beginning of each month, move the divider tab for that month in front of the daily tabs and file all the notes you previously made behind the proper day. Check the file each day for things to put on your daily to-do list.

A personal computer offers a more efficient tickler file. Using the calendar function on the PC to enter your "things to do" provides a quick daily reminder. Just remember to check your PC calendar daily.

The supervisor should make use of planning tools and aids that allow for better use of time, more efficient use of materials and equipment, and more effective use of workers.

COMPETENCY REVIEW

1. Describe eight planning benefits.
2. Cite four planning problems and suggest ways to solve them.
3. Define the two major types of plans.
4. Show the relationship between organizational goals and the environment.
5. Distinguish between the external environments of upper-level and lower-level management.
6. Give an example of goal or objective setting by different levels of management.
7. Explain the planning focus of the supervisor.
8. Describe the process of writing a meaningful objective.
9. Describe forecasting as it applies to supervisors.
10. Explain the process of writing an action plan.
11. Describe four major activities for which supervisors should plan.
12. Describe four types of planning tools and aids a supervisor may use.

APPLICATIONS

1. Sean McGrath completed the following activities on Monday. Analyze the activities, and make suggestions for how he can improve his use of time. Finally, estimate the amount of time that will be saved if your suggestions are implemented.

Activity	Time	Suggestion	Time saved
Prepared budget for next year for equipment/personnel/materials/supplies.	50 min	_____ _____	____
Waited 30 minutes to see personnel director about a possible replacement for Sue. Never did get to see her.	40 min (counting time to and from)	_____ _____ _____ _____	____
Worked on Jane's project while she was at dentist.	60 min	_____ _____	____
Repaired broken piece of equipment. Didn't want to wait for repairman.	30 min	_____ _____ _____	____
Interviewed possible addition to staff. Person not qualified.	30 min	_____ _____	____
Listened to gripes around water cooler.	20 min	_____ _____	____
Helped Jamie reorganize the work area.	30 min	_____ _____	____
Returned 6 telephone calls; received 8; all but 4 were business.	45 min	_____ _____ _____	____
Was to meet with Nathan from the union. Nathan called to cancel, but I did not receive message and went to Union Hall.	60 min	_____ _____ _____ _____	____
Joe, Mike, and Rose dropped by to chat.	45 min	_____ _____	____
Discussed the schedule for next week with Mary. Will try to see John later today and Sam tomorrow morning	20 min	_____ _____ _____ _____	____

Source: Adapted from Elwood N. Chapman, *Supervisor's Survival Kit: A Mid-Management Primer,* 2d ed., Science Research Associates, Chicago, 1980, p. 134.

2. Rewrite the following objectives. Explain why you made the changes.
   a. Increase per capita output by 10 percent.
   b. Improve quality of work life (QWL).
   c. Reduce maintenance costs.
   d. Increase productivity.
   e. Reduce absentee costs.
3. Develop a daily planning calendar for McGrath, using the activities shown in application 1 and using the form shown on page 51 and provided in the Instructor's Manual.
4. Interpret the Gantt chart shown on page 55. What was each worker's output each day? What percentage of the work was actually completed by each worker? What was the cumulative actual production for each worker? For the department? If this is McGrath's department, what actions should he take now?

CASES

Case I

A "GRAND" IDEA

Curry Lawler was delighted when canceled meetings suddenly left him with a free four-day weekend. As president of a hotel chain with seven sites, he traveled often on business, but he looked forward to a short trip "away from it all." Just last week he had told his wife he had always wanted to see the Grand Canyon but had always been too busy. She said, "Yes. My idea of a great trip would be to sit on a lounge chair at the rim and watch the sun rise, then watch the changes, and then watch the sunset, and the next day change the position of the chair and do it all over again." "I'll surprise her," he thought. "I'll get reservations, a chair, and we'll go tomorrow."

Two hours later he dejectedly accepted the fact that there was not a room to be had in the entire Grand Canyon area for the weekend. Suddenly, he called in Jim Nass, vice president, and said, "Jim, I've just had a great idea: let's build a hotel at the Grand Canyon." He recapped his experience. "We've wanted to branch out to a more resortlike concept instead of urban hotels, and there's obviously a need."

"Wait a minute, Curry. It sounds like a grand idea, but there must be some constraints, or else somebody would have done it before. Let me look into it."

1. Can you think of any obvious constraints in the environment?
2. Research the situation. What other constraints to building a hotel at the Grand Canyon can you discover?
3. Is it a "grand" idea?

Case II

WHERE IS MR. GANTT WHEN I NEED HIM?

Marcy Deal is the production supervisor for a large manufacturing company. She has recently been promoted to her present job from unit supervisor. Yesterday (March 15) she received orders for five jobs, which she must schedule among four workers. The jobs and the time required are shown below. Prepare two Gantt charts to schedule (1) the jobs and (2) the workers. All work must be completed by June 1.

Job Name	Time Required	Workers
Sewell	4 weeks	Cozart
Hampton	10 weeks	Williams
McNeal	2 weeks	McNamara
Cooke	6 weeks	Lawson
Roscoe	8 weeks	

REFERENCES

1. Laurence P. Peter and Raymond Hull, *The Peter Principle,* William Morrow & Company, Inc., New York, 1969, p. 159.
2. Anne S. Daughtrey and Betty R. Ricks, "Supervisory Management Survey," 1985.
3. Peter Drucker, *The Effective Executive,* Harper & Row Publishers, Inc., New York, 1967, p. 25.
4. Daughtrey and Ricks, op. cit.
5. Ibid.
6. Dennis L. Mott, "Time Management," *NBEA Yearbook,* chap. 14, no. 18, National Business Education Association, Reston, Va., p. 145.

SUGGESTED READINGS

Allen, Ken: "Managing Time Profitably," Dartnell Human Resources Development Program, 1981.

Bowers, Dan M.: "Up-to-the-Minute Time-Recording Systems," *Office Systems '88,* vol. 5, no. 10, December 1988, p. 52.

"Business Fads: What's In—and Out," *Business Week,* Jan. 20, 1986, p. 52.

Coke, Alfred M.: "Mission Planning at the Operational Level," *Supervisory Management,* May 1985, p. 2.

"Good Managers Manage Their Time," *Front Line Management,* no. 134, The Economic Press, Inc., Fairfield, N.J.

Harper, Stephen C.: "Time: Managing the Most Mismanaged Resource," *Managerial Planning,* July–August 1990, p. 27.

"Here Comes GM's Saturn," *Business Week,* Apr. 9, 1990, p. 52.

Leonard, Joseph W. "Why MBO Fails So Often," *Training and Development Journal,* September 1985.

Mayfield, Dave: "The New Office: Home," *The Virginian Pilot and the Ledger Star,* October 7, 1991, p. 12.

McKenzie, R. Alec, and Theodore Engstrom: *Managing Your Time,* Zondervan Publishing House, Grand Rapids, Mich., 1969.

"Schedules and Deadlines," *Front Line Management,* no. 102, The Economic Press, Inc., Fairfield, N.J.

Simmons-Forbes, Maree: "Facing the Challenge of Space Forecasting," *Office Systems '87,* vol. 4, no. 1, January 1987.

Sloma, Richard S.: "No-Nonsense Planning for Administrators," *Office Administration and Automation,* April 1985.

Smith, Michael G.: "Planning Your Company's Future," *Tidewater Virginian,* January 1986, p. 52.

"These 'Temps' Don't Just Answer the Phone," *Business Week,* June 2, 1986, p. 74.

Warda, Allan: "Key Results Planning," *CA Magazine,* June 1986.

"Who Will Be Where and When: Forecast the Easy Way," *Personnel Journal,* May 1986, p. 51.

Wilson, Dorothy: "Getting Organized: Eight Ways," *Modern Secretary,* August 1982.

GLOSSARY

action plan   Describes how the organization's goals and objectives are to be accomplished.

backward scheduling   The process of beginning with a completion date and scheduling work to meet that date.

core time   The time during the day during which all employees must be on the job.

daily plans   Plans that show a supervisor's actions for a particular day.

flextime   Allowing employees to set their work hours within certain parameters.

forecasting   Looking into the future and predicting future needs.

forward scheduling   The process of analyzing jobs, scheduling tasks, and estimating a completion date based on work to be done.

goals   The "end" to which a company aspires, stated in broad terms.

human resources   The people in the organization, their behaviors, attitudes, skills, motivations, and performance in getting the job done.

just-in-time inventory (JIT)   A control technique that arranges for inventory to be delivered directly to the production facility as it is needed—"just in time" to be used.

nonhuman resources   The organization's technology—its equipment, facilities, materials, information, money, and the processes involved in getting the work done.

objectives   What the company hopes to accomplish, stated in specific terms.

operational plans   Plans that facilitate the accomplishment of the everyday activities of first-level managers.

organizational environment   Encompasses all of the human and nonhuman resources in the organization and the interaction among these resources.

scheduling   Deciding when activities will take place as well as their order.

short-term plans   Plans typically made for 1 to 5 years that become one of the vehicles for accomplishing the long-term organizational plans.

single-use plans   Plans that are made for one activity or project and are "used up" once that project or activity is completed.

standing plans   Plans that seldom change and are used year after year.

strategic plans   Long-term plans formulated by upper-level management that reflect the vision of the organization for its future.

telecommuting   working from a location other than the workplace.

**STUDYING THIS CHAPTER
WILL ENABLE YOU TO:**

1. Define *decision* and *decision making*.

2. Identify and give an example of programmed and nonprogrammed decisions.

3. Explain the types of decisions made by the three levels of management.

4. List, in order, the steps in the decision-making process.

5. Describe a supervisor's internal and external environments.

6. Discuss techniques and sources the supervisor can use to develop alternatives in decision making.

7. Define and describe a decision tree.

8. Identify factors that influence decision making.

9. Describe ethical, legal, and socially conscious decisions.

10. Discuss decision-making styles and approaches.

CHAPTER OUTLINE

ESSENTIALS OF DECISION MAKING
   The Meaning of Decision Making
   Types of Decisions
   Responsibility for Decision Making

STEPS TO MAKING DECISIONS AND SOLVING PROBLEMS
   Identify and Define the Problems
   Develop Alternative Solutions
   Evaluate Alternative Solutions
   Make a Decision and Implement a Solution
   Evaluate and Follow Up the Decision

FACTORS THAT INFLUENCE DECISION MAKING
   Authority
   Company Policies and Procedures
   Available Time

   Personality
   People- Versus Job-Related Problems

MAKING ETHICAL, LEGAL, AND SOCIALLY CONSCIOUS DECISIONS

DECISION-MAKING STYLES AND APPROACHES
   The Rational Style
   The Intuitive Style
   The Individual or Group Decision Approach

Competency Review
Applications
Cases
References
Suggested Readings
Glossary

C H A P

Making Effective Decisions

upervisors must make decisions every day: scheduling decisions, purchasing decisions, staffing decisions, approving decisions, and so on. As workers seek more control over the decisions that affect their jobs and their lives, the supervisor is becoming more of a facilitator of the problem-solving efforts of subordinates than the primary decision maker. In this chapter, we will look at the decision-making process and problem-solving techniques.

Essentials of Decision Making

There are three essentials of decision making that you must know if you want to make effective management decisions. These essentials answer the questions What is decision making? What types of decisions are there? Who in the organization is responsible for making decisions?

The Meaning of Decision Making

Only exception impulse decisions

A **decision** is the choice of a course of action from two or more alternatives. **Decision making** is the process of completing a series of steps to select a course of action. Management is largely a decision-making process. Management decisions are concerned with resources and processes, including people, plant, equipment, strategies, production schedules, work processes, maintenance, compensation, and all other facets of management. Such decisions may have a limited effect on the organization or may be far-reaching, depending on the type of decision.

Types of Decisions

Decisions may be classified by the proportion of the organization involved in making them, the length of time required to make them, and the organizational functions on which the decisions are focused. However, decisions generally are classified into two major types: programmed and nonprogrammed.

Programmed Decisions. Management sets up policies or procedures for handling matters involving the daily operation of a business. Decisions that are routine and repetitive are called **programmed decisions.** For example, when all production supervisors in a particular company follow a standardized procedure for stocking parts inventory for their respective work groups, they are making a programmed decision. Personnel supervisors who follow a policy of coordinating with line managers the performance appraisal schedules for their employees are making a programmed decision. These situations occur regularly and usually affect small groups of people. Because they are routine and recurring, setting policies and procedures for handling them saves the supervisor time when a decision is needed. It also ensures that these decisions, while different, will be made in the same way by the different managers. Most of the decisions made in an organization are programmed decisions.

Nonprogrammed Decisions.   Many decisions in business are not routine and repetitive. **Nonprogrammed decisions** are usually onetime decisions that can affect the entire organization. They are less structured than programmed decisions. Sometimes called *nonroutine decisions,* they usually involve problems requiring a great deal of analysis before a choice of action is determined.

Some problems may be unique, unexpected, or calamitous; for example, an acquisition that will end the corporate life of the acquired organization; new technology that will make current production processes obsolete; a flood that will bring business to a halt for weeks. But nonprogrammed decisions are made regarding opportunities as well as problems. For example, the nonprogrammed decision of 3M management to market its highly successful Post-it Notes came from an employee's idea for an easily removable bookmark coupled with a product that the company had considered a failure—a glue with a low-sticking quality.

Some decisions may be partly programmed and partly nonprogrammed. For example, a company may have a standard procedure for submitting ideas for new products. The procedure may call for submitting the idea first to the unit head and then, in sequence, to the division director, marketing manager, new product development manager, and research director. Results would then be sent back in reverse order and on to upper-level executives, who would make a nonprogrammed decision as to whether or not to market the product. Decisions along the way may be programmed, nonprogrammed, or a combination of the two. Note that several managers are responsible for decisions made between the idea and the successful marketing of the product.

COMPETENCY CHECK
Can you describe and give examples of programmed and nonprogrammed decisions?

Responsibility for Decision Making

Authority for decision making usually is delegated on the basis of the scope of the decision. **Scope of the decision** refers to the breadth of the effect of the decision on the company. For example, a decision to move the company to another city would affect all employees and would, therefore, be broad in scope. A decision to install a conveyor belt on the company's loading pier would affect a limited number of employees, mostly those in the shipping and receiving department. Higher-level managers are responsible for making decisions that are broader in scope. As the scope of the decision decreases, the level of management where the decision is made is lowered.

Another guideline for determining responsibility for decision making is cost. Generally, decisions should be made at the lowest level consistent with the scope, effectiveness, and cost of the decision. This means simply that a president drawing a six-figure salary shouldn't, as a rule, be making decisions about how many reams of paper to order for the copy machine. In some organizations, the amount that managers may request for purchases or other expenditures is determined by their level. For example, an office manager may purchase supplies and equipment up to $1,000. For any purchases above $1,000, approval from the office manager's supervisor is required. At each higher level, the amount authorized is higher.

Time required for making the decision is also a determining factor for decision-making responsibility. Daily operations decisions are made quickly and are decided by first-line managers. Major decisions, such as relocations and downsizings (reductions in the workforce), take months, require much detailed information, and are made by upper-level management.

Upper-level Management.   Broad decisions that have an impact on the whole organization are made by top management. Upper-level managers generally make fewer decisions than do managers at lower levels, and the cost of making decisions is usually greatest at this level. As shown in Figure 3.1, all levels of managers make both programmed and nonprogrammed decisions. Most of the decisions made by upper-level managers, however, are nonprogrammed and may involve several upper-level executives in the process. Examples of the decisions typically made by upper-level management include reorganization and restructuring of all or specific divisions of an organization, closing plants or eliminating divisions, and downsizings.

Middle-Level Management.   Middle-level managers typically are involved with allocating resources within their divisions. They spend the majority of their time managing day-to-day operations. They may make decisions regarding the proportion of the budget to assign to each department or the type and number of people to be employed in each department. Little of their time is spent with clients, customers, or other outside groups; they coordinate the work of groups that are headed by first-line managers who report to them. The decisions of middle-level managers affect a large segment (the division), while the decisions of upper-level management affect all plants in the organization. Middle-level managers make both programmed and nonprogrammed decisions.

or Supervisors

First-Line Managers.   First-line managers make more decisions than do managers at higher levels. However, most of their decisions relate to operational concerns and usually are covered by policies and procedures. A few of their decisions will be nonprogrammed or a combination of programmed and nonprogrammed. Decisions at this level are typically less costly than are those at higher levels.

Figure 3.1
**RESPONSIBILITIES
FOR DECISION
MAKING BY TYPE
OF DECISION**

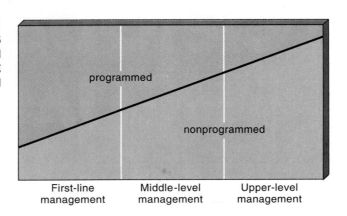

Supervisors make decisions daily regarding individual employee problems. They must also make daily decisions on such operations matters as establishing standards; purchasing supplies and equipment; setting work and vacation schedules; hiring, training, and disciplining workers; making salary and promotion recommendations; planning a budget; measuring productivity; and resolving grievances.

First-line management decisions are usually narrow in scope because they affect only a small segment of the organization. Regardless of the level at which decisions are made, they are generally more effective when managers follow a sequence of steps to arrive at their decisions.

COMPETENCY CHECK

Can you describe the types of decisions made by the three levels of management?

Steps to Making Decisions and Solving Problems

Making a decision can be simple or complex. It can be as simple as deciding whether to work overtime or as complex as determining the mission of the organization. The success of the organization is related directly to the effectiveness of the decisions made by its managers. Theorists have determined that good decision makers follow a sequence of steps, called the *decision-making process,* in making their decisions. Figure 3.2 shows the six steps in the decision-making process.

Not all decisions are made in order to solve a problem. A *problem* is any deviation from an established standard of performance. **Problem solving** is the process of determining the appropriate course of action to alleviate a problem. Problem solving does, therefore, involve decision making; and most managerial decisions involve solving a problem. We will use the terms *decision making* and *problem solving* interchangeably.

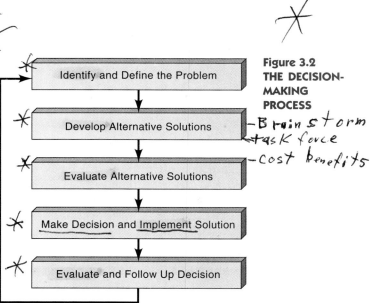

Figure 3.2 THE DECISION-MAKING PROCESS

Identify and Define the Problem

A manager must be aware of a problem in order to solve it. Better still, a manager should be alert to potential problems and make decisions that will prevent a problem from occurring. A problem solver often has a vague feeling that something is not right. Before the problem can be solved, it must first be identified. Problem identification tends to be informal and intuitive.[1]

Managers must also continually monitor the environment to be aware of potential problems that need attention or opportunities for improving the workplace. Effective supervisors will be alert to the *internal environment*—the unit's objectives, plans, policies, procedures, standards, operations, and workers. Any deviation from plans will call for a decision. If workers regularly fail to meet standards, for example, you will need to examine the cause and decide what action to take. Are workers properly selected, trained, motivated, appraised, rewarded? Is equipment adequate? Are procedures efficient? Are standards realistic? Monitoring your internal environment will keep you in tune with problems and opportunities for improvement.

The supervisor's *external environment* is made up of elements within the organization but outside the unit. As pointed out in Chapter 2, these elements include company objectives and policies, other departments, other supervisors, and so on.

The company's external environment also includes forces outside the organization such as customers, suppliers, stockholders, and the general economy. While supervisors are less concerned with the external environment than is upper-level management, the effective supervisor will, through reading and professional associations, keep aware of changes in the external environment that may have an impact on the company.

Before a problem can be solved, it must be identified and defined clearly. To avoid confusing symptoms with the real problem, list everything that is happening that makes you think there is a problem. For example, product quality is resulting in many consumer complaints, several pieces of equipment have broken down recently, employee morale is low. Is the problem outdated equipment, a need for more training, or poor management? Sometimes putting the problem statement in writing helps to clarify it. The problem should be stated in as few words as possible; the more words, the less clear the exact problem. The next step is to find possible solutions.

Develop Alternative Solutions

COMPETENCY CHECK

Can you list several techniques and sources the supervisor can use to develop alternatives in decision making?

Information gathering is a primary activity in this step of the decision-making process. This is the time to be creative. Develop as many alternatives as you can in the time you have available. If you leave out the best alternative, you cannot make the best decision. There are several things a supervisor can do to aid in generating alternatives.

Evaluate Alternative Solutions

At this stage, the manager must compare the costs and benefits of each alternative. The question "What will be the consequences if this action is taken—or not taken?"

WHAT CAN THE SUPERVISOR DO?

Here are several techniques and sources you can use to develop alternatives:

1. *Brainstorm.* Managers and others can get together, concentrate on a problem, and identify as many solutions as they can. Rules for this technique call for rapid-fire identification of any alternatives that come to mind. "Hitchhiking" onto someone else's idea is encouraged. No analysis or negative reactions are allowed until the evaluation stage, no matter how farfetched an idea might seem. At the end of the session, suggestions are evaluated and several alternatives are selected for in-depth study.

2. *Check the files.* Has the situation occurred before? Company history may provide alternatives to try again or to avoid. Has a manager previously made a decision in a similar situation? This experience may provide alternatives to repeat or to avoid. A warning is needed here, however: Relying on past experience alone may be detrimental to finding the best solution in the current environment. Examine experiential alternatives carefully.

3. *Seek advice.* Talk to managers, staff specialists, and others in the organization whose expertise enables them to offer suggestions. However, treat a suggestion from these sources as just one among many as you develop alternatives. Don't feel that you must blindly follow it solely because it came from a member of the organization. Keep in mind that you are developing as many alternatives as you can.

4. *Form a group or task force.* A basic tenet of participative management is that workers should be involved in problem solving and decision making. Who knows more about the problem than the workers who perform the daily tasks? Groups may consist of work teams, workers and supervisors, special task forces, or committees.

5. *Use external sources.* To develop awareness, read extensively and do not restrict your reading to business publications. Branch out to psychology, anthropology, and the social sciences, as well. If your industry has a trade association, read its publications to learn what your competitors are doing. Join a professional association of managers, human resources specialists, or technical specialists. If you are alert, you might find excellent alternatives in unexpected places.

6. *Use your own creativity.* Some people are more creative than others. With a little effort, you can improve your ability to examine things from a different viewpoint. Brainstorming will help; so will reading in different fields. Keep your eyes and ears open. Let your mind wander from your typical thought patterns. When considering the problem at hand, ask yourself some What if? questions.

must be answered as objectively as possible for each alternative. The more important evaluation of a possible solution is "Will it solve the problem?"

The evaluation for problems of small scope and significance may be a simple mental analysis before a choice is made. Or the supervisor may make a written comparison of alternatives, listing their costs and benefits in separate columns and choosing the alternative whose benefits outweigh its costs. As problems broaden in scope and significance, the manager might use other analytical tools and procedures, such as risk analysis, payoff tables, cost-benefit analysis, or decision trees.

A **decision tree** is a graphical representation of the alternatives available to solve a problem. Alternatives available to the decision maker are shown as possible paths in a treelike structure. Branches of the tree indicate possible future conditions after the decision has been made. Figure 3.3 shows a simplified decision tree that might be used by Katherine Farley to evaluate her alternatives in handling Juanita in Case I on page 84. The square in Figure 3.3 represents a *decision point;* the circles correspond to an *event.*

Assume that Katherine's objective is to improve Juanita's performance and productivity and, further, that she has three alternatives: (1) to enforce disciplinary policy, (2) to use positive reinforcement (for example, complimenting her on her progress) and close supervision, or (3) to use a combination of the two. As you can see, the decision tree gives Katherine a graphical display of a range of possible outcomes to the three decisions. It shows the probability of success for the three decisions in terms of meeting the objective and based on three possible reactions of Juanita to each alternative. For example, if alternative 1 (enforce discipline) is used, improvement will be high only if Juanita's reaction is favorable to that decision. It will be low or nil if Juanita responds well only to positive reinforcement and close supervision, because that alternative was not chosen. Improvement will be moderate if Juanita's reaction is a favorable response to a combination of the two, because only part of the combination (discipline) was used. In choosing alternative 1 or 2, there is a one in three (33 percent) risk that little or no improvement will result. Alternative 3, the combination, suggests that at least some improvement will occur, even though the risk is two out of three that the improvement will be moderate.

Using statistical tools in which elements of the problem are given numerical values and analyzed mathematically is helpful in many instances. Remember, however, that the tools do not make the decisions; only the manager can do that, after interpreting the numerical data. As a supervisor, you should have a basic knowledge of analytical tools even if you have limited need for their use.

Make a Decision and Implement a Solution

Making a decision and implementing it are the two sides of the decision-making coin. This is the "buck-stops-here" reality of the process. You must choose one of the alternatives. You may have evaluated a long list of alternatives, using broad-based, quality information and statistical tools, but making the choice is the moment of truth.

Two reasons why some supervisors have trouble making decisions are uncertainty that they may not have all the information and fear of making a mistake and

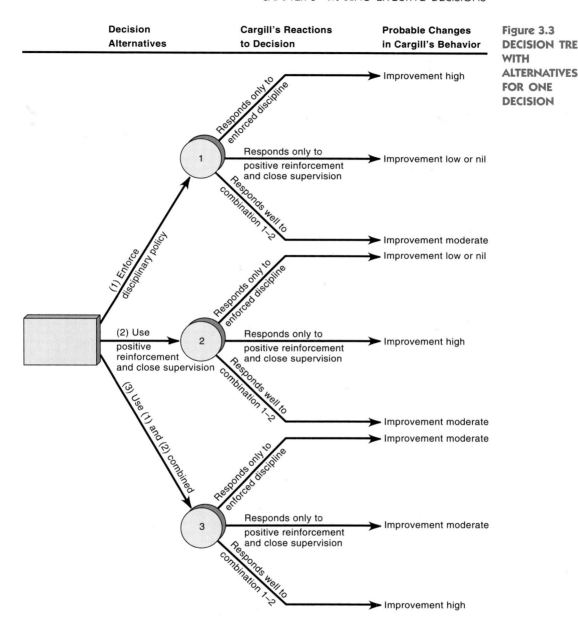

Figure 3.3 DECISION TREE WITH ALTERNATIVES FOR ONE DECISION

Source: Adapted from Lester R. Bittel, *What Every Supervisor Should Know,* McGraw-Hill Book Company, New York, 1985, p. 144.

having to suffer the consequences. If you have carefully followed the steps in the decision-making process, you should not hesitate to choose one of your alternatives. Many problems are brought to you because a subordinate wants your agreement and approval before proceeding. Common sense will provide the correct answer in most managerial situations. You will have more problems by repeatedly refusing to make decisions than by occasionally making an incorrect one.[2] The following checklist may serve as a checkpoint for those who need a final assurance before making the decision.[3]

- ❏ Will the decision actually solve the basic problem, or will it block or divert the solution? Will the problem occur again?
- ❏ Does it form policy, set precedent, or contradict existing policy?
- ❏ Has it been tried by others or tested on a small scale?
- ❏ Has it been thought through all the way to final application, or might unexpected questions arise when the decision is to be implemented?
- ❏ Will it require administrative follow-up? If so, by whom?
- ❏ Is it a permanent solution, or can it be stopped or discontinued? Will it permit switching to other courses of action?
- ❏ What will be the long-term and indirect costs? Will these add to overhead?
- ❏ Has the problem been stated fairly to all persons and interests?
- ❏ Is the solution fair to all concerned, or may it be harmful to someone?
- ❏ Will the solution build goodwill and friendly feelings and provide the basis for good future work relations and business dealings, or might it leave a chain of negative reactions?
- ❏ Will it be profitable?

Most of these questions should have been answered during the evaluation of alternative solutions. Of course, you cannot run through the entire checklist every time you have to make a quick decision, and not every question will always be relevant. But in general, among these questions you will find the ones that may help you make your decision.

Making the decision and implementing it go hand in hand. A decision to change a production process needs to be put into action in order to improve the situation that put the decision process in motion. A decision not acted on may not be applicable later because the situation is no longer the same. As a supervisor, you will be responsible for implementing decisions involving your unit. If persons other than the decision maker implement the decision, it is the decision maker's responsibility to follow up and see that appropriate action is taken.

Evaluate and Follow Up the Decision

How good was the decision? The answer to this question lies in whether or not the objective was met. Was the problem solved? If not, then you were dealing with symptoms and not the real problem. A great deal can be learned from both successes and failures. Of course, situations differ, and a past successful decision may not be totally applicable at another time. But knowing what worked and what did not may provide guidelines in similar circumstances.

Examine the method by which the decision was made as well as the results. Did productivity increase as a result of the new process? Did the training program improve worker performance? Did the hiring of part-time workers smooth out the seasonal workload increase at less-than-overtime costs and without damaging worker morale?

Following up over an extended period of time, perhaps several weeks or more, will give you a clearer picture of the quality of your decision. Certain glitches may show up immediately; some will take longer to surface. The reaction of workers, management, and other members of the organization is an example. The effect on subordinates will probably show up immediately because they and their work will undergo change.

To facilitate acceptance of a decision, the supervisor should maintain open communication with workers and train them properly for the change. The supervisor should observe workers more closely and offer assistance during the early steps of the change. These efforts will assist workers in becoming comfortable with the new process or policy. The change process is addressed more thoroughly in Chapter 8.

Invite feedback from workers and give feedback on their progress frequently. A verbal pat on the back will be welcomed by those who adjust quickly and well. Instead of criticizing those having problems, ask "What can I do to help you with this new process?" This follow-up with workers will help ensure successful implementation of the decision.

Don't forget to communicate the change to other managers in the organization who are affected. Keep the unit manager informed along the way. A memo or short progress report including, if possible, cost savings will alert your manager to the effectiveness of the decision in operations. It will also demonstrate your management skills to upper management.

COMPETENCY CHECK

Can you list, in order, the steps in the decision-making process?

Factors That Influence Decision Making

A variety of factors may influence your decision. Several of the most common ones are discussed here.

Authority

As you learned earlier in this chapter, responsibility for most decisions usually is delegated to the different levels of management. As a plant work-group supervisor, for example, you would not have the authority to make decisions concerning administrative support staff or sales staff. Nor would the heads of these units make decisions concerning your work group. You must know and operate within the limits of your authority for making decisions. Problems you observe outside this boundary should be referred to the appropriate supervisors.

WHAT CAN THE SUPERVISOR DO?

After you have made your decision, be sure to take the following actions, preferably in the order listed:[4]

1. Inform everyone concerned, precisely and clearly, what your decision is.
2. Be sure they all understand it thoroughly; answer any questions.
3. Ensure that the decision is put into effect at the proper time.
4. Supervise carefully how the decision is being carried out, and analyze results as work progresses.
5. Be ready at all times, even immediately after you announce a decision, to listen to any suggestions for, or objections to, your decision. Evaluate these with an eye to improving future decisions.
6. If you find that your decision was not, after all, the best one possible, abandon it at once. Don't fail to let all concerned know about any change. Then make your decision all over again based on the new facts. And, once more, go through all the steps necessary to make a good decision possible.
7. Document carefully everything connected with your decision as an aid to your evaluation of it. You should learn from each previous decision how to make better and wiser ones.
8. Don't hesitate to discuss the results of your decision with other supervisors and with your immediate supervisor.
9. If you're positive you are right about a decision, stick to it.

Company Policies and Procedures

One of the first things a manager should do when a problem is encountered is to determine whether a policy has been established to cover it. When developing alternatives, such a determination is a must. Policies and procedures set standards for action on recurring problems. They save time and maintain uniformity in handling routine matters. Generally, policies and procedures keep the organization operating smoothly and uniformly and serve as a guide for making programmed decisions.

Policies and procedures may become outdated, however, and may actually prevent a manager from making the best decision. They must be kept up to date and also be flexible enough to take care of situations in which they are not clearly appropriate. For example, the company policy for funeral leave for a member of the immediate family is 3 days. But when an employee's father who lives 3000 miles away dies, flexibility may be needed to allow the employee to make arrangements for and attend the funeral and assist in handling the related legal matters before returning to work.

Available Time

Many decisions, particularly routine ones, are made in moments. Others require weeks or months. While most managers would prefer plenty of time for information gathering and detailed analysis before making a decision, few can afford this luxury. If a boiler gauge in a small factory registers a critical steam level, the shop supervisor will not have time to do a detailed analysis of alternatives. He or she would make an on-the-spot decision to evacuate the workers and turn off the boiler. Conversely, a decision as to whether to install a robotic production line will require prolonged investigation and analysis. The process for making a decision will be affected by the time available.

Personality

Perfectionism is a major deterrent to effective decision making. Supervisors who search for the one perfect solution and fail to act out of fear that the decision will be wrong are indecisive. Everyone makes mistakes, but everyone learns from each decision—good or bad. The evaluation and follow-up step provides the opportunity to change and correct a bad or ineffective decision.

In the former Soviet Union, decisions for many years were made at the top. What to produce and how much, what the product should look like, the number of people to employ, their pay, job titles, and promotions were decisions made only at the top. Input from the employees who were supposed to carry out the decisions was minimal. As a result, when President Yeltsin began to introduce capitalism and free enterprise, no one was in the habit of making decisions, and workers became paralyzed by the fear of making a mistake. They would hold endless meetings, ask for more studies, and find a good reason why someone higher up should take the responsibility.[5]

People- Versus Job-Related Problems

People problems deal with disappointments, frustrations, hostilities, and personality conflicts. Job-related problems deal with tangibles or procedures that affect people. People problems may be simple requests concerning work schedules, procedures, breaks, and personal matters important to an individual but not to the total operation of the unit. Usually, you can make a quick yes-or-no answer. If a special request does not violate any company policy, will not damage your relationship with others, and will not endanger the safety of others, it should be granted quickly.

Other people problems may be considered major or potentially major. Only one individual may be involved, and the problem may be highly personal and concern the supervisor because it affects productivity. Two or more people may be involved, another department may be included, and productivity also may be affected.[6]

COMPETENCY CHECK

Can you list the factors that influence decision making?

WHAT CAN THE SUPERVISOR DO?

The following five-step procedure is recommended for both simple and complex people problems.[7]

1. *Listen carefully to all problems or complaints.* Anything important to your employees must be important to you.
2. *People problems usually involve two or more people.* Gather information from both sides before drawing any conclusions or making a decision. Do not choose sides.
3. *Weigh all facts carefully.* Ask: Will the decision be fair to all concerned? Will it violate any company policy? Are there any serious side effects of this decision? Evaluate possible solutions before deciding on one.
4. *Communicate your decision and explain to all parties why you made it.* Encourage a two-way conversation. Listen to any negative reactions, but remain firm in your decision.
5. *Follow up.* Work to restore any relationships that may have been damaged because of your decision.

• Making Ethical, Legal, and Socially Conscious Decisions

From the Wall Street excesses of Michael Milken, Ivan Boesky, and Dennis Levine, to name a few, in the 1980s to the current issue of importing goods made in China's prisons, ethical, legal, and social issues are drawing headlines for many organizations. In a survey of 2000 corporations conducted by the Ethics Resource Center, 92 percent of the companies were found to have codes of ethics on insider trading, bribery, and conflicts of interest. However, another survey revealed that between 1975 and 1984, over three hundred *Fortune* 500 companies were involved in one or more illegal acts.

Some managers interpret ethics as an issue of fairness—fair treatment of people (promotions, benefits, and grievances). For an organization to be fair, it must balance its priorities, giving as much weight to people concerns as it does to economics. Basically, to be fair means balancing your self-interest with the interests of others. The ethical person knows when to put aside selfish, personal needs and act on behalf of many people.

Most companies known for their high ethical standards are also highly profitable. In a study of 25 corporations with reputations for strong ethics and healthy finance, such as Cadbury Schweppes, Corning Glass Works, Diamond Shamrock, Digital Equipment Corporation, IBM, Motorola, 3M, and Southwestern Bell, three traits were found to be common to all: fairness, personal responsibility, and purpose.

The ice-cream maker Ben & Jerry's scrutinizes the ethics of its business every year and issues a social-performance annual report that evaluates how the company has integrated its social goals with the way it conducts business.

When Union Carbide moved its headquarters to Danbury, Connecticut, unequal perks were eliminated. Each of its 2350 private offices was configured to be the same size and furnished with the same items. Executive parking and the executive dining room were eliminated also.[8]

At Turner Broadcasting, owner of CNN—the world's largest global television network—people and capital are devoted to the promotion of social goals. Supplying information is a major ingredient of Ted Turner's sense of social responsibility to the global community. Award-winning documentaries include *Famine in Africa* and *Education Revolution;* live coverage of the Gulf War and the Soviet coup in 1992 and special programming to increase public awareness of problems of the environment are other examples. Turner Educational Services provides a free 15-minute daily news broadcast and accompanying teacher support material to more than 20,000 U.S. schools.[9]

Shoddy ethical practices ultimately result in lower revenues and profits and damaged future earning capacity for individual companies and entire industries. However, as our newspapers report and statistics support, there is an alarming rise in impropriety, questionable practices, and fraud. Recent scandals involving the savings-and-loan industry, defense contractors, and commodity traders reveal dramatic increases in conflicts of interest, paying or accepting bribes, misuse of confidential or proprietary (company-owned) information, violations of antitrust laws, price fixing, and personal enrichment through expense accounts.

On a smaller, personal level, you probably see many unfair, unethical practices every day. Sexual harassment, the boss taking long lunches, or small lies to clients about why a job is not completed are issues of ethics, too.[10]

Decisions are affected by the value system of the organization as well as by legal constraints. The supervisor should be aware of the company's mission and ethical framework and should be guided by them, especially when making nonprogrammed decisions. Blanchard and Peale[11] have proposed a set of questions to serve as guidelines for managers who face an ethical dilemma in decision making. Their "ethics check" is shown in Figure 3.4.

Suppose you learn that one of your workers has access, through a relative, to information about a competitor's bid for a construction job for which your company is also bidding. The worker offers to get the information for you from the relative's files. Getting the contract will mean jobs for you and your workers, yet your conscience says no. What should you do? Using the "ethics check," you find your answer in the first question: Your worker would be stealing proprietary information, which is clearly illegal. When an action is legal but still questionable, you move on to the second question.

When your situation lets you answer yes to the first two questions, your own value system becomes your final guide to making ethical decisions. Everyone has a personal code of ethics—a collection of values and beliefs that form the underpin-

---

Figure 3.4
BLANCHARD AND PEALE'S "ETHICS CHECK"

To guide you in decision making when you face an ethical dilemma, ask yourself these three questions:

Ethics Check	Consider
1. Is it legal?	Will I be violating either civil law or company policy?
2. Is it balanced?	Is it fair to all concerned in the short term as well as the long term? Does it promote win-win relationships?
3. How will it make me feel about myself?	Will it make me proud? Would I feel good if my decision was published in the newspaper? Would I feel good if my family knew about my decision?

Source: Kenneth Blanchard and Norman Vincent Peale, *The Power of Ethical Management.* Text copyright © 1988 by Blanchard Family Partnership and Norman Vincent Peale; illustration copyright © by permission of William Morrow and Company, Inc., New York, p. 27.

COMPETENCY CHECK

Can you describe ethical, legal, and socially conscious decisions?

ning of how we think, react to others, and conduct our lives. Usually our ethics are so ingrained, so much a part of who we are, that we are unaware of them as a code, per se.[12]

 ## Decision-Making Styles and Approaches

As a supervisor, you may use different styles of decision making. Will you make all decisions rationally or intuitively? Or will the situation dictate your style? Will you approach decision making alone or in participation with groups?

 ### The Rational Style

The rational style incorporates the decision-making process described in this chapter. It involves a step-by-step process that examines facts and figures and is sometimes called the *systematic approach* to decision making. The supervisor tries to examine each situation or problem in an orderly manner. Payback analysis, decision trees, and other analysis tools are used to arrive at a rational decision.

 ### The Intuitive Style

Some supervisors prefer to avoid the analysis and step-by-step process and rely on feelings to guide their decision making. The best decisions often are based on a

WHAT CAN THE SUPERVISOR DO?

Regardless of the size of your company or the number of employees you supervise, you can create an atmosphere in which people treat one another fairly and with integrity. You establish this climate through actions, communication, rewards, and written guidelines. Here are several specific ways to do this:[13]

1. *Draft a code of ethics for your immediate work group.* Talk with employees about the ethical issues they encounter while performing their jobs and how they handle them. Train your employees in ways to adjust their reactions and better handle such situations.
2. *Identify ethical conflicts and potential conflicts as early as possible.* Ask: Which action produces the greatest net benefit to all parties? Does the proposed action violate any party's rights or any key ethical principles? Are the benefits and burdens conferred by the action fairly distributed?
3. *Reward and discipline ethical and unethical behavior.* Include an ethics category in the annual performance appraisal. Publicly honor employees for principled behavior. Make clear the consequences of filing false reports, marketing dangerous or defective products, and failing to report such conduct to others.
4. *Institute safe channels for employees to address unfair work practices.* Create a policy and support mechanism for handling complaints and issues raised by whistle-blowers.
5. *Ask prospective employees about their ethics.* For example, "How would you respond to an employee who included a few extra expenses (known as *padding*) that weren't actually related to a business trip on an expense report?"

blend of the decision maker's intuition (based on experience and hindsight) and the rational step-by-step process.[14]

In a survey of executives, 67 percent preferred the rational decision style. When making tough decisions, they enlisted the aid of staff recommendations, statistics, and consultants. The remaining 33 percent relied on "gut feelings."[15]

3 The Individual or Group Decision Approach

For some managers, making decisions alone is an awesome responsibility. Others prefer to decide alone. This chapter has dealt largely with individual decision making. The trend is toward employees having more involvement in decisions that affect their jobs.

most managers use all methods combined

Group decision making brings a variety of skills together to seek a solution to a problem. Because the workers are performing the jobs in which many problems occur, they are better motivated to solve them. The group sets its own norms for behavior, which the supervisor must recognize and deal with.

In participative management, group decision making is often part of the organizational structure. Groups may be given titles such as "work team," "work group," "task force," or "problem-solving team." These groups usually consist of five to seven people who perform similar jobs. Each group may have some autonomy in setting schedules and procedures. Participation typically is voluntary. The supervisor may serve as team leader, coordinating the efforts of the group; in highly participative organizations, the team leader is chosen by the group. The group analyzes a problem, develops and evaluates alternatives, and recommends its chosen alternative to management. Implementation often is under the guidance of the group or its team leader, with support from the supervisor.

Victor Vroom and Phillip Yetton constructed a model that uses a decision tree to help managers decide when and how to allow participation in decision making. Vroom and Arthur G. Yago later added another factor to the model: whether the subordinate has sufficient information to make the decision. Time and whether or not the manager wants to develop a subordinate's decision-making skills are factors also. Time and space do not permit us to review these models here in detail. However, sources where these models may be found are listed in the suggested readings at the end of the chapter.

General Electric has an employee-based decision-making process called *Work-Out*. It's a forum where three things can happen: Participants can get a mental workout; they can take unnecessary work out of their jobs; they can work out problems together. A group of 40 to 100 people, picked by management from all ranks and several functions, goes to a conference center or hotel for a 3-day session. The "boss" opens the session and roughs out an agenda—typically, to eliminate unnecessary meetings, forms, approvals, and other drudge work. The boss leaves, and the group breaks into five or six teams. Aided by an outside facilitator, the groups spend a day and a half listing complaints, debating solutions, and preparing presentations for the final day.

The third day is what gives Work-Out its power. The boss, ignorant of what has happened, returns and takes a place at the front of the room. Each team spokesperson makes a proposal. By the rules of the game, the boss can make only three responses: Agree on the spot; say no; or ask for more information—in which case, a team must be chartered to get it by an agreed-upon date.

By using early Work-Outs to go after minor issues such as excess paperwork, GE gets quick victories. The easy pickings have big benefits. At GE's NBC network, the operations and technical services department eliminated forms that totaled more than two million pieces of paper a year.[16]

In addition to operations work groups, management decisions are often made through group efforts. Upper-level managers often work as a group to make decisions on objectives, strategies, and resource allocations. You might participate with other supervisors and your department manager to set objectives for the department. At whatever level, group decision making has some good and some bad fea-

Figure 3.5
ADVANTAGES AND DISADVANTAGES OF GROUP DECISION MAKING

Advantages	Disadvantages
Provides a broader range of knowledge, ideas, and alternative solutions.	Takes more time to reach a decision Is a more costly process. Takes workers away from their work stations during group deliberations.
Improves communication within work unit as workers understand better the role of the supervisor.	Supervisor generally still accountable for decision made by group; may become resentful.
Improves chances of success because solution is found by workers, who then feel part of the process of management.	Allows strong members to dominate group and exert undue influence on decisions; the less strong may become discouraged and stop participating.
Improves job dimensions by allowing workers to participate in decision making.	Requires a high level of supervisory skills to coordinate, communicate, clarify, and implement group's efforts.
Improves morale of workers.	
Develops leadership potential of workers within group.	

Source: Adapted from Victor H. Vroom and Philip W. Yetton, *Leadership and Decision Making,* University of Pittsburgh Press, Pittsburgh, 1973.

tures that you will need to consider. The advantages and disadvantages of group decision making are summarized in Figure 3.5.

As you have learned, the style or approach selected to make decisions is often determined by the situation. The best approach is the one that will help you make the best decision. Whatever approach is used, implementation of the decision-making process must be followed up to determine long-term effectiveness.

COMPETENCY REVIEW

1. Define *decision* and *decision making.*
2. Identify and give an example of programmed and nonprogrammed decisions.
3. Explain the types of decisions made by the three levels of management.
4. List, in order, the five steps in the decision-making process.
5. Describe a supervisor's internal and external environments.
6. Discuss five techniques and sources the supervisor can use to develop alternatives in decision making.
7. Define and describe a decision tree.
8. Identify three factors affecting decision making.

9. Discuss, in your own words, what constitutes ethical, legal, and socially conscious decision making. Give examples to illustrate your points.
10. Discuss two decision-making styles or approaches.

APPLICATIONS

1. Michi Kimura's company is moving into a new plant in the suburbs. For 5 years, Kimura has walked the five blocks from her apartment to work. The company will now be 7 miles away from home, and she faces a transportation problem. She doesn't own a car, mainly because she has been saving to buy a condo. Develop and evaluate a set of alternatives Michi might consider.
2. Form groups of five to seven students to brainstorm one of the following topics:
    ❏ How can we improve campus parking?
    ❏ How can educational issues such as date rape awareness and prevention and AIDS awareness and prevention be presented to your student body?
    ❏ How can your campus start a recycling program? What can be recycled on your campus?

    Have one student serve as moderator and one as recorder. The moderator will keep the members actively contributing for a predetermined period of time (about 10 minutes); will prevent negative comments or reactions to suggestions, regardless of how farfetched they seem; and will allow one member to "hitchhike" onto another's idea by amending or embellishing it. The idea is to be as creative as possible. The recorder will write down (on paper or on the chalkboard) all suggestions in as brief a form as possible.

    After the predetermined time, all suggestions will cease. The group will then evaluate all suggestions and choose three or four that they would recommend for study as possible solutions to the problem.
3. Divide students into ethics teams to discuss solutions and report their decisions for the following situations:
    a. A baby food company has learned that slivers of glass have been found in several jars of carrots.
    b. An automobile manufacturer has been sued because of inadequate seat belts (lap belts only) in the backseat of one of its cars. A small boy died and his twin brother was paralyzed from the waist down in an accident while riding in a car produced by this automobile manufacturer. Legal research revealed that the company knew about the problem several years earlier and could have corrected it by adding shoulder harnesses for $12 each.
    c. An oil tanker runs aground in Chesapeake Bay, causing millions of gallons of oil to spill into the bay, which is a major fishing area. Miles of shoreline are damaged, and the delicate ecosystem of the bay is upset.

4. The questions regarding your personal code of ethics below should be answered truthfully. Determine your ethics score.

HOW ETHICAL ARE YOU?

Some of our personal values are in a perpetual state of flux, while others are very fixed. But whether fluid or not, our ethics guide us through peaks and valleys of the day. Here are questions to help you unearth your personal code and shed light on how your personal ethics affect your work relationships. Score your answers:

1 Never	3 Sometimes	5 Always
2 Seldom	4 Often	

1. Do you apply different values or standards to situations depending on whom you are talking to?
2. Do you judge and value people according to how much money they earn? Where they went to school? Who they know?
3. Do you consider a verbal commitment—your word—less binding than a legal contract?
4. Do you believe there are degrees of honesty and that a little dishonesty is acceptable?
5. How often have you stolen something?
6. Have you ever told a harmless white lie?
7. Do you use threats as a kind of motivation?
8. Do you believe that everyone has a price—that loyalty and commitment can be bought?
9. Are there some things you would do only if you were paid enough?
10. Do you believe ethics is not something that can be taught but that people must acquire through experience?

What your answers mean. A score of 40 to 50 indicates that you do not have a strong code of ethics but tend to adjust your opinions and reactions to the individual situation; a score of 20 to 40 indicates that your ethics are more or less fixed but may be modified depending on a situation; and a score of less than 20 indicates a firm code of ethics that holds true in almost all situations.

Source: This material is reproduced from *The Healthy Company,* by Robert H. Rosen, Ph.D.; Jeremy P. Tarcher, Publisher, 1991.

CASES   Case 1

MONDAY MORNING HEADACHE

Katherine Farley, a supervisor in the assembly plant of Aztec Systems, Inc., has agonized over the decision about Juanita Cargill, a member of her work group. Juanita has been with the company for 9 years and, until the past year, had been a competent worker. Katherine and Juanita had been in the same work group for 4 years when Katherine was promoted to supervisor a year ago.

Knowing that Juanita, who had more seniority, wanted the supervisory job, Katherine weighed very carefully this and many other factors about the promotion before she decided to accept it. She accepted because she knew she was better qualified and was confident that she could work out any problems that resulted. But she hadn't counted on Juanita's attitude.

Since Katherine's promotion, Juanita's productivity has fallen, she has been absent or late for work frequently, and she has seemed resentful of Katherine's attempts to determine the cause of her behavior and to restore her productivity. Last week, when Juanita was 30 minutes late 2 days in a row, Katherine called her into her office for a conference. When Katherine asked her what could be done about the problem, Juanita responded, "You're the super; it's your problem."

Katherine was angry with Juanita for not seeing that she had been very lenient with her and was trying to salvage her job. She also was angry with herself for having so much difficulty making the decision that now seemed inevitable. At least she was following company policy that the supervisor confer with the worker before recommending suspension or termination.

"Think about the problem over the weekend, Juanita," Katherine said. "See me Monday, 9 A.M.—sharp! We'll make a decision then."

"Well, Monday is here," Katherine thinks as she dresses for work after the stressful weekend, "and I still haven't made a decision."

1. What type of decision must Katherine Farley make? Is it programmed or nonprogrammed?
2. What decision-making style has Katherine used up to this point?
3. How would you evaluate Katherine's decision making at this point? Give reasons for your answer.
4. If you were Katherine, what decision would you make in the Monday session with Juanita?
5. How would you implement your decision?

| Case II |

CAN DOMINO'S DELIVER?

In 1989, Tom Monaghan, founder of Domino's Pizza and inventor of mass-market pizza delivery, stepped back from daily operations in order to try to sell his private company. No one was willing to pay more than half what he considered it to be worth. "I picked the worst time in history to try to sell a company of this size," Monaghan now says. He now has refocused on his pizza delivery business and eliminated the other distractions that once filled his time. A travel agency and a three-masted ship (the *Domino Effect*) are gone. A sports cable network and shopping centers may go, as will most of the 16 board directorships at colleges and organizations.

While Monaghan was away for 2 years, the competition was eating into Domino's business. In 1990, Pizza Hut, Inc., reported a 20 percent jump in overall revenues. However, Domino's posted only a 6 percent gain.

Industry analysts figure that Pizza Hut has captured a quarter of the pizza delivery market. Although Domino's share of the delivery market is still the largest, it fell from 50 percent in 1989 to 46 percent in 1990. Pizza Hut helped the market erosion when it spent half of its TV ad budget in 1991 on Domino's-bashing commercials.

Tom Monaghan's new strategy is to focus on delivery and to back out of experiments with other formats. An effort to sell Domino's pizza at Burger King outlets was canceled by mutual agreement. Take-out stands at airports and other places were eliminated, too. Domino's is testing a joint venture with AT&T to develop a toll-free number that would allow customers to call one number anywhere in the country while a computer routes calls to the nearest outlet. Domino's would then have just one number to advertise, and hungry customers have to remember just one number. Domino's says the new system would produce an annual savings of $2.5 million in Yellow Pages advertising.

Domino's also has been slashing costs internally. The regional offices are down from 16 to 9 and are expected to drop further to 4 or 5. The sale of a corporate jet, a 40-seat prop plane, and a helicopter brought a onetime $6.4 million gain and will save $2 million in annual operating costs. By eliminating sponsorships of an Indy car racing team and national team tennis tournaments, $2.5 million will be saved annually. Finally, a huge Christmas display that attracted 500,000 people to Domino's headquarters in Ann Arbor, Michigan, has been canceled for good.

Some industry executives wonder if Domino's has become too austere or focused to the point of inflexibility. For example, the company underwent a long internal debate in 1990 before deciding to risk complicating operations by offering diet cola. Some outsiders say that Domino's has been slower than other chains in introducing pizzas with extras such as pepperoni or extra cheese to satisfy customers who want something different. Domino's executives figure that they are offering extras at a pace that won't gum up speedy delivery. Franchisees and employees are glad that a clear strategy is emerging after 2 years of drift.

In December 1993, Domino's abandoned its 30-minute delivery guarantee. A jury in St. Louis awarded $79 million to a woman injured in a collision with a Domino's driver who had run a red light. In May 1992, Domino's agreed to pay $2.8 million to the family of a woman killed by a Domino's driver accused of speeding to meet the delivery guarantee, which promised $3 off any pizza delivered more than 30 minutes after it was ordered.

To replace the delivery guarantee, Domino's will offer a new product satisfaction guarantee. Monaghan said that consumers should see no significant change in delivery times. "The speed of driving is a very insignificant part of the process," he said. He stated further that he believes the company's drivers, who deliver more than 5 million pizzas a week and travel 750 million miles a year, still have the safest delivery record in the world.

1. Identify the problem.
2. What external and internal environmental factors affected the decisions Tom Monaghan and Domino's has made in the past and now in trying to turn around the company?
3. What decision-making style was used when the company decided to offer diet cola? Was the decision made on a timely basis?
4. Was the decision to abandon the 30-minute delivery guarantee an ethical and socially responsible decision or a financially prudent one? Discuss.

Source: As reported in Lisa Driscoll and David Woodruff, "With Tom Monaghan Back, Can Domino's Deliver?," *Business Week,* Oct. 28, 1991, pp. 136, 140, and *The Cincinnati Enquirer,* Dec. 21, 1993, p. A1.

REFERENCES

1. James M. Higgins, *The Management Challenge,* Macmillan Publishing Company, New York, 1991, p. 75.
2. Loren B. Belker, *The First Time Manager,* 2d ed., AMACOM, New York, 1986, pp. 21–22.
3. Victor H. Vroom and Phillip W. Yetton, *Leadership and Decision Making,* University of Pittsburgh Press, Pittsburgh, 1973.
4. Robert R. Blake and Jane S. Mouton, *Executive Achievement,* McGraw-Hill Book Company, New York, 1986.
5. Peter F. Drucker, *Managing for the Future,* Truman Talley Books/Dutton, New York, 1992, pp. 145–146.
6. Elwood N. Chapman, *Supervisor's Survival Kit,* 2d ed., Science Research Associates, Inc., Chicago, 1987, pp. 139–141.
7. Ibid.
8. Robert H. Rosen, *The Healthy Company,* Jeremy P. Tarcher, Inc., Los Angeles, 1991, pp. 51–52.
9. From CNN's *Pinnacle,* Sunday, Feb. 23, 1992.

10. Rosen, op. cit., p. 51.
11. Kenneth Blanchard and Norman Vincent Peale, *The Power of Ethical Management,* William Morrow & Company, Inc., New York, 1988.
12. Rosen, op. cit., p. 54.
13. Ibid., p. 58.
14. Warren R. Plunkett and Raymond F. Attner, *Introduction to Management,* PWS-Kent Publishing Company, Boston, 1989, p. 171.
15. Mark Memmott, "It Takes Guts for Executives to Make the Tough Decisions," *USA Today,* July 21, 1987, p. 7B.
16. Thomas A. Stewart, "GE Keeps Those Ideas Coming," *Fortune,* Aug. 12, 1991, pp. 41–49.

SUGGESTED READINGS

Blanchard, Kenneth, and Norman Vincent Peale: *The Power of Ethical Management,* William Morrow & Company, Inc., New York, 1988.

Edwards, Gary: "Workplace Ethics," *Management Solutions,* December 1986, pp. 12–16.

Einhorn, Hillel J., and Robin M. Hogarth: "Decision Making: Going Forward in Reverse," *Harvard Business Review,* January–February 1987, pp. 66–70.

Heirs, Ben, and Peter Farrell: *The Professional Decision-Thinker,* Dodd, Mead & Company, New York, 1987.

Herron, Sue, Larry Jacobs, and Brian Kleiner: "Developing the Right Brain's Decision-Making Potential," *Supervisory Management,* March 1985, pp. 16–22.

Howard, Robert: "Values Make the Company," *Harvard Business Review,* September–October 1990, p. 133.

Nutt, Paul C.: "Decision Style and Strategic Decisions of Top Executives," *Technological Forecasting and Social Change,* 1986, pp. 39–62.

Vroom, Victor, and Arthur Yago: *The New Leadership: Management Participation in Organizations,* Prentice-Hall, Inc., Englewood Cliffs, N.J., 1988.

Vroom, Victor, and Phillip Yetton: *Leadership and Decision Making,* University of Pittsburgh Press, Pittsburgh, 1973.

GLOSSARY

decision   The choice of a course of action from two or more alternatives.

decision making   The process of completing a series of steps to select a course of action.

decision tree   A graphical representation of the alternatives available to solve a problem.

nonprogrammed decision   A onetime decision that can affect the entire organization.

problem solving   The process of determining the appropriate course of action to alleviate a problem.

programmed decision   A routine and repetitive decision.

scope of the decision   The breadth of the effect of the decision on the company. The broader the scope, the more people will be affected by the decision.

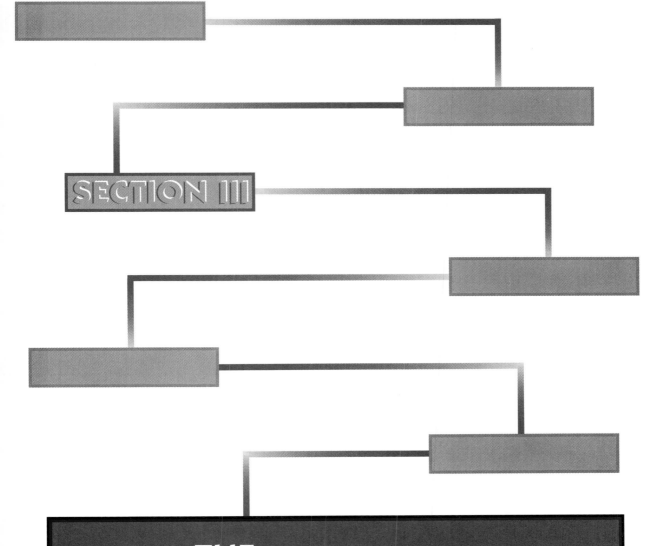

SECTION III

THE
Organizing
Function

STUDYING THIS CHAPTER WILL ENABLE YOU TO:

1. Define *organizing* and explain why it is critical to meeting company objectives.

2. Define *job design* and discuss job scope, job enrichment, and job enlargement.

3. Define *job analysis* and tell why it is important.

4. Describe the differences between a job description and a job specification.

5. Identify the bases for departmentalization.

6. Discuss self-directed work teams and the reasons for organizing them.

7. Describe the concepts of centralization and decentralization in delegating authority and assigning resources.

8. Identify and explain the organizing principles.

9. Define *organization structure* and describe four structures.

C H A P

THE Supervisor's Role IN Organizing

CHAPTER 4

verall organizational design is usually handled by top management. They create the structure, determine the number and nature of management personnel, and establish the lines of authority. However, supervisors also spend a large percentage of their time organizing. Unfortunately, many supervisors focus only on their narrow functions and do not keep in touch with the total organizational framework—the "big picture." To be effective members of the management team, supervisors must be aware of the overall picture. This chapter will help you develop this awareness by describing the fundamentals of organizing.

What Is Organizing?

Organizing is the process of grouping activities to be performed into manageable components and assigning them in such a way as to achieve the organization's objectives. Organizing follows closely—and sometimes overlaps—the planning function. Organizing is critical to achieving company objectives because it:

**COMPETENCY
CHECK**
Can you define
organizing and
explain why it is
critical to
reaching
company
objectives?

1. identifies what is to be done and who is to do it.
2. shows, in organization charts, who reports to whom and who is in charge of whom, and establishes the channels of communication for the process.
3. focuses resources on the objectives to be achieved.
4. provides the basis for coordinating the efforts of personnel in the pursuit of company objectives.

These outcomes of organizing will be grouped into three elements for our discussion. These are (1) dividing the work into jobs, (2) delegating authority, and (3) assigning resources.

Dividing the Work into Jobs

Accomplishing tasks, large and small, depends on the division of the work among individuals or groups. One way to subdivide the tasks is to design specific jobs for individuals or groups to accomplish. For example, an airplane organization must design jobs for contract administrators, engineers, purchasing agents, riveters, welders, and so on. In this first section, the discussion of the subdivision of work centers around job design, job analysis, departmentalization, and subunits within departments.

Job Design

Every job must be specifically created and labeled before a worker is selected to fill it. Jobs are the building blocks of an organization. Creating jobs is an organizing task called *job design.* **Job design** is the process by which job content is identified, work methods to perform the job are delineated, and the job's relationship to certain other jobs in the organization is specified.

In determining the work to be done, the job designer can group together a manageable number of similar tasks. Examples are the movements of a lathe operator, the cleaning and repair tasks of a maintenance worker, the process of writing a computer program, or the supervision of a given number of salespersons. While job design establishes the work to be done to accomplish organizational objectives, it also has a significant impact on the motivation of the worker and the quality of work life in the organization. Job design includes the scope of jobs, job enrichment, and job enlargement.

Job Scope.   Job scope refers to the number and combination of tasks a worker is asked to perform. It also includes the *time cycle* of a job; that is, how long it takes to complete a task before it must be repeated. Deciding on the degree of specialization is the most critical element in designing jobs. Jobs may be generalized or specialized.

Task generalization gives the worker a wide range of tasks to perform in a job. Employees' job satisfaction and morale tend to be enhanced when their job comprises varied responsibilities. Boredom results when work activity is limited to one or two repetitive tasks. When a large number of employees are assigned varied responsibilities, the organization benefits because its workforce becomes better trained. Employees who perform diverse tasks can shift quickly from one job to another when needed.[1]

Task generalization can also mean organizing around outcomes, not tasks—one person performs all the steps in a process. For example, at Mutual Benefit Life, individual case managers perform the entire application approval process. Previously, each application passed through a series of individuals who each performed a single task before passing it on to another person, resulting in a lengthy approval process.[2]

Task specialization gives the worker a limited number of tasks to perform. It allows employees who perform the same task repeatedly to become highly knowledgeable. Some employees experience higher status and enhanced self-esteem from being experts. However, the majority of workers prefer to perform broad tasks that give them a feeling of control over what they are doing.[3]

Specialized tasks may be automated through the use of robots. The automobile industry incorporates robots in a variety of repetitive tasks. Repetitive office tasks, such as keying and mailing the same letter or memo to several people, are automated through the use of the computer and facsimile machines. Many managers routinely transmit various charts, memos, and diagrams by fax.

Job Enrichment.   Job enrichment is any effort that makes work more meaningful or satisfying by adding variety or responsibility to a job. Task generalization is involved because enriching a job usually means adding more planning, decision making, controlling, and responsibility.[4]

Job enrichment may be accomplished by increasing the autonomy and responsibility of employees. Organizing teams and delegating greater authority for self-management to the teams also provides job enrichment.[5] In Chapter 11, you will learn how job enrichment and job enlargement can be used to motivate and empower workers.

Job Enlargement.   Job enlargement is the process of increasing the number of operations an individual performs in a job.[6] The company receptionist's job that consists of answering the telephone and greeting visitors may be enlarged by adding such duties as sending and receiving all faxes, arranging conference calls, and keeping the company calendar updated. Lengthening the time cycle in order to add more tasks to a job is another way of enlarging it. For example, the gardener's job currently consists of mowing and weed-eating a lawn in 2 hours. The gardener's job is enlarged when the additional tasks of trimming shrubs, weeding the flower beds, and watering the flowers are included in a 4-hour job.

The relationship of job design to motivation makes job design a common approach to the search for productivity improvement. As a supervisor, you are responsible for meeting production standards. You therefore need to be aware of the impact job design can have on productivity by increasing or decreasing worker motivation. In an established organization, after jobs are initially designed, you may be asked to participate in the analysis of existing jobs, a process that may result in the redesigning of jobs.

**COMPETENCY
CHECK**
Can you define
job design and tell
why it is
important?

Job Analysis

In today's changing environment, it is unrealistic to assume that any job design is permanent. Designs must be kept up to date. In addition, jobs must be described and communicated to workers so that they will clearly understand their roles in the organization. To do these things, job analysis must be instituted.

Job analysis is the process of determining what tasks make up the job and what skills, abilities, and responsibilities are required of an employee hired to fill that job. In large organizations, job analysis is usually a specialized function of the human resources department. Supervisors usually are involved in the data-gathering process. In smaller organizations, supervisors may direct the collection of data, which may be analyzed by internal personnel or by an outside consultant. The purpose of collecting information for job analysis is to develop a job description and a job specification. The job descriptions and job specifications that result from job analysis are so critical to legally mandated nondiscriminatory employment that most businesses conduct some type of ongoing job analysis.

Data can be gathered by observing the worker on the job, interviewing the worker, having questionnaires completed by the worker or with the supervisor, or having the worker keep a log of tasks performed over a period of time. Work sheets and other instruments used to collect data must be acceptable under the 1978 Uniform Guidelines on Employee Selection. To be acceptable, the procedure must clearly identify the job duties and behaviors necessary to perform the job. Job analysis work sheets usually are designed to answer questions such as:

- ❑ What are the major duties and responsibilities?
- ❑ What tools and procedures are used?
- ❑ What knowledge, skills, and abilities are required?
- ❑ What are the physical requirements of the job?
- ❑ What are the environmental conditions of the job?

Job Description.   The **job description** is a written statement of the duties and responsibilities of any person holding a job. It may be a short statement or a lengthy, formalized one. Whatever the format, job descriptions are important documents for staffing and performance appraisal.

The supervisor will use the job description to orient a new worker to the job. The job description will describe for the worker the tasks to be performed, the tools to be used, and the supervision given or received. It also becomes an important legal document for the organization in case the organization is called upon to show that its personnel decisions and activities are nondiscriminatory.

Job descriptions are sometimes called *position descriptions*. Figure 4.1 shows a position description for a supervisor.

COMPETENCY CHECK

Can you describe the differences between the job description and the job specification?

Figure 4.1
POSITION DESCRIPTION

POSITION DESCRIPTION

Position Title *Word Processing Supervisor*   Position No.:   _2 784-C_

Reports to: *Manager of Information Systems*   Effective Date: _01/01/94_

Approved by: _____   Status: _Exempt_
                        (Must be signed)

I. General Description of Duties/Position:
   Manages the Word Processing Department of 6 WP operators. Receives original work from all managers, establishes priorities, sets production schedules. Provides technical expertise for new and nonroutine applications. Establishes and implements turnaround and accuracy standards. Trains new operators and assists incumbent operators with programming and technical problems. Prepares and submits reports to manager of information systems and works with that position in executing company and department policies. Cooperates with Human Resources manager on personnel matters relating to WP operators.

II. Responsibilities:
   1. Records and logs incoming work from managers. Assigns priorities and establishes method of assigning to operators. Maintains service checks and support communications with originators.
   2. Checks progression of jobs to maintain turnaround/accuracy standards. Communicates with originators when deadlines may not be met.
   3. Maintains knowledge of equipment capabilities and software updates and problems through vendor contacts and professional publications.
   4. Provides or secures expertise on nonroutine applications.
   5. Trains new operators and experienced operators on new applications.
   6. Prepares and submits monthly reports on productivity and cost/budget analysis.
   7. Cooperates with Human Resources manager in performance appraisal schedules and personnel data-gathering activities re WP operators.

III. Knowledge, Skills, and Abilities:
   1. Completion of high school diploma; some college preferred.
   2. Five years' experience as a WP operator.
   3. Knowledge of WP equipment and software.
   4. Excellent oral and written communication skills necessary for communicating with all levels of management and preparing required reports.
   5. Administrative and organizational skills appropriate for preparing schedules and assigning work.

Supervision Received: Has limited supervision. Works under the general direction of the manager of information systems.

Supervision Given: Supervises 6 WP operators and the WP function for the company.

Job Specification.   A **job specification** is a statement of the qualifications necessary for performing a job. The major difference between the two documents is that the job description focuses on the job while the job specification focuses on the individual who will hold the job. The job specification generally shows the job requirements of the worker in terms of education; licensing, experience, and training; and knowledge, skills, and abilities. Job specifications commonly are used in recruiting and staffing activities. A comparison of information contained in a job description and in a job specification is shown in Figure 4.2. Recruiting and staffing are discussed in greater detail in Chapter 6.

Departmentalization

As organizations grow in size, some form of grouping becomes necessary. **Departmentalization** is the grouping of work or individuals into manageable units. The overall departmentalization of an organization is determined by top management. Supervisors usually are concerned with functions within prescribed departments. There are many bases for grouping jobs that can be used by a business of any size. The most common bases are by function, territory, product, customer, and process and are illustrated in Figure 4.3.

Functional Departmentalization.   The most widely used form of departmentalization is by function. A functional department groups together people who perform similar or closely related tasks. For example, production, finance, marketing, and engineering are typical departments in small manufacturing companies. Within specific departments, the work may be further subdivided. For example, accounts

---

Figure 4.2
COMPARISON OF JOB DESCRIPTION AND JOB SPECIFICATION

Job Description	Job Specification
A written statement of the duties and responsibilities of any person holding the job.	A written statement of the qualifications necessary for performing the job.

Information contained in each:

Job title	Education and training
Work location	Experience, licenses
Job summary	Decision-making ability
Duties	Initiative
Tools and equipment	Physical skills and effort
Materials and forms used	Responsibilities
Supervision given or received	Communication skills
Working conditions and hazards	Emotional characteristics
	Unusual sensory skills: sight, smell, hearing

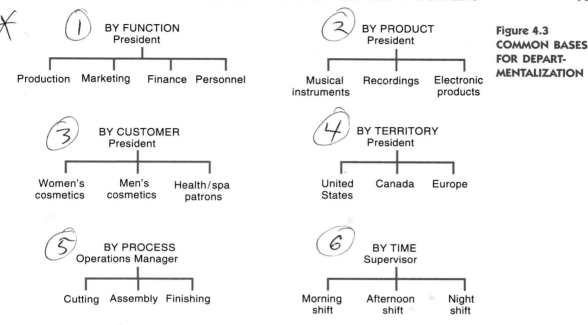

**Figure 4.3
COMMON BASES
FOR DEPART-
MENTALIZATION**

receivable, accounts payable, and payroll may be subunits in the finance department.[7]

Territorial Departmentalization. Departmentalization based on territory often is used by organizations that operate at dispersed locations. Territorial departmentalization often is referred to as *geographic departmentalization.* In this form of departmentalization, all the activities for a given geographic area report to one manager. Territorial considerations may indicate physical separation as remote as different countries, or the division may be by city, state, or region. Businesses with international components would necessarily consider geographic or territorial departmentalization. The Internal Revenue Service is a well-known example of organization by territories. Procter & Gamble (P&G) is a global organization that is organized by countries. Eastern Europe and the Russian Republic are recent additions to P&G's territories.

Product Departmentalization. Departmentalization by product may be used in organizations with several major products. A large discount store, for example, may set up departments for groups of related products such as auto accessories, hardware, health and beauty, housewares, pharmacy, and various clothing departments.

Product departmentalization often is referred to as *divisionalization* because an entire division may be devoted to one product or type of products. Xerox Corporation is a global company that until 1992 had two main products and, therefore, divisions: (1) document processing and (2) insurance and other financial services. Xerox began selling off its financial services companies in 1992 and returned to its main products in document processing.

Customer Departmentalization.   Customer departmentalization takes into consideration the differing needs of customers or clients. A bank often will have separate departments for banking services: investment and trust department, mortgage and home loan department, personal loan department, customer service, etc.

Process Departmentalization.   Some manufacturing organizations find departmentalization by process an appropriate basis for organizing. Manufacturing companies that produce autos, oil products, garments, or furniture use departmentalization by process. A large furniture manufacturer may have separate departments for cutters of wooden parts for a chair, for workers who assemble the parts, and for finishers.

Subunits Within Departments

An organization that is departmentalized by functions, territories, products, customers, or processes may be further subdivided within each department. Supervisors are likely to be involved directly in organizing by time and work teams.

Time.   Organizations that operate 24 hours a day usually organize by workers' time periods. Workers may perform the same or different tasks on each shift.

One of the oldest forms of shift work is the 7 A.M. to 3 P.M., 3 P.M. to 11 P.M., and 11 P.M. to 7 A.M. time periods. There are many variations of this shift format in use today.

Another form is flextime. If, for example, core time is set as 10 A.M. to 3 P.M., some workers may choose to arrive at 7 A.M. and leave at 3 P.M. while others choose to arrive at 10 A.M. and leave at 6 P.M. Besides giving workers some freedom to choose their work hours, flextime can help to alleviate rush-hour traffic in highly industrialized areas.

Departmentalization by time is used in a variety of organizations, including the fast food industry, shipbuilding, auto manufacture, hospitals, and large computer service organizations.

It is quite common for organizations to use overlapping bases for departmentalization. This is called *mixed departmentalization.* A supervisor in a hospital, for example, may supervise only nurses (function) who work on the night shift (time) in the children's ward (customer and territory).

On a larger scale, Procter & Gamble is organized by territories and by products, such as paper, beverages, and soap. Xerox Corporation also uses mixed departmentalization within its document processing division. It is subdivided geographically (U.S.; Eastern Hemisphere countries; Japan, Australia, and New Zealand; Canada, North and South America, the Caribbean, China, and Hong Kong) and by function (corporate research and technology and corporate strategic services; document processing customer operations; and document processing business divisions).

Work Teams.   Organizing work teams is another form of grouping and job redesign to accomplish organizational objectives. Manufacturing companies, such as Xerox Corporation, Best Foods, General Electric Company, IBM Corporation, Corning, Digital Equipment Corporation, Colgate-Palmolive Company, and TRW have pioneered the team concept and are experiencing rapid growth of self-directed teams. At the same time, many white-collar organizations now use self-directed work teams. These include Shenandoah Life Insurance Company, the St. Paul Companies, AT&T, and IDS Financial Services, a division of American Express.[8]

A **self-directed work team** (also called *self-managed team*) is a group of employees who are responsible for an entire work process or segment that delivers a product or service to an internal or external customer. It is not a group brought together for a special purpose, such as a product-launch team, a quality-action team, or a problem-solving team.[9] A term often associated with self-directed work teams is *empowerment*. **Empowerment is passing on authority and responsibility.** Empowerment occurs when control and authority are delegated to employees who then experience a sense of ownership and control over their jobs.[10] Reasons often cited for organizing self-directed work teams include:

 work circles

- ❑ improved quality, productivity, and service.
- ❑ greater flexibility for rapid adaptability to change.
- ❑ reduced operating costs resulting from fewer management layers.
- ❑ faster response to technological change.
- ❑ fewer, simpler job classifications.
- ❑ better response to new worker values.
- ❑ ability to attract and retain the best people.[11]

Problem-solving teams are groups of employees who perform similar tasks and who are responsible for addressing specific issues or problems in their work units. The number of team members varies, but typically 10 to 15 members will volunteer to participate to solve problems related to their work. The supervisor may serve as leader, or the leader may be chosen from the team.

There are also committees, task forces, and ad hoc groups targeted to specific problems. Beth Israel Hospital in Boston has arranged its entire staff into teams and committees. Each employee participates in a departmental work team. Some people serve on standing work teams dedicated to researching and planning hospital missions; others work on single-issue, ad hoc teams.[12] Ethics committees also are used to solve organizational problems. A hospital may use an ethics committee to decide who receives the first available organ transplant or whether or not to treat patients who do not have health insurance.

A task force is a group organized to solve a problem, but the members usually do not give up their regular assignments for the life of the project. Central States Insurance Company in Omaha, Nebraska, uses companywide task forces to solve its future human resources challenges. Employee-led committees examine major concerns, including family support, health care costs, communications, and employee recognition.[13]

People are realizing that empowered teams provide a way to accomplish organizational goals and meet the needs of our changing workforce. The next step in the organizing function is delegating authority to carry out the tasks.

WHAT CAN THE SUPERVISOR DO?

Empowerment is an internal event, not something the supervisor does *to* employees but something they decide to do for themselves. With this point of view, the supervisor's role shifts from trying to delegate empowerment skills to supporting, coaching, and teaching them. To be effective in providing employees with an environment in which they are supported and encouraged to overcome fears and self-doubts that block their own growth and empowerment, supervisors need to:

1. believe in their employees' ability to be successful.
2. be patient and give them time to learn.
3. provide direction and structure.
4. teach them new skills in small, incremental steps.
5. ask questions that challenge employees to think in new ways.
6. share information with employees.
7. give employees timely, understandable feedback and encourage them throughout the learning process.
8. offer alternative ways to do things.
9. have a sense of humor and show they care for each employee.
10. focus on results and acknowledge personal improvement.

Source: Adapted from Richard Hamlin, "A Practical Guide to Empowering Your Employees," *Supervisory Management*, April 1991, p. 8.

Delegating Authority

A primary purpose of organizing tasks and work units is to be able to take the next step—delegation of authority. **Delegation of authority** is the shifting of authority from a manager to a lower-ranking employee. **Authority** is the right to make decisions and use resources (human, physical and material, financial, and time) without getting permission from someone else. As a supervisor, you should have the authority you need to carry out your responsibilities in making decisions, taking action to control costs and quality, and exercising discipline over the workers assigned to you. The continued growth and success of an organization are dependent upon delegation of authority and decentralization.

Centralized decisions are made primarily by upper-level management. As you learned in Chapters 2 and 3, in the traditional organization top management sets objectives and establishes broad policies; middle management focuses on coordinating, with peers and lower management, the strategies for carrying out objectives; and first-line management (supervisors) focuses on operations. The degree to which an organization delegates authority to the various levels depends on management philosophy.

Decentralized decisions are made at the lowest point in an organization where people have the information and skills required to make a decision.[14] A guiding principle is that authority should be delegated to the lowest level of management commensurate with appropriate skill and lowest cost. For example, suppose you are a supervisor for an organization that is considering moving its headquarters from New York to Los Angeles. Your salary would meet the criterion of lowest cost, but normally you would not have the conceptual skill and knowledge of the organization to qualify you to make the decision as to whether to move. Authority for this type of decision should be centralized. Suppose, however, that there is a conflict over the vacation schedule of two members of your work crew. No doubt top management would have the ability to make the decision, but at a six-figure salary compared to first-line management salary, it would be a misuse of resources to centralize authority at the top level for such a decision.

In some instances, essential decision making may be centralized within a decentralized organization. In a highly decentralized company where the product lines range from aerospace to electronics to automotive parts, separate business units are necessary for manufacturing and selling the various product lines. Each business unit reaches entirely different industries, uses different technologies, and pursues different product introduction rates, but they may share a corporate database encompassing all the accounts of vendors used throughout the company. This allows each business unit to negotiate prices and terms with suppliers on the strength of the entire corporate relationship. Creating that database requires coordination with each purchasing segment of each independent business unit and companywide agreement on consolidating thousands of vendor account numbers.[15]

Chapter 5 addresses the supervisor's role in delegating authority. Our concern here is the overall concept of authority delegation as a part of organizing. Determining the centralization or decentralization policy is usually a function of the philosophical climate established at the top. What works for one company may not work for others. What works at one time may not be appropriate at another.

COMPETENCY CHECK

Can you discuss the concepts of centralization and decentralization in delegating authority?

Assigning Resources

A corollary to delegating authority is assigning resources to carry out the responsibility. As you learned in Chapter 2, supervisors are responsible for using the resources available to them in the most efficient way. Human, physical and material, financial, and time resources cannot be used efficiently if the supervisor has no authority for assigning these resources as needed. For example, a data entry specialist calls at 8 A.M. and says she has the flu and will not be at work for two or three days. You, as the accounting supervisor, know that there is an audit report due tomorrow, and you need a data entry person. In order for you to call a temporary service and request a data entry specialist, you must have a budget and the authority to make the decision to request outside help. If overtime is necessary in order to complete the audit report on time, you must be able to make that decision.

Organizing Principles

Management theorists have presented many organizing principles over the years. We shall address three significant ones here: unity of command, authority and responsibility parity, and span of control.

Unity of Command

The **unity of command** principle states that each person should have one, and only one, supervisor. It means that there is only one person in each unit who has the authority to make decisions appropriate to the position. Unity of command is the oldest of the classical principles of management. This principle establishes a two-way relationship for carrying out tasks. It is designed to ensure that directions are transmitted clearly to the worker from the supervisor and that feedback from the worker to the supervisor indicates completion of the task as directed.

Unity of command is violated when there are self-directed work teams, task forces, special projects, and matrix organizational structures (discussed later in this chapter). In these situations, there are two bosses: the team, task force, or project leader and the functional boss. Violations of unity of command generally do not create problems when lines of communication remain open.

Unity of command problems can occur when one employee is assigned to one or more supervisors. The assignment may be justified because the employee doesn't have enough work to do for one supervisor. Disagreements occur, however, when one supervisor demands more than the allotted share of time. An advance designation of a higher authority to resolve disputes can alleviate difficulties.

Authority and Responsibility Parity

As you read above, authority is the right to make decisions and use resources without getting permission from someone else. When the manager or supervisor accepts the task and the authority necessary to carry out the task, an obligation is incurred. **Responsibility** is the obligation to perform assigned tasks and to use the granted authority properly.

Effective delegation requires that the authority granted to a person be sufficient to carry out the assigned responsibility. This is known as **authority and responsibility parity.** Too little authority results in supervisors having to consult with their supervisors before making minor decisions.

Suppose, as a word processing supervisor, you are given the authority by your manager to direct workers in your unit to produce a prescribed number of pages of output per day. You are therefore responsible to your manager for the output. If you have the authority but don't use it to direct the workers to do the tasks, you are not carrying out your responsibility and will, at some point, be held accountable for your failure to act. Trouble will also arise if you are held accountable for producing the daily output of pages but are not given the authority to direct the workers to do it. You will learn more about this disparity in the discussion of delegation in Chapter 5. Here, the point to be made is that efficient delegation requires that authority and responsibility be equal.

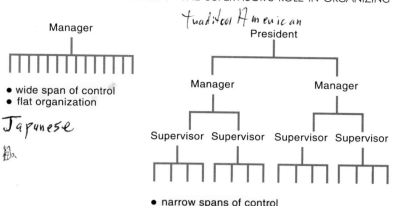

Figure 4.4
SPANS OF
CONTROL

[handwritten: Traditional American]

[handwritten: Japanese]

Span of Control

The number of subordinates reporting directly to one manager is called the manager's **span of control**. While management theorists have searched for the ideal number, no standard has ever been found. Instead, a principle has evolved that states that there is a limit to the number of workers one manager can supervise and that the span of control should be kept within manageable limits.

[handwritten: ✗ about 6 people]

The height of an organization chart is related to span of control. A wide span of control (few levels and many workers per manager) creates a flat organization because there are few managers. Conversely, a narrow span (many levels and few workers per manager) creates a tall organization because more levels of management are needed. These differences are shown in Figure 4.4. American organizations typically have taller organizations than do foreign organizations, especially those in Japan.

Several factors should be considered in determining the manageable span of control. Examine Figure 4.5 to note how these factors affect the span.

COMPETENCY CHECK
Can you identify and explain the organizing principles?

Figure 4.5 FACTORS INFLUENCING THE SPAN OF CONTROL		
Factor	An Increase Occurs in the Span of Control When	A Decrease Occurs in the Span of Control When
1. Type of task	Subordinates have similar tasks.	Subordinates have different tasks.
2. Location of workers	Subordinates are physically close.	Subordinates are physically distant.
3. Complexity of tasks	Subordinates perform simple tasks.	Subordinates perform complex tasks.
4. Coordination	Subordinates' tasks need little coordination.	Subordinates' tasks need much coordination.
5. Planning	Manager spends little time planning.	Manager spends much time planning.

Source: Adapted from Samuel Certo, *Modern Management,* 5th ed., Allyn and Bacon, Inc., Boston, 1992, p. 271.

These principles apply to all areas of the organizing function, whether the consideration is dividing the tasks into jobs, grouping the jobs into departments, or fitting the departments into an overall management structure.

Organizational Structure

After tasks have been assembled into jobs and grouped by jobs into departments, the overall management structure can be formalized to show relationships among all members of the organization. An **organization structure** is a framework of task and authority relationships among the subunits of an organization. The organization structure usually is represented by the organization chart and is determined by top management. The major types of organization structure are line, line and staff, matrix or project, and informal.

Line Organization Structure   *small company*

In most organizations, there is a vertical line of authority that begins at the top—the chief executive level—and goes down through the first level of management—the supervisor's level. The vertical relationship of the line forms the company's **chain of command**—the steps by which authority flows downward in an organization, specifying who reports to whom.

In *line organization structures*—those units of the organization that contribute directly to the creation and distribution of goods or services that the company provides—line authority is exercised. **Line authority** is authority within the chain of command of a given unit.

The purpose of line organization is to direct human and capital resources toward the achievement of company objectives. The **line** is typically referred to as that which organizations cannot do without. Marketing, operations (production or service operations), and finance have traditionally been considered to be the three major functions without which an organization could not survive. The basic idea is that, regardless of the service or product, you have to be able to sell it, make it, and finance the selling and making of it before you have an organization.[16] Small companies often have a pure line structure. Such an organization is shown in Figure 4.6. As the company grows in size and complexity, it may change to another organization structure.

Line-and-Staff Organization Structure

Many factors in the environment today require personnel with specialized technical and professional skills to provide expertise, to advise, and to provide other supportive activities to line managers. Advisory personnel are referred to as **staff**—all in the organization who are not line. **Staff authority** is of an advisory nature and comes from outside the chain of command for a particular unit. However, a staff manager exercises line authority within a specific group. Human resources management, research, corporate planning, and other similar functions usually are considered to be staff functions.[17] Figure 4.7 shows a line-and-staff organization chart.

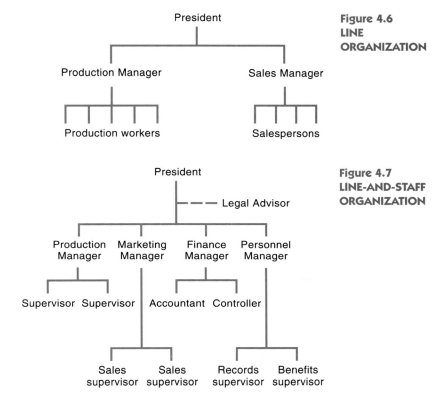

**Figure 4.6
LINE
ORGANIZATION**

**Figure 4.7
LINE-AND-STAFF
ORGANIZATION**

In this chart, the legal advisor and the personnel manager operate as staff. The legal advisor serves as counsel to the president, offering advice regarding the legal aspects of proposals, decisions, and actions. If the production manager wants to use a new manufacturing process, for example, the legal advisor may research the environmental implications and advise whether the process would violate Environmental Protection Agency regulations. If the legal advisor finds that the production manager's proposed new process is illegal, he or she may refuse to approve the line manager's request. As a rule, the refusal would be passed by the attorney to the president, who, in turn, would deny the line manager's request, thereby adhering to the chain of command.

The personnel manager is also considered staff in that he or she serves a support function to all line managers. However, within the human resources department, this manager also has line authority over the subordinates in that department (the records and benefits supervisors, for example).

**COMPETENCY
CHECK**
Can you describe the difference between a line organization and a line-and-staff organization?

Matrix, or Project, Organization Structure

Organizations today must cope with a complex and changing environment and therefore require flexibility to accommodate change. Traditional organizational structure sometimes can result in an inflexible organization that is slow to respond to change. The matrix organization allows the organization to take advantage of new opportunities and solve special problems.[18] A *matrix,* or *project, organization structure* combines features of the functional and product departmentalization and is used on an ad hoc basis to manage specific projects. A matrix structure is designed to use key managers or other specialists where and for the length of time they are needed. After a project is completed, the managers or specialists return to their home bases or are reassigned to other projects. A matrix structure is an **adhocracy**—an organization structure characterized by temporary teams of workers who move from project to project. The term *ad hoc* means "for a specific purpose."[19]

By contrast, the traditional organization is a **bureaucracy**—a rational, systematic, and precise form of organization in which rules, regulations, and techniques of control are defined precisely. It is characterized by a maze of rules, regulations, delays, and pettiness at all levels.[20] The greatest challenge to American business in the 1990s, especially for the large company, may well be its management of people. Restructuring the organization around information—something that will, of necessity, have to be done by large businesses—invariably results in a drastic cut in the number of management levels and, with it, the number of "general" management jobs.[21]

The primary distinguishing feature of the matrix organization is the responsibility of the manager in charge (project or product manager). The manager must complete the project with employees who report directly to one or more other managers. Conflict can occur when an employee reports to more than one manager and when the managers have failed to coordinate and communicate with each other.

A matrix organization may be used, for example, to research, manufacture, and test a new product before it is added to the organization's existing product line. As shown in Figure 4.8, separate organizations would be established for products A and B. The functional organization would continue undisturbed, with one exception: While product A is being developed, workers with special needed skills would be "borrowed" from their regular departments and assigned temporarily to the product A manager. When the product A project is completed, these workers would return to their functional departments. The product A manager, therefore, would be managing a separate organization that functioned concurrently with the company's permanent organizational structure. He or she would direct the activities of the product A workers. Permanent employment relationships, such as personnel records, would continue to be handled for product A workers by their regular functional managers. Careful preparation, clear assignment of responsibilities, and open communication minimize disruption and help to maintain a smooth operation while the project is in progress.

As a supervisor, you might be involved in a matrix, or project, structure within your own division. For example, a new inventory system or a new computer configuration might necessitate setting up a project team. Technical specialists might be borrowed from all work groups, including yours, to facilitate the implementation. You might share authority over one of your workers while he or she is working on the project. In addition, you might need to reassign the project member's workload while the project is active. You might also need to counteract possible resentment if extra tasks are assigned to the remaining work team, as well as the jealousies that

COMPETENCY CHECK

Can you explain the use of the matrix, or project, organizational structure?

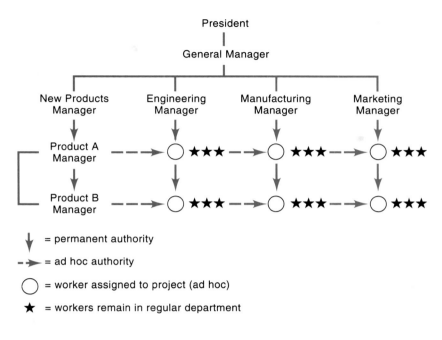

Figure 4.8
MATRIX
ORGANIZATION

may occur as a result of the temporary assignment of one of your workers to a "special project." Coping with a new organizational structure, particularly one that is superimposed on the existing one, calls for a high level of supervisory skill.

Informal Organization Structure

Formal organization structures are the line, line-and-staff, and matrix/project structures discussed in the previous paragraphs. The *informal organization structure* is the pattern of working relationships used to supplement and complete the formal structure—to fill the gaps. For example, a marketing manager has become friends with the accounting supervisor. The accounting supervisor offers to help the marketing manager organize the software programs on her PC—not part of the accounting supervisor's usual duties. If the marketing manager wanted help from someone in the information systems department, she would have to make a formal request for assistance. Assistance from the information systems department then would be part of the formal organization structure.

Informal groups are an important component created within the informal organization. These groups form as a result of individual needs, common interests and values, and desire for friendship and companionship. Informal groups may socialize together, participate in sports together, commute together, or engage in job-related activities.

The organizational structure selected by the organization depends on many things, but the main consideration is the function the structure is expected to provide. A look at some of the tools used in organizing will add another dimension to your understanding of the overall structure of an organization.

COMPETENCY REVIEW

1. Define *organizing,* and explain why it is critical to reaching company objectives.
2. Define *job design* and discuss job scope, job enrichment, and job enlargement.
3. Define *job analysis* and tell why it is important.
4. Describe the differences between job description and job specification.
5. Identify five main bases for departmentalization.
6. Discuss self-directed work teams and the reasons for organizing them.
7. Discuss the concepts of centralization and decentralization in delegating authority and assigning resources.
8. Identify and explain three organizing principles.
9. Define *organization structure* and describe four structures.

APPLICATIONS

1. Assume that you work during the day at Pizza Joe's and have been taking a night course in supervision at a local university. You regularly discuss with your coworkers the new concepts that you learn in class. To help them understand job enrichment and job enlargement, list three ways that the job of delivery person could be enlarged. List three ways that the cook's position could be enriched.
2. In August 1992, the U.S. Postal Service announced a major reorganization plan that would eliminate 30,000 management positions. The new organization will replace the 73 regional divisions with a three-part field structure: (1) marketing and sales, (2) customer services, and (3) processing and distribution, which will oversee mail distribution. What was the previous form of departmentalization? What form of departmentalization will be used in the new organization? Draw an organization chart for the new organization. The postmaster general is at the top of the chart.
3. From your own experiences or from the experiences of an organization about which you have some knowledge, describe a situation that violates the principle of authority and responsibility parity. List the problems caused by the disparity. Describe how you might have corrected the situation.

| Case 1 | | **CASES** |

RETOOLING THE CAR SHOP

Mike Tanaka had been thinking for weeks about how he would tell Steve Howard, his employer and longtime friend, that he was thinking of leaving the young company. He wanted to be sure that Steve would understand there was nothing personal in his decision, even though Sachi, Steve's wife, and Clark, Steve's brother, were involved in the problem. Mike was calm but deliberate as he talked with Steve over coffee.

"Look, Steve. It isn't the work. I like repairing foreign wheels. And I think there is a great future here for Foreign Car ServiCenter. The business is growing like crazy. But I can't work in chaos. Let me give you a few examples.

"For one thing, I don't know who is boss. Sachi tells me to put the Jag ahead of the Honda, and you tell me the Volks is top priority. Then I find that the parts for two jobs weren't ordered on time, and the owners call me at home to chew me out because we didn't deliver as promised. I turn over the job tickets to Clark, and they get lost. So Sachi chews me out because she can't send out the bills. And last week, I even had to cover the front desk and the phone because Clark had to deliver a car and Sachi was at the wholesaler's picking up parts. You and I used to do the repairs, but managing takes most of your time now; and because you're back in college part-time, I'm usually left here with the whole can of worms.

"Kevin [a part-time worker] can't do much in three afternoons a week, and he can't take over a whole job. Roger [an apprentice] has promise, but he's pulled from one car to work on another one right in the middle of a job. So he just throws up his hands and walks out. Then I have to chew him out. It's a circus.

"It's not that we don't have the customers. It's just the opposite—we've grown beyond our ability to handle all the business the way we're set up. I'd like to stay, but I'm losing interest fast. Either we get organized, or I'm going to have to make a change. I'll make a decision by the end of the month."

Mike Tanaka is an excellent worker and runs the repair function of the shop. Steve Howard doesn't want to lose him. Steve knows business has tripled in 3 years and is still growing. He has been thinking about making changes for some time. Based on an analysis of the organization's financial position and its potential, he has decided to expand to larger quarters, hire more workers, and add a parts department. Steve will remain as president. Mike will be repairs manager and will prepare cost estimates and manage all repairs. Steve's wife, Sachi, will become manager for administration. A new sales manager will be hired to handle repair scheduling and counter sales of parts. Steve's brother, Clark, will no longer work for the organization. Other new positions include two repair specialists, an apprentice, an accounts clerk to handle bookkeeping and inventory, a secretary to the president, a receptionist, and a counter salesperson.

1. Draw an organization chart to reflect the changes that will take place at Foreign Car ServiCenter.
2. What will the span of control be for each manager? What problems, if any, do you see in the spans of control?
3. Do you see any assignments that may later cause conflict?
4. If Steve Howard decides to add a full paint shop to the repair service, where would you place the new function in the organization? Explain.
5. What reorganization do you recommend that differs from the reorganization that Steve plans?

HURRICANE ANDREW

Hurricane Andrew ripped through Southern Florida and Louisiana the last week of August 1992. The American Red Cross is a nonprofit organization whose mission includes responding to natural disasters. Many complaints were heard about the slow response of the Red Cross and the lack of organization on site in Florida and Louisiana. One woman in Florida reported that she didn't see much being done locally, just a top-heavy group of bureaucrats standing around and a haphazard, sloppy distribution of food and supplies. In fact, some volunteers took matters into their own hands, rented trucks, found organizations and individuals to donate food, and distributed it themselves. One Red Cross official said, "In the future, I'll have an 'instant readiness team' on location within hours to determine the immediate needs before sending in a large-scale operation." Elizabeth Dole, president of the Red Cross, said that the Red Cross had done an outstanding job of responding to the needs in Florida and Louisiana. She also said, "Hurricane Andrew was a lot worse than anyone expected." ABC Evening News reported on August 29, 1992, that those neat organization charts hanging on the walls in the American Red Cross headquarters didn't do much good after hurricane Andrew.

1. What should be included in the list of immediate needs for responding to a natural disaster?
2. Combining your knowledge of planning with your organizational skills, develop a plan for responding to a natural disaster of the magnitude of hurricane Andrew.
3. How should the tasks necessary for carrying out the plan be divided?

REFERENCES

1. Andrew J. DuBrin, *Essentials of Management,* South-Western Publishing Co., Cincinnati, 1990, p. 161.
2. Michael Hammer, "Reengineering Work: Don't Automate, Obliterate," *Harvard Business Review,* July–August 1990, p. 104.

3. DuBrin, op. cit., p. 162.
4. Bernard J. Reilly and Joseph P. DiAngelo, Jr., "A Look at Job Redesign," *Personnel,* February 1988, p. 65.
5. Herbert J. Chruden and Arthur W. Sherman, Jr., *Managing Human Resources,* 7th ed., South-Western Publishing Co., Cincinnati, 1984, p. 37.
6. Samuel C. Certo, *Modern Management,* 5th ed., Allyn and Bacon, Inc., Boston, 1992, p. 462.
7. Andrew J. DuBrin, R. Duane Ireland, and J. Clifton Williams, *Management & Organization,* South-Western Publishing Co., Cincinnati, 1989, p. 212.
8. Richard S. Wellins, William C. Byham, and Jeanne M. Wilson, *Empowered Teams,* Jossey-Bass Publishers, San Francisco, 1991, pp. 9, 45.
9. Ibid., p. 3.
10. Ibid., p. 22.
11. Ibid., pp. 10–13.
12. Robert H. Rosen, *The Healthy Company,* Jeremy P. Tarcher, Inc., Los Angeles, 1991, p. 92.
13. Ibid.
14. DuBrin et al., op. cit., p. 657.
15. Ernest M. von Simson, "The 'Centrally Decentralized' IS Organization," *Harvard Business Review,* July–August 1990, p. 158.
16. James M. Higgins, *The Management Challenge,* Macmillan Publishing Co., New York, 1991, p. 257.
17. Ibid.
18. DuBrin et al., op. cit., p. 216.
19. DuBrin, op. cit., p. 181.
20. Ibid., p. 165.
21. Peter D. Drucker, *Managing for the Future,* Truman Talley Book/Dutton, New York, 1992, p. 157.

SUGGESTED READINGS

Boyett, Joseph H., and Henry P. Conn: *Workplace 2000,* Penguin Books, New York, 1991.
Bureau of Intergovernmental Personnel Programs: *Job Analysis, Developing and Documenting the Data,* Washington, 1973.
Byham, William C., and Jeff Cox: *Zapp! The Lightning of Empowerment,* University Associates, Inc., San Diego, 1990.
Champion, Michael A., and Paul W. Thayer: "Job Design: Approaches, Outcomes, and Trade-offs," *Organizational Dynamics,* Winter 1987, pp. 66–79.
Dyer, Lee: "How Does Decentralization Affect Human Resource Departments?" *Training and Development Journal,* February 1987, pp. 20–23.
Hoerr, J.: "Work Teams Can Rev Up Paper Pushers, Too," *Business Week,* April 20, 1987, pp. 61–62.
Lawler, Edward E. III: *High-Involvement Management: Participative Strategies for Improving Organizational Performance,* Jossey-Bass Publishers, San Francisco, 1989.
Manz, C. C., and H. P. Sims, Jr.: *Superleadership: Leading Others to Lead Themselves,* Prentice-Hall, Inc., Englewood Cliffs, N.J., 1989.
McCormick, E. J.: *Job Analysis: Uses and Applications,* AMACOM, New York, 1979.
Miner, M. G., and J. B. Miner: *Uniform Guidelines on Employee Selection Procedures,* The Bureau of National Affairs, Washington, D.C., 1979.

National Center of Education and the Economy: *America's Choice: High Skills or Low Wages,* National Center of Education and the Economy, Rochester, N.Y., 1990.

Sims, H. P., and J. W. Dean: "Beyond Quality Circles: Self-Managing Teams," *Personnel,* January 1985, pp. 25–32.

Stayer, Ralph: "How I Learned to Let My Workers Lead," *Harvard Business Review,* December 1990.

U.S. Department of Labor: *Dictionary of Occupational Titles,* 1977.

Vinton, Donna: "Delegation for Employee Development," *Training and Development Journal,* January 1987, pp. 65–66.

GLOSSARY

adhocracy   An organization structure characterized by temporary teams of workers who move from project to project.

authority   The right to make decisions and use resources (human, physical and material, financial, and time) without getting permission from someone else.

authority and responsibility parity   An organizing principle that the authority granted to a person be sufficient to carry out the assigned responsibility.

bureaucracy   A rational, systematic, and precise form of organization in which rules, regulations, and techniques of control are precisely defined.

centralized decisions   Decisions made primarily by upper-level management.

chain of command   The steps by which authority flows downward in an organization, specifying who reports to whom.

decentralized decisions   Decisions made at the lowest point in an organization where people have the information and skills required to make a decision.

delegation of authority   The shifting of authority from a manager to a lower-ranking employee.

departmentalization   The grouping of work or individuals into manageable units.

empowerment   Passing on authority and responsibility. Empowerment occurs when control and authority are delegated to employees, who then experience a sense of ownership and control over their jobs.

job analysis   The process of determining what tasks make up the job and what skills, abilities, and responsibilities are required of an employee hired to fill that job.

job description   A written statement of the duties and responsibilities of any person holding a job.

job design   The process by which job content is identified, work methods to perform the job are delineated, and the job's relationship to certain other jobs in the organization is specified.

job enlargement   The process of increasing the number of operations an individual performs in a job.

job enrichment   Any effort which makes work more meaningful or satisfying by adding variety or responsibility to a job.

job scope   The number and combination of tasks a worker is asked to perform, including how long it takes to complete a job before it is repeated.

job specification   A statement of the qualifications necessary for performing a job.

line   Employees typically referred to as those that organizations cannot do without.

line authority   Authority within the chain of command of a given unit.

organization structure   A framework of task and authority relationships among the subunits of an organization.

organizing   The process of grouping activities to be performed into manageable components and assigning them in such a way as to achieve the organization's objectives.

problem-solving team   A group of employees who perform similar tasks and who are responsible for addressing specific issues or problems in their work units.

responsibility   The obligation to perform assigned tasks and to use the granted authority properly.

self-directed work team   A group of employees who are responsible for an entire work process or segment that delivers a product or service to an internal or external customer. Also called *self-managed team.*

span of control   An organizing principle regarding the number of subordinates reporting directly to one manager.

staff   All employees in the organization who are not line.

staff authority   Authority of an advisory nature that comes from outside the chain of command for a particular unit.

task force   A group organized to solve a problem but the members usually do not give up their regular assignments for the life of the project.

task generalization   A process that gives a worker a wide range of tasks to perform in a job.

task specialization   A process that gives a worker a limited number of tasks to perform.

unity of command   An organizing principle that each person should have one, and only one, supervisor.

C H A P

Delegating Effectively

What Is Delegation?

J. C. Penney, founder of J. C. Penney Co., Inc., said, "The inability to delegate properly is one of the chief reasons executives fail."[1] Many managers at all levels are confused about delegation and its value to them and to the employees they oversee. Some managers believe they must tell each person exactly how to do a job; many employees believe they should be allowed to do the job any way they want to as long as it gets done. Who is correct? Managers? Workers? Both? Neither?

Supervisors delegate work to varying degrees depending on their definition of delegation. First-line managers must know when, to whom, and how to delegate.

Definition

COMPETENCY CHECK
Can you define *delegation*?

Webster's New International Dictionary defines **delegation** as the "act of delegating; or investing with authority to act for another." This definition should be combined with the commonly accepted business principle that the delegation of responsibility (obligation) for performance should never be conferred without the delegation of authority for directing the performance. In everyday terms, this means that when work is delegated by one person to another, the authority granted by that person should equal the responsibility given.

Just as a scale must be in balance to provide an accurate measure, so must authority be in balance with responsibility if a person is to perform effectively. Delegation means more than assigning tasks; it means sharing authority with a subordinate. If you are the type of supervisor who believes that you are the only one capable of making decisions or completing difficult tasks, delegation will not be an easy supervisory technique to master. But keep trying, for the more you delegate, the easier it becomes and the better supervisor you will be.

The level of delegation varies among supervisors. The delegation continuum shown in Figure 5.1 illustrates the degree of authority given to subordinates and the degree of authority retained by the supervisor. This is usually determined largely by the supervisor's philosophy of delegation.

On the first level (L1), the supervisor assigns a job to be completed by the subordinate but is unwilling (or unable) to give more than token authority to the subordinate.

On level 2 (L2), the supervisor allows the subordinate to work on an assigned task but requires supervisory approval before the subordinate can take action.

On level 3 (L3), the subordinate is given the authority to act but must then report to the supervisor.

On level 4 (L4), the supervisor delegates full authority to the subordinate. At this level of delegation, the supervisor steps back and allows the subordinate to accomplish the task entirely on his or her own.

COMPETENCY CHECK
Can you describe the four levels of delegation?

As more and more organizations and their employees move toward participatory management, levels 3 and 4 become more appropriate delegation levels. As worker participation increases, level 4 becomes an ideal toward which to strive. Level 4 is participatory management in action.

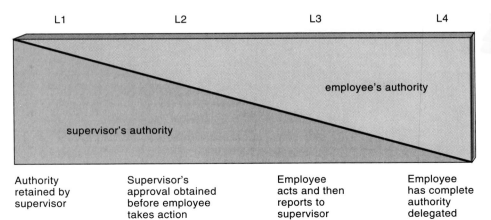

Figure 5.1
LEVELS OF
DELEGATION

| L1 | L2 | L3 | L4 |

employee's authority

supervisor's authority

| Authority retained by supervisor | Supervisor's approval obtained before employee takes action | Employee acts and then reports to supervisor | Employee has complete authority delegated |

Source: Adapted by permission from Tannenbaum and Schmidt's Leadership Model shown in James H. Donnelly, James L. Gibson, and John M. Ivancevich, *The Fundamentals of Management,* 5th ed., Business Publications, Inc., Plano, Tex., 1987, p. 383.

G. David Adams, manager of employee communications for Puget Sound Power and Light Company, says, "I have only one firm rule. I want to be informed. I let my people do their job in whatever way they want. I just want to be given a brief update, either in a staff meeting or when passing someone in the hall." Mr. Adams is approaching level 4, with some remnant of level 3 (reporting).

Why Supervisors Should Delegate

According to J. C. Penney, there are a number of benefits to be derived from delegating tasks to others. The benefits cited by Mr. Penney include:[2]

- ❑ Delegation gives you an opportunity to take on additional work yourself. Of course, the additional tasks should be meaningful ones that lead to your development as a supervisor. Taking on additional work that could be done just as well by others is simply trading tasks.
- ❑ Delegation relieves you of petty, routine details that can probably be done just as effectively by others. A note of caution here: Dumping work on others because you find it petty and boring is not a good motivator for subordinates. The added work and responsibility should be meaningful to the subordinate. The way the work is delegated is very important. Never assign someone a task by saying, "I hate this job—it's so boring. I'm going to let you try it for a while."
- ❑ Delegation can keep your department from becoming a bottleneck, which is likely to happen if you try to do everything yourself. Delegation spreads the work around, shares the challenges, and helps keep work moving through the department.

❏ Delegation <u>improves employee morale</u> by giving employees a feeling of shared responsibility. Workers like to believe that they are important to the organization, and delegation fosters that feeling.

❏ Delegation helps you reduce angst. Sharing the workload is one way of reducing the stress that results from unmet deadlines and too much work.

COMPETENCY CHECK

Can you identify seven reasons for delegating tasks to subordinates?

To Mr. Penney's list of the benefits that accrue from delegation, we might add several others. Delegating assignments to <u>subordinates may improve their decision-making skills</u> by requiring them to examine a task critically and make a decision <u>about how</u> it should be done. In the long run, this develops employees and leads to their growth in the job.

The supervisor <u>may discover some ability in an employee</u> that had not been evident previously, or a problem employee may react positively to the offer of a challenge. Additional benefits of delegation are <u>training</u> workers in unfamiliar tasks, <u>discovering potential leaders</u>, and <u>demonstrating confidence</u> in subordinates.

Any of the benefits cited above should be enough to encourage supervisors to begin to delegate tasks to their subordinates if they do not already do so. If they *have* been delegating work to their subordinates, they should continue to do so, increasing the authority given until they reach the ideal (L4) or the level at which they and their workers are most efficient and effective.

Why Supervisors Do Not Delegate

In general, supervisors do not delegate because they are not comfortable with the philosophy or they don't know how to relinquish control. Some of the specific reasons supervisors are reluctant to delegate are presented below.

Lack of Trust.   Some supervisors <u>do not trust their subordinates</u>' ability to do anything beyond routine assignments. The attitude of the supervisor is "If I want something done right, I have to do it myself."

Perceived Threat.   "If I give all my work away, who will need me?" is a worry expressed by some supervisors. Others are concerned that <u>someone else may do a good job</u> and thus be <u>a threat to their positions</u>—take their jobs. To supervisors secure in their ability to do their jobs, however, subordinates capable of assuming greater responsibility should not represent a threat.

Lack of Tolerance for Ambiguity.   Many managers <u>need to feel "on top of things,"</u> to know what is going on at all times; some even believe they must have their "fingers in all of the pies." Supervisors who feel this way need to know what each subordinate is doing at any given time. They <u>have no tolerance for ambiguity</u>, and thus they delegate very few of their responsibilities.

Loss of Satisfaction That Comes from Work.   Many supervisors, and other managers, receive such satisfaction from doing their own work that they are <u>unwilling</u> to relinquish any part of it. Satisfaction from a job well done, from completing work

WHAT CAN THE SUPERVISOR DO?

The supervisor can learn to let go. Delegation is an important part of supervision. Although delegation can be difficult, if you want your subordinates to grow and develop, delegation is one way to help them in their development.

Do you recognize any of the excuses listed in Figure 5.2? Check the excuses you have used when delegation was an option. If you have used these excuses to keep from delegating, then perhaps you need to reevaluate your supervisory style. No one can do everything. Delegation allows you more time to do other tasks, and, at the same time, it contributes to the growth and development of your subordinates. Try it. You'll like it!

on time, and from knowing that they have the ability to do a task is such a good feeling that it is difficult to share it.

◆ *Aversity to Risk.*   Because the ultimate responsibility always rests with the manager, who will still be accountable if the task is not completed or completed incorrectly, some supervisors are unwilling to take the risk.

COMPETENCY CHECK
Can you identify six reasons supervisors do not delegate?

Figure 5.2
EXCUSES FOR NOT DELEGATING

_____ 1. My employees are too inexperienced to do this. I have to do it myself.
_____ 2. It takes more time to explain the job to someone else than to do it myself. It's not worth the bother.
_____ 3. I can't afford to have a mistake made here.
_____ 4. This job is different. It demands my personal attention.
_____ 5. My staff members are all busy; nobody has time for any additional work.
_____ 6. Nobody else is willing to take on this responsibility.
_____ 7. This is the type of work I'm best at; I'm not going to give it up now to a subordinate.
_____ 8. If I pass it on to a subordinate, I'll lose control of the job. I won't know what's going on.
_____ 9. People will think I'm lazy—that I'm just passing the buck.
_____ 10. No one knows exactly how I want this job done.
_____ 11. If you want the job done right, you have to do it yourself.
_____ 12. This job is too important to trust to someone else.
_____ 13. I've got to approve the final product anyway, so why not do it to begin with?

Source: "Developing Action Plans," *Supervisory Sense,* vol. 7, no. 7, American Management Association, New York, January 1987, pp. 14–15. Reprinted by permission of the publisher. All rights reserved.

Time Concerns.   There are occasions when the time allowed to accomplish a task does not allow for delegation. However, supervisors should not use time as an excuse—"By the time I have explained what this is all about, I could already have the job done."

What Should Be Delegated?

There are some tasks for which delegation is appropriate. Other tasks should *not* be delegated. The effective supervisor knows the difference. One rule of thumb is: If the work does not have a direct bearing on your ability to plan, organize, staff, lead, and control, delegate it; if mistakes would have dire consequences, do it yourself!

Delegate Routine Tasks

Routine tasks can be performed by someone else. Assigning routine tasks to subordinates gives them opportunities to enlarge or enrich their jobs. You should, however, be sure that the tasks assigned have some meaning to the employees; they should not be viewed as meaningless busywork.

Delegate Repetitive Tasks

Repetitive tasks often provide training for more complex jobs. Children crawl before they toddle; they hold your hand before they walk. Subordinates should learn to complete routine and repetitive tasks efficiently with some supervision before they tackle more difficult tasks. Being given that opportunity benefits both the supervisor and the subordinates.

Delegate Tasks That Allow Employees to Grow Professionally

As mentioned earlier in this chapter, tasks that are delegated should be seen as meaningful by the subordinate and provide an opportunity for growth. Learning to do new tasks, becoming involved in departmental operations, experiencing working with others on group projects all lead to employee development. These activities should be encouraged.

Delegate Tasks to More Qualified Employees

People like to believe themselves capable of doing any assigned task and doing it well. But it is important to recognize that sometimes others have greater experience, knowledge, or expertise in a particular area. When this is true, recognize that ability and take advantage of having that capability in your department. For example, if someone in your department is more knowledgeable about the capa-

WHAT CAN THE SUPERVISOR DO?

Smart supervisors evaluate each delegation. Ask yourself the following questions as you evaluate your delegation decisions:

- ❏ Did an emergency or pressure force you to delegate? Or did you plan well in advance?
- ❏ What factors prompted you to select this delegate?
- ❏ Were other subordinates equally qualified? How do you know? If not, was it due to a failure on your part to provide training and development?
- ❏ Did you clearly explain the subordinate's authority? Was it necessary to transmit this information to others? Why?
- ❏ Did the subordinate try to avoid acting as your delegate? If so, why? What do you plan to do about it?
- ❏ When you communicated with the delegate, did you treat him or her as an equal?
- ❏ Did you meet with the delegate to discuss the *completed* delegation? Why? Who took the initiative to arrange the discussion?
- ❏ Did you credit the delegate for what was done? How?
- ❏ Would you give this subordinate another, perhaps more difficult, task? If not, why not?
- ❏ Do you have a written record of what the delegate achieved? Will you use it during a performance appraisal?

Source: Herbert M. Engel, "Understanding Effective Delegation," *Modern Office Technology,* July 1984, p. 18. Reprinted with permission from the July issue of *Modern Office Technology* and copyrighted 1984 by Penton/IPC, subsidiary of Pittway Corporation.

bilities of new equipment, assign the job of comparing equipment for possible purchase to the person with greater ability to make those comparisons. The epitaph engraved on the tombstone of Andrew Carnegie, founder of the American steel industry, reads "Here lies a man who enlisted in his service better men than himself." He always believed there were many people in his organization who had more ability than himself, and he was never unwilling to delegate important jobs to them.

To facilitate delegation, supervisors should divide their current tasks into three categories:

1. work that only the supervisor can perform
2. work that can be delegated immediately
3. work that can be delegated as soon as a worker can be trained to handle the responsibility

COMPETENCY CHECK

Can you cite four categories of tasks that should be delegated?

How Should Delegation Be Accomplished?

There are two sides to the delegation coin—the obligation that workers have to their supervisors and the obligation that supervisors have to their managers. Remember that although you can assign responsibility and delegate authority to a subordinate, you cannot absolve yourself of your own responsibility for completion of the job. Referring to his office, President Harry Truman once said, "The buck stops here." In this case, it is on the supervisor's desk that the "buck stops."

Dale D. McConkey identified the roles of the supervisor (delegator) and the employee (delegatee) as follows.[3] The role of the delegator in the delegation process, he wrote, is to:

1. communicate clearly.
2. specify authority.
3. encourage subordinate participation.
4. review results, not methods.
5. show trust.
6. seek recommendations.
7. delegate credit, not blame.
8. give support.
9. be consistent.
10. know the delegatee.
11. develop the delegatee.

The role of the delegatee is important, too. The delegatee should:

1. take the initiative.
2. relate to the boss.
3. be sure the delegation is realistic.
4. determine if the task is compatible with the delegatee's goal.
5. determine and give feedback regarding results.
6. report periodically to the boss.
7. carry out delegated assignments effectively.
8. develop himself or herself.

Both roles are important to the success of the delegation process. There are many techniques for successful delegation, among them defining the task, assigning authority, setting clear goals, following up, and giving credit.

Define the Task

Tell the person to whom you are delegating a job exactly what you expect. Spell out instructions clearly, including deadlines and any special directions. "Don, this report is due at the vice president for marketing's office on Monday, June 5. Therefore, it must be received by our word processing center by the preceding Wednesday. This is an important report; careful preparation and attractive presentation are critical. I know I can count on you to represent our department in the most positive way." Instructions like these define the task parameters.

2 Provide Necessary Information

The supervisor must provide information regarding the assignment. Initially, all relevant written information should be turned over to the subordinate. In addition, the supervisor will provide any other information that has been received verbally. This is the time for the subordinate to ask any questions or clarify any instructions. For example, the subordinate might want to know if others who will be involved in the assignment have been notified of their roles; if interaction with other departments is expected, if authority has been given to make the contacts and ask for input; how much flexibility there is in time estimates; and so forth.

The supervisor must continue to provide the delegatee with pertinent information as it is received. This routing should be made promptly; information should not be allowed to accumulate on the supervisor's desk. Information received verbally should be transmitted as promptly as that received in written form. However, to minimize misunderstanding, verbal messages should be put into writing before being given to the subordinate.

3 Assign Authority and Responsibility

Delegation should not take place until authority is assigned. Authority is not the icing on the delegation cake; it is the basic ingredient.

Authority should be given in advance so that it can be exercised when required. After-the-fact authority carries very little weight. And when the authority is granted, everyone who will be involved in the action or affected by the results should be made aware of it.

Be specific. Make it clear from the beginning just how much authority and initiative in decision making you are giving. This definition of parameters will spare you from an "I didn't expect you to assume so much authority" situation in the future.

4 Set Clear Goals

Let your subordinate know what results you expect, leaving the means for accomplishing those results to the subordinate's discretion. The goals are the results, and that is where your interests are, not in the methods for achieving the results. An effective delegator will say to the subordinate, "This is what we need to accomplish. What do you think is the most efficient way to achieve these results?" An ineffective delegator might say, "We want to achieve these goals. If you follow this procedure, you can reach the goals," going on to outline steps 1, 2, and 3 in the procedure. Of course, some employees need more supervision and direction than others; but if you expect your subordinates to develop their decision-making skills and to show initiative, you must give them the opportunity to do so.

5 Follow Up on Progress

Following up is not "checking up," or constantly looking over the shoulder of the person to whom you have delegated a task. Rather, follow-up provides the subordinate with the opportunity to let the supervisor know how the task is progressing and allows the supervisor to stay informed.

When the task (job, project, assignment) is originally delegated, checkpoints should be established. This procedure is particularly helpful when responsibility is being delegated to a subordinate for the first time or when an especially difficult task is being assigned. Follow-up is also necessary when it is obvious that the subordinate is getting into serious trouble. Don't let him drown; throw him a life preserver before it is too late!

6 Give Credit for Accomplishment

Weak supervisors often fail to acknowledge good work done by their subordinates while hastily placing blame when someone fails to meet expectations. Good super-

visors, on the other hand, publicly, privately, and promptly recognize and acknowledge good performance and do not advertise blame. Good supervisors also do not leave employees in doubt; nor do they put their workers in the position of the employees in the cartoon on page 124.

As presented in Chapter 11, praise is a powerful motivator. When deserved credit is given to subordinates it encourages them to accept even greater challenges. Blame, on the other hand, should not be broadcast. If a subordinate makes a mistake, try to find out why the mistake was made and give the subordinate support in correcting the error.

What To Do When Delegation Fails

Sometimes delegation does not work. The employee seems to be confused and procrastinates; the result does not seem to be the expected outcome; supervisors perceive a delegation failure. There are some steps that can be used to turn around the failure.[4]

Examine Delegation Techniques

The first step is to review your delegation techniques. Did you follow all of the suggested techniques—clearly defining the task, providing all the necessary information, assigning both the responsibility and the authority for the task, setting clear goals and being sure the goals are understood, and following up on the task? Critically examine your pattern of delegation and, where weaknesses exist, correct them.

Resist Canceling Delegation

When delegation seems to be failing, the first impulse may be to take the task away from the delegatee and reassign it to another employee. This is an overreaction. Rescinding the delegation causes the employee to lose face with both supervisor and peers. The supervisor's ability to select employees for delegation also becomes suspect. And the supervisor projects an image for other employees that says, "If you make a mistake, I'll yank this job from you so fast it will make you dizzy!" The typical reaction from employees, then, is to refuse delegation or to do a careless job knowing that the supervisor will remove the task at the first sign of failure.

Work with the Employee

The first step is to talk with the employee privately and explain why the work is unacceptable. Be specific. Generalities such as "This isn't what I expected" or "Things just don't seem to be working out" are too vague and provide no feedback to the employee.

After the employee fully understands why the work is unacceptable, the supervisor can move on to asking the employee if additional training, preparation, or infor-

COMPETENCY CHECK
Can you discuss six techniques that contribute to successful delegation?

COMPETENCY CHECK
Can you describe three techniques for dealing with delegation failure?

mation is needed. If not, the employee may be asked to propose some solutions to the problem. This meeting is also a good time to review the job again, perhaps going into greater depth in your instructions, if necessary. A model of the final result (in the form of a previous report or procedure) can be provided to help get the employee back on track. Finally, follow-up is essential. The follow-up should take the form of inquiry rather than oversupervision, so that the employee's self-confidence is not undermined.

Nontraditional Delegation Methods

Traditionally, delegation is downward—from supervisor to subordinate. Nontraditional methods of delegation include reverse delegation, lateral delegation, and abdication. Sometimes these nontraditional methods are not even recognized as delegation.

Reverse Delegation

Reverse delegation shifts responsibility upward. Responsibility shifts from the delegatee (subordinate) to the delegator (supervisor). William Oncken and Donald L. Wass use the "monkey on the back" analogy when referring to reverse delegation.[5] Consider the following examples:

1. You approach the door to your office, and Sam greets you with "Good morning. I'm so glad I caught you early this morning. You remember that report you asked me to do last week? Well, we have a problem. You see . . ." Because you just arrived at work and have a number of activities waiting for you, you respond, "Thanks for bringing that to my attention, Sam. Let me give it some thought, and I'll get back to you in the next day or two."
2. Mai says to you, "I have a great idea for a pizza-vending machine to be available at breaks and at lunchtime." Because you are in a hurry, you respond, "Fine. Send me a memo, and I'll consider your suggestion."
3. During a meeting with another subordinate, you agree to support a proposal for better lighting in the work area. As you are leaving, you say, "Let me know how I can help you."
4. You have given a subordinate a rather difficult report to write for a VIP. Because you want to be sure the subordinate gets started on the right track, you say, "I'll do a rough draft so you can get an idea of how the report should be organized. It's just a rough draft, but it should help you get started."

In all the situations described above, the "monkey" has jumped from the backs of the subordinates to you, the supervisor. You have, either wittingly or unwittingly, accepted responsibility for all the delegated tasks. How did this happen? It happened because you and your subordinates did not consider the tasks to be delegated; rather, you considered the tasks to be joint responsibilities.

WHAT CAN THE SUPERVISOR DO?

Let's take a closer look at each of the situations described on page 126 and see what the supervisor can do to prevent these particular monkeys from landing on the supervisor's back.

1. Your initial response to Sam should have been "I'm sorry you have a problem with the report, Sam. Why don't you write down some alternative solutions to the problem and meet me in my office at 4 P.M. tomorrow. I think you should be prepared to suggest a solution at that time."
2. You should not ask for a memo on the suggestion. Asking for a memo clearly makes the next move yours—you are going to have to respond to the memo. Instead, ask Mai to come to your office prepared to discuss her suggestion for a vending machine, but make the appointment only after Mai has had time to collect all the information regarding costs and revenues. Chances are you will not see Mai's name on your appointment calendar.
3. If you think a checkpoint is necessary, tell the subordinate that you will be available for a short discussion on, say, Monday from 2 to 2:30 P.M.
4. Under no circumstances should you have offered to write an initial draft—rough or not. If you have delegated the task to a subordinate, you should have enough faith in your selection of the subordinate and in the subordinate's ability to do the job that it should not be necessary for you to write any part of the report.

How can you avoid reverse delegation? By being aware when a subordinate tries to move the monkey from his or her back to yours and by being prepared for the move, you can prevent the transfer of the monkey from the subordinate's back to yours.

Lateral Delegation

Lateral delegation involves persuading a colleague on a similar level in the organization to do your work. Passive or compliant peers are primary victims—they find it very difficult to say no. Employees who are easily intimidated, vulnerable to peer pressure, or can be manipulated are special targets for lateral delegation. As a supervisor, you should not engage in lateral delegation, nor should you accept it. And you should be aware of your subordinates who try to use a "lateral arabesque" on one of their peers and promptly act to stop the shift.

WHAT CAN THE SUPERVISOR DO?

Respond to the following questions regarding delegation. Analyze your answers to determine your desire to delegate.

	Yes	No
☐ I do the job because I fear that my subordinates lack sufficient experience to assume the responsibility.	_____	_____
☐ I believe my subordinates are already overloaded with work.	_____	_____
☐ I perform the tasks out of long-standing habit; it's *my* job, and I simply can't relinquish it.	_____	_____
☐ I believe no one else is competent to make the required decisions.	_____	_____
☐ I feel it will take so long to explain the work and monitor the performance that it is not worth the effort.	_____	_____
☐ I keep intending to turn the work over "one of these days," but that day never seems to come.	_____	_____
☐ I believe delegating the task will add to the danger of error or misjudgment, and I am unwilling to take the chance.	_____	_____
☐ The work in question is too important for anyone else to do.	_____	_____
☐ I am unable to pinpoint a subordinate who is willing to take on the added responsibility.	_____	_____
☐ I enjoy the particular task too much to relinquish it.	_____	_____
☐ Delegating the work would require revealing more information about the operation than I care to reveal.	_____	_____
☐ Sometimes I feel my security is threatened when I delegate too much.	_____	_____

Source: Ken Allen, *What an Executive Should Know about Managing Time Profitably,* a Dartnell Human Resources Development Program, Chicago, 1981, p. 10. Reprinted with permission.

Abdication

Abdication as it relates to delegation is <u>doing nothing through giving up or shirk-ing responsibility</u>. Supervisors who conveniently "disappear" when a task is to be done or who "forget" when a report is due are delegating by abdication. They simply <u>do not do their jobs</u>, and others must assume the ongoing responsibilities. These supervisors may have reached the first level of management because they were smooth talkers, "con artists" who make people believe they are all they say they are or who were simply not prepared for the promotion. The chances of their maintaining their supervisory positions for any extended period of time are slim; their superiors will eventually begin to understand that they are all talk and no action, and their subordinates will begin to rebel at having to do their work.

The <u>procrastinator is often an abdicator.</u> Putting off tasks and avoiding meeting deadlines shifts the responsibilities to others. If the procrastination is a result of disorganization rather than intentional abdication, the supervisor may be helped. A disorganized supervisor has difficulty setting priorities and anticipating deadlines; these weaknesses can be addressed through time management training and an understanding of what is important in the job.

Reverse delegation, lateral delegation, and abdication are negative forms of delegation. Supervisors must learn to identify and deal with them while, at the same time, learning to use positive forms of delegation.

COMPETENCY CHECK
Can you describe the three non-traditional methods of delegation?

COMPETENCY REVIEW

1. Define *delegation*.
2. List at least six reasons for delegating tasks to subordinates.
3. Identify six reasons supervisors fail to delegate.
4. Describe four categories of tasks that should be delegated.
5. Discuss five techniques leading to effective delegation.
6. Describe three techniques for dealing with delegation failure.
7. Describe the three types of nontraditional delegation.

APPLICATIONS

1. Whose view of delegation do you think is correct: the supervisor who believes each person must be told exactly what to do? the employee who believes each person should be allowed to do the job any way he or she chooses as long as the job gets done? both? neither? Give reasons for your answer as well as reasons for not choosing the other responses.

2. For each of the items in "What Can the Supervisor Do?" on page 128 to which you answered "yes," devise an action plan or strategy to overcome the problem. Use a form similar to the following for each "yes."

   "Yes" statement: _____

   Strategy: _____

3. For the job you currently hold or for a job you previously held, use the levels-of-delegation continuum shown in figure 5.1 on page 117 to identify the level of delegation used by your supervisor. Cite specific incidents to support your decision that your supervisor operated on that level of delegation. Why do you think your supervisor operates or operated at that level?

4. Supervisors must assign and oversee work done by others. Sometimes the work is routine or tedious, such as cataloging new parts, implementing a new filing system, or ordering supplies.

   Jenny, an office supervisor, would like to delegate to Kevin the responsibility for keeping track of supplies and ordering new supplies. The following conversation takes place when Jenny tries to make that assignment:

   Jenny: Kevin, from now on, I want you to inventory supplies and set up a regular time to order new supplies.
   Kevin: But that's a boring job. Who's been doing it up to now?
   Jenny: I have, but it's time somebody else took over. So it's your turn in the bucket.

   With a classmate, write a role-playing skit in which Jenny handles the delegation more effectively. Then, act out the skit showing effective delegation techniques.

Case I

TO DELEGATE OR NOT TO DELEGATE—THAT IS THE QUESTION!

Maury Worth was just promoted to a supervisory position. The promotion became effective when his manager was out of town. Due to the illness of one of Maury's workers, the work schedule was not being met. He decided to pitch in and help, spending about 4 hours daily in the salesroom.

When Maury's manager returns to work, Maury is not available. The manager is upset and tells Maury that it is the function of the supervisor to accomplish work with and through other people, not to do it himself.

1. What was the initial problem in this case?
2. Of the alternatives given below, which would you select to solve future problems when workers are not available?
   a. Let the scheduled work be incomplete or late, and catch up when the worker returns.
   b. Lend a hand, as Maury did in this case.
   c. Prepare backup for emergencies.
   d. Work out an acceptable compromise with the manager.
3. Evaluate each of the alternatives in terms of their advantages and disadvantages to the company, to the workers, to Maury.
4. Develop implementation procedures for the alternative you selected.

Case II

MRS. FIELDS COOKIES COULD HAVE CRUMBLED!

In the 1970s, Debbi Fields, now one of America's best-known makers of chocolate chip cookies, began baking cookies for her husband, Randy, to take to work for his clients. The cookies were so successful that in 1977, Debbi and Randy Fields opened their first store in Palo Alto, California. At 20 years of age, Debbi had no business experience, but she was convinced that people would pay premium prices for freshly baked cookies made with quality ingredients and served with a smile. At first she gave away samples on the street, and business just took off; in 11 years, Mrs. Fields, Inc., had more than $100 million in sales.

When the company was still small, Debbi made all the decisions, many on impulse. She insisted on doing almost everything herself, closely supervising all operations. The company had an ambitious expansion plan, expanding into Hong Kong and London and acquiring a chain of bakery-cafés from PepsiCo. In 1988, partially because of the cost of absorbing the new units and converting the bakery-cafés into "combination" stores, Mrs. Fields, Inc., closed 85 stores.

Even before the closures, the company's board of directors had urged the Fields to develop a management team. Although they had been delegating some of the minor responsibilities, Debbi was leery of sharing her decision-making power. She questioned who could run the company as well as she, who would care as much about product quality as she, who would care as much as she. Debbi admitted that she and Randy were overwhelmed in the organization in terms of details and that they needed to develop their employees so the business wouldn't be so dependent upon the Fields.

1. At what point in Mrs. Fields Cookies was delegation appropriate?
2. What clues in this case show that delegation was needed?
3. What actually happened as a result of the events at Mrs. Fields Cookies? (Go to your library and research Mrs. Fields Cookies.)
4. What decision-making style (Chapter 3) did Mrs. Fields use?

Source: As reported by Alan Prendergast in "Learning to Let Go," *Working Woman,* January 1992.

REFERENCES

1. J. C. Penney, *What an Executive Should Know about Success,* a Dartnell Human Resources Development Program, 1980, p. 14.
2. Ibid., p. 15.
3. Dale D. McConkey, *No-Nonsense Delegation,* AMACOM, New York, 1974, pp. 90–100.
4. Joseph T. Straub, "Delegation Dilemma: What to Do If It Doesn't Work?" *Supervisory Management,* August 1989, p. 7.
5. William Oncken and Donald L. Wass, "Getting Those Monkeys off Your Back," *Management World,* October 1980, pp. 22–25.

SUGGESTED READINGS

Bhasin, Roberta: "Delegating: What and to Whom?" *Pulp and Paper,* February 1991, p. 43.

Bushardt, Stephen C., David L. Duhon, and Aubrey R. Fowler, Jr.: "Management Delegation Myths and the Paradox of Task Assignment," *Business Horizons,* March–April 1991, p. 37.

Calano, Jimmy, and Jeff Salzman: "How Delegation Can Lead Your Team to Victory," *Working Woman,* August 1989, p. 86.

Dorgan, William J. III: "Delegating Does Not Mean Dumping," *Modern Machine Shop,* March 1989, p. 120.

LaMountain, Dennis M.: "Delegated Assignments: How to Cope," *Sales and Marketing Management,* May 1988, p. 78.

Prendergast, Alan: "Learning to Let Go," *Working Woman,* January 1992, p. 42.

Pringle, Charles D.: "Seven Reasons Why Managers Don't Delegate," *Management Solutions,* November 1986, p. 27.

Short, Barbara: "Making the Most of Your Time by Involving Others," *Nursing,* January 1990, p. 99.

Sumner, Sarah: "Delegate Carefully," *Nursing,* January 1990, p. 104.

Yate, Martin: "Delegation: The Key to Empowerment," *Training and Development Journal,* April 1991, p. 23.

GLOSSARY

abdication   The act of doing nothing through giving up or shirking responsibility.

delegation   The act of delegating, or investing with authority to act for another.

lateral delegation   Persuading a colleague on a similar level in the organization to do your work.

reverse delegation   Shifting responsibility upward from the delegatee to the delegator.

THE Supervisor AND THE Staffing Function

AFTER STUDYING THIS CHAPTER, YOU WILL BE ABLE TO:

1. Describe the roles of the supervisor and the human resources (HR) department in the hiring process.

2. Explain the importance of a good match between the applicant and the job.

3. Forecast human resource needs, given basic information.

4. Describe the roles of the supervisor and the HR staff in recruiting.

5. Cite the methods used by the HR staff to screen applicants.

6. Describe the supervisor's activities in planning for the interview.

7. Describe the supervisor's activities in beginning the interview.

8. Describe the supervisor's activities during the interview.

9. Describe the supervisor's activities in closing the interview and after the interview.

10. Explain the role of the supervisor in selection.

11. Name laws that protect against discrimination in employment, and define the protected groups.

12. Identify types of questions that should be avoided during a pre-employment interview.

CHAPTER OUTLINE

THE SUPERVISOR'S STAFFING RESPONSIBILITIES
Sharing Responsibility with the Human Resources Department
Matching the Employee to the Job

THE STAFFING PROCESS
Forecasting Workforce Requirements
Recruiting
Screening Applicants
Interviewing
Selecting the Best Applicant

LEGAL IMPLICATIONS
Equal Employment Opportunity (EEO)
Following Legal Staffing Procedures

Competency Review
Applications
Cases
References
Suggested Readings
Glossary

C H A P

THE
Supervisor's
Role
IN
Staffing

T   E   R   6

At one time, supervisors were not concerned with planning for future staffing needs; staffing consisted primarily of finding a replacement for someone who had left the job. "I quit," "You're fired," or "I'm being transferred" triggered a help wanted advertisement in the local newspaper. This method of staffing is no longer acceptable.

Sharing Responsibility with the Human Resources Department

Staffing responsibilities are shared by the HR department and the supervisor, with the common goal of having the right number of people with the right skills, knowledge, and abilities (SKAs) available at the right time to meet the organization's goals. That's a tall order; and it requires mutual trust, communication, and interaction among the HR department, upper- and middle-level managers, and supervisors.

Supervisors are responsible for forecasting the human resource needs of their departments and for communicating these needs to the HR department. This forecast may be for a period of 6 months, 2 years, or more. Forecasting human resource needs is discussed later in this chapter.

Supervisors are also responsible for communicating their immediate needs to the HR department. When John quits, Marsha is transferred, Mike is fired, or Sue is promoted, a replacement must be found. Large companies usually rely on a formal procedure, requiring the completion of a requisition form such as the one shown in Figure 6.1. This requisition form is completed in triplicate. One copy is used by the interviewer in the human resources department; one is retained by the HR manager until the position is filled and the first copy is returned to the requestor; and the originating department retains one copy. In a small company, a telephone call to the person responsible for hiring may serve as the "requisition."

COMPETENCY
CHECK
Can you differentiate the roles of the supervisor and the HR department in the employment process?

WHAT CAN THE SUPERVISOR DO?

The responsibilities of the supervisor and the HR staff in hiring are summarized in Figure 6.2. on page 140. You will note that the responsibilities are interrelated and dependent on one another.

The roles of the HR staff and the supervisor in other areas of staffing (appraising, rewarding, training, and developing) are described in Chapters 7 and 9.

Figure 6.1
JOB REQUISITION

JOB REQUISITION

CLASS		
☐ PT	☐ OPT	☐ EXEMPT
☐ FT	☐ TEMP	☐ NON EXEMPT

REQUISITION # _____

POSITION TO
BE FILLED _____

HOURS _____

GENERIC JOB #
& GRADE _____

DATE TO
BE POSTED _____

DEPARTMENT
AND NAME

BANK	CENTER	SEC	

REQUEST FOR
START DATE _____

DATE OF TRANSFER
OR TERMINATION _____

HIRING MANAGER _____

MGR'S. PHONE # _____

REASON FOR
VACANCY/OPENING   ☐ RESIGNATION/ TERMINATION   ☐ STAFF INCREASE   ☐ TRANSFER   ☐ LEAVE OF ABSENCE

PERSON TO BE
REPLACED _____

RACE/SEX _____

POSITION VACATED
AND GRADE _____

APPROVAL SIGNATURES:

HIRING MANAGER _____ _____

GROUP HEAD _____
(APPROVAL FOR STAFF INCREASE ONLY)

SPECIFIC REQUIREMENTS: _____
_____

PLEASE ATTACH AN UPDATED JOB DESCRIPTION

NAME OF
REPLACEMENT: _____

START
DATE: _____

RACE/SEX: _____

SOURCE: _____

DATE FILLED: _____

RECRUITER: _____

SEND TO: **PERSONNEL OPENINGS**

White copy: Personnel Openings
Yellow copy: Personnel Openings
Pink copy: Manager

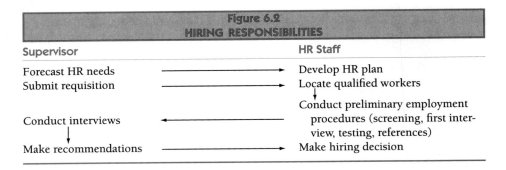

Figure 6.2
HIRING RESPONSIBILITIES

Supervisor		HR Staff
Forecast HR needs	⟶	Develop HR plan
Submit requisition	⟶	Locate qualified workers
		↓
		Conduct preliminary employment procedures (screening, first interview, testing, references)
Conduct interviews	⟵	
↓		
Make recommendations	⟶	Make hiring decision

Matching the Employee to the Job

You will recall from Chapter 4 that a job specification and job description are outcomes of a job analysis. Both the job specification and the job description provide a supervisor with the information necessary to match the applicant and the job.

Using the information from the job analysis and the information about the applicant obtained from the application and from subsequent employment procedures, the supervisor tries to match the job to the person. The match must consider the skills, knowledge, abilities, and interests of the applicant as well as the requirements of the job. For example, if the job to be filled is one in which there is little opportunity for creativity and independent thinking and the applicant has indicated that he or she works best without supervision and is looking for a job that will allow her or him to try new ideas, there is obviously not a match—even if the applicant meets all of the other job specifications.

Matching the job to the applicant—finding a good "fit" between the requirements of the job and the requirements of the applicant—results in a more productive employee. And more productive employees, satisfied with their jobs, remain with the company longer. When the match is bad, either the company will be dissatisfied with the performance of the employee or the employee will be dissatisfied with the job and the company. In either case, the company loses an employee and must go through the entire hiring process once more.

COMPETENCY CHECK

Can you explain why it is important to have a good match between job and applicant in the staffing process?

The Staffing Process

The supervisor's role in the employment process is shown in Figure 6.2. It is important, however, to understand the entire process and then focus on the components that more specifically relate to the duties of the supervisor.

Forecasting Workforce Requirements

Forecasting workforce requirements means projecting future staffing needs in terms not only of quantity of employees but also of skills necessary to perform the jobs of the future.

Forecasting is impossible without data. How can supervisors determine the right number of people and the right skills, knowledge, and abilities needed at the right time for their departments?

Let's look at a forecasting example for the telemarketing arm of a sales department. The supervisor has asked for and received the company sales plan for the next 5 years. Publisher's Promotions, Inc., has set a 20 percent increase in telemarketing sales as one of its sales goals for next year. The increases in telemarketing sales goals for the following 2 years are 20 percent and 15 percent, respectively. The supervisor's charge is to determine how many additional sales associates will be necessary to generate the increased sales and how many clerical workers will be necessary to support the sales associates. At the present sales level, the 20 sales associates are currently working about 6 hours out of 8. The five clerks always have a backlog of orders to process–at least a day's work each week. To determine the number of sales associates and clerks required to meet projected sales levels, the supervisor should take the following steps:[1]

1. Determine the output necessary to meet the goals. The current sales associates make about 2400 telecalls a day (20 sales associates working about 6 hours a day, each making about 20 calls per hour). On the average, 1 phone call in 6 results in a sale. This means 400 sales a day. A 20 percent increase, therefore, would increase sales to a total of 480 a day.

2. Determine how many sales-associate hours would be required to meet the goal of a 20 percent increase in sales.

     2880 calls per day 20 calls per hour = 144 work hours

3. Allow for equipment downtime, coffee breaks, unavoidable delays, and normal level of employee interaction. (An hour to an hour and a half per day is a fair estimate.)

     8 hours −1.5 nonproductive hours = 6.5 productive hours per day per employee

     144 hours ÷ 6.5 productive hours per day = 22.15 sales associates required to reach new sales goals of 20 percent increase

4. Allow for worker absences, vacations, and holidays. On average, the sales associates have been absent a combined total of 80 days for each of the past 3 years. Each sales associate earns 10 vacation days and 5 legal holidays a year.

     10 vacation days + 5 legal holidays for each of 20 employees = 300 days

     80 absences + 300 vacation/holidays = 380 days away from work

     52 weeks × 5 days = 260 days available per year

     380 days off work = 1 year, 120 days, or 1.46 years

     22.15 employees + 1.46 employees = 23.61, or 24 sales associates required to reach goal

5. Determine worker hours for clerks necessary to support the sales associates, keeping in mind that there is a 1-day backlog of work each week. The clerks are now processing 1600 orders a week (four-fifths of the orders generated).

     1600 ÷ 5 clerks = 320 orders processed by each clerk each week

     320 orders ÷ 5 days = 64 orders per day per clerk

     New Target:

     2400 sales ÷ 5 days = 480 orders per day to be processed

     480 orders ÷ 64 orders per day = 7.5 clerks required to process orders

6. Allow for absences, vacations, and holidays for clerks. On average, clerks have been absent from their jobs a combined total of 20 days for each of the past 3 years. They earn the same vacation and legal holidays as the sales associates.

10 vacation days + 5 legal holidays × 7.5 clerks = 112.5 days

112.5 days + 20 absences = 132.5 days away from work

132.5 days = 0.51 of a year

7.5 + 0.51 = 8.01, or 8 clerks required to process the sales resulting from the new target

**COMPETENCY
CHECK**
Provided basic
information,
could you
forecast human
resources needs?

The same kind of analysis this supervisor has made to forecast the needs of her department (24 sales associates, an increase of 4 over the present level and 8 clerks, an increase of 3) can be used to forecast the human resource needs of other types of workers. Substitute "widgets" for number of successful telecalls to determine number of workers required to produce X number of the product. Substitute number of custodial workers or supply workers for the clerks to obtain the required number of support people for production workers. Or substitute the number of documents flowing through a word processing center.

Recruiting

Recruiting is the process of building an applicant pool from which to select employees. The primary responsibility for recruiting rests with the HR department. They may recruit internally and externally to obtain qualified applicants.

Internal Sources

Many organizations prefer to recruit internally before going to external sources. Recruiting internally provides applicants who are familiar with the company and knowledgeable about company politics, and provides a motivation for employees. Internally, applicants may be obtained through:

Job Posting and Job Bidding.   When there is a vacancy, a description of the job and the specifications are posted in an area where employees are most likely to see it. Typical postings are made on bulletin boards, near water coolers, or in the company newsletter, inviting employees to "bid" on a job.

Present Employees.   Present employees provide a pool of applicants, particularly for jobs that represent upward mobility. Present employees may also recommend friends or family members for jobs (if that is permitted in the organization).

Computerized Data Banks.   Many midsize to large companies maintain computerized data banks that identify current employees who are ready for promotion, jobs to which they are now promotable, and jobs in which they are interested.

Former Applicants and Employees. Although these applicants and employees are not presently with the company, they may represent a potential candidate pool for current jobs.

External Sources

Externally, applicants may be obtained through:

Walk-ins. Walk-ins are applicants who "walk in" and inquire if there are any vacancies. They are not responding to a call for applicants. Some companies have so many walk-in applicants that they restrict the time that walk-in applications may be received to one day a week.

Educational Institutions. Students are a good source of applicants, and many companies recruit directly in schools. Depending on the needs of the organization, recruiters may target high schools, vocational schools, community colleges, or colleges and universities.

Employment Agencies. Each state has a state employment agency; the agencies charge neither the applicant nor the employer since they are tax-supported programs. In addition, there are private employment agencies, which charge a fee for placing someone on the job. The fee may be paid by either the applicant or the employer. Temporary help agencies may also add to the applicant pool. The trend among many organizations is to hire temporaries for indefinite time periods to augment the workforce when needed, then let them go when the need has abated.

Media. Advertising jobs through newspapers, periodicals, or radio is another way to obtain applicants. More companies use newspaper advertisements than any other source to generate applicants.

Professional and Trade Associations. Advertisements may be placed in professional and trade journals when applicants are needed for positions requiring specialized technical and professional skills.

Competitors. Some companies raid their competition to get employees. One advantage of this type of recruiting is that the employee needs less training on the job. A disadvantage, of course, is that your company is subject to the same raiding technique.

COMPETENCY CHECK
Can you describe the roles of the HR department and the supervisor in recruiting?

Unions. Labor unions have long been a source of employees for certain types of jobs. The union hall is the contact point between organizations and potential employees.

WHAT CAN THE SUPERVISOR DO?

Supervisors have a role in recruiting, too. They should know the SKA requirements for the job and communicate that information to the HR department. Supervisors may be asked to review advertisements, post job openings, and "sign off" on job bids.

Supervisors can let current employees know that there is (or will be) a vacancy, describe the skills the applicant needs to fill the job, and encourage employees to make recommendations. The supervisor may also recommend that current employees be promoted when they possess the requisite skills.

Screening Applicants

As shown in Figure 6.2, the initial screening process is done by the HR department. The supervisor becomes involved after the initial screening has been completed. In a small company, however, the supervisor might have responsibility for the entire process, which is shown in Figure 6.3.

Applications and Résumés.   The initial screening process begins when the applicant submits an application or résumé to the employment office. The application or résumé itself is a screening device. One application form is shown in Figure 6.4 on page 146. When evaluating the applicant information, both what applicants tell you and what they don't tell you are important. Here are some tips about how to evaluate the applicant based on the information provided in the application.

- ❑ Compare the job description and job specification with the applicant information to see if there is a match and therefore the applicant should go on to the next stage.
- ❑ Look for unexplained gaps in employment that are unaccounted for by education or employment. Gaps in employment may be due to inability to find a job compatible with the applicant's education and experience; the applicant may have been unwilling to accept anything less than the "ideal" job; the applicant may not have been actively looking for work; and so on.
- ❑ Check the reason(s) given for leaving other places of employment. Answers such as "I couldn't get along with my boss," "The other employees were out to get me" will provide some insights into the applicant's ability to work with others. Other explanations such as "My previous employer was hit by the recession and had to lay off many employees. I was one of the newer employees and was let go with the first group" or "I had reached the point at which no other

Figure 6.3
THE SELECTION
PROCESS

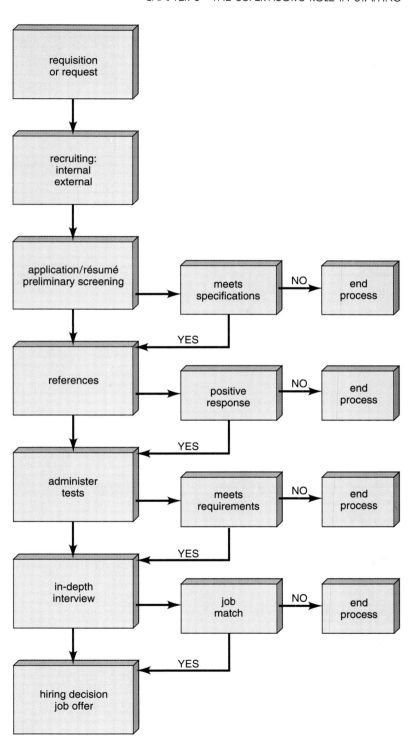

Figure 6.4
EMPLOYMENT APPLICATION

EMPLOYMENT APPLICATION

SOCIAL SECURITY NO _____

NAME _____ STREET ADDRESS _____
     FIRST NAME   MIDDLE INITAL   LAST NAME

APT. NO.
OR BOX _____ CITY _____ STATE _____ ZIP _____
AREA CODE _____
TEL. NO. _____

ARE YOU 18 ☐ YES
OR OLDER? ☐ NO, IF NOT, AGE _____
HAVE YOU WORKED FOR CHICKEN COOP BEFORE?
IF YES, DATES AND LOCATION _____

AVAILABILITY:

			M	T	W	T	F	S	S
TOTAL HOURS AVAILABLE PER WEEK _____	HOURS AVAILABLE:	FROM							
		TO							

ARE YOU LEGALLY ABLE TO
BE EMPLOYED IN THE U.S.? ☐ YES ☐ NO

HOW DID YOU
HEAR OF JOB? _____

HOW FAR DO YOU
LIVE FROM STORE? _____

DO YOU HAVE
TRANSPORTATION
TO WORK? _____

SCHOOL MOST RECENTLY ATTENDED:

NAME _____ LOCATION _____ PHONE _____
TEACHER OR
COUNSELOR _____ DEPT. _____
LAST GRADE COMPLETED _____
GRADE POINT AVERAGE _____

GRADUATED? ☐ YES ☐ NO   NOW ENROLLED? ☐ YES ☐ NO   SPORTS OR ACTIVITIES _____

TWO MOST RECENT JOBS: (IF NOT APPLICABLE, LIST U.S. MILITARY, WORK PERFORMED ON A VOLUNTARY BASIS OR PERSONAL REFERENCES)

COMPANY _____ LOCATION _____

PHONE _____ JOB _____

SUPERVISOR _____ DATES WORKED: FROM _____ TO _____

SALARY _____ REASON FOR LEAVING _____ MGMT REFERENCE CHECK DONE BY _____

COMPANY _____ LOCATION _____

PHONE _____ JOB _____

SUPERVISOR _____ DATES WORKED: FROM _____ TO _____

SALARY _____ REASON FOR LEAVING _____ MGMT REFERENCE CHECK DONE BY _____

PHYSICAL: ANY HEALTH PROBLEMS OR PHYSICAL DISABILITIES WHICH COULD AFFECT YOUR EMPLOYMENT?
☐ YES ☐ NO

DO YOU NOW HAVE OR HAVE YOU HAD, WITHIN THE LAST SIX MONTHS,
ANY CONTAGIOUS OR COMMUNICABLE DISEASES, OR GASTRO-
INTESTINAL INFECTIONS, OR HAVE YOU EVER HAD HEPATITIS OR
SALMONELLA?
EXPLAIN ANY YES ANSWERS IN DETAIL:
☐ YES
☐ NO _____

*DURING THE PAST 10 YEARS, HAVE YOU EVER BEEN CONVICTED OF A
CRIME, EXCLUDING MISDEMEANORS AND TRAFFIC VIOLATIONS? ☐ YES ☐ NO
IF YES, DESCRIBE IN FULL
_____

*A conviction will not necessary bar you from employment

1. I certify that the information contained in this application is correct to the best of my knowledge and understand that deliberate falsification of this information is grounds for dismissal. 2. I authorize the references listed above to give you any and all information concerning my previous employment and pertinent information they may have, personal or otherwise, and release all parties from all liability for any damage that may result from furnishing same to you. 3. I acknowledge that if I become employed, I will be free to terminate my employment at any time for any reason and Chicken Coop retains the same rights. No Chicken Coop representative has the authority to make any contrary agreement.

DATE _____ SIGNATURE _____

Upon termination of my employment, I agree to return all uniforms issued me. It is understood that should these uniforms not be returned the cost of the same will be deducted from my final paycheck.

DATE _____ SIGNATURE _____

YOUR APPLICATION WILL BE CONSIDERED ACTIVE FOR 30 DAYS-FOR CONSIDERATION AFTER THAT YOU MUST REAPPLY

opportunities were available without additional training or education" provide further information.

- ☐ Look at the presentation of the information on the application. Did the applicant complete all parts of the form, or were questions left blank? Was the application completed neatly or sloppily written? Were the responses clearly or poorly expressed? Did the applicant follow directions on the form? For example, if the instructions for one section said "print," did the applicant write or print the responses? Companies that use this technique believe it shows whether the applicant follows instructions, reads and thinks before acting, and is detail-oriented.
- ☐ Check for a pattern of commitment as opposed to a pattern of job-hopping. If there is a pattern of job-hopping, this should be followed up by questions during the interview.
- ☐ See if the applicant's work experience corresponds to the formal education and training.

In some organizations, the applicant has a brief screening interview *before* completing the application form; in others, the brief screening interview follows submission of the application. The purpose of this initial, very brief interview is to determine if the applicant meets the minimum job qualifications.

References.   References may be requested either before or after the supervisor conducts an in-depth interview. Some companies want to have all the preliminary information available before the supervisor's interview; others wait until after the supervisor has indicated an interest in the applicant before asking for references. The advantage of having all the information available before proceeding with the in-depth interview is that if the references do not show that the applicant is a viable one, the process ends and the company's expenses are reduced.

Some employers place little credence in references. Frequently, former employers will provide only limited information. Many organizations limit the information they provide on previous employees to dates of employment and job title or simply acknowledge that the person requesting the reference was, indeed, employed by the organization. Because of possible legal ramifications, former employers are reluctant to give a negative reference and, therefore, give a neutral evaluation of the former employee's performance. The worst-case scenario is one in which a less-than-honest reference is given because it is a way of getting a current employee "out of our hair" and into a new position. While references should continue to be a part of the employment process, it is not wise to overemphasize references when making a decision to employ or not to employ.

Tests

Tests are administered, when appropriate, by the HR department. Typical tests include employment readiness tests and fitness for work tests.

Employment Readiness Tests.   Employment readiness tests include **proficiency tests,** which measure levels of achieved skill or acquired knowledge; **aptitude tests,** which measure an applicant's potential to perform a job; **personality tests,** which evaluate characteristics such as emotional maturity, sociability, and responsibility; **intelligence tests,** which measure a person's knowledge; and **vocational interest inventories,** which evaluate an applicant's likes and dislikes in relation to occupations and hobbies. Because of the decline in basic worker skills, many employers are now administering **literacy tests,** which measure an applicant's reading and writing skills; **basic math skills tests,** which measure an applicant's ability to solve basic math problems such as making change, computing the cost of more than one item, and so on. Tests to measure English as a second language are also being administered because of the increased number of immigrants entering the workforce who do not have English as their first language. Figure 6.5 shows the results of a study, *Basic Skills: An AMA Research Report on Testing and Training,*[2] conducted by the American Management Association, which focuses on literacy and math skills testing of new hires.

If tests are a part of the employment process, they should meet the criteria of **validity, reliability,** and **job relatedness.**

A test is considered to be valid when it measures what it is represented to measure. For example, if a test is to measure an applicant's ability to perform the math functions required on the job but it really measures only the ability to follow instructions, then the test is said to be invalid.

A reliable test produces the same results with repeated use. If Scott, for example, is given a test to measure his manual dexterity and scores very low, and then he is given the same test a week later and scores very high, the test is not a reliable measure of his ability.

Any test given for employment purposes must be job-related—that is, all job requirements must be necessary for the successful completion of the job tasks. For example, if a shorthand test is required for all secretarial applicants when the actual duties of the secretary do not require shorthand, the test is not considered job-related.

Fitness for Work Tests.   Tests designed to measure applicants' fitness to perform the work for which they are applying include drug screening, physical tests, honesty tests, and polygraphs.

Drug screening has become a major part of the testing program for many companies. A drug- and alcohol-free workplace has become one of the targets and is included in the strategic plan of the HR departments.

The employment application for Wal-Mart includes the following statement:

> I understand that Wal-Mart Stores, Inc. has a commitment to maintain an alcohol/drug-free workplace and that Wal-Mart unless prohibited by state law, requires a drug screening test as a part of its selection and hiring process. I understand that such drug screening will consist of the testing of a urine sample or other medically recognized test

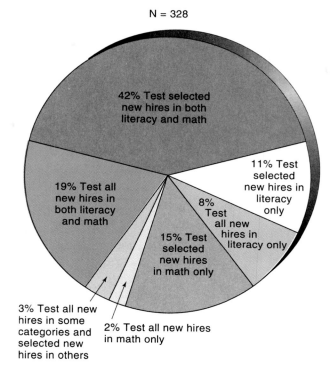

N = 328

Figure 6.5
WHAT ARE NEW
HIRES TESTED
FOR?*

42% Test selected new hires in both literacy and math

11% Test selected new hires in literacy only

19% Test all new hires in both literacy and math

8% Test all new hires in literacy only

15% Test selected new hires in math only

3% Test all new hires in some categories and selected new hires in others

2% Test all new hires in math only

*Sample includes only those firms that do test.
Source: American Management Association; printed in *Management Review,* April 1989, p.57. Reprinted by permission of the publisher. All rights reserved.

designed to detect traceable amounts of a controlled substance in my body. If any detectable amounts are found in my body, a second test, approved by the NIDA, will be performed on the same specimen. If the results of the second test are also positive, I will be disqualified from consideration for employment and any offer of employment withdrawn. I further understand and agree that if I am employed, I may be required to submit to alcohol/drug testing under certain circumstances during my employment. I have read, understand, and agree to the statement above. (please initial here.) _____

Pre-employment medical examinations are prohibited under the 1990 Americans with Disabilities Act. Once an offer of employment has been made, employers may then require a physical examination. Further discussion of the ADA is included in the section in this chapter on "Legal Implications."

Honesty may be tested by either paper-and-pencil honesty tests or by graphology. One honesty test consists of a set of 40 statements that the applicant is asked to mark true or false. Statements such as "Every normal person is sometimes tempted to steal," "If a person steals once, he is likely to steal again," and "I get mad easily and then get over it soon" are examples from honesty tests.

Graphology is the study of handwriting shapes and patterns for the purpose of determining the personality of the writer. One of its potential uses is testing the honesty of the applicant. There is some controversy over whether or not honesty tests and graphology are valid testing tools.

Polygraphs, once often used, are no longer routinely used. The Employee Polygraph Protection Act of 1988 severely limited the use of polygraph examinations by private employees. This act prohibits employers from requesting that job applicants and/or current employees take any lie detector or polygraph test except under narrowly defined conditions. For example, employees may be requested but not required to take a polygraph as a part of an ongoing investigation, but even this type of testing has many limitations.

COMPETENCY CHECK

Can you cite the methods used to screen applicants?

Interviewing

After an applicant has gone through the initial screening and met the basic qualifications for the job, the next step is an in-depth interview by the supervisor. This is the stage at which the supervisor tries to determine, based on all the preliminary information, if this applicant is the person for the job. This is also the time at which the supervisor will describe the job and provide some information about the company.

Before the Interview

The supervisor, as well as the applicant, must prepare for the interview. The first step is for the supervisor to become familiar with the job description, the job specification, and the applicant information. Applicant information will come from the application or from a résumé, from references, from the test results, and from any notes made by the HR staff following the initial interview. Figure 6.6 is a good checklist to follow when becoming familiar with the job requirements.

Set the stage for the interview by creating a comfortable environment. Conduct the interview in a room that is private and in which the atmosphere is pleasant (comfortable temperature, enough light, attractive). If your office doesn't meet these requirements, there may be a conference room available for the interview. Keep in mind that the interview offers you an opportunity to present the company in a positive way to a potential employee who may become an invaluable asset to the company. At the same time, however, be honest about any requirements of the job that may be perceived as negative. For example, if overtime is required, if there is a dress code, or if there is a no-smoking policy, applicants should be made aware of these requirements.

Prepare questions to be asked during the interview. The questions should focus on the applicant's employment history, education, outside activities and interests (if appropriate), strengths and weaknesses. A form that can be used to develop your

Figure 6.6	
WHAT THE INTERVIEWER SHOULD KNOW ABOUT THE REQUIREMENTS OF THE JOB	

Skill/Knowledge/Education

Technical knowledge required
Job expectation—output, quality,
   costs
Special equipment required
Specific experience required
Specific skills required
Formal education required
Job duties involved

Responsibilities

Potential loss to company—
   equipment, products, $$, good will
Supervision of others
Safety of others
Confidential information
Customer contact
Vendor contact
Public contact

Physical

Activity—energy required
Mobility—speed required
Strength
Visual/auditory requirements
Sensitivity of touch/smell
Dexterity
General health
Appearance (if relevant)
Sex (if bona fide requirement)

Environment

Working conditions
Safety hazards
Hours
Location
Travel

Intellectual

Intelligence required
Judgment required
Independent action required
Amount of supervision

Miscellaneous

Pay—benefits
Future potential of job

Emotional

Pressures of job
Variety or monotony of work
Job satisfactions
Adaptability required
Relationships with others
Personality and attitudes of
   supervisors, coworkers,
   subordinates

Source: Sovran Bank, N.A., Norfolk, Va. Reprinted with permission.

questions is shown in Figure 6.7. A list of possible questions is presented later in this chapter.

Many companies use a structured interview format (one that follows a set pattern of questions provided to the interviewer). If this is the case, your preparation for the interview should consist of becoming so familiar with the questions that they will seem to be your own.

During the Interview

When the applicant comes into the room, stand, greet him or her with a firm handshake, and introduce yourself. Indicate where the applicant should sit. Make every

COMPETENCY CHECK

Can you describe the supervisor's activities prior to the interview?

Figure 6.7
STRUCTURED INTERVIEW FORM

Supply questions prior to the interview to be used during the interview to help in selecting the best person for the position.

Applicant's Name _____

Position Applied For _____

Interviewer _____

Employment History

Opening question: _____

Specific questions: _____

_____

_____

Education

Opening question: _____

Specific questions: _____

_____

_____

Volunteer Activities

Opening question: _____

Specific questions: _____

_____

_____

Problem-Solving Skills

Opening question: _____

Specific questions: _____

_____

_____

Personality Factors

Opening question: _____

Specific questions: _____

_____

_____

Other Factors

Opening question: _____

Specific questions: _____

_____

_____

effort to put the person at ease. If the applicant appears to be nervous, offer a beverage and spend a moment in small talk. But be careful to avoid questions that might later be considered discriminatory.

Let the applicant know the purpose of the interview. "You have completed the initial screening process, and our purpose today is to try to establish if there is a proper fit between you and the job for which you have applied." Keep in mind that the interview should provide information about the applicant that may not be completely covered by the application. Therefore, you should talk no more than 20 to 25 percent of the time. Otherwise, you may become the interviewee, and the purpose of the interview will be lost.

Maintain control of the interview. Control means that you establish the direction of the questions and the time spent on the answers. Do not allow the interviewee to wander off in other directions; keep the purpose of the interview in mind. Begin with a leading question such as "How did you learn about this job opening?" or "Why are you interested in this job?"

Once the lead-in has been done, you can get to the heart of the interview. To gain the type of information that will be helpful, however, there are certain types of questions that should be avoided. Try to avoid:

Questions That Can Be Answered with a Yes or No.   "Were your business courses helpful to you?" "Do you think you have the skills to do this job?" Change these yes or no questions to open-ended questions that allow the applicant to respond in more than monosyllables. Perhaps the first question could be changed to "How were your business courses helpful to you?" The second question could be changed to "Describe the skills that you would bring to this job." Open-ended questions also provide the interviewer with an opportunity to see and hear the applicant use communication skills that may not be apparent in yes or no responses.

Leading Questions.   These questions often telegraph the right response. For example, "Would you say that you have good interpersonal skills?" or "Don't you think that it is important to plan for personal growth?" say to the interviewee "Your response should be a very strong yes."

Obvious Questions.   "So you graduated from John Marshall High School?" is a question that is answered on the application and is a waste of time to ask. "You worked for John Cool for 2 years right after college?" is another example of an obvious question. Use the limited time you have to obtain information not available to you prior to the interview.

Questions That Are Not Job-Related.   Confine your questions to ones that are related to the job. "When overtime is necessary, is that a problem for you?" "What kind of lathe have you operated?" "When did you receive your optician's license and in what locality?" are all job-related questions. Questions that are not job-related might include "Are you a Redskins fan?" or "What do you think of [the current 'hot topic']?" or even "What do you do for recreation?"

Questions That May Be Considered Discriminatory.   This issue is addressed later in this chapter.

A major employer has divided the questions to be asked during the interview into these categories: work experience, education and training, leadership, initiative, persistence, motivation, and communication skills.

Work Experience

- ❏ Describe your work experience at your previous position.
- ❏ What additional responsibilities did you have?
- ❏ What was the most fulfilling aspect of that job?
- ❏ What was the least fulfilling aspect of that job?
- ❏ Why did you leave?
- ❏ How do you feel about your progress on that job?
- ❏ Which of your previous jobs did you find most fulfilling?
- ❏ Which of your previous jobs did you find least fulfilling?
- ❏ What recognition for outstanding performance did you receive in your previous job?
- ❏ Why did you choose to work for your previous employer?
- ❏ What skills did you develop in your previous position?

Education and Training

- ❏ What was your major course of study?
- ❏ Why did you select that course?
- ❏ What was your minor course of study, if any?
- ❏ What courses did you prefer? Why?
- ❏ What courses did you dislike? Why?
- ❏ What courses did you find most valuable? Why?
- ❏ What courses did you find least valuable? Why?
- ❏ What training have you had that would help you in this position?
- ❏ What further training or education do you anticipate obtaining?

Note: As the applicant's educational experience becomes less recent, it decreases in relevance. Educational experience is also less important than the amount and quality of the applicant's work experience.

Leadership

- ❏ How do you feel about making decisions? Why?
- ❏ How do you feel about supervising others? Why?
- ❏ How would you evaluate your degree of self-confidence? Why?
- ❏ How do you feel about authority?

Initiative

- ☐ What is your idea of challenging work?
- ☐ How do you feel about working in an unstructured environment?
- ☐ How do you feel about regularly increasing your job responsibilities?

Persistence

- ☐ How do you feel about working in a high-pressure area?
- ☐ How do you feel about working in a position in which there are many obstacles to overcome?
- ☐ How would you react if given an unpleasant task?

Motivation

- ☐ What are your short-term career goals?
- ☐ What are your long-term career goals?

Communication Skills (if Job-Related)

- ☐ What is important to you in communicating with others?
- ☐ What written communication skills have you developed?
- ☐ Have you taken any communication courses? Describe them.
- ☐ What public speaking experience do you have?

The interviewer should be objective during the interview and wait until the interview is over before making a decision about whether to recommend this applicant for the job.[3]

Avoid snap judgments. It has been said that many interviewers make a decision about an applicant within the first 3 minutes of an interview. It is very difficult to overcome an initial negative impression. For example, if the applicant is late for the appointment, the interviewer may decide, justly or unjustly, that this applicant is not dependable. Rather than jumping to a conclusion, a good interviewer will file that bit of information away and evaluate the applicant based on the total interview.

Avoid personal biases. Objectivity is the key; evaluate the applicant on the basis of all the information you have available. You may believe that pregnant women should not be working or that members of minority groups take longer to learn a job. These are personal biases not based on fact. The first step in avoiding decisions based on biases is to recognize that you have biases and that you must put them aside when you make employment decisions.

Avoid the "halo effect." The halo effect occurs when you let one factor influence your assessment of all other factors of an applicant's employability. For example,

Mason scored very high on her aptitude test; therefore, you assume that she is also a good performer and a responsible person. You are guilty of letting the halo effect color your assessment of Mason's entire potential. On the other hand, Jeff is late for his interview and so you assume that he must be irresponsible and lack good thinking skills. Negative halo (sometimes called "horn") effect is at work here.

Avoid emphasizing the negative. One negative can outweigh several positives because the focus is often on the negative rather than the positive. As the song says, "Accentuate the positive, eliminate the negative." This does not mean that you should ignore negatives; it simply means that negative factors should not receive greater weight than positive ones. Keep them in perspective.

COMPETENCY CHECK

Can you describe the supervisor's activities during the interview?

If possible, wait until after the interview to make notes and complete any required forms. It is very distracting to the applicant if you are writing while he or she is talking. Interviewers can also be distracted if they try to take notes while listening to the applicant.

Closing the Interview

When you have all the information you require to make your recommendation, close the interview. You may do that by saying "Is there anything else we should cover?" or "Do you have any additional questions that I can answer at this time?" If there are none, you may close the interview by thanking the applicant for coming in and explaining that he or she will be notified of the employment decision by the HR department within 2 weeks (or whatever time frame has been established).

After the Interview

A written record of the interview should be made immediately following the interview. If you wait until later, you may forget some points you wished to make. Or if you interview several people before making your written report, it is possible to confuse some of the applicants and to attribute qualities to the wrong person. Two examples of applicant interview reports are shown in Figures 6.8 and 6.9 on pages 157 to 159.

COMPETENCY CHECK

Can you describe the supervisor's activities in closing the interview and after the interview?

Interviews play a large role in the staffing process. Most people believe they are a good judge of character, and, therefore, they place great weight on the interview even though studies have shown that the interview is less reliable than believed. Figure 6.10 on page 160 shows the weight that is placed on the various phases of the selection process.

Selecting the Best Applicant

As H. Ross Perot once said, "Eagles don't flock; you have to find them one at a time."[4] And so it is with good employees.

In large organizations, selection will be made by the HR department based on all the information received, with special emphasis on the supervisor's recommenda-

Figure 6.8
APPLICANT INTERVIEW REPORT

SOVRAN FINANCIAL CORPORATION
APPLICANT EVALUATION REPORT
MANAGEMENT ASSOCIATE PROGRAM
INITIAL INTERVIEW

Applicant's Name: _____ Date: _____

Referred by: _____ Interviewer: _____

Rate on scale of 1–5 with	1	2	3	4	5
	Poor		Good		Excellent

1. **IMPACT** – Ability to create a good first impression, to command attention and respect, to demonstrate confidence, and to achieve personal recognition.   _____

    +/– Business Dress   +/– Poise   +/– Maturity   +/– Grooming
    +/– Confidence   +/– Assertiveness   +/– Enthusiasm

2. **ORAL COMMUNICATION SKILLS** – Effectiveness of expression as demonstrated by clarity of speech, vocabulary, and grammar.   _____

    +/– Vocabulary   +/– Syntax   +/– Clarity   +/– Rate   +/– Grammar
    +/– Eye Contact   +/– Animation   +/– /Volume

3. **SALESMANSHIP** – Ability to persuade and to sell oneself in the interview.   _____

4. **LEVEL OF ACHIEVEMENT** – Factors which comprise this person's record, quality of life's experience or indicate commitment to achievement and success.

    College _____

    Major _____

    GPA _____ Date Graduated _____
                                                           (or will graduate)

    +/– Business Coursework   +/– Activities   +/– Leadership
    +/– Community Involvement   +/– Work Experience

5. **INTEREST** – Extent to which this individual is knowledgeable about Sovran, has adequately prepared for a career in banking, and matches up to Soven's current goals.   _____

    +/– Industry Knowledge   +/– Level of Ambition
    +/– Banking Career Interest   +/– Quality of Questions
    +/– Sovran Knowledge   +/– Realistic Expectations
    +/– Management Interest   +/– Business Development Interest

(Continued)

Figure 6.8
(CONTINUED)

GEOGRAPHICAL INTERESTS
(Rank for Priority (1,2,3)

FUNCTIONAL INTERESTS
(Check appropriate areas)

AREA   CITY PREFERENCE

＿＿ Retail	＿＿ Fin. Serv./Invest.
＿＿ Commercial	＿＿ Real Estate Finance
＿＿ Trust	＿＿ Personal
＿＿ Marketing	＿＿ Audit
＿＿ Accounting	＿＿ Systems
＿＿ Operations	＿＿ Mortgage Lending
＿＿ Leasing	

＿＿ Centeral Region   ＿＿＿＿＿＿＿
＿＿ Eastern Region   ＿＿＿＿＿＿＿
＿＿ Hampton Roads Region   ＿＿＿＿＿＿＿
＿＿ Maryland   ＿＿＿＿＿＿＿

＿＿ Mountain Region   ＿＿＿＿＿＿＿
＿＿ Northern/Potomac Region   ＿＿＿＿＿＿＿
＿＿ Skyline Region   ＿＿＿＿＿＿＿
＿＿ Southside Region   ＿＿＿＿＿＿＿
＿＿ Western Region   ＿＿＿＿＿＿＿

OVERALL RATING ＿＿＿＿＿＿＿
(Rate on scale of 1–5)

RECOMMENDATION (check one)

☐ Drop from consideration (circle reason for decision)
   a. applicant not qualified
   b. applicant not interested in M.A. position–do not refer to other areas
   c. competition too stiff

☐ Consider for next step in selection process

☐ Definitely move to next step in selection process

☐ Other: Drop from consideration for M.A. position and refer to: (check appropriate area)

   Commercial (CBA) ＿＿＿   Accounting ＿＿＿
   Real Estate Finance (REFA) ＿＿＿   Systems ＿＿＿
   Other ＿＿＿   (Specify department below)

   ＿＿＿＿＿＿＿＿＿＿＿＿＿＿＿＿
   ＿＿＿＿＿＿＿＿＿＿＿＿＿＿＿＿

APPLICANT IS A CANDIDATE FOR (check one)   ＿＿ February Program   ＿＿ June Program

Interviewer's Signature ＿＿＿＿＿＿＿＿＿＿＿＿＿＿＿＿＿＿＿＿＿＿＿＿＿＿＿＿

Source: Sovran Bank, N.A., Norfolk, Va., used in Betty R. Ricks and Kay F. Gow, *Business Communications: Systems and Applications,* John Wiley & Sons, Inc., New York, 1987, p. 438. Reprinted with permission.

6. *Americans with Disabilities Act of 1990* protects against discrimination based on physical and mental handicaps that substantially limits one or more major life activities. Examples include a condition that requires a wheelchair; visual, hearing, or speech impairments; mental retardation; and chronic mental illness. Under this act, an employer may not ask an applicant if he or she has a disability. An employer may, however, ask how, with or without reasonable accommodation, an applicant would perform the duties of the job. A medical examination may not be required until an applicant is offered a position, but the job offer may be made conditional upon passing a medical examination, if that is a condition of employment for all hires.

Employers are not required to give preferential treatment to a disabled person unless that person is the best qualified. Employers, however, must provide reasonable accommodation, which may include such measures as adjusting work schedules, reassigning some minor tasks, providing adaptive equipment or devices, and modifying the workplace to make it accessible to employees with disabilities. A major communications organization has prepared an excellent description of reasonable accommodations that can be applied to different limitations and jobs. This information is provided in Figure 6.13 on page 166.

According to congressional estimates, the average cost to accommodate a disabled worker will be $304, with 51.1 percent of accommodations made at no cost and 80 percent of the changes costing more than $500.

The ADA also requires equal access for the disabled to all public accommodations.

In addition to the laws discussed, federal contractors or subcontractors may not discriminate against Vietnam veterans. Larger federal contractors may be required to examine their workforce to be sure there is no underutilization of women or minorities. Being aware of the law is the first step toward protecting your company from lawsuits.

All employment decisions should be based on the qualifications of the worker, not on whether the person is black, white, or Oriental; male or female; young, middle-aged, or older; Catholic, Protestant, or Buddhist; from the United States or France; or disabled. The basic question should be "Is this the person most qualified to do the job?"

There are several exemptions to the laws that we discussed above. If there is a seniority clause in a union contract, promotion, transfer, or termination may be determined by seniority. Another exemption is if the company can show that the qualification is a bona fide occupational qualification (BFOQ). A BFOQ may specify, for example, that a model for women's clothes must be female; that someone advertising cosmetics for black females must be both black and female; or that a flight attendant must meet a minimum height requirement in order to reach overhead storage areas.

COMPETENCY CHECK
Can you identify six major federal acts governing equal employment opportunity and describe the groups they protect?

Figure 6.13
TYPES OF REASONABLE ACCOMMODATIONS

The table below:

☐ Specifies various types of reasonable accommodations that can be applied to different limitations and jobs.
☐ Provides a description and example(s) of each type of accommodation.

Type	Description	Example(s)
Job tasks	Modifying the methods of performing a job.	Arranging for a vision-impaired employee to give reports orally or on tape rather than in writing.
Work schedule	Adapting work schedules to meet individual needs.	Arranging for an employee with severe physical limitations to begin and end the workday at non-rush-hour periods.
Work site	Altering the: ☐ Employee's workstation. ☐ Equipment used on the job.	☐ Rearranging furniture. ☐ Raising the height of a workstation. ☐ Rearranging the placement of equipment needed to perform the job.
Aids and devices	Providing aids or devices to help employees perform job tasks.	Providing talking calculators, amplified telephones, audio players and recorders, and/or TDDs (Telecommunications Devices for the Deaf).
Readers, interpreters, and assistants	Providing assistance such as job specialists or coworker volunteers.	☐ Providing sign language interpreters for hearing-impaired employees attending meetings or training. ☐ Providing readers to assist with mail and/or document processing.
Structural modification	Modifying physical facilities to make them accessible to individuals with disabilities.	☐ Installing wider doors. ☐ Modifying elevator controls; e.g., providing pushbuttons in Braille. ☐ Providing reserved parking spaces.

Note: Supervisors should ask employees with known disabilities if they require reasonable accommodations to perform their jobs.

Following Legal Staffing Procedures

In order to follow legal staffing procedures, supervisors must know what constitutes discrimination and must conduct themselves in such a way as to avoid even the perception of discriminating practices. Supervisors have little influence on what is included on the employment application or how preliminary screening is done; these decisions are made at higher levels in the organization. Therefore, the primary staffing responsibility of supervisors is to interview all applicants and make recommendations for hiring in a nondiscriminatory manner.

Nondiscriminatory interviewing means asking only job-related questions. Figure 6.14 was developed by New York State's Division of Human Rights as a guide to which pre-employment questions to ask and which to avoid. It should be noted,

Figure 6.14
LEGAL AND ILLEGAL PRE-EMPLOYMENT QUESTIONS

Here is a series of questions which the New York State Division of Human Rights has compiled as being lawful and unlawful pre-employment inquiries. As New York appears to be stricter than most states and the federal government, by following these recommendations, lawyers suggest that a company may be less likely to find itself in difficulty with the authorities because of pre-employment inquiries. (Verified with N.Y. State Division of Human Rights as of January 1985.)

Subject	Lawful*	Unlawful
Race or Color:		Complexion or color of skin. Coloring.
Religion or Creed:		Inquiry into applicant's religious denomination, religious affiliations, church, parish, or religious holidays observed. Applicant may not be told "This is a (Catholic, Protestant, or Jewish) organization."
National Origin:		Inquiry into applicant's lineage, ancestry, national origin, descent, parentage or nationality. Nationality of applicant's parents or spouse. What is your mother tongue?
Sex:		Inquiry as to gender.
Marital Status:		Do you wish to be addressed as Mr.? Mrs.? Miss? or Ms.? Are you married? Are you single? Divorced? Separated? Name or other information about spouse.
Birth Control:		Inquiry as to capacity to reproduce, advocacy of any form of birth control or family planning.
Age:	Are you 18 years of age or older? If not, state your age.	How old are you? What is your date of birth? What are the ages of your children, if any?
Disability:		Do you have a disability? Have you ever been treated for any of the following diseases . . . ? Do you now, or have you ever had, a drug or alcohol problem?
Arrest Record:	Have you ever been convicted of a crime? (Give details)	Have you ever been arrested?

(Continued)

	Figure 6.14 (CONTINUED)	
Subject	**Lawful***	**Unlawful**
Name:	Have you ever worked for this company under a different name? Is additional information relative to change of name, use of an assumed name or nickname necessary to enable a check on your work record? If yes, explain.	Original name of an applicant whose name has been changed by court order or otherwise. Maiden name of a married woman. If you have ever worked under another name, state name and dates.
Address or Duration of Residence:	Applicant's place of residence.	
Birthplace:		Birthplace of applicant. Birthplace of applicant's parents, spouse or other close relatives.
Birthdate:		Requirements that applicant submit birth certificate, naturalization or baptismal record. Requirement that applicant produce proof of age in the form of a birth certificate or baptismal record.
Photograph:		Requirement or option that applicant affix a photograph to employment form at any time before hiring.
Citizenship:	Are you legally able to work in this country?	Of what country are you a citizen? Whether an applicant is naturalized or a native-born citizen; the date when the applicant acquired citizenship. Requirement that applicant produce naturalization papers or first papers. Whether applicant's parents or spouse are naturalized or native-born citizens of the United States; the date when such parents or spouse acquired citizenship.
Language:	Inquiry into languages applicant speaks and writes fluently, if job-related.	What is your native language? Inquiry into how applicant acquired ability to read, write or speak a foreign language.
Education:	Inquiry into applicant's academic, vocational or professional education and the public and private schools attended.	
Experience:	Inquiry into work experience.	
Relatives:	Name of applicant's relatives already employed by this company, if company policy prohibits this practice.	Names, addresses, ages, number of applicant's spouse, children or other relatives not employed by the company.
Notify in Case of Emergency:		Name and address of person to be notified in case of accident or emergency.

(Continued)

	Figure 6.14 (CONTINUED)	
Subject	**Lawful***	**Unlawful**
Military Experience:	Inquiry into applicant's military experience in the armed forces of the United States or in a state militia. Inquiry into applicant's service in particular branch of United States Army, Navy, etc.	Inquiry into applicant's military experience other than in the armed forces of the United States or in a state militia. Did you receive a discharge from the military in other than honorable circumstance?
Organizations:	Inquiry into applicant's membership in organizations which the applicant considers relevant to his or her ability to perform the job.	List all clubs, societies and lodges to which you belong.

Prima Facie Discriminatory Inquiries

In the absence of business necessity, a selection criterion should not be used if it has a disproportionately burdensome effect upon those of a particular race, creed, color, national origin, gender, age, marital status, or disability group. In Griggs v. Duke Power Company, 401 U.S. 424, 431 (1971) the U.S. Supreme Court said:

"The touchstone is business necessity. If an employment practice which operates to exclude Negroes cannot be shown to be related to job performance, the practice is prohibited."

It is considered prima facie discriminatory to inquire about a subject which, because of its disproportionately burdensome effect, may not properly be used as a basis for selecting employees. The inquirer may justify the making of such inquiry by the showing of a business necessity such as a bona fide occupational qualification.

*Inquiries that would otherwise be deemed lawful may, in certain circumstances, be deemed as evidence of unlawful discrimination when the inquiry seeks to elicit information about a selection criterion which is not job-related and which has a disproportionately burdensome effect upon the members of a minority group and cannot be justified by business necessity.

Source: Adapted from New York State Division of Human Rights, 1985. Reprinted with permission.

however, that although the figure is labeled "Legal and illegal pre-employment questions," it is not the questions themselves that are legal or illegal. For example, if you ask an applicant, "Have you ever been arrested?" you're not going to be charged with a crime, handcuffed, and hauled off to jail. What may be considered illegal is the way the applicant perceives that the information has been used. "I believe I wasn't hired because the interviewer asked if I had ever been arrested and I said yes. Well, I was arrested 10 years ago for a minor offense of which I was later found innocent. But I didn't get a chance to explain. I believe I was discriminated against."

Treat all interviewees the same. Don't ask female applicants if they are free to travel unless you ask the same question of male applicants. Don't ask minority applicants about their credit ratings unless you ask nonminority applicants the same question and then only if job-related. For example, applicants for positions where they will be dealing with substantial sums of money are usually asked about their credit rating. Be consistent in your treatment of applicants.

COMPETENCY CHECK

Can you list 10 questions that should not be asked during a pre-employment interview?

WHAT CAN THE SUPERVISOR DO?

Supervisors should take the following precautions when interviewing job applicants. This list, of course, is not inclusive, but it does provide some guidelines.

1. Age should not be an item for discussion.
2. Female applicants should not be questioned about their child-care arrangements.
3. An applicant's religious preferences are his or her private affair and should not be discussed.
4. It is unwise to seek information about the employment of an applicant's spouse unless the applicant indicates that this is a factor to be considered.
5. Matters related to the applicant's race, ancestry, or national origin are not open for discussion.
6. Value judgments about workplace social life that could be expected to discourage unmarried or minority applicants should not be expressed. Provide only factual information, and leave the appraisals to the applicants.
7. Attempts at "in" jokes related to race, national origin, religion, or gender should be avoided.
8. Discussion of military discharge or rank at time of discharge should be avoided.
9. Asking a handicapped applicant to describe the severity of his or her handicap is unlawful.
10. Questions about civil rights litigation with former employers should be avoided.
11. Questions about arrests are unwarranted because the person is not judged guilty by an arrest.
12. Avoid discussion of political affiliation or membership in any political organizations.

Source: AA/EEO Department, Old Dominion University, Norfolk, Va.

COMPETENCY REVIEW

1. Describe the roles of the supervisor and the human resources department in the hiring process.
2. Explain why it is important that there is a good match between the applicant and the job.
3. Forecast human resources needs, given basic information.
4. Describe the roles of the supervisor and the HR staff in recruiting.
5. Cite the methods used by the HR staff to screen applicants.
6. Describe the supervisor's activities in planning the interview.
7. Describe the supervisor's activities in beginning the interview.
8. Describe the supervisor's activities during the interview.
9. Describe the supervisor's activities in closing the interview and after the interview.
10. Explain the role of the supervisor in selection.
11. Name six laws that protect against discrimination in employment, and define the protected groups.
12. Identify five types of questions that should be avoided during a pre-employment interview.

APPLICATIONS

1. The projections for Publisher's Promotions, Inc., for next year are shown on page 141. Using the information provided on pages 141–142, complete the projections for the following 2 years.
2. Test your equal employment opportunity knowledge by answering the following questions. Answer "Yes" if you believe the question is legally defensible. Answer "No" if you believe the question is not legally defensible.

	Yes	No
1. Are you married?	_____	_____
2. Do you have children?	_____	_____
3. What is your age?	_____	_____
4. Where do you live?	_____	_____
5. How long have you lived there?	_____	_____
6. Tell me a little about yourself.	_____	_____
7. Do you believe in God?	_____	_____
8. Can you speak, read, or write fluently in any language other than English?	_____	_____
9. How did you acquire this ability?	_____	_____
10. What educational experience have you had?	_____	_____
11. Have you ever been arrested?	_____	_____
12. Are you willing to work an evening shift?	_____	_____
13. Are you willing to work on Christmas or Easter?	_____	_____
14. What organizations or clubs do you belong to?	_____	_____
15. What kind of credit rating do you have?	_____	_____
16. What are your height and weight?	_____	_____
17. Do you have friends or relatives employed here?	_____	_____
18. Are you pregnant?	_____	_____
19. What kind of military discharge did you receive?	_____	_____
20. Do you have any handicaps which might affect your ability to perform the duties of the job for which you are applying?	_____	_____
21. How do you feel about working for a woman?	_____	_____
22. What happens if you or your spouse gets a job transfer?	_____	_____
23. Do you feel that your race or color will be a problem in your performing the job?	_____	_____
24. Where were you born?	_____	_____
25. What is your maiden name?	_____	_____

Source: Adapted from "Interviewing Checklist," AA/EEO Department, Old Dominion University, Norfolk, Va., which was adapted from State of Virginia EEO Office Training Program, 1982.

3. Conduct an interview with a fellow student for a telemarketing position, using the interview questions provided on pages 154 through 155.
4. Develop a set of questions that you think are appropriate for interviewing a candidate for a word processor's position. Use the form shown in Figure 6.7. Compare your questions with those developed by a fellow student. Discuss the similarities and differences.

Case I ——————————————————————————— **CASES**

IT'S A MAN'S WORLD

Yesterday, two bus drivers retired, one quit, and one was fired. "Mac" McNeil, the supervisor of bus drivers for Independent Transit Company, is in the process of hiring replacements. The first of two interviews scheduled for this afternoon is in progress.

McNeil: "Hello, Mrs. North. It is Mrs., isn't it? You know, this job is a man's job. You may have to deal with some rowdies and even a few drunks. And this is a big piece of equipment for a little gal like you. Why, you probably can't even reach the pedals. How tall are you, anyway?

"Why don't you sit down and tell me all about your family. You're mighty young-looking to have three kids. How old are you?

"Little lady, don't you think you ought to be home with those kids and not taking a man's job away from him? Well, with all that feminist mumbo jumbo, I guess we'd better go through the formalities. You worked for Union Transit for 5 years?

"Ever been arrested?

"While you're out driving a bus, what does your husband do? And who are you going to get to take care of the kids? You know, we can't have you missing work because one of the kids is sick. You aren't pregnant again, are you?

"What was your maiden name? Kowalsky? Isn't that Polish? I guess if you're Polish you support the Pope? You hear the joke about the Polock who . . .

"Well, honey, I'll let you know about the job. I've got several men, WASPs, to interview first, and then I'll make a decision. Don't call me, I'll call you.

"Oh, by the way. You're kind of bent over in the shoulders. Have you got back problems, or is your front too heavy to carry around?

1. What did McNeil do wrong? List each interviewing mistake he made.
2. What questions *should* McNeil have asked to determine the applicant's qualifications for the job?

Case II

SHE'S TOO FAT FOR ME!

Bonnie Cook, 32, who weighs 300 pounds, sued the state of Rhode Island for discrimination when they failed to give her back her job at a state-run mental hospital. She sought $60,000 in back pay and the next available job at the Joseph H. Ladd School in Exeter, Rhode Island, where she had worked as an attendant from 1979 to 1986. She quit at that time to look after her sick child, reapplied for a job in 1988, and was turned down.

The state argued that Cook's weight would hinder her ability to restrain or help patients, and an attorney representing the state had compared her circumstances to that of Chicago Bears football player William "the Refrigerator" Perry, who was not allowed to play until he reduced his weight to 320 pounds.

Cook's attorney argued that her weight would not hinder her from doing the job because she had done this job before when her weight was estimated to be the same. Her actual weight was recorded in 1988 at 329 pounds, not the 300 estimated pounds shown on her application. Her attorney also stated that there was no reason why Bonnie Cook should be denied the opportunity to earn a living and support her family. The attorney argued that the doctor who denied her application stereotyped Cook when he refused to hire her because she was overweight. Cook testified that she was told she might be considered for the job if her weight dropped below 300 pounds. She said she went on a diet but suffered side effects from taking weight loss pills. Cook also said that she exercises more and eats less than she did during her previous employment at the center. The doctor at the center said he never promised Cook a job if she lost weight.

1. Take a position for either Bonnie Cook or the center. Justify your position.
2. What do you think the outcome was from this jury trial?
3. If this is considered to be discrimination, what is the basis?

Source: Associated Press item printed in *The Virginian-Pilot and The-Ledger Star,* Norfolk, Va., September 19, 1992.

REFERENCES

1. Adapted from Lester R. Bittle, *What Every Supervisor Should Know,* 5th ed., McGraw-Hill, New York, 1985, pp. 189–190.
2. American Management Association, reported by Eric Rolfe Greenberg, "Corporate Testing for the Three R's," *Management Review,* April 1989, p. 57.
3. Betty R. Ricks and Kay F. Gow, *Business Communications: Systems and Applications,* John Wiley & Sons, New York, 1987, pp. 429–430.
4. H. Ross Perot, *Bits and Pieces,* vol. F, no. 4M, The Economic Press, Fairfield, N.J., 1985, p. 23.
5. Peter M. Panken, "The Road to Court Is Paved with Good Intentions," *Nation's Business,* June 1985, p. 46.

SUGGESTED READINGS

Bacas, Harry: "How Companies Avoid Mistakes in Hiring," *Nation's Business,* June 1985.
Clipp, Richard: "Avoiding Legal Hassles When Hiring and Firing," *Office Systems '86,* March 1986.
Essex, Nathan L.: "When Talk Isn't Cheap: Steering Clear of Defamation Suits," *Personnel,* vol. 65, no. 5, May 1988, p. 44.
"Graphology, a Historical Review," *The HRC Newsletter,* vol. VI, ed. 1, Spring–Summer 1990, p. 1.
Hunsicker, J. Freedley: "Ready or Not: The ADA," *Personnel Journal,* August 1990, p. 81.
Keller, Hope: "Rating the Impact of the ADA," *The Virginian-Pilot and The Ledger-Star,* Sept. 29, 1992, p. 10.
Kiechel, Walter: "How to Pick Talent," *Fortune,* Dec. 8, 1986.
Perry, Toni A.: "Staying with the Basics," *HRM Magazine,* November 1990, p. 73.
Phillips, Joseph V.: "Changing the Rules of the Workplace: Civil Rights and Disability Issues," *The Virginian-Pilot and The Ledger-Star,* Apr. 1, 1991, p. 4.
Wickliff, Jay: "Beyond Hiring: Staffing," *Personnel,* vol. 65, no. 5, May 1988, p. 52.
Willis, Rod: "Recruitment: Playing the Database Game," *Personnel,* vol. 67, no. 5, May 1990, p. 24.

GLOSSARY

aptitude test   A test that measures an applicant's potential to perform a job.
basic math skills test   A test that measures an applicant's ability to solve basic math problems.
graphology   Study of handwriting shapes and patterns for the purpose of determining the personality of the writer.
intelligence test   A test that measures a person's knowledge.
job posting/job bidding   Placing a job description and specification in an area where employees are likely to see it and from which they can apply for the vacancy.

job relatedness   All job requirements must be necessary for the successful completion of the job tasks.

literacy test   A test that measures an applicant's reading and writing skills.

personality test   A test that evaluates characteristics such as emotional maturity, sociability, and responsibility.

proficiency test   A test that measures levels of achieved skill or acquired knowledge.

recruiting   The process of building an applicant pool from which to select employees.

reliability   A test that is reliable produces the same results with repeated use.

validity   A test that has validity measures what it is represented to measure.

vocational interest inventory   A test that evaluates an applicant's likes and dislikes in relation to occupations and hobbies.

CHAPTER 7
Training and Developing an Effective Workforce

STUDYING THIS CHAPTER WILL ENABLE YOU TO:

1. Identify elements in the relationship of training and development to the staffing function.

2. Discuss the supervisor's role in training and development.

3. List sources for identifying training and development needs.

4. Discuss conditions that affect learning.

5. Identify ways to encourage participation in training and development programs.

6. Discuss the importance of measuring training and development results.

7. Identify and define methods for training operations personnel.

8. Give examples of training methods used for operations or developmental training.

9. List factors to consider when choosing a training method.

10. Discuss methods by which trainees can evaluate a training program.

11. Give the meaning of the levels of training evaluation.

CHAPTER OUTLINE

THE RELATIONSHIP OF TRAINING AND DEVELOPMENT TO STAFFING
Moving Employees to Productive Status
Providing for Employee Growth
Maintaining Organizational Continuity

THE SUPERVISOR'S ROLE IN TRAINING AND DEVELOPMENT
Identifying Training Needs
Administering Training
Reinforcing New Behaviors
Repeating Training as Needed
Identifying New Training Needs
Retraining and Reassignment

SOURCES FOR IDENTIFYING TRAINING NEEDS
Performance Appraisals
Employee Surveys
Career and Succession Plans
Technological and Procedural Changes
Human Resources Forecasting

ESTABLISHING THE CLIMATE FOR TRAINING AND DEVELOPMENT
Conditions for Learning
Encouraging Participation
Measuring Training Results

TYPES OF TRAINING AND METHODS OF PROVIDING TRAINING
Orientation
Operations Training
Developmental Training
Selecting the Training Method

EVALUATING THE TRAINING AND DEVELOPMENT PROGRAM
Evaluation by the Trainee
Evaluation by the Trainer

Competency Review
Applications
Cases
References
Suggested Readings
Glossary

C H A P

Training AND Developing AN Effective Workforce

By the year 2000, experts say, 60 percent of all new jobs will require a high school education. Unfortunately, 70 percent of labor force entrants will have less than a high school education. In an increasingly competitive and technology-oriented world, the pool of qualified employees is shrinking instead of growing. To build the requisite well-trained workforce, employers will be compelled to:[1]

- ❐ recruit actively to bring in and train marginal candidates, rather than screening them out as in the past.
- ❐ invest heavily in expanded, continuous educational and training programs for all employees.
- ❐ find ways to make employees more productive, especially by tapping their ability to contribute to improvements in the work process.
- ❐ replace adversarial labor relations with an approach that focuses on cooperation.

✴ The Relationship of Training and Development to Staffing

As you learned in Chapter 6, both the supervisor and the human resources staff devote a great deal of time and effort to recruiting and selecting the best candidate for each job. Staffing is an expensive process. Proper training and development must follow selection; otherwise staffing costs are a direct drain on profits. Because profit is essential to effective organizational continuity, any breakdown in the staffing-training-development chain threatens that goal.

Figure 7.1 shows the six elements that graphically portray the relationship of training and development to the staffing function. Recruitment and selection bring the new employee into the organization. Orientation and training help the new worker become a productive member of the organization and the experienced worker adapt to changing job demands. Development programs give workers the opportunity to grow and progress in their careers within—and sometimes outside—the organization. Performance appraisals conducted for both new and experienced workers often identify a need for additional training or development. The

**Figure 7.1
RELATIONSHIP OF TRAINING AND DEVELOPMENT TO THE STAFFING FUNCTION**

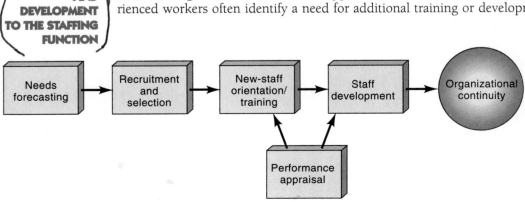

entire process provides the organization with its own high-quality human resources pool from which to fill its job needs and thus provide for organizational continuity. This chapter focuses on the training and development part of the process.

Training refers to company-directed activities and experiences designed to develop the skills, knowledge, and behaviors that will lead to effective current job performance. Training usually relates to a specific job or to related jobs and is designed to teach new skills or upgrade current ones. It includes, for example, the training of a newly hired sanitation worker in the technical and mechanical aspects of the waste collection truck to be driven and on the pickup schedule and route the worker will follow. Training also includes preparing a worker to change to newer methods of performing a job.

Development refers to increasing workers' abilities in order to improve future job performance, with emphasis on interpersonal and decision-making skills. For example, to prepare you to move from supervisor to a higher level of management, your organization may offer management and leadership training as part of its development program.

Training and development (T&D) is a specialized field of management support. T&D programs cover a broad range of sophistication and complexity. In small companies, T&D may be as simple as startup instruction for new employees by the supervisor. At the other end of the spectrum are company-owned training centers like Motorola University, operated by Motorola, Inc., and the customized centers of McDonald's, GE, and IBM. The objectives of all T&D programs are the development and retention of a productive workforce in order to meet company goals. Training new workers to become productive as quickly as possible receives a high priority.

Moving Employees to Productive Status

New employees move from being an expense to the organization to a point where they "earn their keep" by being productive. However, changing the productive status of workers through training is not limited to new employees. Experienced workers often need training or retraining to increase their productivity. Efforts to reduce waste, to cut costs, or to increase productivity often lead to changes in job requirements. New methods, standards, technology, or equipment may necessitate the retraining of workers.

Keeping workers productive through training and retraining is an ongoing activity. In addition, development programs help to motivate productive workers by providing growth opportunities.

Providing for Employee Growth

Effective human resources planning includes providing opportunities for employees to develop beyond the technical demands of their current jobs. Participating in development programs not only makes workers more valuable to the organization but improves their motivation by giving them a feeling of self-fulfillment. It also tends to make them more loyal to the organization. Finally, these programs improve the management of the organization by helping to identify and develop future managers from within.

Development programs are directed largely, though not exclusively, to management. Objectives of these programs are to:

- ❑ identify and develop potential managers from nonmanagerial personnel.
- ❑ improve the skills and abilities of current managers to enable them to manage more effectively.
- ❑ provide for the personal growth of managers.
- ❑ provide for organizational continuity through planned managerial succession.

Because this text is directed to you as a current or future supervisor, it emphasizes the training of nonmanagerial personnel. Preparing you to move from supervisor to a higher level of management is an example of organizational planning for continuity.

Maintaining Organizational Continuity

Through training and development, organizations not only prepare employees for promotion but prepare others to fill the vacancies created by the promotions. Through succession planning, organizational continuity can be maintained. Effective T&D programs help to minimize the disruption caused by personnel changes and keep the organization operating smoothly.

While succession planning usually is associated with managerial development, it also applies in a lesser degree to operations. For example, if one of your group leaders is promoted to section foreman, you should have a plan for moving someone in the group up to become group leader. In operations, a promotion often leaves a vacancy that can be filled only by hiring a new worker.

One of the hallmarks of self-directed teams is that they embrace the concepts of *multiskilling* and *job rotation*. Often in team environments, members are expected to learn every job on the team and, in some cases, to learn jobs on other teams as well. Organizations benefit from the flexibility that provides continuity when team members are promoted, ill, on vacation, or transferred to other units. Most team members see the change as positive because the variety provides greater job challenges and better understanding of the total process.[2]

COMPETENCY CHECK

Can you identify the elements in the relationship of training and development to the staffing function?

The Supervisor's Role in Training and Development

As a supervisor, you will play an active role in the overall training and development program. In a small company, you may be the only trainer available. Your program will be limited to the time you can spare from your other responsibilities. In a large company, you will cooperate with the human resources department (HRD) and/or training department, but you will have specific responsibilities in the training of your workers: (1) identifying training needs, (2) administering training, (3) reinforcing new behaviors, (4) repeating training, (5) identifying new training needs, and (6) retraining and reassigning. Let us look first at your function in finding out what training is needed.

Identifying Training Needs

Because you are considered the technical specialist for the requirements of jobs under your supervision, you are the primary source of information about the qualifications of workers who are to be hired. As workers become experienced, you will, through daily supervision and performance appraisal, be able to identify training that will help them improve their performance. In addition, you will be aware of workers with special skills or abilities who may benefit from development courses to prepare them for promotion.

At all stages of your workers' tenure, your daily contact with them will enable you to identify the training needs that will benefit both the workers and the organization.

Administering Training

In most organizations, the supervisor carries the responsibility for training new workers in the specific jobs for which they are hired. After you have oriented new workers to the work area, introduced them to coworkers, and assigned them to their workstations, you will give instructions on what is to be done and how it is to be done.

In organizations where a training specialist conducts the initial training, the supervisor's responsibility usually is to see that the new worker performs the job according to established procedures. If there is a human resources department, your training and development role is shared with that department. In the orientation of new workers, for example, the HRD carries the responsibility for acquainting new workers with overall aspects of the company while line managers handle information about the immediate work area. You will learn more about orientation later in this chapter.

As Figure 7.2 shows, you and the HRD have some separate and some shared training responsibilities. For example, the human resources department's company-wide T&D needs analysis is one source of information when identifying the training needs of your workers; other sources are discussed in the next section.

Reinforcing New Behaviors

Learning not practiced and reinforced will be forgotten. For example, the supervisor of the customer service representatives trained the reps on a new multiline telephone system. When a rep calmly and courteously handled a call while three lights were flashing indicating calls waiting, recognition of that accomplishment provided much needed reassurance.

Taking time at the beginning or end of each day to mention workers by name who practiced the new skills particularly well is time well spent. Constant encour-

Figure 7.2
TRAINING RESPONSIBILITIES OF SUPERVISOR AND HUMAN RESOURCES DEPARTMENT

HR Department	Supervisor
Conducts companywide training-needs analysis; sets objectives for overall T&D program; designs, implements, and evaluates program.	Orients workers to specific work environment
May assign specialist to teach job-specific skills to new workers based on supervisor's identification of skills.	Reviews and approves training program relating to supervisor's department
Designs and implements training program for general knowledge and ability needs of workers.	Identifies skills to be performed in each job
Provides feedback to supervisors regarding results of training of their workers.	Trains, or supervises training by a senior worker of, new workers in job skills; if training is by a specialist, provides feedback to HR department
Provides feedback to all managers regarding overall T&D program.	Identifies training needs of workers in general knowledge and skills, and communicates these needs to HR department
	Identifies and recommends candidates for developmental programs
	Encourages workers to participate in growth and developmental programs available through HR department
	Provides performance data to HR department relating to training and development

agement of those having difficulty will reinforce the new behavior even though it may not be easy for some workers.

Repeating Training as Needed

Refresher and follow-up training conducted periodically avoids the impression that training is a "onetime thing," not to be taken too seriously. If you notice that some employees who attended a training program practiced the new skills for a while and then returned to the old behavior, retraining may be needed.

Identifying New Training Needs

Developing new skills often creates the need for additional skills. For example, employees in the word processing department learned a new desktop publishing software program so that the company's monthly newsletter could be produced in house. That project was so successful that other departments began to request desktop publishing work. Some of those requests included creative artwork and artistic typefaces. New graphic and typeface software programs were added, and training was conducted for those programs as well.

Too often, workers are trained only in the technical aspects of their jobs—how to operate machines and equipment. Training to work with customers is often overlooked. Supervisors must be alert to the potential for solving productivity and quality problems as well as creating more customer satisfaction through training.

Retraining and Reassignment

A growing number of management experts now believe that downsizing and recession-induced layoffs will turn out to be a seriously misguided policy. Frank Popoff, president of Dow Chemical, says, "The layoff of experienced workers must be seen as an absolute last resort if American industry is to prosper in the long term." After discovering in the mid-1980s that layoffs were very costly in terms of lost morale and trust, Intel determined to avoid any more. In each of the past 2 years, Intel has redeployed about 600 workers whose previous jobs disappeared. When a plant was closed, for example, its employees were retrained and reassigned to other facilities or given desk jobs.[3]

While technology has rendered some skills obsolete, it has created a huge and largely unsatisfied need for others. The prescription for workers who want to ward off obsolescence: Be ready to learn new skills and shift gears at a moment's notice. Organizations must move more quickly to change product lines and adapt technologies in order to compete, which places a premium on the ability to be retrained quickly. People must be prepared for more job changes and more training.[4]

When an organization chooses to retrain its workforce, supervisors are directly involved in the identification of workers to train in specific areas. After supervisors are retrained, they retrain their employees. Organizations that promote the concept and acceptance of an atmosphere of lifelong learning will be better able to stay competitive in the future.

COMPETENCY CHECK
Can you discuss the supervisor's role in training and development?

Sources for Identifying Training Needs

Many sources from which you can identify the need for training and development are available. Several of the most common sources are discussed in this section.

Performance Appraisals

The appraisal system provides information about the degree to which each employee's work is measured against the performance standards established for each job. Productivity deviations are one measure. If you see, for example, that a worker is producing only 8 units per hour in an area where the standard is 12 and the average is 11 to 17, you should try to determine the reason. If the worker's skills are deficient, additional training is in order.

Examining a series of appraisals of this worker will show whether the production rate is typical, is increasing or decreasing, or is erratic. Your findings, together with your observations of the worker, will help you determine what type of training would help improve productivity. The worker may, for example, need additional supervised practice of the job skills taught in orientation or in previous training ses-

WHAT CAN THE SUPERVISOR DO?

Although testing is the best gauge of literacy problems, supervisors need to be alert to mistakes commonly ascribed to stupidity, laziness, or sloppiness:

Accidents—repeated accidents even when guidelines are posted clearly.
Misinterpreted job orders—simple-to-execute orders for products or services frequently not produced as requested.
Customer complaints—resolution of complaints is slow or sloppy.

Additionally, supervisors need to be aware of concealment methods:
- buddy systems that result in ghostwritten forms—an employee never fills out a form; someone, usually a coworker, helps
- watching and listening attentively to instructions
- claiming hand injuries when asked to write
- claiming loss of glasses or inability to decipher someone's handwriting when asked to read

Source: Adapted from "Employee Illiteracy," *Inc.*, August 1992, p. 81; and Claire J. Anderson, Betty R. Ricks, Sally A. Coltrin, and Lynda L. Brown, "The Human Resources Management Implications of Workforce Illiteracy: A SHRM/CCH Study," Norfolk, Va., 1990.

sions or may need training in new skills. The productivity report for all workers will serve as another source of information relating to training possibilities.

Identifying job-related literacy problems is becoming an important part of performance appraisals. **Functional** or **workplace literacy** encompasses reading, writing, speaking, listening, and mathematical skills. Functional illiteracy is often defined as the inability to use reading skills to cope with everyday tasks.

Employee Surveys

Information on the skills, knowledge, and abilities of all workers in the organization provides an inventory of its human resources. In addition to skills information, the inventory may include information on the worker's experience, education and training, special knowledge, time in current job, performance appraisals, compensation record, and career goals. By showing the skills available within the organization, the survey helps identify the skills that must be acquired through outside sources or through training and development programs within the organization.

Career and Succession Plans

The organization's career and succession plans provide information that can help identify training and development needs. Career planning motivates employees by informing them of growth opportunities within the organization; T&D programs help them prepare for these opportunities.

Despite the economic climate or the type of business, treating each worker as a potential career employee reinforces loyalty while improving the workforce. Federal Express and Disney have thrived on strong training programs. Both treat everyone as a potential career employee. The training Federal Express gives its customer service people in Memphis and Disney's training of a 17-year-old would-be jungle boat driver far surpass the training many technical firms give their machinists.[5]

Technological and Procedural Changes

The introduction of new technologies increasingly will require retraining of workers. Jobs are changing, especially in manufacturing. The number of unskilled and semi-skilled jobs is declining. Disparities between the average skill level of workers and the skill level demanded by the work are affecting most manufacturing companies. A survey of 360 companies conducted by the National Association of Manufacturers found that one-third regularly reject job applicants for poor reading and writing skills. Serious deficiencies in basic math and reading skills were reported by 50 percent of the companies. The need for literacy skills in the workforce is increasing.[6]

Workplace literacy classes, known as *basic skills training,* held on site and often on company time, are becoming more common. Companies are learning that illiteracy is their problem as well as that of the public schools. The major reasons that companies conduct basic skills training include the scarcity of qualified entry-level workers (42 percent), upgrading the skills of present workforce (26 percent), and employees with limited English speaking skills (23 percent).[7] Corporate literacy programs are conducted by General Motors at 150 of its plants; at the Adolph Coors learning center in Golden, Colorado; by Exxon at its Baytown-Olefins plant in Texas; by GTE in 10 communities where GTE is based; at Motorola's Mesa, Arizona, plant; and by Eli's Chicago's Finest Cheesecake, Inc.[8]

Statistical process control (SPC), programmable logic control, computerized materials handling, and increasing use of robotics have permanently changed life on the production line. Consequently, at Ford, worker retraining is nearly continuous.[9]

Human Resources Forecasting

As new technology is introduced into more and more industries, it requires changes in both blue- and white-collar work skills and patterns. Most companies already recognize that relationship. They know that they must retrain their workforce to learn, use, and maintain new technologies. Training programs are designed into a company's strategic plans alongside plant modernizations and expansion. Tenneco relates human resources planning to corporate goals and strategies, requiring its vice presidents to submit 5-year "executive resources" projections along with their 5-year business plans.

Entry-level workers of the future will need more technical skills than today if they are to function effectively in the workplace.[10] Organizational planning must include plans for a workforce that can achieve the organization's goals and objectives.

In this section, you have learned the major sources from which to identify training and development needs. Other situations may clue you in to other training needs. New health or safety information may be released, or problems may be spot-

COMPETENCY CHECK

Can you list the sources for identifying training and development needs?

ted by you or by an OSHA inspector. Workers themselves may identify training needs through suggestion systems or task forces.

Identifying training needs, however, is only one of your jobs. Establishing a climate in which training can take place also is necessary if the program is to succeed.

Establishing the Climate for Training and Development

The climate of an organization is established at the top. Both the philosophy and the reward system for implementing that philosophy are set by top management and then passed down through every level and to every member of the organization. For T&D to be successful, top management must "buy" it as a strategy for growth, "sell" it to the entire organization, and reward successful participation in it.

Even in an excellent organizational climate, there is another dimension of T&D that must be considered. The worker-participant is expected to learn in the program. How will that be accomplished?

Conditions for Learning

How do people learn? And why? The psychology of learning is a complex body of knowledge beyond the scope of this text. Our focus here is on an overview that will help you, as supervisor, apply some of the findings of research to your training program.

Research to date has told us more about *why* people learn than about *how* they learn. While we do not yet have complete answers to how people learn, scientists continue to probe the human brain in their search for knowledge about the learning process. Behavioral scientists have already given us considerable insight into *why* people learn.

Learning has been defined as a change in behavior. If we observe behavioral changes, we can assume that learning has taken place. For example, to move from one place to another, an infant first crawls. Then, after being coaxed to walk to parents' outstretched arms, the child learns how to reach the goal in an upright position. From then on, the youngster begins to abandon crawling in favor of walking. The child's behavior has changed through learning. Studying the conditions under which a person learns new behavior provides some insight into why a person learns. An understanding of certain conditions of learning will enable you to plan and implement your training program. Here are some conditions that are now considered basic to learning.

A Desire to Learn

The worker must *want* to learn. You cannot force workers to learn anything. There must be some internal willingness to make the effort. The desire to learn is called *motivation,* and it is discussed in Chapter 11. Motivation is influenced greatly by a person's perceptions, values, and attitudes, which vary from one person to another.

Workers may look at the training program and ask "What's in it for me?" or "Do I want this job enough to learn this new skill?" As supervisor, your job will be to recognize that you must create conditions that will stimulate workers' desire to learn.

The Purpose of Training

Trainees must know the purpose of the training. Why is it being given? Is it designed to improve safety? Increase productivity? Cut costs? Improve quality? Make the task easier for workers? If workers know the purpose and feel that it is worthwhile, they will respond better to the training. For example, if workers know that training in cutting procedures for making wooden chairs is designed to control unit cost and increase the company's and their earnings, they will more willingly respond to training for cutting as many chair legs as possible from a given piece of wood, consistent with standards of quality.

Training Applicability

Knowing that the training will be applicable to their lives will facilitate learning for workers. To be applicable, training should be:

1. *Meaningful*. Requiring all shop workers to take a sales training course would meet with some protest because it would not be meaningful for most of them.
2. *Realistic*. Training assembly-line workers in the procedures for processing insurance claims would not be realistic, nor would training toy salespersons on tactics for selling to senior citizens. Meeting the "real-world" test is an important condition for most work-related learning.
3. *Transferable to the workplace*. Skills training generally is more transferable than some other kinds of training because it can be given either at the workstation or, if given off the job, on identical or closely simulated equipment. Generally, the more similarity between the training and the job, the more transferable the learning.

Learner Involvement

Learning is an active, not a passive, process. The more a worker is involved in the situation, the easier the learning. This suggests that instruction should involve as many of the senses as possible. Let the learner see, hear, touch, smell, and taste. Imagine training people to become chefs by using only their visual and auditory senses! They must touch a tomato to judge its firmness, smell milk to judge its freshness, and taste broth to judge its seasoning. By the same token, lecturing is the least effective way to teach television repair. Lectures with visuals and demonstrations are somewhat better, but hands-on experience by the trainee is the most effective way to teach television repair because the worker is involved in the learning.

Organization of Training

Training materials should be organized in such a way as to make learning easier. Breaking down a skill into small components and arranging these components in the correct sequence is an appropriate way to organize most job-skill training. For example, welding instruction might follow this sequence: (1) an overview of welding technology; (2) safety rules and the protective clothing needed for the task; (3) preparation of materials to be welded; (4) parts of the welding torch, its fuel supply, its operation, its ignition and control; and (5) proper close-down and storage of equipment. Training might extend over a period of time in order to provide for an evaluation of each part of the learning before the worker progresses to the next component.

Timing is important so that learning of the different parts can be assimilated by the worker. The parts serve as building blocks to learning the whole process. Training organization should consider the components of the content, the sequence in the job process, and the interval between training segments.

♦ Feedback to Learners

Learning takes place more readily when learners are given feedback on how they are progressing. Training specialists know the power of a pat on the back for a job done well. They also know that it is important to point out weak points in the learning as they are spotted and to put the learner back on track immediately by explanation or demonstration.

Both positive and negative feedback serve a purpose. Positive feedback gives the learner encouragement to move ahead. Pointing out errors helps the worker get back into the learning sequence and may prevent the compounding of errors into another step of the process. In some situations it may prevent hazardous events. Telling a worker "Go ahead; I'll tell you when you're wrong" does not provide appropriate feedback. Nor does frequent fault finding help a worker progress. If frequent errors are occurring, it might be wise to observe the worker move backward in the steps until you and the learner together find out where the problem originated. You might say, "Let's see if together we can find out where the problem is. Let's go back to the previous step and see if that's where my instruction was not adequate." Negative feedback can be given in a positive way.

Learner Expectations and Rewards

Learning is closely related to the expectations of the learner. Research shows that workers are motivated to act based on their expectations of reward. The questions they ask themselves are: Will I be rewarded for my effort? Is the reward worth the effort involved? Can I be sure the reward will be forthcoming?[11]

Management can offer rewards such as higher pay or promotion for participating in training programs. Reward systems must be established and adhered to as part of the training and development program because expectations often influence the motivation of a worker to participate or not. Individual supervisors may be limited in the rewards they can offer their workers; reward systems usually are standardized to apply throughout an organization.

COMPETENCY
CHECK
Can you discuss
the conditions
that affect
learning?

Encouraging Participation

One of your first tasks in T&D will be to communicate the reward system to the workers. Then you must convince them that personal and near-term benefits will accrue to them as a result of the training. Successful completion of training will further *their* interests, give *them* more salary, prepare *them* for promotion. In addition, you must show them that as they progress, the whole organization progresses. As the company grows, they, in turn, will reap further long-term benefits, and the cycle will continue.

Because most workers today want to progress in their careers, encouraging participation in T&D is not too difficult. But there are always some who, for a variety of reasons, avoid training programs. They may fear the learning situation, fear failure, resent having to learn something new, or simply be satisfied with the status quo.

Research shows that tying pay to performance is a good motivating device. Giving raises or bonuses to those whose training results in improved performance sends a message to nonparticipants. Limiting or withholding pay increases from those who do not meet standards may also move some to get the training. In some cases, especially those involving safety or new systems, you may have to present an alternative—train or be terminated. To the holdout, you might finally have to say, "Alex, you've chosen not to participate in two training programs in the new system. We've discussed this several times, and you've indicated that your only reason for not taking the training is that you don't want to. We can't accept that. We're under OSHA pressure to get all our people certified; we have no choice. So I must notify you that the final program will begin June 1. If you do not take advantage of it, you will be terminated as of that date. As you know, that's company policy. If you want to talk to me about it, I'll be glad to meet with you." Then follow through on your proposal. Hopefully, you'll be able to persuade most workers to participate by emphasizing the benefits to themselves and to the company.

Another way to encourage participation is through career pathing. Today's workers want to know what their opportunities are for growing within the company. Career paths will let them see how they can move up. Career paths may be dual. A quality control technician in plant operations, for example, may move into engineering management. A dual-career ladder would show how this worker might move up in either department.

New technology and new market strategies also create new jobs. Employees on one career path may enter training programs in order to move into one of these emerging careers.

COMPETENCY CHECK
Can you list ways in which you can encourage participation in T&D programs?

Measuring Training Results

In an organization that supports T&D, every employee is aware that the program is available. Internal communications announce T&D opportunities, report results, and feature successful participants. Visibility becomes the fuel for keeping the program alive.

Besides encouraging employee participation, making results visible shows management the effect of the program on profits. This means that results should be measurable. You should follow up on participants after the training to document the benefits to the worker and to the organization.

Let's say that one of your workers produced an average of 20 units per hour before skills training. A month after she completed the training, she was averaging 24 units per hour, a 20 percent increase. She should be commended for her accom-

**Figure 7.3
EFFECTS OF
TRAINING ON
PRODUCT
REJECTS**

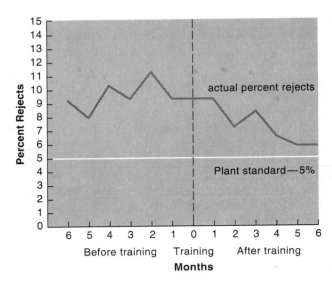

plishment, and her performance appraisal should show her improvement. Her work group and the department should be informed of her and the program's success. Management should be given a report, not only of her personal accomplishment, but also of the increased productivity for the work group and the department.

A graphic presentation often helps to dramatize results. A before-and-after graph of the results of a program aimed at improving quality control will enhance the report to management. Figure 7.3 shows one form that may be posted on a department bulletin board to advertise to all workers how training can improve their performance.

COMPETENCY CHECK
Can you discuss the importance of measuring T&D results?

Wherever possible, training results should be translated into dollars and cents and communicated to management and the employees. The financial results of some types of T&D programs are not immediately visible, but those that the supervisor deals with often are.

Types of Training and Methods of Providing Training

Generally, types of training are orientation, operations, and developmental. The type of training, or the skill or information to be learned, often dictates the method by which the training is delivered.

Orientation

The introduction that workers are given to the organization and their jobs is called **orientation.** Employees form their initial impressions of the company during the first few days. These impressions may be positive or negative. To get the new employee-employer relationship off on a positive note, most organizations

WHAT CAN THE SUPERVISOR DO?

A little extra time spent properly orienting new workers can go a long way toward maximizing their long-term effectiveness on the job. Suggestions for information to include in the orientation of a new worker include:

- ☐ Welcome the new employee to the company and to the department or division.
- ☐ Explain the philosophy and objectives of the organization.
- ☐ Describe the organization's operations, levels of authority, and their relationship.
- ☐ Explain clearly what is expected of the new employee: attitude, reliability, initiative, emotional maturity, personal appearance.
- ☐ Give a brief history of the organization.
- ☐ Explain the rules, regulations, policies, procedures, and city, state, and federal laws if appropriate.
- ☐ Introduce the new worker to fellow workers and people in offices the new worker will visit or work with regularly.
- ☐ Explain the criteria for performance appraisal.
- ☐ Review promotional opportunities.
- ☐ Give the new worker a copy of the employee handbook and explain the specific conditions of employment: working hours, punctuality, attendance, conduct, overtime, termination causes and procedures.
- ☐ Explain pay periods, procedures, and benefits: salary, insurance, sick time, breaks, vacation, recreation facilities, holidays, social activities, educational benefits, pension, etc.
- ☐ Show the location of and demonstrate the use of safety devices, fire prevention, etc.
- ☐ Restate your welcome and give encouragement.

Source: Adapted from Mark A. Truitt, *The Supervisor's Handbook,* National Press Publications, Shawnee Mission, Kans., 1991, p. 41.

provide an orientation to welcome new workers. This not only helps to create a good interpersonal beginning but also helps employees adjust to their new surroundings.

The orientation may consist of a few hours during which the worker is informed about company benefits, pay, and vacations and is introduced to his or her workplace and coworkers. A handbook describing the company history and its employer-employee relations may be given to workers to review after the orientation session. Some orientation programs are spread over a longer period of time and include an in-depth look at the organization.

Topics covered in orientation sessions vary with the nature, size, and complexity of the organization. One comprehensive list shows 130 possible topics.[12] Figure 7.4

Figure 7.4
ORIENTATION CHECKLIST

Name of Employee_____
Starting Date_____
Department_____

Name of Employee_____
Starting Date_____
Department_____
Position_____

HR DEPARTMENT

Prior to Orientation
_____ Complete Form A and give or mail to
 new employee
_____ Complete Form B
_____ Attach Form B to "Orientation
 Checklist—Supervisor" and give to
 the supervisor
Employee's First Day
Organization and Employee Policies
 and Procedures
_____ History of XYZ Inc.
_____ Organization chart
_____ Purpose of the company
_____ Employee classifications
Insurance Benefits
_____ Group health plan
_____ Disability insurance
_____ Life insurance
_____ Workers' Compensation
Other Benefits
_____ Holidays
_____ Vacation
_____ Jury and election duty
_____ Funeral leave
_____ Health services
_____ Professional discounts
_____ Child care
End of Orientation—First Day
_____ Make appointment for second day
_____ Introduce supervisor
Other Items
_____ Job posting
_____ Bulletin board—location and use
_____ Safety
_____ Alcohol/drug usage
_____ Where to get supplies
_____ Employee's records—updating

SUPERVISOR

Employee's First Day
_____ Introduction to coworkers
_____ Tour of department
_____ Tour of company
Location of
_____ Coat closet
_____ Restroom
_____ Telephone for personal use and rules
 concerning it
Working Hours
_____ Starting and leaving
_____ Lunch
_____ Breaks
_____ Overtime
_____ Early departures
_____ Time clock
Pay Policy
_____ Pay period
_____ Deposit system
Other Items
_____ Parking
_____ Dress
Employee's Second Day
_____ Pension retirement plan
_____ Sick leave
_____ Personal leave
_____ Job posting
_____ Confidentiality
_____ Complaints and concerns
_____ Termination
_____ Equal Employment Opportunity
During Employee's First Two Weeks
Emergencies
_____ Medical
_____ Power failure
_____ Fire

At the end of the employee's first two weeks,
the supervisor will ask if the employee has any
questions concerning any items. After all
questions have been discussed, both the
employee and the supervisor will sign and date
this form and return it to the HR Department.

_____
Employee Signature

_____
Orientation Conducted By

_____
Date

Source: Reprinted by permission from page 270 of *Human Resource Management* by Robert L. Mathis and John H. Jackson;
Copyright © 1994 by West Publishing Company, St. Paul, Minn. All rights reserved.

shows, in checklist form, the topics that might be included in a 2-day orientation. Note the follow-up at the end of 2 weeks.

The human resources department usually designs the orientation program and conducts the general sessions. The supervisor handles the part that relates to his or her specific unit. A checklist should be used to see that all planned topics are covered. To ensure that coverage is complete, it is recommended that the person handling each topic initial and date the checklist after completion. Many organizations also require that the new employee sign the checklist to show that instruction was received.

Orientation is the first step in training the new employee. After orientation, training focuses on the worker's specific job. As the employee becomes more experienced, training may focus on developing the worker for growth in the organization. Your involvement in developmental training usually will be limited to recommending workers for these programs or to participating in them yourself. But you will be actively involved in operations training.

Operations Training

Your major role in T&D will be job-intensive training of the operations workers for whom you are responsible. Immediately after orientation, your workers will begin learning their jobs under your direction, usually at their job stations. The operations training methods shown in Figure 7.5 are typically one-on-one sessions in which you, or a senior employee under your direction, shows the worker how to do the job.

In **on-the-job training (OJT)**, the trainer uses the demonstration method to show the worker how to follow the job procedure, operate equipment, handle supplies, and follow safety rules. Key points or "tricks of the trade" in performing the job are explained by the trainer to help the learner master the tasks as quickly as possible. After demonstrating the tasks, the trainer watches the worker repeat the process. While OJT is the term applied to a specific method, all the operations training methods shown in Figure 7.5 occur on the job.

The advantages of OJT are that (1) it is done at the actual workstation, (2) it requires no special equipment, and (3) the worker is producing during the training process. A disadvantage is that when a worker is used as a trainer, the pressures of his or her own job may lead to neglect or shortcuts, which can result in a poorly trained and disenchanted worker. Worker-trainers should be carefully chosen and prepared to do the training. They should also be rewarded for their training efforts.

Job instruction training uses special trainers to train supervisors in a four-step process to teach skills to workers. Job instruction training is a structured on-the-job training method that was developed during World War II to improve production.[13] When this method is employed, special trainers first train the supervisors in a four-step instruction process. This process is printed on a "trainer card" for quick reference by the supervisor. The four-step card is shown in Figure 7.6.

Figure 7.5
COMMON METHODS OF OPERATIONS TRAINING
Operations Training (basically job-intensive)

Apprentice training: Provides on-the-job experience under guidance of a skilled and certified worker. Requirements may be set for training, length of training, equipment, and skill level. Usually for skill crafts. May be monitored by U.S. Department of Labor.

Demonstration: Trainer performs a process or operates equipment while trainees observe. Usually accompanied by an oral explanation of the procedure. Typical in skills training.

Job instruction training : Form of on-the-job training. "Trainer card"–guided instructor. Card lists a 4-step instruction process: preparation, presentation, performance tryout, and follow-up. Still widely used.

Job rotation: Worker rotates through a series of jobs, staying in each a few days or weeks. In operations, worker may rotate through several jobs in a production process. Rotation may also be in different functional areas to enable the worker to learn several phases of the business. Commonly used to develop employee, to expand variety of tasks performed by worker, and to provide organizational flexibility. Sometimes called *cross-training* or *multiskilling.*

Mentor/buddy system: Worker is assigned to another employee recognized for high ability. Mentor serves as role model for new worker. Worker emulates mentor and may seek advice on job or other problems. Buddy system usually operates within work group, where experienced worker serves as buddy or big sister/brother to new worker to teach him or her the job and to guide in adjusting to the job environment.

On-the-job training (OJT): Worker is placed in the job situation. Training is done by supervisor or by an experienced worker. Most common of all types of training.

Vestibule: Training conducted away from the job site in a training simulation created to resemble the employee's actual work area and conditions of the job. Commonly used for skills training and for developing trainees' ability to react to variable conditions. Uses include training for pilots, astronauts, drivers, and police officers.

Apprenticeship is intensive on-the-job training that extends over a longer period of time, ranging from a few months to 2 years or more. The training usually is provided by a skilled worker, who may be certified by the organization, the union, or some other agency. Apprentice training is often required in crafts such as electrical work, plumbing, and shipbuilding.

Apprentice programs may include classroom training in the relevant technology as well as on-the-job training. Apprentices usually are required to progress through prescribed skill levels before they can practice the craft on the job.

Vestibule training simulates actual equipment or conditions that would be hazardous or prohibitively costly in actual use. Teaching the operation of complex

---

Figure 7.6
JOB INSTRUCTION TRAINING

First, here's what you *must do* to *get ready* to teach a job:

1. Decide what the learner must be taught in order to do the job efficiently, safely, economically, and intelligently.
2. Have the right tools, equipment, supplies, and material ready.
3. Have the workplace properly arranged, just as the worker will be expected to keep it.

Then, you should *instruct* the learner by the following *four basic steps:*

Step I—*Preparation* (of the learner)
   1. Put the learner at *ease.*
   2. Find out what he or she already knows about the job.
   3. Get the learner interested in and desirous of learning the job.

Step II—*Presentation* (of the operations and knowledge)
   1. *Tell, show, illustrate,* and *question* in order to put over the new knowledge and operations.
   2. Instruct slowly, clearly, completely, and patiently, one point at a time.
   3. Check, question, and repeat.
   4. Make sure the learner really knows.

Step III—*Performance tryout*
   1. Test learner by having him or her perform the job.
   2. Ask questions beginning with *why, how, when,* or *where.*
   3. Observe performance, correct errors, and repeat instructions if necessary.
   4. Continue until *you know learner knows.*

Step IV—*Follow-up*
   1. Put the employee "on his own."
   2. Check frequently to be sure learner follows instructions.
   3. Taper off extra supervision and close follow-up until person is qualified to work with normal supervision.

Remember—if the learner hasn't learned, the teacher hasn't taught.

Source: Training Within Industry Report, War Manpower Commission, Bureau of Training, 1945.

---

equipment is often conducted through vestibule (entrance) training. Models called *simulators* are used when operation of the actual equipment could be hazardous to the operator or others or prohibitively costly if the real equipment were damaged. Pilots, for example, are trained in cockpit simulators; astronauts are trained in zero-gravity chambers and spacecraft simulators. This training simulates "the real thing" as closely as possible, giving trainees experience in reacting to variables and unexpected events without jeopardizing their safety, the safety of others, or expensive equipment. Vestibule training also is used for workers such as drivers, police and fire personnel, and disaster workers.

The **mentor/buddy training** method extends the learning of the new employee after an initial training period. The mentor serves as a role model and a source of help after new workers are on their own. If the mentor, or buddy, is a willing and effective participant, the relationship can be a positive training support system. The mentor/buddy not only serves as a role model but is also a source of help for new workers after they are put on their own in their jobs.

The mentor/buddy method may be used alone for the initial training or in combination with supervisor training followed by assignment to a mentor/buddy for an extended period.

In **job rotation,** workers are trained in several different jobs within a work unit or department. Job rotation is often referred to as _multiskilling_ because workers become skilled in operating every piece of equipment in the unit or department or learn every aspect of the operation of a unit or department. Workers move from one job to another and work at each for a specified period. Initial training at each rotation is like initial training at any new job. Assignment at each rotation should be long enough for the worker to develop proficiency at the job.

Job rotation also has been used to add variety and interest to routine jobs. After all the stations have been learned, however, monotony tends to return. An advantage is that job rotation helps workers to understand an entire process rather than just a small part of it. Job rotation also increases departmental flexibility; when one worker is absent, another can fill in.

While the methods for training operations personnel discussed here are the most common for on-the-job training, off-the-job and developmental methods may also be used.

COMPETENCY CHECK

Can you identify and define the methods for training operations personnel?

Developmental Training

Although you will not be actively involved in developmental training programs, you should be familiar with the methods used in these programs so that you can (1) recommend workers for them and (2) participate in them yourself.

Figure 7.7 describes 11 developmental training methods. All of them might also conceivably be used for some type of operations training. For example, as you have read, role playing might be used in sales training. Our purpose here, however, is to point out how four of these methods might be used in operations training. While you may occasionally be involved, most training using these methods will be handled by HRD or training specialists.

You certainly will be involved in _counseling and coaching_ your workers in the course of your ongoing relationship with them. The counseling may be strictly informal. For example, you might stop by a workstation on your rounds and say, "I noticed, Megan, that you were late twice this week. That's unusual for you. Is there something I can help you with? I'll be in my office at 4 P.M. today if you'd like to stop by and talk." In a few words, you've called attention to a symptom, alerted the worker that you're aware of the tardiness without condemning her, and offered to help. That combines effective supervision with initial counseling.

You may also use the _lecture_ and _discussion_ methods on occasion when you need to instruct your workers as a group. You may give a brief lecture about a change in

---

Figure 7.7
COMMON METHODS OF DEVELOPMENTAL TRAINING

Developmental Training
(may be current-job related or
preparation for growth within firm)

Assessment center (AC): Management training method used to identify and select management personnel. A potential manager goes through several days of activity, including role playing, discussions, tests, cases, in-basket exercises, simulations, and peer evaluations. Results also help identify areas where participants need further training.

Case study: Written description of a business situation that trainee must analyze and offer solutions to. Often used in management development to give trainee practice in citing good and bad features of the situation in the case; spotting violations of management principles, such as poor organization; and developing alternative solutions.

Conference/seminar/discussion: Training that involves verbal interaction between instructor and participants or among participants. Discussion may be used in operations for problem solving by workers in quality circles; in management for problem solving; or for development of employees at all levels.

Counseling and coaching: Ongoing informal training in which supervisor provides information on improving performance or behavior. May be follow-up coaching to refine skills; counseling workers on group interaction; or giving personal assistance or guidance to workers for individual growth.

In-basket: Written situations based on the company's business activities as they would arrive in the manager's "in" basket daily. Trainee responds, usually in writing, by describing what action he or she would take in the situation. Typically management development.

Lecture: Oral presentation by a person knowledgeable in the topic given to a group of employees. Usually given in "classroom" mode. May or may not include visual illustrations. A "telling" method, the lecture, used alone, is not considered effective for producing lasting results.

Off-the-job training: Training performed away from the workplace. May be in-house training conducted in the company's training facility. May also be off-site training conducted in vendors' training facilities, educational institutions, or commercial training facilities, or by trade or professional associations in a variety of places.

Programmed instruction/computer-assisted instruction (CAI): Learner is given material in a series of small sequential units. He or she must respond correctly to test of each unit before progressing to the next unit. May be in printed form or on a computer. Commonly used for cognitive learning; also used for developing computer skills.

Role playing: Learners assume roles of other people and interact with other learners in acting out a business situation. In sales training, one learner assumes the role of salesperson, another the potential customer. May follow a prepared script or communicate extemporaneously to act out the wrong way and a better way to close a sale, for example. May be used in attitude training to visualize good and bad job behaviors, such as following safety rules or in interpersonal relations. Often used in supervisory training.

Gaming: Using a model of a business situation, including many variables, learner must make decisions and take actions by choosing from among several alternatives. Business simulations and games usually answer "what if" questions; e.g., "If we follow strategy *A*, what market share might we capture?" Gives practice in decision making. Usually developmental.

Video/audio self-directed instruction: Instruction given through TV, videotapes, cassettes, or other audiovisual devices. Commonly used in cognitive learning; may also be used for behavioral learning by depicting right and wrong attitudes or interpersonal relations. May be as diverse as a lecture by an authority on management for developing of managers or one on learning the parts of a new piece of equipment.

company policy or the installation of a new system. A follow-up discussion by workers may be used to further explain and clarify the points presented.

In **computer-assisted instruction (CAI)**, a small part or one step is presented and the learner responds, continuing if the response is correct. This process continues until the entire unit is presented. The instruction is programmed and may be in printed form as well as on a computer. CAI may be used as a preliminary to on-the-job instruction or in conjunction with it. The computer often is used to increase productivity. Workers can learn ways to perform operations faster or why they must perform an operation through a computer program. The more they know about their jobs, the better they can perform them.

Video/audio instruction also is used in cognitive learning, such as learning the parts of equipment for machine operators, recognition of dental problems for dental technicians, or warehouse organization for stock clerks. CAI, video/audio instruction, and programmed instruction may reduce on-the-job learning time and therefore reduce the time the supervisor must spend on training, but they do not substitute for the entire on-the-job training process.

In addition to knowing what operations training and developmental training methods are available, you must also be able to select a method appropriate to your workers' needs.

Selecting the Training Method

When selecting a training method, you need to first examine your *objectives*. If the job is fairly routine and your major objective is to move the worker to productivity as quickly as possible, on-the-job training or job instruction training at the workstation would be preferable to off-the-job methods such as lecture or discussion. On the other hand, if the objective is to improve customer relations among salesclerks, a conference or seminar using role playing, games, and case studies might be appropriate.

On-the-job training is usually the most effective method for developing machine operators' manipulative skills. When the objective is to improve attitude, better personal relations, or enlarge knowledge of the company's product or service, several methods may be used.

Whether to train individually or in groups also would be influenced by objectives. If the objective is to improve a manipulative skill such as keyboarding, for example, the worker would progress faster by working on the actual equipment. Keyboarding could be taught to groups of workers in an off-the-job setting, such as in the company training center or in a community college or technical school. If off-the-job equipment was not available in multiple units so that each trainee could use a keyboard, however, individual on-the-job instruction at the worker's workstation might be used to improve skills.

If the objective is to develop interpersonal skills, training in groups would provide an opportunity for trainees to role-play, discuss, and interact with one another in learning sessions.

COMPETENCY CHECK

Can you give examples of methods that might be used for operations or developmental training?

WHAT CAN THE SUPERVISOR DO?

Getting yourself ready for one-on-one teaching at the job station and the actual teaching when you get there will be easier for you and the worker if you follow these tips:

1. *Do your homework.* Learn the conditions under which workers learn best. Do some reading in the behavioral sciences, especially in the psychology of learning and motivation. Principles of management and human resources management texts will also help you put the behavioral principles into the workplace context.

2. *Prepare the worker for learning.* New workers usually are eager to get started on the job but also have some apprehension. Put them at ease with a pleasant, unhurried manner. You might let the new worker observe coworkers at work. Your attitude should be supportive.

3. *Give an overview of the job and the workstation.* Keep it brief—too much will overwhelm the worker. "Your job will be to fix the picture tube to the frame in the TV cabinet. The tubes will come on the belt from *C* group over there. The cabinets are on the rack in front of you. When you assemble the two, they move on the belt to the spot welders. There's more, but we'll handle that later."

4. *Break the job into manageable components, and demonstrate one part at a time.* "First, let me show you how to seat the tube onto the frame." This is the show-and-tell part. Point out reasons for each step in the process as you demonstrate. Be alert to questions, whether voiced or simply registered on the worker's face. Explain again, if necessary.

   Caution: Workers learn at different paces, so don't bore a fast learner by moving too slowly or laboring over a point. Experience will help you judge pretty closely the learning pace of each worker.

5. *Let the worker perform as you observe.* "Now, let me watch as you seat the tube." Stay with the worker. Let the worker explain each part of the process as she or he performs it. Refrain from interrupting to add new data at this point. Correct only if the worker varies widely from the accepted method. Reinforce the learner's effort.

   Go through steps 4 and 5 for each part of the process. Then let the worker put the parts together by going through the whole process. If a process has many steps, group the steps so the learner won't have to recall them all at once on the first attempt.

6. *Gradually put the worker on his or her own.* As the worker gains confidence and you feel that he or she can do the job without close supervision, let the worker "go it alone." But continue to be supportive. Return occasionally during the first day or so to answer questions and see if there are problems. As far as possible, allow the worker some freedom in making decisions while performing the job, such as sequencing the tasks or scheduling. Don't forget the importance of a verbal pat on the back.

The second factor to consider in choosing a method is *cost*. While you might wish that your machine operators could be trained to high proficiency in vestibule simulations before you risked placing them on plant equipment, it would be far too costly to use that method. On-the-job training by you or a senior employee would be more appropriate. Cost is also a consideration when determining how training time should be divided between personal teaching and written instruction. Your time is limited, and you will not be able to stay by the trainee's side during the entire learning period. After you go through the job instruction training process, for example, an operator's manual might be used by the trainee in the intervals between follow-ups while you are performing other supervisory tasks.

**COMPETENCY
CHECK**

Can you list the
factors to
consider in
choosing a
training method?

A third factor influencing method selection is *resources*. Some organizations have large training staffs and sophisticated facilities. Yours may not be one of them. If it is not, you will need to select an on-the-job method that you or one of your workers can handle. It may also be up to you to train the senior employee who will serve as trainer. An alternative might be a low-cost, off-the-job source such as a public community college or a technical school.

Evaluation of each training program will help you become more adept at selecting methods. Evaluation is the final section of this chapter.

Evaluating the Training and Development Program

How effective was your training and development program? Did it accomplish the objectives you established for it? Improvement in worker performance and increased productivity are critical measures of its success. But you will also need feedback from workers to determine the effectiveness of the program. Did you select the method most appropriate for the type of participant and for your objectives? Answers to these questions should come from an evaluation of the program by trainees and the training staff.

Evaluation by the Trainee

The *degree of participation by workers* is another measure of the success of a program. Word gets around. Successful programs are often the best advertising you can use. Conversely, it doesn't take many boring courses to kill the whole T&D program. Trainees tend to evaluate a program both by the behavior they exhibit after the training and by the judgment they share with their peers.

Before you attempt to measure posttraining performance, you should ask trainees to evaluate their training sessions. A *questionnaire* distributed at the end of training, to be filled in before the trainees leave, is one device used for evaluating a training session. The training questionnaire shown in Figure 7.8 asks participants to rate

Figure 7.8
TRAINING EVALUATION QUESTIONNAIRE

TRAINING QUESTIONNAIRE

Title or Course Number _____ Date _____

Instructor _____ Location _____

1. What is your overall reaction to the training session just completed? *(Please circle one.)*

   Very Good   Good   Fair   Poor

   Comments: _____

   _____

   _____

2. How well did the material presented in this session relate to your job?

   Very Well   Quite a Bit   Some   Very Little

   Comments: _____

   _____

   _____

3. How often will you be able to apply the material presented in your daily tasks?

   All of the time   Often   Some   Very Little

   Comments: _____

   _____

   _____

4. How well did the instructor present this training session?

   Very Well   Good   Fair   Poor

   Comments: _____

   _____

   _____

5. What is your reaction to the visual aids used, if any?

   Very Good   Good   Fair   Poor

   Comments: _____

   _____

   _____

6. What suggestions do you have for improving this training session?

   _____

   _____

   _____

7. What suggestions do you have for additional training sessions?

   _____

   _____

   _____

**COMPETENCY
CHECK**

Can you list the
methods by
which trainees
can evaluate a
training program?

(1) their overall reaction to the training, (2) how well it related to their jobs, (3) the effectiveness of the instructor, and (4) any visual aids used. Employees also are asked to make suggestions for improving the training and to suggest future training.

Combined with your own evaluation, the employee trainee evaluation will assist you in planning future training sessions.

Evaluation by the Trainer

When planning a training session, you establish the criteria by which you will judge the effectiveness of the session. Four levels of training evaluation include reaction, learning, behavior, and results. Questionnaires can be used to evaluate trainee reaction. Tests are commonly used to evaluate learning—knowledge of a topic or concept; i.e., facts, principles, and approaches. Before-and-after training tests can be used to compare growth.

On the behavioral level, evaluation is designed to measure the degree to which training has affected job performance. Behavior is more difficult to measure than are the other levels. A decrease in tardiness and absence can be counted, but other behaviors, such as attitude and teamwork, may be more difficult to measure. Interviews with trainees and their coworkers may reveal behavioral changes. Also, fewer grievances and a better work atmosphere often are observable as a result of improved behaviors.

At the results level, evaluation measures the contribution of the training to the achievement of company objectives. Improved productivity and reduced costs can be measured fairly easily. A cost-benefit analysis will show the degree of effectiveness of training and development to the organization. Figure 7.9 lists the costs and benefits of training.

Figure 7.9 COSTS AND BENEFITS OF TRAINING	
Cost	**Benefits**
Trainer's salary	Increase in production
Materials for training	Reduction in errors
Living expenses for trainer and trainees	Reduction in turnover
Cost of facilities	Less supervision necessary
Equipment	Ability to advance
Transportation	New skills lead to ability to do more jobs
Trainee's salary	Attitude changes
Lost production (opportunity cost)	
Preparation time	

Source: Reprinted by permission from p. 286 of *Human Resource Management* by Robert L. Mathis and John H. Jackson. Copyright © 1994 by West Publishing Company, St. Paul, Minn. All rights reserved.

Some costs and benefits are not easily quantifiable. For example, if a worker who successfully completes a training program leaves a few months later for a better job in another organization, the cost to your organization may be difficult to measure. Some benefits, such as attitudinal changes, also are difficult to translate into monetary terms. Even so, a cost-benefit analysis is a good way to show whether training is cost-effective, and the organization needs to determine the contribution each activity is making to the accomplishment of its objectives.

COMPETENCY CHECK
Can you give the meaning of the levels of T&D evaluation?

COMPETENCY REVIEW

1. Identify elements in the relationship of training and development to the staffing function.
2. Discuss the supervisor's role in training and development.
3. List three sources for identifying training and development needs.
4. Discuss conditions that affect learning.
5. List two ways in which to encourage participation in training and development programs.
6. Discuss the importance of measuring training and development results.
7. Identify and define seven methods for training operations personnel.
8. Give three examples of methods that may be used for either operations training or developmental training.
9. List three factors to consider when choosing a training method.
10. Discuss two methods by which trainees evaluate training programs.
11. Give the meaning of the four levels of training evaluation.

APPLICATIONS

1. For your current job or one you have held in the past, respond to the questions below. If you have not worked, interview someone who now works.
   a. Describe the orientation program the company conducted when you began your job.
   b. List the training methods used by your organization.
   c. Using a format similar to that shown in Figure 7.8 on page 203, evaluate your initial training.
2. In groups of four or five, outline an orientation program for new students at your school. Compare your group's plan to other groups' plans and discuss the differences.
3. "It is necessary for new employees to be trained by the company to perform the jobs for which we hire them; but the company shouldn't spend money on employee development." Do you agree or disagree with this statement by an executive? Defend your position.

4. For each training situation listed in the left column, select a method from the right column that you consider most appropriate. Give your rationale for each selection.

Training Situation	Method
a. Train 10 new pari-mutuel betting window cashiers.	Programmed instruction
b. Train 20 new bricklayers for a large unionized construction organization.	OJT
	Lecture
c. Train 16 employees to teach basic reading and writing skills	Conference or seminar by a local university
d. Train 1 registration clerk in a college to retrieve records on a new display terminal.	CAI
	Vestibule training
e. Train 2 senior workers for possible promotion to group leadership positions.	Case study

ONE DAY IS ENOUGH

Tom Fletcher just graduated from a vocational high school and accepted a job as an administrative assistant in the regional office of a federal supply facility. As he drove to work, many questions were racing through his mind: Can I handle the work? What will be my first assignment? Where will I eat lunch? What if I get sick and have to miss a day? How long will I have to wait before I get a raise? What about a promotion? How long will that take? "All my questions will be answered by my supervisor, I'm sure," he assured himself as he arrived at the receptionist's desk.

Shortly after the receptionist announced Tom's arrival, his supervisor, Mark Conrad, rushed out to greet him.

"Glad to see you, Tom. I'm Mark Conrad, administrative services supervisor. Come with me, and I'll talk about your job on the way. I know you were hired as an administrative assistant, but we're shorthanded today in the document production center, so we're going to start you out there. Human Resources noted that you worked on a Macintosh computer at the vocational school. I think you'll be able to pick up on our Macintosh network without any difficulties."

"Here's your workstation. Have a seat, and I'll show you how to turn it on and get started. All your instructions will be on the screen; just do what it says. Here's the manual in case you need to look up anything. If you have any problems, ask Sylvia Montoya for help. I'll tell her to look out for you. She's doing double duty today, but she'll help if you need her. I'll be in and out all morning. Don't worry about your W-2 and the human resources information. I'll tell HR that I've put you directly to work; they'll get to you shortly. You're on your own."

"Well, so much for answers to my questions," Tom thought as he sat down at the terminal. He was no longer excited. Instead, he was frustrated and scared. He had worked only 2 days on the Mac at his school, just to get acquainted with the keyboard and terminal, a fact he included on his application. He had been hired as an administrative assistant but was told that as he became experienced with government work, there probably would be opportunities for him in the document production center. He was pleased but had no idea that he would be placed into that higher-rated job on his first day.

Tom struggled through the custom-designed menus on the screen, but everything seemed to go wrong. This Mac was a later model than the Mac he had used in the classroom. And the manual might as well have been written in a foreign language. It seemed as though every instruction assumed he already knew a lot about the machine, which he didn't.

Tom tried to get Sylvia's help, but she kept saying that she'd be over as soon as she finished the rush job she was on. The next thing Tom knew, Sylvia had gone to lunch.

Mark Conrad stopped by once and told Tom, "Just use the manual and hang in there."

By 2 P.M., without a break of any kind and hopelessly bogged down with a machine that kept displaying "system error," Tom gave up. Disappointed, he got up, turned off the computer, pushed in his chair, and walked out.

1. List several T&D errors that are evident in this case.
2. Evaluate the on-the-job training method used by Mark Conrad.
3. What would you advise Mark Conrad to do about Tom?
4. If you were Mark's manager, what would you do about the situation?

Case II

TRAINING AND COACHING PAY OFF

Facilities Management and Consulting (FMC) is a turnkey mailroom and copy center services company in Chicago. General manager Carolee Pierce has a unique strategy for coaxing excellence out of the lowest-level worker in the organization—mail clerks. She works at keeping entry-level employees enthusiastic and on the job by offering a career path. Sixty percent of the workers in jobs above entry level started as mail clerks.

FMC needs a variety of positions to run operations at customers' work sites: mail clerks, senior mail clerks, supervisors, site managers, and district managers. In order to have employees who have the experience to promote from within, FMC does three things: it broadcasts upward mobility, conducts extensive initial training, and coaches constantly.

FMC lets employees know they will be moving up in many ways. An ad for FMC's services reads "All of our employees compete within a merit system which rewards job performance with advancement."

The first 3 to 4 weeks of training include switchboard time, audiotapes, videotapes, the customer users' guide, and equipment training. Workers thoroughly learn the mail clerk's job, including how to address a letter properly. The switchboard is ideal for teaching workers how to treat customers, practice vocal tones, and make good first impressions. Videos produced by the U.S. Postal Service are used to cover subjects ranging from pleasing customers to mailroom organization. Audiotapes are used to present other information.

FMC's user's guide provides a description of what a customer can expect from FMC's mail services. Entry-level employees use this guide to learn what FMC does and how it does it. New employees rotate between two or three customer sites during their first month to gain experience on different types of equipment and meet their fellow employees. Then they are assigned to a permanent customer location.

Managers at FMC are responsible for preparing mail clerks and senior clerks to move to the next level by improving computer skills and upgrading written and verbal abilities. Coaching is important for maintaining the interest and encouraging the learning necessary for promotion.

Last year, FMC lost only one of its 30 employees. During the year before FMC took over a client's mailroom, that company had lost 9 out of 15 mailroom employees. Obviously, FMC is doing something right.

1. How important is the emphasis on a career path for new and current employees? Why?
2. Do you agree or disagree with having all new employees start in the mailroom? Explain.
3. What other types of training do you think might be helpful to new employees? Why?
4. What training needs do you think aren't being met for employees beyond the entry level?

Source: As reported in "Giving Dead-End Jobs a Future," *Inc.,* September 1992, p. 31.

REFERENCES

1. Dan Cordtz, "The Changing Nature of Work," *Financial World,* June 23, 1992, p. 66.
2. Richard S. Wellins, William C. Byham, and Jeanne M. Wilson, *Empowered Teams,* Jossey-Bass Publishers, San Francisco, 1991, p. 47.
3. Dan Cordtz, "What's Ahead for Unions," *Financial World,* June 23, 1992, p. 73.
4. Dale Feuer, "The Skill Gap—America's Crisis of Competence," *Training,* December 1987, p. 35.
5. Tom Peters, *Thriving on Chaos,* Alfred A. Knopf, Inc., New York, 1987, p. 325.
6. Troy Segal, Karen Thurston, and Lynn Haessly, "When Johnny's Whole Family Can't Read," *Business Week,* July 20, 1992, p. 68.
7. Lura K. Romei, "If U Cn Rd Ths, U Cn Gt A Gd Job Nd Mor Pa," *Modern Office Technology,* September 1990, p. 10.
8. Segal et al., op. cit., pp. 68, 70.
9. Chris Lee, "Basic Training in the Corporate Schoolhouse," *Training,* April 1988, p. 34.
10. Curtis E. Plott, "Training Programs Available Now," *The Virginian-Pilot and The Ledger-Star,* May 6, 1984, p. K9.
11. Victor Vroom, *Work and Motivation,* John Wiley & Sons, Inc., New York, 1964.
12. Walter D. St. John, "The Complete Employee Orientation Program," *Personnel Journal,* May 1980, p. 377.
13. Fred Wickert, "The Famous JIT Card: A Basic Way to Improve It," *Training and Development Journal,* February 1974, pp. 6–9.

SUGGESTED READINGS

Beardsley, Carolyn: "Improving Employee Awareness of Opportunity at IBM," *Personnel,* April 1987, pp. 58–63.

Brinkerhoff, Robert O.: *Achieving Results from Training,* Jossey-Bass Publishers, San Francisco, 1987.

Gordon, Jack: "What They Don't Teach You about Being a Training Manager," *Training,* June 1986, pp. 22–34.

Magnus, Margaret: "Training Futures," *Personnel Journal,* May 1986, pp. 61–71.

Peters, Tom: *Thriving on Chaos,* Alfred A. Knopf, Inc., New York, 1987.

Peters, Tom, and Nancy Austin: *A Passion for Excellence,* Random House, New York, 1985.

Phillips, Jack J.: *Recruiting, Training, and Retaining New Employees,* Jossey-Bass Publishers, San Francisco, 1987.

Truitt, Mark A.: *The Supervisor's Handbook,* National Press Publications, Shawnee Mission, Kans., 1991.

Waterman, Robert H., Jr.: *The Renewal Factor,* Bantam Books, New York, 1987.

GLOSSARY

apprenticeship   Intensive on-the-job training that extends over a longer period of time ranging from a few months to 2 years or more.

computer-assisted instruction (CAI)   A training method in which a small part or one step is presented and the learner responds, continuing if the response is correct.

development   Increasing workers' abilities in order to improve future job performance, with emphasis on interpersonal and decision-making skills.

functional (workplace) literacy   Reading, writing, speaking, listening, and mathematical skills; the ability to use reading skills to cope with everyday tasks.

job instruction training   A training method that uses special trainers to train supervisors in a four-step process to teach skills to workers.

job rotation   A training method in which workers are trained in several different jobs within a work unit or department.

mentor/buddy training   A training method that extends the learning of the new employee after an initial training period. The mentor serves as a role model and a source of help after new workers are on their own.

on-the-job training (OJT)   A training method in which the trainer uses the demonstration method to show the worker how to follow the job procedure, operate equipment, handle supplies, and follow safety rules.

orientation   The introduction that workers are given to the organization and their jobs.

training   Company-directed activities and experiences designed to develop the skills, knowledge, and behaviors that will lead to effective current job performance.

vestibule training   A training method in which actual equipment or conditions that would be hazardous or prohibitively costly to use to train novices is simulated.

CHAPTER 8
Managing Diversity and Change

STUDYING THIS CHAPTER WILL ENABLE YOU TO:

1. Define *diversity management*.

2. List the diversities commonly recognized in organizations.

3. Describe four fundamentals of managing diversity.

4. Describe ways in which to appreciate and encourage diversity.

5. Describe three adversities in the workplace that you as a supervisor must discourage.

6. Discuss the nature of organizational change.

7. Define *planned change* and *reengineering*.

8. Define the term *change agent* and show how it relates to the supervisor.

9. Illustrate ways through which supervisors can develop in workers a receptive attitude toward change.

10. Give several examples of how supervisors can minimize resistance to change.

11. Identify in order and describe the steps in the change process.

CHAPTER OUTLINE

C H A P

Managing
Diversity
AND
Change

T   E   R   8

he business environment today is one in which change is constant. Not only are manufacturing processes and the ways in which services are delivered changing, but the workforce is changing as well.

The 1990s will bring changes in the social and economic environment and in the strategies, structure, and management of business. Businesses will undergo more radical restructuring than at any time since the modern corporate organization first evolved in the 1920s. Increasing the productivity of the newly dominant groups in the workforce—knowledge and service workers—will be an economic priority and the toughest challenge facing managers.[1]

Domestic and foreign competition have battered many U.S. companies and will continue to force them to scramble for markets. At the same time, U.S. companies also are scrambling for the best talent and searching for ways to get the best from the employees they now have. There is a business rationale for thinking about diversity. In order to thrive in an unfriendly marketplace, companies must create the kind of environment that will attract the best new talent and make it possible for employees to make their fullest contribution.[2]

In this chapter, we will address changes in the workforce and the work environment in general and how to handle these changes. Managing diversity requires managing continuous organizational change.

Recognizing the Diversities

Diversity in the workplace goes beyond gender and ethnicity to include age, background, education, disabilities, lifestyles, and family lives. **Diversity management** means enabling every member of a workforce to perform to his or her potential. Managing diversity doesn't mean "giving *them* a chance." It means creating an environment in which everyone will do his or her best work.[3]

The Hudson Institute in Indianapolis, Indiana, and the U.S. Department of Labor conducted a landmark study and in 1987 issued a report entitled *Workforce 2000*. This report contains dramatic projections of radical demographic changes by the year 2000. One such prediction is that from 1985 to 2000 minorities will make up 85 percent of the growth in the workforce.

Hudson Institute and Towers Perrin, a benefits consulting firm, released a follow-up study report indicating that the changes predicted in the original study are taking place more rapidly than predicted. Qualified workers are in short supply; professionals in general are difficult to recruit; and many companies report having trouble finding secretaries and clerks.[4] Not only is the labor pool changing, it is shrinking. In the 1990s, there will be 4 to 5 million fewer entry-level workers each year than in 1980.[5] These projections were revised again in 1988, as shown in Figure 8.1.

An estimated 40 percent of companies in the United States have implemented some form of diversity training. Companies working toward managing diversity include AT&T, Avon Products, Inc., Bank of Boston, Colgate-Palmolive, Digital Equipment Corp., GTE, Honeywell, Johnson & Johnson, Mobil, and Xerox. Approximately 50 percent of the *Fortune* 500 companies now have diversity man-

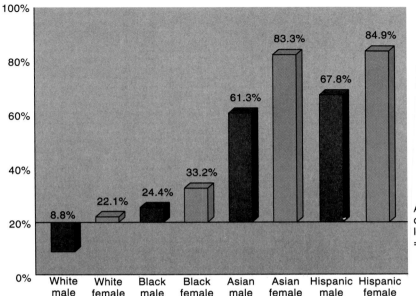

**Figure 8.1
RATE OF
GROWTH OF
LABOR FORCE
COMPOSITION
1986–2000**

Source: Bureau of Labor Statistics.

agers or directors. For example, both Digital Equipment and Honeywell have a director of workforce diversity; Avon has a director of multicultural planning and design; and Colgate-Palmolive has a global diversity manager. As more women and minorities join the labor force, upper management increasingly realizes that diversity is a bottom-line issue. Performance improves when people work well together, and higher productivity is the goal.[6]

Small companies also are experiencing a more diverse workforce. In a survey of small companies conducted by the Olsten Corporation, increases in diversity were reported by 179 companies. The increases in the general workforce and in management in these companies are shown in Figure 8.2.

Diversity issues facing organizations today center around those concerning gender, ethnic minorities, age, educational levels and illiteracy, disabilities, lifestyles, and family lives. A company that wants to encourage, appreciate, and capitalize on diversity may need to change performance appraisal systems, pay and benefits systems, coaching practices, mentoring procedures, development programs, flexible scheduling, job sharing, day care, affirmative action plans, and more.[7]

Gender

Women have entered the workforce in increasing numbers in recent years, and, as shown in Figure 8.1, women will continue to represent a large portion of the workforce in the year 2000.

Figure 8.2
PERCENTAGES OF SMALL COMPANIES REPORTING INCREASES IN THE WORKFORCE AND IN MANAGEMENT

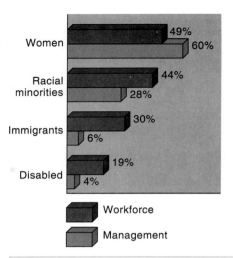

Source: "Workplace Social Issues of the 1990s," the Olsten Forum™ on Human Resource Issues and Trends, copyright © the Olsten Corporation, Westbury, N.Y., 1992.

Gender bias often is presented as a form of protection for women or for other considerations. For example, when a female manager isn't permitted to attend an important seminar in a large city with a high crime rate because it is considered she wouldn't be safe or because she has small children at home, her advancement to higher positions probably is blocked because she hasn't received the same training as her male peers. When a female auditor isn't permitted to travel to out-of-state auditing assignments with male team members because their wives will be upset or "she may cause problems," her advancement probably is blocked.

Anecdotal reports of female professionals and other female workers being ignored and left out of the decision-making process by their male peers and managers are plentiful. In a female-dominated workplace, similar situations often occur. There is evidence that a new wave of women is making its way into upper management, not by adopting the style used by successful men but by drawing on the skills and attitudes they have developed from their shared experience as women. As leaders, these women are more interactive and empowering and have learned to be sensitive to the needs of others. These women are likely to be married and earn the same amount of money as their male peers.[8]

As a supervisor, valuing opinions and suggestions from all workers and providing equal opportunities for participation in training programs and other learning experiences is important for creating an atmosphere in which all workers feel they are accepted and have a chance to advance. On an organizational level, companies that provide child care and flexible benefits for working parents will benefit in the long term.

Ethnic Minorities

Diversity is already a reality at many companies. One-fifth of the workforce at 39 percent of the companies responding to the follow-up study conducted by Hudson and Towers Perrin is made up of minorities. By the year 2000, the workforce will be dominated by nonwhites whose primary language is Spanish and who will make up 29 percent of new hires.[9]

When English is not the native language spoken by an employee, the supervisor must be trained to interview, train, and supervise the worker. An employee lacking skills because of the language barrier presents a new challenge for many organizations. Consequently, in the future an increased emphasis will be placed on training after the employee is hired.

Age

America's aging workforce will change the balance between work and leisure during the next decade. The decline in the number of young workers and the increasing availability of older workers will shift the focus toward a middle-age and older workforce. Older workers now have some of the best opportunities they have ever had. As employers recognize the need for and the value of older workers, they are redesigning jobs to de-emphasize physical labor, arranging paid sabbaticals, and acknowledging the superior performance of long-term employees.[10]

Younger workers often do not have the skills necessary to meet the needs of business. Deficiencies in the basic skills of writing, math, problem solving, and communication will prevent many young workers from obtaining employment. Many companies already have recognized the need for keeping the aging workforce productive. Here are a few examples:[11]

1. Hardee's Food Systems, Inc., KFC, and other quick-service restaurants are turning to older workers to meet the labor shortages caused by the baby bust.
2. Wal-Mart Stores, Inc., employs older workers because they are an important part of the company's future growth.
3. Builders Emporium has learned that older workers understand customer service issues better than younger workers, and that they come from a do-it-yourself generation that makes their employment a good fit.

To many people, younger workers are the mainstream, the competition, and the enemy. Actually, however, they are a hidden minority. Anyone born after 1964, when birthrates began to decline, is a "baby buster." Their relatively small numbers make them a special-interest group with pressures, fears, and feelings different from those of older coworkers. Baby busters were raised in a time free of war, economic pressures, and political uncertainty and therefore have developed unique philosophies and goals for what they want from their work lives.

Younger workers feel little necessity for just putting in time or paying their dues; they want to see immediate signs of success. The young employee wants meaning-

COMPETENCY CHECK

Can you define diversity management and list eight diversities commonly recognized in organizations today?

ful assignments, access to decision makers, and the freedom to balance professional demands with personal interests. Job security means little to younger workers because they are confident their skills will always be in demand. Younger workers also tend to reject authoritarian management styles; they are more questioning, more demanding of explanations, and more pragmatic in their solutions. If they follow directions, it is because an idea makes sense, not because of the source of the idea.[12]

Supervisors of both young and older workers need to learn to build cohesive teams and to motivate both age groups.

Educational Levels and Illiteracy

By the year 2000, 80 percent of all jobs will require 2 years of post–high school education. However, 75 percent of all current employees do not possess this level of education. The changing demographics will create labor shortages among educated and/or skilled workers.[13] A U.S. Department of Labor report released in 1991 concluded that the majority of high school graduates lack the sophisticated information processing, communication, teamwork, and analytical thinking skills that most of the coming decade's jobs will require.[14]

As you learned in Chapter 7, many companies are dealing with illiteracy by providing in-house literacy classes. Other organizations pay the tuition for classes located elsewhere.

Disabilities

With the passage of the Americans with Disabilities Act (ADA) of 1990 and its 1992 amendments, more disabled workers will join the workforce in the future. This act requires employers to hire qualified workers with disabilities and to provide reasonable accommodations for their needs so that they can perform their jobs. By treating each job candidate as a person and not as a diagnosis, businesses are finding that a disabled person with the capability, drive, and determination to succeed can do the job just as well as any nondisabled job applicant. In fact, many people feel that disabled people have underused potential and that making jobs, housing, transportation, and public places more accessible will be a benefit rather than a cost to society.[15]

The most persuasive proof of the wisdom of hiring workers with disabilities comes from employers themselves. Clyde Hopkins, president of Martin Marietta Energy Systems in Oak Ridge, Tennessee, has spent years actively seeking job applicants with disabilities. "The more we do," he says, "the more our people are convinced we should give workers with disabilities the same opportunity as anyone else. Our managers do worry about complying with the law, but that motivation soon wears off when they see how well people with disabilities perform their jobs."[16]

Bill White, president of the Culver City, California, electronic security firm API Security, Inc., states emphatically, "All of the disabled workers we've hired fall within the top 10 percent of our finest employees. If I could staff half my business this way, I would."[17]

Numerous studies regarding the capabilities of disabled people in the workplace have given people with disabilities high marks for work attitudes, attendance, and productivity. Du Pont Company is a national leader in hiring people with disabilities and has measured disabled employees' job performances since 1958. Tabulations from its 1990 survey revealed that managers rated 97 percent of disabled workers as average or above average in job safety; 86 percent, average or above in attendance; and 90 percent, average or above in overall job performance. Other studies reveal similar findings:[18]

- In a 1987 survey by public opinion researchers Louis Harris and Associates, 8 out of 10 department heads and line managers felt that workers with disabilities were no harder to supervise than nondisabled workers, and approximately half rated disabled employees' willingness to work hard, reliability, punctuality, and attendance as better than that of workers without disabilities.
- Data from the U.S. Office of Vocational Rehabilitation reveal that 95 percent or more of disabled workers have the same or lower rates of absenteeism, job turnover, and job-related accidents as nondisabled workers, and that their productivity is at least as high in 90 percent of cases.
- Employees with mental retardation score almost as well as other disabled workers. Among the more than 37,000 people the Association for Retarded Citizens has placed in competitive positions over the last two decades, managers indicate that at least 80 percent have performed their jobs successfully.

Some employers are convinced that workers with disabilities will be their secret weapon in the battle for good workers in the labor-short 1990s. The driving force behind these efforts is a bottom-line belief that employees with disabilities are just as capable of getting the job done as nondisabled people. For example:[19]

- In service-based industries, the number of workers with disabilities has increased 28 percent since 1983.
- In the food-service industry, the number of mentally and physically disabled workers has risen by more than one-sixth since 1986.
- In 1991, Marriott hotels and restaurants employed 8000 people with disabilities; Pizza Hut restaurants, 1000.
- At Sears, Roebuck and Company, 6 percent of the workforce has a disability; 5 percent of U.S. Postal Service workers has a disability.
- Survey results reported in Figure 8.2 indicate an increase of 19 percent in the number of disabled workers in small companies from 1987 to 1992.

Supervisors who work with the disabled will need to be flexible in their training methods, be fair when making task assignments, and allow individuals with disabilities to compete for jobs they are capable of performing.[20]

Lifestyles

Since the mid-1980s, a few private employers, city and state governments, and unions have afforded unmarried couples of the same sex or opposite sex the opportunity to participate in company-sponsored benefits plans on the same basis as married couples. A handful of companies are expanding their definition of "dependent" and liberalizing standards for health insurance coverage and other benefits, such as leaves of absence.

The most frequently used term for these nontraditional dependents is "domestic partner." Also used interchangeably are "partner" and "spouse equivalent." The dependent definition, in some cases, has been broadened to include stepchildren, children of a previous marriage for same-sex couples, and parents.

Organizations such as *The Village Voice,* Ben & Jerry's Homemade, Inc., the cities of San Francisco and Seattle, Lotus Development Corporation, and Levi Strauss & Co. understand that increasing workplace diversity and changing demographics of our society require businesses to implement initiatives that meet the real-life needs of their workforce.[21]

Levi Strauss and Apple Computer, Inc., are among the few companies that specifically ban discrimination against gays; only 20 percent of companies with strong equal opportunity policies explicitly cite sexual preference.[22]

Family Lives

Organizations that want to retain good employees and cut costs are creating or expanding family-friendly benefit programs as a way to retain the best employees. Employees may be caring for elderly parents, have small children who need child care, want to attend a parent-teacher conference or other school event, or want to spend more time with their families. *Flexibility* is a buzzword for benefit programs, and family assistance is growing even as companies struggle to contain overall costs. Flexible work practices are a way to avoid layoffs and keep valued employees while going through cost-cutting activities.[23]

According to a survey conducted by Hay/Huggins Co., in 1987, benefits consultants, none of the surveyed organizations had paternity leave or work-at-home policies. By 1991, approximately one-half offered paternity leaves and 14 percent offered telecommuting options. In the same period, flexible-hours policies increased from 35 to 40 percent.[24]

Du Pont Co. has about 2000 employees working part-time and between 10,000 and 15,000 working flexible hours. Philadelphia Newspapers, Inc., recently offered a special package of voluntary programs to reduce costs including reduced work-week schedules, job sharing, and unpaid leaves of absence. Avon Products, Inc., has launched a new child-care assistance plan and is exploring flexible work options.

IBM also has expanded several family programs, not as another cost-cutting step but as part of a plan to retain its best employees. A flexible work leave of absence program allows employees to work part-time for up to three years with full company-paid benefits, and they can continue the arrangement after the third year by paying part of the benefit costs. The company also has expanded its work-at-home program,

WHAT CAN THE SUPERVISOR DO?

1. Learn about other cultures and their traditions, customs, and beliefs.
2. Solicit opinions from people of other cultures and of different ages.
3. Attend multicultural programs and festivals. Discuss race or ethnicity, religion, gender, sexual orientation, and family so that you can learn and understand more about others.
4. Open channels of communication with people who are different, which includes older workers.
5. Treat each person as a unique individual with unique talents and abilities.
6. Don't laugh at or tell age-related, racist, sexist, ethnic, or disability jokes.[25]

flexible work schedules, and "meal break" option, which lets employees rearrange their workday to attend a child's school function or meet other family and personal needs.[26]

Some innovative organizations provide elder care as part of their optional benefits packages. Supervisors who understand, sympathize, and empathize with family issues and help their employees solve them often see the productivity of affected workers improve rapidly.

The Supervisor's Role in Managing Diversity

Managing diversity is a top-down decision. Because supervisors often have direct contact with diverse work groups, their role in successfully managing diversity is crucial. The greatest challenges to managing diversity, according to the Olsten Corporation survey mentioned earlier, are attitudes/culture, communication, need for more training, providing career opportunities, language barriers, and developing role models/mentors.[27]

Fundamentals of Managing Diversity

Good human resources policies will eliminate many problems resulting from a multicultural and diverse workplace. Policies that prohibit discrimination in hiring, promoting, and making job assignments make the supervisor's job easier because clear guidelines are provided. To assist in the preparation of minorities and women for promotions, role models and mentors often are used.

Equal Hiring Procedures.   The hiring procedures identified in Chapter 6, "The Supervisor's Role in Staffing," need to include procedures for hiring persons with disabilities, minorities, older workers, and workers who do not speak English fluently. Careful job analysis and job design can identify those jobs where persons with diverse abilities can be successful.

Promotion Goals That Include Minorities and Women.   Affirmative action plans get new people into the doors of organizations. Enabling people, such as minorities and women, to perform to their potential is diversity management. The supervisor can help to create an environment where everyone does well and where morale and productivity are high.

 Fair Treatment in Assignments.   Fair treatment applies to the assignment of the challenging and routine tasks, the pleasant and unpleasant tasks, and the conditions under which people are required to work. The Americans with Disabilities Act prohibits employers from assigning individuals with disabilities to stereotyped jobs. For example, a photographic services company should not assign all blind employees to work in the darkrooms. Likewise, deaf people shouldn't be assigned exclusively to work with noisy equipment.[28]

Role Models and Mentors.   Role models are individuals in an organization who are highly respected. They may or may not be aware that others consider them as role models. When an individual is aware of that role, he or she usually takes considerable care to live up to the expectations of others.

Everyone in an organization can benefit personally and professionally from being mentored at different stages in his or her career. **Informal mentoring** begins when an experienced employee takes an active interest in helping a new employee or a new employee approaches a more experienced person for information and help. The active interest of the mentor in the person being mentored, often called a *protégé* or *mentoré*, continues until its purpose is exhausted and the relationship ends. In **formal mentoring,** the organization matches individuals and adds expectations for what should be accomplished.

Mentoring helps make the transition from background, home, and education to work life, and it helps people to acculturate. Going from education to work life is difficult for native-born individuals; it is almost always a major transition for non-native-born individuals. Students have a system to support them. As workers, they may live alone with little, if any, support. Furthermore, they may be assigned to a part of the country with different cultural values. They enter a work culture that has unwritten rules about how things are done, and they need an organizational road map.

Mentoring can be a powerful tool for culture changing and culture transfer from one generation of management to another. In a diverse workforce, mentoring can serve not only to acculturate the new worker but also to make the mentor aware of his or her values and those of the organization.[29]

COMPETENCY CHECK
Can you describe how mentoring can help new employees adapt to a work environment?

Appreciating Diversity

Hiring a diverse workforce provides a diversity of ideas in an organization. It also means supervisors must have the sensitivity and ability to understand people of different cultures.[30]

Figure 8.3
SYMPTOMS THAT MAY SIGNAL A NEED FOR CHANGE

1. Morale is low. Employees are uncooperative, cliquish, unfriendly to new hires, and show no loyalty to the organization.
2. There is a high turnover of personnel.
3. Customer complaints about service have increased.
4. There is an increase in goods returned because of defects.
5. Waste material in production and operation has increased.
6. Equipment maintenance costs have skyrocketed.
7. Workers complain of equipment inefficiency and downtime.
8. Overtime costs have increased.
9. Accident claims have increased.
10. Absenteeism and tardiness have increased.
11. Worker grievances have increased.
12. A sexual-harassment suit has been filed against the company.
13. Productivity has steadily declined.
14. Transfer of company resources to a new acquisition slows down the production of older units, lowering the morale of managers and workers in older units.
15. Little interest is shown in training and development programs.
16. Housekeeping has become lax.
17. Job descriptions rarely portray the actual job being performed.
18. Workers complain that tasks are distributed inequitably.
19. Breaking policies and rules is commonplace.
20. Supervisors often complain that management does not back them up in their decisions.

tastes shifted from large domestic cars to smaller, more reliable Japanese cars. For Sears, its customers moved to discounters such as Wal-Mart and specialty stores like the Gap.[44]

Deciding On and Implementing Changes

In 1986, AT&T decided that a change in strategy was needed to make the company more competitive. One of several planned changes was to restructure its research and development (R&D) function. Although the organization had before and since divestiture used the "baby Bells" for R&D, it decided to break away from the family of Bell companies and buy components from other companies. Such a strategy would have been unthinkable in the old AT&T culture. Now managers found themselves in a different culture—they were being encouraged to think freely about using suppliers other than Bell as well as non-Bell markets for AT&T products. This new concept was accompanied by a complete restructuring of the organization, a refinement of its mission, and a revised set of objectives. Through careful planning and execution of the changes, AT&T's management, by 1988, had already headed the once-great company back onto the road to profitability. Planned changes have been carried out in every aspect of the business, and more are taking place in the 1990s.[45]

All the events at AT&T involved people changes. Layoffs, terminations, reassignments, and transfers affected thousands of workers. When identifying internal targets for change, managers should be aware that any change will affect people. Planned change usually involves some changes in what individual people do and, therefore, in their behaviors at work.[46]

The Supervisor's Role in Managing Change

While major organizational changes usually are initiated at the top level of management, you will be involved directly at the departmental level. Supervisors should participate in planning for any change that involves operations. You will, in fact, be expected to handle the changes that occur on a routine basis. You will also be expected to be innovative in initiating changes that will improve your workers' performance. Making adjustments, as you will learn in Chapter 14, is part of your controlling function.

For larger changes that emanate from top management, you may be expected to serve as the change agent for your department.

The Supervisor as Change Agent

A **change agent** is a person who has responsibility for altering or modifying the behavior both of persons in an organization and of the organization itself. In other words, the change agent is the one who makes change happen. In the future, supervisors will be expected to be change agents for diversity management and cultural change. This means that as a change agent, you will have two responsibilities: (1) identifying departmental needs and initiating appropriate changes and (2) managing the change process when the change is initiated by your superiors.

Much of the first responsibility will be handled through your controlling activities (see Chapter 14). Monitoring the internal and external environment for improvement opportunities will also help. This responsibility should keep before you the question "How can we do this job more effectively?"

COMPETENCY CHECK

Can you define the term *change agent* and show how it relates to the supervisor?

One way to make your job easier is to prepare your workers for accepting change and making changes. Two areas that are the supervisor's major concern in preparing workers for change are: (1) helping workers develop an attitude of receptivity to change as a means of improvement, and (2) minimizing resistance to change. Then you will lead workers through the change process steps of unfreezing, changing, and refreezing.

Helping Workers to Be Receptive to Change

In helping workers become amenable to change, supervisors should first be enthusiastically entrepreneurial in seeking out ways to improve the entire department. Enthusiasm is usually contagious. Workers are more likely to submit innovative suggestions if they know that the suggestions are welcome; that they will be explored and, if feasible, implemented; and, if they are successfully implemented, will be rewarded. Treating suggestions and resultant changes over time under such

WHAT CAN THE SUPERVISOR DO?

Before the change:

☐ Involve employees in discussing the need for change; they will be more accepting if they play a part in creating the change.
☐ Share information that shows how both the employees and the organization will benefit from the change.
☐ Keep communication lines open regarding how the change will affect employees.

During the change:

☐ Give employees progress reports on the planned changes and their implementation.
☐ Provide training so that workers can use the new technology or procedures or adjust to a new organizational structure.
☐ Keep communication lines open while the change is taking place.
☐ Praise employees for progress in adapting to the changes or learning to use new technologies.

After the change:

☐ Reinforce the benefits that have occurred because of the change.
☐ Recognize or reward employees who were instrumental in making the change and those who encouraged others during the change.
☐ Monitor the success of the change and share the results with employees.[47]

a policy will help to develop workers' trust in the supervisor and the organization. Change is always easier to implement in a climate of trust.

Getting started in developing a receptive attitude to innovation and change may be difficult. Talking with and listening to workers will help the supervisor identify those with innovative potential. You might ask workers if they have suggestions for improvement in a specific area, such as waste reduction or work flow. Having them submit proposals and having a work group try them out may motivate others to submit suggestions. Continued encouragement may lead to the attitude you are seeking: receptivity to change as a means of improvement.

COMPETENCY CHECK

Can you illustrate ways through which the supervisor can develop in workers a receptive attitude toward change?

 ## Minimizing Resistance to Change

The second area of concern to the supervisor in preparing workers for change is minimizing resistance to it. If your workers have developed a receptive attitude to change, there will be much less resistance. That will make your job easier. But

---

Figure 8.4
FEARS THAT CAUSE RESISTANCE TO CHANGE

People often resist change because they are comfortable in their present way of doing things. They fear that their lives will be upset and that their future will be uncertain in the changed environment. Below are some of the fears that cause workers to resist change.

Fear

- of the unknown
- of losing their job
- of having their salary reduced
- of losing status, rank, or power
- of not being able to perform the new job
- of new responsibilities
- of required training

- of changes in social/work relationships
- of a required relocation
- of challenges to their values, attitudes, or beliefs
- of change itself

---

human nature being what it is, some resistance will surface when change is introduced. Understanding why people resist change is the first step toward minimizing that resistance.

People resist change for many reasons. The resistance is sometimes overt and sometimes covert. Reasons for resisting changes may be found among the fears listed in Figure 8.4.

Figure 8.5 presents four worker-oriented approaches that can be used to deal with resistance to change. Any new compensation system should be explained thoroughly to all workers. If pay decreases will, in fact, be involved, the facilitation and support approach should be used.

One of the most effective methods of dealing with resistance to change is the participation-and-involvement approach. This participative approach results in longer-term acceptance of and internalization by the workers.[48] Helping to plan and execute the change not only helps dispel workers' fears but also motivates them by increasing their self-esteem. As you will learn in Chapter 11, worker participation in decisions about their work life is one of the best motivators. Here is an example of worker enthusiasm about participation in a team mode at Goodyear Tire and Rubber.

At the morning shift change at Goodyear Tire and Rubber's radial-tire plant in Lawton, Oklahoma, workers crowd into supervisor Bill Jackson's office to check yesterday's production figures against those of the other three shifts. Average tire production time is down to 10 minutes, half that of most other plants in the world. Up the line in the spotless 1.5-million-square-foot plant, tire builders on Ron Wood's team go over personal "business plans" to meet or exceed factory standards, such as 1 percent absenteeism and 1 percent product waste. On the floor, an automatic tire-trimming machine and tread-gluing machine invented by employees do what five employees per shift used to do. "There is so much talent in this plant, it is unreal," says Jackson. "You think of all the years it wasn't used."

Figure 8.5
WORKER-ORIENTED METHODS OF DEALING WITH RESISTANCE TO CHANGE

Approach	Examples	Commonly Used in Situations	Advantages	Drawbacks
1. Education and communication	Use one-on-one discussions, group presentations, and written communications to educate people prior to change and help them see the benefits of change.	Where there is a lack of information or inaccurate information and analysis.	Once persuaded, people will often help with the implementation of the change.	Can be very time-consuming if many people are involved.
2. Participation and involvement	Allow workers to help design and implement change; ask for ideas and advice; form task forces, committees, and teams to work on the change.	Where the initiators do not have all the information they need to design the change, and where others have considerable power to resist.	People who participate will be committed to implementing change; any relevant information they have will be integrated into the change plan.	Can be very time-consuming if participants design an inappropriate change.
3. Facilitation and support	Provide social and emotional support for the hardships of change; actively listen to problems and complaints; provide training in new ways; help overcome performance pressures.	Where people are resisting because of adjustment problems.	No other approach works as well with adjustment problems.	Can be time-consuming and expensive and still fail.
4. Negotiation and agreement	Offer incentives to actual or potential resisters; work out trade-offs to provide special benefits in exchange so that change will not be blocked.	Where someone or some group will clearly lose out in a change, and where that group has considerable power to resist.	Sometimes it is a relatively easy way to avoid major resistance.	Can be too expensive in many cases if it alerts others to negotiate for compliance.

Source: Adapted from John P. Kotter and Leonard A. Schlesinger, "Choosing Strategies for Change," *Harvard Business Review,* March–April 1979, p. 111; and John R. Schermerhorn, Jr., *Management for Productivity,* 2d ed., John Wiley & Sons, Inc., New York, 1986, pp. 519–521.

Harnessing worker power—encouraging pride even in such little things as waxed floors and commitment to big goals such as turning out a high-quality, low-cost product—is one of the keys to Goodyear's success in the global tire market.[49]

Minimizing resistance to change can occur only through effective communication. Workers don't like surprises. Too often in recent years, large groups of workers have been handed pink slips on a Friday morning, to take effect that afternoon. No matter how compelling the reason for the change, workers need a chance to prepare for the economic and emotional trauma that may accompany it. Knowledge of these events has caused workers to lose trust in their organizations. This has made them suspicious of change and has increased their fear of losing their security. Clear, honest, and timely information should precede any organizational change. This applies to companywide change as well as to the routine departmental changes that you, as supervisor, will manage. When your workers trust you and the information you disseminate, they are less resistant to change.

As a change agent executing planned change, you need to understand and be able to lead workers through the change process steps of unfreezing, changing, and refreezing.

**COMPETENCY
CHECK**

Can you give several examples of how supervisors can minimize resistance to change?

The Change Process

Change is complicated. If it involved only moving equipment or installing computers, there would be little difficulty. But as noted above, change involves people. People are creatures of habit, and change upsets habits. Therefore, even when people intellectually accept the reasons for a change, they tend to resist it. How can organizations maintain effectiveness through change under these conditions?

Kurt Lewin says that change should be viewed as a people-oriented, three-step process: (1) unfreezing, (2) changing, and (3) refreezing.[50] A graphic view of the change process is shown in Figure 8.6. A brief discussion of the three steps, based on Lewin's classic thesis, follows.

Unfreezing

The first step in making a change is making workers aware of the need for it and making them receptive to it. They must be made aware that their present behavior is ineffective, and they must be persuaded that the new behavior will make them more effective. This thawing-out process is a difficult one because people usually are comfortable in their present behavior and resist changing.

To encourage the unfreezing, managers must recognize the nature of resistance to change. Resistance stems from the workers' feelings of comfort and security in the status quo and their fears of the unknown. Workers may fear many things, including their ability to handle the new situation, the changes it will make in their social or work relationships, or the change it may make in their economic status. While it may not be possible to eliminate these fears completely, they can be minimized.

A caveat for the unfreezing stage is that the supervisor follow company policy in the change process as in all other functions. Sometimes you may not be made aware

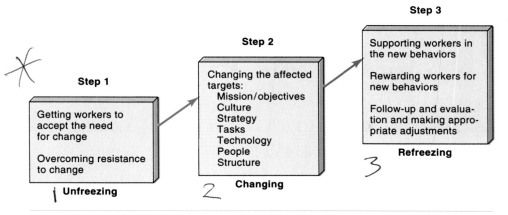

Source: Adapted from Kurt Lewin, "Frontiers in Group Dynamics: Concept, Method, and Reality of Social Sciences: Social Equilibria and Social Change," *Human Relations,* June 1947, pp. 5–14.

of major changes, such as downsizing or plant closings. Or, if apprised by management, you may be sworn to secrecy. Such conditions put supervisors who have tried to create a climate of trust in an awkward position with the workers. The only recourse is to try to persuade management to communicate openly with workers. Failing that, providing emotional support for the affected workers may be all you can do.

A second caveat is that supervisors keep in close touch with workers who are slow to unfreeze. These workers will need additional support throughout the change. If the worker maintains an attitude of resistance, refusing to conform to the change, sooner or later the supervisor will have to make the hard decision to terminate the worker. Continuing the supportive role in the change step that follows will, hopefully, help the supervisor avoid this unpleasant possibility.

Changing

According to Lewin's thesis, workers, once unfrozen, begin to try out the new behavior. This tends to catch on so that one worker follows another in changing. This is especially evident when one worker has some expertise in the new behavior. As you will learn in Chapter 10, expertise can carry the power to influence others. Workers will identify with the expert, who then serves as a role model.

Getting workers to exercise the new behavior over a period of time helps them internalize the behavior; that is, make it a part of their normal behavior. As time passes, the new behavior becomes routine, replacing the old behavior.

Refreezing

Lewin's third step in making a change occurs when the worker has accepted the new behavior experimented with during the second step. At this point, workers' atti-

WHAT CAN THE SUPERVISOR DO?

Understanding the change process is essential if you are going to be an effective change agent. Sometimes you will need to abandon the textbook approach and summon all your creative resources to help you manage change.

tudes should have changed to a point where they support the new behavior as a normal part of their lives.

During this third stage, management should try to maintain the momentum set in motion during the changing stage. Supporting the workers in their new behavioral modes is important in the refreezing process. Encouraging workers who may falter during this stage by providing both emotional support and needed resources will speed refreezing. Rewarding workers who successfully make the change and assimilate it into their work routine is imperative. Workers who were persuaded to change through promised benefits will be turned off quickly if they see no rewards forthcoming. The quality of the refreezing stage will depend greatly on management's reinforcement of the desired outcomes.

COMPETENCY CHECK

Can you identify, in order, and describe the steps in the change process?

Follow-up and evaluation also are essential during the refreezing stage. They not only provide information on the success of the behavioral change but also provide cost-benefit data that will allow management to quantify the value of the change to the organization. Follow-up and evaluation also give management an opportunity to make appropriate adjustments in the new system, if needed. A word of caution regarding adjustments: Too many modifications during this stage may undo progress made in the first two stages. Adjustments themselves constitute change. While some adjustment is to be expected, too many adjustments can create chaos, causing workers to lose confidence in the managers, their planning ability, and the change itself as a means of improvement.

COMPETENCY REVIEW

1. Define *diversity management* and list the diversities commonly recognized in organizations.
2. Describe four fundamentals of managing diversity.
3. Describe ways in which to appreciate and encourage diversity.
4. Describe three adversities in the workplace that you as a supervisor must discourage.
5. Outline the steps for investigating a sexual harassment complaint.
6. Discuss the nature of organizational change.
7. Define *planned change* and *reengineering*.

⑧ Define the term *change agent,* and show how it relates to the supervisor.
9. Illustrate ways in which supervisors can develop in workers a receptive attitude toward change.
10. Give several examples of how supervisors can minimize resistance to change.
⑪. Identify in order and describe the steps in the change process.

APPLICATIONS

1. Complete the following short questionnaire and score your responses as directed below the questionnaire.

WHERE ARE YOUR PREJUDICES?

Each of us possesses a collection of prejudices and stereotypes acquired from parents and friends since childhood. The following questions will help you explore the content of your special biases and evaluate the memories and experiences that generated them. Score your answers:

1 Never   3 Sometimes   5 Always
2 Seldom   4 Often

1. Have you ever felt uncomfortable visiting a foreign country where you were considered different?	1	2	3	4	5
2. As a child, were you ever expected to be seen but not heard?	1	2	3	4	5
3. Do you resent people who live in this country but whose English is imperfect?	1	2	3	4	5
4. Do you discount opinions of people who are female, over 50, short, have a Polish name, speak in a southern accent, have brown skin, or are different from you in any other respect? (Use just one score.)	1	2	3	4	5
5. Are you annoyed by women who swear?	1	2	3	4	5
6. Do you react negatively to men who wear jewelry?	1	2	3	4	5
7. Are you afraid to bring up racial issues with acquaintances of a different race?	1	2	3	4	5
8. Do you believe older people are inflexible and unable to learn new technology?	1	2	3	4	5
9. Do you believe you know who is gay in your office or in your classes?	1	2	3	4	5
10. Do you think black women are emotionally stronger than black men?	1	2	3	4	5
11. Do you believe disabled people would rather not work?	1	2	3	4	5
12. Do you find successful women to be pushy and abrasive?	1	2	3	4	5
13. Do you resent the special opportunities given to minorities?	1	2	3	4	5
14. Do you tell a lot of ethnic jokes?	1	2	3	4	5

Source: This material is reproduced from *The Healthy Company,* by Robert H. Rosen, Ph.D.; Jeremy P. Tarcher, Publisher, 1991, p. 243–244.

2. Add your scores for No. 1. If your score is between 56 and 70, you harbor a number of cultural biases and tend to be fearful or contemptuous of strangers or foreigners. A score between 35 and 55 indicates that while you possess some biases, you also try to avoid stereotypes and regard people more or less equally. If your score is less than 35, you are remarkably free of ethnic or cultural taints and judge everyone individually.
3. Recently a new procedure was implemented for assembling a unit in your department. Everyone but Sheila Raeburn is using it. She is still assembling the unit in the old way. You've talked with her about this several times and have demonstrated the new steps to her. Still she hasn't come around. What do you do? List several actions you might take to handle the situation with Sheila Raeburn.
4. Many events in your lifetime have caused changes in the world of work.
   a. List 10 changes that have occurred in the environment in the last 20 years.
   b. Show how the changes have caused organizational change.
5. Supervisors often are on the front lines when it comes to coping with resistance to change. They may be told by their superiors that a change is to be made and that they must squelch any resistance in their departments. Even when the supervisor is initiating the change, he or she may have to cope with a resister who prefers to do things "like we've always done them." This chapter has given you some guidelines to managing change. But what about your own attitude toward change? The following questionnaire will help you analyze your feelings about change and meeting resistance to it. Respond to the questions by checking under the Yes or No column to reflect your feelings about change. Your instructor will provide directions for scoring.

	Yes	No
1. Do I personally resist change in my life or in my work?	___	___
2. Do I resent being told by superiors that a better way is needed for a process in my department?	___	___
3. Do I offer suggestions for changes up the line as well as down the line to workers?	___	___
4. Have I ever personally tried to sell an idea for change to my superior?	___	___
5. When making changes in my department, do I plan the entire change and then announce it to the workers?	___	___
6. Do I invite suggestions for improvement from workers on a regular basis?	___	___
7. Do I ever assign problems to committees or teams to find solutions?	___	___
8. Do I insist that rules and procedures be followed without exception and without question?	___	___

(Continued)

	Yes	No
9. If I see a worker using a nonstandard procedure to perform a task, do I observe, ask for an explanation, and evaluate the variation according to its effectiveness?	_____	_____
10. Do I provide clear and valid information about a change in departmental procedure?	_____	_____
11. Do I encourage workers to be innovative in improving tasks?	_____	_____
12. Do I demonstrate the benefits of a planned change to workers?	_____	_____
13. Do I try to time changes so that they will occur on Fridays or before holidays to provide workers a cooling-off period?	_____	_____
14. Do I enlist key workers to help in planning changes?	_____	_____
15. Do I provide meet-and-confer time to plan, implement, and evaluate changes?	_____	_____
16. Do I recognize workers' insecurity by clarifying intentions, methods, and expected results of change to relieve their fears?	_____	_____
17. Do my workers freely come to me to offer suggestions for change?	_____	_____
18. Do I usually hear about worker complaints or fears from the grapevine when changes are made?	_____	_____

CASES   Case I

ENGLISH ONLY, PLEASE!

Immigrants bring a variety of languages to the American workforce, and many employers contend that they need English-only policies to prevent the workplace from becoming a Tower of Babel in which safety, productivity, and worker harmony are threatened. However, civil rights groups consider such policies discriminatory because they reflect racist fears of an Anglo-dominated society struggling with an influx of Hispanic and Asian immigrants.

Guidelines published in 1980 by the U.S. Equal Employment Opportunity Commission say that English-only rules cannot be imposed except in cases of "business necessity." Those guidelines, however, are not legally binding, and mixed court decisions haven't helped to clarify what constitutes "necessity." For example:

1. A Puerto Rican warehouse worker in New York City was fired after his supervisor overheard him talking in Spanish about a pizza he had ordered for lunch. The worker won his case, and the EEOC forced the company to abandon its English-only policy.

2. A federal judge sided with Priscilla Garcia, who challenged the English-only policy of Spun Steak Co., a meatpacking plant in south San Francisco, where Garcia had worked 18 years on the assembly line. Garcia overheard her boss telling a coworker: "If you want to speak Spanish, you should go back to your own country." The company claims it was trying to prevent discrimination because, the company's attorney said, Garcia and her coworker had been making fun of a black employee in Spanish. "He knew he was being ridiculed, but he didn't know what they were saying."

3. Puritan-Bennett Corp., a maker of hospital respirators that imposed an English-only rule at its Carlsbad, California, plant, cited safety and productivity reasons for its rule. Personnel Director Elizabeth Peo said, "Communication with your fellow employees is very important, and to have multiple languages makes it difficult at best. We need to assure the integrity of our product. If we don't do our job, a person could die."

   The company settled out of court and agreed to limit its policy to specific circumstances. Workers have to speak English during meetings, while working in teams in which English is the only common language, or when asked by a supervisor to conduct a specific, work-related conversation in English.

4. At Driftwood Convalescent Hospital in Gilroy, California, most of the nurse's aides spoke Spanish as their native language. Jordania Reed's bilingual skills had helped her land the job at Driftwood. She didn't take the new English-only policy too seriously when it was introduced because it made sense to use English when addressing English-speaking patients. However,

the new policy also required employees to use English in private conversations in hallways or other common areas where patients might overhear.

Three days after being caught speaking Spanish to her coworkers for the second time, Jordania was fired. Driftwood's director, Michael Dunn, said he "was simply following federal health regulations that say patients should be cared for in their own language." He also said some elderly residents had complained of being surrounded by foreign-speaking staff; a few senile residents had even asked, "What country am I in?" Jordania is prepared to pursue her case to the Supreme Court if necessary.

1. Divide the class into teams to discuss the issues surrounding English-only rules. Each team should present an oral report as described by your instructor.
2. Discuss the following issues:
   a. valid business reasons for English-only rules
   b. business reasons for not having English-only rules
   c. employee relations reasons for having and for not having English-only rules

Source: Adapted from David Foster, "Do English-Only Rules Aid Prejudice or Prevent Tower of Babel in Office?," *The Arkansas Democrat,* August 30, 1992.

Case II

ORGANIZATIONAL CHANGE AND THE PLANE TRUTH

Regional Airlines had survived airline deregulation through crafty leadership and employee sacrifices. Wages and hiring had been frozen for 2 years, causing morale to go down when workers were asked to do more work for less pay. In 1989, Regional's president announced a companywide program designed to create a positive work environment in which teamwork, creativity, and change could flourish. Four mechanisms—cross-functional task forces, open communication, recognition committees, and individual initiative—would drive the new program.

By December 1990, the program was well under way. Two task forces had completed training and were ready to hold their first meetings; the recognition committee had presented awards to all employees for achieving performance targets companywide; and the *Plane Truth,* a biweekly newspaper started by a group of flight attendants, was in its second year of print.

Just when things seemed to be going well, outside forces began to undermine the new program. The Gulf War caused higher fuel costs and lower passenger miles. So management cut back on workers' hours and set higher quality goals.

Employees were anxious to keep their jobs, so they agreed to management's requests. However, tensions were mounting, and the *Plane Truth* began publishing articles critical of the company.

The president of Regional was not amused. "This is destroying the team spirit and the new program!" he shouted. "We need to make our customers happy, improve our turnarounds and on-times, provide a quality service. We need positive thinking! We need team spirit to make this new program work. One of our board members saw one of these papers that was left in first class. What would customers think if they got their hands on it? Our own employees complaining about slow turnarounds and lost luggage!"

The newspaper was creating tension, but it also was creating unity. One of the flight attendants responsible for publishing the *Plane Truth* said, "Everyone wants to pretend that we're one big happy family, but we're not. We have a lot of problems that will never be solved if we keep our heads in the sand. If the *Plane Truth* hits too close to home, maybe people should think about why. Maybe the machinists see a little too much truth in the reports that they take long breaks and cover for each other. That's not a reason to cancel the paper; that's a reason to continue it."

"Part of feeling positive is believing that we're doing the right things, not denying that some things aren't perfect, and having a little fun. Customers know when employees aren't happy. If we lose this newspaper, it's one more loss for the employees. It will show up in our work; it has to."

1. What is the primary purpose served by the *Plane Truth* during the changes the company is undergoing?
2. What can the president do to alleviate the tensions?
3. Should the *Plane Truth* be discontinued permanently or be put on a temporary hiatus until outside conditions change and internal conditions have a chance to improve? Why?

Source: Adapted from R. Daniel Foster, "The Case of the Team-Spirit Tailspin," *Harvard Business Review,* January–February 1991, pp. 14–25.

REFERENCES

1. Peter F. Drucker, *Managing for the Future,* Truman Talley Book/Dutton, New York, 1992, pp. 18, 93, 108.
2. R. Roosevelt Thomas, Jr., *Beyond Race and Gender,* AMACOM, New York, 1991, p. 4.
3. R. Roosevelt Thomas, Jr., "From Affirmative Action to Affirming Diversity," *Harvard Business Review,* March–April 1990, pp. 112, 114.
4. Lura K. Romei, "Managing the Changing Workforce," *Modern Office Technology,* October 1990, p. 75.
5. Lennie Copeland, "Learning to Manage a Multicultural Work Force," *Training,* May 1988, p. 49.

6. Julie Amparano Lopez, "Firms Elevate Heads of Diversity Programs," *The Wall Street Journal,* Aug. 5, 1992, p. B1; and Thomas Huang, "Piecing Together a Mosaic," *The Virginian-Pilot and The Ledger-Star,* Aug. 1, 1993, p. E1.

7. Jack Gordon, "Rethinking Diversity," *Training,* January 1992, p. 27.

8. Robert H. Rosen and Lisa Berger, *The Healthy Company,* Jeremy P. Tarcher, Inc., Los Angeles, p. 250.

9. Romei, loc. cit.

10. Ibid., pp. 75–76.

11. Catherine Fyock, *America's Work Force Is Coming of Age: What Every Business Needs to Know to Recruit, Train, Manage, and Retain an Aging Work Force,* Lexington Books, Lexington, Mass., 1990, p. 13.

12. Robert H. Rosen and Lisa Berger, op. cit., pp. 252–253.

13. Fyock, op. cit., p. 76.

14. Kevin R. Hopkins and Susan L. Nestleroth, "Where Have All the Workers Gone?," from "Willing and Able," a special advertising section, *Business Week,* Oct. 18, 1991, p. 6.

15. Kevin Hopkins and Susan Nestleroth, "An Able Work Force," *Business Week,* ibid., pp. 35–36.

16. Kevin Hopkins and Susan Nestleroth, "Looking Over the Overlooked," *Business Week,* op. cit., p. 10.

17. Ibid., p. 12.

18. Ibid.

19. Kevin Hopkins and Susan Nestleroth, "Making the Commitment," *Business Week,* op. cit., p. 14.

20. Frank Bowe, *Equal Rights for Americans with Disabilities,* Franklin Watts, New York, 1992, pp. 76–77.

21. Virginia M. Gibson, "Domestic Partners and Employee Benefits," *HR Focus,* June 1992, pp. 1, 6.

22. Keith H. Hammonds, "Lotus Opens a Door for Gay Partners," *Business Week,* Nov. 4, 1991, p. 85.

23. Cathy Trost, "To Cut Costs and Keep the Best People, More Concerns Offer Flexible Work Plans," *The Wall Street Journal,* Feb. 18, 1992, p. B1.

24. Ibid.

25. Adapted from tips written by Greer Dawson as reported in Thomas Huang, "Piecing Together a Mosaic," *The Virginian-Pilot and The Ledger-Star,* Aug. 1, 1993, p. E1.

26. Trost, loc. cit.

27. Ellyn E. Spragins, ed., "The Diverse Work Force," *Inc.,* January 1993, p. 33.

28. Bowe, loc. cit.

29. George F. Simons, Carmen Vazquez, and Philip R. Harris, *Transcultural Leadership: Empowering the Diverse Workforce,* Gulf Publishing Company, Houston, 1993, pp. 162–163.

30. Huang, loc. cit.

31. Copeland, loc. cit.

32. R. Roosevelt Thomas, Jr., "From Affirmative Action to Affirming Diversity," op. cit., p. 111.

33. Susan L. Webb, *Step Forward: Sexual Harassment in the Workplace,* MasterMedia, New York, 1991, p. 49.

34. Ibid., pp. 26–27.

35. Ibid., pp. 53–59.

36. Marilyn Loden and Judy B. Rosener, *Workforce America!: Managing Employee Diversity as a Vital Resource,* Business One Irwin, Homewood, Ill., 1991, p. 58.

37. R. Roosevelt Thomas, Jr., "From Affirmative Action to Affirming Diversity," op. cit., p. 108.
38. Terry L. Paulson, *They Shoot Managers, Don't They?*, Ten Speed Press, Berkeley, Calif., 1991, p. 59.
39. Noreen Hale, *The Older Worker*, Jossey-Bass Publisher, San Francisco, 1990, pp. 102–106.
40. Edward Wakin, "Alternative Workstyles: Jobs à la carte," *Today's Office*, September 1984, p. 44; and Lura K. Romei, "Telecommuting: A Workstyle Revolution," *Modern Office Technology*, May 1992, p. 38.
41. John A. Pearce II and Richard B. Robinson, Jr., *Management*, Random House, New York, 1989, p. 378.
42. Rich Karlgaard, "ASAP Interview with Mike Hammer," *Forbes*, Sept. 13, 1993, pp. 70–72.
43. Jonathan Yenkin, "Author Out to Convert Businesses," *The Cincinnati Enquirer*, Nov. 11, 1993, p. C6.
44. "Fast-Changing Times Left Computer Giant Behind," *The Orlando Sentinel*, Dec. 17, 1992, p. B1.
45. "AT&T: The Making of a Comeback," *Business Week*, Jan. 18, 1988, pp. 56–62.
46. Pearce and Robinson, op. cit., p. 379.
47. R. Bruce McAfee and Betty R. Ricks, "Learning to Handle Change," *The Virginian-Pilot and The Ledger-Star*, July 6, 1992, p. 2.
48. John R. Schermerhorn, Jr., James G. Hunt, and Richard N. Osborn, *Managing Organizational Behavior*, 2d ed., John Wiley & Sons, Inc., New York, 1985, p. 637.
49. "Unleashing Workers," *U.S. News & World Report*, Aug. 24, 1987, p. 44.
50. Kurt Lewin, "Frontiers in Group Dynamics: Concept, Method, and Reality of Social Sciences: Social Equilibria and Social Change," *Human Relations*, June 1947, pp. 5–14.

SUGGESTED READINGS

Argyris, Chris: *Knowledge for Action: A Guide to Overcoming Barriers to Organizational Change*, Jossey-Bass Publishers, San Francisco, 1993.
Boyett, Joseph H., and Henry P. Conn: *Workplace 2000*, Penguin Books, New York, 1991.
Bureau of National Affairs: *The Americans with Disabilities Act: A Practical and Legal Guide to Impact, Enforcement and Compliance*, Washington, D.C., 1990.
Dennis, Helen: *Fourteen Steps in Managing an Aging Work Force*, Lexington Books, Lexington, Mass., 1988.
Dreyfuss, Joel: "Get Ready for the New Work Force," *Fortune*, April 23, 1990, pp. 165–181.
Fernandez, John P.: *Managing a Diverse Work Force: Regaining the Competitive Edge*, Lexington Books, Lexington, Mass., 1991.
Hallett, Jeffrey J.: "Worklife Visions," *Personnel Administrator*, May 1987, pp. 57–65.
Hammer, Michael, and James Champy: *Reengineering the Corporation*, Harper Business, New York, 1993.
Heirs, Ben, and Peter Farrell: *The Professional Decision-Thinker*, Dodd, Mead & Company, New York, 1987.
Jamieson, David, and Julie O'Mara: *Managing Workforce 2000: Gaining the Diversity Advantage*, Jossey-Bass Publishers, San Francisco, 1991.
Jeruchim, Joan, and Pat Shapiro: *Women, Mentors, and Success*, Fawcett Columbine, New York, 1992.

Kanter, Rosabeth Moss: *The Change Masters,* Simon and Schuster, New York, 1983.

Kanter, Rosabeth Moss: "Managing the Human Side of Change," *Management Review,* April 1985, pp. 52–56.

Kanter, Rosabeth Moss, Barry A. Stein, and Todd D. Jick: *The Challenge of Organizational Change,* The Free Press, New York, 1992.

Kogo, S. Kanu: *A Workshop for Managing Diversity in the Workplace,* Pfeiffer & Co., San Diego, 1991.

Laufer, Armand: *Careers, Colleagues and Conflicts: Understanding Gender, Race and Ethnicity in the Workplace,* Sage Publications, Beverly Hills, Calif., 1985.

Loden, Marilyn, and Judy B. Rosener: *Workforce America!: Managing Employee Diversity as a Vital Resource,* Business One Irwin, Homewood, Ill., 1991.

Moores, Tommy: "Making Changes—Smoothly," *Management World,* June 1986, pp. 26–28.

Morrison, Ann M.: *The New Leaders: Guidelines on Leadership Diversity in America,* Jossey-Bass Publishers, San Francisco, 1992.

Morrison, Ann M., and Randall P. White: *Breaking the Glass Ceiling: Can Women Reach the Top of America's Largest Corporations?,* Addison-Wesley Publishing Company, Reading, Mass., 1992.

Morrison, Ann M., et al.: *Breaking the Glass Ceiling,* Addison-Wesley Publishing Company, Inc., 1987.

Mueller, James: *The Workplace Workbook: An Illustrated Guide to Job Accommodation and Assistive Technology,* The Dole Foundation, Washington, D.C., 1990.

Naisbett, John, and Patricia Aburdene: *Megatrends for Women,* Villard Books, New York, 1992.

Payne, Thomas E.: *From the Inside Out: How to Create and Survive a Culture of Change,* Performance Press, Albuquerque, N. Mex., 1991.

Petrocelli, William, and Barbara Kate Repa: *Sexual Harassment on the Job,* Nolo Press, Berkeley, Calif., 1992.

Schoonover, Stephen C., and Murray M. Dalziel: "Developing Leadership for Change," *Management Review,* July 1986, pp. 55–60. This is a special issue on "Managing the Future."

Shea, Gordon F.: *Building Trust in the Workplace,* American Management Association, New York, 1984.

Thiederman, Sondra: *Bridging Cultural Barriers for Corporate Success,* Lexington Books, Lexington, Mass., 1991.

Thomas, R. Roosevelt, Jr.: *Beyond Race and Gender,* AMACOM, New York, 1991.

Thomas, R. Roosevelt, Jr.: "From Affirmative Action to Affirming Diversity," *Harvard Business Review,* March–April 1990, pp. 107–117.

Tucker, Robert B.: *Managing the Future,* G. P. Putnam's Sons, New York, 1991.

Webb, Susan L. *Step Forward: Sexual Harassment in the Workplace,* MasterMedia, New York, 1991.

West, Jane, ed.: *The Americans with Disabilities Act: From Policy to Practice,* Millbank Memorial Fund, New York, 1991.

GLOSSARY

change agent   A person who has responsibility for altering or modifying the behavior both of persons in an organization and of the organization itself.

diversity management   Enabling every member of a workforce to perform to his or her potential.

formal mentoring   A program through which an organization matches individuals and includes expectations of accomplishment.

informal mentoring   A process that begins when an experienced employee takes an interest in helping a new employee, or a new employee approaches an experienced employee for information and help.

planned change   A systematic, deliberate change in the way part or all of an organization functions.

reengineering   Radically changing the way we do our work—how we create value for customers; how we design, invent, and make products; how we sell them; and how we serve customers.

stereotype   A fixed, distorted generalization about all members of a particular group.

CHAPTER 9
Appraising and Rewarding Performance

AFTER STUDYING THIS CHAPTER, YOU WILL BE ABLE TO:

1. Define *performance appraisal*.

2. Discuss who is responsible for providing input and/or conducting performance appraisals.

3. List and describe the major purposes of performance appraisals.

4. Diagram and describe the performance appraisal sequence.

5. Identify uses of performance appraisal information.

6. List and explain types of rater errors.

7. Describe performance appraisal formats.

8. Tell how the supervisor can conduct nondiscriminatory appraisals.

9. Explain the importance of performance appraisal feedback.

10. Describe methods of providing feedback to employees.

11. Explain the importance of the supervisor's role in performance appraisal.

12. Describe planning steps a supervisor should take when preparing for a performance appraisal interview.

13. Cite actions a supervisor should take when conducting a performance appraisal interview.

14. Explain the supervisor's preparation for potentially difficult performance appraisal interviews.

15. List the general types of rewards and give examples of each type.

16. Describe the role of the supervisor in establishing and communicating compensation criteria.

17. Explain criteria for recommending and administering rewards effectively.

18. Explain how a supervisor can implement nondiscriminatory reward systems.

19. Define *comparable worth* and tell how it differs from "equal pay for equal work."

20. Describe how job evaluation is linked to comparable worth.

CHAPTER OUTLINE

C H A P

Appraising
AND
Rewarding
Performance

T   E   R   9

ppraising and rewarding performance is an important role for supervisors. How employees are evaluated determines how they are rewarded for their work. Because workers are motivated by well-done appraisals and well-deserved rewards, supervisors must be knowledgeable in the techniques and tools of appraisals and rewards.

Appraising Performance

Everyone wants to know "How am I doing?" Performance appraisals provide an opportunity to give feedback to workers and to let them know how they are doing.

What Is Performance Appraisal?

COMPETENCY CHECK

Can you define performance appraisal?

Performance appraisal is the process of measuring and reporting employee behavior and accomplishments during a given period for the purpose of improving job performance.

Who Appraises?

Supervisors play a major role in performance evaluation because their input carries more weight than does any other information source. In an American Management Association study, respondents overwhelmingly acknowledged the influence of the immediate supervisor's input. This is shown graphically in Figure 9.1. Note that 96.2 percent of the respondents reported that the immediate supervisor has moderate or extreme influence, with 78.9 percent citing the influence as having extreme weight.

Other sources of input and/or performance appraisals include peers, up-the-line evaluations, self-evaluations, and customer/client feedback.

Peers. Sometimes coworkers are asked to evaluate one another or provide input about their performance. Work teams may evaluate one another or may be evaluated as a group.

Up-the-Line Evaluations. Workers may be asked to evaluate their supervisors, or supervisors may be asked to appraise their managers. This up-the-line evaluation sometimes causes apprehension on the part of the evaluator, who fears that there will be reprisals at his or her own evaluation time. Up-the-line evaluations can be effective only in an open environment in which trust and honesty are valued.

Self-Evaluations. Self-evaluations are discussed later in this chapter. One concern of supervisors and others is that workers will inflate their self-ratings. This has not been shown to be true; on the contrary, most workers tend to undervalue their own efforts.

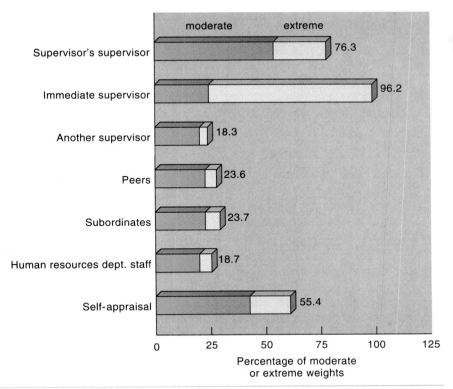

Figure 9.1
SUPERVISOR'S INFLUENCE ON RATINGS

Customers/Clients. To obtain feedback from a number of different sources, customers/clients may be asked their opinions of employees. This is especially true in service industries, where employees often interact with customers and clients outside the organization.

Why Appraise?

Performance appraisal provides information needed to accomplish several purposes important to both the employer and the employee. The information produced by appraisals has many uses in improving organizational productivity.

Purposes

Performance appraisals have two purposes: employee evaluation and employee development. For most companies, evaluation is the more important purpose. Appraisals of employees' performance provide the basis for administrative decisions

COMPETENCY CHECK
Can you cite the importance of the immediate supervisor's input into the performance appraisal process?

Figure 9.2 PURPOSES FOR WHICH RESPONDING COMPANIES USED PERFORMANCE EVALUATION	
Purpose	**Percentage of Respondents**
Compensation	85.6
Counseling	65.1
Training and development	64.3
Promotion	45.3
Human resources planning	43.1
Retention/discharge	30.3
Validation of selection technique	17.2

Source: Evelyn Eichel and Henry E. Bender, *Performance Appraisal: A Study of Current Techniques,* American Management Association, New York, 1984, p. 7. Reprinted, by permission of the publisher, from *AMA Management Briefing,* 1984. Copyright © 1984, the American Management Association, New York. All rights reserved.

about promotions, demotions, terminations, transfers, and rewards. The development purpose—to improve performance on the job—has generally been secondary, but the AMA study referred to earlier shows that the focus of performance appraisals is shifting to a more balanced approach. Purposes for which responding companies use performance evaluation are shown in Figure 9.2.

Uses of Information

As shown in Figure 9.3, appraisal information may be used in five primary ways:

1. To make administrative decisions, such as whom to promote, suspend, terminate, demote, or transfer.
2. To identify training and development needs, such as what kind of training and development is needed and who can benefit by it.
3. To motivate and provide feedback by letting workers know how they are performing, what their strengths are, and in what areas they need improvement.
4. To validate the selection process by comparing worker performance with desired outcomes. For example, if 25 percent or more new employees are performing below desired levels, the selection criteria should be examined to see whether the job description and job specification accurately define the requirements of the job.
5. To make compensation decisions, such as who should receive merit increases, who should receive only minimal increases, and who should receive no pay increases at all.

COMPETENCY CHECK
Can you identify five uses of performance appraisal information?

Accurate, current information is required to make objective judgments that affect workers' careers. Unfair, inequitable, subjective decisions are often made because performance data are incomplete and not reported objectively.

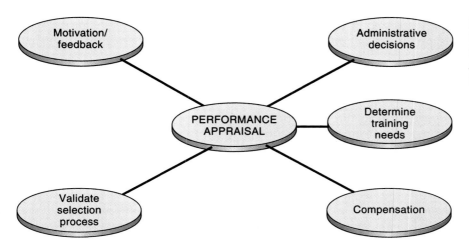

Figure 9.3
**USES OF
PERFORMANCE
APPRAISAL
INFORMATION**

When to Appraise

Performance appraisals are an ongoing, continuous process, not just a semiannual or annual process. Informal appraisals occur every time a supervisor comments on an employee's work, makes a notation of an accomplishment, or suggests ways to improve. However, formal performance appraisals take place during a specified time which is determined by whether the employee is new or experienced at the job.

New Employees

Should

Many organizations have a formal procedure for evaluating new employees at 30, 90, and 180 days. This procedure allows the company to track the employee's progress at regular, specified intervals to determine if the employee is meeting prescribed goals and if it is cost-effective to continue the employment relationship. Feedback is provided to the employee after each appraisal.

Companies that still have a probationary period (a trial period before the employee is "officially" hired) find that it is particularly important to keep both the employee and the company apprised of the new employee's progress. Not all companies continue to have a probationary period as a part of their employment process because employees may incorrectly assume that if they "pass" the probationary period, they are secure in their future employment.

Informal, frequent appraisal and feedback are particularly important to the new employees' success. New to the job, they must be told where they are meeting expectations and where they are not. Only with this information can new employees become productive.

Experienced Employees

Experienced employees are generally appraised on a formal basis annually on their anniversaries—that is, on the date they became employed by the company. Ongoing, informal appraisals are just as important for experienced employees as for new employees. The formal appraisal should hold no surprises for the employee, if appropriate informal appraisal and feedback have been given throughout the year.

There are, however, some exceptions to the annual review. In organizations where change is the norm, such as high-tech industries, fast food companies, or companies where competition is tight, annual reviews and projections may not be frequent enough to maintain competitiveness. In times of recession where downsizing occurs, more frequent reviews may be necessary.

How to Appraise

When performance appraisals are done by the supervisor, the appraisal follows a sequence of activities. Supervisors and others who perform appraisals must know and follow the sequence while being aware of characteristics of their own behavior that may lead to possible errors in the appraisal.

Sequence

Performance appraisal follows a sequence of activities, as shown in Figure 9.4. This sequence consists of (1) setting performance standards, (2) communicating these standards, (3) observing employees doing their work, (4) collecting data, (5) distributing employees' self-appraisals, (6) completing the supervisor's appraisal, (7) evaluating performance, and (8) providing feedback.

Setting Performance Standards. Performance standards provide a benchmark against which to measure employee performance. In some companies, performance standards based on historical data have already been set. For example, a standard day's work may be defined as "produces 1800 widgets with no more than 1 percent rejects," and employees who produce above that average (standard) receive a higher evaluation than do those who produce the average or below the average. Or a sales standard may be "completes 15 calls on potential customers, securing at least two new accounts during the month." Other companies set individual employee standards through a management by objectives (MBO) process, where managers and workers set goals cooperatively. MBO is typically used for management positions and where employees have some flexibility or control over their work. An assembly-line worker, for example, has little control over the quantity of work performed and therefore is not a good candidate for MBO.

Communicating Standards. Employees should know from the beginning what the basis for their evaluations will be. Will they be evaluated on the quality of their work? The quantity? Initiative? Dependability? If so, what do these terms mean, and what is the measure applied to them? What quality is expected? What quantity? What does *initiative* mean, and what behaviors must be exhibited to show initiative? For example, if quality is judged by percentage of rejects, what percent is considered high, acceptable, marginal, and unacceptable?

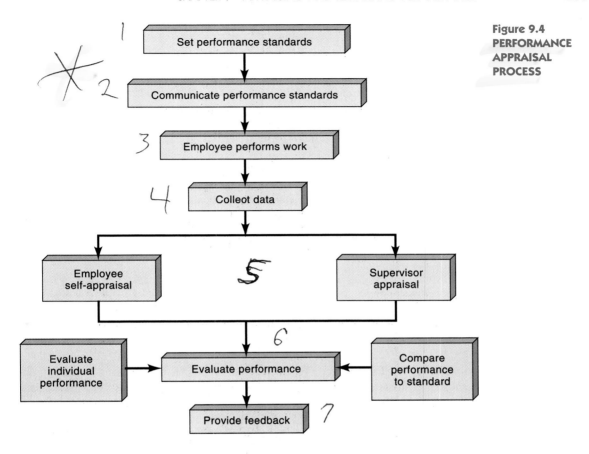

Figure 9.4
**PERFORMANCE
APPRAISAL
PROCESS**

Observing Employees Performing Work.   Employees should be observed as they perform their daily tasks all through the appraisal period (quarterly, semiannually, or annually), and information regarding their performance should be recorded. Observation is a skill that can be learned, and practicing on a daily basis enhances the supervisor's ability to notice and comprehend what is going on within his/her workplace.

Collecting Data.   Data for the performance appraisal should be gathered throughout the appraisal period (quarterly, semiannually, or annually), not in the last minutes prior to the formal evaluation. Supervisors should record both positive and negative incidents on the job. These incidents should be recorded immediately. A notebook is a handy way to record such incidents, which then become a part of the workers' files and can be referred to when evaluating worker performance. Examples of a supervisor's notes are shown on the next page:

4/6
Max's error rate continues despite our discussions and suggestions for improvement.

4/12
Suzanne was on break for an additional 15 minutes today—second time this week.

4/17
John not only finished the special project on time, but it required only minor revisions.

Distributing employees' self-appraisals.   Workers may be asked to complete appraisals of their own performance. This form is typically the same as the form completed by the supervisor. When self-appraisal is a part of the performance appraisal process, this procedure should be followed:

1. Discuss the purpose of the self-appraisal with the employee.
2. Review the format, and clarify what the employee should do to complete the form. Encourage questions and try to ensure that the employee completely understands exactly what is required.
3. Provide the employee with the self-appraisal form at least a week before it is to be completed.
4. Set a specific time when the self-appraisal must be completed.
5. Stress the importance of the self-appraisal to the total performance appraisal system.

Appraising the Employee.   The supervisor needs to plan before beginning the employee evaluation. Plan a time when interruptions will be at a minimum and ask not to be disturbed. Plan to work in a place that is comfortable and where full concentration can be given to the task. Plan the procedure to be used, and follow the same procedure with each worker. Gather all the performance data and place it in each employee's folder. Review all the data before beginning to write. Write a draft copy. Put the draft aside for at least an hour, longer if possible. Then go back to the draft copy, and try to read it as if someone else had written the evaluation. Rewrite as necessary for clarity and objectivity.

COMPETENCY CHECK

Can you diagram and describe the appraisal sequence?

Evaluating performance.   Evaluation should be based on the worker's performance *on the job* and not on traits or characteristics. This is discussed in greater detail later in this chapter.

Providing Feedback.   Feedback may be provided in written form or in oral form and is discussed later in this chapter.

Errors

Sin Yu was a Chinese philosopher of the third century. He discussed the system of using an imperial rater to evaluate the official family of the Wei dynasty. Sin Yu said, "The Imperial Rater of Nine Grades seldom rates men according to their merits, but always according to his likes and dislikes."[1] Sin Yu's criticism is still valid today because performance appraisals are subject to rater errors. Some of

WHAT CAN THE SUPERVISOR DO?

TO AVOID RATING ERRORS, A SUPERVISOR SHOULD:

☐ Put aside personal biases, and evaluate a worker on performance only (personal bias).

☐ Realize that workers have both strengths and areas where they need improvement, and rate each job dimension on its own merits, not on the basis of one strength or weakness (halo effect).

☐ Understand that some workers are more productive than others; not everyone is average. Be willing to make a distinction among above-average, average, or below-average workers (central tendency).

☐ Recognize that *all* workers are not exceptional, nor are *all* workers less-than-satisfactory performers. Acknowledge worker differences, and appraise individuals according to their performance (strictness/leniency).

☐ Be willing to accept people who are different, and don't expect everyone to be like you. Variety in experiences and backgrounds is desirable (similarity).

☐ Keep notes about events that happen throughout the appraisal period, and refer to the entire list of incidents when making an appraisal so that a worker's actions immediately previous to the appraisal will not affect your rating to a greater degree than will all previous actions (recency of events).

the more common rater errors to be avoided when evaluating worker performance include:

1. Personal bias against members of a different race, age, religion, gender, or national origin.
2. The **halo effect,** which lets your rating of one factor affect your rating of all other factors. "John displays an excellent knowledge of nursing techniques; therefore, I judge that he is excellent in all other nursing activities."
3. The **central tendency**—judging most workers as average, thus not making a distinction between high and low performers.
4. Harshness and leniency, which are opposite sides of the same coin. Supervisors who are harsh raters tend to rate everyone at the low end of the scale; supervisors who are lenient raters evaluate everyone at the high end of the scale.
5. Similarity—rating people who are like you higher than those who are different from you.
6. Recency of events—letting what happened yesterday (or last week) affect your judgment of a worker's performance for an entire rating period.

COMPETENCY CHECK

Can you explain common rating errors?

What Format to Use

Appraisal formats may take many different forms and contain very different information. The format of a performance appraisal may be comparative, absolute, or outcome-based.

Comparative Formats

If a **comparative format** is used, the supervisor evaluates employees in relation to one another. The most frequently used comparative methods are *ranking* and *forced choice.*

Ranking requires the evaluator to compare employees on the basis of their overall performance and then to list them in either *ascending* (lowest-to-highest) or *descending* (highest-to-lowest) order. This is frequently done by identifying the best performer and the worst performer, the next-best and the next-worst, and so on until all employees have been placed in rank order. Ranking is the simplest way to do a comparative appraisal.

Forced choice places a predetermined percentage of workers into each of several levels of performance. For example, employees may be "forced" into the following groups:

Excellent	10%	Below average	20%
Above average	20%	Unsatisfactory	10%
Satisfactory	40%		

Although comparative formats are relatively simple, there are problems associated with them. One problem is that they do not provide any measure of the differences between rankings. For example, the employee ranked eighth may be considerably more productive than the one ranked ninth, while there may be very little difference in the performances of the employees ranked ninth and tenth. As you can imagine, as the number of employees increases, ranking becomes much more difficult. Because comparisons are usually made on a *global* (overall) basis, there is very little information available about strengths and weaknesses. For the employee, it is similar to a student receiving a grade of C on a test without being told which questions were answered correctly and which were answered incorrectly. Ranking therefore provides no basis for employees to understand the positive and negative aspects of their performance and thus prevents employee development.

When ranking is used to determine performance among members of different departments, ratings become even more vulnerable to inconsistency. For example, Employee A in Department 1 may be an outstanding employee in a department of outstanding employees, therefore ranking No. 5 among 15 employees. Employee B may be an average employee in a department of average and below-average performers and therefore earns a ranking of No. 1 in the department. If someone who was not knowledgeable about the differences reviewed the two departmental rankings, the logical conclusion would be that Employee B was the better performer, a conclusion that would be incorrect and unfair.

Absolute Formats

pre fered

When **absolute formats** are used, the supervisor evaluates each employee's performance without comparing it to the performance of others. Frequently used absolute methods include *narrative, critical incidents, graphic rating scales, weighted checklists,* and *behaviorally anchored rating scales (BARS)*.

The **narrative method** requires the rater to give a written description of a worker's performance. As its name implies, a narrative describes the worker's strengths, weaknesses, and potential, as well as providing suggestions for improving the worker's performance.

The success of the narrative method depends largely on the supervisor's ability to observe performance and translate that observation into written form. Just as important to a "good" performance appraisal are the supervisor's writing skills and ability to describe the worker's performance clearly. A standardized form may be used to provide some uniformity to the information recorded. One form used for a narrative appraisal is shown in Figure 9.5.

Figure 9.5
NARRATIVE FORMAT

Supervisor's Name _____

3-, 6-, 9-month or annual evaluation   (circle one)

Major accomplishments for the evaluation period.

Major areas in which improvement is required.

Description of major areas of strength.

Description of major areas needing improvement.

Evaluation of job skills.

Signature of supervisor _____   Date _____

The **critical incidents method** is closely related to the narrative method. Under this method, the supervisor records both the positive and the negative actions that employees take in performing their jobs. The supervisor's notes shown on page 256 are examples of positive and negative job behaviors recorded as critical incidents.

The **graphic rating scale** is the oldest absolute appraisal method. A graphic rating scale is a form containing a number of items relating to job performance. The rater simply checks where the employee scores on a continuum. Graphic rating scales have been criticized for lacking definition; that is, the items being used to appraise employees are frequently vague. Figure 9.6 is one example of a graphic rating scale.

All too often, the dimensions included in a graphic rating scale are traits, or characteristics, rather than job behaviors. Traits are difficult to measure unless a job behavior is used to describe the trait. For example, the word *dependability* means different things to different people. What is your definition of the word? If the clue given is the word only and supervisors are expected to rate employees' dependability on a scale of 1 to 5 (or whatever range is used), the responses will differ according to what *dependability* means to the rater. If, however, *dependability* is described as "completing assigned work on schedule" or "arriving at work on time prepared to begin work," raters (and employees) know the basis for the rating. To be used effectively, graphic rating scales should also include a description of the behaviors required to earn a 1, 2, 3, 4, or 5 on the scale.

Figure 9.6
GRAPHIC RATING SCALE FORMAT

Employee's Name _____ Dept. _____

Supervisor's Name _____

3-, 6-, 9-month or annual evaluation   (circle one)

Directions: Circle the number that best describes the employee's job behaviors and performance for the period circled.

	Unacceptable	Average	Good	Outstanding
Job knowledge	1	2	3	4
Quality of work	1	2	3	4
Quantity of work	1	2	3	4
Initiative	1	2	3	4
Cooperation	1	2	3	4
Loyalty	1	2	3	4
Creativity	1	2	3	4
Dependability	1	2	3	4
Responsibility	1	2	3	4
Team player	1	2	3	4

Supervisor's signature _____ Date _____

Like graphic rating scales, **weighted checklists** give traits or job behaviors along with a scale, but weighted checklists assign a value (points) to each of the items. The degrees of performance within a category may also vary according to the value assigned. Figure 9.7 shows a weighted checklist that assigns differing values within each trait rather than weighting the value of each trait. A weighted checklist may also provide a method for valuing each item according to its perceived importance. For example, "quality of work" might be more important than "quantity of work" and therefore count as 20 percent of the total, while 15 percent may be assigned to quantity. Either format may be used.

Behaviorally anchored rating scales (BARS) concentrate on job behaviors, not on personal traits or characteristics. BARS get their name from the "behavioral anchors," or statements that describe each job dimension. The behavioral anchors are usually developed by a committee or task force including managers, supervisors, and workers. Using job analyses as a basis, the committee identifies *job clusters;* that is, jobs that have similar characteristics and requirements. Performance dimensions are then derived by identifying critical aspects of performance for each of the job clusters. For example, in a BARS developed for a hospital, some of the critical nursing dimensions were identified as nursing process, patient and family education, interpersonal relationship skills, and organizational ability.[2] For each of the dimensions of performance, the task force is asked to provide specific behavioral examples of highly effective and highly ineffective performance (critical incidents). The committee then evaluates each of the behavioral descriptors, discarding incidents where unresolved disagreements exist. An example of a BARS from one nursing dimension, organizational ability, is shown in Figure 9.8.

Outcome-Based Formats

When **outcome-based formats** are used, employees are judged on the basis of performance outcomes. Two of the best-known outcome-based methods are standards of performance and management by objectives (MBO).

Standards of performance involve comparing actual accomplishments with a list of conditions that will be fulfilled if the job is considered to be performed well. Figure 9.9 is an example of a standards of performance form for a production supervisor. The standards are established through negotiation between the individual employee and the manager. At the end of the appraisal period, the individuals meet to compare the actual results with the agreed-on standards, recording those that have been fully met, almost met, partially met, and so on. At this meeting, the employee is given an opportunity to explain why any discrepancies occurred, and a revised standard may be agreed on.

Management by objectives (MBO) is similar to the standards of performance method in many ways. Goals are established through negotiation between worker and supervisor. Results are measured by the level of goal achievement. Follow-up at appraisal time focuses on achievements, and an action plan is developed for discrepancies. The difference between these two outcome-based methods is that MBO focuses on specific *goals* (changes) to be achieved within a specified time frame, while the standards of performance method focuses on a level of performance that

COMPETENCY CHECK
Can you identify the three major types of performance appraisal formats?

COMPETENCY CHECK
Can you describe several methods within each of the major performance appraisal formats cited above?

Figure 9.7
WEIGHTED CHECKLIST FORMAT

SUPERVISOR'S APPRAISAL OF EMPLOYEE'S JOB PERFORMANCE

Name of Employee _____ Department _____
Job Title _____ Date of Appraisal _____

	☐ 0 PTS	☐ 1–5 PTS	☐ 6–10 PTS	☐ 11–15 PTS	☐ 16–20 PTS
QUALITY OF WORK	Much of work just gets by. Work requires constant checking to eliminate mistakes he [or she] should recognize. Low standards as to neatness.	Work requires checking due to some lack of care, interest or other reasons. Work not quite as neat as it should be.	Most of work done well. Usually acceptable in both accuracy and neatness.	Very few errors, usually minor in nature. Work seldom has to be done over.	Mistakes extremely rare. Merits complete confidence in ability to do quality work without close supervision. If checking work of others, rarely fails to find existing errors.
QUANTITY OF WORK	Seldom gets work done in required time. Slow.	Output not always up to amount described in performance standard for job.	Turns out the normal amount of work but seldom more.	Output exceeds amount described in the performance standard for this job.	Volume of work is extraordinarily high. Usually does considerably more than expected of average person in job.
JOB KNOWLEDGE	Leans heavily on others for procedures he [or she] should know. Slow learner.	Has acceptable knowledge of most phases of job, but leans on others in some phases of job.	Shows adequate personal knowledge of all parts of job. Can proceed without special instructions on all regular work.	Has very good knowledge of all parts of job. Without special instructions can proceed correctly on many unusual (as well as routine) matters.	Has most exceptional knowledge of job and spends time studying other phases of dept. work. Others in job class look to him [or her] for correct procedures.
APPLICATION TO WORK	Spends much time away from desk. Often interrupts work for idle talk. Usually tardy. Waits for assignments.	Spends more time than necessary in talk or away from desk. Due to own poor planning is idle at some times but unable to handle volume at others. Often tardy.	Spends no more time than necessary in talk or away from desk. Shows fair planning to keep busy. Sometimes tardy.	Usually on the job at all times. Very little idle time. Industrious. Rarely tardy. Does day's work.	Energetic. Loses no time in starting and works right to the last minute. Plans work in advance so as to avoid delays. Never tardy.

Source: Evelyn Eichel and Henry E. Bender, *Performance Appraisal: A Study of Current Techniques*, American Management Association, New York, 1984, p. 40. Reprinted, by permission of the publisher, from AMA Management Briefing. Copyright © 1984 by the American Management Association, New York. All rights reserved.

Figure 9.8
BEHAVIORALLY ANCHORED RATING SCALE FORMAT

RN DIMENSION 4: ORGANIZATIONAL ABILITY

The ability to organize work effectively; to allocate time effectively; to set priorities in the workplace; to complete one's work within reasonable time limits.

HIGHLY EFFECTIVE PERFORMANCE

9 Frequently has time to assume additional responsibilities because she/he organizes and sets priorities so well; usually remains calm and organized and is able to function effectively when emergencies and unexpected events occur; is a resource to other nurses in prioritizing their daily routine.

8 Consistently begins pre-op teaching prior to surgery; organizes and prioritizes activities in order to handle effectively a heavier-than-usual patient assignment.

EFFECTIVE PERFORMANCE

7 Organizes and prioritizes activities in order to handle effectively a standard patient assignment; completes the initial assessment and initiates the care plan when admitting a new patient.

6 Organizes each work day to complete effectively the necessary patient care and other activities within the time at work; consistently completes the necessary care plan; correctly prioritizes activities to allow completion of the essential activities; is able to adapt the day's activities to unexpected events; allocates time effectively.

MARGINAL PERFORMANCE

5 Completes all essential patient care but leaves some nonessential care for the next shift; occasionally forgets about hospital meetings that were scheduled during the shift; has difficulty adjusting the schedule to meet changing patient needs; can organize a workload under usual circumstances, but becomes disorganized when something unusual happens; occasionally needs help prioritizing the day's activities.

4 Completes essential patient care during the shift but rarely completes nonessential patient care; usually misses meetings; consistently stays overtime to get his/her daily work done; usually relies on charge or head nurse to prioritize and organize work.

3 Sometimes leaves essential patient care to be completed by the next shift; makes several trips to the supply room to get what is needed when only one trip should be necessary; can organize and prioritize for small patient assignments, but is unable to do so for standard patient assignments; nursing care plan is frequently incomplete.

INEFFECTIVE PERFORMANCE

2 Must have the charge or head nurse organize the day's activities to complete the nursing care required; leaves work for the next shift and does not care about the problems it might cause; does not finish all care and resists staying overtime to finish; rarely completes the initial assignment and rarely initiates the care plan when admitting a new patient.

1 Never completes the nursing care plan; fails to organize and prioritize the day's activities and needs frequent reminders throughout the day to complete certain activities on time; generally leaves essential patient care undone because of poor organizing of the work; is flustered during the shift if demands are presented.

NOTE: This is one of several dimensions used to evaluate nurses. A separate summary sheet is used to record the ratings and devise an action plan (called PIP, Personal Improvement Plan).

Source: Glenn L. DeBiasi, "The Development, Implementation, and Evaluation of a Nursing Performance Evaluation System," position paper, Norfolk, Va., August 1982. Reprinted by permission.

	Figure 9.9 STANDARDS OF PERFORMANCE FORMAT
Significant Job Segments	**The Job of the Production Supervisor Is Well Done When:**
1. Safety	A. Monthly safety meetings are conducted in accordance with company schedules. B. Safe operating procedures are followed by all employees. C. Regular monthly inspections are held in the department in accordance with the approved checklist. D. Action is taken within 5 days to correct any unsafe conditions. E. Monthly safety reports are submitted by the fifth of the month.
2. Controlling costs	A. Waste and scrap are kept below 2% of total production. B. One cost-saving improvement per month is developed and put into operation. C. Overtime costs are held to a maximum of 3% of direct labor costs. D. Overhead costs are kept within budget limitations. E. Salary controls are exercised in accordance with the salary administration plan. F. At least two team projects a year are undertaken to eliminate causes of significant scrap losses. G. The ratio of productivity to costs is improved by 1% every 6 months.
3. Developing subordinates	A. New employees are inducted and trained in accordance with a definite plan. B. Performance reviews are held with all subordinates on at least an annual basis. C. Discussions are held with subordinates at least quarterly to see that performance improvement takes place according to plan. D. Responsibilities and authority are delegated to subordinates on a planned basis.

Source: Adapted with permission of the publisher, from *How to Improve Performance Through Appraisal and Coaching.* Copyright © 1982 by Donald L. Kirkpatrick. Published by AMACOM, a division of the American Management Association. All rights reserved.

Figure 9.10
MANAGEMENT BY OBJECTIVES (MBO) EXAMPLE

Results listed will be accomplished during FY 199–.

1. Revise sales reporting procedures by October 15 so computerized reports can reach all branch managers by the tenth of each month.
2. Establish a procedure for responding to customer complaints by March 15.
3. Increase market share in the midwest region by 5%.
4. Revise, publish, and distribute new procedures for collecting overdue accounts by August 1.
5. Conduct three regional meetings during November to introduce new reporting procedures.
6. Design a new product bulletin to be mailed to all current customers by May 1.
7. Open two new branches in the Midwest before December 1.
8. Increase direct product profit by 4% for replacement parts sales.
9. Reduce cost of goods sold by 6%.
10. Investigate the potential net gain in sales volume and profit that could be realized if auto parts stores were added to present sales distribution channels.

---

is considered to be acceptable on a continuing basis. Figure 9.10 is an example of MBO goals for a sales manager.

How to Make Nondiscriminatory Appraisals

The key to making nondiscriminatory appraisals is really quite simple—but not always so easy to do. The key is to *evaluate all employees on the basis of job performance only, be consistent in your application, apply criteria objectively to all employees, and document, document, document.*

Evaluating employees on the basis of job performance means judging only the way they do their jobs without regard to their age, race, gender, religion, or national origin and putting aside any personal likes or dislikes. For example, you may have a preconceived notion that older workers are dependable but not open to new ideas and therefore are resistant to change. As an *individual,* you can believe anything you choose; as a *supervisor,* you must put aside your preconceptions about age.

WHAT CAN THE SUPERVISOR DO?

Most supervisors have little control over the types of appraisal formats used in their companies. However, they should be aware of the various formats and the strengths and weaknesses of each, be able to use the current format to its best advantage, and be prepared to suggest alternative methods when appropriate.

Consistency in evaluating performance means that given the same information, the way you evaluate Susie Perkins today is the way you will evaluate her 2 weeks from now—or 2 months from now. Applying criteria objectively to all is simply being fair and not letting your personal feelings interfere with your appraisal.

Documentation is very important, especially when supervisors meet with workers to review the appraisal. If an employee earns a high rating on productivity, the supervisor should be able to say, "Smitty, in March, April, and May you reached your goal of securing five new service contracts each month and in June, July, and August, you exceeded your goals." If an employee receives a low rating on attendance, the supervisor should be able to say, "Jane, you were late on March 10 and 25, on April 2 and 6 you left early, and on . . ."

Providing Feedback

Performance appraisal feedback may be given to employees by providing a copy of the written appraisal and by conducting a postappraisal interview. Either or both methods of providing feedback are acceptable, although a combination of both a written appraisal and face-to-face feedback is preferable.

Written

Feedback through written appraisals is usually provided by making a copy of the supervisor's appraisal available to the employee. The written appraisal may be accompanied by a transmittal note from the supervisor calling attention to the more important points made in the performance appraisal. The note may also include an invitation for the employee to make an appointment with the supervisor to discuss the appraisal.

Oral

Following the performance appraisal, many supervisors conduct postappraisal interviews. The purposes of the interview are to be sure there are no misunderstandings about the performance appraisal ratings, to allow employees to share their attitudes and feelings about their job performance, to provide an opportunity for a straightforward and honest discussion with ample time for questions and answers, and to build a better relationship between supervisors and workers.

Preparing for the Interview

The supervisor's objectives for the performance appraisal interview should be to inform, encourage, and give recognition. To accomplish these objectives, the supervisor must plan. The planning checklist in Figure 9.11 provides some general guidelines for preparing for the appraisal interview.

Conducting the Interview

Most supervisors do not look forward to performance appraisal interviews, especially at the beginning, when they have had no experience in providing feedback.

	Yes	No
Figure 9.11		
PLANNING CHECKLIST		
Find quiet, neutral place for interview	——	——
Review employee's job description, performance standards, objectives, and background	——	——
Give employee sufficient advance notification	——	——
Ask employee to come prepared with completed self-appraisal	——	——
Clarify purpose of interview	——	——
Prepare list of positive behaviors and compliments	——	——
Prepare list of inappropriate actions and behaviors and how to discuss them	——	——
Anticipate reactions to comments and plan how to handle them	——	——
Keep a detailed list of facts to support your appraisal	——	——
Prepare a list of corrective actions you plan to take	——	——
Write down the approach you plan to use to get acceptance of corrective actions	——	——
Make a note of follow-up activities	——	——

The first performance appraisal interviews, and sometimes even subsequent interviews, make supervisors nervous and uncertain. The careful planning described in Figure 9.11 is one way to reduce the apprehension usually associated with appraisal interviews. If you are well prepared for an interview, are confident in your appraisal of the employee's performance, and have reviewed all the information, much of your apprehension will disappear.

Conducting the interview requires planning also. Review what you wish to say to the employee. Define the order in which you will discuss the evaluation. Be prepared to develop an action plan with the employee. Make the performance appraisal interview a productive experience for both you and the employee.

Keys to a productive performance appraisal interview are:[3]

1. *State the purpose, and create a positive attitude.* You might say, "As we discussed when this meeting was arranged, our purpose today is to discuss your performance since the last appraisal and determine how we can help you do your job better or more efficiently. Let's together review our performance appraisals— your self-appraisal and my evaluation. Then we can work on an action plan for both the areas of strength and the areas in which some improvement may be needed."

    By setting the stage in this manner, the supervisor provides a structure for the session. The employee also realizes that the discussion will be a two-way one, with both the employee and the supervisor having an opportunity to state their views. In addition, the employee is aware that the outcome of the discussion will be an action plan for his or her development—one that the employee has played a major part in developing.

2. *Be specific.* Provide specific examples of both positive and negative job performance. It is not enough to say to the employee, "You're doing just fine" or "You just don't seem to be doing as good a job as you could." These appraisals do not give any information that will help the employee improve. More helpful feedback is given when the supervisor specifies performance that is satisfactory as well as performance that could be improved.

3. *Give behavioral feedback.* Behavioral feedback provides information about something the employee does and something over which the employee has control. "You're too tall" is feedback about something over which the employee has no control. "You were five minutes late for work yesterday and again today" describes an employee's behavior and something that can be changed. "You have a poor attitude" is too general; that appraisal could mean any number of things. "You have not been getting along with your fellow workers recently. Can you describe the problem as you see it?" is more specific and behaviorally stated.

4. *Be flexible.* Sometimes your appraisal on a particular dimension may be incorrect because you have not had access to all the information. If you have rated an employee "average" on interpersonal relations and the employee brings to your attention that he has been helping a new employee get acquainted on the job and that he often helps out when another employee is overscheduled, you should be flexible enough to change your rating if the change is justified.

5. *Share responsibility.* Ask "What can I do to help you in the performance of your job?" Make the appraisal a joint venture, offering whatever help it is within your authority to offer.

6. *Listen.* Be an active listener. Encourage the employee to do most of the talking. If you talk 25 percent of the time and listen 75 percent of the time, the performance appraisal interview will be much more productive and informative. The interview should not be a "telling" experience; it should be a "sharing" experience.

7. *Agree on an action plan.* After discussing the performance appraisal and commenting on the employee's strengths and weaknesses, you and the employee should agree on an action plan. The action plan should include notes on the employee's strengths, identify areas in which improvement is needed, specify actions to be taken and who will take those actions, and note when improvement can be expected.

8. *Follow up.* The action plan should include a time frame for follow-up to see if improvement has occurred. Follow-up is vital if improvement or correction is expected. If the action plan specifies that improvement should be noted within 6 weeks, you and the employee should meet in 6 weeks to discuss the outcomes.

COMPETENCY CHECK

Can you cite the keys to a successful performance appraisal interview?

Conducting Difficult Interviews

Ideally, performance appraisals would all go smoothly, as the supervisor and the employee calmly and rationally discuss the employee's performance from their different perspectives. But not all postappraisal interviews are smooth because the employee doesn't play the role expected by the supervisor or the supervisor does not play the role expected by the employee. When this happens, the supervisor needs to be prepared to handle the situation.

Precautions for Minimizing Problems

Some precautions can be taken that will minimize the possibility of a negative reaction from the employee. These include:

1. Never criticize an employee's behavior to another employee. Speak to the person involved, not to others.
2. If the employee has recently made a mistake and you are still angry about it, postpone the appraisal interview until you have calmed down and can objectively discuss your evaluation with the employee.
3. Always conduct the interview in private. People get defensive when they are subjected to criticism in front of their peers.
4. Schedule the interview at a time when the employee is not immersed in a critical job with time constraints. The employee will be in a hurry to get back to the task.
5. Be pleasant, not antagonistic, no matter what feedback you have to give.

Preparations

If the interview may be difficult because you believe the employee will be defensive when the constructive aspects of the appraisal are raised, you must mentally prepare for the discussion. First of all, be absolutely sure that your appraisal is objective and that you have documentation of the behaviors—be sure you are on firm ground. Next, try to anticipate the employee's reactions to your comments and then plan your response. Practice in front of a mirror, if this is your first time to be involved in a potentially difficult appraisal feedback. This way, you can see your expressions as you respond to the employee. Practice until you feel confident that you can respond calmly to the employee, who may strenuously disagree with your evaluation. Role-play with a friend who assumes the position of the employee.

If the discussion gets too heated, stop the interview before you lose your temper and reschedule it for when tempers have had a chance to cool. Continuing an interview that is out of control is counterproductive.

Occasionally supervisors must deal with an employee whom they do not like or who does not like them and who is receiving a deservedly poor evaluation. This is difficult and takes an extra pound of objectivity and self-control. The supervisor *must* try to put his or her own feelings aside and think of this employee as any other employee who is receiving a poor evaluation—one that has been earned. Documentation is extremely important here because good documentation lends credibility to the appraisal and gives the supervisor the confidence required to conduct this performance evaluation in a professional, impersonal manner.

COMPETENCY CHECK

Can you explain the supervisor's preparation for potentially difficult performance appraisal interviews?

WHAT CAN THE SUPERVISOR DO?

After conducting the performance appraisal interview, the supervisor can compare his or her technique with the following checklist:

	Yes	No
❏ **Opening**		
Put the employee at ease?	___	___
Stated the purpose of the interview?	___	___
❏ **Employee Viewpoint**		
Asked how he or she views job and working conditions?	___	___
Asked if there are any problems you need to discuss?	___	___
❏ **Supervisor Viewpoint**		
Made a summary statement only?	___	___
Avoided making comparison to other workers?	___	___
❏ **Desirable Behavior**		
Mentioned one or two such points?	___	___
Emphasized identified strengths?	___	___
❏ **Self-Improvement**		
Mentioned one or two such points?	___	___
Avoided presenting "shortcomings"?	___	___
Discussed work-related topics?	___	___
❏ **Self-Improvement Plans**		
Made it the employee's plan, not yours?	___	___
Played the role of helper or counselor?	___	___
❏ **Advancement Opportunities**		
Mentioned any advancement opportunities?	___	___
Reviewed future possible pay increases?	___	___
Warned poor performers, if necessary?	___	___
❏ **Conclusion**		
Answered questions of general concern?	___	___
Closed interview on a constructive, encouraging note?	___	___

Rewarding Performance

Supervisors give too little salary information to employees, according to a survey of managers in 330 of the 500 largest industrial and service companies.[4] The Towers et al. survey also found that:

❏ 76 percent of the surveyed managers believe supervisors are uncomfortable talking with employees about pay.
❏ 60 percent believe the supervisors in their organizations may not have a clear understanding of the mechanics of the pay system.

❑ 92 percent said supervisors in their organizations do know where they can get answers to pay questions.

Based on the responses to the survey, Towers et al. recommend that companies deal with the sensitive pay issue in a frank and credible way. According to the authors, the key is a thorough, ongoing training program for supervisors that would teach them how to explain the pay program, how to tell employees how their performance affects their pay, and how to respond knowledgeably to questions.

Types of Rewards

As shown in Figure 9.12, rewards may take many forms. The three general types of rewards are those given by the company, those that come from the tasks or the job itself (**intrinsic rewards**), and those the supervisor or manager gives.

Company-established Rewards. Supervisors have no control over company-established rewards except to see that they are administered according to company policy. Note in Figure 9.12 that both monetary compensation and benefits are included in the company-granted rewards. Benefits may include life insurance, health insurance, dental plans, pension plans, child-care centers, and all the other nonmonetary benefits shown in column 1, as well as some others not mentioned. Many companies are offering flexible benefits plans, sometimes called "cafeteria-style" benefits programs. These plans may combine a group of benefits into a package, with workers selecting the cluster that suits their needs, or employees may receive an allowance to apply to the benefits they select.

Intrinsic Rewards. Supervisors have some indirect control over rewards that are intrinsic to the task or job (those shown in column 2 of Figure 9.12). Although the feeling of achievement one gets from performing a job well is internal to the person doing the job, the supervisor can add to this feeling of achievement by assigning additional responsibilities, providing opportunities for growth, redesigning jobs to make them more interesting or provide more variety, and acknowledging work well done. (Refer to Chapter 11 for a discussion of motivation.)

Rewards Given by the Supervisor. The area of rewards over which supervisors have direct control is shown in column 3 of Figure 9.12. These are tools, techniques, and strategies that supervisors can use to reward their employees. Not all these rewards are appropriate for all workers; some workers respond more positively to some rewards than to others. For example, some employees have no interest in advancement but crave attention. Within appropriate boundaries, supervisors can provide that attention. Praise and recognition are powerful rewards if used correctly with those who respond to praise. Praise and other motivators are described in Chapter 11.

COMPETENCY CHECK

Can you list the three general types of rewards and give five examples of each type?

Figure 9.12 TYPICAL EMPLOYEE REWARDS		
Company-given	**Intrinsic to Job**	**Supervisor-given**
Awards	Sense of:	Advancement
Bonuses	Achievement	Attention
Cafeteria	Challenge	Autonomy
Child care	Flexibility	Clear goals/rewards
Clear, consistent policies	Growth	Development
Company car	Interesting work	Feedback
Contests/prizes	Responsibility	Friendship
Dental plan	Self-worth	Honesty
Discounts at company store	Variety	Information
Discounts on company products		Involvement/participation
Elder care		Praise/recognition
Expense account		Support
Flexible working hours		Trust
Free dinners, tickets, etc.		
Gainsharing		
Gifts		
Health insurance		
Legal services		
Life insurance		
Loyalty/appreciation		
Medical insurance		
Offices and furnishings		
Parking space		
Pay		
Pension plans		
Profit sharing		
Promotion		
Security		
Social standing		
Stocks		
Titles		
Use of company equipment and facilities		
Vision plan		

Establishing and Communicating Reward Criteria

Criteria for rewarding employees for their work are usually established by the company and may differ according to the level or position of the employee in the company. Communicating the criteria to employees is a role supervisors need to strengthen. Recall that the Towers et al. survey found that supervisors give too little salary information to employees.

Bases for Rewarding Employees. Companies may choose to reward their employees on the basis of seniority; they may give cost-of-living increases or across-the-board increases; or they may adopt merit-pay or pay-for-performance reward systems. The supervisor's role in seniority, cost-of-living, and across-the-board pay increases is minimal. Supervisors, however, play a major role in reward systems based on pay for performance or merit because supervisors are responsible for evaluating workers' job performance.

Communicating Bases for Rewards.   Employees should know the criteria for compensation decisions. What does an individual employee have to do to receive a pay increase? Changing the criteria for pay adjustments without communicating the changed expectations to the employees is no longer acceptable.

Bases for rewards can be communicated to employees in several ways: through conferences in which the supervisor tells the individual worker what level of performance is expected for what level of pay increase; through group meetings in which the criteria for various levels of pay increases are described; or through a company handbook in which expected performance is clearly described. Whatever the method used to communicate the bases for pay adjustments, the supervisor has a responsibility to provide the information to employees and to ensure opportunities for questions and answers. This, of course, assumes that the supervisors are aware of and understand company compensation policies and practices.

Open- or Closed-Pay System.   Some companies choose to have an **open-pay system,** one in which information is made available to employees who wish to inquire about salaries. A system is considered to be open if salary information is available about either individual pay or pay ranges for a specific job. **Closed-pay systems** provide no salary information, and some companies have a policy prohibiting any discussion among employees about their individual salaries. Employees who violate the policy may be subject to dismissal. Supervisors are obligated to support the company's policy on availability of pay information whether it is an open or a closed policy.

COMPETENCY CHECK
Can you describe the responsibility of the supervisor in establishing and communicating compensation criteria?

Recommending and Administering Rewards

Supervisors play a major role in recommending rewards based on merit or pay for performance. It is therefore important that recommendations for rewards be based on *objective* performance evaluations.

Although merit pay and pay for performance are both based on results of work, the pay method for the two may differ. In a pay-for-performance system, employees' earnings are based on how well they do their jobs. Top performers receive greater monetary rewards than do average performers; average performers receive more than below-average performers. In a merit-pay system, additional compensation is usually awarded only to employees whose work is above average, that is, above the expected standard of performance. The purpose of merit pay, recognition of increased productivity, is defeated if pay increases are given to all employees, regardless of their performance.

To recommend and administer rewards effectively, supervisors should observe the following:

1. Workers should be able to see a relationship between their work effort and their pay. When employees see a relationship between work effort and pay, they are more likely to perform in a way that will give them the rewards they desire.

WHAT CAN THE SUPERVISOR DO?

Supervisors can provide salary information to employees in keeping with company policies regarding how much information is to be made available. Supervisors can also, provided the appropriate systems are in place, make sure that better performance leads to better rewards by maintaining an objective appraisal system. Use the following checklist as a self-check noting the interdependence of the appraisal and reward criteria.

	Yes	No
1. Do job descriptions accurately reflect job content and the skills, effort, and responsibility required?	___	___
2. Are employees accurately classified into jobs based on the work they perform, their skills, and their actual responsibilities?	___	___
3. Are the method and process used to determine job value fair? Do they provide due process?	___	___
4. Are jobs graded accurately, considering skill, effort, responsibility, and working conditions?	___	___
5. Are pay ranges competitive with those of other organizations that employ people in similar jobs?	___	___
6. Do employees understand the criteria used to appraise performance and how the measurement is done?	___	___
7. Are performance criteria appropriate and weighted correctly given their relative importance?	___	___
8. Are employees given an adequate opportunity to review appraisals, and do they have an adequate appeal process?	___	___
9. Are current pay scales equitable, given the skills and performance levels of individuals?	___	___
10. Do employees understand the pay program and how it is supposed to work? If not, what is unclear?	___	___

Source: Robert J. Greene, "Effective Compensation: The How and Why," *Personnel Administrator,* February 1987, p. 115.

COMPETENCY CHECK

Can you cite the four criteria for recommending and administering rewards?

2. Workers should perceive pay recommendations as being equitable. When workers believe that pay recommendations have been based strictly on work performed, there is less conflict among workers and more incentive to perform at higher levels.
3. Workers should perceive salary administration as being consistent and fair. When employees believe salary administration is fair and consistent among workers, there are better relationships among workers and between workers and supervisors. Supervisors are considered to be more objective in the performance of their duties.

4. Supervisors should be sure that all salary decisions are made in a nondiscriminatory way.

Implementing Nondiscriminatory Rewards

Much has been written about our litigious society, and, indeed, more and more employers are being sued by their employees and former employees. It is therefore incumbent upon supervisors to protect both their companies and themselves by being knowledgeable about what is legal and permissible in appraising and rewarding employee performance.

The key to implementing nondiscriminatory rewards is the same as that for administering nondiscriminatory appraisals—make them job-related, consistent, and objective and have good documentation.

All decisions regarding what a worker will earn must be related to job requirements and performance on the job. A supervisor who consistently awards a poor performer satisfactory ratings and average salary increases and then one day says "I can't put up with your poor performance any longer—you're fired!" is placing the company in a vulnerable position if the fired employee chooses to sue the company. Even though the supervisor may have given the poor performer worse appraisals and smaller pay increases than any other worker in the department, the supervisor has still, by giving satisfactory ratings and salary increases, indicated to both the company and the employee that the worker's performance is okay. There is therefore no basis for terminating the employee. For example, one employee was not warned in his annual performance appraisal that his work was so weak he might be terminated. When he was fired, he sued the company and won a judgment for $61,000.[5]

To avoid a situation such as this, both performance appraisals and recommendations for rewards should be based on job performance, criteria applied consistently to all workers, and objective application of criteria.

COMPETENCY CHECK
Can you describe the keys to implementing nondiscriminatory rewards?

Monitoring Comparable Worth

In biblical times, according to Lev. 27:3–4, females of working age were valued at 30 silver shekels while males were valued at 50 shekels.

Comparable worth has been called the "issue of the 1980s," but the controversy associated with it has extended beyond the 1980s and is still a hot topic in the 1990s. **Comparable worth** goes beyond equal pay for equal work, which was addressed in the Equal Pay Act of 1963. That law, a gender-based act, says that people performing essentially the *same* jobs should receive the same pay, except as that pay may be affected by seniority or union contracts. Comparable worth, on the other hand, addresses the issue of pay based on the *value* of the job (as determined by the number of points assigned), whether the jobs are the same or different.

Most working women remain in nursing, secretarial, light-industry, and waitressing jobs that make up a low-paying "pink-collar" ghetto. Supporters of comparable worth say the only way to eliminate the pay bias left from the days of sex-segregated jobs is to revalue all jobs on the basis of the skills and responsibility required. Thus a clerk-typist might seek the same pay as, for example, a warehouse worker, claiming that the jobs are of equal value.[6]

To determine a job's value, a job evaluation must be conducted. A **job evaluation** defines the various factors required, such as job knowledge, communication, accountability, education, planning and decision making, or whatever other factors the company considers important. Typically, the process of doing a job evaluation involves three steps.[7]

1. Developing composite job descriptions, based on information obtained through questionnaires and interviews for the jobs to be evaluated. The use of this information ensures that all job tasks performed by an employee are explicitly stated.
2. Assigning each job a number of points for each of a variety of factors, such as skill, effort, responsibility, and working conditions.

WHAT CAN THE SUPERVISOR DO?

A pay equity problem arises when men and women are employed in such a way as to create male-dominated and female-dominated job classifications and there are pay differentials between them. Usually, a classification or job family is considered to be gender-dominated if 70 percent or more of the employees are male or female. With that parameter in mind, the following measures to minimize the pay equity liability are recommended.

1. *Job design.* Job responsibilities/tasks should be analyzed to minimize the number of stereotypical "male" or "female" tasks: typing, manual dexterity, weight lifting, etc. Dispersing these tasks will assist in integrating the job categories.
2. *Recruiting.* Diligently seek to attract males (or females) into gender-dominated jobs. Equal utilization of males and females in a job negates major pay equity problems. Recruiting specifications need to be scrutinized to eliminate gender segregation in the selection process (heavy lifting, typing, excessive experience or education, and any skill or trait favoring one gender).
3. *Job evaluation.* Examine methods and factors for their impact on sex stereotyping. Evaluators need to be schooled to eliminate their intentional and unintentional biases. Evaluate jobs based on content—not the title of the incumbent—and be sure that both males and females are active in the process. Provide for an independent review of evaluation results by someone sensitive to, and knowledgeable about, pay equity problems.
4. *Market pricing.* Carefully designed market pricing of jobs is still a strong defense against pay equity claims. The selection of surveys—e.g., quality, industry, geographic area covered, number used—must be carefully evaluated.

3. Comparing jobs with similar numbers of points to see whether the salaries are similar and, if they are not, determining whether the difference is related to the gender of those filling the jobs.

Studies show that patterns of discrepancies in pay still exist in the workplace. Job evaluations have uncovered a consistent pattern of undervaluing jobs held by females. Examples of that pattern are in Minnesota, where the category of typing pool supervisor (female) with a calculated job value of 199 points earned $1373 per month while painters (male) with 185 points earned $1707 per month; or in San Jose, California, where both the senior legal secretary (female) and senior carpenter (male) jobs were valued at 226 points but the secretary's pay was $454 less per month than the carpenter's pay. In Washington State, licensed practical nurse

5. *Internal/external reconciliation.* A conflict often arises when trying to reconcile the internal ranking or hierarchical order of jobs with external job worth as measured by market pay levels. Consistency of system application is the key for all levels of jobs. If the external market takes precedence over the internal evaluation of V.P. Marketing (male), it should also be the deciding factor for the typist (female) position.

6. *Upward mobility.* Job-posting programs, career ladders, cross-training and skill-training programs can provide mobility for both genders into and out of gender-dominated positions. The problem of the "glass ceiling" is still present in many organizations. The "glass ceiling" places a cap on how high in an organization women and minorities can go. In December 1993, women who claimed they were stuck in low-paying jobs at a California grocery chain won up to $107 million, which has been described as a wake-up call for an industry that has failed to see women as management material.

7. *Management training.* Sensitivity to the liabilities of pay equity can eliminate current and future problems.

8. *Salary administration.* Analysis of position in salary range, years of experience in the position, starting salaries, promotional increases, merit increases, and performance evaluation by gender assists in identifying historical, current, and prospective problems. Sound policy design and definition should include constant audit mechanisms.

Source: "Human Resource Management Ideas and Trends in Personnel," *Commerce Clearing House,* no. 104, Nov. 18, 1985, p. 182.

(female) and corrections officer (male) jobs were valued at 173 points each, but the pay differential between the two jobs was $416 per month.[8]

Advocates of comparable worth believe it is a fair way to value jobs and establish pay. They try to value jobs that are traditionally female more objectively and equitably and to reward workers based on the value of the jobs they hold. Opponents of comparable worth believe it is an artificial way of elevating pay and that the *marketplace* (supply and demand) should determine the pay for a particular job. Opponents also point to the difficulty of valuing jobs except in an artificial way. As expressed by a Washington, D.C., attorney, "You tell me how to set up a system outside the marketplace that objectively compares rock musicians and brain surgeons, and I'll tell you whether nurses and plumbers should have comparable pay. But I suspect it can't be done in any but an artificial way."[9]

COMPETENCY REVIEW

1. Define *performance appraisal*.
2. Discuss who is responsible for providing input and/or conducting performance appraisals.
3. List and describe the two major purposes of performance appraisals.
4. Diagram and describe the performance appraisal sequence.
5. Identify five uses of performance appraisal information.
6. List and explain five types of rater errors.
7. Describe three performance appraisal formats.
8. Tell how the supervisor can conduct nondiscriminatory appraisals.
9. Explain the importance of performance appraisal feedback.
10. Describe two methods of providing feedback to employees.
11. Explain the importance of the supervisor's role in performance appraisals.
12. Describe eight planning steps a supervisor should take when preparing for a performance appraisal interview.
13. List six actions a supervisor should take when conducting a performance appraisal interview.
14. Explain the supervisor's preparation for potentially difficult performance appraisal interviews.
15. List three general types of rewards and give five examples of each type.
16. Describe the role of the supervisor in establishing and communicating compensation criteria.
17. Explain four criteria for recommending and administering rewards effectively.
18. Explain how a supervisor can implement nondiscriminatory reward systems.
19. Define *comparable worth* and tell how it differs from "equal pay for equal work."
20. Describe how job evaluation is linked to comparable worth.

APPLICATIONS

1. Each of the statements given below is an example of performance appraisal feedback. If you think the statement gives specific behavioral feedback, state your reason(s). If not, rewrite the statement to describe specific behavior. You may make any assumptions about performance standards in your rewrite.
   a. Receptionist: "You get entirely too many personal calls. You should not let personal business interfere so much with your job."
   b. Dental technician: "You seem to be having a problem relating to our patients."
   c. Hotel maid: "The hotel rooms don't look as clean as they should."
   d. Assembly-line worker: "The level of rejects for your part of the line is good. Keep up the good work."
   e. Parts counterperson: "You're not as courteous to our phone customers as you are to our over-the-counter sales customers."
   f. Telemarketer: "You're really doing a good job for a person so new to the job. You've already exceeded our goal by 18 percent."
   g. Welder: "Your safety record is below standard."
   h. Salesperson: "The language you use around your peers as well as our customers is unacceptable. You had better clean up your act—or else!"
2. Suzanne Silverman and several other supervisors are discussing the performance appraisals they conducted last week. Identify the rater errors in the comments made by Suzanne and her colleagues:
   a. "I just don't believe women are capable of handling hard physical labor."
   b. "Personally, I like Julie. She's very much like me."
   c. "All of my employees are pretty much the same, so I give them all a satisfactory rating."
   d. "It's really hard to forget all the times Joe was late. Why, only last week he was late twice!"
   e. "Well, from my point of view, people really have to show me something if they want better than a satisfactory rating from me."
   f. "I'd rather rate everybody 'good' than hassle about it."
   g. "Barbara is so knowledgeable about repairs; she just seems to be good in everything she does."
   Identify the rater errors present in the comments by Suzanne Silverman and her colleagues.
3. You are the sales supervisor in the toy department of a large retail store specializing in children's clothing and toys. There have been complaints about the performance appraisal format currently in use, and you have been asked to recommend a format to be used in evaluating salespersons. Which format would you choose? Why? If you were asked, would you recommend that the same format be used throughout the company in all departments? Why, or why not?
4. You are the supervisor in a company that is being pressured by some of the employees to consider a comparable-worth plan. Take a position on comparable worth, and write a memo providing a rationale for your position.
5. Rate a performance appraisal system, using the checklist in Figure 9.13.

Figure 9.13

PERFORMANCE APPRAISAL CHECKLIST

	YES	NO
1. Is the performance appraisal system based on the measure of effective employee behavior?		
2. Is the performance appraisal based on an accurate reflection of job performance? (The overall measure of job performance is fundamentally related to critical aspects of the job.)		
3. Is the performance appraisal system based on a thorough analysis of the job?		
4. Is the performance appraisal system based on job analysis data pertaining to:		
(a) knowledge and skills?		
(b) specific rates or levels (standards) of performance?		
5. Does the appraisal system meet the criteria of Title VII federal guidelines?		
6. Has empirical data been collected to prove the validity of the method for the purpose for which it is being used?		
7. Does the performance appraisal method differentially discriminate against a specific subgroup of the working population?		
8. Are performance ratings all job related?		
9. Were performance measures developed through job analysis?		
10. Are raters able to observe the performance they are to rate?		
11. Are ratings collected and scored under standardized circumstances?		
12. Have the employees been advised of the critical requirements of their jobs?		
13. Are performance appraisals conducted at least once a year?		

	YES	NO
14. Are the employees evaluated solely on the extent to which they fulfill the critical requirements of the job?		
15. Are rewards tied directly to performance?		
16. Was the job analysis conducted at a time when the job was reasonably stable?		
17. Are criterion measures reliable?		
18. Does the appraisal instrument enable the appraiser to differentiate good from poor performers?		
19. Do appraisers:		
(a) have a thorough knowledge of the job?		
(b) have ample opportunity to see the individual on the job?		
(c) have the expertise in interpretation of what is seen?		
20. Do appraisers have formal training in:		
(a) the appraisal system?		
(b) the appraisal instrument?		
(c) the job of individuals being evaluated?		
21. Are raters trained to reduce rating errors?		
22. Do subordinates have a high degree of participation in the performance appraisal?		
23. Do subordinates participate in the setting of specific goals they are to achieve?		
24. Are subordinates "free" to discuss problems that may be hampering their current job performance?		
25. Do the supervisor and subordinate agree on a plan of action to be taken until the next review?		

Case I

A DIFFERENT TWIST ON COMPARABLE WORTH

According to the June 8, 1992, issue of *The Wall Street Journal*, S. Lichtenberg & Co. was sued by the Amalgamated Clothing and Textile Workers Union for unfair labor practices and alleged violations of equal employment law. The law firm representing the union framed a novel legal argument—that the comparable-worth theory extends to racial discrimination. The theory holds that employers illegally discriminate if they pay women less than men for jobs that are dissimilar but equal in value or that require equal competence. The union alleges that Lichtenberg had discriminated by paying its white male supervisors more than its black female curtain makers, jobs that require similar levels of competence. Lawyers arguing this case have also filed a similar suit against *The Washington Post* on behalf of the Washington-Baltimore Newspaper Guild. The law firm representing Lichtenberg said there was no merit to Mr. Newman's charges.

1. Do you believe there is a legitimate link between racial discrimination and comparable worth? Why?
2. What would your argument be if you were representing the Amalgamated Clothing and Textile Workers Union?
3. What would your argument be if you were representing S. Lichtenberg & Co.?
4. What do you think was the outcome of the suit?

Case II

DISCUSS YOUR SALARY, AND YOU'RE FIRED!

Beach Supplies and Services, Inc. (BSS), has long had a policy of pay secrecy. The employees have generally ignored the policy and, while not discussing individual pay in front of the supervisors, have discussed their salaries with one another. Company policy includes the statement "Any employee overheard discussing salary with another employee may be subject to immediate dismissal."

Miguel Garcia is relatively new to BSS. He was hired 6 months ago as supervisor of the design department. Garcia came to the company with 10 years' experience with a competitor that had a very liberal open-pay policy. Although he read the handbook and is aware of the policy, Garcia chooses to ignore it when he overhears employees discussing their pay. In fact, Garcia believes such a policy is archaic and foolish.

After the performance appraisals last week, when employees were told what their annual pay would be for the next year, there was a lot of grumbling among workers as they openly discussed their salaries. May Wilson, an employee with a great deal of seniority, was particularly upset when she heard that other employees with less seniority had gotten larger pay increases than she had. May even discussed this discrepancy with workers in several other departments. When the other supervisors overheard these discussions, they agreed that Garcia should be told and that he should take action.

1. Should Garcia follow company policy?
2. Do you favor a closed- or an open-pay system?
3. Does your preference depend on whether you are a worker or a supervisor? Why?
4. What are the benefits and what are the potential problems with a closed-pay system? An open-pay system?

REFERENCES

1. Quoted in Evelyn Eichel and Henry E. Bender, *Performance Appraisal: A Study of Current Techniques,* American Management Association, New York, 1984, p. 9.
2. Glenn L. DeBiasi, "The Development, Implementation, and Evaluation of a Nursing Performance Evaluation System," position paper, Norfolk, Va., August 1982.
3. Ibid.
4. Towers, Perrin, Forster, and Crosby survey, reported in "Human Resource Management Ideas and Trends in Personnel," *Commerce Clearing House,* no. 124, Aug. 22, 1986, p. 133.
5. James M. Jenks, brochure, Alexander Hamilton Institute, New York, undated.
6. Iamar Lewin, "Comparable Worth," *The Virginian-Pilot and The Ledger-Star,* Jan. 29, 1984.
7. Robert L. Farnquist, David R. Armstrong, and Russell P. Strausbaugh, "Pandora's Worth: The San Jose Experience," *Public Personnel Management Journal,* vol. 12, no. 4, Winter 1983, p. 397.
8. Lewin, loc. cit.
9. Farnquist, op. cit., p. 398.

SUGGESTED READINGS

Bradt, Jeffrey A.: "Pay for Impact," *Personnel Journal,* May 1991, p. 76.
Brown, Melvin, Jr.: "How Am I Doing?" *Corrections Today,* December 1990, p. 66.
Cameron, Jeffrey R.: "Performance Evaluations Reevaluated," *The Police Chief,* February 1989, p. 53.
Cumming, Charles M.: "New Directions in Salary Administration," *Personnel,* January 1987.
Geis, A. Arthur: "Making Merit Pay Work," *Personnel,* January 1987.
Guinn, Kathleen A., and Roberta J. Corona: "Putting a Price on Performance," *Personnel Journal,* May 1991, p. 72.
Hoevemeyer, Victoria A.: "Performance-Based Compensation: Miracle or Waste?" *Personnel Journal,* July 1989, p. 64.

Kanter, Rosabeth Moss: "The Changing Basis for Pay," *Society,* September/October 1989, p. 54.

Kanter, Rosabeth Moss: "From Status to Contribution: Some Organizational Implications on the Changing Basis for Pay," *Personnel,* January 1987.

Krein, Theodore J.: "Performance Reviews that Rate an 'A,'" *Personnel,* May 1990, p. 38.

Lee, Charles: "Poor Performance Appraisals Do More Harm Than Good," *Personnel Journal,* September 1989, p. 4.

"Let Your People Know Where They Stand," *Front Line Management,* no. 111, The Economic Press, Inc., 1975.

Levy, Martin: "Almost-Perfect Performance Appraisals," *Personnel Journal,* April 1989, p. 76.

"Making It Through the Difficult Performance Review," *Supervisory Sense,* July 1986.

Norman, Carol A., and Robert A. Zawacki: "Team Appraisals—Team Approach," *Personnel Journal,* September 1991, p. 101.

Odiorne, George S.: "The Trend Toward the Quarterly Performance Review," *Business Horizons,* July/August 1990, p. 38.

Phillips, Kenneth R.: "Red Flags in Performance Appraisals," *Training and Development Journal,* March 1987, p. 80.

"The Positive Way to Criticize," *Front Line Management,* no. 105, The Economic Press, Inc., 1976.

Sahl, Robert J.: "Design Effective Performance Appraisals," *Personnel Journal,* October 1990, p. 53.

Sashkin, Marshall. *A Manager's Guide to Performance Management,* American Management Association, New York, 1986, p. 31.

Waldrop, Heidi: "Rating with Mirrors," *Computer Decisions,* September 1986.

Wallach, Arthur E., and Lauren Hite Jackson: "Getting an Answer to 'How Am I Doing?'" *Personnel,* June 1985.

GLOSSARY

absolute format   Evaluating each employee's performance without comparing it to the performance of others.

behaviorally anchored rating scale (BARS)   A rating method that concentrates on job behaviors, not on personal traits or characteristics.

central tendency   Judging most workers as average.

closed-pay system   Compensation system that provides no salary information to anyone other than the individual employee regarding his/her own salary.

comparable worth   Addresses the issue of pay based on the value of the job, whether the jobs are the same or different.

comparative format   Format that allows appraisals through comparisons of workers on their overall performance.

critical incidents method   Recording both the positive and the negative actions that employees take in performing their jobs.

forced choice   Placing a predetermined percentage of workers in each of several levels of performance.

graphic rating scale   A form containing a number of items relating to job performance where the rater checks where the employee scores on the continuum.

halo effect   Letting a rating on one factor affect the rating on all other factors of the performance appraisal.

intrinsic rewards   Compensation that comes from the satisfaction of the job itself.

job evaluation   Defines the various factors required to perform a job well.

management by objectives (MBO)   Establishing goals through negotiation between supervisor and worker and measuring performance by the level of goal achievement.

narrative method   Requires the rater to give a written description of a worker's performance.

open-pay system   A compensation system in which information is made available to employees who wish to inquire about salaries.

outcome-based format   Judging employees on the basis of performance outcomes.

performance appraisal   The process of measuring and reporting employee behavior and accomplishments for a given period for the purpose of improving job performance.

ranking   Comparing the job performance of all employees and then placing them in either ascending or descending order.

standards of performance   Comparing actual accomplishments with a list of conditions that will be fulfilled if the job is considered to be performed well.

weighted checklist   A form similar to a graphic rating scale, but assigns a value to each of the items.

THE
Leading AND
Motivating
Function

STUDYING THIS CHAPTER WILL ENABLE YOU TO:

1. Define *leadership* and *power.*

2. Discuss five kinds of power.

3. Describe briefly several traditional leadership theories.

4. Identify the forces the supervisor should consider when choosing a leadership style.

5. Discuss four contemporary leadership styles.

6. Define *self-leadership* and identify the responsibilities of a supervisor of a self-directed work team.

CHAPTER OUTLINE

C H A P

THE Supervisor's Role IN Leadership

E R 1 0

pper management establishes a foundation of effective leadership by thinking through the organization's mission, defining it, and establishing it clearly and visibly. The organization's leader sets the goals and priorities and sets and maintains the standards. Effective leaders are rarely permissive; but when things go wrong, they do not blame others. Because an effective leader knows that he or she, and no one else, is ultimately responsible, he or she is not afraid of strength in associates and subordinates. An effective leader wants strong associates, encourages them, pushes them, and glories in them. Because a leader holds him/herself ultimately responsible for the mistakes of associates and subordinates, a leader also sees the triumphs of associates and subordinates as personal triumphs, rather than as threats.[1] Effective leaders are on every level; they are not just the CEOs. Supervisors can be effective leaders as well.

Companies that are determined to win over customers from their competitors have learned that the way they treat people makes a big difference. In these companies, "empowerment" and "teamwork" are terms that mean something. Jack Welch of General Electric, who was once nicknamed "Neutron Jack" for eliminating so many people while leaving the buildings standing, announced in GE's 1992 annual report that people skills were now top priority and that "the autocrat, the big shot, and the tyrant" were on their way out.[2]

This chapter focuses on some of the research findings in leadership. Our purpose here is confined to introducing some basic leadership styles and to illustrating the use of different styles in different situations.

Power and Leadership

 Leadership is the process of influencing others to work toward the accomplishment of organizational goals and objectives. Incorporated into that definition are the basic requirements of personal integrity, vision, responsibility, and trust. Leaders influence people through power and authority; but leadership and power are not the same thing. **Power** is the extent to which an individual is able to influence others so they respond to directions. Influencing others on behalf of the organization is the job of an effective supervisor.[3]

Power comes from a variety of sources. Think of the influence of these people: Albert Einstein, Michael Jordan, Barbra Streisand, Lee Iacocca, Bill Clinton, Saddam Hussein, Margaret Thatcher. Each is from a different walk of life, and though all have or have had power, each has had it for a different reason. How does one get power? In the view of J. R. P. French and B. Raven,[4] there are five kinds of power:

1. **Reward power.** You have reward power when your workers see that you have the ability to provide them with something they want, such as pay increases, promotions, or feelings of pride, belonging, or sense of worth.
2. **Coercive power.** As a supervisor, you have coercive power if your workers see you as a source of punishment, such as assigning difficult jobs, isolating a worker from the group, blocking promotions, or giving low ratings on performance appraisals. Coercive power is based on fear.

3. **Legitimate power.** When you are given the job of supervisor and the authority that accompanies it, legitimate power is part of the package. This is sometimes called *position power.* Workers tend to view their bosses as having a certain inherent level of power and the authority to carry out the job.

4. **Referent power.** If workers see in you qualities such as competence, fairness, and consideration, they are likely to accept you as a role model and may even try to emulate you. Workers typically will accept your influence in order to increase their identification with you. This personal power may derive from an attractive personality and charm, sometimes called *charisma.* Sam Walton, founder of Wal-Mart; Lee Iacocca, former CEO of Chrysler Corporation; and Adolf Hitler have often been described as charismatic leaders.

5. **Expert power.** If your workers see you as highly skilled and knowledgeable in your field, you may lead through expert power. Their respect for your expertise will make them more willing to follow your direction on the job.

COMPETENCY CHECK
Can you discuss power in relation to leadership?

Traditional Leadership Styles

There have been many attempts to identify and describe traditional leadership styles. We shall examine several of these styles.

Trait Theory

The perception of leadership is important because leadership style is not what the leader thinks it is but what the followers think it is. Early leadership theories focused on what leaders were like rather than on the actions they took. Researchers tried to identify the personality traits of known leaders that could be used in predicting leadership success in others. Ghiselli and other researchers found certain traits to be common among successful leaders.[5] Among these traits were supervisory ability, occupational achievement, intelligence, self-actualization, self-assurance, and decisiveness.[6]

Personality and social traits, as well as physical characteristics, were examined, and findings seemed to suggest that leaders tended to be more intelligent, more extroverted, more dominant, and more decisive than followers, as well as bigger and taller. Closer examination, however, revealed some contradictions. It was noted that not all the traits were applicable to all situations, leading one researcher to conclude that "the chance of finding a set of universally effective leadership traits is nil."[7]

While it is acknowledged today that certain traits may influence a person's ability to lead, the same traits have not been shown to be reliable predictors of leadership success for all managers or in all situations. More realistic predictors may be what leaders do that makes them effective—their behaviors.

Behavioral Theory

How leaders delegate tasks, communicate with subordinates, motivate subordinates, and carry out their tasks are behaviors that help make a leader effective.

Although behaviors can be learned, those appropriate in one situation may not be appropriate in another. Leadership qualities and behaviors that are effective currently may change as an organization's culture changes. When a business grows from its early entrepreneurial beginning into a medium-size or large corporation, the leadership style that was effective for the entrepreneurs may be inappropriate for the structure and culture of a large organization.

COMPETENCY CHECK

Can you explain the trait and behavioral theories of leadership?

Researchers generally view leadership behavior as focusing on one of two styles when working with subordinates: a task-oriented style and an employee-oriented style. *Task-oriented* supervisors closely supervise subordinates to ensure that the task is performed to their satisfaction. *Employee-oriented* supervisors encourage subordinates to perform tasks by allowing them to participate in decisions that affect them and by being friendly, trusting, and respectful toward subordinates.[8]

Theory X and Theory Y

Some theories of leadership center around the way in which the leader views people in the work environment. A classic among these is Douglas McGregor's theory on the assumptions we make about people in the workplace. This theory often is viewed in both a leadership and a motivation context.

McGregor felt that a leader's views about people and their behavior largely determine his or her style of operating. He cited two sets of assumptions and labeled them *theory X* and *theory Y.*[9]

Theory X leadership style assumes the following:

 1. People have an inherent dislike for work and will avoid it if possible.
2. People must be coerced, controlled, directed, and threatened with punishment in order to get them to work.
3. The average human prefers to be directed, wishes to avoid responsibility, and has relatively little ambition.

Theory Y leadership style assumes that:

1. The expenditure of physical and mental effort in work is as natural as play or rest.
2. People can exercise self-direction and self-control in the service of objectives to which they are committed.
3. The average human learns, under the right conditions, not only to accept responsibility but to seek it, and that the more responsibility the organization is willing to give its people, the harder they will work in pursuing its goals.[10]

If you are a theory X supervisor, you assume your workers are unwilling to accept responsibility; therefore, you don't assign tasks that require a high level of responsibility for the outcome. This can become a self-fulfilling prophesy—your workers have no major responsibilities, and so, in your view, they are not responsible workers. On the other hand, if you are a theory Y supervisor, you assume that your workers want responsibility and want to be included in important decisions. Therefore,

WHAT CAN THE SUPERVISOR DO?

You can start learning about yourself by examining your assumptions about people at work. Respond to the following questions and analyze your tendencies toward theory X and theory Y. Your instructor will help you determine and interpret your score.

	Strongly Agree	Agree	Disagree	Strongly Disagree
1. Almost everyone could probably improve his or her job performance quite a bit if he or she really wanted to.	__	__	__	__
2. It's unrealistic to expect people to show the same enthusiasm for their work as for their favorite leisure-time activities.	__	__	__	__
3. Even when given encouragement by the boss, very few people show the desire to improve themselves on the job.	__	__	__	__
4. If you give people enough money, they are less likely to worry about such intangibles as status or individual recognition.	__	__	__	__
5. Usually when people talk about wanting more responsible jobs, they really mean they want more money and status.	__	__	__	__
6. Being tough with people will usually get them to do what you want.	__	__	__	__
7. Because most people don't like to make decisions on their own, it's hard to get them to assume responsibility.	__	__	__	__
8. A good way to get people to do more work is to crack down on them once in a while.	__	__	__	__
9. It weakens a person's prestige whenever he or she has to admit that a subordinate has been right and he has been wrong.	__	__	__	__
10. The most effective supervisor is one who gets the result management expects, regardless of the methods used in handling people.	__	__	__	__
11. It's too much to expect that people will try to do a good job without being prodded by their boss.	__	__	__	__
12. The boss who expects his or her people to set their own standards for superior performance will probably find they don't set them very high.	__	__	__	__
13. If people don't use much imagination and ingenuity on the job, it's probably because relatively few people have much of either.	__	__	__	__
14. One problem in asking for the ideas of subordinates is that their perspective is too limited for their suggestions to be of much practical value.	__	__	__	__
15. It's only human nature for people to try to do as little work as they can get away with.	__	__	__	__
Total Checks	__	__	__	__

COMPETENCY
CHECK
Can you compare
the assumptions
made by theory X
and theory Y
leaders?

you assign them responsible tasks and allow them freedom in making decisions that affect their work.

McGregor's theory X and theory Y are not "polar opposites; X is not bad and Y is not necessarily good."[11] Where workers *do* behave irresponsibly, are lazy, and respond only to coercion, the supervisor should examine all the elements of the situation to find the reason for the behavior and to find the best leadership "fit" among people, tasks, and the organization.[12]

✗ The Leadership Continuum *or Range*

Leadership often has been portrayed in terms of the degree of decision-making input the supervisor allows from followers. According to Robert Tannenbaum and Warren H. Schmidt, there is a continuum, or range, of leadership behavior available to supervisors when making decisions. Each type of decision-making behavior has a corresponding degree of authority used by the supervisor and a related amount of freedom available, or delegated, to subordinates. The leadership continuum is illustrated in Figure 5.1 on page 117.[13]

At the extreme left side of the model is the authoritarian or autocratic leader who makes all decisions, maintains high control, and allows little subordinate freedom. At the extreme right side of the model is the democratic leader who encourages participation in decision making, exercises little control, and allows much subordinate freedom and self-direction.   *lazze faire*

The leadership continuum theory holds that different situations require different leadership styles. Tannenbaum and Schmidt stress that factors, or forces, that influence a supervisor's determination of which leadership behavior to use in making decisions include the following:

1. *Forces in the leader.* Forces in the supervisor that influence the leadership style include his or her value system or feelings about delegating and degree of confidence in subordinates; personal leadership tendencies—authoritarian or participative; and feelings of security in uncertain situations, or tolerance for ambiguity.
2. *Forces in subordinates.* Subordinates are different, and their preferences for leadership vary according to their need for independence—need and want direction or not; readiness to assume responsibility; tolerance for ambiguity (need specific or general directions); interest in the problem and perception of its importance; understanding of and identification with company goals; expectation of sharing in decision making.
3. *Forces in the situation.* Leadership style is influenced by the type of organization—centralized or decentralized; how effectively the group works together; the work group's knowledge and experience relevant to the problem; time pressure; demands from upper levels of management; and outside demands from government, unions, and society in general.[14]

Using the continuum and these forces, for an authoritarian supervisor who is accustomed to directing dependent workers under boss-centered leadership in a centralized organization, a leadership style near the left end of the continuum may be the most appropriate. But if you are a new supervisor with a participative orientation and come to a workplace that has the other conditions described, you will have some adjusting to do to prevent confusion among workers who are accustomed to receiving orders. Before your participative style can be effective, both the workers and the work climate will have to be changed; this will take planning and must occur over time. Chapter 8 addresses the change process.

The Leadership Grid®

A classic leadership model is the Managerial Grid® theory of Blake and Mouton.[15] As shown in Figure 10.1, the Managerial Grid (republished as the Leadership Grid® Figure in 1991 by Robert Blake and Anne Adams McCanse) is a two-dimensional

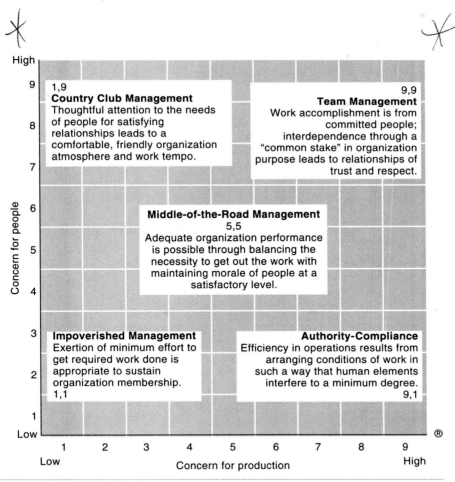

**Figure 10.1
THE LEADERSHIP
GRID® FIGURE**

Source: The Leadership Grid® Figure from *Leadership Dilemmas—Grid Solutions,* by Robert R. Blake and Anne Adams McCanse (formerly the Managerial Grid Figure by Robert R. Blake and Jane S. Mouton), Gulf Publishing Company, Houston, p. 29. Copyright © 1991 by Scientific Methods, Inc. Reproduced by permission of the owners.

display of seven leadership styles.[16] Through an interactive process with feedback, managers are assisted to locate their own leadership assumptions regarding their concern for people and concern for production in relation to these seven styles, including paternalism and opportunism, which are not shown. Although there are 81 points on the grid, Blake and McCanse used the corners to show the extremes and the center for a balanced position.

A supervisor who is primarily concerned with production and shows little concern for people is a 9,1 leader (9 in concern for production; 1 in concern for people). These leaders want to maintain a tight control over their workers in order to complete tasks efficiently; human relations are unnecessary. This is the *authority-compliance* or *task management style*.

A supervisor who is primarily concerned with people and shows little concern for production is a 1,9 leader. These leaders avoid conflicts and try to be well liked. The task is less important to these leaders; they are more interested in good interpersonal relations and keeping people happy. This is the *country club management style*.

The supervisor who tries to balance the concerns for people and production, though this leader provides only an adequate level of concern for the two dimensions, is a 5,5 leader. This center position on the grid is called the *middle-of-the-road management style*.

A 1,1 leader does only enough to keep his or her job. These leaders have little concern for people or productivity and avoid conflicts. This is the least productive leadership style and is called the *impoverished management style*.

The 9,9 leader has a high level of concern for both people and production. A 9,9 leader believes that when people are committed to the organization and feel a part of it, the resultant atmosphere of mutual trust and respect will lead to high productivity. These leaders are flexible and responsive to change and understand the need for change. This *team management style* has a participative focus and is the ideal toward which managers should strive.

Through the Leadership Grid, you can determine your supervisory style and develop a plan to work toward a 9,9 style, if that style is appropriate to your situation.

Contemporary Leadership Styles

As organizations have grown and changed, leadership styles have adapted to the changes dictated by the workplace. We will look at four contemporary leadership styles: the Japanese style, participative style, situational style, and self-leadership style.

Japanese Style

The Japanese recognize that there are really only two demands on leadership. One is to accept that rank does not confer privileges; it entails responsibilities. The other is to acknowledge that leaders need to impose on themselves congruence between

agreeing

deeds and words and between behavior and professed beliefs and values—personal integrity.[17]

The style of leadership used by many Japanese managers incorporates consensus decision making, development opportunities, employee recognition, management by wandering around, and long-term results orientation.[18] Another Japanese management principle, called *kaizen,* is organized work on improvement with specific goals and deadlines. For example, a goal may be a 10 percent reduction in cost within 15 months and/or a 10 percent improvement in reliability within the same time period.[19] In the United States, the concept of continuous improvement is known as *total quality management (TQM),* which is covered in depth in Chapter 15.

The consensus process of decision making used by Japanese managers goes beyond the usual concept of participative management. Everyone who would be affected by an important decision is involved, regardless of the number of people. Employees therefore support the decision, understand it better, and are committed to implementing it. One drawback, however, is the time that is often required to reach a consensus. When hundreds of workers are involved, reaching a consensus may take months or years.

Japanese managers recognize that employees can perform their work without close supervision and numerous rules. Employee-involvement groups called *quality circles* originated in Japan in the 1970s for the purpose of suggesting ways to improve quality and cut costs. Quality circles are groups of employees who work together on specific quality, productivity, and service problems. Because quality circles are temporary and circle members often don't have the power or authority to translate their ideas into action, they have fallen into disuse in the United States.[20] However, quality circles are still used in Japan to recognize employees as experts.

Japanese supervisors and executives wander around the office, factory, and at social events. They become involved personally with the lives of their employees and offer solutions to personal problems when necessary. Communication is improved by the personal contact.

Employees are valued by their supervisors and are provided an abundance of coaching, training, and development opportunities. A people-oriented style of leadership is effective in accomplishing long-term results. Japanese workers typically are positive toward technological improvements and are willing to take risks for long-term results.

Lifetime employment for all workers once was the rule for Japanese companies. The Japanese economy was booming, and no one considered that it might change. However, economic conditions began to change in the late 1980s and early 1990s, and companies began to lay off workers. Tactics similar to those used in many American companies for forcing no-longer-needed employees to resign also have been used. For example, a manager might be moved to a new office where he or she has no real duties or responsibilities. Bored and frustrated because he or she no longer feels useful, the manager eventually resigns. Another worker may be reassigned from a white-collar position to cleaning the offices or plant. That worker, too, eventually will resign.

Participative Style

You learned in Chapter 1 that participative management means employee involvement, often in teams, in making decisions on such matters as setting goals, production processes, schedules, assignment distribution, and problem solving. Participative management is not a democracy in which employees make all the decisions. The philosophy of participative management is related to McGregor's theory Y assumptions about people. This philosophy is that, under proper conditions, employees should have the opportunity to make a significant contribution to solving problems, controlling costs, contributing to objectives, and assisting in the management of the business. Managers, supervisors, and workers must be trained thoroughly before they can participate effectively.[21]

A **participative leader** is one who shares decision making with team members. The participative leader regularly coaches subordinates, negotiates their demands, and collaborates with others.[22] In order for participative management to succeed, the leader needs employees who want to participate and who have worthwhile input. Equally important is a supervisor who is willing to accept employee contributions. Some supervisors use participation as a tool to make people feel important and to lower their resistance to formal authority. They see it as a way to gain cooperation and acceptance of their decisions. In other words, these supervisors have no problem with participative management as long as decisions go their way. Other supervisors believe that employee participation in important decisions leads to improved decision making and to increased departmental effectiveness. These supervisors see employees as a vast untapped resource. Employees also are more satisfied when their decision making and control participation is meaningful.[23]

With true participation, all workers have a right and a responsibility to contribute, to stay informed, and to share the rewards of their efforts. Participation makes people feel validated because their work has meaning, they can influence the outcome, and they can have a positive impact on others.

Participation in decision making is involved in several other leadership styles, as you will see.

Situational Style

The **situational approach to leadership** assumes that successful leadership varies and requires a unique combination of leaders, subordinates, and situations. It attempts to (1) identify the factors that are most important under a given set of circumstances and (2) predict the leadership style that will be most effective under those circumstances. One of the most popular approaches to situational leadership is the Hersey-Blanchard model, which examines the subordinate in the situation.[24,25] Paul Hersey and Kenneth Blanchard term the leadership characteristics *task behavior* and *relationship behavior*. These behaviors generally correspond to the autocratic and participative dimensions of Tannenbaum and Schmidt's leadership continuum. Task behaviors include giving directions, following up, and taking corrective action. Relationship behaviors include providing people with support, giving them positive feedback, and asking for their opinions and ideas.

Distinctive features of the Hersey-Blanchard model are the maturity level of the followers and the mix of task and relationship behaviors in the leadership style. Hersey and Blanchard define *maturity* as the employee's desire for achievement, willingness to accept responsibility, and task-related ability and experience. The relationship between a supervisor and workers moves through four phases as workers develop and mature. Supervisors need to vary their leadership style with each phase. Figure 10.2 shows the four phases or styles of leadership.

In Phase 1, when workers first enter the organization, a high-task orientation by the supervisor is most appropriate. Workers are told what tasks to perform and how to perform them, and they are expected to learn the organization's rules and procedures.

In Phase 2, employees are not willing or able to accept full responsibility. The supervisor can, however, show more trust in them and begin to ask for employee input. Relationship behavior is increased as task behavior is somewhat decreased.

In Phase 3, employees' abilities and confidence have increased, and they are ready for more responsibility. As employees gradually become more confident and experienced, they need more support and encouragement.

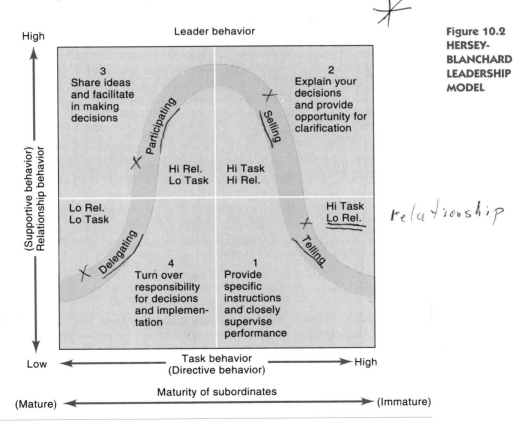

**Figure 10.2
HERSEY-
BLANCHARD
LEADERSHIP
MODEL**

Source: Adapted from Paul Hersey, *The Situational Leader,* Warner Book, New York, 1984, p. 63.

In Phase 4, employees are able to perform independently and no longer need a directive relationship with their supervisor. Highly competent workers who are also willing to take responsibility for their tasks might prefer the freedom to work on their own. This combination of skill and willingness greatly reduces their need for direction and support.

Self-Leadership Style

The concept of a self-directed work team—a group of employees who are responsible for an entire work process or segment that delivers a product or service to an internal or external customer—was introduced in Chapter 4. The use of self-directed, or self-managed, work teams usually includes a complete task; members who possess a variety of relevant skills; workers with the power to determine methods of work, schedules, and task assignments; and compensation and feedback about performance for the group as a whole.[26] Through the use of self-managed teams, the development of individual strategies for completing tasks is replaced by a focus on group methods for task completion.[27]

About one in five U.S. employers operates self-managed teams today. Charles Manz predicts that by the year 2000, 40 to 50 percent of all U.S. workers will be managing themselves through teams. Companies with teams find that labor costs drop, morale rises, and signs of alienation ease.[28]

There will always be managers; even teams rotate leaders periodically. However, highly competitive companies have discovered that they can do with far fewer bosses than they once had. Those bosses who remain in team-based operations are no longer bosses in the traditional sense. Titles such as consultant, facilitator, or coach are very common. The role of the manager in a team setting is to help the frontline worker, not to ask the frontline worker to help the manager.

CIGNA Corp.'s customer service center in Virginia Beach, Virginia, is an organization in which the management team focuses on supporting those people who are interacting with the customer. A customer service manager at General Electric oversees about 35 people, four times as many workers as before the conversion to teams in 1988. One reason why workers can operate with so little supervision in team environments is that they typically have access to more information such as profit-and-loss statements, production data, and quality charts.[29]

Charles Manz and Henry Sims suggest that the leadership styles that emerge from the self-managed teams are more effective than the more traditional styles. **Self-leadership,** as defined by Manz and Sims, is the ability of workers to motivate themselves to perform unappealing, but necessary, tasks as well as attractive tasks. When employees are allowed to use strategies on the basis of self-leadership and to behave on the basis of self-management, they are more likely to develop behavior that does not deviate from the organization's behavior standards.[30] Manz and Sims found that self-led leaders encouraged others to practice self-reinforcement, self-observation, and evaluation; to value and act on self-expectations; to set goals for themselves; to rehearse critical procedures; and to engage in self-criticism when necessary.[31]

It is likely that in view of all the leadership theories available, you are now asking yourself, "How can I choose the right style?" What are the forces within you—your

COMPETENCY CHECK

Can you briefly describe three contemporary leadership styles?

WHAT CAN THE SUPERVISOR DO?

A supervisor in an organization in which self-directed work teams are utilized may wonder what his or her responsibilities are. The functions of the supervisor in self-directed work teams include the following:

1. Supervising a larger number of direct reports. Supervising 50 to 75 employees would be virtually impossible in a traditional organization.
2. Being the administrative liaison with higher levels. The supervisor communicates with higher levels by completing performance appraisal forms, salary administration forms, required legal reports, budgets, and safety and accident reports, for example.
3. Monitoring and advising on the legal requirements of affirmative action and other employment law issues. Although teams may choose the entry-level team members, compliance with employment laws must be monitored by the supervisor.
4. Facilitating interpersonal relationships among team members. The supervisor often coaches and counsels team members and entire teams. Training members in group processes, assessing the skill levels of teams, solving team management problems as a counselor and mediator, and occasionally arbitrating conflicts are important functions of the supervisor.
5. Supporting the work teams in ways that enhance goal achievement. For example, the supervisor can serve as an advocate for teams by obtaining physical facilities that provide adequate work space, computer access, technicians, and generally favorable working conditions.
6. Removing obstacles. The supervisor can protect against interference and bottlenecks as well as represent the teams to higher levels.
7. Managing the information flow. Horizontal communication of routine information among several work teams needs to be fast and efficient. The supervisor might communicate common goals and strategies, changes in customer and client demands, and recognition for achievement of goals to the teams that produced the desired results.
8. Assessing and measuring overall team success. The supervisor surveys, collects, and summarizes individual team members' opinions and recommendations about how the team is functioning. Questions the supervisor may ask include: Do the teams and all members know their tasks? Are the members clear on which processes do and do not work? How are interpersonal relationships going? Are the leadership and facilitation of the work team supportive? Responses to these questions can be fed back to the teams, thus providing the basis for continuous improvement.[32]

values, your personality, your abilities—that influence your leadership style? What type of leader are you now? Is your style effective? Can it be improved? Can you change your style? Are you willing to do so? These questions suggest that you do a self-appraisal to learn more about yourself. Application 3 will help you answer some of these questions.

COMPETENCY REVIEW

1. Define *leadership* and *power.*
2. Discuss five kinds of power.
3. List the common leadership traits that Ghiselli and other trait theory researchers identified.
4. Compare the behavioral style of a task-oriented supervisor to the behavioral style of an employee-oriented supervisor.
5. Describe McGregor's theory X and theory Y leadership styles.
6. Describe briefly the leadership continuum theory and identify three forces the supervisor should consider when choosing a leadership style.
7. Describe the five styles of leadership identified on the Leadership Grid.
8. Describe briefly the following contemporary leadership styles: Japanese style, participative style, situational style, and self-leadership style.
9. Define *self-leadership* and identify the responsibilities of a supervisor of a self-directed work team.

APPLICATIONS

1. Which leadership style is reflected in the following statement? How can this style be improved? "I have to let them know I'm checking. We've got a job to do. That lazy Mark Howard would never get here on time except for payday."
2. Which leadership style on the Leadership Grid is indicated by the statement in No. 1? How can this style be improved?
3. Assess your own leadership competencies by taking the Leadership Assessment Test on page 301. Answer each question realistically rather than in terms of how you wish you were. If you feel you can't reply to a question, skip it. There are no right or wrong answers; this is simply a means of understanding your leadership potential.

LEADERSHIP ASSESSMENT TEST

1	2	3	4	5
Strongly Disagree	Disagree	Neither Agree Nor Disagree	Agree	Strongly Agree

JOB PROFICIENCY
1. I set high standards for myself. 1 2 3 4 5
2. I am competent in my job. 1 2 3 4 5
3. I work hard to improve my job knowledge. 1 2 3 4 5

COMMUNICATIONS
4. When speaking, I explain ideas and concepts so all can understand. 1 2 3 4 5
5. I listen closely to others and pay attention to what they have to say. 1 2 3 4 5
6. I write effectively and am able to organize and explain thoughts clearly. 1 2 3 4 5
7. I convey appropriate enthusiasm to motivate mysuburdinates. 1 2 3 4 5

PROFESSIONAL ETHICS
8. I accept responsibility for my decisions and the impact they have on others 1 2 3 4 5
9. I am a credible role model and set the proper example for others to follow. 1 2 3 4 5
10. I demonstrate moral courage and stand firm on my values, moral principles and convictions. 1 2 3 4 5
11. I am open, honest and candid when dealing with others. 1 2 3 4 5

PLANNING
12. I am proficient in developing courses of action, scheduling and organizing. 1 2 3 4 5
13. I establish clear priorities and goals. 1 2 3 4 5
14. I am flexible, able to handle uncertainty, and do not become easily frustrated. 1 2 3 4 5
15. I allow others to help me develop plans when appropriate. 1 2 3 4 5

USE OF AVAILABLE SYSTEMS
16. I actively seek information needed to solve problems or develop recommendations. 1 2 3 4 5
17. I know how to organize things so information flows efficiently throughout the group or company. 1 2 3 4 5

18. I know how to use analytical techniques to solve problems or arrive at conclusions. 1 2 3 4 5
19. I can estimate the time it takes to get a job done and effectively manage time and competing priorities. 1 2 3 4 5

DECISION MAKING
20. I know which decision to make and which decisions to delegate to subordinates. 1 2 3 4 5
21. I know how to build commitment for the decisions I make. 1 2 3 4 5
22. I include others in the decision-making process when appropriate. 1 2 3 4 5
23. I develop creative and imaginative solutions when faced with unfamiliar problems. 1 2 3 4 5

TEACHING AND COUNSELING
24. I understand and accept my responsibility to teach, coach and counsel. 1 2 3 4 5
25. I am an effective teacher. 1 2 3 4 5
26. I demonstrate the patience and concern necessary to be an effective counselor. 1 2 3 4 5
27. I use good judgment with personal information and maintain confidentiality when appropriate. 1 2 3 4 5

SUPERVISION
28. I give clear and concise instructions; others know what to do after receiving my directions. 1 2 3 4 5
29. I do not oversupervise or "micromanage." 1 2 3 4 5
30. I don't undersupervise or give too little guidance. 1 2 3 4 5
31. I know how to evaluate performance to determine whether standards are being met. 1 2 3 4 5

TEAM BUILDING
32. My actions will help develop a healthy leadership climate. 1 2 3 4 5
33. I ensure that others receive credit for their contributions and accomplishments. 1 2 3 4 5
34. I accept the honest mistakes of others as a normal part of learning. 1 2 3 4 5
35. I help others learn by sharing my experience and expertise. 1 2 3 4 5

Source: Reprinted by permission of James G. Patterson.

CASES | Case 1 |

ANDREW'S NATURAL STYLE WON'T CUT IT ANYMORE

Andrew Santiago's voice on the telephone sounded strained. "I can't believe it," he said. "Only a few months ago, I felt confident as a manager; I loved my job. Today, I dread coming to work and doubt my own ability. I think it might be best just to throw in the towel."

Andrew Santiago has been working for the same company for more than 15 years. Less than a year before he called me, he had been promoted from production manager at one of the company's plants to plant manager in another. I'd been a consultant to Santiago's company for a number of years, and I respected his competence; he was a good choice for plant manager.

When I first met Andrew, he was in his first management job: production supervisor. He gave me a tour of his shop and was obviously proud of it all: the high-tech assembly line he had installed and supervised from start-up, the outstanding productivity figures of his group, and, above all, his people.

Often when managers tour their plants, the workers spread the word down the line to shape up. Not so with Andrew. His employees continued working but often paused to make friendly comments to their boss. They were genuinely glad to see him. If Andrew stopped to bring to my attention some detail of the production process, he always included a line worker in the demonstration by asking one of them to explain it to me. He asked questions of everyone, and, most important, he praised their work, their ideas, and their contributions to the company. It was a team effort that seemed easy and natural.

The plant has now grown to over 600 employees, and, although most other plants in the corporation are union shops, this plant isn't one of them. The plant supervisors still make major plant decisions through "town meetings," at which managers encourage employee opinions and seek consensus.

When Andrew Santiago was promoted to a new job as manager of another plant 3 years ago, however, he seemed to face a new labor grievance nearly every day, and relations with his supervisors were awful. His predecessor, Frank White, had been a tough manager who knew what he wanted and was willing to go "toe to toe" with the union. The plant never had a strike while Frank was plant manager, and he retired with a reputation of having been a "tough cookie," feared as much by the supervisors under him as by his employees.

Andrew's leadership style seemed a perfect replacement for Frank's. But when Andrew took over with his same natural, communicative style, trouble began immediately. For example, Andrew talked with one of his supervisors about the dangerous clutter in the work area. The supervisor claimed the problem was a lack of people, so Andrew arranged to have an employee moved over to the supervisor's department. A few weeks later, the situation hadn't changed. This time, the supervisor said the mess was caused by insufficient equipment.

Andrew had story after story like this one. He couldn't trust his supervisors to level with him. Grievances with workers were mushrooming, and Andrew was frustrated and bewildered.

1. What do you think is the reason for the problems Andrew Santiago is having in his new job?
2. What leadership theory or theories seem to be operating in this case? Explain.
3. If you were Andrew, what would you do?

Source: Adapted from Marge Yanker, "Flexible Leadership Styles: One Supervisor's Story," *Supervisory Management,* January 1986, pp. 2–6.

HILLARY McKORKIN NEEDS HELP!

Absenteeism has become a particularly acute problem among the programmers and systems analysts in the management information systems (MIS) department at Hall-Mason Company. MIS supervisor Hillary McKorkin is being pressured from upper management because of delays in system upgrades and special programming projects. She has tried using the company's disciplinary system to discourage absences. Six months ago, she instituted an incentive program that would reward employees for perfect attendance records for 1 month, 3 months, 6 months, 9 months, and 12 months. Successful employees would receive items such as coffee mugs and T-shirts bearing the Hall-Mason Company logo as well as a special MIS department motto: "Information Systems Does It Better!" Not one employee qualified for the 1-month perfect attendance award; forget about the other awards.

1. What leadership approach might encourage and result in improved attendance as well as timely completion of work projects?
2. Are the rewards adequate? Discuss.

REFERENCES

1. Peter F. Drucker, *Managing for the Future,* Truman Talley Book/E. P. Dutton, New York, 1992, pp. 121–122.
2. Jolie Solomon, "A Touching Presidency," *Newsweek,* February 22, 1993, p. 44.
3. R. Wayne Mondy, *Supervisory Management,* January 1986, p. 37.
4. J. R. P. French and B. Raven, "The Bases of Social Power," in D. Cartwright (ed.), *Studies in Social Power,* The University of Michigan Press, Ann Arbor, 1959, pp. 150–161.
5. See, for example, Edwin E. Ghiselli, "Managerial Talent," *American Psychology,* October 1963, pp. 631–641; J. D. Barrow, "The Variables of Leadership: A Review and Conceptual Framework," *Academy of Management Review,* April 1977, p. 232; and R. M. Stogdill, "Historical Trends in Leadership Theory and Research," *Journal of Contemporary Business,* Autumn 1974, p. 5.
6. Edwin E. Ghiselli, *Explorations in Management Talent,* Goodyear Publishing Co., Santa Monica, Calif., 1971.
7. C. A. Schriesheim, J. M. Tolliver, and O. C. Behling, "Leadership Theory: Some Implications for Managers," *Business Topics,* Summer 1978, p. 35, cited in Leslie W. Rue and Lloyd L. Byars, *Management: Theory and Applications,* 4th ed., Irwin Publishing Co., Homewood, Ill., 1986, p. 385.
8. James A. F. Stoner and R. Edward Freeman, *Management,* 4th ed., Prentice-Hall, Inc., Englewood Cliffs, N.J., 1989, pp. 462–464.
9. Douglas McGregor, *The Human Side of Enterprise,* McGraw-Hill Book Company, New York, 1960, pp. 16–48.
10. John A. Pearce II and Richard B. Robinson, Jr., *Management,* Random House, Inc., New York, 1989, p. 755.
11. Daniel A. Wren and Dan Voich, Jr., *Management Process, Structure, and Behavior,* 3d ed., John Wiley & Sons, Inc., New York, 1984, pp. 399–400.
12. John J. Morse and Jay W. Lorsch, "Beyond Theory Y," *Harvard Business Review,* May–June 1970, pp. 61–68.
13. Robert Tannenbaum and Warren H. Schmidt, "How to Choose a Leadership Pattern," *Harvard Business Review,* May–June 1973, pp. 162–180.
14. Leslie W. Rue and Lloyd D. Byars, *Management Theory and Application,* 4th ed., Irwin Publishing Co., Homewood, Ill., 1986, p. 391.
15. Robert R. Blake and Jane S. Mouton, *The New Managerial Grid,* Gulf Publishing Company, Houston, 1978.
16. Robert R. Blake and Anne Adams McCanse, *Leadership Dilemmas—Grid Solutions,* Gulf Publishing Company, Houston, 1991, p. 29.
17. Drucker, op. cit., pp. 116–117.
18. Bernard J. Keys and Thomas R. Miller, "The Japanese Management Theory Jungle," *Academy of Management Review,* April 1984, pp. 342–353.
19. Drucker, op. cit., pp. 181–182.
20. Ibid., pp. 8–9.
21. Donald C. Mosley, Leon C. Megginson, and Paul H. Pietri, Jr., *Supervisory Management,* 3d ed., South-Western Publishing Co., Cincinnati, 1993, pp. 274–297.
22. Ibid., p. 295–297.
23. Edward Glassman, "Leadership Style's Effect on the Creativity of Employees," *Management Solutions,* November 1986, p. 24.

24. Paul Hersey and Kenneth Blanchard, *Management of Organizational Behavior,* 4th ed., Prentice-Hall, Inc., Englewood Cliffs, N.J., 1982.

25. Paul Hersey, *The Situational Leader,* Warner Books, New York, 1984.

26. Thomas Cummings, "Self-Regulated Work Groups: A Socio-Technical Synthesis," *Academy of Management Review,* 3, 1987, p. 120.

27. Charles C. Manz, "Self-Leadership: Toward an Expanded Theory of Self-Influence Processes in Organizations," *Academy of Management Review,* 11, 1986, pp. 589–590.

28. Joann S. Lublin, "Trying to Increase Worker Productivity, More Employers Alter Management Style," *The Wall Street Journal,* February 13, 1992, p. B1.

29. Dave Mayfield, "Managers Often Are Leery of Work Teams," *The Virginian-Pilot and the Ledger-Star,* Mar. 29, 1992, p. E2.

30. Ibid.

31. Charles C. Manz and Henry P. Sims, Jr., "Leading Workers to Lead Themselves: The External Leadership of Self-Managing Work Teams," *Administrative Science Quarterly,* 32, 1987, p. 120.

32. Adapted from Olga Myers, "Enhancing a Supervisory Style," *Supervision,* December 1990, pp. 16–17.

SUGGESTED READINGS

Bellman, Geoffrey M.: "The Quest for Staff Leadership," *Training and Development Journal,* January 1986, pp. 36–44.

Bennis, Warren.: *On Becoming a Leader,* Addison-Wesley Publishing Co., Inc., Reading, Mass., 1989.

Blanchard, Kenneth, Patricia Zigarmi, and Drea Zigarmi: *Leadership and the One Minute Manager,* William Morrow and Company, Inc., New York, 1985.

Conger, Jay A., Rabindra N. Kanungo, and Associates: *Charismatic Leadership,* Jossey-Bass Publishers, San Francisco, 1988.

DePree, M.: *Leadership Is an Art,* Doubleday & Co., Inc., New York, 1987.

Haas, Howard: *The Leader Within,* HarperBusiness, New York, 1992.

Kotter, John P.: *The Leadership Factor,* The Free Press, New York, 1988.

Kouzes, James, and Barry Posner: *The Leadership Challenge: How to Get Extraordinary Things Done in Organizations,* Jossey-Bass Publishers, San Francisco, 1987.

Manz, Charles C., and Henry P. Sims, Jr.: *Super-Leadership,* Berkley Books, New York, 1990.

Nanus, Burt: *Visionary Leadership,* Jossey-Bass Publishers, San Francisco, 1992.

Orsburn, Jack D., Linda Moran, Ed Musselwhite, and John H. Zenger: *Self-Directed Work Teams,* Business One Irwin, Homewood, Ill., 1990.

Peters, Tom, and Nancy Austin: *A Passion for Excellence,* Random House, Inc., New York, 1985.

Stayer, R.: "How I Learned to Let My Workers Lead," *Harvard Business Review,* November–December 1990.

Terry, Robert W.: *Authentic Leadership,* Jossey-Bass Publishers, San Francisco, 1993.

Vercillo, Tony: *Passionate Leadership,* Delta Sales, Chino Hills, Calif., 1991.

Vroom, Victor H.: "Reflections on Leadership and Decision-making," *Journal of General Management,* Spring 1984, pp. 18–36.

Waterman, Robert H., Jr.: *The Renewal Factor,* Bantam Books, New York, 1987.

GLOSSARY

coercive power   Power derived from workers' perception that the leader is a source of punishment such as assigning difficult jobs, isolating a worker from a group, blocking promotions, or giving low performance appraisals.

expert power   Power derived from workers' seeing the leader as highly skilled and knowledgeable in a particular field and being willing to follow directions out of respect for the leader's expertise.

leadership   The process of influencing others to work toward the accomplishment of organizational goals and objectives.

legitimate power   Sometimes called *position power* because workers view the leader as having the power and authority to carry out the job.

participative leader   One who shares decision making with team members.

power   The extent to which an individual is able to influence others so they respond to directions.

referent power   Power derived from workers' seeing in the leader qualities such as competence, fairness, and consideration and possibly wanting to emulate the leader. Sometimes called *charisma*.

reward power   Power derived from workers' seeing that the leader has the ability to provide something they want such as pay increases, promotions, feelings of pride, belonging, or sense of worth.

self-leadership   The ability of workers to motivate themselves to perform unappealing, but necessary, tasks as well as attractive tasks.

situational approach to leadership   An assumption that successful leadership varies and requires a unique combination of leaders, subordinates, and situations.

CHAPTER 11
Motivating Employees

STUDYING THIS CHAPTER WILL ENABLE YOU TO:

1. Describe Maslow's hierarchy of needs.

2. Explain Herzberg's two-factor theory.

3. Define the needs for achievement, power, and affiliation identified in McClelland's acquired needs theory.

4. Describe Vroom's expectancy theory.

5. Discuss behavior modification.

6. Discuss motivating employees through job enlargement and job enrichment.

7. Describe the motivational aspects of gainsharing and profit sharing.

8. List factors important for worker job satisfaction.

C   H   A   P

Motivating Employees

he workplace of the 1990s is vastly different from that of only a decade earlier. Organizations are downsizing, reorganizing to eliminate layers of management and other supervisory positions, and freezing promotions, pay raises, and hiring. Consequently, fewer promotional opportunities are available, and fewer dollars are available for raises. Motivating employees during these changes as well as after the changes have occurred is particularly challenging. In this chapter, you will study some of the motivational theories that have been useful in the workplace for many years and still serve as guidelines for supervisors of today. Understanding human behavior on the job is essential for the successful supervisor.

As you will see in the discussion on gainsharing and profit sharing, empowerment is the key to motivation and, therefore, company advancement and profits for many companies, large and small. As Tom Peters says in *Liberation Management,* "empower until you're blue in the face."[1] The idea of turning to the workers for help often happens in a crisis situation, when the organization is on the verge of collapse. However, using an organization's most important resource—its workers—to help solve production problems is perhaps the best approach to motivation in today's workplace. Given the opportunity, workers often have better ideas for improvement than their supervisors or upper management.[2] Leadership and motivation are closely related. The leader who is capable of influencing workers to accept ownership of their roles in the organization is a leader who understands motivation. You will study more about employee involvement in Chapter 15, "Implementing Total Quality Management."

Motivational Theories

Leadership was defined in Chapter 10 as the process of influencing others to work toward the accomplishment of goals and objectives. **Motivation** is the desire or drive within a person to achieve some goal. *Within* is the operative word here, for motivation is an internal condition based on a person's values, perceptions, and needs. What can you do as a leader to ignite this internal flame? Creating a climate in which your workers will be motivated on a continuing basis probably will be your greatest challenge as a supervisor.

The purpose of this chapter is to help you develop an understanding of human behavior so that you can create a workplace climate in which workers willingly strive to achieve the company's goals as well as their own. First, let us look at a few popular motivation models, selected from the large volume of research in the field.

Maslow's Hierarchy of Needs

A great deal of research has been conducted to try to find out why people behave as they do. An interesting disclosure from these efforts is that human beings are all alike and yet they are all different. From this contradictory assumption, we know what, in general, "makes us tick." For example, all human beings need food, clothing, and shelter, and most find some way to get these things. But to use this knowledge of similarity, we must recognize that people have their individual views of those basic needs. The amounts and types of food, clothing, and shelter needed differ from person to person, depending on their individual perceptions, values, goals, and even other needs. Psychologist A. H. Maslow put these concepts into a model of human motivation.

The behavior of human beings is based on their needs, according to Maslow.[3] The first of two principles of Maslow's theory is that needs can be classified into five groups and arranged in a hierarchy; when one need is satisfied, another need emerges to be satisfied. His hierarchy of needs became a widely accepted model of human behavior. Maslow's hierarchy of needs is shown in the left section of Figure 11.1.

The most basic needs are the physiological, or survival, needs (food, clothing, and sex). Next is the need for safety or security (such as protection from physical harm and financial ruin). Third, people need to interact with other humans and to have a sense of belonging; these Maslow called "social needs." The fourth level is the need for esteem (to be considered by oneself and by others as a worthwhile human being). Finally, there is the need for self-actualization (to develop to one's full potential). Maslow studied the needs of people in general. The second principle of his theory is that since one's needs depend on what one already has, only unsatisfied needs can motivate human behavior. For example, a person who has satisfied his or her survival needs will no longer be motivated by these needs and so will move up the hierarchy to satisfy his or her need for feeling safe and secure.

The other side of this theory is that until the basic physiological needs are met, higher needs won't motivate behavior. Maslow explains that "a person who is lacking food, safety, love, and esteem probably would hunger for food more strongly than anything else."[4]

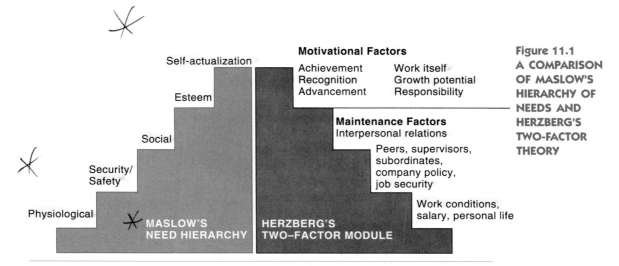

Figure 11.1
A COMPARISON OF MASLOW'S HIERARCHY OF NEEDS AND HERZBERG'S TWO-FACTOR THEORY

Source: Adapted from "Hierarchy of Needs" from *Motivation and Personality*, 2d ed., by Abraham H. Maslow. Copyright 1954 by Harper & Row Publishers, Inc. Copyright © 1970 by Abraham H. Maslow. Reprinted by permission of HarperCollins Publishers, Inc.

WHAT CAN THE SUPERVISOR DO?

Use the hierarchy of needs to help you examine the work environment and develop procedures, programs, and conditions that will apply generally to workers. The list shown in Figure 11.2 will serve as a starting point to check your management's status in providing for worker needs. Compare the list to the programs and procedures used in your department. What about the worker who has been efficient and faithful for some time but for whom there has been no suitable spot for promotion? Perhaps that person could become a trainer of other workers, with recognition given to his or her expertise in company publications *along with* a bonus at payday.

While Maslow's theory does present a broad generalized view of human behavior, it has not been without criticism. This has led to qualifications of the theory over the years. You should be aware of the changed view of Maslow's hierarchy. Among the qualifications are these:

- ❑ The theory does not take into account varying needs among cultures and individuals. Such variations are critical in the management of people on the job.
- ❑ The satisfaction of one need does not occur independently of other needs. One need does not have to be completely satisfied before another need seeks satisfaction. Moreover, higher-level needs are probably never fully satisfied. The desire for esteem, for example, is a lifelong need and will continue to motivate even after some satisfaction is achieved.

COMPETENCY CHECK

Can you describe Maslow's hierarchy of needs?

The supervisor should consider Maslow's hierarchy-of-needs theory as a guideline for understanding human behavior in general but should emphasize individual differences in applying it in the workplace.

Herzberg's Two-Factor Theory

Another explanation of human behavior was proposed by Frederick Herzberg.[5] While Maslow's theory applied motivation to people in general, Herzberg studied the motivation of people in the workplace. Based on a study of engineers and accountants, Herzberg developed a motivational theory of two dimensions: *dissatisfiers,* which he called "hygiene, or maintenance, factors," and *satisfiers,* or motivators.

Herzberg found that workers feel dissatisfaction about things *outside of* but related to their jobs such as their relationship with supervisors, salary, and working conditions. While these are dissatisfiers when they are absent or are not effective, their presence does not satisfy. In other words, workers *expect* certain basic working conditions; because they are expected as a part of the job, they do not motivate.

Figure 11.2 WHAT MANAGEMENT CAN DO TO PROVIDE FOR WORKER NEEDS IN THE MASLOW CATEGORIES	
Needs Categories	**What Management Can Do**
Self-actualization	Provide growth and career opportunities. Provide training and development programs. Encourage creativity. Encourage achievement. Encourage participation in community betterment programs.
Esteem	Praise high performance. Publicize individual achievement. Give frequent and prompt feedback for accomplishment. Provide for greater worker responsibility. Promote to higher jobs.
Social	Provide for working in groups. Provide for interaction among different levels. Sponsor recreation and company social events. Encourage participation and cooperation in both formal and informal structures.
Safety/security	Provide safe working conditions. Provide a broad benefits program. Provide job security. Provide for fair and equal treatment of all workers.
Physiological	Pay fair and equitable wages. Provide comfortable workstations. Provide rest breaks. Provide proper space, light, heat, and air conditioning.

Herzberg labeled these dissatisfiers as "hygiene, or maintenance, factors." They are shown on the right in Figure 11.1.

In Herzberg's view, certain conditions about the job itself tend to cause satisfaction when they are present and to serve as motivators. Their absence, however, does not prove highly dissatisfying. Note in Figure 11.1 the job-content nature of the six conditions that Herzberg called *motivational factors.*

As you can see, Figure 11.1 is a comparison of Maslow's hierarchy of needs and Herzberg's two-factor theory. The hygiene features in the Herzberg model generally coincide with Maslow's lower-order needs: physiological, safety, security, and social. Herzberg's motivational factors relate closely to Maslow's higher-order needs: esteem and self-actualization. In general, the Herzberg study of worker motivation tends to validate Maslow's hierarchy of needs.

WHAT CAN THE SUPERVISOR DO?

As a supervisor, you can use the Herzberg model in many ways. In the maintenance-factor area, you can:

- ❑ communicate departmental policies to workers and administer the policies equitably.
- ❑ improve your supervisory abilities.
- ❑ monitor working conditions to see that they provide adequately for accomplishing the assigned task.
- ❑ maintain workplace safety.
- ❑ provide fair, equitable, and objectively determined salary recommendations.
- ❑ improve relationships with peers and workers.
- ❑ keep workers informed about what is going on, as far as confidentiality will allow.

In the motivational-factor area, you can:

- ❑ analyze jobs to see whether they can be enriched or enlarged.
- ❑ praise workers for their accomplishments.
- ❑ publicize worker achievements via bulletin boards, company publications, and the media.
- ❑ let workers know that you feel they are competent and you expect high achievement from them.
- ❑ delegate more authority to workers.
- ❑ provide training and development programs and encourage (recognize and reward) participation in them.
- ❑ assign workers to special projects and recognize results.
- ❑ encourage worker participation in problem solving within their work units or within the department.
- ❑ assist workers with career planning.
- ❑ make objective recommendations for promotions.
- ❑ rotate jobs or cross-train workers to provide broader experience.

**COMPETENCY
CHECK**

Can you explain
Herzberg's two-
factor theory?

The Herzberg model is very useful to management. An organization that wants to recruit and retain competent workers should examine its workplace, its administrative and supervisory practices, and its salary and benefits plan. But to motivate workers to high productivity, the organization also has to look at the design of its jobs. Job content should provide workers with a feeling of pride of accomplishment and a sense of contribution to the total organization. In addition, the organization should examine its growth and development programs for workers. Employees should have some input into the jobs they perform and should be able to grow and develop on the basis of their potential for and contributions to the organization's growth.

McClelland's Acquired Needs Theory

In the 1960s, David C. McClelland identified the needs for achievement, power, and affiliation. His theory was based on the assumption that people learned or acquired certain needs from their culture and life experiences. When a need is strong enough, a person will engage in work-related activities that will satisfy the need.[6]

The **need for achievement** is the desire to do something better than it has ever been done or to accomplish something difficult just because it is difficult. People with a high need for achievement often contemplate on how they can do their jobs better, seek responsibility, take calculated risks, complete difficult assignments, and advance their careers. In other words, they do not want to fail and will avoid tasks that require too much risk. Money is the measure of success for people with a high need for achievement. Entrepreneurs and others who enjoy developing programs or companies from the ground up have a strong need for achievement.

The **need for power** is the desire to control, influence, or be responsible for others as well as to control money and real estate. A person with a strong need for power often concentrates on finding ways to advance him/herself to gain a position of authority and status. These individuals seek increasingly responsible tasks, are comfortable in competitive situations, and are comfortable with decision making.

The **need for affiliation** is the desire to maintain close, friendly personal relationships. Supervisors with a high need for affiliation typically work toward developing a cooperative, team-oriented work situation. Some individuals with a high need for affiliation may avoid supervisory roles because of the conflicts that will undoubtedly occur. The desire for approval and personal relationships may interfere with the ability to make necessary decisions. On the other hand, a supervisor with a low need for affiliation may not express adequate concern for the needs of subordinates.

COMPETENCY CHECK
Can you define the needs for achievement, power, and affiliation?

Vroom's Expectancy Theory

motivation = matter of choices

A different approach to motivation was presented by Victor H. Vroom. Unlike the Maslow and Herzberg theories, which focus on the inner forces of the individual and the conditions in the workplace as explanations of behavior, Vroom's expectancy theory explains worker motivation as a matter of choices.[7] Vroom asserts that individuals choose to exert work effort or not depending on what the rewards are. Put in the vernacular, this is the "What's-in-it-for-me?" theory.

To simplify the expectancy theory, consider these questions:

❏ Will my efforts lead to successful performance? This is the *effort-performance expectancy*. It asks, in other words, Do I have the skills and abilities necessary to perform the job well enough to get the reward? *Can I do it*

- ❏ If I perform the task successfully, will I get the reward? This is called the *performance-reward expectancy.* What evidence is there that the reward will be forthcoming? Does the company live up to its word in giving promised rewards?
- ❏ Is the reward worth the effort? This is called *reward attractiveness,* or *valence.*

As an example, let's look at Ramon Mendoza, who works as a counter clerk in a large photo processing firm. A vacancy is expected in the processing department; it is for a higher-paying, entry-level job in the technical phase of the business. To get the job, Ramon must take a processing course.

Knowing that Ramon might wonder whether he could do the job even after taking the course, the manager might reassure him by pointing out his success in his present job, his personal interest and experience in photography, and the success of others. Ramon might wonder whether he will get the job even if he completes the course successfully. The manager could point to the organization's record of promotions to reassure him. Finally, under the expectancy theory, Ramon might wonder if the job is worth the effort involved in taking the course and making the change from his present job. The manager could point out the career opportunities available in the technical phase of the business, opportunities that would open up to him through the change. Interviews might be arranged for Ramon with others in the firm who have moved up the ladder through the processing department.

Knowing how the expectancy theory operates to motivate the individual, you can advise the worker through his or her thinking about career or other opportunities within the organization.

COMPETENCY CHECK

Can you briefly describe Vroom's expectancy theory?

Motivating Through Behavior Modification

Behavior modification is a method of encouraging appropriate behavior through the consequences resulting from that behavior. In other words, appropriate behavior is rewarded, and inappropriate behavior results in punishment. Consequently, the rewarded behavior is repeated, and inappropriate behavior tends to be eliminated. *Positive reinforcement,* or rewards, is preferable because it is more effective in achieving positive results. Workers perform better and feel better about their jobs when they receive recognition for their efforts and feel that what they do is valuable and appreciated by the organization. The supervisor, because he or she is in close contact with individual workers, establishes the atmosphere for motivation through praise.

Negative reinforcement can be the punishment for inappropriate behavior or the elimination of the punishment when the inappropriate behavior is eliminated (also called *extinction*). For example, when a worker consistently calls in sick on Mondays and consistently receives verbal and/or written reprimands or his or her pay is docked, these consequences are negative reinforcement or punishment. When the worker consistently reports for work on Mondays, he or she no longer receives the

WHAT CAN THE SUPERVISOR DO?

When strong punishments are used on a long-term basis, behavior modification may result in additional undesirable results such as increased absenteeism or high employee turnover. Therefore, establishing clear guidelines for a behavior modification program is essential. A supervisor may incorporate the following procedures:

- establishing varying levels of rewards related to varying levels of performance
- telling workers what they are doing wrong
- punishing workers privately to avoid public embarrassment
- giving rewards and punishments consistently when earned to emphasize the seriousness of management's commitment to the behavior modification program[8]

reprimands or reduction in pay, which is also a negative reinforcement because the consequences have been removed.

Sam Walton, founder of Wal-Mart, used a straight-forward form of behavior modification that he described as follows:

> Keeping so many people motivated to do the best job possible involves a lot of different programs and approaches we've developed at Wal-Mart over the years, but none of them would work at all without one simple thing that puts it all together: appreciation. All of us like praise. So what we try to practice in our company is to look for things to praise. Look for things that are going right. We want to let our folks know when they are doing something outstanding, and let them know they are important to us.
>
> You can't praise something that's not done well. You can't be insincere. You have to follow up on things that aren't done well. There is no substitute for being honest with someone and letting them know they didn't do a good job. All of us profit from being corrected—if we're corrected in a positive way. But there's no better way to keep someone doing things the right way than by letting him or her know how much you appreciate their performance. If you do that one simple thing, human nature will take it from there.[9]

COMPETENCY CHECK

Can you describe behavior modification?

Motivating Through Reorganizing Tasks

Workers in jobs that quickly become routine and repetitive often feel "stuck" and unoptimistic about their futures. Reorganizing tasks through job enlargement and job enrichment are motivational techniques that can be cost-effective. Job enlargement, job enrichment, and their relationship to effective organizing were discussed in Chapter 4. We can now see that these same organizational tools also are motivational tools.

Job Enlargement

Job enlargement was defined in Chapter 4 as the process of increasing the number of operations an individual performs in a job. Workers soon become bored with routine, monotonous activities. Through job enlargement, a job can be expanded to include additional tasks. For example, tasks that were performed by several workers may be combined and assigned to one or two employees.

Generally, employees are amenable to taking on additional responsibilities because they feel that their jobs are then more important. Additionally, they consider their jobs to be less monotonous, which increases workers' job satisfaction. Supervisors often must spend considerable time working out the organizational problems associated with job enlargement; i.e., whose jobs are to be combined, who is to take on which new responsibilities, and what to do with those employees who like their jobs just as they are.

Job Enrichment

Job enrichment was defined in Chapter 4 as any effort that makes work more meaningful or satisfying by adding variety or responsibility to a job. With company downsizings and the need to effect financial savings, promotions may be few and far between. Outstanding performance doesn't guarantee a promotion when there are no promotions to be made. How, then, does the supervisor keep bright, hardworking employees satisfied with their jobs?

Using job enrichment, a supervisor can ensure through careful scheduling and job assignments that everyone in a department has an equal number of challenging and routine jobs. Job enrichment also may be accomplished through committee assignments, task force assignments, and other unusual experiences that will break up the routine daily activity. As the supervisor and employees become more comfortable with job enrichment, employee involvement in planning, scheduling, and decision making may be implemented. The supervisor, however, must be comfortable with giving up some power when employees become involved in planning and decision making. Although employees may assume some of the supervisor's responsibilities, the supervisor is still held accountable for overall departmental performance.

COMPETENCY CHECK

Can you describe how job enlargement and job enrichment can be motivational tools?

> ## Motivating Through Gainsharing and Profit Sharing

As a result of company reorganizations, downsizings, and buyouts designed to save the company from financial ruin or a hostile takeover, many companies are instituting incentive programs that relate pay to performance. These programs, however, usually require employee involvement in and acceptance of the responsibility of setting goals and achieving them. Although not all employees are interested in or willing to learn how to run a company, employee involvement generally leads to organizational success.

Gainsharing

A practice that has become increasingly popular is known as **gainsharing**—a program in which employees are rewarded financially for productivity gains they have achieved. Annual bonuses are the typical form of reward for productivity improvements—a positive reinforcement. Gainsharing programs usually involve employees in setting the productivity goals as well as developing the plans for achieving them and recognize the motivational aspects of money.

Jack Stack reports in *The Great Game of Business* how Springfield Remanufacturing Corporation in Springfield, Missouri, established a bonus program that resulted in moving the company from a loss position in the first year of the program to pretax earnings of $2.7 million in its fourth year. No one was laid off.

The supervisors and managers of this small International Harvester factory bought it from Harvester when Harvester was in a crisis. Jack Stack believes that a good bonus system can help by emphasizing job security and reminding workers what it takes to protect their jobs and by showing them how they can get more out of those jobs. The bonus system at Springfield Remanufacturing provides for holding base salaries at a level that gives workers job security and shares, through bonuses, whatever additional money they generate. Educating its workers about business helps them get involved in the major goals of making money and generating cash. Overcoming basic ignorance about business has paid off for Springfield Remanufacturing.[10]

Profit Sharing

Another method of allowing employees to share in the financial results of their efforts is called **profit sharing**—a program by which employees share part of the risk and, therefore, share in the resulting profits. Profit-sharing program payoffs can range from annual checks to deposits in tax-sheltered retirement plans or stock ownership plans. Different plans work best for different companies; there isn't necessarily one best method of providing employees with a financial stake in their organization's achievement. FourGen Software, near Seattle, offers stock options that are redeemable at the vested employee's discretion. Jamestown Advanced Products Inc., a metal-fabricating company in Jamestown, New York, distributes large checks to employees when labor-cost targets are beaten.[11]

A typical profit-sharing plan limits each employee's share to a certain percentage of total compensation. However, if a company that has an employee stock ownership plan (ESOP) grows, its stock increases in value, and employees at all levels can do very well. Employee stock ownership plans distribute the rewards for long-term growth. When the ESOP is invested with sizable amounts of stock and employees understand their rights and responsibilities, it can be a powerful tool for molding individuals into a cohesive group with a common purpose. Because stock plans require long-term growth, employees tend to direct their attention away from short-term personal or departmental goals and toward company objectives. The average 5-year ESOP participant at RLI Insurance Co. in Peoria, Illinois, owns 8000 company shares, which are worth approximately $160,000. Teaching employees how to track their company's financials allows them to keep up with their personal investment and helps to make them feel like the owners.[12]

The number of U.S. companies turning to employee ownership has increased since 1974, when legislation granting tax benefits for investment vehicles known as ESOPs was passed by Congress. At first, ESOPs were used primarily to provide employee benefits or to enable the owners to generate cash by selling stock to employees. In the 1980s, however, employee buyouts became popular as a way to rescue struggling companies. The Avis car rental company boasts of one of the biggest success stories after employees acquired it for $1.7 billion.

COMPETENCY
CHECK

Can you discuss
how gainsharing
and profit sharing
may be
motivators?

Typically, employee ownership provides workers with only a minority interest in the company and has a mixed record of reviving businesses. In some cases, employee buyouts have failed because of high debt or because the companies involved were in declining industries. In late 1993, United Airlines' two largest employee unions presented a proposal to buy most of the air carrier in return for major wage and work-rule concessions. United's unionized pilots and machinists proposed to buy 53 percent of the carrier at an estimated cost of $4.55 billion or more, a landmark agreement because of its size. At this writing, the buyout has not yet been approved by the unions and the company's board. If it is approved, the employee buyout trend is likely to spread as a way to extract wage concessions from unions.[13]

Job Satisfaction

Job satisfaction has been a topic of research for many years, and researchers have had difficulty identifying factors that consistently result in job satisfaction. The results obtained from this research have been just about the same throughout the years: Employees want the same things they have always wanted. According to C. J. Cranny of Bowling Green State University, employee satisfaction is a "function of the difference between what employees want or think they should get, and what they're really getting."[14]

As shown in Figure 11.3, the items at the top of the list of importance to today's workers—health insurance, benefits, and job security—can be expected in today's economic environment of layoffs, cost-cutting measures, and increased health care expenses. Also ranking high is "interesting work." Noting the relatively low level of importance of high income in Figure 11.3, a supervisor needs, therefore, to recognize the value of interesting work and strive to meet that important need.

Similar results are shown in Figures 11.4 and 11.5. A wide gap exists between

Figure 11.3
HOW IMPORTANT IS EACH OF THE FOLLOWING CHARACTERISTICS TO YOU? HOW SATISFIED ARE YOU WITH IT IN YOUR CURRENT JOB?

	% of Workers Who	
	Ranked It as Very Important	Said They Were Satisfied
Good health insurance and other benefits	81%	27%
Interesting work	78	41
Job security	78	35
Opportunity to learn new skills	68	31
Having a week or more of vacation	66	35
Being able to work independently	64	42
Recognition from coworkers	62	24
Regular hours (no weekends, no nights)	58	40
Having a job in which you can help others	58	34
Limiting job stress	58	17
High income	56	13
Working close to home	55	46
Work that is important to society	53	35
Chances for promotion	53	20
Contact with a lot of people	52	45
Flexible hours	49	39

Source: Reprinted with permission, *Inc.* magazine, November 1992. Copyright 1992 by Goldhirsh Group, Inc., 38 Commercial Wharf, Boston, MA 02110.

Figure 11.4
WHAT DO YOU MOST PREFER IN A JOB?

	% of Workers Saying Aspect Was the Most Important			
	1973	1980	1985	1990
Important and meaningful work	52%	52%	48%	50%
High income	19	20	19	24
Chances for advancement	18	19	22	16
Job security	7	6	7	6
Short work hours	5	3	3	4

Source: Reprinted with permission, *Inc.* magazine, November 1992. Copyright 1992 by Goldhirsh Group, Inc., 38 Commercial Wharf, Boston, MA 02110.

Figure 11.5 HOW SATISFIED ARE YOU WITH THESE ASPECTS OF YOUR JOB?				
	% of Workers Saying They Were Satisfied			
	1984	1988	1990	1992
Type of work	78%	80%	77%	79%
Coworkers	76	77	77	76
Benefits	81	77	74	71
Being treated with respect and fairness	64	62	60	58
Job security	63	64	59	58
Chances to contribute ideas	54	55	56	54
Pay	57	50	47	46
Recognition for performance	44	48	45	39
Advancement opportunities	33	36	34	27

Source: Reprinted with permission, *Inc.* magazine, November, 1992. Copyright 1992 by Goldhirsh Group, Inc., 38 Commercial Wharf, Boston, MA 02110.

Figure 11.6 SELECT FROM THE FOLLOWING LIST THE TWO FACTORS THAT ARE MOST IMPORTANT TO YOU IN YOUR CURRENT JOB			
	% of Respondents Who Chose Each Factor, by Educational Level		
	High School Graduate or Less	Some College or Less	College Graduate
Pay	46%	42%	29%
Amount of independence	31	35	40
Pleasant working environment	30	23	17
Liking the people at work	29	24	19
Gratifying work	25	32	43
Contribution to public good	11	14	23
Important career step	10	15	19

Source: Reprinted with permission, *Inc.* magazine, November 1992. Copyright 1992 by Goldhirsh Group, Inc., 38 Commercial Wharf, Boston, MA 02110.

"important and meaningful work" and "high income." These results reveal that benefits and pay are less important when workers enjoy their work.[15]

What workers want depends on who they are. Differences in expectations are related more to levels of education than to any other factors, as shown in Figures 11.6 and 11.7. Gender doesn't seem to make a difference; men and women view the same aspects of the workplace as rewarding or not rewarding.[16]

	Overall	Professionals/ Managers	Tech.	Sales/ Admin.	Blue Collar
Figure 11.7 WOULD YOU SAY YOU ARE ENJOYING YOUR WORK MORE, LESS, OR ABOUT THE SAME AS YOU WERE FIVE YEARS AGO?					
More	52%	60%	55%	51%	44%
Less	19	14	18	22	24
About the same	27	24	26	26	31
Don't know/ no answer	2	2	1	1	1

Source: Reprinted with permission, *Inc.* magazine, November 1992. Copyright 1992 by Goldhirsh Group, Inc., 38 Commercial Wharf, Boston, MA 02110.

Figure 11.8 WHICH ONE OF THE FOLLOWING WOULD MOST GIVE YOU THE FEELING OF SUCCESS IN YOUR LIFE?	% Choosing Each Factor
Happy family life	62%
Ability to do some good in the world	15
Earning lots of money	10
Position and prestige in your work	6
Involvement in some creative activity	4
Fame	1
Don't know/no answer	2

Source: Reprinted with permission, *Inc.* magazine, November, 1992. Copyright 1992 by Goldhirsh Group, Inc., 38 Commercial Wharf, Boston, MA 02110.

Another factor important to the satisfaction of workers is a "happy family life." In Figure 11.8, "happy family life" is the first job-related answer. Employers who are astute enough to write policies that help employees balance work and family responsibilities are more likely to attract and keep employees committed to their company. The company becomes more than "just a place to work."[17]

The marketplace has changed dramatically in the last 20 years, and with those changes the next generation of companies, both large and small, has developed new ways of thinking. Some of these companies are Wabash National, LifeUSA, Springfield Remanufacturing Corp., Wal-Mart, Southwest Airlines, Jamestown Advanced Products, and the Baltimore plant of Chesapeake Packaging Co. What these companies have in common is a new way of thinking about how people work together. The traditional roles, obligations, and expectations of the conventional organization structure are eliminated. The responsibility of the business is no longer centered at

COMPETENCY CHECK

Can you list factors that make workers' jobs more satisfying?

the top; the CEO and everyone else have undergone a kind of liberation. An important aspect of these new changes is that managers don't have to figure out how to motivate employees, and employees don't sit around waiting to be told what to do next. The goal is to have everyone thinking like an owner.

Within some of these companies, chaos has resulted from the emotional and organizational strain. Foremen and supervisors find their customary jobs and status abolished. Some will survive the change; others won't. Change, as presented in Chapter 8, will direct the companies of the twenty-first century to organize in ways that allow employees to take responsibility as well as to share in the risks and rewards of their efforts. New ways of motivating workers will develop with the new ways of doing business.[18]

COMPETENCY REVIEW

1. Describe Maslow's hierarchy of needs.
2. Explain Herzberg's two-factor theory.
3. Define the needs for achievement, power, and affiliation identified in McClelland's acquired needs theory and describe how these needs typically affect individuals.
4. Describe Vroom's expectancy theory.
5. Discuss behavior modification.
6. Discuss how job enlargement and job enrichment can be motivators.
7. Describe the motivational aspects of gainsharing and profit sharing.
8. List three factors identified in this chapter as being important to worker job satisfaction.

APPLICATIONS

1. Using Maslow's hierarchy of needs, give an example of an action the supervisor can take to motivate workers at each level. On the lines below try to supply an example not shown in the text.

Need	Motivating Action
Self-actualization	_____
Esteem	_____
Social	_____
Security & safety	_____
Physiological	_____

2. According to Vroom, what aspect of his expectancy theory would be demonstrated by the following statements?

    a. "There aren't any guarantees that I'll be able to reach that sales goal by the end of the year. It's a lot higher than I've ever done before."

    b. "Now, let's figure this out. If I want to make $1 million in sales next year, how many sales calls will I have to make each day and month? And how much will each sale have to average? That's too hard; I'd be killing myself for a lousy trip to Hawaii."

    c. "Who says we'll actually get a $25,000 bonus? Remember five years ago, when Kurt Bidwell was general manager? He proposed a $30,000 bonus for each sales rep who brought in $1.5 million in sales. Then, when 15 of us made it, he said the company couldn't afford it."

3. Some supervisors think that motivational tools must be created by upper management or that these tools are expensive. The following items cost under $10 and may be effective with the "plateaued" employee. List five more inexpensive items that may be used to motivate and to boost morale.

    a. Take the employee out to lunch.

    b. Ask the employee to redesign a form.

    c. Show sincere concern for the employee's career and personal life when it is especially important to the employee.

    d. Assign the employee to a special task force.

    e. Bring snacks or doughnuts to say "thanks" for a job well done.

    f. _____

    g. _____

    h. _____

    i. _____

    j. _____

Source: Adapted from Richard A. Payne, "Motivating the 'Plateaued' Employee," *Piedmont Airlines,* August 1986, pp. 81–85.

4. Which of McClelland's acquired needs is demonstrated in each situation below?

    a. Mack Fischer supervises 20 assemblers in the circuit board section of Vaxco Corporation, a small computer manufacturing company. He has established a friendly working atmosphere within the plant by getting to know each of the workers, asking about their families, sharing family photos, and sincerely caring about each of them. After work on Fridays, most of the assemblers and Mack go to a nearby café for snacks before going home. Recently, some quality control problems have arisen with a few of the circuit boards produced. Mack has tracked the problems to Beth Baker, whose husband was injured in an auto accident and has been in the hospital for 6 weeks. She has been taking care of their three children, working full-time, and visiting her husband in the hospital daily for 6 weeks. Mack stops by Beth's station daily to ask how she and her husband are doing. However, he doesn't want to bring up the quality issue now and maybe create more stress for Beth.

b. Monica Diaz has been a document processing supervisor for six months. She started working at Palmento Industries 3 years ago as a mail clerk and soon advanced to a word processing specialist position in the document processing department. She is constantly checking the bulletin board for new positions that may be posted and for which she may be qualified. Monica has made it clear to the word processing specialists that she now supervises that she won't be their supervisor forever—she has plans.

c. C. J. Frost, supervisor of the plastic materials processing plant, has been with Unique Manufacturing Co., for 11 years. He started out as a finisher in the final-stage section of the plant and quickly became recognized for his creativity. CJ developed new procedures for sanding and smoothing the exposed cut edges of Plexiglas consumer products that saved time and money and resulted in smoother edges. During his tenure as supervisor, he was the first to volunteer his work group to develop new procedures whenever the need arose. He also encouraged his team members to look for ways to improve procedures. CJ and his team had an impressive array of awards displayed in a showcase outside CJ's office on the shop floor. CJ and his team have been rewarded financially as well. CJ is the highest-paid plant supervisor in the company, and his team members have received the highest annual bonuses the last 5 years.

Case I

CASES

BLOCKED CAREER

Jim Morris was a 61-year-old supervisor in the die-casting department at a leading truck plant. Jim had worked 22 years for the company, the last 9 in the same position, and he was considering retirement. He was tired of the routine and just did his job, filed his reports, and went home. However, after he thought about having to pay for college for his two children, he reconsidered retirement.

When Jim announced that he would stay beyond early retirement, his boss was noncommittal; it really didn't matter. A year later, however, Jim's boss was transferred. The new manager, John Malone, recognized Jim's situation, and, more important, he recognized Jim's knowledge of the machines he used. John attended a company-sponsored seminar for managers with similar motivational problems and learned how he might help Jim become interested in his job again.

John asked Jim to develop a task force to study a machine that was not operating properly and to develop a solution within 2 months. Jim was allowed to select the personnel he needed, and he assembled the task force in only a few days. Manufacturers' specifications were reviewed and the equipment functions analyzed within 1 month. Jim and his task force identified a way for the company to save almost $2 million.

Jim's enthusiasm continued after the project was completed. He was proud to announce that he would not retire until age 65 because his job was more challenging than it had been in years.

1. What motivators did John Malone use with Jim?
2. Explain how other motivators might have worked in this situation as well.

Case II

THE TOPPED-OUT DIRECTOR

Cynthia Goodman had been director of product packaging in the lightbulb division of Smithfield Corporation for almost 10 years. During her 16 years at the plant, she had moved rapidly through the ranks. She was now in charge of the packaging for all new lighting products.

In the past year, however, she was consistently behind schedule by as much as 2 to 3 months on every project. Other departments criticized her for unresponsiveness, and the stack of paperwork on her desk multiplied daily. She was convinced that nothing would ever change. Her staggering workload and the feeling of never catching up had destroyed her motivation and her morale. Instead of confronting Cynthia, her boss, Kevin Short, decided to introduce motivators to see if she could regain her previous performance levels.

Kevin gave Cynthia the freedom to hire all the temporary help she needed to get her work up to date within 1 month. He asked her to analyze the work flow to see if new products or systems could prevent the overload from occurring again. Kevin also took Cynthia to a regional meeting so that she could explain to all those who had been complaining what an insurmountable task she was faced with. She told them that they should be grateful for the volume of work she *did* get done under the circumstances.

Cynthia's work-flow analysis resulted in shortening new packaging turnaround from 3 months to 10 days. With the package development process streamlined, computer and employee time was saved.

1. What methods did Kevin Short use to motivate Cynthia?

2. Why were these methods effective with Cynthia?

Source: Both cases are adapted from Richard A. Payne, "Motivating the 'Plateaued' Employee," *Piedmont Airlines,* August 1986, pp. 81–85.

REFERENCES

1. Tom Peters, *Liberation Management,* Alfred A. Knopf, Inc., New York, 1992, p. 13.
2. Olga J. Myers, "A Basic Managerial/Supervisory Tool Often Overlooked," *Supervision,* October 1990, p. 8.
3. A. H. Maslow, *Motivation and Personality,* Harper & Row Publishers, Inc., New York, 1954.
4. Ibid., p. 82.
5. Frederick Herzberg, Bernard Mausner, and Barbara Block Synderman, *The Motivation to Work,* 2d ed., John Wiley and Sons, Inc., New York, 1959.
6. David C. McClelland, *The Achieving Society,* Van Nostrand Reinhold, New York, 1961; and "Business Drive and National Achievement," *Harvard Business Review,* July–August 1962, pp. 99–112.
7. Victor H. Vroom, *Work and Maintenance,* John Wiley & Sons, Inc., New York, 1964.
8. W. Clay Hamner and Ellen P. Hamner, "Behavior Modification on the Bottom Line," *Organizational Dynamics,* no. 4, Spring 1976, pp. 6–8.
9. Sam Walton, *Made in America,* Doubleday & Co., Inc., New York, 1992, p. 140.
10. Jack Stack, "The Great Game of Business," *Inc.,* June 1992, pp. 53–66.
11. John Case, "The Best Small Companies to Work for in America," *Inc.,* November 1992, p. 96.
12. Ibid., pp. 97–98.
13. "Buyouts to Follow United Model," *The Cincinnati Enquirer,* December 18, 1993, p. B5.
14. Christopher Caggiano, "What Do Workers Want?" *Inc.,* November, 1992, pp. 101–102.
15. Ibid.
16. Ibid.
17. Ibid.
18. John Case, "A Company of Businesspeople," *Inc.,* April 1993, pp. 79–93.

SUGGESTED READINGS

Blanchard, K., and Johnson, S.: *The One-Minute Manager,* William Morrow Company, New York, 1982.

Cranny, C. J.: *Job Satisfaction: How People Feel about Their Jobs and How It Affects Their Performance,* Lexington Books, Lexington, Mass., 1992.

Peters, Tom: *Liberation Management,* Alfred A. Knopf, Inc., New York, 1992.

Stack, Jack: *The Great Game of Business,* Doubleday/Currency, New York, 1992.

Tarkenton, Fran: *How to Motivate People,* Harper & Row Publishers, Inc., New York, 1986.

Truitt, Mark R.: *The Supervisor's Handbook,* National Press Publications, Shawnee Mission, Kans., 1991.

Walton, Sam: *Made in America,* Doubleday & Co., Inc., New York, 1992.

GLOSSARY

behavior modification   A method of encouraging appropriate behavior through consequences resulting from that behavior.

gainsharing   A program in which employees are rewarded financially for productivity goals they have achieved.

motivation   The desire or drive within a person to achieve some goal.

need for achievement   The desire to do something better than it has ever been done or to accomplish something difficult just because it is difficult.

need for affiliation   The desire to maintain close, friendly personal relationships.

need for power   The desire to control, influence, or be responsible for others as well as to control money and real estate.

profit sharing   A program in which employees share part of the risk and the resulting profits.

STUDYING THIS CHAPTER WILL ENABLE YOU TO:

1. Define *communication*.

2. Describe the basic communication components.

3. Identify major sources of current information and relate those to the preferred sources.

4. Define *grapevine*.

5. Identify methods of communicating information upward.

6. Explain horizontal communication and Fayol's bridge.

7. List ways to communicate information downward.

8. Describe the supervisor's role in problem-solving teams.

9. Describe ways a supervisor can contribute to a meeting as a participant.

10. Describe activities a supervisor should engage in before, during, and after a meeting.

11. List guidelines for effective verbal communication.

12. Describe actions the supervisor can take when supervising employees for whom English is a second language.

13. Describe the functions of nonverbal communication.

14. Explain types of nonverbal communication.

15. Explain the importance of written communication.

16. Identify tips for effective writing.

17. Describe how technology aids communication.

C H A P

Communicating Effectively

The Communication Process

An anonymous author once wrote, "I know you think you understand what you thought I said, but what you heard is not what I meant." **Communication** is the process of exchanging information, and the message is *understood*. The following incident actually occurred—as explained by one of the authors:

> My secretary, Melody, was to mail a hundred certificates of completion to participants in a training course. The 8½″ × 11″ certificates were very attractive, printed by the sponsoring agency and signed by the superintendent, the supervisor, and the instructor. Melody was not at her desk when I left the office, so I wrote a note that read, "Fold these as little as possible." Melody did! She folded the certificates to fit into small, personal-sized envelopes.

Did communication take place here? No! There was no mutual understanding (and the certificates had to be redone).

Communication Components

Communication is attempted when one person (the *sender*) wants to convey something (a *message*) to another person (the *receiver*) and the second person acknowledges that the message has been received (*feedback*). As illustrated in Figure 12.1, these are the four basic components of the communication process.

The sender initiates the communication because he or she has something to convey to someone through language that may be oral, written, or nonverbal. The message is encoded and then transmitted through a medium (words, numbers, illustrations, or actions) that puts the sender's thoughts into a form that can be transmitted. The receiver *decodes* (interprets) the message based on her or his background and experiences and responds to the message through feedback. **Feedback** lets the sender know whether or not the message was understood. The feedback that Melody

COMPETENCY CHECK
Can you define *communication?*

B.C.

Source: By permission of Johnny Hart and Creators Syndicate, Inc.

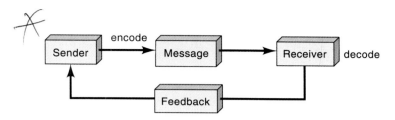

Figure 12.1
**COMMUNICATION
PROCESS**

gave when she folded the certificates and inserted them into small envelopes was action feedback that gave a clear signal that the message had not been understood and communication had not taken place. Feedback may also be in oral or written form.

Throughout the communication process, "noise" is present. Noise is anything in the environment that detracts from or confuses the message. For example, a receiver may be distracted by a quiet conversation nearby; a sender may be distracted by the telephone ringing; both sender and receiver may be distracted by people walking by.

**COMPETENCY
CHECK**
Can you describe the four basic components of communication?

Sources of Information

Employees want to know what's going on in their company. Most employees believe that they are entitled to information because they have a vested interest in the company. Where do employees get their information? Where do they *want* to get their information? The answers to these two questions are shown in Figure 12.2. These

Figure 12.2		
EMPLOYEE SOURCES OF INFORMATION		

Preferred Sources		Actual Sources	
Rank	Source	Rank	Source
1	Immediate supervisor	1	Immediate supervisor
2	Small group meetings	2	Grapevine
3	Top executives	3	Small group meetings
4	Annual business report to employees	4	Bulletin board(s)
5	Employee handbook/other booklets	5	Employee handbook/other booklets
6	Orientation program	6	Regular general employee publication
7	Regular local employee publication	7	Regular local employee publication
8	Regular general employee publication	8	Annual business report to employees
9	Bulletin board(s)	9	Mass meetings
10	Upward communication programs	10	Top executives
11	Mass meetings	11	Orientation program
12	Audiovisual programs	12	Union
13	Union	13	Mass media
14	Grapevine	14	Audiovisual programs
15	Mass media	15	Upward communication programs

Source: Karen Rosenburg, survey by Towers, Perrin, Forster, and Crosby in *Human Resources Management—Ideas and Trends in Personnel,* no. 97, Aug. 12, 1985, p. 123. Reproduced with permission from *Human Resources Management—Ideas and Trends,* published and copyrighted by Commerce Clearing House, Inc., 4025 W. Peterson Ave., Chicago, IL 60646.

COMPETENCY
CHECK
Can you identify
five of the major
sources of current
information and
relate these
sources to the
preferred ones?

responses are from a survey of 10,000 employees conducted by Towers, Perrin, Forster, and Crosby, management consultants. Survey employees were asked to list their major preferred sources for job-related information and their actual sources. The list on the left makes it clear that employees would like to rely on their immediate supervisor for their information and not on the grapevine, but the list on the right shows that the actual sources are the immediate supervisor and the grapevine, in that order.

Making the Grapevine Work for You

Every company has an informal communication channel called a *grapevine*. Note that in Figure 12.2, the grapevine is listed as one of the *least* preferred sources but one of the *most* used current sources of information. The grapevine is particularly active in firms where the formal communication channels are inactive or ineffective. Employees want to know what's happening in the workplace, and if they aren't given the information through the usual formal channels, the grapevine takes over. The grapevine is typified by "Did you hear about the RIF?" "Sam told Marie that Jim is getting comp time for the extra hour we worked last Friday" and so on. As the grapevine spreads information, distortion occurs, but 70 to 90 percent of the details communicated through the grapevine are correct.[1]

Until employees are given organizational information directly through formal communication channels, supervisors must learn to make the grapevine work *for them and the employees.*

COMPETENCY
CHECK
Can you define
grapevine?

grape vine
Second

WHAT CAN THE SUPERVISOR DO?

The supervisor is making progress as a communicator of job-related information. Perhaps even more important, a growing percentage of employees acknowledge the supervisor as their *preferred* source of information (see Figure 12.2). To capitalize on the confidence placed in them, supervisors must know what information employees want and need. Employees are concerned about organizational plans for the future, especially as they relate to mergers, downsizing, reorganization, expansion in other countries; new technology and how it would affect employees; how the organization is performing in terms of profitability; job-related "how-to" information; how jobs fit into the organization; productivity improvement; and personnel policies and practices, to mention some of the concerns expressed.

WHAT CAN THE SUPERVISOR DO?

Supervisors should feed the grapevine not with rumors but with facts. Since grapevines flourish in information voids, it's best to keep them well fed. This is especially true during troubled times, when the fears and anxieties of employees often result in false and unproductive grapevine information. To avoid such perils and pitfalls, it is best to do the following:

- ☐ Keep employees informed about key issues by using the formal channels. The formal channels are staff meetings, posted notices, and announcements in company newsletters and fliers.
- ☐ Keep employees informed informally through the grapevine. To do this, pass information to the key people on the grapevine, sometimes called *liaison communicators*. These are the employees who receive information and pass it on to other staff members.[2]

liaison - respected & liked

Overcoming Communication Barriers

Employees often say, "What we have here is a failure to communicate." Communication is often blocked because some barriers are difficult to penetrate. While there are many barriers to effective communication, this discussion is limited to the more common communication barriers: (1) differing frames of reference, (2) technical language and jargon, (3) information overload, and (4) conflicting signals. Other barriers include not thinking through what you hope to accomplish through your communication; poor timing; physical barriers such as temperature, noise, and so forth; distrust or fear of the communicator; and using attacking and judgmental language.

Differing Frames of Reference

Supervisors are in daily contact with people who have varied experiences, education, and backgrounds, which means that they also have differing frames of reference. The expression "I know where you're coming from" has, of course, no relationship to geography. The expression refers to understanding how another individual feels about something based on his or her frame of reference. Sometimes it is difficult to understand someone whose background is entirely different from yours. For example, a supervisor with 10 years' experience on the job, an associate's degree from a technical school, and a middle-class, suburban background might have difficulty communicating with a dropout from an urban high school. Their experiences, educations, and backgrounds are very different, and people use their pasts as their frames of reference.

Technical Language and Jargon

Jargon is pompous, trite, and abstract language or, as Webster defines it, unintelligible talk. Jargon is also specialized language of a trade or profession. An example of the former occurred during World War II, when President Franklin D. Roosevelt asked an aide to write a memo on the subject of blacking out federal buildings. The aide submitted the following memo for the president's signature:

> Such preparations shall be made as will completely obscure all federal buildings occupied by the federal government during an air raid for any period of time from visibility by reason of internal or external illumination. Such obscuration may be obtained by blackout construction or by termination of illumination. This will, of course, require that in building areas in which production must continue during the blackout, construction must be provided so that internal illumination will continue. Other areas may be obscured by terminating the illumination.

President Roosevelt revised the memo to read:

> In buildings where you have to keep working, put something across the windows. In buildings where you can afford to let the work stop for awhile, turn out the lights.

Some people use technical language and jargon to try to impress others. The saying "Express, don't impress" is a good one. The goal of communication is to deliver your message in a way that the receiver understands. You rarely achieve that goal when you use technical language with those who are not in your field or when you use jargon.

Information Overload

Almost all employees today, whatever their level, get too much information and have too little time to evaluate it. This barrier to effective communication becomes greater as the tide of information increases.

The information overload problem is partly a result of our reluctance to voluntarily decrease the amount of information we receive. We hesitate to say, "Take me off the distribution list. I rarely use this report, and if I need the information, I know where it is available." Perhaps this is because we do not want to admit there is some information we neither need nor use, or perhaps it is because the overflow of information (overwhelming as it may be) makes us feel important.

One organization decided to see whether its managers really used all the reports they were sent and whether they would even notice if the reports were discontinued. First, notices were attached to the tops of all the reports. The notices asked (1) if the managers used the information in the report, (2) if they wished to continue to receive the report, and (3) if the report could be distributed less frequently and still provide the necessary information in a timely manner. Those who returned the notices responded (1) yes, (2) yes, (3) no.

A follow-up was conducted several months later. This time, the notice was placed about three-quarters of the way through the report. The notice read: "If you wish to continue receiving this report, please return this notice to the computer center within 10 days." What do you think the response was this time?

Conflicting Signals

When senders convey one message in words and a different one through actions, they are guilty of sending conflicting signals. For example, your supervisor may say, "We have an open-door policy here, and I encourage you to drop by at any time to talk to me." Then, when you come by to discuss a problem, not only is the door shut, but the secretary says, "She's busy." When you finally do get in the door, the supervisor shuffles papers, answers the phone several times, and is generally inattentive. Conflicting signals have been given. Supervisors should be aware that conflicting signals cause employee confusion and uncertainty. Which message is to be believed? Care should be taken to send the same messages each time, whatever the form used.

Communicating with Individuals

Supervisors communicate both formally and informally with their superiors, their peers, and their employees. The communication may be upward, horizontal, diagonal, or downward.

Superiors

Upward communication—communication from employee to manager—is declining, according to a Towers, Perrin, Forster, and Crosby survey. Perhaps with the trend toward more participative management, upward communication will receive more emphasis. Upward communication is important to employee morale and should be encouraged.

Upward communication can also be diagonal. For example, look at the following situation:

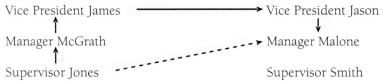

Under normal conditions, if Jones in production needs to discuss a problem with Malone in quality control, she would go up the chain of command through McGrath to James to Jason and then down the chain of command to Malone. Using the diagonal communication channel, however, Jones would go directly to Malone. Called "bypassing the chain of command," this practice is not generally encouraged. But if the practice is approved, it saves time, and, because the communication is direct, there is less chance of distorting the message. Some managers do not like workers to use diagonal channels because managers may not always be informed of the communication and their perception is that their control is diminished. Bypassing the chain of command also occurs when an employee goes over the supervisor's head with an issue, or when a manager bypasses the supervisor and gives directions to employees. This type of bypassing the chain of command should be avoided; it creates, rather than solves, problems.

The purpose of upward communication is to pass information from employees to managers. This information may be communicated in a number of ways, including:[3]

- ❑ *Reports.* This is the most frequently used method of upward communication. Reports may be oral or written, formal or informal.
- ❑ *Grievance procedures.* This form of upward communication allows employees a formal channel of appeal beyond the authority of their immediate supervisors.
- ❑ *Complaint or suggestion boxes.* Boxes for depositing complaints and suggestions are effective when both employees and managers view them as legitimate sources of information.
- ❑ *Questionnaires and surveys.* Information about employee attitudes, morale, views of the organization, and relationships between managers and employees may be obtained through questionnaires and surveys.
- ❑ *Open-door policy.* The availability of managers to workers through an open-door policy reflects the degree of managerial commitment to open communication among all levels of employees.
- ❑ *Grapevine.* The grapevine information may originate at a lower level in the organization and be communicated upward.
- ❑ *Liaison communicators.* Employees may supply information to managers, either voluntarily or by request. Sometimes coworkers resent this method of upward communication and consider the source an "informer," a "snitch," or the manager's favorite. When liaison communicators are used, they must be objective and resist rumor-mongering.
- ❑ *Special meetings.* Employees may call special meetings to discuss items of interest with managers. If these meetings allow for a mutual exchange of information, they may be an effective means of upward communication.
- ❑ *Problem-solving groups and teams.* These employee groups are described in Chapters 4 and 10. As management styles have become more participative, problem-solving groups and teams have become a more legitimate way to communicate with upper levels of management through worker presentations of their suggestions for improvement.

COMPETENCY CHECK

Can you identify methods of communicating information to superiors?

The effectiveness of upward communication is determined by the attitudes of managers toward participative management and the confidence that is placed in the employees. When participation is encouraged, more upward communication results.

Peers

Horizontal (or lateral) communication—communication between peers—presents unique opportunities and challenges. It allows employees to bypass the formal structure and address problems at the level at which they appear. In 1916, Henri Fayol, an early management authority whose contributions to the classical era were discussed in Chapter 1, identified this form of communication and illustrated it with a chart shown in Figure 12.3 that became known as "Fayol's bridge."

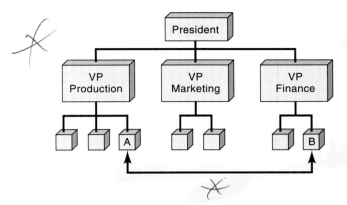

Figure 12.3
FAYOL'S BRIDGE

Horizontal communication is fast. It works in much the same way as diagonal communication. To solve a problem that involves A and B in Figure 12.3, it is not necessary to go through the formal layers of the organization—upward through the chart at the left and then downward through the chart at the right. The directness of this form of communication also helps to reduce the information loss and distortion that often occur when information travels through many different people.

According to a survey reported in *Personnel Journal,* more than 60 percent of employees in a variety of organizations say that lateral communication is ineffective. More specifically, 45 percent say that communication between peers within departments is inadequate, and 70 percent claim that communication between departments must improve.[4]

One of the greatest dangers of horizontal communication is that it may become a substitute for both upward and downward communication. When this happens, two major channels of communication are bypassed, and information that should be shared is not available to these channels.

COMPETENCY CHECK

Can you explain horizontal communication and Fayol's bridge?

Employees

Most of the information flow within an organization is downward. Managers at different levels within the company communicate with the people they manage. Information may be communicated from managers to employees in many different forms, including:[5]

- ❑ *Directives.* Company policies and procedures are communicated to employees through directives. Directives may be sent only to employees who are affected or may be distributed widely for information purposes.
- ❑ *Bulletin boards and posters.* These communication devices are most effective when placed where employees typically congregate. To be effective, bulletin boards and posters also must be attractive and contain up-to-date information on topics of interest to employees.
- ❑ *Company publications.* Well-written articles placed in company publications are another method of making information available to workers. As reported by Towers, Perrin, Forster, and Crosby, however, workers do not always consider these publications the best source of company news.

❐ *Letters and pay inserts.* Most employees pay attention to what is put into a pay envelope; inserts may therefore be an effective way to communicate with employees.

❐ *Employee handbooks.* When workers are hired, they may be given employee handbooks. Employees should be encouraged to read these handbooks because they usually contain information regarding employee responsibilities and benefits. Many companies require new employees to sign a statement to show that they have actually read the handbook.

❐ *Memos.* Memos are one of the most frequently used forms of communicating in-house information, especially among departments. Memos are an efficient way to communicate in-house information.

❐ *Information racks.* Like bulletin boards, information racks should be placed in areas where employees congregate—next to a water fountain, near a drink machine, or close to a snack bar. Information racks should also be kept current and neat and contain information of interest to employees.

❐ <u>*Loudspeakers.*</u> The effectiveness of a loudspeaker as a method of communication depends largely on how often and where it is used and for what purpose. If the loudspeaker often interrupts work with unimportant messages, it simply becomes a part of the background noise and even an object of ridicule. Loudspeakers are inappropriate in most office and sales settings and are primarily used in industrial settings.

❐ <u>*Grapevine.*</u> As described earlier, the grapevine is also used to send information from managers to employees.

**COMPETENCY
CHECK**
Can you identify
ways to
communi-
cate information
from manager to
employee?

The effectiveness of downward communication is determined largely by the willingness of managers to share information with workers. Sharing information builds trust and emphasizes teamwork between managers and employees.

Communicating with Groups

Supervisors interact not only with individuals—superiors, peers, and workers—but also with groups. Although a group is simply a collection of individuals, communicating with a group requires skills different from those used when communicating with individuals on a one-to-one basis.

Two major components exist in all group settings—content and process. *Content* is the task with which the group is charged; *process* is what happens between, among, and to group members as they go about the activities necessary to accomplish the task. Process looks at the interactions of the members of a group—*group.dynamics.*

 ## Working with Committees

Supervisors are frequently asked to work with committees as either committee members, chairpersons, or facilitators. As a member of a committee, it is <u>important</u> that the supervisor <u>be on time for meetings,</u> <u>be prepared,</u> and <u>be an active participant</u>.

To prepare for a meeting, the supervisor should review the committee's charge; note some ideas for reaching the goal as well as questions or items that need clarification; and conduct any research necessary to make a contribution to the work of

WHAT CAN THE SUPERVISOR DO?

Supervisors are looked upon as a major source of information. They provide information to superiors, to peers, and to workers. There are many ways to communicate with each group, and supervisors should learn to use all the tools and techniques effectively. Not all companies have all of the communication tools and techniques available, nor are all the formal communication channels used. Supervisors, however, should take advantage of any opportunity to keep their superiors informed about developments in the department, to communicate with their peers when such communication will expedite work, and to keep their workers informed.

the committee. For example, if a task force has been formed to deal with the problem of employee turnover, the supervisor would want to bring information to the meeting about the turnover in his or her department, any trends that might have been observed, any actions that may have been taken to reduce employee turnover, and specific results that can be attributed to those actions.

Working with Problem-Solving Groups and Teams

With the increase in employee involvement and participation in issues related to the workplace, a supervisor may be asked to serve as a facilitator for a problem-solving group or to work with a team within the department.

Problem-Solving Groups.   The supervisor's role in a problem-solving group may be as the chairperson, as the facilitator or as a resource person. Some companies prefer to have the supervisor act as a resource person and facilitator and have a member of the work group serve as chairperson. Still others believe the supervisor should act as the chairperson. As a resource person and facilitator, the supervisor is an observer, stepping in only when it is necessary to keep the group on track or at the request of the chairperson. The role of chairperson of the problem-solving group is somewhat different from the role of the traditional chairperson. Even when serving as the chairperson, the supervisor is a part of the group and has the same vote—one—and the same influence as each of the other members of the group.

Teams.   Some organizations are using the team approach—dividing the workforce into groups, each group responsible for all phases of a particular segment of the work. When the team approach is used, the groups are empowered to make all decisions for that segment. The supervisor's role in a team is to act as coach and counselor and team member.

Working Effectively in Meetings

Supervisors play several roles as they attend meetings, whether as a participant or as chairperson.

COMPETENCY
CHECK
Can you discuss
each of the roles
a supervisor may
play when
working with a
problem-solving
group or a team?

As a Participant

When supervisors participate in meetings, they should observe the common courtesies of arriving on time, projecting interest, being attentive, and not leaving before the meeting is adjourned.

In addition, the supervisor will contribute more and gain more from the meeting if he or she practices good listening skills. One often-cited study found that adults in various occupations spend 45 percent of their communicating time listening. Listening is not the same as hearing. *Hearing* is the act of perceiving sound(s) ("She's hard of hearing."). *Listening* is the act of attaching meaning to the sound(s) ("He never listens!"). Listening skills can be improved if you:[6]

- ❏ listen for key words and concepts.
- ❏ weigh important points and supporting facts.
- ❏ take selective notes.
- ❏ form opinions only after hearing all the information to be presented.
- ❏ increase your vocabulary to increase your understanding.
- ❏ avoid mental debates with the speaker.
- ❏ are attentive.
- ❏ avoid preconceptions or prejudgments.

Of course, good listening skills are an essential part of the supervisor's daily tools. Effective listening to workers should be an ongoing technique as supervisors work to build strong relationships with their workers.

When making comments to the group, the supervisor should speak so that other participants can hear. Speaking too softly, trailing off at the ends of words or sentences, or not speaking clearly diminishes the contribution. A great idea that no one can understand may be rejected or, at best, met with little enthusiasm.

There is seldom universal agreement on anything. So if you disagree with a suggestion, discuss the merits of the idea without attacking the person who made the suggestion. One positive way to disagree with another group member's suggestion is to suggest an alternative.

COMPETENCY CHECK

Can you describe how the supervisor can contribute as a participant to the success of a meeting?

As a Chairperson

As the chairperson of a meeting, the supervisor's responsibilities will vary according to the size, composition, location, and purpose of the meeting. The supervisor may be responsible for securing the meeting room, notifying the participants, arranging the seating, controlling the physical environment, and generally overseeing the meeting arrangements as well as for conducting the meeting and for any postmeeting activities.

Before the Meeting.   If the supervisor is responsible for all the premeeting arrangements, as many of the routine arrangements as possible should be delegated. However, the supervisor should come to the meeting early and check the room before other participants arrive to be sure all arrangements are complete. A premeeting checklist is provided in Figure 12.4.

Figure 12.4
PREMEETING CHECKLIST

Participants
_____ Number invited
_____ Number accepted
_____ Agenda distributed

Facilities
_____ Room reserved
_____ Number of chairs required
_____ Add/remove chairs
_____ Temperature
_____ Lighting
_____ Seating arrangement
_____ Lectern required
_____ Microphone required

Audio-Visual Equipment/Aids
_____ Overhead projector
_____ Slide carousel projector
_____ Film projector
_____ Screen
_____ Tape recorder/player
_____ Videotape player

Refreshments
_____ Coffee
_____ Tea

Refreshments (cont.)
_____ Danish, doughnuts
_____ Cream, sugar, artificial sweetener
_____ Spoons, napkins
_____ Cold drinks
_____ Other

Amenities
_____ Notepaper
_____ Pens
_____ Pencils
_____ Name cards

Miscellaneous Requirements
_____ Videotape recorder
_____ Flip chart
_____ Transparency pens
_____ Chalk/eraser
_____ Extension cord
_____ Handouts _____ #
_____ Other (list)
_____
_____
_____

One of the responsibilities of a chairperson is to prepare and distribute an agenda to all participants. The order of the agenda should reflect the importance of the items to be discussed, with the most important ones first. Everyone is more creative; more alert; more prepared to make careful, considered decisions; and more willing to participate in the entire process early in the meeting than later (especially if the meeting is long, runs overtime, or is scheduled for late Friday afternoon). Agendas speed meetings along and keep them on track. They also force the person who called the meeting to specify clearly the items to be covered. Agendas also make participants aware of the items for discussion and give them time to prepare for the meeting by completing assignments and gathering and reading background information prior to the meeting. Agendas minimize the "If I had known we were going to discuss . . ." excuse.

Distribute the agenda far enough in advance of the meeting for some preplanning to be done. An agenda is also a tool for handling digressions tactfully: "That's a good idea, Charlie, but we should defer that discussion either to the end of the meeting, if time permits, or to another time so that we can complete today's agenda."[7]

The temperature must be comfortable for most participants, the lighting adequate for reading and writing. The seating arrangement should be appropriate to the number of people and the meeting's purpose. If the meeting was called to provide information, make sure everyone can see and hear the speaker. If the purpose of the meeting is to provide an arena for discussion, place chairs so that interaction is possible. Make the environment one that invites group members to participate.

During the Meeting.   As the meeting leader, there are actions you can take to make the meeting more productive. These actions are summarized in Figure 12.5, and several of them are discussed here.

The chairperson should begin the meeting at the time scheduled, whether everyone is present or not. If you develop a reputation for starting on time, participants will soon realize that you respect the value of their time (and your own), and they will be encouraged to arrive at future meetings on time. State the purpose and time frame of the meeting. End on time. Keep the meeting moving along; if members want to ramble or digress, courteously but firmly return the discussion to the issue. Allow all members to participate in the discussion, but keep the meeting orderly; do not allow it to become noisy or disorganized. Take charge!

After the Meeting.   Most postmeeting activities are writing activities and are the responsibility of the chairperson. One of the most important postmeeting activities is to prepare a follow-up summary. Minutes are sometimes recorded, but since min-

---

Figure 12.5
WHAT TO DO AT THE MEETING

The following actions taken during the meeting will help you have a more productive meeting.

_____ Distribute an agenda before the meeting
_____ Be prepared by having reread the agenda and by being informed about the items to be discussed
_____ Have additional background information reproduced (if appropriate) or be prepared to give the information orally (if necessary)
_____ Start on time
_____ Give a short, warm welcome
_____ Introduce new or unknown members (if group size allows)
_____ State purpose of meeting
_____ State amount of time meeting should take
_____ Stop on time
_____ End on a positive note
_____ Be in charge
_____ Know your participants

WHAT CAN THE SUPERVISOR DO?

Meetings often lack mutually understood goals. Some goals aren't even stated; they are merely implied. Meetings may have several goals, some in conflict with others. All the goals listed below may be legitimate at one point or another in one meeting or another. As a supervisor, can you identify the goals of the meetings you call? Of the meetings you attend?

_____ To block, retard, delay, or confuse action

_____ To fill up time and avoid pressing issues back at the job

_____ To fill a meeting quota

_____ To keep the group divided

_____ To diffuse decision responsibility so that decision failure will be shared

_____ To meet the social needs of the group

_____ To use the meeting arena to impress the boss

_____ To share significant information openly

_____ To set goals, priorities, and plans

_____ To learn some new skill or approach

_____ To coordinate activities

_____ To clarify issues and reach understanding between individuals and with other groups

_____ To identify a problem, assign action to a person, and set a time target

_____ To solve a problem and assign implementation responsibilities

_____ To hear announcements from the boss

_____ To provide mutual assistance

_____ Other (specify)

Source: Richard J. Dunsing, *You and I Have Simply Got to Stop Meeting like This*, AMACOM, New York, 1978, p. 61.

utes include only actions taken, a summary is extremely helpful to all participants. Summaries serve these four important functions:

1. Everyone receives identical written confirmation of the proceedings. Because people have selective memories, recollections of events often differ.
2. Written confirmation of task assignments eliminates any confusion about responsibilities.
3. A clear statement of decisions reached and votes taken is provided.
4. A record for both participants and absentees is provided.

COMPETENCY CHECK
Can you describe the activities a supervisor should engage in before, during, and after a meeting?

Supervisors should make an effort to obtain feedback from participants regarding the effectiveness of the meeting. Feedback on meeting productivity can be obtained from several sources and in several ways. Verbal feedback may be obtained, but this kind of feedback is often distorted because only positive comments may be heard directly with indirect sources relied on for the negative comments. A formal meeting evaluation may be conducted, using an evaluation form that addresses the way the meeting was conducted, the value of the meeting, the physical facilities, and the overall achievement of the meeting goals. While it would be unusual to conduct formal meeting evaluations of routine meetings, managers may want to evaluate an important meeting to be sure the goals of the meeting were accomplished.

Every meeting is a miniature management cycle. You *plan* the meeting, you *organize* the tasks, you *lead* the group, and you *control* through feedback from the evaluation process.

Verbal and Nonverbal Communication

Communication may be verbal, written, or nonverbal. This section discusses *verbal communication* (what we say) and *nonverbal communication* (what we communicate by our behaviors).

Verbal Communication

Because verbal communication is a <u>primary method of providing information</u>, supervisors must make every effort to ensure that communication (understanding) takes place. One of the problems with verbal communication is that no written record exists and each individual's recollection is dependent upon his or her memory of the event.

Making Verbal Communication More Effective

To make verbal communication more effective, the following guidelines should be observed.[8] These guidelines are appropriate whether you are speaking to one individual, to several individuals, or to a group.

Know What You Want to Say.   Whether you are speaking to one person or to a large group, you should have a definite idea of what you want to convey, how you are going to say it, and what you hope to accomplish. You may want to rehearse mentally how you are going to approach a subject, particularly if it is a sensitive one or one that is likely to cause a confrontation.

Consider Your Listener's Point of View.   Your listener may have a viewpoint entirely different from yours, so you should be open to the possibility of another opinion. And it is important to listen to the opinions of others and to be open to other views.

Move from the Simple to the Complex.   If you want to convey more than routine information, plan the order of the items to be discussed. Any background information required for understanding should precede the presentation of new ideas or topics for discussion. Moving from the simple to the complex allows ideas to be developed. Begin with a basic concept, and then expand the information.

Select Your Words Carefully.   When communicating orally, you do not have the luxury of reviewing and rephrasing your words as you do when communicating in writing. Therefore, before you speak, know your listeners' backgrounds, and select your words carefully so as to send your message clearly without offending your listeners. Try to be sensitive to the way your words may be interpreted.

Enunciate Clearly.   Speak clearly and naturally in a tone that will be understood. Failure to pronounce words clearly and correctly or mumbling may cause your listeners to lose interest or to feel that you are so unsure of what you are saying that it probably has no value.

Use the Active Voice.   The active voice is more easily understood because it is more direct. Using the active voice will help you speak more concisely, too, because it puts the action right up front. For example, "Tom called me" is more direct than "I was called by Tom."

Be Courteous and Natural.   No one likes to listen to people who are artificial, pompous, or rude. A natural, forthright manner is the most effective way to communicate. Your listener will appreciate courtesy in communication, just as you do.

Repeat if Necessary.   One way to be sure that your message was both received and understood is to summarize briefly the points made. You may also ask the listener to confirm the message by repeating it.

 Establish Eye Contact, and Be Aware of Body Language.   Establishing eye contact with your receiver encourages communication. Eye contact keeps your mind from wandering and has the additional benefit of making the listener feel more important because of your obvious attention.

COMPETENCY CHECK

Can you list guidelines for effective verbal communication?

Working with English as a Second Language (ESL)

English as a second language is becoming more prevalent in the workplace as employees come from more diverse geographical backgrounds. According to a Society of Human Resource Management/Commerce Clearing House[9] study, firms on the West Coast of the United States are more likely to experience difficulties arising from language barriers. Immigrants, as new employees whose English language skills are minimal or nonexistent, must depend initially on coworkers and supervisors. Initiating a buddy system, using icons, pictures, and gestures to enhance communication, being patient, and never embarrassing anyone who lacks English-language skills are actions that help non-English-speaking employees adjust to their jobs. Supervisors who encourage their companies to offer ESL classes and promote employee participation help to minimize problems resulting from lack of English-language skills.

Nonverbal Communication

Everyone engages in communication that is neither verbal nor written; it is communication through action. Sometimes it is difficult to understand nonverbal communication because it is subject to interpretation by the receiver.

Functions

Nonverbal communication serves to reaffirm or emphasize, to contradict, to substitute, to complement, and to control.[10] Nonverbal communication may be used in conjunction with verbal communication, or it may be used by itself.

Gestures and facial expressions may serve to restate or emphasize a particular point. Sometimes a nod of the head emphasizes verbal agreement; a smile may reaffirm "How good to see you"; the type of clothing worn may reaffirm the importance placed on a particular event.

Sometimes nonverbal behavior may contradict verbal communication. You may say, "Yes, I have time to meet with you" and then continue to work on something else instead of listening. The verbal message "I have time" is contradicted by your actions, which clearly say, "I'm too busy for you right now."

Nonverbal behavior may substitute for a verbal message. For instance, if you ask someone how the weather is and the response is a flip of the hand, you understand that to mean "so-so."

Complementary nonverbal behavior is often used in speaking. These nonverbal cues serve to reinforce a verbal message. A supervisor may hold up a defective part as she explains how to spot a particular defect.

Nonverbal cues may also be used to control the behavior of others. For example, a lifted finger may call for quiet.

Nonverbal communication is an important part of the communication process. Supervisors need to recognize that their actions speak as loudly as their words, regardless of whether the words are communicated orally or in writing.

COMPETENCY CHECK

Can you describe functions of nonverbal communication?

Types

How can communication be achieved without words—either written or verbal? What specific nonverbal behaviors can be used to communicate a message?

The seven types of nonverbal communication are: (1) silence, (2) body language, (3) gestures, (4) facial expressions, (5) touch, (6) space and distance, and (7) personal appearance.[11]

Silence is a very powerful communication tool that can have both positive and negative meaning. Through your silence, you can communicate displeasure, lack of interest, or failure to understand. Silence may be used for emphasis, as when a speaker pauses, or it may indicate that you are listening carefully, attentively.

A popular subject in recent years, *body language* as nonverbal communication takes two forms: (1) unconscious movements and (2) consciously controlled or altered movements. When bored, you may yawn or shift positions frequently. When nervous, you may fidget or bite your nails. These movements are usually made unconsciously. Conscious movements may communicate, too. You may cross your arms in a "show-me" attitude, look at your watch, or gaze around the room.

A *gesture* is a deliberate body movement intended to convey a message. A thumbs-up gesture shows that things are under control; a wave of the hand may indicate "you go first"; standing when introduced to people who are older or in higher-ranking positions shows respect.

Facial expressions are important in nonverbal communication because faces express a great range of emotions. The entire face is expressive, especially the eyes. Awareness of how a smile, laugh, frown, or scowl may be interpreted is important; you do not want to send the wrong message through your facial expression.

The first nonverbal communication we have in life is *touch*. Communication by touch should take into consideration both cultural patterns and individual preferences. Some people prefer a handshake to a pat on the back or a verbal greeting to an arm around the shoulder. You must be aware of cultural differences and individual preferences when using touch as a communication tool.

Distance is a communication tool which, like touch, expresses degrees of intimacy and of cultural and individual acceptance. Better communication is possible at closer ranges because the verbal message is clearer and the nonverbal messages more readily observed. The space you place between yourself and others also communicates a message. If you sit behind a large desk and place your employee in a chair in front of the desk, you have communicated that you want the conversation to be formal and that you are in charge. Seating yourself and your employee closer together and side by side says that the conversation is to be informal and on an equal level.

Personal appearance and dress communicate a message because there are accepted and expected grooming and dress standards. Those who disregard the accepted standards send the message that they do not choose to conform to company standards and group norms.

COMPETENCY CHECK

Can you describe types of nonverbal communication?

Written Communication

Many people believe that written communication is more difficult than face-to-face verbal communication because it provides no immediate feedback to the sender, no opportunity to explain unclear messages or answer questions immediately, no way to reinforce the message with nonverbal cues, and no advantage of seeing the reaction of the receiver.

Importance

Written communication is important because it not only sends the message in written form but provides an ongoing record of the communication. At a later date, one cannot say, "But that is not what I said" or "I never agreed to that," as may often happen with verbal messages.

Tips for Effective Writing

When sending messages in written form, you must be careful to use the five Cs of good writing—clarity (the message is easy for the reader to understand); conciseness (the message contains enough words to make the meaning clear without sacrificing courtesy); completeness (the message provides the reader with enough information to enable him or her to take appropriate action without having to ask for additional information); correctness (the message has the facts straight, is free of typographical errors and misspelling, and is grammatically correct); and courtesy (the message conveys the information in a way that creates and maintains goodwill). But that is not enough! Here are some tips that will help the reader understand the message.[12]

Write for the Reader.   Use vocabulary appropriate for the reader, neither overestimating nor underestimating your reader's ability to understand.

Keep Sentences Short.   Long, run-on sentences lose the reader's interest quickly. If most of your sentences are longer than 15 to 20 words, consider breaking them up into shorter sentences. Remember, a sentence is a group of words conveying a *single* thought.

Use Paragraph Breaks.   Paragraph breaks divide the message into readable units, separating the text into main and supporting ideas. Paragraph breaks also improve the message's appearance through making the message less cluttered by leaving white space.

Use Short, Simple Words.   Look at the difference between the memo written by Roosevelt's aide and the revised memo. Long words are rarely necessary and should never be used in an attempt to impress—they rarely do.

Avoid Jargon.   The key here is to ask yourself, "Is this the way I would express myself if I were speaking rather than writing to this person?"

Avoid Trite Words and Phrases.   Some expressions are used because they have been around for a long time. When words and phrases become outdated, they should be discarded for more crisp, clean, contemporary language. For example, "as per your request" should be replaced with "at your request," "at the present time" with "now," and "notwithstanding the fact that" with "although." One check for trite words and phrases is, Do your phrases often begin and end with little words such as *by, in, as, it, is, of, to,* or *with,* or with words ending in *-ing*? If so, you may want to evaluate your use of these words to see if they are lead-ins to outdated words and phrases.

Use Action Words.   Action words move your message along briskly. For example, "It is our belief that this change will be of interest to you" is read more easily if action words such as "We believe this change will interest you" are used.

Avoid Redundancies.   Redundancies are repetitions. For example, the phrases "surrounded on all sides," "new beginner," "refer back," "and etc.," "past history," and "consensus of opinion" all contain redundancies.

Use a Natural Style.   Business letters do not have to be formal, stilted, or long. They can be warm, natural, and brief. Write in the style that is natural for you and in a tone that considers the reader.

Use Personal Pronouns.   When we talk to others, we use *I, we,* and *you.* Although this is often not the case in business writing, the informality associated with personal pronouns makes communication more natural. Instead of saying, "It is the opinion of the company," say "We believe"; instead of "The association with your company has been a pleasant one," say, "We have enjoyed our association with you and your company."

Use Correct Punctuation.   Punctuation can make a difference in what the message actually says. For example:

Mrs. Jones, said the secretary, was late.
Mrs. Jones said the secretary was late.

Proofread Carefully.   Sometimes an error in preparing a letter can be very costly to the company; sometimes an error creates such an impression of incompetence that the customer loses faith in the company; sometimes an error is just a nuisance. As one person remarked, however, "As long as the document is in your hands, a mistake is a keying error; when it is in someone else's hands, it is a *gross error!*" The person who initiates the message has the responsibility for checking its accuracy.

    In a study by the American Assembly of Collegiate Schools of Business, communication skills were identified as one of the most important skills required of first-line and middle managers.[13] Supervisors therefore must develop their oral and written communication skills as they strive to improve the performances of their employees as well as their own performances.

COMPETENCY CHECK
Can you cite techniques for writing effective messages?

Technology-Based Communication

More and more companies are using technology to communicate information more efficiently. Computers, electronic mail (e-mail), voice mail, and video are used to generate and receive messages to individuals and groups. As the technology becomes more available to first-line managers, supervisors will be required to understand and use the technology to enhance communication and to improve productivity. A personal computer or terminal on each manager's desk is becoming more the norm than the exception.

Computers

Computers have become an important tool for communication, and managers at all levels need to be able to use the computer for document origination. As recently as 1988 and 1991, at least two studies showed that longhand was the technique most used to create written communication. However, a study of managers ranging from senior- to first-level published in 1993 showed that using the computer to keyboard and send their own messages is the method most often used.[14] Figure 12.6 shows this information.

According to Figure 12.7, respondents to the 1993 study believed that more and more managers will choose to prepare their own documents on a microcomputer and will be *expected* to prepare their own documents on a microcomputer. However, knowing how to use the computer is not enough; managers must also know how to communicate. Basic communication skills, as described in this chapter, are transferred to the computer, and the computer then provides the vehicle for more efficient message generation. Once the document has been keyed into the computer, paper copies are produced using a printer.

The saying "Garbage in, garbage out" has been around as long as computers have been in existence. And it is still true. Computers only process what is input and provide no safety net for poor writing skills.

Electronic Mail

Electronic mail (e-mail) uses the computer to generate, send, and receive messages electronically, both internally and externally. A user types a message into the computer and codes the message for access only by the intended receiver(s), and the message is then stored in the receiver's computer. Many e-mail systems allow the user to create distribution lists to identify a group of receivers whose names and e-mail addresses are automatically used for distribution of particular types of messages. For example, a supervisor may want to send an invitation to all other supervisors to attend a seminar in her department. She keys in the invitation and tells the computer to distribute the message to all other supervisors on site according to a prestored list.

To be effective, users of electronic mail need to be aware of some format differences between printed and electronic messages. Some suggestions for better communication using e-mail include:[15]

1. Because computer screens are limited to 24 or fewer lines, all related information should be presented within one screen size or less. This format allows readers to see related information together, eliminating the need to scroll through the entire message to link information.

Figure 12.6 FREQUENCY AND PERCENTAGE OF ALL DOCUMENT ORIGINATION METHODS			
Often	Occasionally	Seldom	Never
Keyboard yourself and send:			
Letters 62 (38.7%)	27 (16.2%)	12 (7.5%)	23 (14.4%)
Reports 66 (41.2%)	27 (16.9%)	10 (6.3%)	30 (18.8%)
Memos 63 (39.4%)	25 (15.6%)	9 (5.6%)	23 (14.4%)
Forms 40 (25.0%)	21 (13.1%)	12 (7.5%)	41 (25.6%)
Other 15 (9.4%)	1 (0.06%)	2 (1.2%)	12 (07.5%)
Handwrite for someone to complete:			
Letters 37 (23.1%)	27 (16.9%)	37 (23.1%)	24 (15.0%)
Reports 33 (20.6%)	26 (16.2%)	32 (20.0%)	36 (22.5%)
Memos 35 (21.9%)	27 (16.0%)	28 (17.5%)	47 (29.4%)
Forms 30 (18.8%)	33 (20.6%)	19 (11.9%)	47 (29.4%)
Other 6 (3.7%)	5 (3.1%)	8 (5.0%)	15 (9.1%)
Rough draft keyed for someone to complete:			
Letters 15 (9.4%)	31 (19.4%)	21 (13.1%)	31 (19.1%)
Reports 18 (11.2%)	29 (18.1%)	21 (13.1%)	44 (27.5%)
Memos 13 (8.1%)	33 (20.6%)	24 (15.0%)	49 (30.6%)
Forms 14 (8.7%)	27 (16.9%)	17 (10.6%)	57 (35.6%)
Other 3 (1.9%)	7 (4.4%)	3 (1.9%)	17 (10.6%)
Dictate to machine:			
Letters 7 (4.4%)	5 (3.1%)	9 (5.6%)	93 (58.1%)
Reports 6 (3.7%)	5 (3.1%)	6 (3.7%)	103 (64.4%)
Memos 8 (5.0%)	7 (4.4%)	13 (8.1%)	95 (59.4%)
Forms 5 (3.1%)	2 (1.2%)	5 (3.1%)	106 (66.2%)
Other 1 (0.6%)	1 (0.6%)	1 (0.6%)	27 (16.9%)
Dictate to secretary:			
Letters 3 (1.9%)	8 (5.0%)	14 (8.7%)	74 (46.2%)
Reports 3 (1.9%)	3 (1.9%)	12 (7.5%)	100 (62.5%)
Memos 6 (3.7%)	12 (7.5%)	13 (8.1%)	94 (58.7%)
Forms 3 (1.9%)	3 (1.9%)	10 (6.3%)	99 (61.9%)
Other 1 (0.6%)	1 (0.6%)	1 (0.6%)	26 (16.3%)
Other:			
Letters 1 (0.6%)	—		4 (2.5%)
Reports 2 (1.2%)	2 (1.2%)	—	6 (3.7%)
Memos —		—	
Forms 2 (1.2%)	2 (1.2%)	—	9 (5.6%)
Other 1 (0.6%)	1 (0.6%)	—	5 (3.1%)

Source: Linda Henson Wiggs, "Document Origination and Factors Contributing to Selection of Origination Method: Implications for Business Curricula," *The Delta Pi Epsilon Journal*, vol. 35, no. 2, Spring 1993, p. 106.

Figure 12.7 TRENDS IN DOCUMENT ORIGINATION METHODS ANTICIPATED BY RESPONDENTS		
Anticipated Changes in Methods of Document Origination	2–3 years	4–10 years
Will communicate more through electronic mail	89 (55.6%)	94 (58.7%)
Less administrative support	67 (41.9%)	56 (35.0%)
Will choose to prepare own documents on microcomputer	66 (41.2%)	54 (33.7%)
Expected to prepare own documents on microcomputer	52 (32.5%)	58 (36.2%)
Expected to prepare own documents on mini- or mainframe computer	40 (25.0%)	42 (26.2%)
More administrative support	15 (9.4%)	14 (8.7%)
Expected to use centralized dictation system	10 (6.3%)	12 (7.5%)
Will have voice recognition input technology	15 (9.4%)	62 (38.7%)
Other	2 (1.2%)	4 (2.5%)

Note: Respondents were asked to check all responses that applied.
Source: Linda Henson Wiggs, "Document Origination and Factors Contributing to Selection of Origination Method: Implications for Business Curricula," *The Delta Pi Epsilon Journal,* vol. 35, no. 2, Spring 1993, p. 109.

2. Subject lines need to be definitive, not general. Unless the general subject is something of particular interest to readers, such as "Overtime," readers of e-mail use the subject lines to decide whether to read the entire message. For example, "Cafeteria" may not attract the reader's attention, but "New Cafeteria Hours and Meal Costs" might.
3. The beginning of the message should explain the contents as quickly as possible. It is easy for a reader of a printed message to scan several pages of printed material easily and quickly; multiple screens are not as easy to scan.
4. E-mail has a greater need for subheads. These are aids to readers as they scroll through the document.
5. E-mail should include a signal to the reader when additional pages are included, and the last screen should carry a symbol such as ### or END that lets the reader know he or she has reached the last screen of the message.

E-mail allows messages to be sent and read at the convenience of both the sender and the receiver and eliminates the need for paper copies. If paper copies are required, the originator and/or the receiver can print them out on their printer.

Voice Mail

Voice mail uses the telephone to send messages from one person to another using "mailboxes." Voice mail sends a verbal message to a mailbox, where the message is recorded. Typically, the sender dials a company telephone number and receives a verbal message such as "You have reached the Ace Company mailbox system. At the tone, dial the mailbox number of the person for whom you want to leave a message." After the mailbox number is dialed, the sender may hear "You have reached Marge Miller's mailbox. Please leave your message at the tone, and I will return your call as soon as possible." Recipients access their messages by entering a personal code from a Touch-Tone telephone. The code preserves the confidentiality of the message. Voice mail has the advantage of overcoming time zone differences when communicating internationally or from coast to coast and minimizes "telephone tag."

Video

Videotaped messages delivered via satellite are being used more and more to distribute personalized messages to groups of people. Videotaped messages can be used effectively to address large groups of employees, a method used by Sam Walton and Wal-Mart to explain changes, to motivate employees during downtimes, to give a pep talk, and so forth. This method is as close to one on one as many employees will ever get to their boss. Pepsi-Cola Co. used videotaped messages in 1993 when consumers claimed to have found objects such as syringes in their Pepsi cans. Pepsi's chairman made a video explaining the situation that was available by satellite to any television station that wanted to air the video. Some companies are now using videotaped messages as a training device—to explain how to do a job or to upgrade skills.

Although it is unlikely that supervisors will participate in making videotaped messages for satellite distribution, it is very likely that they will be called upon to introduce a taped message and to do a follow-up on its showing. How seriously the taped message is received by the viewers may depend partially on how well the supervisor introduces, listens to, and follows up on its contents. The supervisor who says, at the end of the videotape, "Well, that's it—back to your work" diminishes the message. The supervisor who follows up with a short "What can we do?" discussion will enhance the message.

COMPETENCY CHECK

Can you describe how technology aids in communication?

COMPETENCY REVIEW

1. Define *communication*.
2. Describe the four basic communication components.
3. Identify five major sources of current information and relate those to the preferred sources.

4. Define *grapevine*.
5. Identify six methods of communicating information upward.
6. Explain horizontal communication and Fayol's bridge.
7. List six ways to communicate information downward.
8. Describe the supervisor's role in problem-solving groups and teams.
9. Describe five ways a supervisor can contribute to a meeting as a participant.
10. Describe activities a supervisor should engage in before, during, and after a meeting.
11. List seven guidelines for effective verbal communication.
12. Describe actions the supervisor can take when supervising employees for whom English is a second language.
13. Describe four functions of nonverbal communication.
14. Explain six forms of nonverbal communication.
15. Explain the importance of written communication.
16. Identify at least 10 tips for effective writing.
17. Describe computers as a document-origination method.
18. Explain how electronic and voice mail aid communication.
19. Describe the differences in format of electronic mail and printed messages.
20. Describe videotaped messages as a communication tool.

APPLICATIONS

1. Each of the following statements violates one of the five Cs of good writing (clarity, conciseness, completeness, correctness, and courtesy). Identify the "C" that is violated. Then rewrite the statement to correct the error.
   a. As much as I hate to lose her, I can't recommend her too highly for promotion.
   b. In the event that we find ourselves in disagreement on the issue, it may be necessary that we seriously consider the advisability of continuing to do business with your company.
   c. Can we meet on Wednesday at 8:00 in the conference room?
   d. The stationary you delivered on Tuesday, March 29, 1993, is exactly what we wanted.
   e. It is obvious that you have made little attempt to meet your obligations. It is also obvious that you do not care about your credit standing with our company.
2. The following form will help you evaluate a working meeting (as opposed to an informational meeting). Select any meeting to evaluate. Circle the number on the scale that best expresses your view of the typical level of that behavior or characteristic. You may want to survey the entire group, the leader, or a few participants.

   To establish your own meeting model, you can place another symbol—a check mark, perhaps—at the number on each item as you believe it should be to best fulfill the meeting needs of your group.

MEETING CHARACTERISTICS AND BEHAVIORS

Goals

0	1	2	3	4	5

None set; irrelevant or trivial items only.

Well defined, clear, sharpened by the group.

Roles of Participants

0	1	2	3	4	5

Not known what to contrbute, extent of involvement

Meeting output known, limits known

Value of Meeting in Reaching Goals

0	1	2	3	4	5

Goals best achieved outside a meeting

This meeting and this group best for purpose

Priorities Set

0	1	2	3	4	5

None set; all have equal weight

Clear delineation of relative importance

Sense of Time

0	1	2	3	4	5

Much time wasted on trivia

Best time-fit between group focus and issue needs

Straight Talk

0	1	2	3	4	5

Much fuzzy talk, undefined motives

Issues set up, positions and wants clearly stated

Closure of Topics

0	1	2	3	4	5

Topics end, but decisions and action left unstated

All debate ends with a conclusion, decision, or assignment

Leadership Assumed

0	1	2	3	4	5

Left in the air, with goals and roles not in focus

Assumed by leader or led as needed

(Continued)

Participant Commitment

0	1	2	3	4	5

Each marks time, stays aloof, protects self-interest only

Each supports group effort, accepts decision

Participant Utilization

0	1	2	3	4	5

Some dominate continually; quiet ones never tapped

Each shares skill and insight as appropriate

Procedures and Rules

0	1	2	3	4	5

Many applied to excess, with high need to control behavior

A few used to set boundaries, keep on track

A Setting for Human Habitation

0	1	2	3	4	5

Uncomfortable, "cold" environment; distracting, dull setting

Basic air, heat, comfort needs met; seating arrangement facilitates contact

Source: Richard J. Dunsing, *You and I Have Simply Got to Stop Meeting Like This,* AMACOM, New York, 1978, pp. 64–65.

3. What messages do you receive when you see people using the following nonverbal communication?
   a. leaning forward
   b. crossing their arms
   c. sighing
   d. pushing their chairs back
   e. rolling their eyes upward
   f. yawning
   g. arriving late
   h. coming unprepared
   i. whistling
   j. putting their hands on their hips
   k. raising their eyebrows
   l. looking at their watches
   m. slinging a leg across a chair arm

4. Write a memo on any subject that you would like to bring to the attention of the dean of your school. If a computer is available to you, key the memo and print it out. Then assume that the memo is going to be transmitted to your dean via e-mail. What changes, if any, would you make in the format of the memo? Why these changes?

| Case I | | **CASES** |

BUT IT WAS JUST ANOTHER OF THOSE MEETINGS!

Jerry Malone is the new supervisor of the infants, children, and young teens department of the Merchandise Mart and in that position supervises a full- and part-time sales staff of 32. As supervisor, he will rotate with other departmental supervisors as chairperson of the Merchandise Mart weekly sales meetings. On Monday, September 1, Jerry sees this notation on his calendar:

> *Second reminder:* Chair of September 8 meeting. Regular meeting room is not available due to renovation.

The following is a calendar of Jerry's actions following his seeing the second reminder.

> *September 1.* Panicked.
> *September 2.* Asked around to see if anyone had suggestions.
> *September 3.* Wondered if other supervisors had business to include at the meeting.
> *September 4.* Asked other supervisors informally if they had any business to be included.
> *September 5.* Roughed out an agenda for the meeting. Gave the rough copy to the store manager's secretary to be typed when she had time. Jerry emphasized to her, however, that the agenda had to be in everyone's hands by closing time today.
> *September 5.* Found a room that would do for the meeting. Counted the stacked chairs and decided that there were enough to accommodate everyone who would be attending the meeting. Thought the room was a little cool but decided that with everyone in the room on Monday, it would be warm enough. The lighting was from one overhead light fixture but seemed to be adequate.

1. Critique Jerry's actions.
2. Write a memo to Jerry detailing how his preparations could have been more helpful to the meeting participants. Suggest to Jerry a better timetable for meeting preparations.

Case II

WHAT THE HECK DOES *THAT* MEAN?

According to *The Wall Street Journal* (5/20/92 and 11/19/92), some countries that now use English in their advertising and instructional materials are finding that the translation from their native language to English suffers from inaccuracy. A sign in a Paris hotel says, "Please leave your values at the front desk," while in Japan hotel guests are invited to "take advantage of the chambermaid." If you're hungry, a Polish menu allows you to select "roasted duck let loose" or "beef rashers beaten up in the country people's fashion." A Swiss restaurant warns, "Our wines leave you nothing to hope for." In Acapulco, a hotel gives new meaning to quality control when it boasts that "The manager has personally passed all the water served here."

Some other translations include one in a Norwegian cocktail lounge where ladies are requested not to have children at the bar; in Moscow a hotel sign across from a cemetery reads, "You are welcome to visit the cemetery where famous Russian and Soviet composers, artists, and writers are buried daily except Thursday"; a sign in Bucharest on an elevator that was being repaired explained, "The lift is being fixed for the next day. During that time we regret that you will be unbearable."

In Japan, Douter Coffee Co. has a special brew for those who are "tense in the breasts," while the City Original Coffee Company has "Ease your Bosoms" on their packets and boasts that "This coffee has carefully selected high quality beans and roasted by our all the experience." A sports bag has a tag that says, "A drop of sweat is the precious gift for your guts." A Tokyo hotel advises guests that it "is forbidden to steal hotel towels, please," but politely adds, "If you are not a person to do such thing, please not to read notice." A car rental agency offered these instructions to clients: "When passenger on foot heave into sight, tootle the horn. Trumpet him melodiously at first but if he still obstacles your passage then tootle him with vigor."

"Drop your trousers here," suggests a Bangkok dry cleaner, while a laundry in Rome says, "Ladies, leave your clothes here and spend the afternoon having a good time."

1. Which of the components of the communication process are not properly implemented?
2. As a manager, what do you think of the effectiveness of this type of communication?
3. What is your interpretation of some of these translations?
4. As a consultant asked to make a recommendation about the use of these advertising and instructional materials, what would your response be?

REFERENCES

1. Donald B. Simmons, "How Does Your Grapevine Grow?" *Management World*, February 1986, p. 18.
2. Keith Davis, Arizona State University, in ibid.
3. Betty R. Ricks and Kay F. Gow, *Business Communication: Systems and Applications*, John Wiley & Sons, Inc., New York, 1987, pp. 9–10.
4. Valerie A. McClelland and Richard E. Wilmot, "Improve Lateral Communication," *Personnel Journal*, August 1990, p. 32.
5. Ricks and Gow, op. cit., pp. 7–8.
6. Ibid., pp. 292ff.
7. Ibid., p. 230.
8. Ibid., pp. 225ff.
9. Claire J. Anderson and Betty R. Ricks, *1990 SHRM/CCH Survey*, Commerce Clearinghouse, June 26, 1990.
10. Ricks and Gow, op. cit., pp. 236–237.
11. Ibid., p. 232.
12. Ibid., p. 30.
13. Lyman W. Porter and Lawrence E. McKibbon, *Management and Development: Drift or Thrust into the 21st Century?*, McGraw-Hill Book Company, New York, 1988, p. 112.
14. Linda Henson Wiggs, "Document Origination and Factors Contributing to Selection of Origination Method: Implications for Business Curricula," *The Delta Pi Epsilon Journal*, vol. 35, no. 2, Spring 1993, p. 100.
15. Raymond V. Lesikar, John O. Pettit, Jr., and Marie E. Flatley, *Basic Business Communication*, 6th ed., Richard D. Irwin, Inc., Homewood, Ill., 1993, p. 274.

SUGGESTED READINGS

Foster, R. Daniel: "The Case of the Team-Spirit Tailspin," *Harvard Business Review*, January–February 1991, p. 14.

Gonring, Matthew P.: "Communication Makes Employee Involvement Work," *Public Relations Journal*, November 1991, p. 40.

Kiechel, Walter: "Breaking Bad News to the Boss," *Fortune*, April 9, 1990, p. 111.

McKeand, Patrick J.: "AT&T Revamps Employee Communications to Emphasize 'New Direction' for 90s," *Public Relations Journal*, November 1990, p. 26.

McKeand, Patrick J.: "GM Division Builds a Classic System to Share Internal Information," *Public Relations Journal*, November 1990, p. 24.

Mishra, Brenda: "Managing the Grapevine," *Public Personnel Management*, vol. 19, no. 2, Summer 1990, p. 213.

O'Connor, James V.: "Building Internal Communications," *Public Relations Journal*, June 1990, p. 29.

Ray, Eileen Berlin: "The Relationship among Communication Network Roles, Job Stress, and Burnout in Educational Organizations," *Communication Quarterly*, vol. 39, no. 1, Winter 1991, p. 91.

Ward, Mark: "Swing on the Company Grapevine," *EDN News*, Apr. 18, 1991, p. 1.

GLOSSARY

communication   The process of exchanging information and making the message understood.

decode   Interpret.

downward communication   Information sent from managers to workers.

electronic mail (e-mail)   Uses a computer to generate, send, and receive messages electronically.

encode   Organize thoughts.

ESL   English as a second language.

feedback   Communication component that lets the sender know whether the message was understood; may be in oral, written, or behavioral form.

grapevine   An informal communication channel.

horizontal communication   Communication between and among peers.

jargon   Pompous, trite, abstract language—unintelligible talk.

lateral communication   Communication between and among peers.

liaison communicator   Key people on the grapevine who receive information and pass it on to other staff members.

nonverbal language   Information communicated by behaviors.

upward communication   Communication from employee to manager.

voice mail   Uses the telephone to send messages from one person to another to a "mailbox," where the message is recorded.

CHAPTER 13

Turning Problem Employees into Productive Workers

STUDYING THIS CHAPTER WILL ENABLE YOU TO:

1. Recognize behavioral or attitudinal indicators that point to a potential problem employee.

2. Name other methods of identifying potential problem employees.

3. Describe strategies for preventing undesirable behavior.

4. Describe methods for correcting undesirable behavior.

5. Explain reasons for having disciplinary actions overturned.

6. Describe the planning involved in preparing for a counseling interview.

7. Describe pitfalls to avoid in the counseling interview and suggest alternative actions.

8. Discuss special types of problems and suggest actions a supervisor might take to correct these problems.

9. Describe how immediate dismissal procedures differ from dismissal following progressive discipline.

10. List primary actions a supervisor should take to avoid legal problems as a result of employee termination.

CHAPTER OUTLINE

Turning Problem Employees INTO Productive Workers

Recognizing Problem Employees

It is a rare supervisor who does not experience the frustration associated with supervising employees whose work is less than satisfactory, who are absent from or late to work, insubordinate, or involved with substance abuse. Typically, such employees exhibit behavioral or attitudinal responses that are different from those shown by productive and motivated workers.

Behavioral and Attitudinal Indicators

Like the proverbial chicken and egg, it is hard to tell which comes first, the behavior or the attitude. Does the behavior cause a change in attitude, or does the change in attitude cause the behavior? Because of the difficulty in answering this question and the "blurring" that sometimes occurs when trying to differentiate actions associated with behavioral and attitudinal problems, the problems will be described here without attempting to differentiate the inappropriate behavior from the attitude.

Problem employees reported by managers include those with high lost-time rates, those who do not notify the supervisor when they must be late or absent, those who are continually late or chronically absent, and those who use drugs or alcohol. Other problem employees reported include those with above-average accident rates or safety violations and those with substandard quality and quantity of work. Managers also complain about insubordinate workers, those with "bad attitudes," gripers, gossipers, and those who, in other ways, damage group morale.[1]

COMPETENCY CHECK

Can you identify behavioral or attitudinal indicators that should alert a supervisor to a potential problem employee?

A generally accepted estimate of the number of problem employees in the workforce at any one time is approximately 10 percent, as shown in Figure 13.1. Of this 10 percent, approximately one-half are hard-core problem employees who will be very difficult to turn into productive workers. To avoid creating your *own* stress and subsequent behavioral, attitudinal, and motivational problems, you should recognize the fact that you may not be able to save everyone. Give it your best shot, and then expend your energy on employees who will benefit from your efforts.

Other Indicators

Other methods for identifying potential problem employees include observation, surveys and diagnostic tests, direct employee appeal, and feedback from co-workers.

Observation.   As you go about your daily supervisory activities, you may notice symptoms of employee distress, confusion, or even hostility. Employees may report to work late, not follow the rules, or become surly and rude.

As you read in Chapter 10, management-by-walking-around is a great way to get to know your workers better. Observing employees as they go about their jobs will give you an opportunity to observe their behavior without being intrusive. If workers are used to seeing you walk around, they are more apt to continue doing their jobs in their usual way when you are present. If, however, you enter their space only

DARK CLOUD OVER PROBLEM EMPLOYEES

Figure 13.1
DISTRIBUTION OF PROBLEM EMPLOYEES

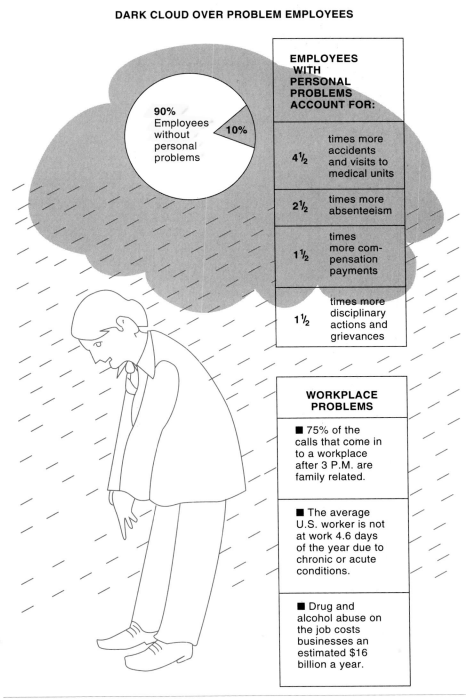

90% Employees without personal problems

10%

EMPLOYEES WITH PERSONAL PROBLEMS ACCOUNT FOR:

4½	times more accidents and visits to medical units
2½	times more absenteeism
1½	times more compensation payments
1½	times more disciplinary actions and grievances

WORKPLACE PROBLEMS

■ 75% of the calls that come in to a workplace after 3 P.M. are family related.

■ The average U.S. worker is not at work 4.6 days of the year due to chronic or acute conditions.

■ Drug and alcohol abuse on the job costs businesses an estimated $16 billion a year.

Source: Article by Gordon Borrell, graphics by Judy Jordan-Valloria, *The Virginian-Pilot and The Ledger-Star,* Norfolk, Va., Feb. 9, 1986, p. E1.

when there is a problem or when you are getting ready to complete the scheduled performance appraisals, they may react in an artificial way. They will be more intent on impressing you than on doing their jobs.

Surveys and Diagnostic Tests.   It is unlikely that you, as a supervisor, will decide to administer, on your own, any questionnaires or surveys relating to worker behavior or attitudes. This is usually the responsibility of the HR department. You may be asked, however, to administer a survey or a diagnostic test to the employees in your department as part of a companywide effort to gather information. If so, your responsibility is to introduce the instrument to the employees, explain its purpose, gain their cooperation, and follow the instructions given to you by the HR department.

For an organization to gain any benefit from a survey or diagnostic test, the participants must take the activity seriously. As their supervisor, you must set an example by doing your part in a professional manner. You would not introduce a questionnaire by saying, "Listen, people, the front office sent this questionnaire for you to fill out in your spare time. I know it's just another piece of busywork, but let's humor them. When you've finished, drop the thing on my desk." Instead, be sure that everyone understands its purpose, understands that the responses to the questionnaire will ultimately benefit both the organization and the workers, and that their input will be considered seriously. Convey the message that you are counting on them to respond openly and honestly to the questions. For the best response, a specific time (company time) should be set aside to complete the survey in a place that is relatively comfortable and quiet.

WHAT CAN THE SUPERVISOR DO?

First of all, be an observant supervisor. Be aware of what is happening in the workplace, particularly of any changes in worker behavior. Develop a reputation for being a caring supervisor by displaying an interest in the well-being of all the workers you supervise.

Practice an open-door policy, and make workers aware that you are available when they need to see you. This does not mean that if you are in the middle of an important task with an immediate deadline, you have to drop everything to see a worker at the very moment he or she asks to see you. Unless the worker has a true emergency, you can explain that you are in the midst of an important project with a deadline that can't be changed but you will be free by, say, 2 P.M. and will clear your calendar so the two of you can spend whatever time is necessary to talk out the problem. To make workers feel at ease in coming to you and not as though they are taking up your valuable time, you must learn to balance your own needs with those of the workers to the benefit of both.

Direct Employee Appeal.   Sometimes an employee will make a direct appeal for help. This will happen only if workers feel free to talk to you and know, by your previous actions, that you are available to them and interested in their well-being. Employees must also be confident that anything they tell you will be kept in the strictest confidence and that you will never break that confidence without their permission.

Feedback from Coworkers.   Just as the employee who comes to you with a problem must believe that you are trustworthy and can keep a confidence, so must the coworker who approaches you on behalf of a friend or perhaps someone who is not a friend. The coworker may feel, on the one hand, that this person needs help. On the other hand, he may feel that he is "telling tales" and might be getting someone in trouble if he approaches the supervisor. Assure the coworker that you have a mutual interest in helping a valued employee, and encourage him to give you any information he feels comfortable sharing with you. You may not get the full story, but you will probably get enough of it so that you can make a judgment about how to proceed in your effort to help the employee.

COMPETENCY CHECK

Can you name other methods of identifying potential problem employees?

Problem Employee or Problem Management?

Before labeling an employee a *problem,* consider the possibility that the root cause may be poor or ineffective management. One study found that about half of the employees labeled *problems* by their managers were victims of poor management.[2] These employees had not been adequately trained, had not been provided with counseling when they needed it, and had not received written warnings, as provided according to company policy. Some managers have neither the patience nor the ability to develop employees or to change their behavior.

Managers think they have a problem employee when, in reality, the employee simply has a different operating style. The outcome of this employee's efforts (productivity) may be acceptable; it is simply the process that is disturbing to the supervisor. Some examples of process concerns include the following:[3]

- ❐ *Physical appearance.* Some supervisors prefer a particular type of dress and are disdainful of employees who lack what they consider to be "style consciousness." However, not all jobs require a clean-shaven face or a suit and tie. Even in jobs that do not require certain dress standards, employees who refuse to conform to the supervisor's *perceived* requirements are usually deemed problems.
- ❐ *Work hours.* Some employees are more productive when they work outside the traditional work time. Biological clocks, family responsibilities, and personal preferences all affect an employee's productivity. If flexible work hours can be used to reduce tardiness or absenteeism, some problem employees may be turned around.
- ❐ *Extra hours and weekends.* Some supervisors find that they must work overtime and on weekends to catch up. If this is a regular pattern, perhaps the supervisor needs to evaluate the work habits that cause the overtime. In any event,

these supervisors may equate extra work with high productivity and expect their workers to put in the same overtime. If they don't, these supervisors may perceive the employees as being insufficiently committed to their jobs—or "problem employees."

- *Participation in activities after work hours.* Christmas parties, July Fourth picnics, and "thank-God-it's-Friday" celebrations all contribute to group cohesiveness and morale. However, employees who choose not to participate should not be penalized or considered "problem employees" just because they are less social than others or have other obligations.

- *Differences in values, attitudes, and lifestyles.* Supervisors may find themselves objecting to the lifestyles, attitudes, or values of the employees they supervise. Some supervisors have difficulty separating what employees do on the job—their productivity—from the opinions they express.

- *Demographic differences.* While we like to think that we are free of bias, prejudice still exists. And where demographic differences (differences in age, gender, race, or ethnic origin) occur, some supervisors may believe that the differences are associated in some way with the employee's ability to do the job. Diversity is to be valued, not denigrated (see Chapter 8).

Preventing Undesirable Behavior

The old adage has it that "An ounce of prevention is worth a pound of cure." Clearly, preventing problems is preferable to correcting them.

Establish, Communicate, and Maintain Expectations and Policies

One of the ways to prevent undesirable behavior is to be sure that each employee knows what is expected in terms of job performance (standards) and that workers are made aware of all company policies that directly or indirectly affect them.

The first step is to be sure that you have a clear policy on discipline. The policy should include the behavior employees are expected to observe as a condition of continuing employment. The rules should cover all the usual practices the organization considers important in the conduct of the job. There should be a general statement, too, that allows action to be taken for any negative behavior not specifically covered in the policy. Not every situation can be covered by a policy; the supervisor needs the discretion to take action when any inappropriate behavior is observed, whether that behavior is specifically defined in the company policy or not.

Management has a reasonable right to expect employees to be on time, to attend regularly, to give a fair day's work, to be physically and mentally able to perform the work assigned, to respond positively to direction, to learn the total job as well as any new jobs, to adjust to changes, to get along with fellow employees, and to know and observe the rules and procedures of the organization.[4]

In addition, the supervisor must recognize that some policy violations are more serious than others—stealing is more serious than lateness, for example. This means that policies should specify whether violations are major or minor and that the consequences of violations will vary according to the seriousness of the offense. Serious offenses may include possession or use of illegal or intoxicating substances on company property, possession of an unauthorized weapon, theft, fighting, sabotage, gross negligence, and repeated insubordination. Less serious offenses—such as failure to follow directions, leaving the job without permission, minor safety-rule infractions, horseplay, gambling, absenteeism or tardiness, or failure to maintain work standards—may be handled by a progressive discipline approach (discussed later in this chapter). An example of a policy in use by a major health care organization is shown in Figure 13.2.

Merely having a discipline policy does not prevent negative employee behavior. The policy must be disseminated and clearly communicated to all employees by whatever means are available to the supervisors—orientation meetings, bulletin boards, staff meetings, and so forth. Having employees sign to verify that they have read the handbook is a helpful tool and places some of the responsibility for being informed on the worker.

Clear standards, strictly maintained and communicated to employees, with specific policies for dealing with nonproductive or disruptive workers, discourage substandard work and increase morale and overall productivity. Setting and maintaining standards is one of the topics dealt with in Chapter 14.

Provide Ongoing Training

Preventive action would include providing the necessary instruction, using one or more of the techniques described in Chapter 7, at the time of employment. Sometimes, people are hired who do not have all the requisite skills or who have the aptitude for the job but do not yet possess the ability to do the job efficiently. Training is designed to overcome these deficiencies. When too little or inadequate training is provided, work performance is usually substandard. It is important to differentiate between employees who *can't* do and those who *won't* do. The "can't-do" worker benefits from training; the "won't-do" worker doesn't.

Provide Assistance in Personal Problem Solving

At some time in their employment lives, all employees have personal problems. Some are serious, some less so, but all are important to the employees themselves. If the organization does not provide a way for its employees to try to solve their problems, the problems will spill over into the workplace as workers seek their own solutions, often in ways unacceptable to the organization. For example, if a company does not offer any way for employees to take care of personal business that cannot be conducted outside work hours, employees may call in sick rather than lose a day's pay. Stress management training, wellness programs, employee assistance programs, day-care centers, and other types of organizational support systems provide avenues for workers to solve their personal problems before the problems

**Figure 13.2
POLICY NUMBER: 401
CORRECTIVE ACTION POLICY**

TYPE "A" RULES: Offenses of this type are handled in a *four-step* procedure:

- **First Step:** Documented verbal notice, valid three (3) months from the date of discovery of the infraction.
- **Second Step:** Written notice, valid six (6) months from the date of discovery of the infraction.
- **Third Step:** Disciplinary time off of one (1) day, valid six (6) months from the date of discovery of the infraction.
- **Fourth Step:** Termination.

EXAMPLES OF OFFENSES SUBJECT TO TYPE "A" RULES

1. Absenteeism and/or tardiness based on the specific policies of your department.
2. Abuse of sick leave; i.e., using the sick leave program for other than income protection at the time of an illness.
3. Leaving assigned work area without permission.
4. Unauthorized extension of breaktime or mealtime.
5. Failure to use safety measures prescribed by your supervisor.
6. Smoking in unauthorized areas.
7. Creating or contributing to unsanitary conditions.
8. Failure to sign in or out on time sheet.
9. Failure to receive authorization from the appropriate supervisor or manager prior to working overtime.
10. Soliciting and distributing unauthorized materials in patient-care areas and/or working areas where patients or visitors are present, other than the cafeteria or coffee shop.
11. Eating food from patient trays or kitchens.
12. Failure to display properly or misuse of your I.D. badge.
13. Inappropriate attire and/or appearance. Employees may be sent home to change without pay for the time absent.

TYPE "B" RULES: Offenses of this type are handled in a *three-step* procedure:

- **First Step:** Written notice, valid six (6) months from the date of discovery of the infraction.
- **Second Step:** Disciplinary time off of two (2) days, valid (6) six months from the date of discovery of the infraction.
- **Third Step:** Termination.

EXAMPLES OF OFFENSES SUBJECT TO TYPE "B" RULES

1. Using profane or abusive language.
2. Engaging in heated arguments.
3. Negligent use or defacement of organization property.
4. Horseplay, scuffling, or throwing objects.
5. Wasting worktime.

(Continued)

Figure 13.2 (Continued)
POLICY NUMBER: 401
CORRECTIVE ACTION POLICY

6. Accepting money, gifts, or other forms of remuneration from patients or vendors.
7. Failure to notify the immediate supervisor of inability to report to work according to departmental policy procedures. If on sick leave, the employee must call in daily, unless otherwise indicated by the supervisor.
8. Failure to report injuries or incidents involving patients, visitors, or employees.
9. Failure to maintain acceptable standards of work performance.
10. Making false and/or malicious statements concerning other employees or the hospital.
11. Violation of organizational safety, security, fire, traffic, or parking regulations.

TYPE "C" RULES: Offenses are handled in a *one-* or *two-step* procedure:

■ Disciplinary time off of three (3) days.

■ On Type C Rules, immediate suspension is required pending an investigation of the alleged offense. The suspension must be immediate and not at the convenience of the department. Upon completion of the investigation, if the employee is cleared of the offense, then the employee shall be reinstated and paid at the regular rate of pay for all scheduled work time during the suspension. If it is found that the employee has committed an offense, the suspension will remain valid, or where warranted, the offense may result in termination.

EXAMPLES OF OFFENSES SUBJECT TO TYPE "C" RULES

1. Committing an act of violence.
2. Unauthorized possession, use, or distribution of intoxicating liquors or drugs on organization property, or reporting to work under the influence of intoxicants or drugs.
3. Possessing explosives, firearms, or dangerous weapons on the premises.
4. Unauthorized use, removal, theft, or intentional damage to organization property and/or the property of a patient, visitor, or employee.
5. Gambling on organization premises.
6. Sleeping or the appearance of sleeping on the job.
7. Failure to maintain acceptable standards of work performance.
8. Subjecting patients, visitors, or employees to physical or verbal abuse.
9. Failure to report injuries or incidents affecting patients, visitors, or employees.
10. Willful or idle conversation concerning patients, their records, or other confidential information.
11. Falsification of the organization records such as personnel records, time records, organization/hospital records, or other forms of dishonesty.
12. Insubordination or refusal to follow reasonable requests or assignments of supervisor. The employee should perform the request or assignment and then express any complaint via the Employee Grievance Policy.
13. Any absence of three consecutive workdays or more during which the employee failed to notify the appropriate supervisor.
14. Conviction of a criminal offense.

become workplace problems. Many of these support systems are described in Chapter 16.

Provide and Encourage Feedback

Feedback from supervisor to employee and from employee to supervisor opens lines of communication that may be conducive to identifying potential problems and preventing their occurrence. If workers feel free to ask their supervisor for assistance when they need it, or for tips for doing their work more efficiently, many problems may be prevented. When employees are informed early on that their behavior or job performance is unacceptable and are given help in correcting the problem, troublesome situations may be avoided.

Maintain Consistent, Equitable Supervisory Action

One of the outcomes of equitable and consistent supervisory action is that workers perceive that their supervisors are being fair and that any action taken, whether positive or negative, will be the same, regardless of who the worker is. Employees tend to be less dissatisfied and to exhibit less undesirable behavior in an atmosphere of fair and consistent supervisory treatment.

Correcting Undesirable Behavior

Sometimes the possibility of turning a poor performer into a superstar is slim. Could it be possible that the employee does not know how to do her job and that is the reason she makes excuses for her work, doesn't do her share, and doesn't want to admit to the number of errors she makes? If this is the case, giving instruction on how to do the job would be appropriate. At this point this constitutes corrective action.

While it is desirable to prevent unwanted behavior, it is not always possible to do so. Sometimes it is necessary to correct undesirable behavior through disciplinary measures. The purpose of employee discipline is to correct undesirable behavior. This assumes that the employee is well-intentioned and willing to change when shown the correct course of action.

Progressive Discipline

Many organizations have adopted a policy of *progressive discipline,* a policy that imposes increasingly severe penalties as violations are repeated. The steps in a progressive discipline policy may range from three to five levels of severity, with correspondingly severe penalties. A typical five-step system would follow these steps:

1. *Verbal reprimand.* On the first occasion of substandard work or violation of a work rule, the employee is given a verbal warning. Nothing is put into writing in the employee's record, but he or she is told that the offense should not be repeated. The supervisor, of course, would keep a record of the oral warning.

2. *Written reprimand.* On the second occasion of substandard work or violation of a work rule, the employee is notified in writing, with a copy put into the employee's work record.
3. *Second written reprimand.* On the third violation, the employee is issued a second written reprimand, which is also placed into the employee's work record.
4. *Suspension.* On the occasion of the fourth work violation, the employee is placed on suspension, usually for a period of from 1 to 3 days.
5. *Discharge.* The fifth repeated violation brings immediate discharge.

Organizations that elect the three-step progressive discipline policy shorten the chain of events by giving a verbal warning followed by one written reprimand and finally suspension or discharge.[5]

Figure 13.2 shows disciplinary action using progressive discipline. Note that the disciplinary action depends on both the type of offense and the number of previous offenses.

The "Hot Stove" Rule

Douglas McGregor, who is credited with the theory X, theory Y perceptions of employee behavior (see Chapter 10), is also credited with the hot stove analogy to disciplinary action (called the **"hot stove" rule**). The analogy equates touching a red-hot stove with experiencing disciplinary action. When one touches a hot stove, the reaction is immediate, there was warning, and the result is both consistent and impersonal. Similarly, disciplinary action should be immediate, with warning, consistent, and impersonal (directed toward the act and not against the person).

Immediate

When an employee violates a work rule, whether related to job performance or behavior, the result of that violation should be immediate—just as the result of touching a hot stove is immediate. If the violation calls for immediate dismissal (assuming all facts are known and all disciplinary procedures have been followed), the employee should be dismissed immediately and required to leave the premises, escorted if necessary. If the violation calls for a verbal warning, it should be given as immediately after the act as possible, and given privately. In some cases, not all facts are known, and the appropriate action may be temporary suspension. Later, when the investigation is complete, if the recommendation is that disciplinary action was not warranted, the employee should be returned to the job with back pay and all privileges restored.

With Warning

Does a red-hot stove give a warning "If you touch me, you're going to be burned"? Of course. Employees should be aware that if they violate company policy, standards, or rules, they will be disciplined. Warning can be provided through posted rules, supervisory information, policy handbooks, orientation, and other types of communication.

What about a policy that has been in existence and clearly communicated to employees at the time of employment but has never been enforced? For example, there may be a policy requiring workers in a particular construction area to wear safety shoes but the supervisors have given tacit approval to not wearing safety shoes by ignoring those who choose not to wear them. Let's assume that a new manager is employed and this manager believes strongly that safety precautions are important. She communicates to the supervisors that from now on, all safety rules will be strictly enforced. The supervisors have an obligation to warn their employees that while the safety-shoe rule has been on the books but not strictly enforced, from this day on, noncompliance will bring about disciplinary action.

Consistent

When a hot stove is touched, one is burned—the stove is consistent no matter who touches it or when it is touched. Discipline should be administered with the same consistency. Consistency in discipline means that all violations will receive the prescribed disciplinary action. Consistency does not necessarily mean, however, that everyone will receive the same measure of discipline. Individual circumstances must be considered before discipline is administered. For example, one employee has a record of arriving late to work and has been previously warned about tardiness and its consequences. Another employee who could always be depended on to be at work on time—even early—has been late twice this week due to a family emergency. The penalty should be different for the two workers, based on the previous work record. This inconsistency in a rule of consistency can also be related to the hot stove. Someone who touches a hot stove repeatedly will receive a more serious burn than will the person who touches the stove only once.

Impersonal

A hot stove isn't selective about whom it burns. The stove doesn't care if you are the one who shined it last week or if you are the one who burned the peas onto its surface. The hot stove punishes *the act of touching*.

Discipline should also be impersonal, based on the current violation and applied against the *act*. It should not depend on the supervisor's personal feelings about the employee. It should also be applied without resentment toward the employee who has been disciplined. Impersonal discipline means that the *behavior* is undesirable, not the person.

Nonpunitive Discipline

Nonpunitive discipline is discipline without punishment. This more contemporary approach encourages a disciplined workforce by recognizing that workers themselves must be the real source of discipline and by reinforcing self-discipline.

The traditional disciplinary system assumes that all violations must be punished and that the supervisor must be sure that the punishment fits the crime. Proponents of nonpunitive discipline feel that the traditional system forces the supervisor to play the "heavy" and wear a black hat. According to the traditional approach, supervisors are supposed to monitor workers, note the black marks in their records, and ultimately build a case for dismissal, if that is appropriate.

Like progressive discipline, <u>nonpunitive discipline follows a series of steps</u>. The difference is in the approach. These steps are as follows:[6]

Oral Reminder. An oral reminder is given to the employee in a private meeting between the supervisor and the employee. The purpose of the meeting is <u>to gain the employee's agreement to solve the problem</u>. Instead of warning the employee of the consequences if the offense is repeated, the employee is reminded that he or she has a personal responsibility to meet reasonable standards of performance and conduct. Documentation of the meeting is made in a working file only.

Written Reminder. If the problem continues, the supervisor and employee meet again. The supervisor reviews the good business reasons for the desirable behavior, discusses, without threats, the employee's failure to abide by the original agreement, and, through counseling, again gains the employee's agreement to solve the problem. Together, the supervisor and employee create an action plan, which is then summarized in a memo to the employee with a copy placed in the employee's personnel file. Note the difference between "warnings" of future consequences and "reminders" that restate the need for the rule and the individual's responsibility to abide by the rule. Figure 13.3 summarizes the differences between warnings and reminders.

Further Action. If the above steps are ineffective in correcting the behavior, the <u>employee may be placed on a 1-day paid decision-making leave</u>. The company pays the employee for this day, with the understanding that she or he will return on the following day either to make a total commitment to the job and to change the undesirable behavior or to quit and find another job that will be more in keeping with his or her philosophy. The employee does not begin work immediately on returning to the work site. First, there is a meeting with the supervisor to announce the decision. If the decision is to stay, the supervisor and employee set specific goals and

Figure 13.3 WARNINGS VS. REMINDERS		
	Warnings	Reminders
Timing	Before the conversation	After the conversation
Focus	Next step	Individual responsibility
Purpose	Threaten further negative consequences	Remind employee of performance standard
Time perspective	Past	Future
Responsibility for action	Supervisor	Employee
Supervisor's role	Judge	Coach

Source: David N. Campbell, R. L. Fleming, and Richard C. Grote, "Discipline Without Punishment—At Last," *Harvard Business Review*, July–August 1985, p. 169.

develop an action plan and a timetable. The employee clearly understands that if a change is not made and the requirements of the action plan are not met, the result will be termination.

According to its proponents (John Huberman, David Campbell, R. L. Fleming, Richard Grote, and others), nonpunitive discipline, properly implemented, is successful in terms of retaining potentially good employees and reducing turnover, disciplinary incidents, grievances, and sick leave. These benefits are shown in Figure 13.4, along with the company experiencing the benefits.

Team Discipline

Some companies have adopted **team discipline,** a disciplinary policy that is devised and implemented by the people who work together as a group.[7] The group sets its own standards and rules and enforces them. The group determines the appropriate penalties for rule violations and administers the penalties to the offenders.

Team discipline can be remarkably effective for it allows employees greater control over what they do, leading to greater productivity. Allowing the group to express its disapproval via discipline also places the outcome with the social or group control, whichever is stronger. Most employees react strongly to disappointment in their behavior expressed by their coworkers and enforced by penalties administered by their work group.

Instituting team discipline is not easy, for the supervisor must relinquish control over the traditional disciplinary function to workers. Supervisors must be careful not to "jump in" and solve a problem when they see workers experiencing some difficulty, or when termination is the only option and the workers do not want to wear "the black hat."

Before a company decides that team discipline is the route it wishes to take, training in how and when to discipline others is a *must.* When training programs are not instituted, team discipline will fail—not for lack of interest and enthusiasm by workers, but for lack of knowledge.

COMPETENCY CHECK

Can you describe methods of correcting undesirable behavior?

Guidelines for Effective Discipline

Having established guidelines is helpful particularly for those new to supervision. Experienced supervisors can use a little refresher course, too. The following checklist can be used to help you develop more effective disciplinary practices or to serve as a check on your current method.

DO YOU:

- understand the disciplinary policies, procedures, and rules and why they are important?
- clearly communicate the policies and rules to all employees under your supervision?
- support the company policies by following the rules yourself and by being verbally supportive?

Figure 13.4
BENEFITS OF NONPUNITIVE SYSTEMS

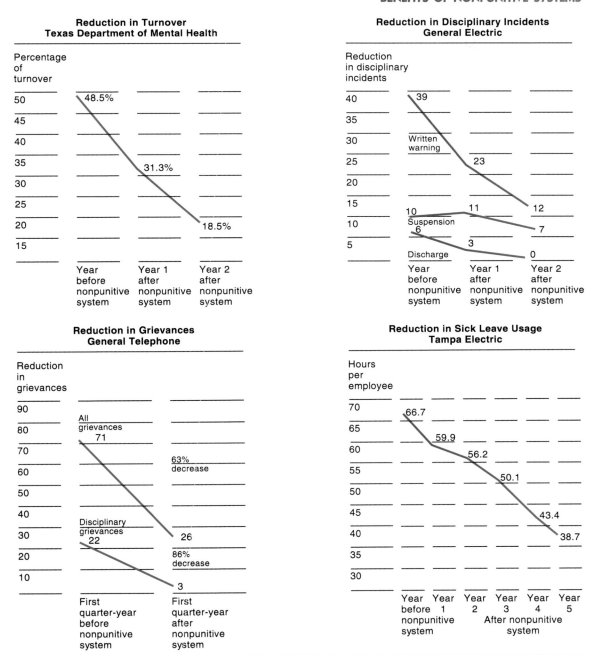

Reduction in Turnover
Texas Department of Mental Health

Percentage of turnover

50 — 48.5%
45
40
35 — 31.3%
30
25
20 — 18.5%
15

Year before nonpunitive system | Year 1 after nonpunitive system | Year 2 after nonpunitive system

Reduction in Disciplinary Incidents
General Electric

Reduction in disciplinary incidents

40 — 39
35
30 — Written warning
25 — 23
20
15 — 10 — 11 — 12
10 — Suspension 6 — 7
5 — 3
Discharge — 0

Year before nonpunitive system | Year 1 after nonpunitive system | Year 2 after nonpunitive system

Reduction in Grievances
General Telephone

Reduction in grievances

90
80 — All grievances 71
70
60 — 63% decrease
50
40
30 — Disciplinary grievances 22 — 26
20 — 86% decrease
10 — 3

First quarter-year before nonpunitive system | First quarter-year after nonpunitive system

Reduction in Sick Leave Usage
Tampa Electric

Hours per employee

70 — 66.7
65 — 59.9
60 — 56.2
55 — 50.1
50
45 — 43.4
40 — 38.7
35
30

Year before nonpunitive system | Year 1 | Year 2 | Year 3 | Year 4 | Year 5 After nonpunitive system

Source: David N. Campbell, R. L. Fleming, and Richard C. Grote, "Discipline Without Punishment—At Last," *Harvard Business Review,* July-August 1985, p. 178.

- ◻ understand the extent of your authority?
- ◻ get all the necessary facts before taking disciplinary action, not relying on hearsay or jumping to conclusions?
- ◻ take action when violations occur?
- ◻ document violations and action taken?
- ◻ share the documentation with the offender?
- ◻ ensure that the penalty fits the violation?
- ◻ return to normal work relations when the disciplinary action is over?
- ◻ discipline in private?
- ◻ follow the "hot stove" rule?

Bases for Overturning Disciplinary Action

Disciplinary action can be overturned if not properly conducted. When any of the following conditions existed, previous court and arbitration rulings have overturned the disciplinary penalty:[8]

Insufficient Evidence.   When there were no witnesses, no production records, and no lost-time records, the supervisory action was overturned.

Inadequate Warning.   When there was no policy, the policy was not publicized and enforced, or the employee received no warning that there was a violation of a rule prior to the penalty being imposed, courts ruled that the warnings were either nonexistent or inadequate.

Too-severe Punishment.   When the penalty did not fit the offense, the disciplinary action involved a first offense, and the worker had an otherwise good work record, courts did not respond favorably to the organization administering the penalty. When the organization did not have a progressive discipline policy (that is, it went directly to suspension or discharge without due process), courts exhibited an unwillingness to support the organization's actions.

Actions Based on Prejudice.   Prejudice rears its ugly head in many guises. Prejudice and bias are not limited to issues such as gender, age, race, religion, and

WHAT CAN THE SUPERVISOR DO?

When employees exhibit performance or behavioral problems, using a uniform method of recording the incident is helpful. Figures 13.5 and 13.6 show two forms used to differentiate performance violations from behavioral misconduct. A uniform format allows the same type of information to be recorded regardless of the person being disciplined.

Figure 13.5
CORRECTIVE ACTION FORM: BEHAVIOR-STANDARD VIOLATIONS

Employee's
Name _____ Department _____ Date _____

Violations of behavior standards are corrected through a progressive disciplinary procedure.

( ) 1. Excessive absenteeism.
( ) 2. Excessive tardiness.
( ) 3. Job duties performed below standard.
( ) 4. Abusive physical behavior.
( ) 5. Sleeping on the job.
( ) 6. Disregarding personal hygiene or standards of dress and appearance.
( ) 7. Unauthorized personal visits or telephone calls.
( ) 8. Discourteous or inappropriate interpersonal relations.
( ) 9. Parking in unauthorized parking zone/failure to display parking sticker.
( ) 10. Failure to follow safety practices.
( ) 11. Other behavior problems.

DISCIPLINARY STEP	First Discussion ( )	Second Discussion ( )	Probation ( )	Suspension ( )	Discharge ( )
DATE	___/___/___	___/___/___	___/___/___	___/___/___	___/___/___
TIME					
ACTION TO BE TAKEN					
EMPLOYEE'S COMMENTS					

The employee's signature indicates that this matter was discussed with him/her and does not necessarily mean that the employee agrees with what is stated.

Employee's Signature _____ Date _____
Supervisor's Signature _____ Date _____

For probation, suspension, and discharge actions:
Reviewed by:
Human Resources Director _____ Date _____
Department Director _____ Date _____
Vice President _____ Date _____

Figure 13.6
CORRECTIVE ACTION FORM: WORK-RULE VIOLATIONS

Employee's
Name _____ Department _____ Date _____

Violations of work rules are regarded as major infractions subject to immediate termination of employment.

( )   1. Mistreatment of patient.
( )   2. Theft, reasonable basis for suspicion of theft, or attempted theft.
( )   3. Willful destruction of property.
( )   4. Assault with intent to do bodily injury.
( )   5. Insubordination: refusal to perform assigned work.
( )   6. Willful breach of confidentiality.
( )   7. Sexual harassment.
( )   8. Use of alcohol or drugs on hospital premises or reporting to work under the influence to the extent that job performance is in any way impaired or to the extent that others are aware of their use.
( )   9. Willful falsification of personnel, time and attendance, or other hospital records.
( ) 10. Solicitation or distribution.
( ) 11. Possession of firearms or other dangerous weapons on hospital premises.
( ) 12. Violation of major safety rules.
( ) 13. Any absence without notification to supervisor prior to shift start.

DISCIPLINARY ACTION	Suspension ( )		Discharge ( )
	Date _____	Time _____	

INVESTIGATION RESULTS _____
_____
_____

EMPLOYEE'S COMMENTS _____
_____
_____

The employee's signature indicates that this matter was discussed with him/her and does not necessarily mean that the employee agrees with what is stated.

Employee's Signature   _____ Date _____
Supervisor's Signature   _____ Date _____
Reviewed by Human Resources Director _____ Date _____
Department Director's Signature   _____ Date _____
Vice President's Signature   _____ Date _____
For additional space, use the reverse of this form.

national origin. They may also include unwarranted preferences for educational or experience levels, physical appearance, or attitudes and values. Any act of discrimination places the supervisor's recommendations for discipline in jeopardy.

No Clear-cut Violation of Policy.   If a policy did not specifically prohibit the action for which the employee was penalized, it is difficult to persuade the courts to uphold the disciplinary action.

Inadequate Documentation.   A supervisor who hopes to uphold a penalty imposed for substandard work performance or for poor attitudes affecting the employee's performance or the performance of other members of the group must have *documentation* (written evidence) to show that the discipline was justified. Unable to produce documentation, the supervisor may find that the case is considered suspect.

COMPETENCY CHECK

Can you describe reasons for overturning disciplinary action?

Disciplinary Counseling Interview

For disciplinary counseling sessions to be effective, they must be planned, keeping in mind certain pitfalls that must be avoided if the sessions are to be successful.

Planning

Plan your counseling objective. What is your desired end result? When the employee leaves the conference, what do you want him/her to have decided to do? Plan your timing, setting, and opening. Meet with the employee as soon as possible following the infraction. The best time to meet is early in the shift and early in the workweek. If you wait until just before the worker's shift is over, you will both be tired and tempers may be short. You also might not have enough time to complete the discussion, and an already disgruntled employee will become more so because the shift is over and he or she cannot go home. An early meeting also allows you to note whether there is a change in behavior or performance during the shift—in other words, to see if your counseling had any effect. Late sessions mean that the worker leaves soon after the meeting and the effect may be minimized by the next day. The same rationale is true for sessions on Friday. If the discussion is held on Monday, Tuesday, or Wednesday, you will have an opportunity on Thursday and Friday to observe any change in behavior or work performance.[9]

The setting must be private. If your office is glass-enclosed and therefore visible to other workers, go to a conference room or to another office. Privacy is a must. Make arrangements for uninterrupted time, and unless the plant is on fire, allow no one to interrupt your privacy.

Review the employee's work record. However, deal with the current problem, not with the past. Prepare your opening comments. For example, "Come in, Joe. I asked you to come in today to try to find out why you are not meeting your goals and to offer my help. Are there any problems I should know about?" This could lead in to a discussion about problems with equipment, supplies, coworkers, goals, process, family, and so on. This should not, however, turn into an excuse-finding session or one in which the blame is placed everywhere except where it belongs. If you are rel-

**COMPETENCY
CHECK**

Can you describe
planning actions
taken for an
effective
disciplinary
counseling
interview?

atively inexperienced in conducting a disciplinary counseling interview, you may wish to role-play so you are prepared. Anticipate the employee's reaction and be prepared to deal in facts. Be serious. This is not the time to begin the meeting with a joke to put the employee at ease. Be professional in attitude and appearance.

All meetings need a sense of closure, and in the disciplinary counseling interview closure is provided by clarifying the standards that will be used to measure improvement, set a deadline for corrective action, and emphasize that you plan to follow up and evaluate the employee's progress to confirm that performance has improved.

Pitfalls to Avoid

Some pitfalls to avoid in disciplinary counseling sessions include the following:[10]

- ❏ Avoid historical absolutes, such as "You're never on time" or "You're always arguing with me." These absolute statements put the receiver on the defensive. Focus on the present situation and how to correct it.
- ❏ Avoid public scenes in which you openly discipline an employee in front of others. Publicly humiliating others accomplishes nothing in terms of improving performance. Correct in private; praise in public.
- ❏ Avoid emotional reactions. Nothing is accomplished by emotional outbursts other than the triggering of an emotional response. Stay in control of your own emotions, even if you have to take a deep breath and count to 10.
- ❏ Avoid rejecting the person. Putting employees down and attacking their self-esteem only makes a bad situation worse. Focus on specific behaviors and ways to correct those undesirable behaviors.
- ❏ Avoid "garbage dumping." "Not only did you make five mistakes on the report you completed, but last week you made two mistakes on the financial statement. And last month, you neglected to send that memo on the new policy to two of the supervisors." This is *garbage dumping*—piling criticism on top of criticism when one does not relate to the other. Deal with one issue at a time.
- ❏ Avoid "shrinkspeak." "You're a perfectionist because you could never get approval from your father unless everything was just right. You're still insecure and trying to get approval the same way." Unless you are a psychiatrist, psychologist, or trained therapist, this is out of your area of expertise. Focus on describing the unacceptable behavior and attempting to correct the deficiencies.
- ❏ Avoid closing your mind. "Don't confuse me with facts; I've made up my mind." Take the time to listen and talk out the dimensions of the problem. You could be wrong!
- ❏ Avoid indirect communication. Don't give critical communication through the grapevine or through a second person. Give the message yourself, no matter how unpleasant you anticipate its being.
- ❏ Avoid doing all the talking. Let the worker have an opportunity to talk about his or her frustrations.
- ❏ Avoid distracting tactics employed by the worker. Keep the discussion on track with comments such as "What we're discussing is your performance, why it's inappropriate, and what you must do to correct it."

**COMPETENCY
CHECK**

Can you cite
pitfalls to avoid
and suggest
alternative
actions?

Counseling Employees with Special Problems

Employees with special problems require counseling. The counseling may be provided by the supervisor, if she or he is trained in counseling, or it may be provided by counseling professionals. In trained hands, counseling is a powerful tool for helping employees deal with problems they encounter at work and problems outside the workplace that affect their ability to perform effectively on the job. Some say that counseling is an art. Fortunately, it is an art that can be learned.

Supervisors should be trained before they attempt to counsel employees. Too often, well-meaning but untrained people do more harm than good when they try to counsel others. Irreparable harm can be done if a supervisor gives advice that is (1) uncalled-for, (2) inappropriate to the situation, or (3) of a clinical nature. Even good advice can be given in the wrong way.

A supervisor trained in counseling is the best person to counsel workers within his or her department. Employees know their supervisor, are comfortable talking with him or her, and realize that their supervisor is interested in their mental and emotional well-being.

Absenteeism and Tardiness

Employee abuse of sick leave results in an estimated loss of $10 billion to $20 billion a year to American industry. Controlling the abuse requires a continuous effort.

Absentee Policy

"I believe that having a formal absenteeism policy makes employees accountable for their attendance," says Pat Iannatti, human resources manager at Kasei Memory Products, Inc., a division of Verbatim Corporation. Located in Chesapeake, Virginia, Kasei Memory Products, Inc., produces computer disks.

Managers in many organizations agree with Mr. Iannatti, and as a result formal absenteeism policies have been implemented. As a part of the policy, a warning letter such as the one shown in Figure 13.7 may be sent to the employee so he or she understands the consequences of continued absenteeism.

The number of absences or instances of tardiness can be tallied for each employee either by computer or by hand. A portion of a manual form used by one large banking institution is shown in Figure 13.8, but such a form may be easily computerized.

Penalties

Kasei Memory Products, Inc., has a no-fault attendance policy, eliminating the need to judge employees' excuses for being absent or tardy. Regardless of the reason for an unscheduled absence, employees receive points for missing work. And because the points result in prescribed corrective actions, they ensure consistency across departments and within the company.

Points are assigned for failure to work all or part of a scheduled workday, including scheduled overtime and volunteer overtime. Tardiness, early departures, and

---

Figure 13.7
SAMPLE WARNING LETTER

Re: *Absenteeism*

During the past four months, beginning _____, you have been absent from work for three periods; these periods of absence are outlined below.

	DATES OF ABSENCE	REASON FOR ABSENCE
First Period	_____	_____
Second Period	_____	_____
Third Period	_____	_____

Any further periods of absence before _____ will lead to a formal probation.

You will not be paid for any additional absences incurred before _____.

Listed below are some facts you should know about probation.

1. You will be terminated if you are absent while on probation.
2. While on probation, employees are not eligible to apply for a job through Job Posting. The employee must also complete a period of satisfactory attendance equal to the probationary period before being eligible for Job Posting.
3. While on probation, employees are not eligible for salary increases.

_____
Signature of Supervisor

_____
Date

BLIND NOTE: A copy of this memo should be included in the employee's permanent personnel file.

Figure 13.8
ABSENTEE CALENDAR

Code	Reason for Absence	Code	Reason for Absence
2	Short Term Absence (STA)	6	Conferences, Seminars & Workshops
3	Vacation	7	Other Paid Absence (explain)
4	Holiday	J	Unpaid Absence (explain)
5	Short Term Disability (STD)		

☑   USE FOR UNEXCUSED ABSENCE

☒   USE FOR EXCUSED ABSENCE

◯   TARDY

◩   VACATION

NAME _____

DATE _____

ADDRESS _____

HOME PHONE _____

DEPT. _____

POSITION _____

JANUARY

Sun.	Mon.	Tues.	Wed.	Thur.	Fri.	Sat.

leaving and returning to work during the same shift are also considered absences. Employees do not receive points for scheduled absences, including company holidays, jury duty, funeral leave, vacations, military leave, or those due to injury. Points are assigned in the following manner:

- Half a point is given for any partial workday absence or late arrival of more than 10 minutes but less than half a day. Repeated tardiness of less than 10 minutes can also result in half a point.
- 1 point is assigned for a full day of absence with a call-in before the shift starts.
- 1½ points are given for a full day of absence with a call-in after the shift begins.
- 4 points are assigned for a full day of absence with a call-in by the end of the shift.

The type of counseling received depends on the number of total points earned. Employees with 3 points receive a verbal warning; 5 points leads to a written warning; 8 points results in a suspension; and 10 points within 12 months can lead to discharge. However, before an employee is terminated, the employee's supervisor, department manager, and the HR director will review any extenuating circumstances. Employee appeals may be made to a panel of at least four department managers.

Employee points remain in the file for 12 months. After that time, the points for that particular absence are expunged from the file and are not considered in future disciplinary action.

Rewards

Kasei Memory Products, Inc., also provides an incentive for those with perfect attendance. Employees with no unscheduled absences for 6 months have their names and pictures posted on the employee bulletin board. Those with no absences for 1 full calendar year each receive a $25 gift certificate to use at a nearby mall. New employees with perfect attendance for 6 months receive $10 certificates; 9 months' perfect attendance earns a $15 certificate.

The combination of rewards for perfect attendance and a no-fault attendance policy makes Kasei's disciplinary policy unique. Does this approach work? "Yes," says Mr. Iannatti. "In prior years, there were employees with high absenteeism. Their attendance has improved as a result of the new policy."[11]

Usually, a supervisor tries to remedy the absenteeism problem by counseling. Some absentees respond to counseling; others do not. Counseling will probably benefit employees whose:[12]

- pressures off the job are so strong that they affect the employees' commitment to work.
- work appears to them to be disagreeable and dissatisfying.
- working relationships with others are unpleasant and distasteful.
- absence or tardiness is not based on an underlying serious problem and who could benefit from a straightforward "word to the wise."

On the other hand, counseling will probably *not* work with employees for whom:

WHAT CAN THE SUPERVISOR DO?

Supervisors will find helpful suggestions in the 12-point absenteeism checklist shown below. Are you following these suggestions in your department?

❐ Insist on prompt notification *always* when someone in your department must be absent unexpectedly.

❐ Insist on prior discussions about necessary absences for personal reasons, rather than explanations *after* the stay-away. In any event, call for *real* explanations rather than imaginative stories and "phony" excuses.

❐ What is the "Blue Monday" situation in your department? Keep a running record of absences on Monday or the day after each holiday, compared with absences on the best-attendance day (which will probably be payday!). The difference is a good indicator of "phony" absenteeism.

❐ Avoid crises due to unexpected absences by having standard operating procedures and standard backstop procedures: who is to be kept informed of what details, who is to pinch hit for whom.

❐ Be sure to give prompt notification to other departments that may be affected by delays caused by unexpected absences in your department.

❐ Maintain good departmental and individual absence records. Make periodic checks to see who are the "Absence-proners."

❐ Have heart-to-heart discussions with the ones who cause most of your absentee problems. See if there are personal problems on which counsel by you or someone in the HR or Medical Department can help.

❐ Is a group meeting in your department called for? Collect some facts and figures on actual costs of absenteeism to the department and to the company, including *related costs* as well as direct costs, to drive home the seriousness of the problem.

❐ Check your departmental record with that of other departments. Is yours out of line? Where does the basic fault lie? *Turn the mirror on yourself!*

❐ Know your employees. Without prying, show an interest in their personal lives. Encourage after-hour discussion of problems that affect attendance and productivity.

❐ Wear "mental safety goggles" periodically: Look for safety hazards in equipment and operations, and for poor housekeeping that can cause accidents.

❐ Insist that every employee report to you *any* injury, no matter how minor it may seem. It's your responsibility to see that every injured employee gets proper first-aid and/or medical treatment. This applies even to minor injuries, to prevent infection and possibly serious after-effects.

❐ the pay level or the job itself holds no strong attraction.

❐ off-hour activities have a greater appeal than do on-the-job activities.

❐ the whole purpose of being absent is to inconvenience, punish, or disrupt the organization.

For this latter group, discharge may be the only appropriate course of action.

Substance Use and Abuse

While substance abuse is not new, the number of substances, the number of workers involved, and the extent of abuse have increased in recent years. Businesses were developing alcohol abuse programs in the 1940s; drug abuse programs began increasing in the 1960s.

A complicating factor is that the *use* of some substances—alcohol, tobacco, and prescribed drugs—is not illegal, while the *use* of other substances—cocaine and heroin—is illegal. Alcohol abuse has long been a problem in the workplace. The National Council on Alcoholism and other agencies estimate that about 10 percent of workers are alcoholics.[13] While some of these can perform their jobs satisfactorily, at least for a time, many cannot. Typical employee behavior changes related to a drinking problem are shown in Figure 13.9. Alcoholics are typically absent more often and are involved in more job-related accidents than are nonalcoholics.[14]

Organizations may address substance abuse in any of several ways. They may offer in-house counseling, rehabilitation programs, referrals to medical or other specialized agencies, employee assistance programs, or educational programs.

The formation of a company policy toward substance abuse should be a top priority. Figure 13.10 shows one company's policy. The role of the supervisor is part of the policy, which expressly tells the supervisors that their responsibility is to closely and accurately monitor employee *performance and work habits*, to refer workers who have observable signs of substance use to the Personal Assistance Program, and to leave diagnosis to trained professionals. Note that guidance is given to the supervisor in recognizing signs that may point to substance abuse. Supervisors should be extremely cautious about making charges that cannot be substantiated and should refer employees who are suspect to the appropriate persons in the organization charged with the responsibility of employee assistance.

The term *drug use* usually refers to the use of substances such as marijuana, heroin, and cocaine. The cost of drug use to the U.S. economy is estimated to be over $25 billion per year.[15] The impairment of skills, decision-making ability, and reaction time by users makes the potential for danger in certain jobs enormous. Think of the possible disastrous results of drug abuse by pilots, workers in chemical or nuclear power plants, doctors, bus drivers, and the military.

Drug use creates the same kinds of problems in the workplace as alcoholism, plus some of its own. One of these is the increased potential for theft, to which many addicts resort to support their habits. Unlike alcohol, the use of these drugs is illegal. The legal difference has a significant impact on company policy. Commonwealth Edison Corporation has the following policy on drug abuse at work. Note the specific penalties for policy violation.[16]

The illegal use, sale, or possession of controlled substances while on the job or on company property is a dischargeable offense.

Off-the-job illegal drug use that can adversely affect an employee's job performance or that can jeopardize the safety of others is cause for administrative or disciplinary action up to, and including, termination of employment.

Figure 13-9
TYPICAL EMPLOYEE BEHAVIOR CHANGES RELATED TO A DRINKING PROBLEM

EMPLOYEE BEHAVIOR PATTERN	EMPLOYEE'S RESPONSE TO CRISIS	OBSERVABLE SIGNS

Early Stage
• drinking to relieve tension
• increase in tolerance
• memory lapses
• lying about drinking
	90%
	Criticism from boss Family problems
	Supervisor's Evaluation
	Actual Job Deterioration
		Absenteeism
		  tardiness (at lunchtime)
		  absent from post
		General Behavior
		  complaints from fellow workers
		  overreacts to real or imagined criticism
		  complains of not feeling well
		  makes untrue statements
		Performance on Job
		  misses deadlines
		  errors due to inattention or
		    poor judgment
		  lowered job efficiency

Middle Stage
• sneaking drinks
• feeling guilty
• tremors
• loss of interest
	75%
	Loss of job advancement
	Financial problems, e.g., wage garnishment Warning from boss
		Absenteeism
		  frequent days off for vague ailments or
		    implausible reasons
		General Behavior—Marked Changes
		  statements are undependable
		  begins avoiding associates
		  exaggerates work accomplishments
		  hospitalized more than should
		    be expected
		  repeated minor injuries on and off job
		Performance
		  generally deteriorating
		  spasmodic work pace
		  lapses of attention—cannot concentrate

Late Middle Stage
• unable to discuss problems
• efforts for control fail
• neglect of food
• drinking alone
	50%
	Typical Crisis
	In trouble with law
	Punitive disciplinary action
	Serious family problems, separation
	Serious financial problems
		Absenteeism
		  frequent time off (maybe for several
		    days)
		  does not return from lunch
		General Behavior
		  grandiose, aggressive and/or
		    belligerent
		  domestic problems interfere with work
		  seems to lose ethical values
		  financial problems (garnishments)
		  more frequent hospitalization
		  will not discuss problems
		  problems with the law
		Performance
		  far below what is expected

Approaching Terminal Stage
• now thinks "my job interferes with my drinking"
	25%
	Final warning from boss
	Termination
	Hospitalization
		Absenteeism
		  Prolonged unpredictable absences
		General Behavior
		  drinking on job
		  completely undependable
		  repeated hospitalization
		  physical deterioration visible
		  serious financial problems
		  serious family problems—divorce
		Performance
		  uneven
		  generally incompetent

Job Performance

Years of Alcohol Addiction

7   11   14

Source: Reproduced with permission from *Human Resources Management—Ideas and Trends,* published and copyrighted by Commerce Clearing House, Inc., 4025 W. Peterson Ave., Chicago, Ill. 60646.

> **Figure 13.10**
> **POLICY ON ALCOHOLISM**

Policy.

The underlying concept of Kemper's personnel policies is regard for the employee as an individual as well as a worker. Reflecting this concern, the company has devised a policy with six principles.

1. We believe that alcoholism, drug addiction, and emotional disturbances are illnesses and should be treated as such.

2. We believe the majority of employees who develop alcoholism, other drug addiction, or emotional illness can be helped to recover, and the company should offer appropriate assistance.

3. We believe the decision to seek diagnosis and accept treatment for any suspected illness is the responsibility of the employee. However, continued refusal of an employee to seek treatment when it appears that substandard performance may be caused by any illness is not tolerated. We believe that alcoholism, other drug addiction, or emotional illness should not be made an exception to this commonly accepted principle.

4. We believe that it is in the best interest of employees and the company that when alcoholism, other drug addiction, or emotional illness is present, it should be diagnosed and treated at the earliest possible date.

5. We believe that the company's concern for individual alcohol drinking, drug taking, and behavior habits begins only when they result in unsatisfactory job performance, poor attendance, or behavior detrimental to the good reputation of the company.

6. We believe that confidential handling of the diagnosis and treatment of alcoholism, other drug addiction, or emotional illness is essential.

The objective of this policy is to retain employees who may develop any of these illnesses, by helping them to arrest its further advance before the condition renders them unemployable.

Supervisory Practices.

Supervisors are instructed not to attempt to identify alcoholics or drug abusers among their employees, since diagnosis is the job of trained professionals. The firm's Personal Assistance Program provides training and assistance to supervisors and handles such problems through referrals. Supervisors' responsibility is to closely and accurately monitor employee *performance and work habits.* They should concern themselves only with job performance except when there are observable signs that the employee is drinking or taking illegal drugs on the job, is under the influence of alcohol or drugs, or is behaving in an abnormal manner. Supervisors are told to discuss referral with the Program's staff when an employee has a serious problem in any job area or difficulties in two or more of these job areas: sporadic performance, periods of poor judgment and confusion, increased sick time and tardiness, irritable attitudes toward other employees, quick or unreasonable anger, and strained relations with agents, policyholders, and the general public. Supervisors are warned to beware of three don'ts: don't play the expert, don't feel guilty about referring, and don't get emotionally involved.

The Program staff uses a variety of internal and external sources for consulting, counseling, and treatment for employees with alcohol, drug addiction, or other living problems.

Source: The Kemper Approach to Alcoholism, Drug Addiction, and Other Living Problems, Kemper Group, Long Grove, IL 60049, pp. 13–19.

Employees who are arrested for off-the-job drug activity may be considered to be in violation of the company policy.

Employees undergoing prescribed medical treatment with a controlled substance should report this to their supervisor or the company medical department.

As a supervisor, your top priority will be to know company policy and to communicate it to workers. The policy is the company's standard for disciplinary action in cases of drug use.

Insubordination

The general rule in industry is that employees have an obligation to obey a legitimate order unless it would be unsafe to do so. Workers are to do what they are told, even if they do not want to. Failure to follow a legitimate order is one form of insubordination.

Insubordination can take two forms: (1) An employee may willfully refuse or refrain from carrying out a direct order or instruction given by a supervisor and (2) an employee may direct threats, abusive language, or physical violence at the supervisor.

Before accusing a worker of insubordination based on a refusal to carry out a direct order, the supervisor should mentally reconstruct the conversation to recall if a direct order was given. "Anne, I think this layout would be more attractive if the colors were more distinct" is not a direct order; it is a suggestion, an opinion. If Anne fails to change the colors on the layout, her supervisor may be upset; but Anne did not refuse to carry out a direct order.

Even when a direct order is refused, it is wise to try to determine the reason for the refusal before charging insubordination. Was the refusal based on an inability to comply? Was the box too heavy to lift, for example? Was the refusal based on religious convictions? Were you asking someone to work on a religious holiday? Was the refusal based on the employee's perception that the order was irrationally conceived?[17] Was the order reasonable? For example, in a steel-fabricating plant, renovation was taking place during the winter so the heat was turned off. Employees were told to work in the plant although the temperature dipped down to 20 degrees.

Schedule a face-to-face conversation, *not a confrontation,* with the employee whom you believe has been insubordinate. Ask for an explanation. Explain the consequences of insubordination in your organization again. The employee should have been made aware of the policy on insubordination and the consequences of violating the policy at the time of hiring and orientation.

Insubordination that takes the form of physical violence toward the supervisor is not so easily handled. The policy of many organizations is that physical violence or a threat of physical violence in the presence of others is grounds for immediate dismissal. No counseling is required or expected when the supervisor's personal safety is threatened.

COMPETENCY CHECK

Can you discuss several special types of problems and suggest actions a supervisor might take to correct these problems?

The Last Resort

There comes a time when, having exhausted all the means available and having expended as much time as is economically sound, you may have to discharge a worker. This is sometimes referred to as "terminate," "fire," "let go," "permanent lay-off," "dismiss," or even "derecruit." Whatever the act is called, it is an unpleasant event for both participants—the person being discharged and the person who does the discharging.

Terminating Problem Employees

Before making a decision to discharge an employee, a review should be made of the employee's work history and all the efforts that have been made to date to turn this problem employee into a productive one. After the review, if the decision is made to discharge the employee, the process must be carefully planned and executed to protect the supervisor and the organization's image and legal position and to allow the employee to leave without loss of self-respect and dignity.

Immediate Dismissal.   As explained earlier in this chapter, because of the seriousness of the offense, it is sometimes necessary to discharge an employee immediately. When this is the case, the discharge should be clean and swift. As a procedural matter, keys or other security devices should be collected by the supervisor prior to the employee's leaving the premises. Personal passwords and codes used by the employee should be deleted from the access list. General passwords and codes should be changed immediately. As with any dismissal, careful documentation should be made and the files made available to the HR department.

Dismissal Following Progressive Discipline.   Dismissal, even when conducted in a professional manner, is unpleasant. Most employees who are discharged feel rejected, shocked, and often bitter toward the company. And these feelings are projected toward the company representative who has the responsibility for dismissing the employee. Because this is an emotion-charged situation, the supervisor should remain objective and avoid emotionalism in order to defuse the situation as much as possible.

The meeting in which the employee is told of his or her termination should be planned with the help of the HR department. The staff of the HR department can make available information that should be a part of the discharge meeting. For example, a written benefits package should be prepared for the discharged employee, including any outplacement services or counseling that is available. The supervisor should also review the company policies and procedures for termination to be sure that he or she is operating within the boundaries prescribed by the company.

The meeting should take place in a private location when the supervisor has ample time to devote exclusive attention to the employee who is about to be discharged. It should *not* take place 10 minutes before quitting time with an "I'm sorry, Joe, but this is it. We've tried everything with you, so there's nothing else we can do.

You can pick up your paycheck and not come back." Instead, the supervisor, prior to the meeting, should have reviewed all the documentation and be prepared to tell the employee exactly why the discharge is necessary, giving specific documented examples of substandard performance or unacceptable behavior.

Once you have planned thoroughly what you are going to say and how you are going to say it, you are ready to face the employee. The discharge meeting typically lasts about 30 minutes, with the termination being given first. It is cruel to subject an employee who is about to be discharged to idle chitchat about the weather or the health of the economy. Get to the issue at hand. Without being defensive or emotional, convey the fact that this employee has not been performing up to the standard expected, review the progressive discipline procedures, and then give the termination message. The remainder of the time should be spent providing the employee with information about the benefits package and other services available through the company and explaining what the employee should do next. Most of the time, the discharged employee is unaware of what follows a discharge. For example, you should tell the employee how the final paycheck will be handled (mailed or picked up), remind the employee to collect personal belongings, and explain how references will be handled. This meeting is not a discussion; it is an announcement of a decision and the format for carrying out the decision. A termination checklist is shown in Figure 13.11.

COMPETENCY CHECK
Can you describe how immediate dismissal procedures differ from dismissal following progressive discipline?

Legal Considerations

Throughout this chapter, the actions that supervisors should take in regard to problem employees have been described. Many of these actions also keep the supervisor from making illegal discharge decisions or from implementing the discharge in a way that might later be deemed illegal.

Employee Termination Rights

Employees have certain rights connected with employment-termination practices. An employee's discharge may be declared invalid if any of the following conditions exist:[18]

- ❏ The employee was discharged for a reason specifically prohibited by federal or state standards. For example, termination in direct violation of Title VII of the Civil Rights Act of 1964, the National Labor Relations Act, or the Occupational Safety and Health Act is specifically prohibited by law.
- ❏ The employee was discharged for complying with a statutory duty. Courts have refused to uphold an employee's discharge for performing jury duty, for example; for refusing to commit perjury as requested by the employer; for objecting to violating the law; or for complaining to public authorities about illegal activities of employers.
- ❏ The discharged employee had an implied contract under the terms of employment. Some courts have ruled that employee manuals containing statements such as "You can be dismissed only for sufficient cause" or "Termination is based on unsatisfactory performance" are implied commitments. On June 5,

Figure 13.11
EXIT CHECKLIST

Employee Name: _____   Years of Service _____

Social Security No: _____   Responsibility Unit No: _____

                                                      Name: _____

	Action Taken By (Initial)	Date	Not Applicable
Payroll Notified	_____	_____	_____
Exit Interview Scheduled	_____	_____	_____
Termination Data Checklist Mailed	_____	_____	_____
Benefits Department Contacted for Retirement Estimate to be Calculated (Vested with 10+ Years of Service)	_____	_____	_____
Notice of COBRA Eligibility Sent to Benefits	_____	_____	_____
COBRA Material Provided	_____	_____	_____
Application for Thrift & Profit Sharing Benefits Upon Termination of Employment Mailed	_____	_____	_____
Application for Thrift & Profit Sharing Benefits Upon Termination of Employment Received	_____	_____	_____
Exit Survey Mailed	_____	_____	_____
Exit Survey Received	_____	_____	_____
Manager Contacted	_____	_____	_____
Other Action Taken (Specify)	_____	_____	_____
Parking Card Received; Card # _____ and mailed to Prop. Mgmt.	_____	_____	_____
P.C. Loan Cleared	_____	_____	_____
RETURN OF PROPERTY:			
Identification Card	_____	_____	_____
Benefits Card	_____	_____	_____
Corporate Visa	_____	_____	_____
Company Pin	_____	_____	_____
Attache Case	_____	_____	_____
PC Software, etc.	_____	_____	_____

1985, the Wisconsin Supreme Court ruled that an employee handbook is an offer by management of a set of employment terms and conditions; if a Wisconsin employee accepts management's offer, a contract has been formed.

The American Society for Personnel Administrators has suggested that to avoid the perception of an implied contract, employers use the following disclaimer:

> I understand that this employment application and any other company documents are not contracts of employment, and that any individual who is hired may voluntarily leave employment upon proper notice, and may be terminated by the employer at any time for any reason. I understand that any oral or written statements to the contrary are hereby expressly disavowed and should not be relied upon by any prospective or existing employee.

Disclaimers, when used, should be inserted into the employee manual or be included in the employment application. Any employer using a disclaimer, however, should make sure that its rules and regulations and other policy statements do not conflict with the disclaimer. Some companies are using the statement "No employee has any contract with this company except for documents titled Employment Contract."

Oral statements made during an employment interview, or even during a performance appraisal interview, may constitute an implied contract. In one case, a person being hired was told that "she could stay and grow with the company." When she was let go several months later, she sued for breach of contract—and won. Any comment that suggests that passing a probationary period leads to job security should be avoided. Even "Don't worry, Ms. Daily, no one ever gets fired around here" can be held as a valid promise of guaranteed employment.

❑ The discharged employee has been deprived of due process rights guaranteed under the Fourteenth Amendment. Arguments have been made that dismissal from employment can be regarded as the taking of liberty or property. "Due process" therefore gives a discharged employee the right to certain procedural steps, including a hearing and the right to know the reason for dismissal.

❑ The employee's discharge was motivated by bad faith or malice or based on retaliation that violates public policy. The primary determinant of public policy protection is the court's judgment as to what type of conduct violates public policy and the determination that an employee's discharge was wrong and actionable.[19]

Supervisory Action

Perhaps two of the most important precautionary measures a supervisor can take to protect the company from charges of illegal termination are (1) to carefully and regularly document any action taken and (2) to be sure that there is no discrimination involved in any termination decision.

Document Performance.   Documentation means keeping records of every time you speak to a problem employee about deficiencies in work performance and any subsequent actions you take to help improve the individual's performance. These records may take various forms, including the following:[20]

- ❑ A memo to file stating that you spoke to the employee about a certain matter on a certain date. Note the specific actions or efforts you agreed to take and those the employee agreed to make. A memo to file can also be written when someone makes a major complaint to you about the employee's performance.
- ❑ A copy of any performance agreement you and the employee work out and a memo to file on whether or not the agreement was followed through satisfactorily.
- ❑ Any memos written in conjunction with the progressive discipline procedures.

Whatever form of documentation you use, it is important that you keep a copy of the communication in the employee's personnel file. Except for a memo to file, the employee should receive a copy of all correspondence directed to his or her attention. In addition, all appropriate people should receive copies of the documentation. For later support, your supervisor and the HR department should be aware of the situations leading to an employee's termination.

Avoid Discriminatory Termination.   Be sure there is no discrimination involved in the termination action. Carefully review the procedure. Did you have any bias against the employee's age, gender, race, color, religion, or national origin? Did the fact that the employee was pregnant have anything to do with your decision? You have to be able to answer no to all these questions. Be aware of any actions that might later be called discriminatory. For example, it is unwise to say to an employee, "Joan, now that your children are in high school, wouldn't you feel better if you were at home with them? You know how the high school drug scene is" or "Jack, you're getting along in years, and the pressures of this job are increasing every day. Think of how great it would be to be fishing instead of what you're having to put up with in this job." Any comments along these lines are open to an interpretation of discriminatory termination of employment.

COMPETENCY CHECK

Can you cite the two primary actions a supervisor can take to avoid legal problems as a result of employee termination?

COMPETENCY REVIEW

1. Identify five behavioral or attitudinal indicators that point to a potential problem employee.
2. Name four other methods of identifying potential problem employees.
3. Describe four strategies for preventing undesirable behavior.
4. Describe four methods of correcting undesirable behavior.
5. Give five reasons why disciplinary actions may be overturned.

6. Describe the planning involved in preparing for a counseling interview.
7. Describe eight pitfalls to avoid in the counseling interview and suggest alternative actions.
8. Discuss several special types of problems and suggest actions a supervisor might take to correct these problems.
9. Describe how immediate dismissal procedures differ from dismissal following progressive discipline.
10. List two primary actions a supervisor should take to avoid legal problems as a result of employee termination.

APPLICATIONS

1. Obtain a policy statement on absenteeism, substance abuse, insubordination, or discipline. Identify what you consider to be strengths and weaknesses of the policy statement. How would you change the policy statement?
2. In groups of five to six, using the policy statements you have collected as guidelines, write a policy on the topic of your choice. The groups will exchange final policy statements and critique each in writing, returning the critique to the original authors.
3. Obtain an employee handbook from any available source. Review it carefully and respond to the following questions:
   a. Does the handbook relay information about company policies, procedures, and rules relating to disciplinary action and termination? Can you think of any questions the handbook fails to cover?
   b. Can you find any statements that might be interpreted as implied contracts? Give specific examples.
   c. Is the language appropriate to its audience? Why or why not? Give specific examples.
   d. In what ways would a handbook for employees of a fast food restaurant differ from that of one intended for insurance representatives?

CASES

Case I

GIVE ME MY REPRIMAND WITHOUT PENALTY!

The company you work for has no policy about absenteeism. The newly hired director of HR is "appalled" at the lack of formality in what he considers to be a serious problem. He has scheduled a meeting with all supervisors to discuss the no-fault absentee policy that was used by the company he formerly worked for. He has distributed the information found on pages 388 and 390 (Kasei Memory Products, Inc.) for your review.

1. Make a list of questions you want to ask at the meeting.
2. Would you support the change? What is your basis for accepting or rejecting the no-fault absentee policy?
3. List the pros and cons of both the traditional approach to absenteeism and the no-fault approach.

Case II

BUT I'VE BEEN SICK!

Patricia Mangan was described by management at the metalworking plant as a "fine individual with good work habits when present on the job." She was, unfortunately, absent more than she was on the job.

Of the 210 working days in the 10 months preceding her discharge, Mangan was able to work only 43 days. The balance of that period was devoted to surgery and convalescence during excused absences and leaves of absence. There was no question that her ailments were genuine; what troubled her supervisor was that Mangan was usually unfit to perform her work even when she was present, and her doctor did not anticipate that her condition would improve to the point where she would be able to do her job anytime in the near future. She was therefore discharged.

Mangan challenged her discharge with a grievance, charging that the discharge was not for just cause. Management countered that it had no choice but to discharge her because her absences seriously disrupted production and no change for the better could be expected. The case was taken to arbitration.

The union argued that every one of the grievant's absences had been for a valid health reason and had been excused by management. It conceded that the year preceding the discharge had been a particularly severe one because it had included surgery—first on a hand and then on a dislocated shoulder. A statement from Mangan's doctor confirmed the nature of her medical problems. Management did not dispute the genuineness of the ailments and emphasized that the discharge had not been for disciplinary reasons. Instead it presented, as exhibits, the following record of the woman's employment with the company:

She failed to reveal, on her job application 4 years earlier, a mishap prior to that time that caused a recurrent shoulder-separation problem. She was hired; 7 months later, she quit on the advice of her doctor. Two months later, she reapplied, again failing to note her preemployment injury, and was rehired. For better than a year thereafter, her attendance was satisfactory; then, toward the end of the following year, there was a sharp increase in her absences, on an erratic basis.

Early in the year that preceded her discharge, she requested and was granted a leave of absence for surgery, indicating, at the time, that she expected to return after 6 weeks. But she did not return for 3 months beyond that anticipated date, asking for and getting two extensions of the leave. One week following her return, she again sought and was granted a leave, which lasted an additional 2 months. Then, for the first 6 weeks after the next return to work, she had some irregular daily absences. One month later, she asked for another leave, at which time she was terminated.[21]

1. Was the discharge for good cause?
2. If you were the arbitrator, how would you rule?

REFERENCES

1. George Odione, *Strategic Management of Human Resources,* Jossey-Bass, Inc., San Francisco, 1984.
2. Clayton V. Sherman, *From Losers to Winners: How to Manage Problem Employees . . . and What to Do if You Can't,* AMACOM, New York, 1987, p. 13.
3. Ibid., p. 14.
4. Rodney P. Beary, "Discipline Policy—A Neglected Personnel Tool," *Administrative Management,* November 1985, p. 21.
5. Sherman, op. cit., p. 105.
6. David N. Campbell, R. L. Fleming, and Richard C. Grote, "Discipline Without Punishment—At Last," *Harvard Business Review,* July–August 1985, p. 162.
7. Walter Kiechel III, "How to Discipline in the Modern Age," *Fortune,* May 7, 1990, p. 179.
8. Sherman, op. cit., p. 166.
9. Ibid, p. 130.
10. Bruce A. Baldwin, "Critical Communication: Giving Negative Feedback with Positive Results," *PACE Magazine, Piedmont Airlines Inflight Magazine,* November–December 1982, p. 12.

11. Betty R. Ricks and R. Bruce McAfee, "Managing 101," *Business Weekly, The Virginian-Pilot and The Ledger-Star,* Norfolk, Va., Mar. 15, 1993, p. 5.
12. Sherman, op. cit., p. 93.
13. Christine A. Flipowicz, "The Troubled Employee: Whose Responsibility?" *Personnel Administrator,* vol. 24, June 1979, p. 18.
14. Frank E. Kuzmits and Henry E. Hammonds II, "Rehabilitating the Troubled Employee," *Personnel Journal,* April 1979, p. 239. Reprinted with permission. All rights reserved.
15. Peter Bensinger, "Drugs in the Workplace," *Harvard Business Review,* November–December 1982, pp. 48–50.
16. R. Bruce McAfee and Arno F. Knapper, *Employee Relations Management,* Old Dominion University, Norfolk, Va., 1983.
17. Stuart A. Youngblood and Gary L. Tidwell, "Termination at Will: Some Changes in the Workplace," *Readings in Personnel and Human Resource Management,* 2d ed., West Publishing Company, St. Paul, Minn., 1984, p. 406.
18. Thomas H. Williams, "Fire at Will," *Personnel Journal,* June 1985, p. 76.
19. George E. Stevens, "Firing Without Fear," reprinted from *Management World,* March 1984.
20. Peter Wylie and Mardy Grothe, *Problem Employees,* Pittman Learning, Belmont, Calif., pp. 203–204.
21. "Discipline and Grievances," National Foreman's Institute, Waterford, Conn., 1979.

SUGGESTED READINGS

Foxman, Loretta D., and Walter L. Polsky: "HR Skills Help Managers Turn Around Poor Performers," *Personnel Journal,* May 1991, p. 28.
Grove, Andrew S.: "What to Do with Pain-in-the-Neck People," *Working Woman,* June 1991, p. 32.
Jacobs, Deborah L.: "How to Fire Someone Without Getting Sued," *Working Woman,* January 1990, p. 24.
Luke, Robert A., Jr.: "How to Give Corrective Feedback to Employees," *Supervisory Management,* March 1990, p. 7.
Lyons, James: "You Can't Fire Me," *Forbes,* September 16, 1991, p. 164.
Ricks, Betty R., and R. Bruce McAfee: "Absence Makes the Boss Grow Crosser," *Business Weekly, The Virginian-Pilot and The Ledger-Star,* March 15, 1993, p. 5.
Ricks, Betty R., and R. Bruce McAfee: "Handling Difficult Employees," *Business Weekly, The Virginian-Pilot and The Ledger-Star,* May 17, 1993, p. 2.
Shaller, Elliot H.: "Avoid Pitfalls in Hiring, Firing," *Nation's Business,* February 1991, p. 51.
Sharifzadeh, Mansour: "Dealing with Your Absenteeism Problem," *Management Solutions,* October 1988, p. 35.
Siegel, Alexandra: "The New Thinking on Firing: Do It Quickly," *Working Woman,* August 1991, p. 12.
Straub, Joseph T.: "Disciplinary Interviews: The Buck Stops with You," *Supervisory Management,* April 1991, p. 1.
Weiss, Donald H.: "How to Deal with Unpleasant People Problems," *Supervisory Management,* March 1992, p. 1.

GLOSSARY

hot stove rule   Equates touching a red-hot stove with experiencing disciplinary action.

insubordination   Failure to follow a legitimate order and directing threats, abusive language, or physical violence toward the manager.

nonpunitive discipline   Discipline without punishment.

progressive discipline   A policy that imposes increasingly severe penalties as violations are repeated.

team discipline   Policy in which the group sets its own standards and rules and enforces them.

THE Supervisor AND THE Controlling Function

STUDYING THIS CHAPTER WILL ENABLE YOU TO:

1. Define *control.*

2. State characteristics of effective standards.

3. Describe the steps in the control process.

4. Define and give examples of types of control.

5. Identify areas in which the supervisor is responsible for control.

6. Describe benchmarking.

7. Compare fixed, flexible, and zero-based budgets.

8. Describe scheduling techniques.

9. Describe the difference between 100 percent inspection and sampling, and explain sampling techniques.

10. Describe types of time controls.

11. Distinguish between economic order quantity and "just in time," explaining the purposes of each.

12. Describe uses of the computer as a control tool.

13. Describe General Electric's frontline control concept.

CHAPTER OUTLINE

THE CONTROL PROCESS
Setting Standards
Observing and Measuring Performance
Comparing Results to Plan
Taking Corrective Action

PHASES OF CONTROL
Preliminary Controls
Concurrent Controls
Feedback Controls

WHAT TO CONTROL
Time
Behavior
Materials and Equipment
Processes
Costs
Quality and Quantity

CONTROL TOOLS AND TECHNIQUES
Benchmarking
Budgets
Scheduling Techniques
Quality Controls
Time Controls
Materials Controls
Computer Controls
Frontline Control

Competency Review
Applications
Cases
References
Suggested Readings
Glossary

C H A P

THE
Supervisor's
Role
IN
Controlling

E R 1 4

The Control Process

One of Murphy's laws states, "Anything that can go wrong, will go wrong. Leakproof seals—will; self-starters—will not; interchangeable parts—won't." And Murphy is often correct! The controlling function provides the opportunity to minimize and correct these mistakes before the company's opportunities for reaching its goals are affected.

**COMPETENCY
CHECK**
Can you define
control?

Control is the function of comparing actual performance with planned performance and taking corrective action when necessary. One of the major responsibilities of supervisors is controlling. However, the word *control* conjures up visions of manipulation and is often resented, because many people reject the idea that they are being controlled. Control is seen as a negative force (using authority to exercise command over their entire work life) rather than as a positive force (using certain activities to produce a quality product or service in the quantity planned for).

A study of the controlling activities of supervisors by the authors revealed that supervisors believe they spend more time on measuring productivity than on any other controlling activity. A ranking of the responses by time spent on specific activities is shown in Figure 14.1. Note that supervisors reported spending a large percentage of their time controlling a varied range of activities.

There are four steps in the control process: (1) setting standards, (2) observing and measuring performance, (3) comparing performance with standards, and (4) taking corrective action when necessary.

Figure 14.1 CONTROLLING ACTIVITIES OF SUPERVISORS		
Activity	% Ranking Activity as No. 1	% Ranking Activity among Top Five Activities
Measuring productivity	14.7	64.6
Evaluating departmental objectives	14.7	55.9
Quality control of output	14.7	49.9
Reporting control results to management	11.8	50.0
Comparing planned with actual budget expenses	8.8	47.3
Salary administration	8.8	35.3
Appraising performance	5.9	61.8
Follow-up of training program	5.9	32.3
Evaluating standards	2.9	38.3
Measuring plant & equipment efficiency	—	1.7
Other (expense reduction, controlling stock)	8.8	8.8

Source: Anne Scott Daughtrey and Betty Roper Ricks, supervisory management survey, 1985.

Setting Standards

Chapter 2 described how setting standards of performance is a part of the planning process. Standards provide the link between planning and controlling, as shown in Figure 14.2. Knowing what is expected provides the basis for the control function.

Setting standards provides a yardstick against which to measure the organization's movement toward its goals. To serve as effective yardsticks, standards themselves must be effective, and to be effective, they must possess certain characteristics.

Standards Must Be Realistic

For example, let's suppose that your marketing firm set a new standard of 100 "cold" sales calls and 50 scheduled sales calls per month for each salesperson on the staff. Is that expectation realistic? Is there enough time in the month for the salespeople to logistically carry out the activities? Is adequate leadership on board to motivate salespeople to that level of productivity? Is there support staff available to handle the orders that may result from the increased sales activity? Are the standards so high that, instead of being motivated, the sales staff will simply throw up their hands, say "I can't possibly do that," and give up? Are the standards so low that they can be met with little effort and therefore provide no challenge? Will the sales staff require some additional support in making phone calls and completing paperwork? Will the sales staff require some additional training if they are to succeed?

These and other questions must be addressed by management. If the answers to most of the questions show that the standard cannot be met, the standard is not realistic and should be reviewed and revised.

Standards Must Be Stated Clearly

A **standard,** by definition, is a "stated level of acceptable performance." The standard should be as precise as possible. Quantitative standards lend themselves to precise statements (200 units per hour per machine with a 5 percent scrap rate, for example). Behavioral standards, such as "No profanity may be used in dealing with customers," are more difficult to quantify. Words that may be considered profane by some people may be considered "colorful" by others. Figure 14.3 shows that some behavioral standards *can* be quantified. Fuzzy statements provide no yardstick for measuring and are therefore a waste of time. "Good attendance is required" is a fuzzy statement. What is "good attendance"? Open to a variety of interpretations by different supervisors, this may lead to differing treatment of workers. Stated qualitative and quantitative tolerances, showing allowable deviations from a standard, will make standards clearer and measurable.

Figure 14.2
**LINKING
PLANNING AND
CONTROLLING**

Figure 14.3 QUALITATIVE AND QUANTITATIVE STANDARDS	
Standard	Tolerance
10-minute car wash	2 minutes more
4.1" pipe	+/− 0.05"
9 P.M. starting time	5 minutes late
Quality customer relations	Two complaints per month
Clean, polished surface	Two visible defects
125/75 blood pressure	+/− 20 points
Perfect attendance	One absence per month
100,000 tool parts	+/− .05 percent

Standards Must Be Communicated

Workers need to know what is expected of them. Knowing on what basis their performance will be appraised increases workers' confidence by removing their uncertainties. Confident workers perform better than do those who are frustrated by wondering how they are doing or how they will be judged.

Standards should be communicated to the appropriate people through the appropriate channels. For example, if attendance standards are imposed on all workers alike, the standard should be printed in the company handbook or communicated orally during orientation sessions, or both. Standards for sales, however, need be communicated only to the people involved in that activity. Communication of standards for specific activities may be done through line management, that is, from headquarters to division manager, to supervisors, and, finally, to workers.

Telling workers what is expected of them sets up the controlling process. In participative management, workers may be involved in setting the standards, as well as judging how well the standards are being met.

COMPETENCY CHECK
Can you cite three characteristics of effective standards?

Observing and Measuring Performance

Observing and measuring performance is not limited to the performance of employees. Supervisors must observe and monitor equipment, materials, processes, costs, and the quality and quantity of the output. This is the information-gathering phase of the control process—the activity through which supervisors gain the information needed to compare performance with standards. The tools and techniques used to generate the information are explained in a later section of this chapter.

Comparing Results to Plan

Comparing the actual performance to the planned performance is the third step in the control process. Comparison is the step in which deviations from the standard are identified. A comparison of actual performance to planned performance may reveal deviations that bring into question the standard itself in addition to—or rather than—actual performance. The supervisor is responsible for measuring performance and noting deviations from the standard.

Taking Corrective Action

Taking corrective action to revise the standard may or may not be within the supervisor's purview. Let's look at an example.

In a tool-and-die factory, a standard for a new stamping machine is to stamp out 100,000 tool parts per week, with a tolerance of plus or minus 5 percent. The parts move from the stamper to the assemblers. During the first week, the supervisor observes that some assemblers are idle. The problem is traced to the stamping machine, which is found to be producing only 15,000 parts per day—or 75,000 per week. Acceptable performance would be between 95,000 and 105,000 (100,000 plus or minus 5 percent). The supervisor tries to determine whether the cause is the training or performance of the operator; the process, including the work flow and the layout; the new stamping machine; or the standard.

If the worker's performance is causing the deviation, the supervisor might have total responsibility for bringing the worker up to the expected standard. In some cases, additional training will be required. If so, the supervisor's responsibility might be simply to refer the worker for retraining and to work cooperatively with the HR staff until the worker's performance is up to par. In other instances, the supervisor may provide the additional worker training. If the process is identified as the problem, the supervisor would review the work flow, the layout, and the process and make suggestions for redesign. In cases where the technology is beyond the supervisor's skills, his or her responsibility might be limited to reporting the deviation to the division heads. If the standard for the machine is found to be unrealistic, the appropriate level of management should take the matter up with the vendor. Whatever the cause of deviation from expectations in operations, the supervisor plays a critical role in early detection and either takes corrective action or refers it to someone who can. The correct analysis or diagnosis must be made, however, to lead to appropriate corrective action.

COMPETENCY CHECK

Can you describe the four steps in the control process?

Phases of Control

There are three major opportunities for exercising control: (1) before the product is manufactured or the service provided, (2) during the time the product is manufactured or the service is rendered, or (3) after the product is manufactured or the service is provided. These types of controls are referred to as *preliminary controls, concurrent controls,* and *feedback controls.*

Preliminary Controls

Preliminary controls (sometimes shortened to precontrols) are the controls that are in place before the product is manufactured or the service is performed. These controls are preventive in nature; that is, their purpose is to prevent problems that may occur rather than to correct problems. Preliminary controls are directed at the resources coming into the organization (*input*)—resources such as people, material, and money.

One way to prevent problems with human resources would be to have an effective selection process that carefully screens potential employees in order to select those who have the knowledge, skills, and ability necessary to perform the jobs. Ensuring that the materials purchased are of the correct quality for the job and that they are available in the quantity required is the way to prevent problems occurring because of inadequate materials. Preliminary controls that can prevent money problems include ensuring that enough money is available to pay for items ordered or that the amount spent does not exceed the amount budgeted.

Concurrent Controls

Concurrent controls are the controls that are exercised during the manufacture of the product or when the service is provided. These controls are primarily implemented through observation of the activity. The purpose of concurrent controls is to spot errors when they occur and to correct them at their origin. Concurrent controls are directed at the activity or transformation process, as shown in Figure 14.4. As the word implies, *transformation* is the process by which inputs are used to produce a product or to provide a service (*output*).

Identifying problems as they occur allows the supervisor to take immediate corrective action. For example, if a floor supervisor notices that a salesperson is experiencing problems with the computerized register, the floor supervisor (using concurrent controls) would discuss the problem with the salesperson, demonstrate correct use of the register, and have the salesperson show, through operation of the register, that the problem is resolved. Or if a foreman sees that a worker is not wearing the required safety equipment, he or she would bring this violation to the worker's attention immediately and correct it at that time.

Feedback Controls

Feedback controls are controls exercised after the product is manufactured or the service provided. These controls are directed at the results of the process (*output*) and are primarily implemented through reporting and other feedback.

**Figure 14.4
PRELIMINARY
AND
CONCURRENT
CONTROLS**

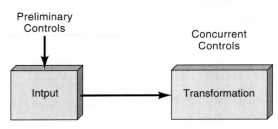

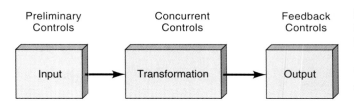

Preliminary Controls   Concurrent Controls   Feedback Controls

Input   Transformation   Output

Figure 14.5 CONTROL PROCESS USING PRELIMINARY, CONCURRENT, AND FEEDBACK CONTROLS

The process from preliminary controls to feedback controls is shown in Figure 14.5.

When a supervisor receives a report from quality control on the number of rejects for a given period, the supervisor is exercising feedback control. When a service supervisor receives reports from the service representatives each week on the number of service calls made, the supervisor is exercising feedback control. When a supervisor compares expenses with the budget, the supervisor is also using feedback control. Information received after the product is manufactured or the service is rendered provides the basis for feedback controls. Did we meet or exceed our goals? Were customer complaints down? Were we within budget? These questions are answered through feedback controls. Of course, when deviations are found during the feedback control process, the supervisor must then make plans (or implement plans already in existence) to correct the problems. A recap of the major points about preliminary control, concurrent control, and feedback control is shown in Figure 14.6. These three types of controls provide three opportunities to identify problems and correct them.

COMPETENCY CHECK
Can you define and give examples of the three types of control?

WHAT CAN THE SUPERVISOR DO?

The supervisor can make sure that all three types of control are in place and that each control is exercised regularly and consistently. Remember that the purpose of the three controls is to provide three opportunities to check on the quality and quantity of the goods and services produced. Preliminary control allows the supervisor to check the resources that go into producing the goods or providing the service. When this control is not properly exercised, there is little check on the quality and quantity of the resources used. Concurrent control is primarily a supervisory responsibility, for this control is exercised through observation of day-to-day operations. Supervisors must be aware of deviations from standards and be prepared to take immediate corrective action. Feedback control is the final check on goods and services. This is the supervisor's last opportunity to put the stamp of approval on the department's output. Supervisors must take advantage of each of these opportunities to detect deviations from the standard and to take the necessary corrective action.

	Figure 14.6		
	SUMMARY OF DIFFERENCES IN THE THREE TYPES OF CONTROL		
	Preliminary Control	**Concurrent Control**	**Feedback Control**
Directed at	Resources	Activity	Results
Process	Input	Transformation	Output
When	Before	During	After
How	Preventive measures	Observation	Feedback
Purpose	Preventing problems	Observing and correcting problems	Identifying deviations and taking corrective action

What to Control

Supervisors have responsibility for exercising control over all the activities in their departments. Total quality management (TQM) endeavors to control the quality and quantity of all resources in a synergistic way. (See Chapter 15, "Implementing Total Quality Management.") For our purposes here, however, we will categorize separate control responsibilities as time, behavior, materials and equipment, processes, cost, and quality and quantity of output.

Time

Exercising control over time is a critical element in keeping work schedules on track. When employees don't report to work on time, if they leave before the end of the workday, or if they take breaks or lunch periods that exceed those provided, time control is not being exercised effectively.

Behavior

Behavior refers to the way in which employees conduct themselves in the performance of their jobs. Exercising control over behavior means, first, providing employees with standards against which their actions can be compared. As discussed earlier, these standards may be qualitatively or quantitatively expressed. For example, "working cooperatively with others" may be defined as "helping coworkers complete their jobs if they require such aid." This is a qualitative standard. Qualitative standards are more subjective than are quantitative standards, but, if they are based on observation and critical-incident reports (recall this from Chapter 9), qualitative behavioral standards can be effective.

Materials and Equipment

Using materials wisely and equipment efficiently is vital if a company expects to make a profit. Supervisors are the people most closely involved in day-to-day operations and, therefore, the ones who will see materials wasted or equipment improperly used. Their responsibility, then, is to ensure that controls are in place to prevent waste and improper use of equipment, to be aware of any of these undesirable actions, and to take whatever corrective action may be necessary (training, retraining, and so on).

Processes

Sometimes the process used to convert inputs into outputs (transformation) is flawed. Perhaps the flow of work is inefficient. Work is not moving through the organization in a smooth flow; it is bottlenecked and slowed at one or more stations. Or perhaps the distribution of work is skewed, resulting in one person having too much work while another has too little. When this occurs, the supervisor needs to examine the situation and look for a more efficient method (process).

Costs

Costs refer to the amount of money expended to produce a good or a service. Costs are usually stipulated in the expense budget for the department. When preliminary controls are not in place, too much may be spent for materials, for example. The materials may be of a higher quality than that required for the job, or the quantity ordered may be greater or less than needed (leaving materials unused or causing a slowdown in production when materials are not available). Observation of waste as a cost is also a supervisor's responsibility. Finally, comparing the costs for a period with the budget for that period provides the information needed for feedback control of cost. In the case of costs, however, taking corrective action for the past period is impossible. The expenditure has already been made.

Quality and Quantity

Perhaps the supervisor's greatest concern is meeting the standards of quality and quantity of goods produced or services provided. Certainly if there are too many defective goods produced or too many services rendered that require repeat calls, then the unit, department, and, ultimately, the company will not be profitable. Quality has become a focus of many U.S. companies as they compete with other countries for consumer dollars. The slogan used by Ford Motor Company, for example, is "Quality is Job 1." Other companies, both large and small, are emphasizing quality as they promote their product or their service.

Quantity is the other side of the coin. Quality without quantity does not make profits, nor does quantity without quality. The supervisor is responsible for maintaining a balance between the two by ensuring that one is not sacrificed for the other. In an effort to increase production and turn out greater numbers of widgets, workers cannot ignore the importance of maintaining a quality product. On the other hand, if workers are trying so hard to produce a 100 percent defect-free product that it is taking them twice as long to produce the number required by the standard, quantity is being sacrificed for quality. It's quite a balancing act for supervisors; but it's their job.

COMPETENCY CHECK

Can you name activities a supervisor is responsible for controlling?

Control Tools and Techniques

Many employees are concerned over how a change to a formal control system would affect their jobs. Much of the concern is a result of lack of information about control systems and the tools and techniques used to implement and operate the process.

Benchmarking

Benchmarking is a technique that allows companies to measure themselves against the top performers in their industry and then establish their goals to exceed those of their competitors. Although a relatively new technique, benchmarking has the potential to aid companies in meeting the challenges of their global competitors. According to recent studies by Towers Perrin, the Massachusetts Institute of Technology, and the American Productivity and Quality Center,[1] most major companies will have some type of benchmarking system within five years.

The idea behind benchmarking is to research and find practices or performances that have proved to be the most successful in their business and that can lead to improvements for a department or a company. By using these "best practices" of their competitors, companies can streamline their own practices and become more effective and efficient. The information they gather is an invaluable tool in their mission for quality.

Budgets

A **budget** is a statement that specifies anticipated revenues and expenses for a given period. Some supervisors may submit only an **expense budget,** which specifies only the costs the supervisor expects to incur as the product or service is produced. This is because some departments are not profit-generating in themselves but are part of a process that ultimately produces the product or the service that generates the revenue. **Profit centers** are the departments or units that actually bring in revenue to the company.

For example, on an assembly line, the department responsible for wiring refrigerators is not a profit center; the sales department of the plant is a profit center.

Budgets, like standards, also link the planning and control processes. As a planning tool, the budget identifies anticipated revenues and expenses. As a control tool, it is used to compare planned revenues and expenses with actual revenues and expenses. An example of a budget used as a control tool is shown in Figure 14.7

The budget shown in Figure 14.7 is a **fixed budget,** that is, a budget that does not change with the number of units produced or the number of services rendered. A **flexible budget** is one that allows for fixed expenses for costs that remain constant even as production or service levels change (property taxes, basic overhead expenses, and depreciation) and for different levels of expenditures based on the level of production. Costs that vary according to level of production or service include direct labor, materials, and some general and administrative expenses.

Figure 14.7 BUDGET FOR OPTICAL DEPARTMENT (JANUARY–MARCH 199__)				
	Budget	Actual	Over	Under
Expected Revenues:				
Glasses	$93,750	$98,674	$4,925	
Services	350	200		$150
Miscellaneous	200	250	50	
Expected expenses:				
Frames	$56,000	$60,000	$4,000	
Lenses	3,000	3,400	400	
Miscellaneous materials	3,000	2,500		$500
Labor	13,500	13,500		
Machine maintenance	500	200		300

Regardless of the type of budget used—fixed or flexible—supervisors should be realistic as they project their expenses and revenues. At the end of the budget period, supervisors should examine the budget deviations, both over and under budget projections. Let's look at Figure 14.7 again. Note that revenue from the sale of glasses was greater than anticipated, by $4925; expenses for frames and lenses were also greater than anticipated, by $4400. The supervisor should try to determine why there were deviations. Perhaps the cost of frames and lenses increased during the 3-month period. Maybe the opticians were careless and broke frames or dropped lenses, requiring reorders and thereby increasing expenses. Or perhaps the supervisor was on target for the expenses as they related to the projected revenues, but, as revenues increased, so did expenses. Did expenses increase in proportion to revenues?

The **zero-based budget** was developed by Texas Instruments, Inc., and used by President Carter's administration in his Office of Management and Budget. Unlike traditional budgets, which allow departments to build their current budget based on previous years' budgets including an inflation adjustment, a zero-based budget starts from scratch, or zero. It requires each program to be justified each year.[2] Every program, whether new or ongoing, is put to the same test. No supervisor can take the continuation of a program for granted simply because "We've always had it." For example, assume that your company has a program that pays employees for courses taken at the local community college. Each year at budget time, this program starts with a clean slate and is proposed along with all other programs. These proposals are placed in priority order, and if the reimbursement program does not compete successfully with all other programs, it may be modified or dropped.

COMPETENCY CHECK
Can you describe fixed, flexible, and zero-based budgets?

Scheduling Techniques

A **schedule** is a plan that specifies time periods for completing specific activities. A number of techniques may be used to schedule activities, but we will limit our discussion to Gantt charts, the critical path method (CPM), and program evaluation and review technique (PERT).

Gantt charts were described in Chapter 2 as they related to planning. They may also be used as control tools when a comparison is made of scheduled output and actual output. Figure 14.8 shows such a use of the Gantt chart as it relates to task completion. The Gantt chart in Chapter 2 focused on scheduling human resources, while the Gantt chart in Figure 14.8 focuses on activities. Note that in Figure 14.8, the design phase took longer than planned, but scheduling, ordering, and materials delivery were accomplished in less time than planned. Note also that a period of time planned for was not available. Assembling, inspecting, and shipping have not begun.

Figure 14.8
GANTT CHART

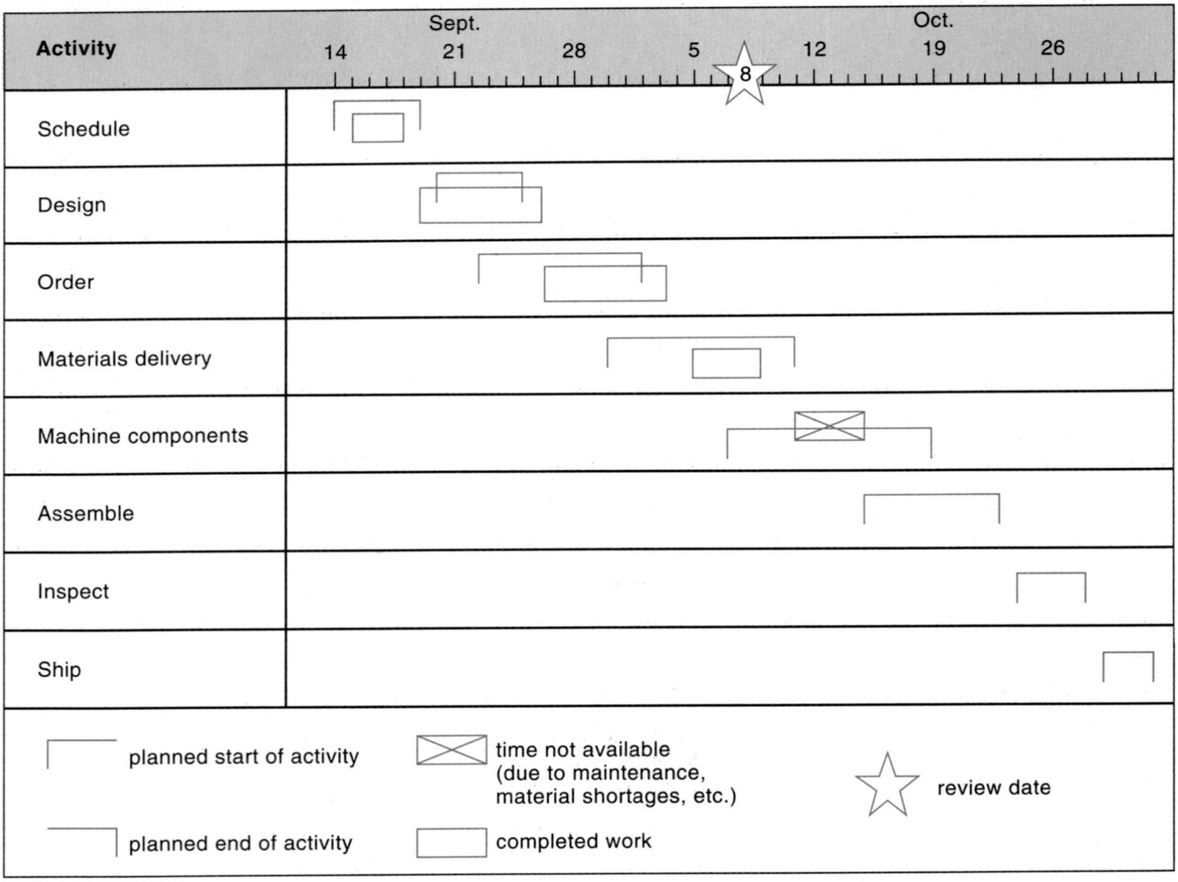

Source: John R. Schermerhorn, *Management for Productivity,* John Wiley & Sons, Inc., New York, 1984, p. 529. Copyright © 1984. Reprinted by permission of John Wiley & Sons, Inc.

The **critical path method (CPM)** and **program evaluation and review technique (PERT)** are time-scheduling techniques for projects that require a sequence of activities; some activities can be performed concurrently, while others have precedence requirements. CPM and PERT charts show a network of time requirements and relationships for all activities necessary to complete a project. The activities are the tasks that must be performed and are represented by arrows. Activities are the time-consuming elements in the network chart. The circles in the chart represent events—decision points or the accomplishment of some activity. Events do not consume time or resources. Figure 14.9 shows a critical path method network. The term **critical path** denotes the sequence of activities that requires the longest period of time to complete. The path is critical because a delay in it means a delay in the project itself. Delays in other paths are not necessarily critical because there is some additional time built into the paths taking less time than the critical one. Let's look at Figure 14.9 first and then determine the critical path for this activity.[3]

The figure shows, in network form, the work activities necessary to construct an electric power plant. Note that it is necessary to complete some activities before others. For example, the plant design, as shown in activities 1–2, must be completed before any other activity can take place. However, site, vendor, and personnel selection can take place concurrently. The installation of the generator shown in activities 5–7 cannot begin until the site preparation has been completed (activities 3–5) and the generator has been manufactured (activities 4–5). There are really four paths through the network from first event to last (events 1–8). The site preparation

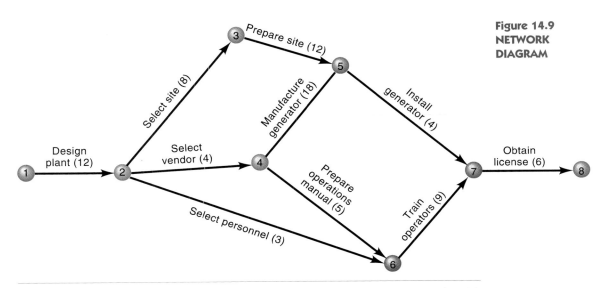

**Figure 14.9
NETWORK
DIAGRAM**

Design plant (12)

Select site (8)

Prepare site (12)

Manufacture generator (18)

Install generator (4)

Select vendor (4)

Prepare operations manual (5)

Obtain license (6)

Select personnel (3)

Train operators (9)

Source: David R. Hampton, *Management for Productivity*, McGraw-Hill Book Company, New York, 1986, p. 702.

(activities 3–5) and the generator manufacture (activities 4–5) are on different paths, but since they converge at event 5, either activity could delay the generator installation.[4] Note that the estimated time to complete an activity is shown on the line between events.

Now let's look at Figure 14.10 and determine the critical path, or the path estimated to take the longest time to complete. If you add the time required to complete the paths, path 2 becomes the critical path.

The major difference between CPM and PERT is in the way estimated time is calculated. CPM uses one estimate of the time required to complete an activity. PERT uses three estimated times to arrive at a time requirement. PERT time is calculated by determining expected time from (1) optimistic time (the time required if everything goes as planned), (2) pessimistic time (the time required if Murphy's law is at work—what can go wrong will go wrong); and (3) most likely time (the time required when some activities go as planned and others do not). The formula for calculating expected time is:

$$\frac{OT + 4(MLT) + PT}{6}$$

Therefore, if optimistic time for activity 1 is 9 weeks, pessimistic time is 15 weeks, and most likely time is 12 weeks, expected time would be calculated as follows:

$$9 + 4(12) + 15 = \frac{72}{6}, \text{ or } 12 \text{ weeks}$$

COMPETENCY CHECK
Can you describe three scheduling techniques?

Use of PERT in scheduling the development and construction of the Polaris missile is said to have reduced the time required to produce Polaris by more than 2 years.

Computers are used to generate CPM and PERT charts and to update information in a timely manner, making network scheduling techniques more available to other than top-level managers.

 ## Quality Controls

To maintain high-quality output, goods or services must be evaluated in terms of how they meet quality standards. Products may be evaluated by 100 percent inspection or by sampling.

Figure 14.10	
DETERMINING THE CRITICAL PATH	
Path	**Times**
1. 1–2–3–5–7–8	12+8+12+4+6
2. 1–2–4–5–7–8	12+4+18+4+6
3. 1–2–4–6–7–8	12+4+5+9+6
4. 1–2–6–7–8	12+3+9+6

Source: David R. Hampton, *Management for Productivity,* McGraw-Hill Book Company, New York, 1986, p. 682.

WHAT CAN THE SUPERVISOR DO?

Although supervisors may not be called upon to generate a CPM or PERT chart, they may be held responsible for providing some of the input. It may therefore be important for them to know the basics of network scheduling so they can provide the information required to schedule their departments as a part of a network (CPM, PERT) schedule.

100 Percent Inspection

Inspecting every product or evaluating every service may not be feasible. Suppose you checked every flashbulb to be sure it worked or tasted every cookie to be sure it was done. What would you have left to sell? However, 100 percent inspection is appropriate for some products and services. Custom-made suits and handmade furniture are examples of products for which 100 percent inspection is not only feasible but recommended. Expensive automobiles such as Rolls-Royces and Bentleys are also 100 percent inspected.

Sampling

Sampling is used when 100 percent inspection is not a feasible or cost-effective method for determining quality. Sampling may be conducted randomly (choosing an item to be inspected on a random basis) or statistically (choosing an item to be inspected on a mathematical basis; for example, every fiftieth item). Sampling assumes that if 95 percent of the items tested are acceptable, then 95 percent of the total output is acceptable.

A sample may be judged on either an **acceptability standard** (sampling by attributes) or on a **variability standard** (sampling by variables). If sampling is done by attributes, the product or service sampled is determined to be either acceptable or unacceptable; there is no maybe. For example, a lightbulb either lights or it doesn't; a microwave oven is either repaired and working properly or it is still not working. The acceptability standard is often referred to as "go/no go."

Sampling by variables allows for some leeway from the standard. A watch may gain or lose up to a given number of seconds per day; a tire tread may be within plus or minus $\frac{1}{16}$ of an inch; eyeglass lenses may be plus or minus 0.012 diopters. As long as the sample is within the tolerances, it is considered to be within the quality standard.

COMPETENCY CHECK

Can you describe the difference between 100 percent inspection and sampling, and can you explain two sampling techniques?

Time Controls

Most large and many small firms have some means of recording employee work attendance, including, in some organizations, detailed accounts of times of arrival, breaks, and times of departure. Factories have always been leaders in timekeeping, using a time clock in most cases for keeping track of worker time. Since the early days of time clocks, other options have become available for keeping employees' time records. Nick Kinnie and Alan Arthurs have identified three options they label "old tech," "no tech," and "new tech."[5] Old tech retains the traditional electro-mechanical time recorder; no tech has discarded automatic time recording and replaced it with supervisory recording or an employee honor system; and new tech uses a computer to record time and to provide a range of other information beyond simple timekeeping.

The more sophisticated new-tech devices can provide a supervisor with information about an entire department, an individual employee, or even a particular workstation. This information can then be made available via a computer screen or hard copy to both the supervisor and others in the organization who need this information for various planning and decision-making purposes. Figure 14.11 shows the three methods of recording employee time and the benefits and costs of each. The

COMPETENCY CHECK

Can you describe three types of time control?

Figure 14.11
BENEFITS AND COSTS OF ALTERNATIVE TIME-RECORDING METHODS

	Benefits	Costs
1. Time clock	Low cost of purchase, installation, and maintenance	Administration costs
	Permanent record for payroll and discipline	Possible abuses
Time clocks Clock cards	Acceptable and established	Feelings of inequity
2. Manual	Very low costs of purchase, installation, and maintenance	Possible abuses
	Harmonization of timekeeping arrangements	Time-consuming for supervisors
Logbooks Time sheets Honor cards	Reinforces supervisor's authority	Inconsistent treatment of employees?
3. Computerized	Simplified payroll and lower administration costs	Cost of purchase, installation, and maintenance
Cards or badges	Improved management information	Will it work?
Micro, mini, or mainframe computers	Fewer errors and abuses	Is it acceptable?

Source: Nick Kinnie and Alan Arthurs, "Clock, Clock, Who's There?" *Personnel Management,* August 1986, p. 45. Reprinted by permission of Personnel Publications, Ltd.

choice of method is dependent on the needs of the organization and of the individual departments.

Materials Controls

Supervisors have the primary responsibility for ensuring that materials are available in the quantity and of the quality required and that these materials are on hand when needed. Materials not needed for the job must be stored somewhere; workers must be assigned to account for and distribute materials as needed. On the other hand, if materials are not available when needed, workers are idle—an expensive delay. One technique used to ensure that materials are ordered in the least expensive quantity is **economic order quantity (EOQ).** EOQ takes into consideration (1) the cost of maintaining materials and (2) the cost of ordering materials to determine the least expensive amount to order. The formula for determining economic order quantity is the square root of (two times actual demand for inventory use times ordering cost) divided by carrying cost:

$$EOQ = \sqrt{\frac{2DO}{C}}$$

where D = actual demand for inventory use
$\quad\quad\quad O$ = ordering cost of inventory
$\quad\quad\quad C$ = carrying cost of inventory

Figure 14.12 shows an inventory driven by economic order quantity. Let's suppose that the demand for a particular part for your department is 200 per year, the cost of each order is $60, and the carrying cost is $10 per unit annually. The EOQ is determined by calculating the square root of 2 times 200 times $60 divided by $10. This shows that the supervisor should order 50 units of this particular part to

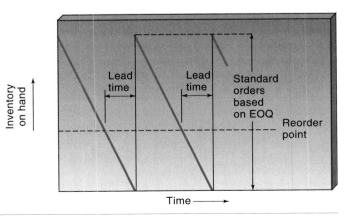

**Figure 14.12
ECONOMIC
ORDER
QUANTITY**

Source: John R. Schermerhorn, *Management for Productivity,* 3d ed., John Wiley & Sons, Inc., New York, 1989, p. 498. Copyright © 1984. Reprinted by permission of John Wiley & Sons, Inc.

minimize inventory cost. When materials are ordered more frequently, ordering costs go up and carrying costs go down. Conversely, when orders are placed less frequently, ordering costs go down and carrying costs go up. Therefore, supervisors should try to balance the costs by using economic order quantity to arrive at the most economical amount of inventory to keep on hand.

The second problem, mentioned earlier, is that of having excess materials or not enough materials. *Kanban,* a technique developed in Japan for controlling inventory, requires that parts be supplied **"just in time" (JIT)**. JIT is now used by many firms in the United States. Don't confuse this with the JIT (job instruction training) described in Chapter 7. The "JIT idea is simple: Produce and deliver goods in time to be sold, subassemblies just in time to be assembled into finished goods, fabricated parts just in time to go into subassemblies, and purchased materials just in time to be transformed into fabricated parts."[6]

The following describes how one Ford Motor Company assembly plant uses "just in time."[7]

On a typical day, at least 25 railcars and 30 tractor-trailers laden with parts pull into the Ford Motor Company's light-truck assembly plant. "A couple of years ago, we could have survived 4 days, maybe 5, without this daily replenishment," said Percy Eason, the plant's material manager. "These days," said Eason, "Ford's assembly line here would be starved for parts within 24 hours if deliveries did not arrive daily."

"You can't keep a large inventory when it's costing you 20 cents on the dollar—the combined cost of insurance, interest, and other expenses of maintaining inventory." Eason was quoted as saying, "Having a leaner inventory of parts has uncovered assembly-line snags that had been masked by a comfortable cushion of spares." However well *kanban* works for the Japanese, U.S. automakers have to allow some flexibility. The companies that supply Japan's automakers with parts tend to be concentrated around the assembly plants and are able to deliver their products in a matter of hours. Because suppliers in the United States are dispersed throughout the country, the flow of parts is more susceptible to interruptions. Therefore, U.S. automakers are often forced to maintain reserves that would be unnecessary in Japan.

Eason also commented that the concern with inventory levels has focused attention on several less visible matters, including the accuracy and timeliness of inventory records. Ford has installed video display terminals in the plant that allow supervisors to refer more quickly to inventory information in the computer.

Both EOQ and JIT are techniques supervisors can use to better manage the material resources for which they are responsible.

COMPETENCY CHECK

Can you distinguish between EOQ and JIT and explain the purpose of each?

Computer Controls

Computers are used as control tools to provide information about the progress being made toward accomplishing the objectives of the organization, the department, and the individual. Computers may be used for counting, reporting, and updating to help supervisors make comparisons between what was planned and what was achieved for a given period, for <u>monitoring employee performance</u>, and for operating controls.

Counting

Computers may be used to count work and compare the results against a standard. For example, in a word processing center, standards may be established for (1) the number of pages, lines, or documents to be produced during a standard workday, (2) turnaround time, and (3) errors. As work is received in the word processing center, it is logged in on a computer. When the work is completed, it is logged out. From this information, a weekly employee performance report such as the one shown in Figure 14.13 can be generated.

Reporting

The information stored in the computer may be used to generate a variety of reports in a variety of formats, depending on the needs of the supervisor. If an analysis of individual work is required, a report similar to Figure 14.13 can be requested.

At a General Electric facility, six weekly printouts derived from job forms provide information on the number of jobs handled for various word originators. One report summarizes a week's output by one operator, with totals provided for dictation, longhand manuscript, and cut-and-paste methods of input.[8]

Different reports for different management levels can be generated. For example, in a word processing center, a higher-level management report can be created for a longer period of time than that shown in 14.13. The average performance, coverage, and effectiveness of the center can be tabulated, showing how many workers were used compared to how many should have been used to produce the indicated volume of work.

Updating

Use of the computer makes updating files relatively easy and allows supervisors to make changes in a timely manner. Reports can then be generated based on the most up-to-date information available and sent electronically to the appropriate levels of management.

Operating

Many factories are becoming automated, with computer networks handling diverse operations. Materials are checked in at the loading dock by computer and placed on conveyor belts that carry them to storage areas, from which they will be distributed by automated carriers. Computers are used to check inventory automatically, flag items that need to be reordered or that have been on the shelf for a given period, and print out order forms.

Monitoring

A U.S. House of Representatives subcommittee estimates that as many as 26 million U.S. office workers may be monitored through their computers.[9] The practice of

Figure 14.13
WEEKLY EMPLOYEE PERFORMANCE REPORT

EXHIBIT 1a

EMPLOYEE PERFORMANCE SUMMARY   BRUCE PAYNE & ASSOCIATES, INC.

DEPARTMENT/BRANCH NO. ___   SECTION SYSTEMS & DATA PROCESSING NO. ___   UNIT WORD PROCESSING NO. ___   FOR WEEK ENDING 10/5

EMPLOYEE NUMBER	S	NAME	PERFORMANCE % 13 Week	PERFORMANCE % Cur. Wk.	CHARGEABLE HOURS Standard Allowed Hours	MEASURABLE Measured	MEASURABLE Unmeas.	Delay	Errors	Paid Not Worked	Service and Admin.	Total Available	NONCHARGEABLE HOURS Loaned	Approved Activity	Absence Vacation Holiday	Total Straight Hours	Overtime Hours Incl.
9231		M. Holms		147	1.5	1.0	—	—	—	—	37.5	38.5		1.3		39.8	1.0
3653		J. Sammons		80	14.6	18.2	7.0	.3	—	—	12.0	37.5		1.3		38.8	
6275		D. Boger		74	17.8	27.1	8.8	—	—	—	1.3	37.2		1.6		38.8	
4628		D. Smith		72	29.5	40.7	1.9	—	—	—	—	42.6		1.3		43.9	5.1
3241		S. Engle		68	22.2	32.6	4.2	—	—	—	—	36.8		2.0		38.8	
1352		D. Kellogg		64	10.8	16.9	8.4	—	—	—	0.4	25.7		1.3	11.8	38.8	
4158		C. Richardson		63	21.6	34.3	2.8	—	—	—	0.4	37.5		1.3		38.8	
8573		V. Grennel		48	15.9	32.8	4.1	—	—	—	0.6	37.5		1.3		38.8	
1478		L. Alton		42	15.9	37.9	3.7	—	—	—	1.0	42.6		1.3		43.9	5.1
8756		M. Music		—	—	—	—	—	—	—	—	—		—	38.8	38.8	
TOTALS					149.7	241.5	40.9	.3			53.2	335.9		12.7	50.6	399.2	11.2

Adjusted Total SAH 175.0

COVERED BY STANDARDS   GOAL 90   ACTUAL 86

AVERAGE STAFF PERFORMANCE   GOAL 100   ACTUAL 62

STAFF EFFECTIVENESS   GOAL 89   ACTUAL 52

Source: Walter Kleinshrod, Leonard Kruka, and Hilda Turner, Word Processing Operations, Applications, and Administration, The Bobbs-Merrill Company, Inc., Indianapolis, 1980, p. 179.

WHAT CAN THE SUPERVISOR DO?

A checklist can be developed to help decide the measures best suited for evaluating performance. From such a list, the supervisor can select the appropriate measures needed to supervise effectively. These measures can then be used to design a customized measurement system. A portion of such a chart for a word processing supervisor is shown in Figure 14.14.

secretly monitoring employees' work electronically began in the 1970s, when telephone companies began installing eavesdropping devices to help in training new operators and for quality control.

Under an agreement reached in April 1992 with the communications workers' union, Centel ended undisclosed eavesdropping. U.S. West says its supervisors now always sit within sight of employees who are being monitored. AT&T's self-managed work groups allow some phone operators to decide when their supervisors can listen. In May 1993, legislation was introduced offering protection to workers whose telephone calls and computer activities are monitored. The bill, the Privacy for Consumers and Workers Act, would not actually outlaw monitoring but would place stringent requirements on employers to notify workers when monitoring occurs. Businesses are opposed to the bill, contending that secretly monitoring employees is one of the few accurate ways of monitoring quality and gauging performance.

COMPETENCY CHECK

Can you describe uses of the computer as a control tool?

Frontline Control

Frontline control, a process developed at General Electric, focuses on the people costs resulting from pressure to complete work and meet schedules. Frontline control makes it easier for supervisors to formulate daily objectives for their units and to develop a plan to meet them, communicate expectations to workers, check performance frequently against the plan, take corrective action before it's too late, and report interference promptly.[10]

The seven basic principles of this approach are:

1. Each work element must have a time standard or target that is current and reasonable. The standard should reflect expected output from a qualified employee working at a normal pace without interruption.

2. Specific performance expectations for every job must be communicated to every worker. Accepting these targets, even tacitly, amounts to a contract between the supervisor and worker. It is therefore important that employees understand what is expected, have an opportunity to agree or disagree, and know how performance will be measured.

Figure 14.14
WORD PROCESSING PERFORMANCE MEASUREMENT AND CONTROL SYSTEM

Measures that could be developed in a Word processing performance measurement and control (PMC) system:		For your center the measure at the left is (check one):				
Description of measure	What the measure indicates or how used: *Ref:*	5	4	3	2	1
		Degree of importance 5 high-1 low				
1 Productivity (A) Productivity of total center, e.g., work units/keyboard hours	1 (A) Indicates performance rate or efficiency for overall center I (A)					
(B) Productivity of each secretary	1 (B) Same as I (A), calculated for each secretary I (B)					
2 Turnaround (A) A single turnaround average for all documents processed by the center	2 (A) Indicates overall level of service as it relates to II (A) speed of getting documents back to users					
(B) Turnaround average by secretary for all documents processed by that secretary	2 (B) Same as II (A), calculated for each secretary II (B)					
(C) Turnaround average by user department for user department's documents	2 (C) Same as II (A), except indicates service provided to each user department II (C)					
(D) Turnaround averages for original, revision, and rush work. Total of three averages for overall center	2 (D) Indicates level of service provided by center on three classes of work. Recognizes differences in priority II (D) of the three classes					
(E) Turnaround averages by secretary for original, revision, and rush work. Three averages for each secretary	2 (E) Same as II (D), calculated for individual secretaries II (E)					
(F) Turnaround averages by user department for original, revision, and rush work. Three averages per department	2 (F) Same as II (D), except indicates service provided to each user department II (F)					
3 Work Volume (A) Total volume of work processed by the center, e.g., pages, documents, or other units of work	3 (A) Indicates quality of work produced or through-put of center—how much was III (A) done					
(B) Total volume of work processed by each secretary	3 (B) Same as III (A), calculated for each secretary III (B)					
(C) Total volume of work processed for each user department	3 (C) Same as III (A), except indicates work done for each user department III (C)					
7 Quality (A) Volume of secretary-made errors. Total for center	7 (A) Indicates level of quality for work leaving center VII (A)					
(B) Volume of secretary-made errors. Total for each secretary	7 (B) Same as VII (A), calculated for individual secretaries VII (B)					
8 Other						

Suggested frequency for preparing above measures	(A) Prepare these measures on a regular basis, e.g., weekly. (B) Prepare on an irregular basis. (C) Do not include these measures in PMC system.	A	B	C

Source: Walter Kleinshrod, Leonard Kruk, and Hilda Turner, *Word Processing Operations, Applications, and Administration,* The Bobbs-Merrill Company, Inc., Indianapolis, 1980, p. 198.

3. The unit must be staffed at the level needed to meet current output requirements. Staffing at historical performance levels can only perpetuate inefficien-
   cies. If units are staffed to meet the peak loads, they will be operating ineffi-
   ciently in the slack periods.

4. Every supervisor, at the beginning of every shift, must have a production plan
   that he or she can reasonably expect to meet. The plan must reflect scheduling
   priorities based on today's "hot" lists and reflect today's resource availability—
   the materials, tools, and people available to do the job. For long-cycle and
   white-collar operations, the planning period may be a week rather than a shift,
   but the planning principle still stands.

5. At frequent intervals during the scheduled period (every hour or two in the
   shop, perhaps daily in the office), progress must be evaluated against the plan.
   This means monitoring output either from every worker or just from key
   checkpoints. If the plan is not being met, corrections can be made before the
   end of the shift.

6. Problems must be identified, addressed, and resolved. Lost time or variances
   from the plan are documented and classified, and a formal problem-solving
   procedure is put in place.

7. Every supervisor, every day, should be able to specify what his or her productivity is. This daily indicator reflects performance today. If you are asked, "How
   did you do yesterday?" instead of answering, "I met schedule," you should be
   able to say, for example, "I met schedule, and I achieved 90 percent labor utilization." Let's look at GE's plan for implementing front-line control.[11]

Planning

The first thing, planning, entails deciding what time values are appropriate for
each work activity in the unit. If good time standards exist, or if percentage factors can be applied to the time standards to bring them up to date, use them. But
if time standards are nonexistent or hopelessly outdated, develop an estimate for
each product family at each workstation. The target should not be based on what
is currently being produced from the workstation but on what should be produced if it operates without interruption. To formulate the target, consider what
constitutes a normal machine cycle with allowances for setups and material handling and what represents a good hour's production.

Next, develop a target table for each workstation and include on your tables
the common tasks that make up 80 percent of the operations. Incidental tasks or
product varieties can often be grouped with the common tasks or can be added
to the tables as the need occurs. But if there is a large variety of operations or
products, select a limited number of key volume indicators–those operations or
output measurements that are representative of the whole unit's output.

The Daily Schedule Control

The best format to use for the tables is the schedule control sheet. For short-cycle
operations, use Figure 14.15. Under "work assignment," express the "target" in

---

Figure 14.15

SCHEDULE CONTROL SHORT-CYCLE OPERATIONS

Supervisor _____　　Area _____　　Date _____

Work Assignment					Follow-up								Report		
					PERIOD 1		PERIOD 2		PERIOD 3		PERIOD 4				%
Name	Station	Job	Quantity	Target	Plan	Actual	Plan	Actual	Plan	Actual	Plan	Actual	Planned	Actual	Productivity
												Totals			

---

units per hour. Under "follow-up," document "actual" performance against "plan" at regular intervals throughout the shift. And under "report," the productivity percentage per worker can be generated by dividing the "actual" quantity produced for the day by the "planned" quantity. Finally, the productivity percent for all the workers on the shift combined can be generated by dividing the total "actual" quantities by the total "planned" quantities.

For long-cycle operations, use Figure 14.16. Under "work assignment," express the "target" in hours per unit. Under "follow-up," document target "hours earned" against actual "hours worked" at regular intervals throughout the shift. And under "report," generate the productivity percentage for each couple of workers by dividing the "hours earned" by the "hours worked." Finally, generate the productivity percentage for all the workers on the shift by dividing the total "hours earned" by the total "hours worked."

On the back of the control sheets is a variance summary (see Figure 14.17) codifying the causes of lost time to highlight repetitive problems, explaining each problem, and listing immediate and future corrective actions.

Figure 14.16

SCHEDULE CONTROL LONG-CYCLE OPERATIONS

Supervisor _____   Area _____   Date _____

Work Assignment				**Follow-up**									**Report**	
				PERIOD 1		PERIOD 2		PERIOD 3		PERIOD 4				
Job	Names	Operation	Target	Hours Worked	Hours Earned	Hours Worked	Hours Earned	Hours Worked	Hours Earned	Hours Worked	Hours Earned	Hours Worked	Hours Earned	% Productivity
										Totals				

Now let's look at how you could utilize the control sheets when you make each work assignment.

Recording Assignments

Before shift start-up, fill out the first part of the schedule control. It might read like Figure 14.18 or 14.19. Then make sure the specific assignments and your expectations are communicated to your workers. For Jones and Smith, do this by posting the target tables at the presses. For Black and White, say to them, "I want you to wire Unit 2 completely. Let me know how it goes during the day today because it should be ready for test by the end of the shift tomorrow."

Follow-Up

Next, follow up on the worker's performance. In the pressroom, for example, if after checking performance every hour you find that by noon Smith has produced the expected 200 parts, note 200 planned and 200 actual in the period 4

Figure 14.17

VARIANCE SUMMARY

Supervisor _____   Area _____   Date _____

Work Station	Codes	Hours Lost	Problems	Corrective Action	Action Complete (Y/N)

Variance Codes:
A–Materials Quality   C–Tooling and Equipment   E–Operator
B–Materials Availability D–Design and Planning   F–Other

Figure 14.18
PRESSROOM SCHEDULE CONTROL

Name	Station	Job	Quantity	Target
J. Jones	Press #1	Part A	400	100/hr
S. Smith	Press #2	Part B	200	50/hr

	Figure 14.19		
	ASSEMBLY HOUR SCHEDULE CONTROL		
Job	Names	Operation	Target
Unit 1 assm.	B. Brown	Pipe complete	16 man-hours
	G. Green		
Unit 2 assm.	W. White	Wire complete	32 man-hours
	B. Black		

Source: Harlan R. Jessup, "Front Line Control," *Supervisory Management*, October 1986, p. 18.

"follow-up" column on the schedule control sheet (Figure 14.15) and comment to Smith, "Looks good!"

On the other hand, if Jones has produced only 300 parts against the 400 planned, record the results in the Period 4 "follow-up" column (Figure 14.15) and ask him why. If it was a materials, equipment, or operator problem, record the lost time (1 hour) and its cause on the variance report.

On the assembly floor, if everything goes according to plan, Black and White should be 25 percent through their wiring job at noon. If they both lost an hour trying to find the engineer in order to get the latest revision of the wiring diagram, record 6 hours earned against 8 hours worked in the Period 2 columns of the "follow-up" section (Figure 14.16). Then talk to Black and White to find out what caused the problem and to determine how to correct it. Did they act appropriately, or did they just put in a call and then sit and wait? Can they recover the time, or should other action be taken? On the variance report (Figure 14.17), record the problem and document actions taken and future action needed.

At the end of the shift, enter the final data for each worker or pair of workers and talk to the operators about the day's performance. Then summarize the results for all of them combined and calculate the shift's productivity performance against plan. To cite two other examples: If you have a total of 20 operators, their performance might be recorded as 140 hours earned against 160 hours worked for a productivity factor of 88 percent. And if you have an assembly line with a total of 10 operators, their performance might be recorded as 800 units produced against 1,000 units planned for a productivity factor of 80 percent.

Reporting

Once all the forms have been completed, discuss your unit's performance with your manager, making sure he or she understands what you are doing and what real problems need his or her attention. You can never win by concealing the real situation until the last day of the shipping period. But if you reveal a current problem, you will gain some understanding.

Track performance trends for yourself. Day-to-day calculations won't mean much without a trend comparison, especially if you haven't had good measure-

WHAT CAN THE SUPERVISOR DO?

If you want your plan to work, you have to take control of your resources and, perhaps by using General Electric's frontline control approach, be a supervisor actively involved in the daily control activities that help to ensure that your unit or department does, indeed, meet its goals.

ments in the past. Tracking trends will help you to understand and communicate real performance gains. It will also help to reveal some of the chronic problems that look insignificant today but that will lead to significant lost opportunity if they persist.

The Bottom Line

Frontline control can be a powerful tool for improving the performance of any unit. But to really improve productivity, you must go one step further and increase the workload or reduce the workforce.

If more work is coming, figure out how to do it without a proportionate increase in head count. But if work levels are staying the same, reduce overtime, take advantage of attrition, and perhaps ask your boss to help transfer employees out of your unit.

Your new control procedure, your improved communication, and your problem-solving routines should give you confidence that you can do it. You might set yourself a goal of 10 percent or 15 percent more output per employee and take the necessary steps, painful as they may be, to achieve this goal in the next 3 months. If you succeed, you can congratulate yourself for a job well done.

COMPETENCY CHECK

Can you describe GE's frontline control concept?

COMPETENCY REVIEW

1. Define *control*.
2. State three characteristics of effective standards.
3. Describe the four steps in the control process.
4. Define and give examples of the three types of control.
5. Identify at least five areas in which the supervisor is responsible for control.
6. Describe benchmarking.
7. Compare fixed, flexible, and zero-based budgets.
8. Describe three scheduling techniques.
9. Describe the difference between 100 percent inspection and sampling, and explain two sampling techniques.

10. Describe three types of time controls.
11. Distinguish between EOQ and JIT, explaining the purposes of each.
12. Describe five uses of the computer as a control tool.
13. Describe GE's frontline control concept.

APPLICATIONS

1. **a.** Name six situations in which 100 percent inspection is appropriate (other than the examples given in the chapter). Explain why you selected these situations.
   b. Name six situations in which "go/no go" sampling is appropriate (other than the examples given in the chapter). Explain why you selected these situations.
   c. Name six situations in which variable sampling is appropriate (other than the examples given in the chapter). Explain why you selected these situations.
2. Construct a CPM or PERT network diagram for getting up in the morning and getting to class. Mark the critical path in a different color.
3. Given the following information, determine the economic order quantity for this particular situation: Jimmy Monroe, supervisor of the printing department, must determine the most cost-efficient inventory of paper. The department uses 1000 reams of paper per month at a cost of $2.40 per ream. The carrying cost per ream is 15 cents per month.

CASES   Case I

YOU GOT THE RIGHT ONE, BABY UH HUH

In June 1993, PepsiCo, the nation's second largest soft drink maker, went through a marketer's nightmare. Reports came in from across the country that syringes and other objects had been found in Pepsi-Cola. The first reports came from the Seattle-Tacoma, Washington, area, where syringes were found in Diet Pepsi cans. One week later, the media reported that similar complaints had been filed in about half the states. Many consumers reacted the same way Stephen Hoch's wife did—urging her husband to make sure their children didn't drink Diet Pepsi. Dr. Hoch, a marketing professor at the University of Chicago, "went and shook the cans" as a precaution. While he found nothing amiss, that scenario was probably played out all over the country.

"This is a particularly acute problem in the soft drink business, where advertisers dwell so heavily on image," Dr. Hoch said. So what can Pepsi do?

Marketing experts say the company should demonstrate its concern for public safety, treat each complaint seriously, cooperate with appropriate regulators, examine its own operations, and publicize its findings. Said Clive Chajet, chairman of the consulting firm Lippincott & Margulies, Inc., "The first thing one does is to prove that it couldn't possibly be their fault. Then they must be aggressive in demonstrating that regardless of whose fault it is, the company will be relentless in solving the problem."

Contrast this proposed action with that of Johnson & Johnson and the Tylenol scare. In 1982, after spending $85 million on advertising over the past 4 years, Tylenol had 37 percent of the painkiller market and was increasing that share by 2 to 3 percent each year. Then, in October 1982, seven people died in Chicago from cyanide-laced Extra-Strength Tylenol capsules. Although it was proved that the tampering was done on retail store shelves and not at the factory, Tylenol's sales dropped 80 percent—to 12 percent of the market—in 1 month.

At that point, management had three options: (1) to do nothing and hope that people would buy the product again after the crisis was over, (2) to bring the product out under another name, and (3) to do everything possible to protect Johnson & Johnson's good name and reputation and recover Tylenol's lost customers. They chose the third option. First, a three-way safety-sealed package was designed. Then, the chairman took to the airwaves to reassure the public and to reiterate that the FDA had cleared J&J of any negligence or wrongdoing. Retailers and customers were reimbursed for capsules thrown away, and a discount was given to both retailers and consumers who purchased Tylenol, with the company paying the entire $100-million-plus cost of the activities. Within 15 months, Tylenol had recaptured over 30 percent of the total market. Another scare, though not so serious, caused J&J to stop producing capsules, and now Tylenol is produced in only tablets and caplets.

1. How is this case an example of the control function?
2. What was the result of the Pepsi-Cola episode?
3. Why do you think the two companies took two different routes to resolve this problem? Was one preferable to the other?
4. What other similar cases have been reported in the media? How were they resolved?

Source: "Pepsi Caught in a No-Win Situation," and "Pepsi Suspects Tampering; A Hoax, Some Experts Say," *The Virginian-Pilot and The Ledger-Star,* Norfolk, Va., June 27, 1993.

AND THE BELLS TOLLED!

Chief Inspector Ben Halley boarded bus 41 and dropped a token into the fare box. It gave the usual satisfying "ting" as it passed through the mechanism. He sat in the first seat to the right of the driver and watched.

Halley is responsible for checking fare thefts for City Suburban Transit. He likes his job, which involves traveling extensively to subsidiary companies and making sure that drivers are not taking cash fares instead of reporting them. None of the drivers know who he is, and at times his job is much like a detective's.

The company has fare boxes that register the fares with a small meter and a "ting." The meter is deliberately designed so that inspectors like Halley can unobtrusively observe it from the front seat. At the moment, this meter showed 27 fares collected.

The bus stopped, and six people boarded. One gave a transfer, the others dropped tokens and coins into the box. There were five "tings" as they did so, but the man with the transfer blocked Halley's view of the fare box. When he moved away, the register showed only 30 fares collected.

Halley was on the scent now. He carefully noted the next stops, mentally keeping track of the fares collected by counting the "tings." At the end of the run, he had counted 226 fares, but the meter showed only 122. He recalled that Jake Jackson, the supervisor, had complained about the low earning power of this run, considering its traffic potential.

Halley got up to leave the bus as five people boarded. He deliberately situated himself so that he could watch the driver. There was a slight bulge in the driver's jacket pocket. The driver took four fares in his hand and held his hand over the box. Four "tings" registered, but the meter moved only once. Halley's trained ear caught several "tings" coming from the driver's pocket. It was the old, familiar game in the transit business—the bell machine in the pocket. This one was quite small and pretty good. Halley smiled as he got off the bus to phone in his preliminary report to the main office and prepare the written report that would be the basis for action against the driver.[12]

1. Identify two to four preliminary controls that might be used to prevent this type of behavior.
2. Identify two to four concurrent controls that might be used to stop this type of behavior.
3. Identify two to four feedback controls that might be used to correct this type of behavior.
4. What action would you take against the bus driver?

REFERENCES

1. Jeffrey A. Schmidt, "Following the Leader Competitive Benchmarking as a Tool for Survival," *Management Digest*, reported in *Newsweek*, June 1, 1992, p. 6.
2. David R. Hampton, *Management for Productivity*, McGraw-Hill Book Company, New York, 1986, p. 702.
3. Ibid., p. 681.
4. Ibid.
5. Nick Kinnie and Alan Arthurs, "Clock, Clock, Who's There?," *Personnel Management*, August 1986, p. 40.
6. Richard J. Schonberger, *Japanese Manufacturing Techniques: Nine Lessons in Simplicity*, The Free Press, New York, 1982, p. 16.
7. Tom Shean, "Ford Is Geared Up to Achieve Leaner Inventories," *The Virginian-Pilot and The Ledger-Star*, Nov. 21, 1982.
8. Walter Kleinshrod, Leonard Kruk, and Hilda Turner, *Word Processing Operations, Applications, and Administration*, The Bobbs-Merrill Company, Inc., Indianapolis, 1980, p. 181.
9. *The Wall Street Journal*, May 26, 1992.
10. Harlan R. Jessup, "Front Line Control," *Supervisory Management*, October 1986, pp. 12–13.
11. Ibid., p. 15.
12. Richard N. Farmer, Barry M. Richman, and William G. Ryan, *Incidents in Applying Management Theory*, Wadsworth Publishing Company, Inc., Belmont, Calif., 1966.

SUGGESTED READINGS

Bar-Ilan, Avner: "Monitoring Workers as a Screening Device," *Canadian Journal of Economics*, May 1991.
Berry, Waldron: "The Human Side of Control," *Supervisory Management*, June 1985, pp. 34ff.
Johnson, Samuel E.: "Benchmarking Facility Management Practices," *Modern Office Technology*, June 1992.
Schmidt, Jeffrey: "Following the Leader: Competitive Benchmarking as a Tool for Survival," *Management Digest*, June 1, 1992.

GLOSSARY

acceptability standard   A yardstick by which a product is determined to be either acceptable or unacceptable.

benchmarking   A technique that allows companies to measure themselves against the top performers in their industry and then establish goals that exceed their competitors'.

budget   A statement that specifies anticipated revenues and expenses for a given period.

concurrent controls   The controls that are exercised during the manufacture of a product or when a service is provided.

control   The function of comparing actual performance with planned performance and taking corrective action when necessary.

critical path   The sequence of activities that requires the longest period of time to complete.

critical path method (CPM)   A time-scheduling technique for projects requiring a sequence of activities.

economic order quantity (EOQ)   A technique that ensures that materials are ordered in the least expensive quantity.

expense budget   A budget that specifies only the costs the supervisor expects to incur as the product or service is being produced.

feedback controls   Controls exercised after the product is manufactured or the service provided.

fixed budget   A budget that does not change with the number of units produced or the number of services rendered.

flexible budget   A budget that allows for fixed costs that remain constant as production or service levels change and for different levels of expenditures based on the level of production.

preliminary controls   Controls that are in place before the product is manufactured or the service is performed.

profit centers   Departments or units that bring revenue into the company.

program evaluation and review technique (PERT)   A time-scheduling technique for projects requiring a sequence of activities.

schedule   A plan that specifies time periods for completing specific activities.

standard   A stated level of acceptable performance.

variability standard   A sampling technique that allows some deviation from the standard.

zero-based budget   A type of budgeting process that starts from the beginning each year, requiring each program to be justified.

STUDYING THIS CHAPTER WILL ENABLE YOU TO:

1. Define total quality management.

2. Describe Philip Crosby's system for implementing a quality improvement program.

3. Provide an overview of the Deming Management Method.

4. Describe the deadly diseases that can hinder a quality management effort.

5. Explain the purposes of the Malcolm Baldrige National Quality Award.

6. Describe how statistical methods are used in total quality management.

7. Discuss the primary purposes and uses of control charts and run charts.

8. Explain the difference between special and common causes of variation in products and services.

9. Explain why it is necessary for supervisors to identify and eliminate special causes.

10. Describe the problems many supervisors face in terms of their role in total quality management.

CHAPTER OUTLINE

PROCESS FOR QUALITY IMPROVEMENT
Management Commitment
The Quality Improvement Team
Measurement
The Cost of Quality
Quality Awareness
Corrective Action
Zero Defects Planning
Employee Education
Zero Defects Day
Goal Setting
Error-Cause Removal
Recognition
Quality Councils
Do It All Over Again

THE DEMING MANAGEMENT METHOD
The Fourteen Points
The Seven Deadly Diseases
The Malcolm Baldrige National Quality Award

STATISTICAL METHODS FOR DETERMINING QUALITY
Run Charts
Control Charts

THE SUPERVISOR'S ROLE IN TOTAL QUALITY MANAGEMENT
Providing Quality Education
Implementing the Quality Improvement Culture
Empowering Employees
Providing Recognition

Competency Review
Applications
Cases
References
Suggested Readings
Glossary

C H A P

Implementing Total Quality Management

orporate America has begun an ambitious effort to improve the quality of goods and services offered by U.S. companies. These efforts seem destined to continue in the face of strong and continuing competition from foreign producers, most notably Japan. Quality is a universally acknowledged factor in successful business. Indeed, as Allen F. Jacobsen, chairman of the board and CEO of 3M Company, puts it, "I'm convinced that the winners of the 90s will be companies that make quality and customer service an obsession in every single market [in which] they operate."[1]

The list of companies that have implemented quality improvement programs in recent years is extensive. It includes organizations in virtually every type of industry from manufacturing to service to the public sector. Giants such as AT&T, BMW, NEC, H. J. Heinz, Canon, and Corning are on it, as well as small organizations such as Amarillo Hardware and Dana Corp.

**COMPETENCY
CHECK**
Can you define
total quality
management?

The notion that a company can manage quality is rooted in the experience, research, and writings of prominent individuals, especially Philip B. Crosby and the late W. Edwards Deming. In this chapter, we will present an overview of total quality management as a technique for improving organizational effectiveness. Simply defined, **total quality management** is a method of conducting business for producing a product or providing a service that gets it right for the customer the first time and every time. Quality has meaning only in terms of the customer; customers are all persons both inside and outside the organization who use (consume) the commodity or service an employee is producing.

Process for Quality Improvement

Quality improvement, according to Philip Crosby, requires that somebody actually does something. "Doing something" in this context requires that actions be taken to actually change the culture and the management style of the company.[2]

Clearly, this is easier said than done, and all too often corporate executives believe that the organization can be "vaccinated" against quality problems. However, there is, as Crosby points out, no such serum. Rather, the process of installing quality improvement is ongoing and never-ending. Changing a culture so that it never regresses is not something that is easily or quickly accomplished. To do this, Crosby recommends that organizations implement what he calls the fourteen steps for quality improvement.[3] These are actions that constitute an orderly system for modifying the culture and improving organizational effectiveness.

Management Commitment

Initially, says Crosby, senior management must be truly committed to systematic quality improvement. Obviously, some faith in management at lower levels is required, as well as actions that support that confidence. These actions include issuing a corporate policy on quality, making quality the first agenda item at meetings, and having the CEO (chief executive officer) and the COO (chief operating officer) compose quality speeches in their minds and, as they go around the company, deliver them to everyone they meet. Let's look at each of these actions in more detail.

Writing the policy is the first act; getting everyone to understand that top management is serious is the second. Crosby recommends that the policy say this: "We will deliver defect-free products and services to our clients on time." However, every company will have its own way of saying this, and, ultimately, the only rule is that the policy be so clear that it cannot be misunderstood. Figure 15.1 shows several examples.

After the policy has been made clear, a usable quality status report must be provided at important organizational meetings. Quality should be listed as a specific agenda item in order to reaffirm its seriousness.

Finally, as a way of continually reaffirming dedication to the process, the chief executive officer will have to get used to making a short speech regularly that tells everyone, in no uncertain terms, that the company intends to deliver defect-free products and services and that there will be no compromise when it comes to quality.

Figure 15.1
TYPICAL QUALITY IMPROVEMENT POLICIES

3M
Commercial Tape Division
3M Commercial Tape Division is committed to a policy of conformance to requirements for each function of the organization and for customer satisfaction, or we will change the requirements to what we and our customers really need.

Implementation of this policy makes it essential that each person be committed to performance exactly as required.

It is our basic operating philosophy to concentrate on prevention methods to make quality a way of life and perpetuate an attitude of "Do It Right the First Time."

IBM
Research Triangle Park, Raleigh
We will deliver defect-free competitive products and services on time to our customers.

Armco, Inc.
Midwestern Steel Division
The policy of the Midwestern Steel Division of Armco is to provide products that conform to our customers' requirements and deliver them on time and at a competitive price. Our name must represent quality to our vendors, ourselves, and our customers.

Burroughs
We shall strive for excellence in all endeavors.

We shall set our goals to achieve total customer satisfaction and to deliver error-free competitive products on time, with service second to none.

Bechtel
Ann Arbor Power Division
In order to improve quality we shall provide clearly stated requirements, expecting each person to do the job right the first time, in accordance with those requirements or cause the requirements to be officially changed.

Source: Philip B. Crosby, *Quality Without Tears*, Plume Books, New York, 1984, p. 102.

This message has to be clear from the top to the bottom of the organization. The first time the boss agrees to make an exception, everyone in the company will know about it. However, it works the other way as well. People will soon learn that any current urgency will not override the decision to do it right each and every time.

The Quality Improvement Team

Upper management should designate a quality improvement team to guide the process and help it along. The team is not to create red tape, to solve everyone's problems, or to absolve others of responsibility for their actions. It is there to coordinate and support the employees.

The quality improvement team should be made up of people who can clear roadblocks for those who want to improve. These individuals represent the company to the outside world and also represent all functions of the organization. Finally, the team needs to have authority to make commitments without concurrence from higher authority.

The chairperson of the team should be someone who has easy conversational access to upper levels of management. In addition, the overall process needs a full-time coordinator who is there to make certain that the chairperson and the team work together. Top management, the coordinator, and the team chairperson lay out the overall strategy, usually with the help of a consultant. This strategy is agreed upon with the team and varied as necessary to meet the practical needs of the team members.

Ultimately, the team has to understand that the goal is to change the attitudes and practices of supervisors, not those of workers. Employees must also become committed to quality, but that comes later.

Measurement

Many quality improvement teams and many companies are tentative when it comes to measurement. Unfortunately, they look upon it as the ultimate hassle, when, in fact, measurement is a normal part of doing business.

As Crosby sees it, measurement is just the habit of seeing how we are going along. He cites the case of one company that ran into problems with measurement from employees who maintained that there was no way to measure their jobs. In response the quality team issued each supervisor a measurement chart of standard size and color and asked each of them to think of one thing that could be measured. There was a long period of silence, but finally one supervisor wrote "getting to meetings on time." Soon another wrote "articles of mail left over at end of day" on his chart. Another supervisor put "times secretary needs me and cannot find me." Before long everybody had a measurable behavior.

The point here is that all work is a process; you can identify the inputs to work for a bank teller, a cement pourer, or a computer programmer. You receive inputs to your work from other people, other functions, other suppliers. Then you apply your process to it. Your job changes that input in some way, and that results in the output. So any job has input, process, and output, and each lends itself to measurement.

✗ The Cost of Quality

The cost of quality has been a subject of discussion for 25 or more years. However, it has mainly been used as a way of measuring defects in a manufacturing environment and has generally not been used as an across-the-board management tool. That, says Crosby, is because it hasn't been presented to management in an understandable way.

Basically, the cost of quality can be divided into two areas—the price of noncomformance (PONC) and the price of conformance (POC). The former includes all the expenses involved in doing things wrong. Examples of these expenses include efforts to correct a salesperson's orders when they come in, to fix the product as it goes along, to do work over again, to pay warranty claims, and so on. When all of these costs are added together, the total amount can often be rather significant, representing, says Crosby, 20 percent or more of sales in manufacturing firms and over 35 percent of operating costs in service organizations.

The price of conformance, on the other hand, is the cost of making things come out right the first time. This includes professional quality functions, all prevention efforts, and quality education activities. Again, according to Crosby's calculations, this frequently represents 3 to 4 percent of sales in a well-managed company.

Clearly, it makes sense to pay for conformance rather than nonconformance. If the company looks at quality improvement from this point of view, it will realize that dollars invested in making the product or service work, rather than fixing or replacing it later, are well worth it.

✗ Quality Awareness

Many companies use special publications and information systems to explain quality and make their workers aware of it. While these methods are useful, the more effective awareness systems use existing company media. For example, rather than having a separate quality bulletin, make quality awareness part of the regular company newsletter. The word *quality* needs to be widely used, and people need to be reminded regularly. The Milliken Company designs and produces floor mats that carry messages such as "Do It Right the First Time" and other quality slogans. These slogans are one of the most effective ways to remind people about quality.

In the final analysis, quality awareness must become part of the corporate culture. It has to fit in, and people need to know about management's commitment. When quality as conformance to specifications becomes part of the lexicon of the company, then—and only then—does it begin to take hold.

COMPETENCY CHECK

Can you describe the first five steps of quality improvement?

Corrective Action

Even though most companies believe they have a corrective action system, they still have an array of problems that don't seem to be resolved. The reason, according to Crosby, is that all too often corrective action systems are not established to improve quality but rather to return nonconforming items to conforming status. For example, erroneous computer runs are reprogrammed, credit card errors are corrected, or undersized holes are redrilled to proper size. All these are done with great intensity, but none contributes to the real goal of quality improvement.

The purpose of corrective action should be to identify and eliminate problems, not fix mistakes. Corrective action systems have to be based on data that show what the problems are and analyses that show the causes. Once the root cause has been clearly identified, it can be eliminated. That's what corrective action is truly all about.

Zero Defects Planning

Most companies start and operate with defined standards of acceptable quality. In other words, a certain number of errors are planned and accepted as inevitable. They then develop indices that tell everyone how many nonconforming items will be tolerated without penalty or how many field service people will be needed to respond to complaints.

This, unfortunately, may convince people that the determination to get things done right just isn't there, and as long as errors are part of the performance standard, this becomes a self-fulfilling policy. The concept of zero defects establishes a very different standard. It says that work must be done right the first time, no excuses accepted and no exceptions made. When ITT introduced this concept in 1965, it worked very well. As Crosby points out, people will perform to the standard they are given, provided they understand it. When the standard is unclear, like "excellence" or "pride," their work varies from day to day. When the standard is specific, like zero defects, defect free, or DIRFT (Do It Right the First Time), people will learn to pay attention to detail and thus prevent problems. Therefore, one of the basic absolutes of quality management is that the performance standard must be zero defects, not "close enough." This must be planned into the process.

COMPETENCY CHECK
Can you describe the concept of zero defects?

Employee Education

Once management really understands the process of quality improvement, it is time to educate all employees of the company. Traditionally, this is done with a program developed by training and development specialists, possibly working with outside consultants. This is not the recommended approach.

The education system developed by Crosby and his associates provides a standard message that can be taught by anyone trained to use it. The entire system requires 30 classroom hours plus on-the-job assignments. Each session consists of a video, a workshop to bring the subject home to the participants, and then a discussion to personalize the subject to that company. In addition, there are reading assignments. An organized educational program shows everyone that quality is the concern of each and every employee, not just another program mandated by upper-level management.

Zero Defects Day

There are still those in the field of quality who think the purpose of Zero Defects Day is to get all the employees together so that they can sign off on a commitment to improve. This does happen, but it is not what the day is all about. **Zero Defects**

Day is a formal occasion designed to allow management to make its commitment to quality a matter of public record. It is a formal program to show all employees that management is serious. An annual Zero Defects Day should be held to reinforce the importance of quality for all employees.

Goal Setting

Even though zero defects is the ultimate goal, other more intermediate goals need to be established as the program moves forward. It is unrealistic to think that any supervisor can expect to go from the current situation, in which a certain number of mistakes are believed to be inevitable, to a state of few if any defects. Anyone with a basic knowledge of goal setting would know that this expectation will likely lead to frustration and conflict. Still, supervisors need to make it clear that constant improvement is the only thing that will be rewarded.

The goals should be chosen by the employees themselves, not imposed on them by the quality improvement team. Charts and graphs displayed around the work area will keep people aware of their progress.

COMPETENCY CHECK
Can you describe the next five steps of quality improvement?

Error-Cause Removal

Error-cause removal is a process that allows employees to state the problems they have in their work areas so that something can be done about them. It is not a suggestion system in which people have to come up with answers. However, most problem statements contain suggestions that in turn help resolve the issues.

Quality improvement teams are responsible for evaluating the error causes submitted by employees. They must determine what procedure will be followed, how they are going to tell the employee that his/her information has been received, how the problem will be analyzed and acted upon, and how employees will know when a solution has been implemented.

Recognition

A basic principle of behavior is that nobody does something for nothing, or as B. F. Skinner put it many years ago, "behavior is a function of its consequences." If you expect employees to work hard to achieve goals such as zero defects, they must be rewarded and their efforts recognized. Never assume that people know that you appreciate their efforts.

Rewards can take various forms, including cash bonuses, merchandise, plaques, employee-of-the-month notices, systematic praise by supervisors, and so on. The point, however, is that efforts need to be explicitly recognized.

Quality Councils

The idea of quality councils is to bring together managers and supervisors from across the organization and let them learn from one another. They can also support the quality improvement process. Crosby's experience is that there seems to be a very clear demarcation in companies when it comes to the way quality councils operate. They either become actively involved in helping to eliminate hassles and believe that zero defects is achievable or they are skeptical and never become committed to the concept of quality improvement. However, the quality councils can be an effort to involve the skeptics in the process and let them see for themselves that the proposals to improve quality really do make sense.

Do It All Over Again

Quality improvement is not a "program" used by a company to eliminate certain problems. If it is to be truly effective, it must become a way of life, and, as was noted earlier, the basic culture of the organization has to change. This last step, in Crosby's view, means that as quality improvement becomes more and more an enduring way of life and as it becomes the culture of the company, the process gains speed and permanence. Consequently, supervisors have to tell employees continually what is expected in terms of performance. Education has to be a vital part of the relationship.

In order to have meaningful education, it is necessary to have clear, worthwhile goals. They have to be specific, measurable, attainable, relevant, time-framed, and challenging. Employees need to know how to improve performance on their jobs now and also have a sense of how this fits into a bigger picture in terms of broader corporate objectives.

COMPETENCY CHECK

Can you describe the last four steps of quality improvement?

WHAT CAN THE SUPERVISOR DO?

To become more directly involved in the total quality management effort, a supervisor should:

❑ Put aside personal biases and fears of being displaced.
❑ Realize that efforts to improve quality are in everybody's best interest and learn as much as possible about total quality management approaches.
❑ Adopt a goal of zero defects even though some error is inevitable.
❑ Shift the focus from catching errors after production to improving processes in order to avoid mistakes in the first place.
❑ Learn to rely more heavily on the people (both line and staff) who actually perform the hands-on work of the company to identify procedural defects and suggest systematic improvements.
❑ Embrace the concept of total quality management and invite as much participation from employees as possible.

✶ The Deming Management Method

The work of the late W. Edwards Deming has been revered in Japan since the late 1940s, yet until recently he was relatively unknown in this country. Deming first brought his statistical quality control techniques and management philosophy to Japan in 1947. He found the Japanese eager students. By 1951, the Deming Prize, which recognized superlative achievement in quality, was established in Japan. In 1960, Deming became the first American to receive Japan's Second Order of the Sacred Treasure Award because of his effect on Japanese industry. One television show changed Deming's status in the United States. On June 24, 1980, NBC broadcast "If Japan Can . . . Why Can't We?" The final quarter hour of the show focused on Deming's contributions to Japan as well as on business improvements at Nashua Corporation, a U.S. company following the Deming quality philosophy.[4]

✗ The Fourteen Points

Deming claimed that many firms cannot perform well from a long-term perspective because their managers and supervisors do not know what to do. During his seminars he was fond of repeating, "There is no substitute for knowledge!" vigorously and frequently.

American managers, he said, cannot provide answers to their problems because they don't know what questions to ask. Asking the right questions is a skill Deming's method attempts to teach. He believed that effective management hinges on the application of an awareness process that he labeled "profound knowledge." Essentially, this means that managers and supervisors must (1) become more aware of the organization as a system; (2) have some understanding of statistical theory as it applies to product or service variation; (3) be willing to test and validate ideas in order to understand cause-and-effect relationships; and (4) understand that every person is unique and try to optimize and enhance each one's individual abilities. Deming's famous Fourteen Points provide a method for developing profound knowledge in the workplace as well as a way to guide long-term plans and goals.[5]

 Point 1: Create constancy of purpose for improvement of product and service. The continuation of a business requires that it have a clear mission and statement of purpose that is stable over time. In Deming's view, organizations should define their purpose as service to customers and employees. This would require top managers to adopt a long-term view and invest in innovation and employee training, plus research and development activities.

 Point 2: Adopt the new philosophy. The new corporate philosophy advocated by Deming seeks to maximize organizational effectiveness by creating an atmosphere of true cooperation among employees and managers at all levels. It rejects traditional management practices, which often cause supervisors and employees to view themselves as adversaries.

 Point 3: Cease dependence on mass inspection. The problem with inspection to improve quality, said Deming, is that while it may uncover defects, it does not guar-

COMPETENCY CHECK
Can you describe why adopting a new philosophy is critical to the Deming management method?

antee quality. In fact, it can encourage defects because workers feel that "someone else" will catch and fix the problems. Deming maintained that true quality is a function of employees' taking responsibility for their own work and improvements in the way things are done. Inspections can be a useful tool for gathering information about products and services, but by themselves they do not ensure quality.

Point 4: End the practice of awarding business on the basis of price tag alone. Purchasing decisions traditionally have been driven by cost through competitive bidding, not by considerations of quality. Unfortunately, reliance on price alone can lead to inferior materials and products, and this, according to Deming, is counterproductive. Instead he urged that companies establish long-term relationships with a few suppliers. This should decrease variation and allow purchasers and suppliers to become more cooperative and stop dealing with one another as adversaries.

Point 5: Improve constantly and forever the system of production and service. The Japanese describe total quality management with one word, *kaizen*, and for them it means continuous improvement involving everyone. U.S. companies need to adopt this perspective and seek continuous, small incremental improvements in design and production. Statistical tools and operational definitions (definitions determined by use in practice) can be extremely useful in implementing this point. They can provide the means with which to measure improvement.

Point 6: Institute training. Employees need the proper knowledge to do the job right, and training provides this. Under the Deming method, however, training is more than just providing basic job knowledge. It is literally a springboard from which workers can develop pride of workmanship. Training should provide supervisors and workers with the tools they will need to evaluate processes and improve organizations. Deming believed that all employees should receive some training in statistical thinking so that they can understand and appreciate product and service variation.

Point 7: Adopt and institute leadership. Supervisors should be coaches, not police, and supervision should provide a link between management and the workforce. True leadership empowers employees and allows them to inform upper-level management about conditions that need correction. Upper-level management must then act on this information. According to Deming, leadership is the engine that drives organizations toward optimal performance.

Point 8: Drive out fear. Deming often claimed that "no one can put in his best performance unless he feels secure."[6] Fear of reprisal or failure leads to short-term thinking, misinformation, hidden agendas, and padded numbers. It may induce workers to satisfy a rule or a quota at the expense of the company's best long-term interests.

Point 9: Break down barriers between individuals and departments. Barriers between individuals and departments lead to poor quality because "customers" (both inside and outside the organization) do not get what they need from "suppliers." As a result, real quality improvement is difficult if not impossible because people are working at cross-purposes. Organizations should do everything possible to eliminate these barriers through teamwork. This will allow everyone to focus on the needs of customers as the ultimate goal.

X   *Point 10: Eliminate slogans, exhortations, and targets for the workforce.* Unlike Crosby, Deming believed that posters and slogans will not motivate employees. These devices, he said, operate under the erroneous assumption that workers could, if they simply worked harder, accomplish the goals set by management. Instead, managers and supervisors must learn that the responsibility for improving the organization is theirs, not the workers'. In fact, if posters and slogans ask people to do things that are not allowed or rewarded by the organization in which they work, the only results will be disillusionment, frustration, and performance that is further diminished.

X   *Point 11: Eliminate work standards that prescribe numerical quotas.* Deming viewed a quota as "a fortress against improvement of quality and productivity." As he put it, "I have yet to see a quota that includes any trace of a system by which to help anyone do a better job."[7] Quotas do not consider quality. They cannot provide data that are valuable in improving the organization; they destroy pride in workmanship.

Numerical goals and quotas reflect short-term perspectives and do not encourage long-term improvements. In fact, employees may shortcut quality to reach the goal, and once the quota is met there is no incentive to go further. A better approach is for management to understand that every organization has cycles of good and bad times and always to do what will improve the company in the long run.

X   *Point 12: Remove barriers that rob people of pride of workmanship.* This point recommends that all workers be given greater control of their jobs so that they can take real pride in what they do. In other words, supervisors should empower employees by listening to and implementing their suggestions and ideas for quality improvement. This listening and follow-up action, said Deming, needs to be reinforced by upper-level management through specific feedback and rewards. Unfortunately, too many organizations seem more interested in bureaucratic procedures than in improving the quality of their products and services, and as a result, employees have little interest in doing the job right.

X   *Point 13: Encourage education and self-improvement for everyone.* Organizations improve when the employees believe in self-development. As Deming put it, "In respect to self-improvement, it is wise for anyone to bear in mind that there is no shortage of good people. Shortage exists at the high levels of knowledge; this is true in every field."[8] Deming recommended investing in people through lifelong learning, whether in formal or informal settings. Committed, knowledgeable people have the best chance of making the organization in which they work as effective as it can possibly be.

X   *Point 14: Take action to accomplish the transformation.* If total quality management is to become a reality, everyone must be involved. For many organizations, this requires a major cultural change, and Deming, like Crosby, recognized that this can be difficult. Still, managers have to lead the way and show others that they are serious about adopting the new approach. They must demonstrate their concern for worker interests, provide adequate training, and recognize efforts to improve the organization.

As you can see, the Fourteen Points are not a list of action items. They are a code of conduct or a value system that provides a new frame of reference with which to

COMPETENCY CHECK

Can you explain the Fourteen Points?

view the world. In a sense, they are similar to the Ten Commandments—statements of principles that are considerably easier to list than to implement.

Deming offered managers a philosophy of organizational life that is much like that of major religions: continuous, lifelong improvement from conversion to new core beliefs. The Deming philosophy does require a transformation in thinking. In effect, the organization is being asked to adopt a whole new approach to business and employee relations that takes time and perseverance. There is no quick fix, no instant pudding.[9]

The Seven Deadly Diseases

Dr. Deming once told the U.S. Agency for International Development to "export anything to a friendly country except American management." Management in the United States is, he believed, suffering from several deeply entrenched diseases that are potentially fatal. Overcoming these problems will, said Deming, require no less than "a complete shakeup of Western style management."[10]

Lack of Consistency of Purpose. A company without consistency of purpose is unlikely to think beyond the next quarterly dividend and probably has no long-range plan for staying in operation. Obviously, this is a major problem in terms of implementing total quality management.

Unfortunately, employees in many companies have been exposed to a succession of improvement plans. They have seen these programs come and go, often coinciding with the term of the CEO. Disenchanted, they require proof that the company is serious this time, and, certainly, concrete activities such as investing in training and equipment can help convince employees. Still, there is no secret formula, and management must take the time to explain the Deming method in full.

Emphasis on Short-Term Profits. As we have noted above, too many organizations emphasize short-term profits, as demonstrated by the focus on quarterly dividends and the effect they will have on the financial status of the corporation. The problem, according to Deming, is that this short-range mentality can easily promote inconsistency of purpose and cause managers to make decisions that are more likely to reduce quality than to improve it. As the quarter ends, everything on hand is shipped regardless of quality, orders for materials and equipment are deferred, and the company cuts back on research, education, and training.

Evaluation of Performance, Merit Rating, and Annual Review. Many, if not most, companies have systems by which all employees receive an annual rating and then a merit pay raise. The problem here, said Deming, is that the performance appraisal or merit rating typically focuses on individual achievement, and as a result it induces people to engage in behaviors that promote their own short-term interests rather than the long-run goals of the organization. Appraisals and merit ratings discourage risk taking, build fear, undermine teamwork, and pit people against one another as they compete for the same rewards.

In addition, appraisals and merit systems tend to increase management's reliance on numbers. There is a tendency to consider only evidence that can be counted, for example, the number of designs an engineer turns out with no consideration as to their quality.

4   ***Mobility of Management.***   Business seems dedicated to the idea that you can train a good manager in universally applicable techniques. But how can a manager be expected to accomplish anything or engage in long-term programs when he/she is there for only a few years before moving on? Mobility, said Deming, leads to résumé building and implementation of programs that lead to quick results but have very little positive effect over time.

5   ***Running a Company on Visible Figures Alone.***   Visible figures are important, but a company cannot measure its success by them alone. Sure, there is a payroll to meet, vendors to pay, taxes, pension funds, and so on. But, said Deming, the figures that are unknown or unknowable are even more important.

It is, for example, impossible to measure the effect on sales of a satisfied customer or the boost in quality and productivity all along the line that comes from success in improving quality at any workstation. Only in time do these results become apparent.

6   ***Expensive Medical Costs.***   For many U.S. organizations today, premiums for employee health insurance are their single largest expenditure. With the average annual cost of health insurance now averaging about $3500 per employee (and rising), it is not hard to see that large amounts of money that could be used for other purposes will no longer be available.

7   ***Excessive Costs of Warranties, Fueled by Lawyers Who Work on Contingency Fees.***   The United States is the most litigious country in the world. The fact that people are so likely to sue when a product fails causes firms to tie up large sums of money for warranty service, and it leads to a great deal of defensive behavior. Again, this reduces risk taking, leads to short-term thinking, and often disrupts constancy of purpose.

Suppose an organization accepts the Deming method and wants to implement the concepts. Where does it start? The answer, said Deming, is to follow the Shewhart cycle (see Figure 15.2). This involves a step-by-step process that leads to continuous improvement of methods and procedures.[11] It was originally developed in the 1930s by Walter Shewhart, a Bell Laboratory physicist who wanted to develop a zero defects mass-production process for complex telephone exchanges and telephone sets.[12]

The first step in the cycle is for managers to study a process in order to decide what change might improve it. Do not proceed without a plan for action. Step 2 is to carry out the change on a small scale. The company then observes the effects and determines what was learned (step 3), repeats the test if necessary, and looks for side effects (step 4).

COMPETENCY CHECK
Can you describe the seven deadly diseases that may prevent implementation of total quality management?

Figure 15.2
THE SHEWHART
CYCLE

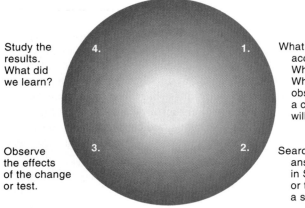

Study the
results.
What did
we learn?

4.

1.

What could be the most important
accomplishment of this team?
What changes might be desirable?
What data are available? Are new
observations needed? If yes, plan
a change or test. Decide how you
will use the observations.

3.

2.

Observe
the effects
of the change
or test.

Search for data on hand that could
answer the question propounded
in Step 1. Or, carry out the change
or test decided upon, preferably on
a small scale.

Step 5. Repeat Step 1, with knowledge accumulated.
Step 6. Repeat Step 2, and onward.

Source: Reprinted from *Out of the Crisis* by W. Edwards Deming by permission of MIT and W. Edwards
Deming. Published by MIT, Center for Advanced Engineering Study, Cambridge, MA 02139. Copyright
1986 by W. Edwards Deming, p. 88.

In addition to the use of the Shewhart cycle, accomplishing the necessary transformation also requires that everyone becomes mainly and primarily concerned
with customer satisfaction. Ask yourself: Who is the person who receives your
work? Whom must you satisfy? These questions will make you be more quality conscious because you are more concerned about how your actions now will affect others later.

The Malcolm Baldrige National Quality Award

Recognizing that American productivity was declining, President Ronald Reagan
signed legislation in October 1982 mandating a national study/conference on productivity. The final report on these conferences recommended that "a National
Quality Award similar to the Deming Prize in Japan [should] be awarded annually
to those firms that successfully challenge and meet the award requirements."

The Baldrige Award, named after the U.S. Secretary of Labor, was signed into law
in August 1987. Its purposes are to:[13]

- ❏ help stimulate American companies to improve quality and productivity for
  the pride of recognition while obtaining a competitive edge through increased
  profits.
- ❏ formally recognize those companies that improve the quality of their goods and
  services.

❑ establish guidelines that can be used by organizations in evaluating their own quality improvement efforts.

❑ provide specific guidance for other American companies that want to improve quality by giving them detailed information on how award-winning companies were able to change their cultures and achieve eminence.

A number of Baldrige Award winners have been quite successful in reducing customer service response time, reducing defects and costs while improving overall output. The list here is quite extensive and includes large manufacturing companies such as Motorola, Xerox, Milliken Co., and Selectron Corp., service organizations including Federal Express and the Ritz-Carlton Hotel Co., and several small businesses including Globe Metallurgical, Marlow Industries, and Granite Rock Co.

However, receiving the Baldrige Award does not guarantee success, as the Wallace Company found out.[14] This company achieved the award in 1990 in the "small business" category. "It was like winning the Super Bowl," said Judith Sanders, a quality consultant and an architect of Wallace's program. Within a year, however,

WHAT CAN THE SUPERVISOR DO?

In terms of implementing the Deming management method, a supervisor should:

1. Be open to the new philosophy and not view it as a personal threat. Empower employees to control quality.
2. Recognize that quality techniques have to become enmeshed in every operation of the organization. Quality becomes a part of business activities, not something apart from business activities.
3. Learn that continuous improvement is a never-ending journey that requires time, effort, and perseverance.
4. Understand that groups not truly converted to Deming's value system may well abandon the Fourteen Points when initial enthusiasm wanes.
5. Work to break down barriers between units and educate employees. See that all are well trained.
6. Forgo the emphasis on short-term profits and look for long-range effects. Think in terms of years, not months.
7. Reward employees for team accomplishments and shift the focus of annual performance review systems.
8. Understand and communicate to employees that total quality management is not a panacea. It will not solve every problem, but it is an effective method if properly implemented.

the company was drowning in a sea of red ink, and ultimately it filed for Chapter 11 bankruptcy protection. The problem was that even though service was improved following implementation of a total quality management program, the costs associated with the changes caused overhead to go up by $2 million a year and customers balked at the price hikes that were necessary to offset the costs. Many of them cut back orders as a result.

The thing to remember here is that total quality management is not a panacea. Companies like Xerox, Motorola, Federal Express, and Harley-Davidson have been successful because they have had patience and a long-term commitment.[15]

Statistical Methods for Determining Quality

"In God we trust. All others must use data." If there is a credo for supervisors, it is that all total quality management programs must be data based.[16] Critical to the Deming method or, for that matter, that of Crosby or any of the quality experts, is the need to make decisions by using accurate, timely data rather than wishes, hunches, or "experience." A training manual for Komatren Ltd., a Japanese competitor of Caterpillar Tractor Company, puts it this way:[17]

> The first step in quality control is to judge and act on the basis of facts. Facts are data such as length, time, fraction defective, and sales amount. . . . Views not backed by data are more likely to include personal opinions, exaggeration, and mistaken impressions. . . . (Data have nothing to do with the accuracy of judgement.) Data without context or incorrect data are not only invalid but sometimes harmful as well. It is necessary to know the nature of that data and that proper data be picked as well.

COMPETENCY CHECK

Can you explain why statistical methods are critical to total quality management?

Statistical methods are a tool companies can use to better understand and control variation in their products and services. Essentially, this means that not all of the finished products and services are meeting established quality control parameters. Too many such deviations will clearly lead to costly problems.

Variations can result from both special (random) and common (controllable) causes. **Special causes** arise from external sources that are not inherent in the process, while **common causes** come from factors that are present as a natural part of the process. A bad batch of material purchased from a supplier, excessive tool wear, and miscalibration of instruments are examples of special causes. A systematic deficiency in lighting could be a common cause. Generally, about 80 to 90 percent of the observed variation in a production process can be traced to common causes. The remaining 10 to 20 percent result from special causes.[18]

If the special causes of variation can be identified and eliminated, the company can concentrate on managing the common causes. Statistical methods of quality control allow an organization to identify and isolate the special causes, thus reducing the random variation in the company's product or service.[19]

Consider, for example, the excess (waste) plastic, called *flash*, that must be trimmed off plastic parts coming out of injection-molding machines.[20] Suppose you were to collect and weigh the flash for every piece. If the weight is tending up or down or there are occasional pieces with a great amount of flash or none, there is no consistency, variation is occurring randomly, and the process is out of control.

Bringing it under control means searching for the special cause(s) of the variation. Perhaps the machine is experiencing a heat buildup, which might explain the problem. Maybe the hopper gets low on raw material now and then, which might explain the variability. Or possibly, the person running the machine has a bad habit, like adjusting the timer now and then instead of leaving it alone. Whatever the special cause, it must be identified and eliminated. But even when greater consistency has been attained, there will still be some variability in the weight of flash from piece to piece. However, this variability will be resulting from common causes instead of special causes.

Once special causes have been eliminated and the process is more in control, management should give thought to improving the process. Note that control is a measure of consistency, not quality. Improving quality requires an affirmative decision by the organization. In the case of the plastic parts, the mold might be improved, a more precise way of feeding raw material could be developed, or the quality of the plastic pellets could be upgraded. In addition, if the operator is consistent but not an especially good machine operator, training may be the answer. On the other hand, if the problems persist after training, a new person should be assigned to the job.[21]

The problem with this example is that even though the injection molding process may be improved, overall product quality has not been mentioned. Rather than being on the plastic parts, the company's emphasis has been on the flash (or waste). While this is not insignificant and reducing waste will definitely reduce product cost for the producer, it does not ensure that a better part is being produced or that the injection-molded parts are conforming to specifications. Doing this requires more analysis, using run charts and/or statistical process control charts.

COMPETENCY CHECK
Can you describe the difference between special and common causes of variation from standards?

Run Charts

A **run chart** is a statistical tool used for tracking data over a period of time in order to look for trends. Sales per month over a period of a year is a typical use of a run chart.[22]

Suppose, for example, that you want to track employee attendance and promptness in arriving at work.[23] A simple run chart such as that shown in Figure 15.3 would allow you to do this for each employee. In this case you find that employee X is more likely to be late for work on Monday than any other day. You could then speak with the person to identify causes and seek appropriate solutions.

If we return to the example of the injection molded plastic parts, we can see how a run chart could be quite useful. Assume that the specifications for the part call for an outer diameter of 5.0 cm, plus or minus .05 cm. In other words, 4.95 to 5.05 cm is the acceptable tolerance. As Figure 15.4 shows, a running plot of measurements, piece by piece, as the process continues allows management to determine how many pieces are exceeding the tolerance and take action as necessary.

COMPETENCY CHECK
Can you describe how a simple run chart is used?

**Figure 15.3
RUN CHART:
"GETTING TO
WORK ON TIME"**

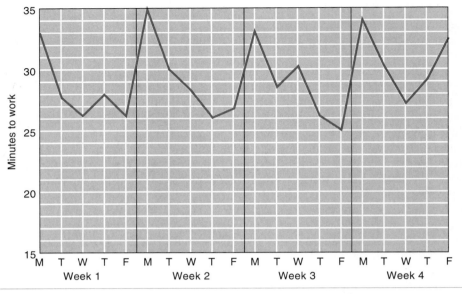

Source: Mary Walton, *The Deming Management Method,* New York: Perigee Books, 1986, p. 108.

**Figure 15.4
RUN CHART:
OUTER
DIAMETERS OF
30 PIECES**

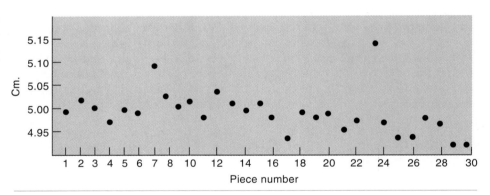

Source: Richard Schonberger and Edward Knod, Jr., *Operations Management,* Business Publications, Inc., Homewood, Ill., 1988, p. 579.

Control Charts

The use of control charts generally goes by the name of Statistical Quality Control (SQC) or Statistical Process Control (SPC). Entire books have been devoted to the different kinds of control charts, but our purpose here is to give you a brief overview.

In essence, a **control chart** is a run chart with statistically determined upper and lower limits (standard deviations) drawn on either side of the process average.[24]

Figure 15.5
CONTROL CHART
SCHEMATIC

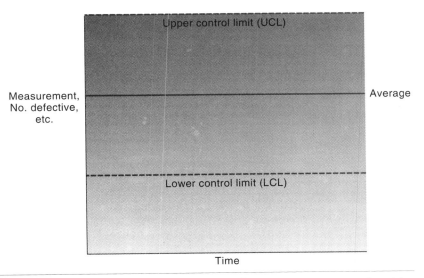

Upper control limit (UCL)

Measurement,
No. defective,
etc.

Average

Lower control limit (LCL)

Time

Source: Mary Walton, The Memory Jogger: A Pocket Guide of Tools for Continuous Improvement. Copyright
© GOAL/QPC 1988, p. 51. Used with permission from GOAL/QPC, 13 Branch Street, Methuen, Mass.
01844–1953. Tel.: 508–685–3900.

Figure 15.5 is a typical example. In SPC, the control limits are generally—but not always—set at three standard errors above and below the center line. These limits have nothing to do with specification tolerance limits. Rather, they tell a supervisor whether or not the process is in control. If it is not, supervisors should look for common and special causes that are resulting in unacceptable variations. These charts come in two broad varieties to be used depending on the nature of the data. One is

COMPETENCY CHECK
Can you list the functions of a control chart?

WHAT CAN THE SUPERVISOR DO?

The use of statistical methods requires a supervisor to:

❏ Become more conversant with simple statistical concepts.
❏ Learn how to identify special versus common causes of variation.
❏ Be constantly vigilant for special causes of variation and control them when they are identified.
❏ Learn how to interpret run charts, control charts, and other statistical process control mechanisms.
❏ Recognize that quality improvement is not a method to be imposed on employees. Statistics are useful tools, but quality improvement must be done through employees.

for the data that can be measured: lengths, temperatures, volume, pressure, and voltage. The other is for data that can be counted: defective components, typographical errors, mislabeled items.[25]

The Supervisor's Role in Total Quality Management

Clearly, total quality management requires a systemwide effort involving all employees from top management down. Upper-level management is responsible for creating a corporate culture consistent with the principles and practices of total quality management. It is at this level that the decision to institute Deming's Fourteen Points or Crosby's process will be made and where systems designed to eliminate the deadly diseases and obstacles must be developed. Middle-level managers must adopt the new philosophy, understand the systems for which they are responsible, implement the quality improvement process or Fourteen Points, and target for attention significant roadblocks to performance. First-line supervisors also have important roles to play. These include providing necessary quality education, implementing (together with middle managers) specific quality improvement programs, empowering employees to control quality, and providing appropriate recognition.

Providing Quality Education

Supervisors must be instructed in the new philosophy and receive training on how to measure system performance and recognize special causes of variation. This has to be translated into day-to-day practice, and all employees have to become involved. A supervisor has a significant role to play in instructing employees and becoming an agent for change within the organization.

Implementing the Quality Improvement Culture

Many business leaders have been frustrated by their inability to follow through on their public commitment to service or product quality. The problem here is often resistance on the part of employees to the new culture. If, for example, zero defects is the goal, everyone in the organization needs to "buy into" this concept. Supervisors are an important part of this process. They are, after all, the ones who will ultimately be responsible for overseeing the program and who, by example, can affect its success or failure.

Too often supervisors have trouble with the major cultural changes that total quality management programs require. They like the idea, but when they realize the magnitude of the change, they back off. Many supervisors have been trained to be somewhat autocratic in dealing with employees, and they don't know how to be more participative. In addition, U.S. managers and supervisors have grown up in organizations that accept defects as inevitable. They don't know how to work any other way. These are problems that must be overcome if total quality management is going to succeed.

Empowering Employees

Critics of participatory management claim that many supervisors and managers adopt only those aspects of employee empowerment that suit their personality and basic management style. As a result, these leaders project inconsistency, and employees conclude that they aren't serious about change. To truly empower employees, supervisors must carefully analyze how they interact with employees and then modify their behavior accordingly. They have to delegate power and decision making to lower levels and use concepts like shared visions of the future to engage all employees so that employees develop a sense of pride, self-respect, and responsibility.

Employee involvement and empowerment attempt to move the organization from the traditional "I just work here, I don't make the rules" type of culture to one of shared vision and goals. The idea is to have the individual's purpose and vision congruent with those of the organization.

Experts agree that first-line supervisors have the toughest time of all with employee involvement programs. That's because generally they are required to give away a lot of power, and, unlike managers further up the ladder, they rarely get any back. Unfortunately, if supervisors don't buy in, the entire process can be subverted.[26]

Providing Recognition

Behavior is a function of its consequences, or, as stated in the parlance of Kenneth Blanchard's *One Minute Manager,* what gets rewarded gets done. People need to see tangible outcomes. As Crosby points out, if a supervisor expects employees to commit to quality, then he/she must recognize their efforts—not only their accomplishments—with timely and specific rewards.

Recognition is an important activity for supervisors. Because you are the person who sees day-to-day activity, you are in a perfect position to provide timely and specific feedback and tell employees how they are doing.

COMPETENCY CHECK

Can you explain why supervisors often resist total quality management and describe what can be done to create more involvement?

COMPETENCY REVIEW

1. Define *total quality management.*
2. Describe Philip Crosby's system for implementing a quality improvement program.
3. Provide an overview of the Deming management method.
4. Describe the deadly diseases that can hinder a quality management effort.
5. Explain the purposes of the Malcolm Baldrige National Quality Award.
6. Describe how statistical methods are used in total quality management.
7. Discuss the primary purposes and uses of control charts and run charts.
8. Explain the difference between special and common causes of variation in products and services.

9. Explain why it is necessary for supervisors to identify and eliminate special causes.
10. Describe the problems many supervisors face in terms of their role in total quality management.

APPLICATIONS

1. Refer to the syllabus handed out at the beginning of the course and respond briefly to each of the following questions.
   a. What do the basic course objectives mean to you? How do you feel about them?
   b. What specifically have you done or can you do to become more directly involved in learning about supervision?
   c. How do you feel about the grading system? Does it promote autonomy or passive dependence?
   d. In your own words, briefly summarize the instructor's grading philosophy. Do you agree that it is appropriate in terms of this course?
   e. In your own words, briefly describe what you perceive to be your rights and responsibilities in this class.
   f. What elements of the syllabus do you most like (dislike)?
   How are these questions related to total quality management?
2. One of the keys to total quality management is employee empowerment. Unfortunately, this concept is a lot like love. We know it when we find it, but we don't ask for a precise definition. In fact, empowerment has been discussed in so many contexts that one of the biggest barriers supervisors face is getting rid of the misconceptions that impede the introduction of an organizational climate conducive to total quality management. Consider each of the following statements. How do these "myths" hinder the implementation of empowerment?
   a. Empowerment means no status differences among people.
   b. Empowerment means no rules, regulations, or sanctions.
   c. Empowerment guarantees operational effectiveness and error-free performance.
   d. Empowerment comes from the top down.
   e. Empowerment means that people are free to pursue their own personal ideas/agendas.
   f. Empowerment means laissez-faire leadership.
   g. Empowerment is desired and will automatically be accepted by all employees.
   h. Empowerment is fully achieved or completed at some time.

Case 1

WINDSOR EXPORT SUPPLY

Windsor Export Supply is a division of Ford Motor Company, employing 250 people who primarily take orders for parts from Ford's foreign manufacturing plants, most of which are located in South America. Once an order is placed with Windsor, it purchases parts from Ford's North American plants, arranges shipment, and collects payment. In the early 1980s, orders began diminishing as Ford's overseas manufacturing capacity grew and demand for North American parts declined. Although Windsor was still profitable, Ford executives sought advice from W. Edwards Deming on improving Windsor's performance.

Windsor was the first service group at Ford to receive training in the Deming philosophy. The initial efforts with Deming focused on the factory floor. There were many barriers to pride of workmanship at Windsor. Managers were surprised to learn that white-collar service employees felt the same kind of frustrations in their jobs as blue-collar factory workers. Harry Artinian of the Ford statistical methods office noted, "If you took the white shirts and ties off those people and put them in overalls, you'd hear the same words."

Deciding where to intervene at Windsor was a complicated procedure. In manufacturing, the accounting system highlights scrap, rework, and excess inventory. But in service functions such figures do not exist. The process of targeting significant inhibitors to performance at Windsor depended upon the knowledge and experience of the company's managers. The management team responsible for instituting the Deming method began with training and flow diagrams, hoping to get one good project as a consequence. Worker response was encouraging, and six projects were initiated.

One unsuccessful project involved freight auditing. Windsor would receive invoices from freight carriers through a contracted auditor, who completed the company paperwork and issued instructions for payment to the Ford accounts payable office in Oakville, Ontario. The contracted auditor was chosen to take advantage of state-of-the-art methods, but late payments and missing information were routine occurrences. Past-due bills mounted, occasionally for months. Almost everyone involved in the system was frustrated.

The freight auditing quality improvement team measured elapsed time between the date Windsor received an invoice and the date Oakville issued a check. Using control charts, they found that the system was stable with an average response time of 14 days, but as many as 35 days might pass between invoice receipt and issuance of a check. The team used cause-and-effect diagrams to identify the reasons for delay. They found keypunch errors, misfiling, missing codes, and misplaced bills. Attempts to resolve those problems with the contracted auditor proved unsuccessful, so Windsor took over the auditing function, making a number of changes to correct problem areas. The result of these efforts was a drop in average response time to 6 days and a reduction in the proportion of rejected bills at Oakville from 34 percent to less than 1 percent.

1. How does this case illustrate the broad applicability of total quality management concepts?
2. How has this organization specifically implemented the ideas of Crosby and Deming?

Source: Adapted from Thomas F. Rienzo, "Planning Deming Management for Service Organizations," *Business Horizons,* May–June 1993, pp. 23–24.

PARKVIEW EPISCOPAL MEDICAL CENTER

Parkview Episcopal Medical Center is one of two hospitals serving Pueblo, Colorado. In 1988, Hospital Corporation of America, which manages the facility, designated it as a "role model" hospital for quality improvement. The basic problem facing the hospital was a strict limitation in revenue in that 95 percent of its patient base was made up of Medicare and Medicaid beneficiaries, HMO members, and the medically indigent. As CEO Michael Pugh put it, "With that amount of fixed payment, it's clear that we have to do something different to survive."

Pugh was introduced to total quality management for the first time in the spring of 1988. By autumn, many Parkview senior managers had received quality training. Pugh established a Quality Improvement Council of senior managers to help guide the implementation of the "new philosophy." Quality improvement teams were formed to address hospital problems under the direction of a group of managers trained specifically to lead them. Almost all department managers attended a week-long course on statistics taught by a consultant. All hospital employees were scheduled to attend a quality awareness course.

Pugh estimates that it should take several years to integrate total quality management methods into the organizational culture, and he has advised managers to expect problems. Still, as Parkview has moved further into its new philosophy, there have been definite improvements in employee morale. In addition, the turnover rate was less than 12 percent in 1990, compared with rates of 15 to 18 percent in previous years. Finally, even though cost savings are more difficult to quantify, quality improvement teams in operating room (OR) scheduling and food service delivery provided the hospital with more than $10,000 in annual savings in each department during 1990.

Parkview's approach to surgery scheduling provides an excellent example of the quality process in action. This hospital had historically not met early-morning surgery schedules; 48 percent of morning surgical procedures began late, affecting operating times for the remainder of the day. In order to address this problem, an OR quality improvement team composed of physicians, nurses, and technicians was formed. The group tracked actual causes for delays, finding two common causes: either the surgeon was late, or the OR was not ready. The team tried to encourage surgeons to arrive on time by (1) reminding physicians that they were expected to be on time for surgeries; (2) not permitting any surgeon who was late to surgery two times in one month to schedule the first case of the day; and (3) posting the names of late doctors in the physicians' lounge.

When the team examined instances when the OR was not ready to begin surgery at the scheduled 7:30 A.M. starting time, it discovered that extensive surgeries, such as total knee or hip replacements, were most likely to start late. The OR staff, coming in at 7:00 A.M., was unable to prepare the operating room for extensive operations in 30 minutes. The team suggested moving starting times for major surgeries to 8:00 A.M. As a result of these efforts, the number of late surgeries dropped from 48 percent to 8 percent.

1. How does this case illustrate the broad applicability of total quality management concepts?
2. How has this organization specifically implemented the ideas of Crosby and Deming?

Source: Adapted from Thomas F. Rienzo, "Planning Deming Management for Service Organizations," *Business Horizons,* May–June 1993, pp. 24–25.

REFERENCES

1. Thomas F. Rienzo, "Planning Deming Management for Service Organizations," *Business Horizons,* May–June 1993, pp. 19–29.
2. Philip B. Crosby, *Quality Without Tears,* Plume Books, New York, 1984, pp. 101–124.
3. Ibid.
4. Rienzo, loc. cit.
5. This material is drawn from several sources but mainly W. Edwards Deming, *Out of the Crisis,* MIT Center for Advanced Engineering Study, Cambridge, Mass., 1986, ch. 2, pp. 18–96; Mary Walton, *The Deming Management Method,* Perigee Books, New York, 1986, pp. 55–80; James W. Dean, Jr., and James R. Evans, *Total Quality,* West Publishing Co., St. Paul, Minn., 1994, pp. 42–46.
6. Deming, loc. cit.
7. Ibid.
8. Ibid.
9. Rienzo, loc. cit.
10. Walton, loc. cit.
11. Rienzo, loc. cit.
12. Peter F. Drucker, *Managing for the Future,* Truman Talley/Dutton, New York, 1992, p. 302.
13. Dean and Evans, op. cit., pp. 52–53.
14. "The Ecstasy and the Agony," *Business Week,* Oct. 21, 1991, p. 40; see also "The Cost of Quality," *Newsweek,* Sept. 7, 1992, p. 48.
15. "The Cost of Quality," *Newsweek,* Sept. 7, 1992, p. 48.
16. Walton, loc. cit.
17. Ibid.

18. Dean and Evans, op. cit., pp. 39–40.
19. Walton, loc. cit.
20. Richard Schonberger and Edward M. Knod, Jr., *Operations Management,* Business Publications, Inc., Homewood, Ill., 1988, pp. 577–585.
21. Ibid.
22. Walton, op. cit., pp. 107–108.
23. Ibid.
24. Schonberger and Knod, loc. cit.
25. Walton, op. cit., p. 115.
26. Donald F. Harvey and Donald R. Brown, *An Experiential Approach to Organization Development,* Prentice-Hall, Inc., New York, 1992, p. 293.

SUGGESTED READINGS

Crosby, Philip B.: *Quality Without Tears,* Plume Books, New York, 1984.
Dean, James W., Jr., and James R. Evans: *Total Quality: Management, Organization, and Strategy,* West Publishing Co., St. Paul, Minn., 1994.
Deming, W. Edwards: *Out of the Crisis,* MIT, Center for Advanced Engineering Study, Cambridge, Mass., 1992.
Juran, Joseph M.: *Juran on Quality by Design,* The Free Press, New York, 1992.
Schonberger, Richard, and Edward M. Knod: *Operations Management,* Business Publications, Inc., Homewood, Ill., 1988.
Walton, Mary: *The Deming Management Method,* Perigee Books, New York, 1986.

GLOSSARY

common causes of variation   Factors causing variation in product or service quality that are a natural part of the process.

control chart   A run chart with statistically determined upper and lower limits drawn on either side of the process average.

error-cause removal   A process that allows employees to state the problems they have in their work areas so that something can be done about them.

run chart   A statistical tool used for tracking data over a period of time in order to look for trends.

special causes of variation   Causes of variation that arise from external sources that are not inherent in the process.

total quality management   A method of conducting business for producing a product or providing a service that gets it right for the customer the first time and every time.

zero defects day   A formal occasion designed to allow management to stand up and make its commitment to quality a matter of public record.

CHAPTER 16
Maintaining a Safe and Healthy Workplace

STUDYING THIS CHAPTER WILL ENABLE YOU TO:

1. Discuss the reasons for maintaining a safe and healthy workplace.

2. Discuss management's role in safety and health programs.

3. Describe legislation that has had an impact on workplace safety and health.

4. Define the role of OSHA in workplace safety and health.

5. Discuss the elements in the work environment that might cause accidents.

6. State ways through which the supervisor can develop safety awareness among workers.

7. Explain the importance of observation and inspection in maintaining safety.

8. Discuss the supervisor's role in investigating and reporting accidents.

9. Define methods of measuring worker safety.

10. Explain the role of ergonomics in the workplace.

11. Define cumulative trauma disorders and describe some measures that companies may take to reduce CTDs.

12. Identify sources of organizational stress and define several stressors within each source.

13. Describe several actions that organizations, supervisors, and individuals can take to reduce employees' job-related stress.

14. Discuss the issue of smoking in the workplace.

15. Describe methods companies can use to provide assistance to employees.

16. Explain employees' rights in a safe and healthy workplace.

CHAPTER OUTLINE

EMPLOYEE SAFETY IN THE WORKPLACE

Management Commitment
Legislation
The Role of OSHA
The Role of the Supervisor

EMPLOYEE HEALTH IN THE WORKPLACE

The Ergonomic Approach
Health Hazards—Cumulative Trauma
    Disorders
Health Hazards—Stress
Health Hazards—Smoking
Providing Assistance

EMPLOYEE RIGHTS IN A SAFE AND HEALTHY WORKPLACE

Acquired Immune Deficiency Syndrome
    (AIDS)
Workplace Choice
Worker Response to an Unsafe Environment

Competency Review
Applications
Cases
References
Suggested Readings
Glossary

C H A P

Maintaining A Safe AND Healthy Workplace

Management concern for employee well-being is still evolving. There was a time when the entire emphasis was on production efficiency, with only a minimal regard for employee safety; in fact, workers were considered to be expedient—simply another cost of doing business. Today, however, companies realize that it is in their best interests as well as those of their employees to provide a safe and healthy environment for workers.

Businesses have a responsibility to take into consideration their effects on society as they plan and operate their organizations. Whatever the degree of social responsibility they assume, effective organizations today recognize that their workers are their greatest resource and give employee safety and health a high priority in their planning. Caring for the safety and health of employees is simply the right thing to do.

Even in the unlikely absence of ethical and social concern, the costs to the company of job-related accidents and illnesses would force today's managers to plan a safe and healthy workplace. While safety statistics differ, research reports invariably show staggering costs. According to the Office of Technology Assessment,[1] stress-related illnesses alone cost business between $50 billion and $75 billion a year. Overall, every year 1 in every 15 workers is injured on the job.[2] A severe case of carpal tunnel syndrome—a nerve injury resulting from repeated bending of the wrist, excessive pressure, and unnatural positions—can cost $100,000 in medical and administrative expenses and lost productivity.[3]

Among the many costs for the organization are production stoppage or slowdown; damaged equipment, products, supplies, and materials; medical and insurance costs; and worker replacement costs. Intangible costs, which eventually translate into dollar costs, include worker morale and motivation, public image, and recruitment ability. There are also hidden costs, such as dispensary services, which are sometimes not directly assigned by an organization to a particular accident or illness.

In addition, employers who do not have a comprehensive multilevel health and safety program may be subject to fines. In the last few years, OSHA has slapped a number of companies, including Sara Lee, John Morrell Co., and Wickes Manufacturing, with substantial fines, some in excess of $1 million.[4]

Suing employers for any number of reasons has become commonplace. A word processing specialist sues because of job-related stress; a warehouse worker sues because of a leg injury; a baker sues because of an equipment injury. Eight journalists filed a $270 million lawsuit against Atex Publishing Systems, a major supplier of word processing systems for newspapers. According to *The Wall Street Journal* (May 19, 1992), disability claims accounted for nearly 12 percent of more than 2400 Ohio employment discrimination cases between 1985 and 1990, as reported by Wright State University researchers. Supervisors have a responsibility to their employers to provide a safe workplace to reduce legal action brought by workers injured on the job.

COMPETENCY CHECK

Can you discuss the reasons for maintaining a safe and healthy workplace?

Employee Safety in the Workplace

The climate of an organization is reflected in the behavior of its members. The climate is a mirror image of morale. A good climate can produce vigor, enthusiasm, a cooperative spirit, and a supportive "family" feeling. A bad climate can result in a dull, lackadaisical, uncooperative, even apathetic organization. Whatever the climate, it is set by management.

Management Commitment

Upper-level managers must have a personal commitment to improve employee safety and health and must include that commitment in the organization's mission and objectives. Moreover, the commitment cannot be just lip service. Management must show, by its actions as well as its words, that it believes in employee safety and health, that it will implement a program and personally participate in it, and that it will hold every member of the organization responsible for participating in the program.

The commitment must also be sustained. Consider the upper-level manager who approves a program and then responds to a request for funds in the following way: "Of course I believe in safety. But we don't have any money for such things as training and posters. Tell the supervisors to find a way to enforce the safety rules—that's what will improve our safety." Workers will take such a short-term commitment as a sign that management isn't really concerned about safety. Sustained commitment requires allocation of resources to carry out the objectives.

COMPETENCY CHECK
Can you discuss management's role in safety and health programs?

Legislation

Federal, state, and local governments have, over the years, passed many laws directed toward improving worker safety and health. Perhaps the most significant state laws were the worker compensation laws. All 50 states now require organizations to pay workers' compensation insurance premiums. This insurance protects workers from loss of income and from other costs related to occupational injuries.

Various federal labor laws, such as the Walsh-Healy Act of 1936, incorporated safety provisions. That act prohibited companies involved in government contracts from placing workers in unsanitary or unsafe working conditions to perform their contract work.

Among other federal laws concerned with worker health are those affecting a particular industry, such as the Coal Mine Health and Safety Act of 1969, later broadened to the Federal Mine Safety and Health Act of 1977. These laws were aimed at reducing the risk of dust inhalation, said to cause black lung disease; explosions; structure or ceiling collapse; and improper ventilation. The act established standards for inspections and emergency procedures.

In 1970, Congress passed the Occupational Safety and Health Act (OSHA), which went into effect in April 1971. It supersedes several safety and health acts, such as Walsh-Healy, that are administered by the U.S. Department of Labor.[5]

COMPETENCY CHECK
Can you discuss the impact of legislation on workplace safety and health?

The Role of OSHA

The Occupational Safety and Health Act is the most significant and pervasive legislation on safety and health yet passed. Some of your activities as a supervisor that relate to this act will be presented later in this chapter.

Purposes

Under provisions of this act, the Occupational Safety and Health Administration was created within the U.S. Department of Labor to:[6]

- ❐ encourage employers and employees to reduce workplace hazards and to implement new, or improve existing, safety and health programs.
- ❐ provide for research in occupational safety and health.
- ❐ establish "separate but dependent responsibilities and rights" for employers and employees.
- ❐ maintain a reporting and recordkeeping system.
- ❐ establish training programs.
- ❐ develop and enforce job safety and health standards.
- ❐ provide for the development, analysis, evaluation, and approval of state occupational safety and health programs.

While OSHA continually reviews and redefines specific standards and practices, its basic purposes remain constant. During some government administrations, OSHA is relatively inactive, only to be revived again when another administration takes office.

In 1991, the OSHA reform act was introduced in Congress. This would require companies with 11 or more employees to set up employee-employer safety and health committees and grant employees the right to act—which includes the rights to refuse hazardous work and to be involved in OSHA enforcement proceedings against employers. The bill also proposes to expand OSHA's authority to public employees and incorporates previous proposals to stiffen criminal penalties. Fines for willful violations would jump from $10,000 to $250,000 for individuals and to $500,000 for corporations. By early 1994, this proposed reform act was still being considered in Congress.

Administration

OSHA is administered out of the U.S. Department of Labor. There are 10 regional offices with 1200 inspectors charged with the task of trying to protect the health and safety of 58 million workers at 3.6 million work sites. The agency's function is to establish and enforce occupational safety and health standards. This function is carried out through workplace inspections; citations for infractions and resultant penalties, where appropriate; data collection and analysis; consultation services; and training programs.

Every business is subject to inspections by the Compliance Safety and Health Officers (CSHOs) of OSHA. States may also conduct inspections. Almost without exception, inspections are conducted without advance notice to the company.

With so many workplaces to inspect, OSHA has had to set up inspection priorities. They are, in decreasing order: imminent danger, catastrophes and fatal accidents, employee complaints, programmed high-hazard inspections, and follow-up inspections.[7]

During inspections, CSHOs determine the route of the tour and talk with workers along the way. They examine recordkeeping; check for posting of required OSHA materials; and inspect for unsafe or unhealthy conditions, noting especially any violations of OSHA standards. CSHOs report their findings to an area director, who determines what, if any, citations or penalties will be imposed. When violations are found, they can be costly. After some years of relative inactivity, OSHA has stepped up its enforcement, with a goal of collecting $1.5 billion in fines from employers by 1995, up from $180 million in 1991.[8]

The act encourages states to develop and operate, under OSHA guidance, state job safety and health plans. More than half of the states now have state occupational safety and health plans, and where these are in place, the public sector as well as the private sector is covered. Once OSHA certifies a state plan, OSHA funds up to 50 percent of the program's costs and relinquishes authority to the states in areas over which the states have jurisdiction.

Rights and Responsibilities

Employers and employees have certain rights and responsibilities under the act. These are shown in Figure 16.1. Employer rights and responsibilities in states that have their own programs generally conform to the federal list.[9]

COMPETENCY CHECK
Can you define the role of OSHA in workplace safety and health?

WHAT CAN THE SUPERVISOR DO?

Remember, you are a manager, too. You will also be feeling the pressure from the factors presented above. In some cases, the pressure may be more acute at your level than it is at the top. You might start by upgrading your own understanding of safety and health.

1. Check out local sources for help. If you have a human resources director and a safety specialist in your organization, talk with them.
2. Learn about the training programs offered through the OSHA Training Institute. For information, write to the institute at the U.S. Department of Labor, 1555 Times Drive, Des Plaines, IL 60018. Or check with your regional or the federal office of OSHA.
3. Learn the rights and responsibilities of both the employer and the employee as shown in Figure 16.1. In situations in which more knowledgeable employees try to assert their rights on safety matters, you not only will not be caught by surprise, you probably will have addressed a potential problem before employees call it to your attention.
4. Get acquainted with the *Federal Register* and other publications that report on safety standards and regulations. OSHA standards and revisions are reported in the *Register*. You can, if you wish to and have the time, read the original standards there, but be prepared to read some very small print in a voluminous document. Most managers wait for OSHA's interpretation, but knowing where official standards are printed should be a part of your knowledge base. Your human resources department may receive the *Register* by subscription and thus help you keep in touch with what is happening in OSHA regulations.
5. Other organizations publish summaries and updates on safety matters. Two such organizations are the National Safety Council, which publishes *Accident Facts* annually, and the Commerce Clearing House, which publishes a biweekly bulletin called *Human Resources Management Ideas and Trends in Personnel*.

Figure 16.1	
EMPLOYER AND EMPLOYEE RIGHTS AND RESPONSIBILITIES—OSHA	

Employer Rights

❑ Seek advice and off-site consultation as needed by writing, calling or visiting the nearest OSHA office. (OSHA will not inspect merely because an employer requests assistance.)

❑ Be active in your industry association's involvement in job safety and health.

❑ Request and receive proper identification of the OSHA compliance officer prior to inspection.

❑ Be advised by the compliance officer of the reason for an inspection.

❑ Have an opening and closing conference with the compliance officer.

❑ File a Notice of Contest with the OSHA area director within 15 working days of receipt of a notice of citation and proposed penalty.

❑ Apply to OSHA for a temporary variance from a standard if unable to comply because of the unavailability of materials, equipment or personnel needed to make necessary changes within the required time.

❑ Apply to OSHA for a permanent variance from a standard if you can furnish proof that your facilities or method of operation provide[s] employee protection at least as effective as that required by the standard.

❑ Take an active role in developing safety and health standards through participation in OSHA Standards Advisory Committees, through nationally recognized standards-setting organizations and through evidence and views presented in writing or at hearings.

❑ Be assured of the confidentiality of any trade secrets observed by an OSHA compliance officer during an inspection.

❑ Submit a written request to NIOSH for information on whether any substance in your workplace has potentially toxic effects in the concentrations being used.

Employer Responsibilities

❑ Provide medical examinations when required by OSHA standards.

❑ Report to the nearest OSHA office within 48 hours any fatal accident or one which results in the hospitalization of five or more employees.

❑ Keep OSHA-required records of work-related injuries and illnesses, and post a copy of the totals from the last page of OSHA No. 200 during the entire month of February each year. (This applies to employers with 11 or more employees.)

❑ Post, at a prominent location within the workplace, the OSHA poster informing employees of their rights and responsibilities.

❑ Provide employees, former employees, and their representatives access to the Log and Summary of Occupational Injuries and Illnesses at a reasonable time and in a reasonable manner.

❑ Cooperate with the OSHA compliance officer by furnishing names of authorized employee representatives, who may be asked to accompany the compliance officer during an inspection.

❑ Do not discriminate against employees who properly exercise their rights under the Act.

❑ Post OSHA citations at or near the work site involved. Each citation, or copy thereof, must remain posted until the violation has been abated, or for three working days, whichever is longer.

❑ Abate cited violations within the prescribed period.

❑ Meet your general duty responsibility to provide a workplace free from recognized hazards that are causing or are likely to cause death or serious physical harm to employees, and comply with standards, rules and regulations issued under the Act.

❑ Be familiar with mandatory OSHA standards and make copies available to employees for review upon request.

❑ Inform all employees about OSHA.

❑ Examine workplace conditions to make sure they conform to applicable standards.

❑ Minimize or reduce hazards.

❑ Make sure employees have and use safe tools and equipment (including appropriate personal protective equipment), and that such equipment is properly maintained.

❑ Use color codes, posters, labels or signs when needed to warn employees of potential hazards.

❑ Establish or update operating procedures and communicate them so that employees follow safety and health requirements.

(Continued)

Figure 16.1		
EMPLOYER AND EMPLOYEE RIGHTS AND RESPONSIBILITIES—OSHA (CONTINUED)		

Employee Rights

Employees have a right to seek safety and health on the job without fear of punishment. That right is spelled out in Section 11(c) of the Act.

The law says employers shall not punish or discriminate against workers for exercising rights such as:

❏ Complaining to an employer, union, OSHA or any other government agency about job safety and health hazards;

❏ Filing safety or health grievances;

❏ Participating on a workplace safety and health committee or in union activities concerning job safety and health;

❏ Participating in OSHA inspections, conferences, hearings or other OSHA-related activities.

Other Rights

❏ Review copies of appropriate OSHA standards, rules, regulations, and requirements that the employer should have available at the workplace.

❏ Request information from your employer on safety and health hazards in the area, on precautions that may be taken, and on procedures to be followed if an employee is involved in an accident or is exposed to toxic substances.

❏ Request the OSHA area director to conduct an inspection if you believe hazardous conditions or violations of standards exist in your workplace.

❏ Have your name withheld from your employer, upon request to OSHA, if you file a written and signed complaint.

❏ Be advised of OSHA actions regarding your complaint and have an informal review, if requested, of any decision not to inspect or to issue a citation.

❏ Have your authorized employee representative accompany the OSHA compliance officer during the inspection tour.

❏ Respond to questions from the OSHA compliance officer, particularly if there is no authorized employee representative accompanying the compliance officer.

❏ Observe any monitoring or measuring of hazardous materials and have the right to see these records, as specified under the Act.

❏ Have your authorized representative, or yourself, review the Log and Summary of Occupational Injuries at a reasonable time and in a reasonable manner.

❏ Request a closing discussion with the compliance officer following an inspection.

❏ Submit a written request to NIOSH for information on whether any substance in your workplace has potentially toxic effects in the concentration being used, and have your name withheld from your employer if you so request.

Employee Responsibilities

❏ Read the OSHA poster at the job site.

❏ Comply with all applicable OSHA standards.

❏ Follow all employer safety and health rules and regulations, and wear or use prescribed protective equipment while engaged in work.

❏ Report hazardous conditions to the supervisor.

❏ Report any job-related injury or illness to the employer, and seek treatment promptly.

❏ Cooperate with the OSHA compliance officer conducting an inspection if he or she inquires about safety and health conditions in your workplace.

❏ Exercise your rights under the Act in a responsible manner.

Source: All about OSHA, U.S. Department of Labor.

The Role of the Supervisor

You are the key person in a safety and health program because you are right there, where most occupational accidents happen. What are your functions? If you learn the six responsibilities presented here, you will be well on your way to becoming an effective safety supervisor.

Implementing Company Policy

Supervisors carry out company policies at the operational level. That is their main function. Do you know what the company safety and health policies are? The manager to whom you report should provide you with this information and cooperate in developing or approving your plans for administering the policies. You may also need to work with the HR manager or the company's safety specialist.

Company policies should be in writing, but sometimes they are communicated only verbally or by the actions of superiors. If that is the case in your organization, you may have to do a bit of research to find out what is expected of you. Unless you, as the key person, promote safety among workers, the company might as well forget the safety program.

A safety consultant, Dan Petersen, suggests that supervisors assess where they are now in terms of safety and health by taking the quiz shown in Figure 16.2. It helps to show where the supervisor needs to be headed in safety management. Try it; then check your score with the scoring system at the end of this chapter.

Understanding the Causes of Hazards and Accidents

An old adage tells us, "An ounce of prevention is better than a pound of cure." Prevention should be the primary thrust of safety and health programs. To promote prevention, you must be aware of what causes accidents and whether these causes are present in your workplace.

There are differing approaches to the prevention of accidents. Too often, the approach is far too simple. If a worker receives an electric shock when using a defective drill, for example, we might look simply at (1) the unsafe act, which was using the defective drill, and (2) the unsafe condition (the defective drill). In this case, we would simply repair or discard the defective drill.

If we explored the event further, however, we might begin to ask questions such as:

- ❑ Why was the defective drill not found in inspection?
- ❑ Why did the supervisor allow its use?
- ❑ Did the employee know he or she should not use the drill?
- ❑ Was the injured employee properly trained?
- ❑ Was the injured employee reminded of the hazard?
- ❑ Did the supervisor examine the job before the event?

Looking at the accident from this perspective, we find that there may be a number of root causes, among them poor inspection, procedures, or training; ill-defined responsibilities; poor job planning by supervisors; or poor equipment maintenance.[10] Note that these causes are all related to management.

> **Figure 16.2**
> **WHERE ARE YOU NOW IN SAFETY?**

When you begin your job as supervisor, you might want to take stock of where you stand in safety. These 15 questions will direct your thinking. Choose for each question the answer that best describes your situation. (Scoring suggestions appear at the end of this chapter.)

1. Do I have a job description that indicates precisely what I am to do in regard to safety?
   (a) No
   (b) I have a job description, but it doesn't mention safety.
   (c) Yes
2. Do I know exactly how much authority I have in safety?
   (a) No
   (b) Yes
   (c) I've discussed it with my boss, and we've reached some decisions.
3. Do I know exactly how I'm going to be measured in safety?
   (a) No
   (b) Yes
   (c) I've discussed it with my boss, and we've come to some agreements.
4. Do I know exactly what I am expected to do in safety?
   (a) No
   (b) All that counts are results—no accidents.
   (c) Yes
5. Do I know what is considered acceptable performance in safety?
   (a) No
   (b) No accidents, I guess.
   (c) Yes
6. How much time do I spend on safety?
   (a) No time
   (b) It's a constant job.
   (c) A few hours a week
7. Have I read the Federal Register?
   (a) What's a Federal Register?
   (b) Yes
   (c) Those sections that apply to me

8. Have I made a list of all violations of the law in my area?
   (a) No
   (b) Once
   (c) Regularly
9. Have I set up a system of priorities?
   (a) No
   (b) Yes
   (c) Yes. It's in operation.
10. Have I kept my boss aware of my status in OSHA compliance?
    (a) Heaven forbid.
    (b) Once I did.
    (c) Regularly
11. Have I documented everything I've done in safety and in OSHA preparation?
    (a) No
    (b) In part
    (c) Yes
12. Do I know what turns my people off?
    (a) Who cares?
    (b) Everything, I think.
    (c) Yes, I know.
13. Do I know what turns them on?
    (a) Who cares?
    (b) Nothing
    (c) Yes, I know.
14. Do I know when to use discipline?
    (a) Always
    (b) Never
    (c) Yes, I know.
15. Do I know how to work with problem people?
    (a) The same way as with anyone else
    (b) No, I don't.
    (c) Yes, I do.

Source: Dan Petersen, *Safety Supervision*, AMACOM, New York, 1976, pp. 2–3.

Another way to look at causes is to look at the three elements in the work environment: people, products, and processes.

People. Are the workers properly selected, trained, motivated, and supervised? Do some workers seem to be accident-prone? Are they careless? Do they take unnecessary chances? Do they use the prescribed protective garments and equipment? Is the supervisor (a person, too!) properly selected, trained, and motivated? Does the supervisor use effective controls?

Products. Does the product contain hazardous materials such as toxic chemicals or explosives? Does its use involve hazardous procedures (detonation, high-voltage current, testing of cars or planes)?

Processes. Does the manufacturing process include potentially hazardous steps such as mixing minerals or chemicals; sequencing electronic or electrical components; applying extreme heat, as in smelting; construction; or lifting? Does the process involve the use of equipment? (Any equipment is potentially dangerous if improperly maintained or used.) Does the process generate waste that is potentially hazardous (fumes, particles that can be inhaled or absorbed into the skin, water or liquids that can burn or cause slippery floors)?

COMPETENCY CHECK

Can you discuss the elements in the work environment that might cause accidents?

Accidents happen in all kinds of businesses, but statistics show that the accident potential is greater in some industries than in others. The U.S. Department of Labor shows that in 1990, the industries with the 10 highest incidence rates for injuries involving lost workdays were in manufacturing. The top three rates were reported in shipbuilding and repairing, special-product sawmills, and meatpacking plants.[11] Workers need to be made aware of potential dangers and encouraged to take safety precautions.

Developing Safety Awareness

Understanding the causes of accidents will better prepare you to develop safety awareness among your workers. A workforce with safety awareness will have fewer accidents because the workers will be more likely to practice safe work habits and avoid potentially dangerous behavior. But how do you develop awareness?

The first step is proper training (see Chapter 10). Each new employee must be thoroughly trained in the company's safety policy and procedures, including, especially, procedures for performing his or her job safely. Experienced employees need refresher courses and information on new products, processes, and equipment. The training should emphasize prevention. Adopting a safety slogan (preferably selected by the workers) can create interest and keep the training alive. Remember that slogans can become boring, so unless it is a company tradition, you might want to change it periodically.

The second step is making workers' jobs more interesting. It is generally agreed that workers whose jobs are satisfying, who feel "in on things," and who have some decision-making authority over their jobs are better motivated. Motivated workers are less prone to the negative behavior that leads to accidents. Consider job design, which you studied in Chapter 4 as an approach to making jobs more interesting: add task variety; let workers perform the whole job rather than parts of it; make the job significant to others; and give feedback on performance of the job.

The third step is using safety committees. These committees provide worker involvement. This participation will develop the committee members' awareness, which through them will spread to their peers. The following activities have been suggested for safety committees:[12]

- ❐ Make regular inspections of the work areas.
- ❐ Sponsor accident-prevention contests.
- ❐ Help prepare safety rules.
- ❐ Promote safety awareness.
- ❐ Review safety suggestions from employees.
- ❐ Supervise the preparation and distribution of safety materials.
- ❐ Make fire prevention inspections.
- ❐ Supervise first-aid equipment maintenance.

Some firms display "accident-free days" signs on the premises. Safety committees often use this as a project. The sign might read: "Koling Steel Works—204 accident-free days." Other signs might be posted on bulletin boards or in the work area. The board might feature awards for safety records, including a photo of the workers who won the awards. Safety committees might maintain the bulletin boards. Developing and maintaining safety awareness among workers will be a continuing challenge.

COMPENTENCY CHECK
Can you state the ways through which the supervisor can develop worker safety awareness?

Observing and Inspecting

Observing is an informal way to keep informed about safety practices and conditions. As you do your routine "walk-around" supervision, you should be alert to safety and health conditions that may need attention. Unsafe conditions found through observation should be corrected immediately. Quick response may not only prevent an accident, but also confirm for the workers your sincerity about safety. Of course, no place can be made 100 percent safe. But the supervisor's job is to reduce risk to a minimum consistent with human ability and company resources.

Another point to remember is that you have many other responsibilities and you can't watch workers all the time, even if that were desirable. Instead, try to instill in the workers the feeling that each is a "safety specialist." General Electric's Columbia, Maryland, plant uses a "participative safety management system".[13] When a worker sees a fellow employee doing something unsafe, the worker silently hands that person a card (shown in Figure 16.3) and walks away. These cards give employees the message that they are responsible not only for themselves but also for fellow workers.

Routine observation by workers will augment observation by the supervisor; together, they will fill in the gaps between inspections. Safety inspections are usually a more formal way to maintain safe working conditions. Inspections have several objectives:

Figure 16.3
GE SAFETY CARD

SAFETY AWARENESS

THE BEST ACCIDENT PREVENTION

I JUST NOTICED YOU DOING SOMETHING THAT COULD HAVE CAUSED AN ACCIDENT. THINK ABOUT WHAT YOU'VE DONE IN THE LAST FEW MINUTES AND YOU WILL PROBABLY RECALL WHAT I SAW.

I AM GIVING YOU THIS CARD AS PART OF OUR CAMPAIGN TO MAKE ALL OF US SAFETY CONSCIOUS. KEEP IT UNTIL YOU SEE SOMEONE DOING SOMETHING IN AN UNSAFE WAY AND THEN PASS IT ON.

P.S. I HOPE I DON'T GET IT BACK.

Source: John A. Jenkins, "Self-Directed Work Force Promotes Safety," February 1990. Reprinted with the permission of *HR Magazine* (formerly *Personnel Administrator*), published by the Society for Human Resource Management, Alexandria, Va.

- ❏ to compare results to plans
- ❏ to evaluate and improve safety standards
- ❏ to note and correct unsafe worker behavior
- ❏ to note and correct unsafe equipment or procedures
- ❏ to check out new facilities, equipment, processes, and materials
- ❏ to spot training needs
- ❏ to gather safety data
- ❏ to reinforce interest in safety

A newer approach to observation and inspection is monitoring through video terminals called Computerized Supervision Systems (CSS). Taking advantage of the networking of computer terminals, CSS allows supervisors to monitor employees who use computer terminals in their jobs or operate sophisticated machine tools.[14]

These systems have both positive and negative sides. They obviously provide management with more information on how employees are using their time and thus allow for greater control over the workplace. Some workers see it as a more objective evaluation than a boss's personal and sometimes biased opinion. On the negative side, some employees consider it a "Big Brother is watching" technique and an invasion of privacy. "I can't even go to the bathroom without being watched," says one telephone operator who is under electronic surveillance. "I have to put up a flag, wait my turn, sign out, sign in, and remove my flag." Others are concerned about the nature and use of the data collected through CSS.

Along with internal inspections, organizations may have OSHA inspections, as described earlier in this chapter. The supervisor can prepare for OSHA inspections by using a checklist derived from the last inspection for the current inspection. The record will provide valuable data on your safety program by giving dated notations of conditions and provide cumulative information on all elements of the workplace under your supervision. Comparing a report to a previous one will alert you to deteriorating conditions, such as loosening floor tiles or corroding pipes, so that the condition can be corrected before it becomes hazardous.

The checklists will also serve as evidence of your ongoing attention to safety in the event that your firm is called on by OSHA or your insurance agency to provide it.

Develop a checklist tailored to your own needs. Figure 16.4 can serve as a pattern. Since OSHA requires you to display the OSHA poster on employee rights and responsibilities, you might want to include "bulletin board" on your list.

COMPETENCY CHECK

Can you explain the importance of regular observation and inspection in maintaining safety?

Investigating and Reporting Accidents

OSHA requires that accidents resulting in death or illness or certain accidents in which injuries are incurred be reported. Note in Figure 16.5 that OSHA guidelines for reporting include almost every work-related death, illness, or injury. It is usually the supervisor's job to fill out the accident report of injured workers in his or her department. The report may then be checked by a safety director or department manager.

Knowing your reporting responsibility will help you in investigating the accident. The accident should be investigated immediately, while observers can recall all the particulars clearly and while the supervisor can examine the accident site. Get the

Figure 16.4 **MONTHLY SAFETY CHECK**		

Dept. _____   Date _____
Supervisor _____
Indicate discrepancy by ☒

General area		**First aid**	
floors condition		first-aid kits	
special purpose flooring		stretchers, fire blankets, oxygen	
aisle, clearance/markings		**Fire protection**	
floor openings, require safeguards		fire hoses hung properly	
railings, stairs temp./perm.		extinguisher charged/proper location	
dock board (bridges plates)		access to fire equipment	
piping (water-steam-air)		exit lights/doors/signs	
wall damage		other	
ventilation			
other			

(Continued)

Figure 16.4
MONTHLY SAFETY CHECK (CONTINUED)

Illumination—wiring		**Security**	
unnecessary/improper use		doors/windows, etc., secured when required	
lights on during shutdown		alarm operation	
frayed/defective wiring		dept. shut down security	
overloading circuits		equip. secured	
machinery not grounded		unauthorized personnel	
hazardous location		other	
wall outlets		**Machinery**	
other		unattended machines operating	
Housekeeping		emergency stops not operational	
floors		platforms/ladders/catwalks	
machines		instructions to operate/stop posted	
break area/latrines		maintenance being performed on machines in operation	
waste disposal		guards in place	
vending machines/food protection		pinch points	
rodent, insect, vermin control		**Material storage**	
Vehicles		hazardous & flammable material not stored properly	
unauthorized use		improper stacking/loading/securing	
operating defective vehicle		improper lighting, warning signs, ventilation	
reckless/speeding operation		other	
failure to obey traffic rules			
other			
Tools			
power tool wiring			
condition of hand tools			
safe storage			
other			

Keep on file as evidence of on-going safety program.

Source: Reprinted from *Safety and Security for Supervisors,* published by Business Research Publications, 817 Broadway, New York, N.Y. 10003, 1980, pp. 20–21.

views of more than one observer, if possible, to give you a complete picture and to verify the accuracy of observers' information.

A copy of the OSHA report should be kept in your files. Your organization may also wish to develop and use its own form, tailored to its own needs for research, safety history, and insurance information. Figure 16.6 shows an accident investigation report form developed by the National Safety Council. Note the information on supervision requested in item 24.

COMPETENCY CHECK
Can you discuss the supervisor's role in investigating and reporting accidents?

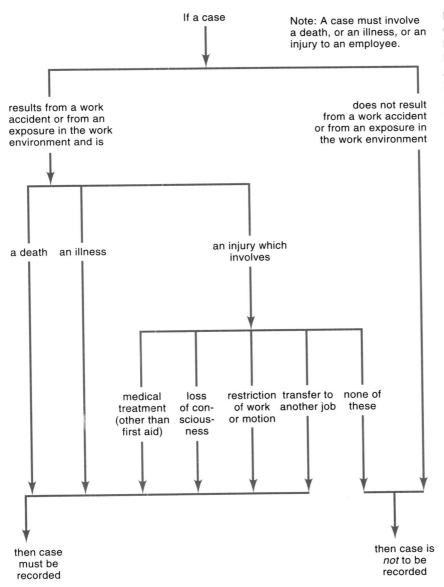

Figure 16.5 GUIDE FOR REPORTING/ RECORDING ACCIDENTS, ILLNESSES, AND DEATHS TO OSHA

Figure 16.6
ACCIDENT INVESTIGATION REPORT

ACCIDENT INVESTIGATION REPORT

CASE NUMBER

COMPANY _____ ADDRESS _____

DEPARTMENT _____ LOCATION (if different from mailing address) _____

1. NAME OF INJURED	2. SOCIAL SECURITY NUMBER	3. SEX ☐ M ☐ F	4. AGE	5. DATE of ACCIDENT

6. HOME ADDRESS	7. EMPLOYEE'S USUAL OCCUPATION	8. OCCUPATION at TIME of ACCIDENT

11. EMPLOYMENT CATEGORY
☐ Regular, full-time
☐ Temporary   ☐ Nonemployee
☐ Regular, part-time   ☐ Seasonal

9. LENGTH of EMPLOYMENT
☐ Less than 1 mo.   ☐ 6 mos. to 5 yrs.
☐ 1–5 mos.   ☐ More than 5 yrs.

10. TIME in OCCUP. at TIME of ACCIDENT
☐ Less than 1 mo.   ☐ 6 mos to 5 yrs.
☐ 1–5 mos.   ☐ More than 5 yrs.

13. NATURE of INJURY and PART of BODY

12. CASE NUMBERS and NAMES of OTHERS INJURED in SAME ACCCIDENT

14. NAME and ADDRESS of PHYSICIAN

15. NAME and ADDRESS of HOSPITAL

16. TIME of INJURY
A. _____ A.M.   P.M.
B. Time within shift
C. Type of shift

17. SEVERITY of INJURY
☐ Fatality
☐ Lost workdays—days away from work
☐ Lost workdays—days of restricted activity
☐ Medical treatment
☐ First aid
☐ Other, specify _____

18. SPECIFIC LOCATION of ACCIDENT

ON EMPLOYER'S PREMISES? ☐ Yes ☐ No

19. PHASE OF EMPLOYEE'S WORKDAY at TIME of INJURY
☐ During rest period   ☐ Entering or leaving plant
☐ During meal period   ☐ Performing work duties
☐ Working overtime   ☐ Other

20. DESCRIBE HOW the ACCIDENT OCCURRED

21. ACCIDENT SEQUENCE: Describe in reverse order of occurrence events preceding the injury and accident. Starting with the injury and moving backward in time, reconstruct the sequence of events that led to the injury.
A. Injury Event _____
B. Accident Event _____
C. Preceding Event #1 _____
D. Preceding Event #2, #3, etc. _____

(Continued)

Figure 16.6
ACCIDENT INVESTIGATION REPORT (CONTINUED)

22. TASK and ACTIVITY at TIME of ACCIDENT

   A. General type of task _____

   B. Specific activity _____

   C. Employee was working:

    ☐ Alone ☐ With crew or fellow worker ☐ Other, specify _____

23. POSTURE of EMPLOYEE

_____

24. SUPERVISION at TIME of ACCIDENT

   ☐ Directly supervised   ☐ Not supervised

   ☐ Indirectly supervised   ☐ Supervision not feasible

25. CAUSAL FACTORS. Events and conditions that contributed to the accident. Include those identified by use of the Guide for Identifying Causal Factors and Corrective Actions.

_____

_____

_____

_____

_____

_____

_____

_____

_____

26. CORRECTIVE ACTIONS. Those that have been, or will be, taken to prevent recurrence. Include those identified by use of the Guide for Identifying Causal Factors and Corrective Actions.

_____

_____

_____

_____

_____

_____

_____

_____

_____

_____

_____

PREPARED BY _____

TITLE _____

DEPARTMENT _____ DATE _____

   Developed by the National Safety Council

APPROVED _____

TITLE _____ DATE _____

APPROVED _____

TITLE _____ DATE _____

Source: Reprinted with permission of the National Safety Council Accident Prevention Manual for Business & Industry: *Administration Programs,* 10th ed. National Safety Council, Itasca, Il., 1992, pp. 306–307.

Cost analysis is important. Without cost data, management would be unable even to estimate the savings realized through accident control. As a supervisor, you will be involved in this cost analysis. To gather cost data, you may be asked to report on a form like that shown in Figure 16.7. Examine the form; note that the questions include the hidden costs of an accident.

Measuring Safety

The U.S. Department of Labor periodically issues data on many areas of U.S. life. OSHA safety and health information is one segment. Data from supervisors from all over the country are compiled and published. Industries, unions, and private agencies such as the National Safety Council also publish safety and health statistics. Data from the various sources are not always comparable because different methods of collecting and reporting are used. Two common measures of safety and health are the injury and illness incidence rate and the lost workday incidence rate. The OSHA formulas for these rates are shown below.

A. Injury and illness incidence rate $= \dfrac{\text{number of injuries and illnesses} \times 200,000^*}{\text{total hrs worked by all employees for the year}}$

B. Lost workday incidence rate $= \dfrac{\text{number of lost workdays} \times 200,000}{\text{total hrs worked by all employees for the year}}$

*OSHA uses a base of 100 full-time employees working 40 hours a week for 50 weeks ($40 \times 50 \times 100 = 200,000$).
Source: Accident Facts, 1993 Edition, National Safety Council, Itasca, Il. Reprinted with permission.

Assume that United Energy Company's 150 employees worked fifty 40-hour weeks during a recent year and reported 6 injuries/illnesses for the period. Using formula as given, the company's injury and illness incidence rate would be 4; i.e., 6 $\times$ 200,000/300,000 = 4. United would find its safety record a bit worse than the national average, which in 1992 was 3.9.

COMPETENCY CHECK

Can you discuss the methods of measuring worker safety?

Now, suppose the 6 injured or ill workers lost a total of 12 working days. United's lost workday incidence rate, using formula B, would be 8; i.e., 12 $\times$ 200,000/300,000 = 8.

Incidence rates can be measured fairly easily; the health part of employee safety and health is much less amenable to measurement, as you will see in the next section.

Employee Health in the Workplace

What is *health?* How can it be measured? And what is the responsibility of business to promote health in the workplace? There are many different answers to these questions.

Since the 1980s, health and fitness have become a national pastime. We have become preoccupied with diets, health foods, nutrition clinics, aerobics, and jogging. Health has reached megabusiness proportions. At the same time, the costs of

Figure 16.7
DEPARTMENT SUPERVISOR'S ACCIDENT COST REPORT

DEPARTMENT SUPERVISOR'S ACCIDENT COST INVESTIGATION REPORT

Injury/Accident _____

Date _____ Name of Injured _____ Dept. _____

Time Lost

1. How much time did other employees lose by talking, watching, or helping at accident? Number of employees _____ × hours =

2. How much productive time was lost because of damaged equipment or loss or reduced output by injured worker?
Estimate hours =

3. How much time did injured employee lose for which he was paid on the day of the injury? Estimate hours =

4. Will overtime be necessary? Estimate hours =

5. How much of the supervisor's or other management's time was lost as a result of this accident? Estimate hours =

6. Were additional costs incurred due to hiring and training or replacement? Training time estimate hours =

7. Describe the damage to material or equipment. _____
_____

8. If machine and/or operations were idle, can loss of production be made up?
Yes _____ No _____

9. Will overtime be necessary? Yes _____ No _____

10. Any demurrage or other cost involved? Yes _____ No _____

ADDITIONAL ACCIDENT COSTS
To compute the total costs of this accident, it is necessary to complete the following costs. Should the supervisor have access to this information it is advised he complete as much as possible. Safety Department will develop those costs not known by supervisor.

11. Estimate of demurrage or other costs. $_____

12. Costs associated with giving medical attention, first-aid, ambulance costs, etc. $_____

13. Workers compensation costs. $_____

14. Hospital medical costs. $_____

15. Costs associated with placing injured on other work when unable to perform regular work. $_____

16. Costs associated with questions 1 through 6.

16-1	$_____
16-2	$_____
16-3	$_____
16-4	$_____
16-5	$_____
16-6	$_____

17. Company dollars lost on accident: TOTAL $

Source: Reprinted with permission from the National Safety Council: *Accident Prevention Manual for Industrial Operations,* 9th ed., National Safety Council, Chicago, 1988, pp. 160–161.

employee injuries are soaring. General Motors' employee medical benefits cost the company more than it pays for the steel it buys from its main supplier.[15]

Robert H. Rosen points out that the healthy company takes an integrated view of health and the organization. He cites four critical elements in that concept. These are the impact of:[16]

- ❐ the employee's lifestyle on his or her own health.
- ❐ the work environment on the employee's health.
- ❐ employee health on the organization's profitability.
- ❐ the larger environment—family, peers, leisure—on employee health and organizational profits.

The author lists 39 costs to show the impact of employee health on the organization's profitability.[17] This implies that one way to measure employee health is by measuring the health of the company, including worker morale, absenteeism, and productivity that translates into profit.

The Ergonomic Approach

Ergonomics is a science that tries to design the work, the workplace, and the tools to fit the worker. Ergonomics goes beyond safety in the workplace, taking into consideration technological, psychological, and aesthetic factors, and is one proactive approach to improving safety, productivity, and quality.

Reynolds Metals Company includes selection of workers as part of its ergonomic approach to safety and health. The company uses "ergonomic testing" as part of its screening process for industrial workers. Administered by the company's medical department, the objective of the testing is to identify workers who are physically and psychologically able to meet the physical stress demands of the job.[18]

Some organizations take an ergonomic approach to improving the work environment because the approach has been shown to improve the quality of work life, thus resulting in improved worker motivation and productivity. Therefore, taking the ergonomic approach to environmental planning in the workplace is not just altruistic. Milton Bradley, the games manufacturer, experienced a 90 percent increase in quality in a packaging area after implementing an ergonomic approach; Textron, Inc., reported that at one plant, improvements—including ergonomics—resulted in a 42 percent reduction in OSHA-recordable incidents.[19]

According to G. Gordon Long of Rhone-Poulenc, Inc., "ergonomics can show the way to efficiency and productivity."[20] He describes four factors—utilities, lighting, acoustics, and furnishings—to be considered in the ergonomic planning of a facility. Note in the following summary of the four factors the safety and health implications for the workers.

Utilities

A properly balanced heating and cooling system, providing a properly maintained air environment, promotes higher productivity, better work quality, improved morale, and a lower rate of absenteeism.

Lighting

Since vision is improved when light is directed toward the actual work surface—such as a desk—the majority of light should be used where it is most needed. This concept of task-ambient lighting should take into consideration problems such as glare, the technical factors involved in fluorescent lighting and computer terminals, and possible eyestrain as workers move from one degree of lighting to another. Color is also related to proper lighting.

Glare adversely affects worker productivity. Glare is produced by brightness within the field of vision that is sufficiently greater than the light to which the eyes are adapted. It can cause annoyance, discomfort, or loss of visual performance and visibility.

Acoustics

The characteristics of sound—pitch, intensity, quality, and reverberation—must be taken into consideration in designing the work environment. Selecting quieter machines, using sound shields for equipment and sound-absorbing materials for room surfaces, providing proper maintenance, and adding controlled music are techniques of managing the acoustical environment.

OSHA requires employers to make available hearing protection devices to all employees who are exposed to noise levels exceeding 85 dBA. For workers whose noise levels exceed 90 dBA, such protection is mandatory.

Furnishings

The workstation design, the type and comfort of the furniture, and the relationship between the employee and the equipment should be reviewed in selecting furnishings. As a general rule, when designing a suitable workstation the following should be avoided:[21]

- ❏ many repetitions
- ❏ prolonged or repetitive exertion of more than 30 percent of the operator's available muscle strength;
- ❏ positioning body segments in extreme or awkward postures, such as severely bending the wrist;
- ❏ maintaining the same body posture for a long duration;
- ❏ vibrating the body or part of the body with tools; and
- ❏ combinations of the conditions described above.

The problem with most workstations turns on two design-related problems.[22] First, businesses employ multicultural workers who include a range of body types, sizes, shapes, and genders. A workstation that fits a 4-foot, 10-inch Vietnamese-American woman on the day shift would be uncomfortable for a 6-foot, 3-inch German-American man on the night shift. Figure 16.8 illustrates the difference in requirements for most women and men.

The second problem is that the human body was meant to flex. People who study back injuries emphasize the need to move, to shift, rather than to sit in one position. Anything that encourages a person to break away from an intense task helps. Unfor-

Figure 16.8
WORK STATION
DESIGN

HEIGHT RANGE OF ADJUSTABLE DESK, SEAT AND VDT (in/cm)

DESK PLATFORMS		SEAT	VDT UNIT	
VDT	Keyboard		Display*	Keyboard**
23–35 58.4–81.3	23–31 58.4–78.7	15–22.5 38.1–57.2	8–18 20.3–45.7	0.67–3 1.7–7.6

* Height from the base to the top line of the screen
** Height from the base to the top of A.S.D...key row

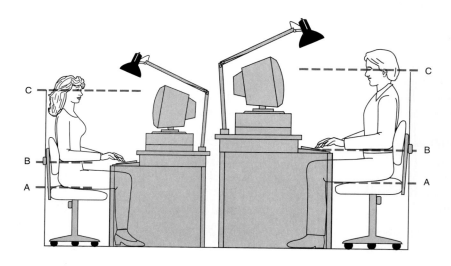

	HEIGHT in/cm	MALE 95 Percentiles	FEMALE 5 Percentiles	RANGE
A	SEAT	19.7./50.0	14.1/35.8	5.6/14.2
B	ELBOW	26.7/67.8	18.3/36.5	8.4/31.3
C	EYE	53.8/136.5	41.5/105.3	12.3/31.2

Anthropometry of seated 5 percentiles female and 95 percentiles male.

Source: Boris Povlotsky, "How to Enjoy the Benefits of Ergonomic Work Stations," *Office Systems '86,* August 1986, p. 45.

tunately, most workstations and chairs limit movement, as does the nature of a given job.

The computer has been described by many workers who use it all day as "one big pain in the neck." A computer operator's ergonomic chair is designed to alleviate the neck and back stress that often results from long periods of sitting at a terminal. Most computer users do not know precisely how high the keyboard platform should be to avoid back and shoulder strain. Neither do they know how to position the chair back at an angle that can help avoid long-term problems. Users need to learn how to properly choose and use equipment. New hires at United Services Automobile Association's mid-Atlantic regional headquarters are measured and then custom-fitted with ergonomically correct desks and computer terminals. A spokesman for USAA says this practice cuts down the risk of eyestrain, back problems, and carpal tunnel syndrome.[23]

While there are no formal regulations governing the safety of today's high-tech workplace, OSHA has published draft guidelines for workplace safety. OSHA hopes the components of good ergonomic management programs will become workplace standards:[24]

- *Worksite analysis.* Take a hard look at the job, analyze the workplace, survey the workers, look into employees' medical backgrounds, and find out what the recurring problems are.
- *Hazard abatement.* Perform an engineering analysis and redesign the job using ergonomic approaches. Change the job to support the basic tenets of ergonomics.
- *Medical management program.* Support a medical management program for workers. Allow employees to get the proper help early when symptoms begin to flare up.
- *Training and education awareness program.* Develop training and education programs to help supervisors and their employees analyze the job and see how problems can be resolved early on.

As a supervisor, you will not be expected to be an ergonomist, but knowledge of the science will make you more alert to stress points in the workplace. You will also be better prepared to suggest improvements in the environment to increase worker safety and health.

COMPETENCY CHECK
Explain the role of ergonomics in the workplace.

Health Hazards—Cumulative Trauma Disorders

According to the Occupational Safety and Health Administration, at least 30 to 40 percent of all workers' compensation cases today stem from **cumulative trauma disorders** (CTDs; sometimes called repetitive-motion or repetitive-stress injuries)—disorders that affect the musculoskeletal and nervous systems, most commonly the lower back and wrist, as well as tendon injuries such as carpal tunnel syndrome. Computer users, meat cutters, workers in poultry processing plants, sewing machine operators, and others who perform repetitive tasks for long periods are the most affected.

The National Institute of Health (NIOSH) estimates that 5 million Americans suffer from CTDs, and that by the year 2000, 50 percent of the workforce will be at risk of developing repetitive-motion disorders. Some studies suggest that the figure is even higher—61 percent in 1991. The American Academy of Orthopedic Surgeons estimates that repetitive-motion injuries cost the nation $27 billion annually in medical treatment and lost income. For low back pain alone, the total compensable cost is more than $30 billion, up $14 billion since 1979.[25]

Carpal tunnel syndrome complaints, believed to be caused by the use of computer keyboards, are flooding the courts, just as in the 1980s asbestos-related injuries did. One judge has ruled that all of the cases of CTS may be consolidated, allowing lawyers to pool their resources. Among the companies named in this consolidated suit are Northern Telecom Inc.; Apple Computer, Inc.; American Telephone & Telegraph Company and its NCR Corp. subsidiary; Eastman Kodak Co. and its Atex unit; IBM Corp.; and Wang Laboratories, Inc., all makers of the equipment at issue. The lawsuits allege that the design of data processing equipment, including computer keyboards and grocery scanners, is flawed and causes injuries when used over extended periods. The lawsuits allege that the companies knew, or should have known, that their product design was defective and, further, that they failed to warn the workers who would use them.[26]

What is the solution? Many researchers say that a good ergonomics management program will help relieve these repetitive trauma injuries. An ergonomics audit, such as the one shown in Figure 16.9, is an effective tool for identifying problem areas. Although this ergonomics audit is specifically for a manufacturing facility, it can be adapted to fit different organizations.

**COMPETENCY
CHECK**

Define cumulative
trauma disorders
and describe
some measures
that companies
may take to
reduce CTDs.

At Milton Bradley, where workers who packed the games accounted for 10 percent of the carpal tunnel disorders, the solutions consisted primarily of engineering controls: raising the height of the belt conveyor, repositioning the belt conveyor, installing a packing table, decreasing the tilt of shipping cartons, and other modifications.[27] At General Motors' Oklahoma City assembly plant, an active ergonomics committee was established that works to redesign jobs and tools.[28] Some fairly simple actions can also minimize injuries. Shoppers at Sam's Club Members Only stores will notice that the employees there all wear back braces to reduce back strain.

Health Hazards—Stress

Stress is not an event or a circumstance; it is a response to it. The actual event or circumstance that demands a response and produces stress is the stressor. Stress is an unconscious reaction to a stressor.[29]

Contrary to a somewhat popular belief, stress is not associated solely with unpleasant events such as losing your job, receiving an unsatisfactory performance appraisal, or losing a loved one. Stress is also present when good things happen. When you get a promotion, meet the "perfect" mate, move to a new location after landing a new job, or even when an anticipated holiday approaches, various levels of stress will be present.

Figure 16.9
ERGONOMICS AUDIT

Workplace characteristics
1. Is the worker able to keep horizontal stretches within the range of normal arm reach? (reach should not exceed 16–18 inches)
2. Does the workstation have adequate space to perform the work comfortably?
3. Does the work activity permit the worker to adopt several different, but equally healthy and safe, postures without reducing the capability to do the work?
4. Is it possible for the worker to choose between sitting or standing when performing a task?
5. Is the design of the chair satisfactory? (i.e., adequate back support and vertical adjustability)
6. Are footrests available, if needed?
7. Are hand supports available, if needed?
8. Are back supports available, if needed?
9. Does the height of the work surface permit satisfactory arm posture? (acceptable hand height is 2–6 inches below elbow height)
10. Is the work surface height adjustable?
11. Are containers in the work area properly labeled?
12. Are the operators exposed to toxic chemical fumes?
13. Is the work area clean and uncluttered?
14. Is the work floor clear of clutter and obstructions which could create the risk of slips, trips, or falls?
15. Are exit signs properly posted?
16. Are warning signs properly posted?
17. Is the fire hose located for easy access?
18. Are fire extinguishers in place?
19. Is the worker subjected to repetitive motion tasks?

Work environment
1. Is there adequate lighting? (illumination of 500 lx or 50 fe is acceptable)
2. Is there visual discomfort from glare that interferes with reading and inspection?
3. Does the noise level interfere with the performance of the job? (more than 85 dBA is unacceptable for memory tasks)
4. Is the noise level high enough to cause hearing loss? (more than 95 dBA is unacceptable)
5. Is the temperature frequently uncomfortable enough to interfere with the job? (acceptable range is 75 to 80 degrees Fahrenheit)
6. Is air circulation too low?
7. Is the ventilation system functioning properly, especially in areas that have a high incidence of unacceptable substances?
8. Are suspended dust, mists, and other particulates present in the air?
9. Are there wet locations that may produce shock hazards for work with electrically powered equipment?
10. Are the floors uneven?
11. Are the floors slippery?
12. Is housekeeping poor?
13. Are there hot surfaces which may cause burns?
14. Are warning labels on equipment to inform the user of potential dangers resulting in improper usage?

(Continued)

Figure 16.9
ERGONOMICS AUDIT (CONTINUED)

Protective clothing and equipment

1. Is eye protection, such as safety glasses, worn as required in designated areas?
2. Is eyewash equipment available in convenient locations?
3. Is proper footwear, such as safety-toe shoes, worn as required?
4. Is a proper protective apron worn as required?
5. Are safety gloves worn as required?
6. Are hearing protective devices worn as required?
7. Are head protection devices worn as required?
8. Are face protection devices worn as required?
9. Are respirators worn in designated areas, such as paint shops?
10. Is first-aid equipment available?

Physical performance

1. Does the task require lifting heavy loads? (55 lb. for males and 33 lb. for females are acceptable in the age group of 20 to 35)
2. Does the job require twisting while lifting?
3. Are the lifting capacities marked on containers?
4. Are safe manual lifting techniques utilized by workers?
5. Does the job require continual handling of materials?
6. Does the job require two-person lifting?
7. Must force be exerted in an awkward position? (e.g., to the side, overhead, or at extended reaches)
8. Is there aid available for heavy lifting or exerting force?
9. Is the pace of the material handling determined by a machine? (e.g., feeding machines, conveyors, etc.)
10. Does the job lack material handling aids? (e.g., air hoists or tables)
11. Does the job involve using hand tools that are hard to grasp?
12. Is there a high level of hand tool vibration? (accelerations greater than 5 mls^2 for an 8-hour shift are unacceptable)
13. Must the worker stand on a hard surface for 45 percent or more of the work shift?
14. Is the worker subjected to frequent daily stair or ladder climbing?

Source: Nanda K. Kittusamy, O. Geoffrey Okogbaa, and A. J. G. Babu, "A Preliminary Audit for Ergonomics Design in Manufacturing Environments," Reprinted from *Industrial Engineering,* July 1992, p. 48. Copyright © 1992, Institute of Industrial Engineers, 25 Technology Park/Atlanta, Norcross, Ga. 30092.

Not all stress is "bad." Some level of stress does, in fact, stimulate performance, as shown in Figure 16.10. Note that when there is little stress, performance is low, but when stress is present in appropriate amounts, performance increases. High stress levels, however, are counterproductive, and performance decreases. Therefore, both too little and too much stress are harmful in terms of employee performance.

Some occupations are more vulnerable to stress than others. The National Institute of Safety and Health (NIOSH) studied 23,300 workers in 130 different job categories and ranked the jobs according to their degree of stress. The top five high-level stress jobs are laborer, secretary, inspector, clinical lab technician, and office

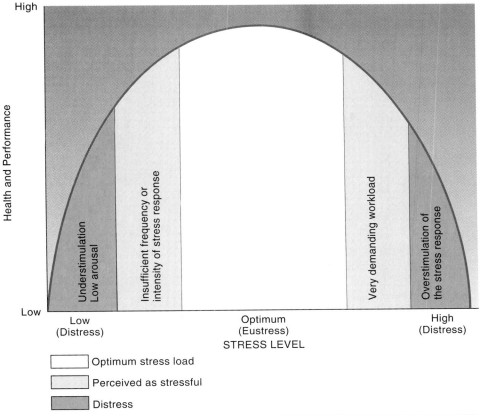

High

Health and Performance

Low

Understimulation
Low arousal

Insufficient frequency or
intensity of stress response

Very demanding workload

Overstimulation of
the stress response

Low
(Distress)

Optimum
(Eustress)

High
(Distress)

STRESS LEVEL

Optimum stress load

Perceived as stressful

Distress

Figure 16.10
STRESS AND
PERFORMANCE

Source: James C. Quick and Jonathan D. Quick, *Organizational Stress and Preventive Management,*
McGraw-Hill Book Company, New York, 1984, p. 154.

manager. The five jobs having the lowest stress levels are clothing sewer,
checker/examiner, stock handler, craft worker, and maid.

Sources of Stress

The four major sources of stress in the workplace are (1) task demands, (2) role
demands, (3) physical demands, and (4) interpersonal demands.[30] Task demands
are specific work activities that must be accomplished. Stressors that result from
task demands include:

- □ occupational category (high-stress versus low-stress jobs).
- □ managerial jobs (when time and decision-making activities are restricted and
  managers are given little latitude in their activities).
- □ career progress (major job changes or lack of career progress).

❒ routine jobs (lack of variety, underutilization of skills).
❒ boundary-spanning activities (working with other departments both within the organization and between organizations).
❒ negative performance-appraisal feedback (negative feedback that must be given and received).
❒ work overload (too much work assigned; too little time).
❒ job insecurity (especially in economic downturns).

Role demands are related to the behavior others expect of us as we fulfill our organizational roles. Organizational stressors resulting from role demands include:

❒ role conflict (when a worker's perception of his or her role is in conflict with the expectations of others).
❒ role ambiguity (when the worker has inadequate, unclear, or confusing information about what behaviors are expected).

Physical demands emanate from the physical environment in which we work. Stressors related to physical demands include:

❒ temperature extremes (too hot or too cold).
❒ illumination and other rays (not adapted to the needs of the particular job).
❒ sound waves and vibrations (excessive noise and vibration).
❒ office design (settings that do not serve the basic office functions).

Interpersonal demands are concerned with the normal course of social, personal, and working relationships found in the organization. Stressors resulting from interpersonal demands include:

❒ status incongruence (actual status and personal expectations do not agree).
❒ social density (too much or too little closeness).
❒ abrasive personalities.
❒ leadership styles of supervisors.
❒ group pressures.

COMPETENCY CHECK

Can you identify the sources of workplace stress and cite several stressors within each source?

According to Ken Pelletier in *Healthy People in Unhealthy Places,* certain sources of stress are more common to managers, while other sources are more common to secretaries, computer terminal operators, and blue-collar workers. Figure 16.11 lists the sources of stress for each of these categories. In some cases, managers and white- and blue-collar workers share the same stressors. There are different stress sources at different levels of the organization for different people.

Measures of Stress

How can supervisors determine that stress is present in the workplace? One way is to notice the employees who exhibit observable behavioral changes for no apparent reason. An increase in tardiness or absenteeism, a rise in the number of grievances

Figure 16.11 CAUSES OF STRESS FOR MANAGERS AND FOR WHITE- AND BLUE-COLLAR WORKERS	
Managers	**White- and Blue-Collar Workers**
Work overload and excessive time demands and rush deadlines	Work stagnation and helplessness
Erratic work schedules and take-home work	Erratic work schedules and frequently changing shifts
Ambiguity regarding work tasks, territory, and role	Rigidity regarding work tasks
Constant change, daily variability	Monotony; deadening, routinized stability
Role conflict (with immediate superior)	Too little contact or conflict
Job instability and fear of unemployment	Job instability and fear of unemployment
Responsibility, especially for people	Little responsibility or influence
Negative competition (cutthroat, one-upmanship, zero-sum game, and hidden aggression)	No competition or stimulation
Type of vigilance required in work assignments and team building toward goals	Type of vigilance required in inherently stressful work (police, firefighters, pilots)
Ongoing contact with stress carriers (workaholics, passive-aggressive subordinates, anxious and indecisive individuals)	Social isolation and lack of support
Sexual harassment	Sexual harassment
Accelerated recognition for achievement (Peter principle)	Inadequate recognition for achievement
Detrimental environmental conditions of lighting, ventilation, noise, and personal privacy	Detrimental environmental conditions of lighting, ventilation, noise, and personal privacy

Source: Kenneth Pelletier, *Healthy People in Unhealthy Places,* Delacorte Press/Seymour Lawrence, New York, 1984, pp. 44–45.

filed, an increase in the rate and severity of work-related accidents, a rise in inter-departmental transfers, an increase in employee turnover, or a change in employee performance may be an indication of abnormal levels of stress. Of course, behavioral changes may indicate problems other than employee stress. However, the presence of any of these behavioral changes should trigger an investigation into the possible causes.

There are also some objective measures that may be used to identify the existence of stressors. Questionnaires or diagnostic surveys may be administered.

Figure 16.12
AN EXAMPLE OF A LIFE EVENTS SCALE

THE LIFE CHANGE SCALE

Score Yourself on the Life Change Scale

What events have happened to you in the past 12 months?

Event Rank	Event Value	Happened (√)	Your Score	Life Event
1	100	_____	_____	Death of spouse
2	73	_____	_____	Divorce
3	65	_____	_____	Marital separation
4	63	_____	_____	Jail term
5	63	_____	_____	Death of close family member
6	53	_____	_____	Personal injury or illness
7	50	_____	_____	Marriage
8	47	_____	_____	Fired from job
9	45	_____	_____	Marital reconciliation
10	45	_____	_____	Retirement
11	44	_____	_____	Change in health of family member
12	40	_____	_____	Pregnancy
13	39	_____	_____	Sex difficulties
14	39	_____	_____	Gain of new family member
15	39	_____	_____	Business readjustment
16	38	_____	_____	Change in financial state
17	37	_____	_____	Death of a close friend
18	36	_____	_____	Change to different line of work
19	35	_____	_____	Change in number of arguments with spouse
20	31	_____	_____	Mortgage over $100,000
21	30	_____	_____	Foreclosure of mortgage or loan
22	29	_____	_____	Change in responsibilities at work
23	29	_____	_____	Son or daughter leaving home
24	29	_____	_____	Trouble with in-laws
25	28	_____	_____	Outstanding personal achievement
26	26	_____	_____	Spouse begins or stops work
27	26	_____	_____	Begin or end school
28	25	_____	_____	Change in living conditions
29	24	_____	_____	Revision of personal habits
30	23	_____	_____	Trouble with boss
31	20	_____	_____	Change in work hours or conditions
32	20	_____	_____	Change in residence
33	20	_____	_____	Change in schools
34	19	_____	_____	Change in recreation
35	19	_____	_____	Change in church activities
36	18	_____	_____	Change in social activities
37	17	_____	_____	Mortgage or loan less than $100,000
38	16	_____	_____	Change in sleeping habits
39	15	_____	_____	Change in number of family get togethers
40	15	_____	_____	Change in eating habits
41	13	_____	_____	Vacation
42	12	_____	_____	Christmas
43	11	_____	_____	Minor violations of the law

This scale shows the relative weight that can be attributed to stress-producing situations. For example, the death of a spouse is a great deal more stress-producing than a change in sleeping habits. After you have added up your score, take a close look at it. If your score is high, you are under a lot of stress. Try to think of ways you could decrease your score. Circle those checked events over which you have some control. Consider the importance to you of exercising control over these events.

Source: Thomas H. Holmes and Monoru Masuda, "Social Readjustment Rating Scale," *Journal of Psychosomatic Research,* vol. 11, 1967, p. 213, Reprinted with permission from Elsevier Science Ltd., Pergamon Imprint, Oxford, England.

Work performance may be affected by stressful events occurring primarily outside the workplace. Questionnaires such as the one shown in Figure 16.12 are available for assessing the general level of stress among a group of individuals to predict the possibility that illness will result from the present stress levels. It should be noted that different people respond to stress in different ways, and the possibility of an individual becoming ill as a result of stress levels will vary according to the coping skills each possesses.

COMPETENCY CHECK
Can you describe three measures of stress?

Strategies for Dealing with Stress

Stress can be dealt with on the organizational level, the supervisory level, or the individual level. You will recall that the sources of workplace stress are task demands, role demands, physical demands, and interpersonal demands. Organizations have a responsibility to respond to these demands on workers in an effort to reduce these stressors. Figure 16.13 suggests some strategies for dealing with task and physical demands. While strategies for dealing with task demands and physical demands primarily focus on reshaping the formal organization, strategies for dealing with role and interpersonal demands focus on both the formal and informal organization. Some of these strategies are also shown in Figure 16.13.

Supervisors have a responsibility and an obligation to implement company policy. Beyond that, however, there are some actions that supervisors can take to reduce stress within their departments.

1. Set well-defined objectives. Supervisors should be sure that their workers are fully aware of what is expected of them and what their responsibilities are. Supervisors should also communicate clearly what kinds of work and work behaviors are rewarded.
2. Have more clarity and consistency in policies. Supervisors should communicate to their employees what the policies mean and should be consistent and equitable in their application.
3. Develop workers' individual talents as much as possible. Supervisors should help their employees feel important about what they do.
4. When possible, even on production lines or with routine clerical work, allow employees to make choices that will give them some control over their work environment.
5. Define interoffice and interdepartmental relations so that workers are not confused about their roles within and outside their departments.
6. Establish a climate in which employees can meet their objectives without unnecessary conflict, distraction, and interruption.
7. Give a direct and immediate response to workers' concerns.
8. Help employees sort out priorities and work within their comfort zones. Too light or too heavy a workload causes stress.
9. Encourage use of company-sponsored exercise facilities. It is commonly accepted today that maintaining an appropriate level of exercise will help a worker work off frustrations and thereby reduce stress.

Figure 16.13
STRATEGIES FOR DEALING WITH TASK AND PHYSICAL DEMANDS

TASK DEMANDS

Task Redesign

Redesigning jobs to improve the person-job fit and to increase the job incumbent's motivation level is one method of reducing stress caused by task demands. This redesign is accomplished by restructuring one or more of the core job dimensions (see Chapter 4).

Participative Management

Increasing worker participation gives employees greater amounts of discretion and autonomy by decentralizing decision making and increasing participation in the decision-making processes, thus reducing stress caused by lack of personal control over how a task is performed.

Flexible Work Schedules

Giving increased discretion over work time enhances individual worker control and discretion in the work environment, leading to reduced stress.

PHYSICAL DEMANDS

Design of Physical Settings

Properly designed physical work environments reduce stress levels and facilitate task accomplishment. Some possible alterations in the physical setting include

Structural changes:
Points of entry and exit	Furniture, fixtures, and placements	Wall placement and height
Ceiling height and angle	Floor angles and elevations	Opening for vistas and lighting

Acoustical changes:
Wall coverings, finishing, and insulation	Ceiling coverings and finishing	Floor coverings and finishing
	Cushions and draperies	Plants and natural additions

Lighting changes:
Natural openings	Placement of artificial lights
Intensity of lighting	Color of interior furnishings

ROLE DEMANDS

Role Analysis

Clarify individual work roles to reduce stress. A "role profile" may be developed based on the expectations of superiors, peers, subordinates, and other key people with whom the individual works. When the conflicts between these different expectations are resolved, the employee understands his or her role, and that role is in agreement with his or her role perception, stress is reduced.

Goal Setting

Identify individual's major areas of responsibility and specify performance goals in each area. Clarification of performance expectations and agreement between the individual and immediate supervisor reduces role stress and increases motivation.

INTERPERSONAL DEMANDS

Social Support

Giving emotional, informational, appraisal, and instrumental support needed by individual employees provides a buffer for the impact of stress.

Team Building

Confronting, working through, and resolving natural interpersonal conflicts that evolve within any work group provides a basis for effective team building.

Source: Based on James C. Quick and Jonathan D. Quick, *Organizational Stress and Preventive Management,* McGraw-Hill Book Company, New York, 1984, pp. 184, 188, and "Participative Management," from Rensis Likert, *New Patterns of Management,* McGraw-Hill Book Company, New York, 1961.

Individuals must also assume some responsibility for their own stress levels and for engaging in activities that will help reduce stress. As an individual, you can:

1. Deal with the cause of the stress; ignoring the problem will not make it go away.
2. Use time management techniques to help avoid the stress caused by missing a deadline or having to redo work because of inaccuracies.
3. Realize your limits, and plan around them; don't take on more than you can handle and still do a professional job. Learn to say no.
4. Learn flexibility, and accept imperfection both in yourself and in those with whom you work.
5. Talk out your troubles with someone you trust.
6. Develop a positive attitude. There is some evidence that positive emotions help fight disease, while negative emotions produce or intensify illness.
7. Learn to distance yourself. If you find yourself in a heated disagreement, stop and ask, "Is this something worth fighting for?" Act accordingly.
8. Streamline your work procedures. Break big jobs down into small components that can be handled more easily.
9. Refuse to fight the inevitable. Stand up for what you believe in, but recognize that there are some things that cannot be changed and must be accepted.
10. Use relaxation techniques such as meditation, breathing exercises, and so on, if you find them helpful in reducing stress.

An example of an individual stress management plan is shown in Figure 16.14. Of course, each individual will react to the different factors in different ways; therefore, each stress management plan must be tailored to the individual.

Because the consequences of too much stress are so costly in terms of worker health and organizational profitability, steps must be taken to control the stress levels present in the workplace. Individual and organizational consequences are itemized in Figures 16.15 and 16.16.

> **COMPETENCY CHECK**
>
> Can you describe several actions that organizations, supervisors, and individuals can take to reduce job-related stress?

Health Hazards—Smoking

During the 1970s, 1980s, and early 1990s, the Surgeon General's reports on smoking and its effects on the smoker and the nonsmoker, through secondary-smoke inhalation, made smoking a highly emotional health issue. Disclosure of the hazardous effects of secondary smoke to the nonsmoker has caused upheaval in the workplace and elsewhere. The Environmental Protection Agency concluded in 1992 that every year 3000 nonsmokers die of lung cancer caused by secondhand smoke.[31] Further, one research group estimates that smoking-related illnesses cost the U.S. health care system more than $65 billion annually to treat.[32]

Remedies are hotly debated by smokers and nonsmokers. Each thinks his or her rights are being violated if the remedy favors the other's view. This creates a dilemma for organizations that wish to treat employees equally. Many states and localities prohibit smoking in public buildings, airlines do not permit smoking on domestic

Figure 16.14
AN EXAMPLE OF AN INDIVIDUAL STRESS-MANAGEMENT PLAN

STRESS MANAGEMENT PLAN

Name: *Jon Dickinson*   Date: *11–20–9–*

Personal Perceptions of Stress
(1) *Practice constructive self-talk*
(2) *Learn to recognize the inevitable*
(3) _____

Personal Work Environment
(1) *Learn to say No! (nicely)*
(2) *Each day make a do list*
(3) *and daily plan*

Lifestyle Choices
  Leisure time use:
(1) *Take an out-of-town 3-day weekend every 2 months*
  Other:
(2) *Don't forget vacations*

Relaxation Method(s)
(1) *Practice progressive relaxation each evening*
(2) *Use momentary relaxation at work*
(3) _____

Physical Outlets
(1) *Jog 30 minutes every other day*
(2) *Tennis or golf each weekend*
(3) _____

Emotional Outlets
(1) *Take time to talk out work frustration with spouse*
(2) *Practice controlled expression of anger at supervisors*
(3) _____

Professional Help
(1) *None now*
(2) _____

Source: Joseph W. Kertesz, "Stress Management Plan," unpublished worksheet, Duke-Watts Family Medicine Center, Durham, N.C., 1982, in James C. Quick and Jonathan D. Quick, *Organizational Stress and Preventive Management,* McGraw-Hill Book Company, New York, 1984, p. 269.

Figure 16.15 INDIVIDUAL CONSEQUENCES OF STRESS		
Behavioral Consequences	**Psychological Consequences**	**Medical Consequences**
Smoking	Family problems	Heart disease and stroke
Alcohol abuse	Sleep disturbances	Backache and arthritis
Drug abuse	Sexual dysfunction	Ulcers
Accidents	Depression	Headaches
Violence	Psychogenic disability	Cancer
Appetite disorders	Burnout	Diabetes
		Cirrhosis
		Lung disease
		Skin disease

Source: James C. Quick and Jonathan D. Quick, *Organizational Stress and Preventive Management,* McGraw-Hill Book Company, New York, 1984, p. 301.

Figure 16.16 ORGANIZATIONAL CONSEQUENCES OF STRESS	
Direct Costs	**Indirect Costs**
Participation and membership: Absenteeism Tardiness Strikes and work stoppages Turnover	Loss of vitality: Low morale Low motivation Dissatisfaction
Performance on the job: Quality of productivity Quantity of productivity Grievances Accidents Unscheduled machine downtime and repair Material and supply overutilization Inventory shrinkages	Communication breakdown: Decline in frequency of contact Distortion of messages
	Faulty decision making: Communication breakdown Impaired judgment
	Quality of work relations: Distrust Disrespect
Compensation awards: Court-awarded Workers' compensation	Opportunity costs

Source: James C. Quick and Jonathan D. Quick, *Organizational Stress and Preventive Management,* McGraw-Hill Book Company, New York, 1984, p. 301.

WHAT CAN THE SUPERVISOR DO?

The supervisor can have a major impact on stress reduction in the workplace. In addition to the supervisory actions discussed above, there are other ways supervisors can personally affect stress levels within their departments. When the company offers stress management programs, be the first to sign up, and encourage others to join you. Perhaps the most important action a supervisor can take is to get his or her own stress under control. A supervisor's stress level is easily picked up by employees and serves to reinforce and elevate employee stress.

We have said that certain levels of stress are healthy and promote greater productivity. The supervisor should recognize the appropriate stress level for the job (there's one stress level for rotating tires and another for playing professional tennis, for example). Among the skills needed by a supervisor is the ability to key the stress level to the demands of the job, retain worker interest, and keep productivity levels high.

flights, McDonald's is testing a ban in dozens of its 9000 restaurants nationwide, and in Los Angeles smoking is no longer permitted in restaurants.

With so much emphasis on health and safety, many managers feel the risks of smoking are great enough to take action. Approaches usually take one of four forms: (1) a total ban—no smoking on the premises, (2) a ban on smoking at the workstation, (3) a ban on smoking other than in designated areas such as lounges, and (4) voluntary quit-smoking programs to help workers stop smoking. In the 1970s, only a brave company would have banned smoking; more and more are doing so today.

**COMPETENCY
CHECK**
Discuss the issue
of smoking in the
workplace.

Providing Assistance

To improve employee health and to reduce health care costs, businesses are using a variety of approaches. One that encompasses the broader view of employee health is the wellness program.

Wellness Programs

A national health insurance trade association defines **wellness** as a "freely chosen lifestyle aimed at achieving and maintaining an individual's good health."[33]

Wellness goes beyond accident prevention and the absence of disease to a state of vitality in the individual. An employee's state of health can affect his or her productivity, motivation, and creativity. Wellness programs offer management an approach to improving these employee contributions and to reducing the costs accruing from absenteeism, fatigue-related accidents, medical claims, and apathy. Hartman and Cozetti report a high degree of participation in wellness programs because employees:[34]

❑ perceive it to be a quality program because it is sponsored by the company.
❑ see it as a fringe benefit and feel they should take advantage of it.
❑ feel it is a convenient way to take care of their health.

Wellness programs take many forms. Among them are physical fitness programs (PFPs); others emphasize drug and alcohol rehabilitation, stress management, counseling, or detection of illnesses such as hypertension or cancer. Among the most popular are the PFPs. The National Industrial Recreation Association estimates that over 50,000 firms have PFPs and that more than 70 percent of these have been formed since 1975.[35] Figure 7.10 shows some of the benefits of physical fitness programs to participants and to the organization. Central States Health & Life Co. of Omaha has a wellness program called the SANE approach—smoking, alcohol, nutrition, and exercise. Bill Kizer, Central States' chairman, says that Central States' impressive growth is not because of his leadership but because Central States is a wellness workplace in which employees pursue personal and career goals in a supportive environment. Such large companies as Johnson & Johnson, AT&T, Coors, and Control Data point to real dollar savings from health-promotion programs for their employees.[36]

Johnson and Johnson has instituted a "Live for Life" program. In an effort to evaluate the cost-effectiveness of the program, J&J is collecting data to determine:

❑ employee biometric changes (changes in blood lipids, blood pressure, body fat, weight, and maximum oxygen uptake.)
❑ employee behavioral changes (changes in smoking, alcohol use, physical activity, nutrition, heart behavior patterns, job performance, and human relations).
❑ employee attitudinal changes (changes in general well-being, job satisfaction, company perception, and health attitudes).

A systematic cost-benefit study is possible because Johnson & Johnson is a self-insured company. Any substantial decrease in illness-care claims attributable to a health maintenance program will be of importance to both the employees and the company. Other measures to be analyzed are absenteeism, turnover rates, accident rates, and a host of employee and management attitudes toward themselves, their work, and one another.[37] Johnson & Johnson tested wellness just as the company would experiment with a new drug, with both a test group and a control group. The company tracked medical costs and productivity of 5,000 workers at three subsidiaries. During the first year, a wellness program cost more than it saved; in the second year, it broke even. In the third year, it saved enough money to pay back the losses incurred during the first year.[38]

The supervisor's role in wellness programs, other than personal participation, is mostly supportive. Encouraging employee participation, commenting on individual progress, and communicating to employees and to other managers any reduced costs or improved productivity by participants will provide positive reinforcement.

Employee Assistance Programs (EAPs)

Employee assistance programs (EAPs) are company-sponsored programs directed toward improving the quality of work life of their employees. EAPs can assist employees in a variety of ways: by improving their physical fitness, by combating substance abuse, by controlling stress, by teaching them to deal with financial problems, and in a host of other ways. For example, Xerox's employee assistance program (XEAP) provides assistance to company employees and their families in areas such as marital counseling, substance abuse, and financial counseling.

Other companies have invested significant amounts of money to begin their EAPs. Kimberly-Clark's health management program began in 1977 with the stated goal of significantly reducing absenteeism, health care costs, and cardiovascular risk factors. Kimberly-Clark's program includes a physical fitness program; health education programs and activities including nutrition counseling, smoking control, exercises for low back pain, and diet management; and a series under the heading of Self-Instruction Classes.[39]

Supervisors should encourage employees to take advantage of company-sponsored employee assistance programs to help them become more physically, mentally, and emotionally healthy individuals. If the company studies cited above are any indication, healthy employees are more productive workers. As a supervisor, you should also take advantage of the programs offered.

Other Groups and Agencies

Sometimes employees need assistance beyond that which is available in the workplace. Perhaps the problems are beyond the capability or expertise of the supervisor or even the company's professional counselor, if such a counselor is even available. Employee assistance programs may not be available when or where the worker needs them. In these situations, the supervisor should know about outside sources of assistance and should direct employees to them.

**COMPETENCY
CHECK**

Can you describe
three ways in
which supervisors
can provide
assistance to
employees with
problems?

There are numerous governmental agencies and private groups that offer their services and assistance at no cost or for a nominal fee. Supervisors should try to maintain a list of local agencies or groups to which employees may be referred. In addition, many organizations offer booklets and pamphlets that offer assistance or provide information. For example, the Center for Medical Consumers and Health Care Information in New York offers publications as well as a free phone-in library called "Tel-Med." The Office of Health Information and Health Promotion and the National Health Information Clearinghouse, both in Washington, D.C., provide consumers with information. Supervisors should be aware of the many services offered by these outside agencies or groups and refer workers to them when appropriate.

Employee Rights in a Safe and Healthy Workplace

It would be great if all the health issues that a supervisor faces were as positive as wellness and employee assistance programs. Unfortunately, they are not. Negative issues that have an impact on the worker and on the work environment continue to emerge. They are often emotionally charged, involving feelings and emotions as well as health issues.

Acquired Immune Deficiency Syndrome (AIDS)

No health issue in recent history has so frightened the world as has AIDS. A virulent viral infection with no known cure, AIDS is not only a death sentence to those who acquire it but it is also spreading at an alarming rate. While the major methods of transmission have been identified, the Centers for Disease Control and Prevention have been unable to classify a likely method of transmission in 6 percent of the cases studied.[40] The disease is causing generalized fear throughout society.

AIDS is different from the communicable diseases that businesses have had some experience in handling. It causes many new problems, and businesses are learning to handle these problems mostly by trial and error. Concerned for the health of their other workers, in the past some companies fired AIDS victims. Others refused to do so. With the passage of the 1992 revisions to the Americans with Disabilities Act, AIDS sufferers are now protected from discrimination based on their disability.

One of the greatest problems stems from the stigma attached to the disease. Although it has recently been acknowledged that AIDS can be contracted by anyone, the majority of victims so far have been homosexual males or intravenous drug users, who suffer from a social stigma as well as the life-threatening illness. Victims are often shunned by their fellow workers, their friends, and even their families out of fear of contagion. One worker refused to work on a computer keyboard that was used by an AIDS patient on another shift. Some will not even shake the hand of an AIDS patient. These fears of the unknown, along with lack of public education, make combating the stigma more difficult. To get the known facts about AIDS to the public, the Surgeon General in 1988 mailed a brochure explaining the disease to every household in the United States. The media, medical and health agencies, schools, and other organizations offer programs to educate the public about the facts, to allay fears, and to promote prevention.

Most companies have now adopted policies that deal with AIDS. Figure 16.17 illustrates one such policy.

COMPETENCY CHECK

Can you describe how AIDS has affected workers' perceptions of a healthy workplace?

Workplace Choice

Prior to the March 1991 Supreme Court ruling in the case of *Automobile Workers v. Johnson Controls, Inc.,* many companies had very strict industrial fetus protection policies. These policies excluded fertile females from certain high-risk jobs because of the potential harm to unborn babies. Some companies included in their policy the demand that women either quit their jobs, be transferred to other jobs typically paying less money, or be sterilized when there are risks to the health of the unborn child. For example, in the early 1980s, Johnson Controls, Inc., makers of batteries, began rejecting new female hires and transferring women off the factory floor at its plants around the country. The policy was sweeping, including every women under the age of 70 who couldn't prove that she was sterile.[41] Before American Cyanamid relaxed its fetus protection rules, five women at its Willow Island, West Virginia, chemical plant submitted to sterilization—the only form of birth control deemed effective by the company.[42]

Figure 16.17

ACQUIRED IMMUNE DEFICIENCY SYNDROME (AIDS) POLICY NO. ER 20

POLICY

Maintenance of a safe work environment is a fundamental value of ABC Corporation. ABC Corporation also believes that employees with AIDS should be allowed to continue gainful and active employment to the extent their conditions can be reasonably and safely accommodated. We believe that we have a role in educating employees and their families to address concerns that may arise regarding AIDS in the workplace.

PROCEDURES

EMPLOYEES AFFECTED BY AIDS

Employees are encouraged, for their safety, as well as the safety of others, to inform the company that they have AIDS. This will enable the Company to provide reasonable accommodation to the employee's condition and take appropriate safety precautions. The employee's decision to continue working will be supported by the Company, so long as safety can be maintained and reasonable accommodations can be provided. As in the case of any illness, an employee's privacy will be respected.

LOCAL AIDS PROCEDURES

Each location is expected to develop procedures to implement the Company's policy/procedures on AIDS. Locations should follow current return-to-work rules and practices regarding physician's certification of an employee's ability to return to work and reasonable accommodations or precautions that may be required. Each location should seek appropriate medical advice where there are questions about the employee's ability to continue working or the availability of reasonable accommodations in conformity with the AIDS policy. Supervisors will be informed of restrictions on the duties of persons with AIDS and of necessary accommodations. Locations should also develop procedures for confidentiality, and become familiar with and follow developments in state and local laws and regulations pertaining to AIDS and their implications in the workplace. Questions concerning the Company's AIDS policy or its application to a particular situation should be directed to your Human Resource Director.

EDUCATION/COMMUNICATION

Corporate will provide all locations with educational materials that address issues relating to AIDS and its impact on the workplace. The materials provided should not necessarily be considered all inclusive, and in no case should be considered a substitute for medical advice. Available information and materials can be expected to change as medical knowledge develops. Employees should be encouraged to consult their personal physicians for advice on medical questions.

All first aid/medical personnel are expected to remain current in proper techniques for handling emergencies. In order to promote consistency in first aid procedures and training with respect to AIDS, locations are encouraged to use Red Cross training consultants and services.

WHAT CAN THE SUPERVISOR DO?

Learn as much as you can about the disease. You will be serving as a role model for your workers, whether you intend to or not. Attend company-sponsored educational seminars. Stay as objective as possible in your dealings with your workers. Remember that your job is to supervise the *performance* of your workers; the workers should know that you are doing so.

Most important, follow your company policy strictly not only to the narrow interpretation but also to its intent.

The Supreme Court Justices ruled that companies cannot exclude females from high-risk jobs because of the potential harm to unborn babies. "Women as capable of doing their jobs as their male counterparts may not be forced to choose between having a child and having a job," wrote Justice Harry Blackmun in a majority opinion.[43] The justices clearly saw the fetus protection policy as sex discrimination and a violation of Title VII of the Civil Rights Act of 1964 and the Pregnancy Discrimination Act. One of the arguments made was that men were allowed the choice of working under conditions that were not risk-free and that might impair their ability to father healthy children, but women were denied the right to choose.

Companies have argued that employers are confronted with two rather untenable alternatives regarding female employees who perform jobs that might cause birth defects should the employee become pregnant. The company can refuse to employ women for these positions, in which case, if sued, they would certainly lose; or the employer can hire women in those positions and face a potential lawsuit if children are born impaired. While the employee can waive her right to sue, she cannot waive the rights of the unborn child. When born, the deformed child will have a cause for action against the employer. Whether the suit will be successful will depend on many factors; businesses are thus deeply concerned about the potential impact on their survival.

Worker Response to an Unsafe Environment

Each employee is entitled to a safe work environment. The Williams-Steiger Occupational Safety and Health Act of 1970 legally encoded what employers had long accepted as a moral contract with their employees. In addition to the specific safety requirements, OSHA's "general-duty" clause protects employees from unsafe and unhealthy conditions in areas in which no standards have yet been adopted. Therefore, the absence of specific standards does not negate the overall necessity of providing workers with a safe and healthy work environment.

What can employees do if they believe their employer is violating a job safety or health standard? Each employee has the right to request from the Department of Labor (DOL) an inspection of any perceived safety or health problem. The request must identify specific violations rather than general ones. A copy of the request must be sent to the employer. While the request to the DOL must be signed by the complainant, no signature is required on the copy that goes to the employer.

Do employees have the legal right to refuse to work or perform an assigned task if the work itself or the work environment is perceived by them to be unsafe? The following are legal conditions for refusing to work when safety is the issue:[44]

1. Normal procedures to resolve the problem(s) resulting in unsafe work conditions have not been successful.
2. The employee(s) notified the appropriate management officials and tried to have the condition(s) corrected, but the unsafe condition(s) remains.
3. The workers' fears are supported by objective physical evidence, and workers show a good-faith belief that the conditions are, indeed, unsafe.

COMPETENCY CHECK
Can you explain employee rights in a safe and healthy environment?

Employees have a right to a safe and healthy workplace. It is in the best interests of both the employer and the employee to provide one.

COMPETENCY REVIEW

1. Discuss three reasons for maintaining a safe and healthy workplace.
2. Discuss management's role in safety and health programs.
3. Describe legislation that has had an impact on workplace safety and health.
4. Discuss the role of OSHA in workplace safety and health.
5. Discuss three elements in the work environment that might cause accidents.
6. State three ways through which the supervisor can develop safety awareness among workers.
7. Explain the importance of observation and inspection in maintaining safety.
8. Discuss the supervisor's role in investigating and reporting accidents.
9. Define two methods of measuring worker safety.
10. Explain the role of ergonomics in the workplace.
11. Define cumulative trauma disorders and describe some measures that companies may take to reduce CTDs.
12. Identify sources of organizational stress and define several stressors within each source.
13. Describe several actions that organizations, supervisors, and individuals can take to reduce employees' job-related stress.
14. Discuss the issue of smoking in the workplace.
15. Describe methods companies can use to provide assistance to employees.
16. Explain employee rights in a safe and healthy workplace.

APPLICATIONS

1. As a supervisor, your top responsibility is the safety and health of the employees reporting to you. It is not only a managerial responsibility but a moral one.

Equally important, it is a responsibility that, if fulfilled conscientiously, will ensure your peace of mind.

If you are a supervisor, answer the questions on the questionnaire that follows based on your present situation. If you are not a supervisor, assume the role of a former supervisor or manager you have had and answer as you perceived his or her safety and health actions. Your instructor will help you determine and analyze your score.

<u>Yes</u>   <u>No</u>

___ ___ a. Do you try on a continuing basis to create and sustain employee awareness with regard to the importance of safety?

___ ___ b. Are you firm and consistent when it comes to the enforcement of safety regulations and rules?

___ ___ c. Are you constantly on the alert to track down hazardous conditions in your department?

___ ___ d. If an accident occurs, or if you uncover a safety hazard, do you always make the best effort you can to track down its cause and take steps to prevent its recurrence?

___ ___ e. Do you make special efforts to indoctrinate new employees in such a way that they will be conscious of the importance of safe performance from the first day they start working?

___ ___ f. Do you give all your people the training they need to ensure safe job practices and conduct?

___ ___ g. Do you promptly make a written report of all accidents?

___ ___ h. Do you encourage first aid for every injury no matter how minor it may be?

___ ___ i. Do you firmly insist on good housekeeping practices?

___ ___ j. Do you inspect your operation on a regular basis to make sure drawers are kept closed, flooring is in good repair, objects do not protrude from shelves, etc., so that the possibility of tripping and falling is kept to a minimum?

___ ___ k. Do you check all machines to make sure they are properly grounded and that electric cords are in good condition?

___ ___ l. Do you rigidly enforce NO SMOKING regulations in areas where flammable liquids or combustibles are stored?

___ ___ m. Where machine guards or shields are called for, do you always insist on their use?

___ ___ n. Do you also insist that employees wear safety goggles, safety shoes, helmets, and safety gloves as required?

___ ___ o. Do you encourage your people to report hazards as soon as they are spotted and give you suggestions for safer performance?

Total number of Yes answers _____

Source: "Safety: You're Responsible," Dartnell Corporation, Chicago, Il., Apr. 26, 1983.

2. Morgan Santos, Inc. (MSI), filed OSHA reports for five accidents involving missed workdays during the past year. The injured employees missed a total of 15 days as a result of the accidents. The company's 125 full-time employees worked 40 hours per week for the full year, less 2 weeks of vacation time.

   MSI is preparing its annual safety and health report and wishes to know its incidence and severity rates. Using the OSHA formulas, calculate the two measures.

3. Smoking is a hotly debated issue. Headlines such as the following, which appeared in *Life* in January 1988, are even more common in the 1990s:

AS A RESULT OF A NATIONAL ANTISMOKING CAMPAIGN, A FEDERAL RULING RESTRICTED SMOKING BY 890,000 GOVERNMENT EMPLOYEES IN 6,800 U.S. BUILDINGS. IN ALL, SOME 40 STATES REGULATED SMOKING IN PUBLIC PLACES. LOS ANGELES PROHIBITS ALL SMOKING IN RESTAURANTS.

   In addition to federal antismoking regulations, many states and cities have enacted antismoking laws. Find out what the regulations are in your city and state. What are the regulations in your school and in your workplace?

Case I

"BUT I DIDN'T SAY I *SAW* THE ACCIDENT"

Part A

Assume that you are preparing to report this accident: Peg Sutton watched the ambulance carrying Julio Rivera, a stock clerk, pull out and head for the hospital. "Poor Julio," she said. "His vacation is scheduled to start next week." Then, turning to the five stock clerks who had gathered, she said, "Okay, back to the scene of the accident, everybody. We need the facts for the accident report." On the way back to the produce section, she thought about the accident. She had been a produce supervisor for this giant supermarket chain for 3 years and had recently been chosen over several other candidates for the job in the big new showplace store.

"Two accidents in the first month," she thought. "My safety record is shot. All that training . . . all the pep talks . . . all the work with the union rep to develop safety procedures. And for what? How could Julio slip on a grape and trigger a bone-breaking avalanche of coconuts on his hand? And why in my department?" She mentally ran through the version of the accident she had heard from Sean Bailey, an assistant supervisor, while they waited for the ambulance. Julio had pushed the loaded cart from cold storage to produce at his usual fast clip. To save a trip, he had placed a crate of coconuts on the back of the loaded cart, partly resting on the handlebars. As he turned the corner at produce, his foot found the grape. As he fell, one of his feet hit the cart, bumping it into the display case. The impact sent the coconuts crashing to the floor onto Julio's hand and foot. That was it, as she recalled.

On the way back, she picked up her accident report. Back at produce, she stepped over the rope blocking the area off from customer traffic. "Okay, Sean, you were in charge here when Julio fell. Let's hear again what happened."

Use the form below to identify the facts of the incident. Was there a part of the accident for which you found no appropriate term? If so, explain that part in brief terminology like that on the checklist.

IDENTIFYING ACCIDENT FACTS

What part of the body was injured? (Description: right/left, location, etc.)

Head _____	Shoulders _____	Hips _____
Eyes _____	Arms _____	Legs _____
Ears _____	Hands _____	Knees _____
Teeth _____	Chest _____	Feet _____
Face _____	Abdomen _____	Other _____
Neck _____	Back _____	

(Continued)

IDENTIFYING ACCIDENT FACTS (CONTINUED)

Identify and describe the nature of the injury.

Cut _____   Puncture _____   Skin eruption(s) _____
Fracture _____   Bruise _____   Hernia _____
Sprain _____   Burn _____   Other _____
Amputation _____   Foreign body _____

Identify and describe the cause of the injury.

Fall _____   Exposure to temperature extremes/burns _____
Collision with or struck by moving object(s) _____   Caught in/by/between objects _____
Inhalation/absorption of toxic substance(s) _____   Other _____
Electric shock _____

Identify and describe the hazardous condition that caused the injury. If none, check here. _____

Defective tools/equipment _____   Improperly guarded or unguarded area _____
Faulty design/construction _____   Inadequate ventilation _____
Workplace arrangement _____   Improper clothing _____
Inadequate lighting _____   Improper housekeeping _____

Identify the equipment/facilities involved. If none, check here. _____

Machines/equipment _____   Elevators _____   Ladders _____
Tools _____   Doors/windows/walls _____   Electrical apparatus _____
Materials/supplies _____   Floors _____   Other _____
Vehicles _____   Stairs _____

Identify and describe the human act that caused or contributed to the accident. If none, check here. _____

Using equipment/tools unsafely _____   Unsafe loading/mixing _____
Failure to follow correct operating procedure(s) _____   Improper lifting/carrying _____
Failure to report unsafe condition(s) _____   Horseplay _____
Operating without authority _____   Poor housekeeping _____
Using unsafe speed _____   Being in an unsafe area/position _____
Using defective equipment _____   Other _____

Identify and describe other factors that contributed to the accident. If none, check here. _____

Failure to follow instructions _____   Lack of training _____
Lack of skill/knowledge _____   Late or no report to medical staff _____
Involvement of other persons _____   Other _____

Part B

Sutton has met the produce group back at the scene of the accident to continue her investigation. She has reviewed the account of Bailey, one of the assistant supervisors, and thinks she has a clear picture of the mishap. On her way back, within earshot of produce, she stops briefly to let a loaded bread dolly pass and overhears an interesting conversation between Bailey and Quan, a new produce clerk.

> Quan: Why did you give her the impression you were here, Sean? You know you were back at the Coke machine.
> Bailey: Oh, knock it off, Ann. I didn't say I saw Julio fall. She just asked me how it happened. Besides, you know every clerk is responsible for watching the floor. I can't do it all. Why didn't you pick up the grape?
> Quan: Don't put the blame on me! You were on duty, and . . .

Seeing Sutton approach, Quan stops. Sutton ignores the conversation for the moment—she will handle that problem later.

"Let's hear it, Sean," she says as she dates her report. Bailey gives essentially the same story, and the others corroborate it.

"Was there any horseplay before the accident?" she asks. All agree there was none. She examines the cart and the display case. Except for a few scratches and some mashed fruit, there is no damage. Coconuts are all over the floor, but only a few are cracked.

"Well, Julio seems to have suffered the worst of this," Sutton says as she looks over the accident report she has to fill in. She will complete items 20 and 21 first, while her memory and notes are fresh.

"Okay," she says. "Let's get the place cleaned up and get back to work. Sean, get maintenance out here to do the floor." As she turns to leave, she says, "And Sean, see me in the produce office when your shift ends, please."

1. Using the following Accident Investigation Report on pp. 516 & 517 and the information in the case, carry out Sutton's responsibility for items 20 and 21.
   a. Describe how the accident occurred (item 20).
   b. Report the accident sequence in reverse order (item 21).
2. What suggestions can you make for improving the safety of the produce operation? Consider people, processes, and equipment. (You might want to review the checklist for identifying key facts to help here.)
3. If you were Sutton, what would you say to Bailey about item 24 when he came to your office?

Figure 16.6
ACCIDENT INVESTIGATION REPORT

ACCIDENT INVESTIGATION REPORT

CASE NUMBER

COMPANY _____ ADDRESS _____

DEPARTMENT _____ LOCATION (if different from mailing address) _____

1. NAME OF INJURED	2. SOCIAL SECURITY NUMBER	3. SEX ☐ M ☐ F	4. AGE	5. DATE of ACCIDENT

6. HOME ADDRESS	7. EMPLOYEE'S USUAL OCCUPATION	8. OCCUPATION at TIME of ACCIDENT

11. EMPLOYMENT CATEGORY
☐ Regular, full-time
☐ Temporary   ☐ Nonemployee
☐ Regular, part-time   ☐ Seasonal

9. LENGTH of EMPLOYMENT
☐ Less than 1 mo.   ☐ 6 mos. to 5 yrs.
☐ 1–5 mos.   ☐ More than 5 yrs.

10. TIME in OCCUP. at TIME of ACCIDENT
☐ Less than 1 mo.   ☐ 6 mos to 5 yrs.
☐ 1–5 mos.   ☐ More than 5 yrs.

13. NATURE of INJURY and PART of BODY	12. CASE NUMBERS and NAMES of OTHERS INJURED in SAME ACCCIDENT

14. NAME and ADDRESS of PHYSICIAN

16. TIME of INJURY
A. _____ A.M. P.M.
B. Time within shift
C. Type of shift

17. SEVERITY of INJURY
☐ Fatality
☐ Lost workdays—days away from work
☐ Lost workdays—days of restricted activity
☐ Medical treatment
☐ First aid
☐ Other, specify _____

15. NAME and ADDRESS of HOSPITAL

18. SPECIFIC LOCATION of ACCIDENT

ON EMPLOYER'S PREMISES? ☐ Yes ☐ No

19. PHASE OF EMPLOYEE'S WORKDAY at TIME of INJURY
☐ During rest period   ☐ Entering or leaving plant
☐ During meal period   ☐ Performing work duties
☐ Working overtime   ☐ Other

20. DESCRIBE HOW the ACCIDENT OCCURRED

_____
_____
_____
_____

21. ACCIDENT SEQUENCE: Describe in reverse order of occurrence events preceding the injury and accident. Starting with the injury and moving backward in time, reconstruct the sequence of events that led to the injury.
A. Injury Event _____
B. Accident Event _____
C. Preceding Event #1 _____
D. Preceding Event #2, #3, etc. _____

(Continued)

Figure 16.6
ACCIDENT INVESTIGATION REPORT (CONTINUED)

22. TASK and ACTIVITY at TIME of ACCIDENT

A. General type of task _____

B. Specific activity _____

C. Employee was working:

☐ Alone ☐ With crew or fellow worker ☐ Other, specify _____

23. POSTURE of EMPLOYEE

_____

24. SUPERVISION at TIME of ACCIDENT

☐ Directly supervised   ☐ Not supervised

☐ Indirectedly supervised   ☐ Supervision not feasible

25. CAUSAL FACTORS. Events and conditions that contributed to the accident. Include those identified by use of the Guide for Identifying Causal Factors and Corrective Actions.

_____

_____

_____

_____

_____

_____

_____

_____

26. CORRECTIVE ACTIONS. Those that have been, or will be, taken to prevent recurrence. Include those identified by use of the Guide for Identifying Causal Factors and Corrective Actions.

_____

_____

_____

_____

_____

_____

_____

_____

_____

_____

PREPARED BY _____

TITLE _____

DEPARTMENT _____ DATE _____

Developed by the National Safety Council

APPROVED _____

TITLE _____ DATE _____

APPROVED _____

TITLE _____ DATE _____

Source: Reprinted with permission of the National Safety Council Accident Prevention Manual for Business & Industry: *Administration Programs,* 10th ed. National Safety Council, Itasca, Il., 1992, pp. 306–307.

Case II

"BUT I DON'T LIKE TO EXERCISE, AND I DON'T EAT BROCCOLI"

Many companies have implemented employee health programs, in which workers are provided with information and facilities designed to increase their physical and emotional fitness. Some of the programs come with bonuses for participation, some with penalties for nonparticipation.

If you are employed by Inner-View Ltd. in Chesapeake, Virginia, and you decide to spend your evening drinking in bars, become drunk, and smash up your car on the way home, Inner-View is not going to pay your hospital bill. The company also caps medical payments for people who get hurt riding motorcycles or all-terrain vehicles. Employees of Jonathan Corp. in Norfolk, Virginia, can smoke if they wish, but their health insurance is going to cost smokers 10 percent more than nonsmokers.

In 1991, Dominion Resources, headquartered in Richmond, Virginia, decided to pay $10 a month extra to employees there who wear seat belts, don't smoke, and keep their weight, blood pressure, and cholesterol within prescribed limits. Metro Machine Corp. of Norfolk, Virginia, gives a company-paid membership in an athletic club as long as the employee uses it regularly. It also provides reimbursement for completing weight management or smoking cessation programs. Included, too, is an hour of free on-site dental care every 6 months, no matter what the care involves, and annual flu shots.

USAA encourages its employees to take periodic stretch breaks, bans smoking completely on site, and insists on low-fat additions to its cafeteria menu.

1. What is your opinion of these components of the companies' wellness programs?
2. Should employees be penalized for their actions off the job? Why or why not?
3. Should bonuses be given for employee actions that are clearly for the good of the employees' health? Why or why not?
4. Why are many companies using the strategies suggested above?

Source: Dave Mayfield, "Sweating Out Rising Health Costs," *Business Weekly* section of *The Virginian-Pilot and The Ledger-Star,* Apr. 20, 1992, p. 12.

Scoring System for Quiz, Figure 16.2:

Give yourself 3 points for any *c* answer, 2 points for a *b* answer, and 1 point for an *a* answer. If you scored 45, you have no worries and probably no accidents. If you scored between 35 and 44, you need to work at it still. If you scored between 25 and 34, you're not quite there, and if you scored under 24, maybe you ought to see the boss about a transfer.

REFERENCES

1. Curt Suplee, "The Electronic Sweatshop," *The Washington Post,* Jan. 3, 1988, p. C1.
2. "Our Jobs More Than Just Pain in the Neck," AP, *The Virginian-Pilot and The Ledger-Star,* July 28, 1993, p. 6.
3. Robert Furger, "Danger at Your Fingertips," *PC World,* May 1993, p. 10.
4. Marilyn Joyce, "Ergonomics Will Take Center Stage During '90s and into New Century," *Occupational Safety and Health,* January 1991, p. 32.
5. *All about OSHA,* U.S. Department of Labor and OSHA, 1985, rev. ed., p. 3.
6. Ibid., p. 2.
7. Ibid., pp. 18–23.
8. William H. Miller, "Back in the Spotlight," *Industry Week,* Aug. 5, 1991, p. 11.
9. The discussion of OSHA is based on *All about OSHA,* op. cit.; *Occupational Safety and Health Act of 1970,* 91st Cong., Pub. L. 91–596, 5.2193, Dec. 29, 1970; and *OSHA: Safety and Health Is Our Middle Name, Four Ways OSHA Can Help,* OSHA 3076, 1984.
10. Based on Petersen, op. cit., pp. 46–47.
11. Martin E. Personick and Ethel C. Jackson, "Injuries and Illness in the Workplace, 1990," *Monthly Labor Review,* April 1992, p. 37.
12. George Terry, *Self Review in Supervision,* Learning Systems, 1975, p. 73.
13. John A. Jenkins, "Self-directed Work Force Promotes Safety," *HR Magazine,* February 1990, p. 55.
14. Discussion based on Ravinder Nath and Barry Gilmore, "Managing Computer Supervision Systems," *Management Solutions,* July 1987, pp. 5–11.
15. Michael R. Carrell and Frank E. Kuzmits, *Personnel-Human Resource Management,* 2d ed., Charles E. Merrill Books, Inc., Columbus, Ohio, 1986, p. 399.
16. Robert H. Rosen, *Healthy Companies, A Human Resources Approach,* American Management Association, New York, 1986, p. 17.
17. Ibid., pp. 20–21.
18. J. Vernon Glenn, "Ergonomic Testing," *Human Resources Management Ideas and Trends,* May 2, 1986, pp. 70–72.
19. Joyce, op. cit., p. 31.
20. G. Gordon Long, "Ergonomics Can Show the Way to Efficiency and Productivity," *Office Systems,* December 1985, pp. 65–68.
21. Nanda K. Kittusamy, O. Geoffrey Okogbaa, and A. J. G. Babu, "A Preliminary Audit for Ergonomics Design in Manufacturing Environments," *Industrial Engineering,* July 1992, p. 47.
22. Patricia M. Fernberg, "Tailoring the Workstation to the Worker," *Modern Office Technology,* June 1993, p. 26.
23. Dave Mayfield, "Sweating Out Rising Health Costs," *Business Weekly* section of *The Virginian-Pilot and The Ledger-Star,* Norfolk, Va., Apr. 23, 1992, p. 12.
24. Aileen Kantor, "Making the Workplace a Fit Place," *Business and Health,* July 1991, p. 70.
25. Joyce, op. cit., p. 31.
26. Jonathan M. Moses, "Carpal-Tunnel-Syndrome Suits Are Consolidated by U.S. Judge," *The Wall Street Journal,* June 3, 1992, p. B6.
27. Joyce, op. cit., p. 34.
28. Ibid., p. 37.
29. James C. Quick and Jonathan D. Quick, *Organizational Stress and Preventive Management,* McGraw-Hill Book Company, New York, 1984.
30. Ibid., p. 155.
31. "Job Strategies," *Glamour,* June 1993, p. 96.
32. Timothy Noah, "EPA Declares 'Passive' Smoke a Human Carcinogen," *The Wall Street Journal,* Jan. 6, 1993, p. B1.

33. *Your Guide to Wellness at the Worksite,* Health Association of America, 1983, p. 3.

34. Stephen W. Hartman and Janet Cozzeto, "Wellness in the Workplace," *Personnel Administrator,* vol. 29, no. 8, August 1984, pp. 108–109. Copyright 1984, The American Society for Personnel Administration, Alexandria, Va.

35. Jack N. Kondrasuk, "Corporate Physical Fitness Programs: The Role of the Personnel Department," *Personnel Administrator,* vol. 29, no. 12, December 1984, pp. 75–80.

36. Fred W. Schote and Sandra Wendel, "Wellness with a Track Record," *Personnel Journal,* April 1992, pp. 98–104.

37. Kenneth Pelletier, *Healthy People in Unhealthy Places,* Delacorte Press/Seymour Lawrence, New York, 1984, p. 144.

38. Neal Templin, "Johnson & Johnson 'Wellness' Program For Workers Shows Healthy Bottom Line", *The Wall Street Journal,* May 20, 1990, pp. B1 & B5.

39. Pelletier, p. 147.

40. *AIDS—The Workplace Issues,* American Management Association, New York, 1985, p. 9.

41. "Health," *Vogue,* May 1990, p. 202.

42. Ibid., p. 203.

43. Jill Smolowe, "Weighing Some Heavy Metal," *Time,* Apr. 1, 1991, p. 60.

44. John J. Hoover, "Workers Have New Rights to Health and Safety," *Readings in Personnel and Human Resource Management,* 2d ed., Randall S. Schuler and Stuart A. Youngblood (eds.), West Publishing Company, St. Paul, Minn., 1984, pp. 396ff.

SUGGESTED READINGS

"AMA Takes a Stand on Seating," *Modern Office Technology,* February 1992, p. 14.

Blanchard, Kenneth, and Norman Vincent Peale: *The Power of Ethical Management,* William Morrow & Company, Inc., New York, 1988.

Holder, Harold D., and Donald W. Cunningham: "Alcoholism Treatment for Employees and Family Members: Its Effect on Health Care Costs," *Alcohol Health and Research World,* vol. 16, no. 2, 1992, pp. 149–153.

LaBar, Gregg: "What If Your Workers Had the 'Right-to-Act'?" *Occupational Hazards,* February 1990, p. 49.

Mahone, David B.: "Review of System Designs Employs Ergonomics Prior to Work Injuries," *Occupational Health and Safety,* May 1993, pp. 88ff.

Miller, William H.: "Back in the Spotlight," *Industry Week,* Aug. 5, 1991, p. 11.

Polakoff, Phillip L.: "Ergonomics: Diagnosis and Treatment for Ailing Workplace Performance," *Occupational Health and Safety,* 1992, pp. 64–66.

Rosen, Robert H.: *The Healthy Company,* Jeremy P. Tarcher, Publisher, Los Angeles, 1991.

"Thousands Face Danger on Job as OSHA Fiddles," *The Virginian-Pilot and The Ledger-Star,* Norfolk, Va., Sept. 11, 1991, p. A2.

Templin, Neal: "Johnson & Johnson 'Wellness' Program for Workers Shows Healthy Bottom Line," *The Wall Street Journal,* May 20, 1990, p. B1.

GLOSSARY

cumulative trauma disorder   A disorder that affects the musculoskeletal and nervous systems, most commonly the lower back, wrists, and tendons.

ergonomics   A science that tries to design the work, the workplace, and the tools to fit the worker.

stress   A patterned, unconscious response to a stressor.

wellness   A freely chosen lifestyle aimed at achieving and maintaining good health.

APPENDIX
A Career in Supervision

When an employee has worked hard and shown evidence of being a team player who is dependable and creative and possesses those interpersonal skills important to getting along with others, the time often comes when the manager says, "You're being promoted!"

Businesses can hire supervisors directly from outside the organization, but most companies find it in their best interest to provide career development programs for their employees. Consequently, most supervisors move up from within the ranks; they have proved themselves on the job. Through career planning, workers and the organization can match career aspirations with opportunities available in the organization. When a vacancy occurs, the organization can identify workers whose aspirations, skills, and experiences qualify them for the job. In this way, the organization retains a good worker and minimizes staffing costs.

When vacancy notices (sometimes called *job bids*) are posted in the organization, qualified workers should apply immediately. Success in performing the technical aspects of the job should have been documented in performance appraisals. Workers who are ready to transfer from the dependency stage of working under a supervisor's direction to working independently and directing the work of others probably have been identified.

Another common avenue into a management career is through a management-trainee program. A worker may use this entry method to move from operations into management, but the management-trainee method is more common as the entry route for recent college graduates. The financial industry routinely hires recent college graduates as trainees. In banking, management trainees move through several departments, spending 2 to 6 weeks in each. This rotation gives them an orientation to the entire organization and also helps identify the special interests and aptitudes of individual workers.

The management-trainee method also gives the new employee an opportunity to work with several managers and to observe different management styles. This is a valuable experience, especially if the employee is preparing for his or her first managerial job.

Prepare to Become a Supervisor

Many people do not prepare for a career in supervision, but when an opportunity presents itself, they take it. Effective supervisors plan for advancement and a career in supervision. *Career planning* is the process of choosing an occupation and organization(s) that will lead to the achievement of career goals.

Many people who become supervisors start their careers in operations. Office supervisors often begin as secretaries, plant supervisors as line workers, accounting supervisors as accountants, building maintenance supervisors as janitors.

The first function of management is planning. The aspiring supervisor should consider planning as an essential step to entering management as a profession. Here are some ways you might prepare to become a supervisor:

1. Develop a career plan based on your own realistic appraisal of your interests, aptitudes, and abilities.
2. Study industry job trends to learn where opportunities will likely be available in the future. For example, the number of knowledge workers and service workers is rapidly surpassing the number of workers in manufacturing, agriculture, and mining. Concentrate on industries in which future job growth is predicted.
3. Obtain information on the U.S. Department of Labor projections of which occupations can expect job growth in the future. For example, more job growth is anticipated for technicians, service personnel, and sales and marketing personnel than for unskilled laborers or agricultural workers.
4. Take advantage of a career development program if your organization provides one.
5. Seek the advice of a career counselor to help you determine your career potential.
6. Inform your supervisor that you are interested in participating in any internal job trial programs that may be available. For example, some organizations offer operations workers or junior managers occasional supervisory assignments, short-term rotations to other departments, or short-term assistant assignments to upper management.
7. Participate in management training courses and seminars that may be offered by your own management, by colleges and universities, by professional organizations, and by professional consultants.
8. Read books and magazine articles on career development and advancement. Read books in which successful businesspeople tell about their careers and how they reached their personal and professional goals. Some local newspapers routinely print articles on conducting a job search, writing résumés and letters of application, interviewing for jobs, and succeeding on the job.
9. Ask for job information interviews. Network with friends and family to find successful businesspeople who will give you a sample interview. Prepare a list of questions to ask the interviewer. Ask for suggestions for jobs or careers for someone with your background. Ask the interviewer to look at your résumé

and make suggestions for improvements. Ask the interviewer how he or she reached his or her current position. Finally, ask if there are any jobs available in his or her company for which you are qualified. Be prepared for a no answer.

10. Pursue a college education. Having a college degree is more important for managers than for many other occupations. Many organizations offer tuition reimbursement programs as part of their employee benefit packages.

Make the Transition

The transition from being led to leading requires a shift in perspective. Rather than depending on others to provide motivation, a supervisor must be self-motivated and provide a motivational atmosphere for the workers he or she supervises.

WHAT CAN THE SUPERVISOR DO?

Become acquainted with the new positions. Learn about the specific responsibilities, the employees in the department, and the department's relationship to the entire organization. Being prepared is the first step.

1. *Take inventory.* You need to study the employees as well as prior departmental outcomes. Examine everything about the department, including the departmental structure and the jobs within the department.
   a. Pull last year's (quarter's) production or service records. Determine if the records show that the department is on target or if there is a problem that needs solving.
   b. Examine staffing levels and skills of department members to determine if the staffing levels are adequate or under/overstaffed and if the employees' skills are appropriate for the jobs.
   c. Define the strengths of individual employees so you can develop those strengths. At the same time, if there are obvious weaknesses, be aware of those as well.
2. *Use your own style.* You can learn to temper abrupt responses, to be more patient, and to work better with others. However, you cannot change your basic personality. You were promoted because of your knowledge, skills, and abilities. Changing your style after the promotion is unwise.
3. *Have confidence.* You were selected over other candidates. Understanding that and recognizing your ability to rise above others should provide you with the confidence to do the job.

Redefine the Role

A new supervisor must perceive and accept him- or herself as a supervisor and understand that his or her role will change. Redefine the role in a way that is comfortable for you and will be accepted by the staff members whom you will now supervise.

Learn to Delegate

You cannot do everything yourself. And, even if you could physically accomplish everything, this fosters neither your own growth nor the growth and development of your staff. There are some tasks for which delegation is appropriate. Other tasks should *not* be delegated. The effective supervisor knows the difference. One rule of thumb is: If the work does not have a direct bearing on your ability to plan, organize, staff, lead, and control, delegate it; if mistakes would have dire consequences, do it yourself!

Learn to Communicate

Many new supervisors fail because they don't communicate with their employees. Workers want to know what you expect from them, what changes will be made and how they will be affected, when they are doing a good job, and when they need to change their behaviors.

Recognize the Importance of Team Effort

Before becoming a supervisor, you probably concentrated on your own contribution to the team effort and genuinely worked to be a part of the team. As supervisor, while still a member of the team, you will now serve in the role of coach. As a coach, you will develop workers' individual talents targeted toward team achievement. To create teamwork, all employees must accept and embrace the philosophy of working for the group rather than for oneself. Your efforts, then, will be directed toward team building and maintenance.

Set an Example

One of the best ways to gain acceptance as a supervisor is to set an example for those whom you supervise. If you expect workers to come to work on time; to start work immediately; to treat others with respect; to follow organizational policies, procedures, and rules; and generally to be an exemplary employee, you must demonstrate these qualities as well. When you step into management, you become a role model—be a positive example of a good employee.

Work with Other Employees

Supervision often has been defined as working with and through other people and using the allocated resources to reach the goals of the organization. You must learn to work with your former peers (if you have been promoted from within) or with a whole new group of people (if you have moved to a different company).

Dealing with a variety of people with backgrounds different from your own requires some effort on your part. If you have not worked with older workers; workers of different cultural, ethnic, or religious backgrounds; workers of a different gender; or people with disabilities, you must carefully examine any biases or stereotypical beliefs you may have.

Working with a variety of people with differing values, background, and experiences is a challenge—one that should be met in the knowledge that each of us brings special talents and capabilities to the job. This variety gives supervisors a larger talent pool than if we were all alike, all with similar values and talents. Make good use of the opportunity.

Dealing with former peers is also a challenge. Perhaps this provides a greater concern for new supervisors than dealing with people with whom no previous contact has been made. Some former peers may have negative attitudes, and you must be prepared to deal with them. How are you going to deal with

- the employee who is loyal to the previous supervisor and is convinced no one can take his or her place?
- the employee who applied for and lost the position to you?
- the employee who views the change in supervisors as an opportunity to do nothing?
- the employee who tests you to see how much he or she can get away with or how far he or she can go before you will say something?
- the inadequate employee who was sheltered by the former supervisor?
- the employee who was overrated by the former supervisor in his or her performance appraisals?

There are no standard answers to these questions, because personalities will affect the way you approach each person. For example, if you know that the worker who applied for your position is resentful and is known to have a hot temper, your approach would be much different than with the person who, though disappointed by not getting the job, is still interested in doing the best job so that when another opportunity presents itself, he or she will be ready.

Some problems common to new supervisors in dealing with employees include:

- feeling guilty about asking employees to do low-level work. Many new supervisors have difficulty asking employees, especially former peers, to perform mundane, though necessary, routine tasks. Remember, however, that certain tasks must be performed and that some people are more appropriate than others to perform those tasks. It is obviously not good judgment for the supervisor to make reams of copies, clean office machines or plant equipment, or stuff envelopes, rather than assign those tasks to others.

☐ being too bossy and overbearing with employees. If you flaunt your new authority, become "bossy," and generally are a tyrant, you quickly alienate employees and lose their respect and cooperation.

☐ playing favorites. All supervisors should treat all employees fairly and equitably. It is sometimes tempting to single out an employee who is especially helpful and cooperative, and those employees should be rewarded, but not at the expense of others. Nor should they receive special treatment—just fair treatment. What about those people with whom you were friends before you were promoted? Alienating them is certainly not the answer. But you cannot afford to go to lunch regularly with former colleagues or to carry on non-work-related conversations while on the job. To the extent possible, be friendly with all employees. Remember, however, there is a difference between *friendliness* and *friendship*. Friendliness implies a warm and sympathetic attitude, while friendship involves intimacy and special consideration. As Auren Uris, in his book *The Executive Deskbook,* advises, "If you have developed a job friendship, you must make it clear to your friend that you cannot allow that relationship to interfere with your judgment on the job."

☐ being indecisive. Employees look to management for direction and support. Employees must sense that you are confident, even if you are not. When dealing with questions or decisions for which you lack sufficient information or are unsure of the answer, you may not be able to give an immediate answer. There is nothing wrong with saying "I don't know, but I will find out and get back to you by a certain date," as long as that is not your only answer. Give yourself enough time to research the answer, but be sure to provide the employee with the answer in a timely manner. Employees respect honesty and effort; they do *not* appreciate or respect those who try to bluff their way through.

☐ refusing to use employee know-how. Employees have a great deal of knowledge that you may initially lack. New supervisors cannot have all the answers immediately—there is a learning curve. Make use of the knowledge and experience that employees bring to the job. In the process, you will begin to develop *their* confidence and loyalty and *your* expertise. When an employee asks a question that you can't answer or you want to teach the employee, turn the question back to the employee. Say, "That's a good question; what do you think we should do?"

Remember, you don't have to know everything in order to be an effective supervisor. However, when you plan your future, set career goals, and strive to be a good supervisor, your chances of fulfilling your goals are much greater. Good luck!

WHAT CAN THE SUPERVISOR DO?

The following general guidelines for establishing yourself as an effective supervisor may assist you in making the transition.

- ❏ Set well-defined objectives. Be sure that workers are fully aware of what is expected of them and what their responsibilities are. Communicate clearly what kinds of work and work behaviors will be rewarded.
- ❏ Make policies clear and consistent. Communicate to employees what the policies mean and apply them consistently and equitably.
- ❏ Develop workers' individual talents as much as possible. Help employees feel important about what they do.
- ❏ Encourage and allow employees to make choices that will give them some control over their work environment whenever possible.
- ❏ Define interoffice and interdepartmental relations so that workers are not confused about their roles within and outside their departments.
- ❏ Establish a climate in which employees can meet their objectives without unnecessary conflict, distraction, and interruption.
- ❏ Give a direct and immediate response to workers' concerns.
- ❏ Help employees sort out priorities and work within their comfort zones. A workload that is too light or too heavy will cause stress.
- ❏ Support organizational policies and convey that support to the employees.

Index